ALSO BY PETER BAKER

*The Breach: Inside the Impeachment and
Trial of William Jefferson Clinton*

KREMLIN RISING

Vladimir Putin's Russia and the End of Revolution

Peter Baker

AND

Susan Glasser

A LISA DREW BOOK
SCRIBNER
NEW YORK LONDON TORONTO SYDNEY

ADG 3422

A LISA DREW BOOK/SCRIBNER
1230 Avenue of the Americas
New York, NY 10020

SCRIBNER and design are trademarks of
Macmillan Library Reference USA, Inc., used under license
by Simon & Schuster, the publisher of this work.

A LISA DREW BOOK is a trademark of Simon & Schuster Inc.

For information about special discounts for bulk purchases,
please contact Simon & Schuster Special Sales:
1-800-456-6798 or business@simonandschuster.com

Designed by Kyoko Watanabe
Text set in Minion

Manufactured in the United States of America

1   3   5   7   9   10   8   6   4   2

Library of Congress Control Number: 2005044157

ISBN 0-7432-6431-2

For Theodore

CONTENTS

Tatyana's Russia

In this country, something happens and you never know where
it will lead.
—TATYANA SHALIMOVA

A bit of this, yet also half of that.
—YEVGENY YEVTUSHENKO

TATYANA SHALIMOVA's high heels sank into the mud as we rounded the corner to her brother's house. To our left, four chickens feasted in a large, open garbage bin. Ahead, her brother's wife stood alone in the kitchen, a gigantic pot of slops simmering on the stove to feed their pig, Masha. Inside the house, there was no toilet, no hot water, and no telephone. Pulling on her Ray•Bans, Tatyana shook her head as she considered the gap separating her life in Moscow from her brother Misha's in the "workers' settlement" of Mokshan. "I can't stay here for more than a few days at a time," she said. Then came a question, *the* question: "Why don't the people here change their lives?" Her unspoken rebuke hung in the air: "I did."[1]

It was nearly ten years to the day after the failed coup by hard-line Communists in August 1991 set in motion the collapse of the Soviet Union. Russia was now a family divided by differing post-Soviet realities, struggling to come to terms with a painful decade of dislocation. For some like Tatyana, there were new hopes and expanded horizons—"the appetite," she explained to us, "grows while eating." For the majority like her brother, there were the ruins of an old system and no more than rare glimpses of something new to replace it.

In the Kremlin, a onetime KGB spy who had sat out the implosion of the Soviet empire in a backwater posting in East Germany had become president of Russia. Few knew what to make of Vladimir Putin, a political cipher who came into office speaking of democracy while preparing to dismantle democratic institutions. Fewer still had a sense of where Russia was headed after its first tumultuous post-Soviet decade. The age of Boris Yeltsin, with all the attendant drunken antics and economic crises, had ended. The age of Putin, whatever it would be, had begun.

We had arrived in Russia as correspondents for the *Washington Post* on the eve of Putin's election as president in 2000 and would stay on through nearly four years of change in a country the world thought it had gotten to know under Yeltsin. We found the place in the throes of a nationalist reawakening, cheered on by a proud, young leader, and yet such a weakened shadow of its former superpower self that it faced an epidemic of young conscripts running away from an army that couldn't properly feed them. It was a time of economic boom as oil revenues floated Russia out of the bank runs and ruble collapses of Yeltsin's presidency. And yet it was also a place ruled by ambivalence and anxiety, when fears of the future crowded out memories of the brutalities in the not-so-distant Communist past. This was a newly assertive Russia, rejecting international loans instead of defaulting on them, glorifying its lost empire rather than exulting in the downfall of dictatorship, a Russia where the clichés of the 1990s, of begging babushkas, gangster capitalism, and oligarchic excess, were no longer operative. The grinding, brutal war in the breakaway region of Chechnya—and the spill-over wave of gruesome terror attacks against subway riders and airline passengers, schoolchildren, and theatergoers—became a grim constant linking the two eras.

A friend of a friend we first met at an Italian café in the center of Moscow, Tatyana would turn out to be one of our first and most reliable guides to Putin's Russia, helping us explore the post-Soviet fault lines that fissured the vast country. Hers was a Russia banking on the promises of an unfinished capitalist revolution; her brother remained behind in the crumbled wreck-age of their childhood, trapped in isolation and the unforgiving legacy of the past. Tatyana's was the world of Moscow's emerging, tenuous middle class, a whirl of European vacations and after-work aerobics classes, supermarkets and traffic jams, rising expectations and perpetual insecurity. Brother Misha's Mokshan, 440 miles to the southeast, was a place of rusting factories and Communist-era bosses, where money remained more concept than reality and the summer harvest of cabbage and potatoes supplied food for the long winter.

"All the positive changes that happened in my life are the consequences of the new system," she said.

"Things are harder now," he countered. "There's not enough jobs and not enough money."

On the overnight train from Moscow to Mokshan, a twelve-hour-and-forty-five-minute journey from one country to another, Tatyana told us her story of wrenching change in Russia's decade of upheaval. At thirty-four, she was part of the transitional generation, the last to receive a fully Soviet education and the first to work mostly in the free market. She grew up with Leonid Brezhnev's stagnation in the 1970s, came of age during Mikhail Gorbachev's perestroika in the 1980s, and became an adult amid the democratic chaos and corrupted capitalism of Boris Yeltsin's 1990s. Now she had forgotten her mandatory classes on Marxism and worked for a foundation trying to reform the Russian judiciary. Ten years earlier, she had never been outside the country. Today, she was fluent in world capitals, most recently Paris and London, a connoisseur of beaches from Spain to Egypt. Where once she lived in a crowded communal apartment with four roommates, one grimy kitchen, and no shower, now she rented a tiny studio and dreamed of owning her own home.

The gulf between her Moscow and her family's Mokshan had always existed. But never had it been so wide—the difference between the $1,500 a month that Tatyana considered "normal" for herself and her Moscow friends and the $70 monthly salary of her brother, between the French cognac she now preferred and the home-brewed vodka he kept in his cupboard. On the short walk from Misha's house to the polluted river where they had swum as kids, he described the berry-picking season just ended, the mushroom-hunting soon to begin, and the cow he wanted to purchase that fall. Tatyana, meanwhile, was looking back at his crooked wooden outhouse. "I am between two worlds," she told us.

So, too, was Putin's Russia, no longer Communist yet not quite capitalist, no longer a tyranny yet not quite free. The heady idealism of the day that Yeltsin had clambered atop a tank in 1991 and brought down the Soviet Union was long since dead and often unmourned. "Democracy" was not now—if it had ever been—a goal supported by much of the population, and the very word had been discredited, an epithet that had come to be associated with upheaval rather than opportunity. Polls consistently found that no more than a third of the population considered themselves democrats a decade into the experiment, while an equally large number believed authoritarianism was the only path for their country.[2] Yeltsin had, in other words, succeeded in killing off Communism but not in creating its successor.

Instead, the Russia we found on the eve of the Putin era remained a country in between, where strong-state rhetoric played well even as the state collapsed, where corruption and the government were so intertwined as to be at times indistinguishable, and where the president from the KGB set as his

main priority the establishment of what he euphemistically called the "dictatorship of the law." Like everyone else, we were left to wonder where these
slogans would in reality lead, certain only that the Putin presidency would
be very different from what had preceded it.

For Tatyana and her friends, there was respite but no real refuge from the
uncertainty. And this perhaps was the most useful introduction for us to Russia, a reminder that while Moscow was now a place of sushi for the few and
new cars for the many, of seemingly unlimited freedoms and a decade's worth
of openness to the West, there were no guarantees. One Sunday afternoon,
at the health club that was her favorite hangout, Tatyana sipped freshly
squeezed pear juice at the sports bar after changing out of her neon yellow
leotard and electric blue spandex shorts. She and her friends were preoccupied with the minutiae of life in the big city at the turn of the millennium,
with Internet dating and vacations abroad and families in the provinces who
couldn't relate. But unlike the pre–September 11 cocoon of Americans who
felt free to ignore the realities of the wider world, Russians did not have the
luxury of completely tuning out.

"In this country, something happens and you never know where it will
lead," Tatyana told her friends.

Heads nodded and soon the conversation broke up. Two of the women
were late for appointments to get their legs waxed.

FROM OUR first trip there together, the Russia that we experienced was
Putin's. During his election campaign in 2000, in a grim March that was neither winter nor spring, we had our initial encounter with what would
become an ever more artfully "managed democracy"—a term that came into
wide use for the first time that political season as Moscow's intelligentsia
struggled to understand the political goals of the little-known secret police
chief who on New Year's Eve, 1999, had become Boris Yeltsin's handpicked
successor.[3]

Trying to understand the Putin appeal, we flew to Magnitogorsk, the rusting steel town straddling Europe and Asia in the Ural Mountains whose
founding had been the proudest achievement of dictator Joseph Stalin's first
five-year plan back in 1929. When we got off the plane late at night, we were
met on the tarmac by a local police official who had been informed that the
Washington Post was coming to town and insisted on checking our documents—an echo of a Soviet past we thought long gone. After negotiating our
way through that encounter, we found a city where the plant managers themselves organized Putin's campaign and workers shrugged at the inevitability

of the anointed president's victory. As the sky turned a hideous orange out-side the mammoth steel plant's gates in a daily light show of environmental hazard, we talked to Soviet leftovers who were so indifferent to politics they told us that it did not matter to them that Putin refused to offer a program for governing the country. If anything, they said, it was a positive. "Stalin's words—that each person is just a small wheel in a big state machine—are still in our psyche," mused the editor of the local newspaper, founded like the rest of the gritty town by Stalin's political prisoners. "That is why people are con-tent with slogans and don't feel they need detailed programs."[4]

On television, on billboards, in the newspapers, were all the apparent hall-marks of democracy—a large field of competing candidates, genuine differ-ences over the country's future, shamelessly pandering photo ops. But rather than being the flourishes of a vibrant new political culture, these proved to be deceptive, reflecting Russian expertise in the arts of *pokazukha*—displays meant only for show. In the end, what struck us about the election was not only the absence of real choice but the mystery of Putin's appeal. After not yet a decade of democratic experimentation, how could it be that this product of the KGB was the best the country had to offer itself?

On election day, when Putin would become Russia's second elected pres-ident in its thousand-year history in an election marred by vote fraud, media manipulation, and irregularities politely overlooked by the world's other great powers, we spent the afternoon in Moscow asking voters about the spy who became president. Their answers surprised us then and still do.

"He knows what order is," Putin voter Tatyana Gosudareva told us, a sen-tence we heard so often in the coming years it would come to seem a refrain. We found a young couple huddled together in the sculpture garden of fallen Soviet statues outside the House of Artists, paying homage to the stern vis-age of Feliks Dzerzhinsky, founder of the Soviet secret police. The monu-ment had been pulled off its pedestal outside KGB headquarters in August 1991 in one of the signal moments of the revolution that spelled the end of the Soviet Union. But more and more these days, the curious who came to glance at the fallen spymaster were not democrats thrilled at his symbolic toppling but Russians like Sergei and Lena, who idolized the strong hands that ruled a state they were barely old enough to remember. Sergei, twenty-four, worked for the latest incarnation of the secret police, the Federal Secu-rity Service, the domestic successor to the KGB that was known by its Russian initials as the FSB. He and his teenage girlfriend, Lena, had voted for Putin because of his background. "Absolutely it prepared him to be president," Sergei said before patiently explaining to us why Russians would be proud of Putin's past. "They like it. They see [the KGB] as strong. They see it as severe, harsh."[5]

It was the first of many times we were to be confronted with a version of recent Russian history so radically opposite to what we thought we understood that it might as well have been about a different country. In the revisionist variant we started to hear that day, there was nothing about the crippling legacy of totalitarianism or the follies of Communist central planning. The gulag was a minor bump in the road, an error in 1937 long since acknowledged and forgotten. History, in this view, did not really begin until 1991 with the tragic sundering of the Soviet empire. All chaos, crises, bank collapses, crazy corruption, and crony capitalism came from this disaster. And this, we eventually came to learn, was no minority view but the sentiment of a majority rarely represented in Western portraits of the new Russia.

It was also the groundwork laid for what Putin's deputy campaign manager called Project Putin, an ambitious effort to reshape Russian politics starting with the election of an unknown secret police chief.[6] The goal was consolidating power back in the Kremlin, where Putin and his advisers firmly believed it belonged by virtue of centuries of Russian history. To do so, Putin would, over the coming years, methodically go after all possible sources of alternative views, from independent media and fiefdom-seeking governors to national legislators and even the very same oligarchic tycoons who had helped orchestrate his rise to power. He could be brutal, as in waging a war in Chechnya that fueled his surprising ascension in 1999 and cost tens of thousands of lives. And he could be subtle, as when he was wooing his counterparts in the West, who embraced him as a new-generation leader only to be surprised by his old-style tendencies.

Through it all, we were on hand to watch as the project unfolded, an effort combining the tools of modern politics with timeworn tactics from the playbook of the fallen dictatorship. It was not Soviet but neo-Soviet. The Communist manifestos were gone, the borders were open, the surface attributes of free speech seemed intact. But the project was clearly aimed at resurrection of Russia as the superpower it had been in Soviet times, if through economic and political means rather than military might. "There is no ideology at all," as one senior official told us, just a belief in the value of seizing power and holding on to it.[7] There was no empty rhetoric about the proletariat this time, but there were Komsomol-style pro-Putin youth groups ordered up by the authorities and trumped-up spy cases and even the revival of the Soviet national anthem first introduced by Stalin. "USSR" T-shirts were all the rage, and old habits of subservience to the authorities, never unlearned, guided political responses to the reempowered president even as a new market world of consumerism took shape in Moscow and a handful of other big cities.

At the start of Putin's presidency, few understood the scale and scope of the Kremlin's Project Putin. Instead, experts debated the question "Who is Mr. Putin?" Western-oriented democrats claimed him as one of their own and took comfort from the team of Yeltsin holdovers and economic liberals Putin assembled to lead further modernization of the Russian economy. Nationalists cheered his war in Chechnya and his vow to end the "disintegration" of the state. Soviet nostalgists—some of them still Communist stalwarts, others simply those who thought back wistfully to the country's former superpower status—welcomed his embrace of symbols like the Soviet red star he ordered back onto the army's banners and the disgraced KGB coup plotter he invited to his Kremlin inauguration.

Putin carefully cultivated these uncertainties about his intentions. As a politician, he had the gift of seeming to be all things to all people, of uniting an otherwise fractured society with soothing words about stability and order. At least initially, that was all that most people had to judge him by. "Putin has said he wants to end the revolution," his political consultant Gleb Pavlovsky told us early on in the presidency, "not to start a new one."[8]

One afternoon, we sat with the president's pollster, Aleksandr Oslon, in his Moscow office on the southwestern outskirts of the burgeoning city, where new American-style malls jostled with concrete apartment towers. We were trying to understand, years later, the appeal of Project Putin. "Putin was a break from the time of chaos. The word *chaos* was the key word in people's understanding," Oslon told us. Yeltsin and his young band of reformers, the new team in the Kremlin believed, had embraced a course of democratic and economic transformation that Russians never really wanted. But Putin came to office determined not to force-feed democracy to Russia; he would, in the metaphor Oslon used with us, simply let the river revert to its authoritarian course and ride along with it. "If you think about politics and culture as a huge river, and there is a person in it going against the tide, you can swim that way, but not for long," the pollster said.[9] In other words, the counterrevolution had begun.

Project Putin was not entirely a surprise, although it may have seemed that way to outsiders who hoped Russia would turn out otherwise. Back in 1989, amid the hopes and anxieties unleashed by the beginning of this latest Russian revolution, when Gorbachev's policy of glasnost, or openness,

offered the novelty of free speech to the people, the popular bard poet
Yevgeny Yevtushenko had written of the dangers of incomplete reform, of
freedom only partially won, and of a Soviet state only partially dismantled. In
his poem "Half Measures," written when Vladimir Putin was still a nobody
spy, Yevtushenko foresaw the failure of democracy in Russia if its central pre-
cepts were never fully embraced. The poem was meant as an exhortation to
Gorbachev to continue on his course of restructuring Soviet society, but
when we read it, many years of partially executed reforms later, it served also
as foreshadowing, a rendering of Russia as we would find it:

> . . . [W]ith every half-effective half measure
> Half the people remain half pleased.
> The half sated are half hungry.
> The half free are half enslaved.
> We are half afraid, halfway on a rampage . . .
> A bit of this, yet also half of that
> . . . Can there be with honor
> A half motherland and a half conscience?
> Half freedom is perilous,
> And saving the motherland halfway will fail.[10]

BY THE TIME we began to write this book, the Kremlin had already carried
out much of its takeover. All three national television networks were once
again controlled by the state, Russia's richest man was in jail after challenging Putin's rule too openly, and his oil company, the country's largest and best
run, was on its way to being renationalized. National elections criticized by
international observers as free but not fair had produced a pocket parliament
unswervingly loyal to the president. Putin had surrounded himself at the
upper echelons of power with a cadre of like-minded KGB and military
veterans—so many so that one-quarter of the political elite was now composed of such *siloviki*, as Russians called these "men of power," compared
with just 3 percent under Gorbachev. The military budget had tripled, and
the secret services received their long-awaited first increases since the
breakup of the Soviet Union. In March 2004, Putin won his second term as
president after a campaign so pointless the only real suspense was whether his
challengers would drop out en masse or let the farce play itself out with their
names still on the ballot.

By then, the debate was no longer over who Putin was, but just how far
he intended to take things.

And the answer would come not long after the president's pomp-filled second-term inauguration at the Kremlin, when, standing underneath the golden tsarist sunburst of St. Andrew's Hall, Putin began his next four years in office with a speech that no longer even mentioned the word *democracy*. Just as it had vaulted him to power, Chechnya would provide the clarifying moment. As the conflict there hit the decade mark, a new wave of Chechen-related mayhem broke out across Russia, starting with the assassination of Putin's handpicked president for the region within days of the viceroy's inauguration and culminating in September 2004 with the seizure of School Number 1 in the town of Beslan not far from the Chechen border.

When the grim standoff ended with the spectacle of hundreds of tiny dead, burned bodies pulled from the rubble, the world watched in horror. For Putin, it was the moment finally to reveal his hand. For three days, his government had lied about everything having to do with the siege, from the number of children trapped inside to the identity of the hostage-takers, who authorities insisted were led by Al Qaeda–affiliated Arabs rather than home-grown Chechen terrorists, a claim swiftly debunked by the evidence but never officially disavowed. Putin chose to blame unnamed nefarious forces in the West in a return to Cold War–style rhetoric that would increasingly mark his statements from that point on. Then, within days, he announced a sweeping Kremlin power grab—the cancellation of gubernatorial elections in all of Russia's eighty-nine regions, with the governors from now on to be appointed by the president, and the end of independent representatives in parliament, with only his puppet parties picking future candidates. He justified the moves as an antiterrorist step "to prevent further crises." When governors rushed to endorse the proposal with statements so fawning that even a tsarist courtier might have blushed, Russia was suddenly as clear as it would ever be. The counterrevolution was over, and Putin had won.

Our book, then, begins and ends with Beslan—a bloodbath of innocents that was also a horrendous unanticipated consequence of Project Putin, when state television broadcast soap operas rather than risk airing the battle, and the president deflected criticism onto Westerners and elected politicians rather than fire a single senior officer in his own corrupted, bloated security forces responsible for handling the hostage-taking.

On the pages between, we hope to provide a wide-ranging tour of Putin's Russia as the Kremlin rose again, from vantage points as varied as the rock music nationalists at Moscow's Nashe radio station to the high school students in Irina Suvolokina's history class who were pretty sure that Lenin had been right after all. Organized roughly chronologically, the book moves from the unlikely rise of Putin through key moments of his tenure, from the early disastrous sinking of the submarine *Kursk* and his decision to take over Russia's only independent television network, to the thoroughly "managed" elections in 2003 and 2004. Putin himself is a presence throughout, whether thwarting efforts to reform Russia's calcified behemoth of an army or charming George W. Bush with a skillfully chosen cross around his neck.

But this is not just a book about politics. Our goal was also to provide a sense of a place where many people have long since given up on politics, where parties of any ideology are permanently discredited after seven decades of one-party rule, and where the modest but tangible economic improvements of the last few years have turned many into at least reluctant Putin converts. If the trade-off of the time has been framed as greater stability but less freedom, many Russians have proved willing to accept that deal. Our guides to this other Russia were many and varied, from a would-be nuclear physicist turned ambivalent underwear salesman in Nizhny Novgorod, who helped us understand Russia's halfhearted embrace of capitalism, to the forgotten residents of the desolate arctic towns of Kolyma, the graveyard of the gulag where many dislocated by the recent turmoil profess longing for the Soviet rulers who sent them there.

One chapter reconstructs the war in Chechnya from the perspective of the most wrenching case to arise from it—that of Colonel Yuri Budanov, a tank commander who admitted strangling a young Chechen woman to death but whose long-running trial became a Rorschach test of the political divisions fracturing Russia in the Putin era. Boomtown Moscow itself is the protagonist of another chapter, as we look at the smart, cynical tastemakers who made the city a place of restless innovation and yet one so indifferent that the band of Chechen terrorists who seized a theater there in 2002 told their hostages they did so in order to shake the city out of its complacency about the war down south.

Along the way, we had encounters with hundreds of Russians who helped us understand Putin's Russia: AIDS patients in Siberia whose government has devoted a total of five Health Ministry staffers to stopping an epidemic spreading more rapidly in Russia than anywhere else in the world; anguished mothers like Natasha Yaroslavtseva, whose only son, Sasha, killed himself after serving his mandatory two years in the troubled Russian military; and brash Kremlin political "technologists" like Marat Gelman, who thought nothing of creating artificial opposition political parties dreamed up in the Kremlin and turning state television into Putin's personal election machine.

To try to understand the KGB tactics and mentality that Putin brought to the Kremlin, we spent many hours interviewing more than a dozen of his fellow former agents now in high-ranking positions in business, politics, and government, a fascinating exercise that revealed to us the enormous sense of entitlement and absolute lack of remorse on the part of Russia's once and present ruling class. These "servants of the state," as they called themselves, fervently believed Putin would rescue Russia from the corruption and liberal permissiveness that had taken hold in the 1990s—and saw nothing wrong with the police state methods that they, and Putin, had learned back in the time of Brezhnev. We spent time as well with the dwindling ranks of Soviet-era dissidents who opposed the Communist regime and now fought an increasingly marginalized fight against its successor. The day after parliamentary elections, in December 2003, evicted Russia's two Western-oriented democratic parties from parliament, we spoke with one of them, a courageous human rights activist named Lev Ponomaryov. "For democrats now," he warned us, "a period is coming very similar to Brezhnev times. They are going to be dissidents now."[11]

Kremlin Rising: Vladimir Putin's Russia and the End of Revolution is also the story of how Project Putin came to pass with the world only offering a passing nod of puzzlement or occasional mild criticism. When we first arrived in Moscow, the new president's mantra of stability had seemed like a code word for boredom, and Western news outlets were scrambling to relocate their correspondents. Then came September 11 and the war in Afghanistan. Putin and President George W. Bush proclaimed themselves not just allies but friends. For a while, in the run-up to the U.S.-led war in Iraq, we began to hear about the Bush administration's plans to declare that Russia had "graduated" from its transition away from Communism, to a full-fledged democracy no longer in need of assistance. It had been more than a decade, after all, and these were monies that would soon be desperately needed in Baghdad. But Putin's Russia had hardly graduated to anything resembling the Western-style liberal democracy of the 1990s collective fantasy. If anything, Russia could serve as a textbook study in how not to reform a dictatorial political system and how not to wage a war on terror. The country's retreat from democracy was a cautionary tale more relevant than ever at a time when Washington spoke of bringing democracy to the Middle East and wrestled with the painful questions of how to balance the freedoms of an open society with the constraints of fighting a shadowy foe. Bush began his second term vowing to promote freedom everywhere, confront "every ruler and every nation" about internal repression, and work toward the goal of "ending tyranny in our world"—and then had to begin with his friend Vladimir at an awkward summit in February 2005. Certainly, Russia was a more open society, with a considerably shrunken state role in the economy and a new web of connections to the outside world that had started to reshape a place warped by decades of isolation and willful ignorance. But the counterrevolution launched by Putin and his circle was not about completing the transition to democracy; it was about rolling it back.

For many still shaped by the past, this was not a bad idea at all, as we started to learn right from the start of our tour in Putin's Russia, when we accompanied Tatyana Shalimova on her trip home to a very different country from the one we had expected to find.

TATYANA's father was standing in the kitchen in Mokshan, bragging about his potatoes again. "I am proud that these are my own potatoes. That we have them through our own labor," said Gennady, an engineer at the phone company who counted on his garden, not his paycheck, to supply their food for the winter.

"I don't agree," Tatyana interrupted. "I've offered to buy them three sacks of potatoes, which is enough for the whole winter."

She turned to her father. "Why do you need to do this work? It's not good for you at your age."

"No, no, no," he sputtered. "It's our work. We are proud of it."

For Tatyana, every visit to her parents' apartment on Engels Street was a series of such confrontations between their Russia and hers. Although she was close to her mother, Valentina, their everyday lives had little in common, from the way they spent their time to the food they ate. ("I like something low-fat, not fried," she told us on the train; within hours, her mother was frying fish and potatoes for us.)

The black-and-white photos from Tatyana's high school that we pored through after lunch could have been a hundred years old: somber, unsmiling girls in frilly white aprons and uncomfortable black woolen dresses, sitting behind wooden desks. They were taken in 1984. Out of her class of thirty or so, Tatyana was the only one to have made it to Moscow. Her high school boyfriend was now buying food in the nearby city of Penza and reselling it in Mokshan. They broke up during her first year in the city, she recalled as we flipped through the photo albums her mother kept carefully in the tiny bedroom that was Tatyana's when she was growing up. "He didn't like all these things—foreigners, foreign languages. 'It's anti-Russian,' he said."

Such thinking still echoed in Mokshan, a town of twelve thousand that was founded in the seventeenth century but retained a Soviet look and feel. Economic problems were easier to talk about in a place where average wages were officially just $35 a month at the start of Putin's tenure, among the lowest in the country. Tatyana's brother Misha was an army veteran who worked as a phone company repairman—and considered himself lucky to have any work at all. Her father would soon retire from the same company with a $70-a-month pension. No one in her family, or most others there, had ever owned a car, and travel in Mokshan for them was exclusively on foot, down muddy, rutted lanes, dodging stray dogs.

The town lived with old fears as well, habits of totalitarianism that influenced Russia's tenuous stabs at democracy. While Tatyana said she felt free to say what she thought, her parents and their friends were wary of talking to a foreigner, citing fear of retribution from the FSB.

One family friend proudly told us that she was never afraid in Soviet times. "My whole life, I always said what I thought. I never thought that something was forbidden," she said in an indignant huff. The next day, she begged Tatyana's mother to make sure we did not quote her by name, saying she could be fired. Another man, asked to describe life there when he pulled up in a truck on the mud-rutted track outside Tatyana's brother's house, replied immediately that he could not answer. "The FSB wouldn't like that," he explained.

Later, back in the city, Tatyana struggled to make sense of these encounters, precursors to many more we would have in the coming years. "Moscow is speaking one language about democracy," she said, "but everybody in the provinces, they are speaking another language, an older one."

Tatyana objected to anyone connected with the old state-security apparatus. "I don't accept any former KGB leaders, including Putin," she said. "People had no real choice; they were offered Putin and they accepted him." But she knew that hers was a minority view. Both in Moscow and Mokshan, she heard regular praise of Putin as the antidote to what was missing from Russia's post-Soviet decade. "My mom used to say, 'You are in Moscow, you can look for the truth and find it. But here we don't have many choices,'" Tatyana said. "There are no jobs in Mokshan, and if you lose yours, you will not find another one. The boss there rules like a king. These people say they are not Communists anymore, but they still have this mentality."

Tatyana, for one, had left that fear behind. "I am not very much afraid. If I were to lose my job, I am sure I could be a teacher. I can be a nurse. I can wash the floor," she reflected. "In Moscow, you have so many choices. You can control your life."

But she was also aware that this was a luxury in Putin's Russia, a privilege available to the small minority that truly believed themselves to be living in a new country of openness and opportunity. For the rest, there was Mokshan, and new iterations of an old past.

Fifty-two Hours in Beslan

She looked like death walking around with a scythe.
—ALEKSANDR TSAGOLOV

EVERY FEW WEEKS, the Totiyev children would gather for another party around the plain wooden table under the single bare lightbulb hanging by a wire from the ceiling. There were eleven of them, the sons and daughters of two brothers living in adjoining houses in the southern Russia town of Beslan, two families sharing a single bustling household. With so many children, birthdays arrived all the time, but if the parents occasionally grew weary of the celebrations, the children never did. They simply organized the parties themselves and prepared all the food—sausages, cheeses, chicken, one of those mayonnaise-laden mixes of meat and unidentifiable vegetables called "salads" throughout the former Soviet Union, sweet, dense cake, and, this being North Ossetia, warm, round, cheese-filled bread that was the local specialty. With all eleven at the table, they were a community unto themselves. "They would say, 'Why do we need anybody else?'" said Raya Tsolmayova, mother of five of the children.

The outside world intruded mainly in the form of school. As the summer of 2004 came to an end, Tsolmayova's children returned from a vacation at the Black Sea and soaked up the last days of freedom before the fall term would begin. The youngest, a buoyant eight-year-old named Boris with a mischievous habit of uprooting the neighbor's flowers to present his mother a fresh bouquet, seemed unenthusiastic about the start of another school year. Tsolmayova bought him some new clothes and had him put them on for his sisters to admire. The four girls played their part. "The girls were telling him, 'Oh, how handsome you look,'" Tsolmayova recalled. "And so I asked him, 'Do you want to go to school now?' And he said, 'A little.'"

Tsolmayova smiled as she told the story. She had a happy face and smiled often even in the midst of great adversity. Theirs was not a wealthy family. Her husband, Taimuraz Totiyev, was an out-of-work baker, struggling to start his own business. They had none of the luxuries of the new Russia, none of the flat-screen televisions or fancy cars or other consumer totems becoming so common in faraway Moscow. But they cherished the first day of school, an event the Soviets had long ago turned into a virtual secular holiday, a tradition that had continued even after the collapse of the system that had established it. In Beslan, as in most Russian towns, the first day of school was considered a communitywide event with little boys decked out in crisp white shirts and little girls in floppy white bows. They would carry flowers to school and, more likely than not, would be accompanied by a mother, perhaps a father, and brothers and sisters who had already graduated or were still too young to attend.

On the morning of September 1, 2004, as Beslan's School Number 1 prepared to start another term, Tsolmayova cooked celebratory blini for breakfast. All five of her children were going, as well as three of her brother-in-law's. Tsolmayova planned to take them, but first her husband asked her to iron a shirt for him. She thought that was a little strange—he had other shirts already ironed—but he was insistent that he wanted to wear this particular one. It meant Tsolmayova would be a little late, so she let the children go ahead of her. As devout Christians, they said a prayer together before the little ones left the house. Then the children kissed her on the cheek one by one and rushed out into the muddy street in their finest clothes to head across the railroad tracks to school. "They told me, 'Mama, catch up with us.' I said, 'Wait for me. Why are you going so early?' They said, 'We want to go.'" Lyuba, age eleven, realized she had forgotten to kiss her mother good-bye and rushed back to peck her on the cheek. "Then she ran away."[1]

The extended Totiyev family was a reflection of Beslan itself, a small town of thirty thousand that seemed even smaller, a place where dawn really was greeted by the crowing of roosters, and dusk could easily find a woman taking the family cow for a walk through downtown. School Number 1 was just short of sacred. Constructed in 1899 as the larger forces of the times were still beginning to gather against centuries of Romanov rule, the two-story red-brick schoolhouse had outlived both the tsars and the commissars who replaced them, surviving to become an expanded horseshoe-shaped landmark near the center of town that served as much as a community center as a place of learning. Five years earlier, its gymnasium had been rebuilt into a showcase, with two-story-tall windows and a basketball court that became the envy of other schools. "It was the best gym in the region," boasted Aleksandr Tsagolov, the physical education teacher who tended it like a garden. "Everyone envied us that we had such a big gym." Burly, balding, and powerfully built even at five foot five, Tsagolov got to the school gym at 6:30 a.m. on the first day of the new fall term, opened all the windows and doors to clear out the air, did his workout, then closed the gym doors and went home for a quick shower before returning for the official opening ceremonies. "Everything was ready," recalled Tsagolov, who went by the nickname Alik. "Three bells rang. For us, that always means gathering. I went out to the courtyard. There were no cars yet. We started to line up."[2]

The principal, Lydia Tsaliyeva, had been there since 7 a.m., personally vacuuming the floors. At the age of seventy-two, Tsaliyeva had made School Number 1 her life. An ethnic Ossetian born in the nearby Chechen capital of Grozny, her family had moved to Beslan when she was nine and enrolled her in School Number 1. For the previous fifty-two years, she had worked there, first as a geography teacher and later as an administrator. Soon after 9 a.m., Tsaliyeva shuffled the students into place for the opening ceremony, still holding a bouquet of flowers one of the children had handed her. Balloons were everywhere. A song from the 1980s played on the speakers, something about childhood and innocence. As the song ended, the balloons started popping. Or rather that's what it sounded like.[3]

"We heard some sort of clapping sound," said Tsagolov. "I thought they were balloons popping. I thought to myself, 'What kind of balloons would be so loud?' I didn't understand at first what was going on. Then the shooting began. Panic. I could hear clearly there was machine gun fire. I thought there was some maniac at first. They cut us off and herded us into the courtyard."[4] Strange men were rushing toward the school wearing camouflage uniforms and black masks. A UAZ-66 military truck screeched to a stop and a gunman went to the back of the vehicle and flipped open a canvas tarp, revealing another two dozen men with Kalashnikov assault rifles. Other guerrillas were firing weapons and trying to direct children into the school gym. A man carrying flowers was shot down. Another man, shouting, "My family is in there," ran toward the building, only to be hit by a bullet.[5] Hundreds of students, parents, and teachers were herded into the gym.

"There was a lot of yelling, panic, shouting," recalled deputy principal Olga Sherbinina. "They said, 'Sit down! Sit down!' We all sat down. Children, parents, teachers. It was so crowded, we couldn't stretch our legs."[6] The guerrillas dragged the body of a man they had killed into the gymnasium and across the floor, streaking blood along the way, then dropped him in the middle of the room for all to see. The message was clear.

One of those who managed to bolt when the first shots were fired was a quiet fifteen-year-old named Kazbek Dzaragasov. He had run so fast he had made it out of the eyesight of the intruders. But then he remembered his eight-year-old sister, Agunda, was still inside. He ran back to the school to find her, giving up his escape to become a hostage himself. Inside the jammed gymnasium, Raya Tsolmayova's five children—Larisa, age fourteen; Madina, twelve; Lyuba, eleven; Albina, ten; and Boris, eight—stumbled around until they were able to find each other, then huddled on the floor together, terrified.

The guerrillas demanded silence.

"We've taken you hostage and our demand is that Putin withdraw the troops from Chechnya," one of them announced. "Until the Russian army is withdrawn from Chechnya, you're going to sit here."

The crowd reacted with horror. Chechen fighters? Here in their little town? Taking children hostage?

As the crowd's predicament sank in, the terrorists became increasingly angry at the noise. "If you don't calm down," one of them said, "we'll shoot at the crowd, and it doesn't matter to us if children, women, men, old women, are killed."

In the local Ossetian language, the principal called on the children to quiet down.

"Speak Russian!" one of the terrorists hissed.

Ruslan Betrozov, the father of two students, also tried to shush people around him. A gunman grabbed Betrozov and put a pistol to his head. "If you don't calm down," the gunman told the children, "we'll shoot him."

A few seconds passed and the frightened children did not quiet down enough. The man pulled the trigger and Betrozov crumpled to the floor dead in front of his two sons.

Then the terrorists grabbed Alik Tsagolov, the gym teacher, and put a pistol to his head. "If you don't calm down," one of them shouted at the hostages, "we'll shoot him next."[7]

THE SEIZURE of a school with hundreds of children came as a shock to Russia but hardly a surprise. Over ten years and two wars, the conflict to control the rugged mountainous territory of Chechnya barely thirty miles to the east of Beslan had evolved from a nationalist struggle for independence into a blood feud in which both sides terrorized civilians with wanton cruelty. Any sense of moral boundaries had long since evaporated. Vladimir Putin renewed the war in the days after his appointment as prime minister in 1999, promising it would be over in two weeks. Yet five years later, it wore on, bitter and unrelenting, deadly and indiscriminate. Putin's bombers flattened the Chechen capital of Grozny, dropping more ordnance than any European city had endured since World War II, indifferent to the civilians huddling in their basements, and leaving behind a hollowed-out shell of a city where not a single building was still standing fully intact. Soldiers regularly conducted *zachistki* (or "cleansing operations"), sweeping up virtually any Chechen man between his teens and retirement age, many of whom wound up tortured and killed or simply went missing forever. Outgunned on the traditional battlefield, the Chechen resistance had long since turned to terrorist attacks against civilian targets, the farther from Chechnya the better. Increasingly they were using female suicide bombers dressed head to toe in black chador and face-covering *hijab,* women known as *shakhidki,* a feminized Russian version of the Arab word for martyrs, but dubbed by the Moscow press "black widows." In the two years before Beslan, Chechen terrorists had bombed trains, planes, and subways, taken over a Moscow theater, slammed a truck bomb into a hospital, and attacked a rock concert. Even before the bloody summer of 2004, more Russians had died in terrorist attacks over the previous two years than in Israel or virtually any other country in the world.

Then starting in May, the Chechens unleashed a new wave of violence. First they assassinated Putin's puppet leader in Chechnya, Akhmad Kadyrov, with a bomb in a reviewing stand during a World War II Victory Day parade. A month later, they staged a daring nighttime raid on the neighboring republic of Ingushetia, briefly taking over the main town of Nazran, setting up their own checkpoints, and shooting any police officer who unwittingly stopped and presented his identification papers. About ninety people died that night. They launched a similar strike into Grozny itself in August as the Kremlin prepared another rigged election to ratify its choice for Kadyrov's successor, this time killing another fifty people in a matter of hours as Russian troops remained sheltered inside their nearby base, unwilling to come out and confront the enemy. A week later two *shakhidki* boarded separate planes at Moscow's refurbished Domodedovo Airport—one by paying a modest bribe of just one thousand rubles (about $34) to an airline official—and set off explosives aboard the passenger jets within minutes of each other, killing all ninety aboard in the world's first multiple-plane terrorist attack since the September 11, 2001, assault on the United States. The night before Beslan, another *shakhidka* blew herself up outside a Moscow subway station, killing herself and nine other people. The government responded with its old instinct—it lied. The Federal Security Service, or FSB, discounted terrorism and suggested that the two planes fell out of the sky at the same time because of human error or mechanical malfunction. Perhaps only in Russia would it seem plausible, much less more comforting to the public, to explain away the simultaneous crashes of two airplanes by blaming aviation incompetence.

The traces of hexogen explosive found at both crash sites exposed the deception.

Russians immediately understood what was happening. This was Chechnya, again, the never-ending war that kept interrupting Russia's dreams of capitalist normality with reminders of its feudal horrors—a war propelled by some of the very people charged with ending it. The country had grown so crooked from top to bottom that many Russians assumed the attacks on the subway or the Moscow theater might actually have been orchestrated by the secret services, or at least abetted by shady cops. They had good reason for their cynicism. When a hostage in Beslan asked one of the guerrillas how they had managed to smuggle a small army equipped with an arsenal of guns and bombs to the school, he replied, "As long as your militia takes bribes, we're going to be able to get anywhere we want."[8]

Putin invariably characterized the war in Chechnya and the suicide bombings it spawned as an extension of the international war on terrorism, emphasizing the foreign financing and the Arab fighters who had come to the region to join the jihad. Indeed, Chechnya had become linked to the broader Islamic fundamentalist cause. Osama bin Laden used it as part of his rallying cry to the Muslim world against the United States. "America and its allies are massacring us in Palestine, Chechnya, Kashmir, and Iraq," he told a Pakistani journalist two months after September 11. "The Muslims have the right to attack America in reprisal."[9] Bin Laden's top deputy, Ayman al-Zawahiri, once traveled to Russia to explore the possibility of relocating operations to Chechnya, only to be arrested on a visa charge by Russians who had no idea who he was and released him after six months.[10] Mohammed Atta and the other soon-to-be terrorists in the Hamburg, Germany, cell who participated in the September 11 hijackings initially wanted to join the jihad in Chechnya, but were told it was too hard to get in and advised to go to Afghanistan instead.[11]

Yet at its root, the Chechnya conflict had little to do with Al Qaeda, and there was scant evidence of large numbers of foreign guerrillas actually involved in the war. Russia was fighting its own people on its own territory in a conflict anchored in hundreds of years of history and repression. Like many Russian leaders before him, Putin thought he could simply eradicate these mountain men with the full force of a once-great empire, only to mire his nation in another endless struggle. Rather than resolve the underlying political grievances and remove the popular mandate for the rebels, he had demonized, victimized, and consequently radicalized an entire people.

Just an hour before the terrorists arrived at Beslan, Putin was issuing another muscular statement stemming from the plane crashes and subway bombing. "We shall fight them, throw them in prison, and destroy them," he had said.[12] Now that hubris was coming home again with devastating consequences on the basketball court of a little school in a little town called Beslan.

THE MOBILE phones started buzzing urgently all around the Russian republic of North Ossetia shortly after the terrorists arrived. Taimuraz Mansurov, the regional parliament speaker who had helped secure funds to renovate the Beslan school gym, was at a local university greeting new students when his son-in-law called. "I couldn't believe it," he recalled.[13] Two of his own children were students at the school.

Mansurov raced to Beslan, arriving around the same time as the region's president, Aleksandr Dzasokhov, a former Soviet official, and a delegation from the State Duma, the lower house of parliament, that happened to be in the area. They found chaos, parents running around screaming, police uncertain what to do, terrorists shooting from the school's windows and roof at anything that moved within range of their rifles. From the beginning, it was clear that a hostage crisis of unprecedented scale was developing. Authorities at the scene were told by witnesses that some eight hundred people were inside the gym. Officials outside the school questioned a man who had escaped. "His lips were shaking," recalled Mikhail Markelov, a Duma deputy. "He was completely white. He was so scared. We asked him how many children were in there. He said, 'The whole city is there.' We asked specifically how many children and he said, 'More than five hundred, plus the parents.'" Even that would prove an underestimate, but Russian officials decided to lie about how many were inside. When Markelov went on the radio shortly after hearing the escaped man's account, he reported just one hundred people taken hostage. "I knew there were a lot more inside," he told us, "but in the first few minutes if we stated the exact figure, there could have been a panic."[14]

Since even before the Soviet era, the first habit of the government has always been to lie to its own people. But that would not work in Beslan. With at least twelve hundred children and adults crammed into the gym, virtually everyone in town had a loved one there or knew someone who did. Among those who raced to the school was Taimuraz Totiyev, Raya Tsolmayova's husband and father of their five children inside. "When I drove out, I heard shooting. I thought it was a special day, maybe they had some fireworks. I didn't think it could be what it was. When I got close, I could see panic. I got out of the car. 'What's happening?' I asked. 'The school's been taken hostage.' 'By who?'" No one knew for sure. Totiyev approached the school courtyard. "I could see there wasn't a single person there. They had gotten everyone into the gym. When they told me some of the kids escaped, I drove around look-ing for one of ours, hoping maybe one of them ran away. But none of them did." Like the others, Totiyev found the government disinformation about the number of hostages outrageous. "Of course, everybody was angry. Who would like that? They knew perfectly well how many people were inside."[15]

For a while, no contact came from the school. Then a woman, shaking and petrified, was sent out with a note. In poor Russian, it announced that the guerrillas who had seized the school were demanding negotiations with Dzasokhov, the North Ossetian president; Murat Zyazikov, an FSB general who had been installed by the Kremlin as president of next-door Ingushetia in a manipulated election two years earlier to replace a less pliant local leader; and Leonid Roshal, a famous children's doctor who had played intermediary with Chechens in the past. The note did not identify the hostage-takers or lay out any demands, but, as Markelov recalled, it warned ominously, "If you try to shut off the electricity or the water at the school, several hostages will be shot. If one of us is shot, fifty hostages will be shot."[16] The note listed a mobile telephone number, but when authorities called, they got only a recording say-ing the phone was blocked.

Inside the school, the children had quieted down after the first man was shot, saving Alik Tsagolov from the same fate, then watched wide-eyed as the gunmen wired the room with more than a dozen bombs. Explosives were placed along the metal rims of the basketball hoops and a wire was strung between them, holding heavy bombs as if they were Christmas lights. The biggest bomb was connected to spring-loaded trigger devices that resembled pedals on the floor. Two terrorists kept their feet pressed on the pedals at all times; if either let up, they told the hostages, the bombs would explode.[17] Two *shakhidki,* draped in black, wore explosives around their waists, one carry-ing a gun in one hand and a button to set her bombs off in the other. "She looked like death walking around with a scythe," Tsagolov remembered. "As soon as there was noise, she put a gun to the heads of babies."[18] Their leader was hardly more humane. Tall and bearded, he inspired fear not only in the hostages but also in his troops, who called him the Colonel.

The guerrillas picked out men from the crowd, forcing them to help set up barricades around the school. As soon as they were done, the terrorists marched their brigade of fathers and older brothers upstairs to Classroom 15 on the sec-ond floor. On the wall was a portrait of Soviet poet Vladimir Mayakovsky and a wooden plaque featuring the quote that had made him obligatory reading for Soviet students: "I would study Russian if only because Lenin spoke it."

The room quickly became an execution chamber. One after the other, the terrorists gunned down the men, as many as twenty-two by some estimates. Then they ordered a hostage named Aslan Kutsayev and another man to throw the bodies out the window. Blood smeared the wall as the men dragged their fellow hostages and shoved them out. When the gunman watching them turned away to change a magazine in his assault rifle, Kutsayev took advantage of the moment and jumped out the window himself. He broke his leg in the fall and began crawling away from the building as his captor raced to the window and started shooting. Russian troops positioned nearby saw what was happening and lobbed several smoke grenades to cover him. Kutsayev, a thirty-three-year-old hardware store manager, escaped, but left behind his wife, two young daughters, and sixty-five-year-old mother-in-law.[19]

By then, authorities had set up a command center at the town hall, divided into two sections, one for civilian officials like Taimuraz Mansurov, the parliament speaker, and the other for law enforcement and military officers, led by the head of the regional FSB, General Valery Andreyev. But that did not answer the question of what to do.

Back in Moscow, the Kremlin dithered, uncertain how to handle a situation involving so many children. Negotiate? Storm the building? The men who had seized the school had not come prepared for serious talks—that was clear. They had come to kill. And storming offered little hope for success. The terrorists had placed snipers on the roof and mined the building. Putin interrupted his vacation in the Black Sea resort of Sochi and returned to Moscow. "When he flew in at night, it was enough to see his face to see that this person was grieving," Aslambek Aslakhanov, Putin's chief Chechnya adviser, told us later. "He was terribly upset. He had very tough discussions about the breakdowns that had occurred."[20] But he had these discussions in private and remained out of public view. He sent none of his cabinet ministers or other senior officials to Beslan. A presidential aide finally called Leonid Roshal, the children's doctor sought by the terrorists, and arranged for a government plane to send him to the scene.

Inside the headquarters in Beslan, the authorities still could not get through on the mobile phone number they had been given. Mansurov, the local parliament speaker, threw himself into the assignment of calling local utility officials to ensure that electricity and water would not be cut off to the school, in accordance with the terrorists' note. Privately, he was anguished. "I would walk somewhere where nobody could see me and I would cry like all the other parents," he told us. His aging mother told him not to come home without his children—dead or alive.[21]

Finally, four hours after the siege began, the hostage-takers called the headquarters, explaining they had written down the wrong mobile phone number on the note. They reiterated that they wanted to speak to Dzasokhov, Zyazikov, and Roshal and added a fourth name, Aslambek Aslakhanov. But the terrorists were growing angry at what they saw on television. The government was still saying there were only a few hundred hostages inside. The guerrillas assumed that meant the Russians were preparing to storm the building and lying in order to minimize the situation. They told the hostages that their leaders were sacrificing them. Then they brought Lydia Tsaliyeva, the principal, to the teachers' lounge they were using as a base. She was shocked at the mess they had made.

"Look what you've done," she scolded one of the gunmen. "You've ruined my school."

"I was a bad student," he said defiantly. "I had bad marks at school."

"You look like it."

They told her to talk to Dr. Roshal and handed her a phone. "Dr. Roshal," she said, "please help save the children." She told him there were twelve hundred hostages inside and the terrorists were furious at the government lies. Then they took the phone back.[22]

By nightfall, the first planes of Alpha commandos, Russia's most elite troops, landed at the nearby airport. They unpacked their guns and body armor and began preparing for battle.

WHEN WE arrived in Beslan late the first day, we found practically the entire town gathered around the local Palace of Culture, a cavernous hall lit by a glittering disco ball. Thousands of people milled in front or sat inside the building, waiting for word, among them Raya Tsolmayova and Taimuraz Totiyev, anxious about their five children. Since the moment the school had been seized, they had heard sporadic but frequent gunshots and rocket-propelled grenades. The parents pacing at the palace were never sure which shot might have been aimed at their little boy or girl. The crowd was angry at the obvious deception about how many children were inside and assailed every official who chanced into their midst. Their top regional leader, Aleksandr Dzasokhov, never dared come near them.

The state's response had been disorganized and dishonest. On state television, the Kremlin maintained tight control over what was said, refusing to allow anyone even to speculate that there were more people inside the school than the 354 that authorities had announced. Some Beslan residents grew so frustrated they attacked a state television crew; others tried to get the word out surreptitiously, holding up handwritten signs in the background of live shots informing viewers that there were more hostages than the state was admitting. Even independent journalists found themselves stymied. Anna Politkovskaya, an intrepid reporter for the newspaper *Novaya Gazeta* whose exposés on Russian abuses in Chechnya had earned her the lasting enmity of the Kremlin, raced to the region, only to find herself doubled over in pain after drinking tea on the plane flight down. She wound up in a hospital and never made it to Beslan, convinced that the tea was poisoned. Radio Liberty's Andrei Babitsky, who had drawn Putin's personal wrath for his gutsy reporting from the Chechen side years earlier, found himself arrested at a Moscow airport after several men picked a fight. The men who provoked him later whispered that they had been told to do so by airport security guards.

At the command center in Beslan, officials remained almost paralyzed with uncertainty. Only two of the four negotiators the guerrillas' Colonel had demanded were even in town, Dzasokhov and Roshal. Aslambek Aslakhanov, the Putin Chechnya adviser, remained in Moscow, unable to speak with the president directly, and Murat Zyazikov, the president of Ingushetia, was in hiding, ducking telephone calls.

Roshal offered to go in alone with food and water. The terrorist spokesman refused. "If you come by yourself without them," he said, "we will kill you."

Roshal tried to appeal to the man's sense of humanity. "These are kids."

"I'm from the mountains," the guerrilla answered, referring to Chechen honor.

"You're not a highlander if you seized women and children."[23]

The intelligence experts in the command center concluded that the hostage-takers had been ordered to take the school but never given instructions on what to do next and were still waiting for direction from the outside. The hostages noticed the guerrillas arguing among themselves, apparently because some were having second thoughts about taking children hostage. According to some accounts, the Colonel enforced a harsh discipline, shooting one of the dissenters to death. By the second day, the two female *shakhidki* had disappeared; the hostages assumed they had blown up, possibly by remote control triggered by the Colonel.

Back in Moscow, Putin broke his public silence more than twenty-four hours after the school seizure to vow that he would do all he could to free the children. "Our principal task in the current situation is of course to save the lives and health of the hostages," he said on state television.[24] By then, the Alpha commandos had begun preparing for a rescue operation, but the idea seemed impossible. Negotiations, officials in the command center decided, might be the only way. Uncertain what the terrorists wanted, officials tried to guess. An end to the war in Chechnya, they figured. But was there anything concrete that the authorities could offer them to end the siege peacefully? They decided to provide the terrorists a safe corridor to escape unharmed. They would offer them money, a plane, the release of thirty guerrillas who had been arrested after the recent raid in Ingushetia. "We were ready to propose anything," said Lev Dzugayev, an aide to the region's president.[25] It wasn't working. "We started to send them messages saying, 'Leave everything like it is and go away, we'll give you a corridor,'" said Taimuraz Mansurov, the parliament speaker. "But they didn't want to talk about it."[26]

Other officials were trying hardball. They rounded up forty relatives of Chechen rebel commanders Shamil Basayev and Aslan Maskhadov—in effect taking their own hostages. Some of them were children, including a five-month-old baby. The men were forced on their knees with sacks pulled over their heads and over the next twenty-four hours were kicked if they moved. The relatives were put on Grozny television to make sure everyone knew they were being held.[27] At one point, they brought to Beslan the wife and three children of one guerrilla inside the school. "She called her husband at the school and told him she was being held by the federal troops and told him not to kill children," said Mikhail Markelov. "He asked her to give the telephone to one of the officers, and when she did, he said, 'Kill her and all three of my kids.'"[28]

At an impasse, authorities turned to Ruslan Aushev, a Soviet Afghan war hero and former president of Ingushetia who had good contacts with Chechen figures. For Putin, calling in Aushev was not easy. Aushev had been a long-time skeptic of Putin's war in Chechnya, and the Kremlin had pressured him into resigning in Ingushetia in 2002, then rigged the election to replace him with Murat Zyazikov. But when a Putin lieutenant called to ask him to fly to Beslan, Aushev immediately said yes. By the time Aushev arrived, he was stunned to find that nearly a day and a half had gone by and no one had figured out even who should talk with the terrorists. Aushev was put on a phone with their spokesman. The spokesman told Aushev he would check with "the emir" and call back. Within fifteen minutes, the phone rang and Aushev was told he could come into the school.

The scene awaiting him inside the stifling hot school gym was increasingly desperate. The terrorists had given the hostages no food since the start and had now stopped giving them water. Many children had stripped down to their underwear and begun urinating into bottles to drink. Kazbek Dzaragasov, the boy who had escaped on the first day only to run back to be with his sister, worried that she was fading. He took his shirt off, peed on it, and gave it to her to squeeze the liquid onto herself.[29] "I could feel the moisture draining out of me," recalled Alik Tsagolov, the gym teacher. "Tension was rising. People became more and more nervous. Hope disappeared by the hour."[30]

Lydia Tsaliyeva, the principal, tried to reason with their captors. "Let the kids go and the adults stay," she pleaded with one of the leaders. "Feel mercy for the young."

"Who felt mercy for my children?" he growled back. "My house was bombed and five of my children were killed."[31]

When Aushev entered the building, the terrorists tried to put a black sack on his head, but he refused. He asked for their demands and the commander handed him a piece of notebook paper addressed, "To his Excellency, President of the Russian Federation Putin, from the servant of Allah, Shamil Basayev." Basayev was the shaven-headed, long-bearded, one-legged master terrorist of Chechnya. To the Russians, he was everything Osama bin Laden was to the Americans, the evil force behind suicide bombings, hostage-takings, and other attacks on civilians that had left hundreds dead. Once nearly a decade before he had stormed into a hospital and taken the entire building hostage, including more than a thousand doctors, nurses, and patients, a siege that would later end up with more than a hundred deaths.

Aushev read the note. In scrawled handwriting, it listed a series of demands: Russian troops should withdraw from Chechnya, which would be granted independence. Chechen and Russian authorities would work together to restore order in the Caucasus and prevent third parties from intervening. And, oddest of all, it stipulated that the newly liberated Chechnya would remain in the "ruble zone," meaning it would continue to use Russian currency. As soon as state television announced that Putin had signed a decree ordering a troop pullout, they would start releasing hostages. The commander added one more warning: if the Russians captured their relatives, half of the hostages would be killed.

Seeing no point in arguing about the demands, Aushev decided he had to see the hostages. He was led into the gym. "It was like a steam bath," he said. "Children there were almost naked because it was stuffy there, there was no water, and they had no food for more than two days. We were afraid that they would start dying there, suffering heart attacks and so on."[32]

At the sight of Aushev, a surge of excitement rippled through the room and some hostages clapped. "I asked them to hold on, told them that I would continue to negotiate and try to resolve this problem."[33] Then he was ushered out of the gym. The principal told him there were twelve hundred hostages, then got down on her knees. "Please, Ruslan, save our children," she begged.[34]

Aushev insisted that the terrorists release the nursing infants in the gym along with their mothers, and they agreed to let him take out twenty-five women and children. Among them was Fatima Tsgayeva, who was still breast-feeding her infant, Alyona. But Fatima had two other children in the school, ten-year-old Kristina and three-year-old Makhar. Fatima tried to have Kristina carry out little Alyona but one of the terrorists refused to let the older girl go and insisted that Fatima take her own baby out. For any mother, this would be a Sophie's choice—rescue your baby but leave two other children? Fatima handed the baby to Aushev, but stayed behind herself.[35]

When Aushev returned to the command center, he made clear how dire the situation was. Not only were there far more than 354 hostages, but conditions in the sweltering gym were deteriorating rapidly. They had to do something. Finally someone suggested contacting Aslan Maskhadov, the Chechen guerrilla commander seen as less radical than Basayev. For five years, the Russians had refused to talk with Maskhadov, refused to try to find any kind of peace with him and labeled him a terrorist. Now they reached out. With Putin's permission, Aushev and Dzasokhov called Akhmed Zakayev, Maskhadov's emissary living in asylum in London. Zakayev agreed to talk to Maskhadov but explained that he had only one-way communications with him; Maskhadov could call him but not the other way around. Zakayev told his callers that if Maskhadov came to Beslan to try to talk the hostage-takers out of the school, the Russians would have to guarantee his safety. Even though the Russians had been seeking his extradition, Zakayev then offered to come to Beslan himself without guarantees to talk to the gunmen. The callers hung up to think it over.[36]

ALIK TSAGOLOV, the gym teacher, did not sleep that night. Many adults were staring vacantly in the distance, the children were listless. No one even flinched anymore when the terrorists shot in the air. "I was completely convinced that we wouldn't live through the night," Tsagolov said. The hostages turned to each other increasingly fraught with fear. "They would get offended if someone wouldn't share their urine with them," the gym teacher remembered. Some students asked Tsagolov to urinate in a bottle for them; he could not bring himself to do it. "'But we're dying without water, please!'" he recalled one saying. "I wanted to do it but I just couldn't."[37]

The terrorists appeared to be more anxious as well. They came again for Lydia Tsaliyeva and ordered her to call the authorities. The principal knew Taimuraz Mansurov's children and went to find them so she could call the local parliament chief. Moments later, the mobile phone rang in the Russian command center. "I started speaking in Ossetian," she recalled, "just saying a word or two: 'We are dying. Please help us.'" Then the Colonel ordered her to speak Russian. She asked the Colonel to let Mansurov's eleven-year-old son, Zelim, speak with his father.[38]

"Papa," the boy said into the phone, "they are saying that there should be no storm. They said if there is a storm, they would blow us all up."

Mansurov was struck by the strength in his son's voice. "You're a man and you should be brave," he told the boy. "You have a sister there. And we are trying to take care of you." Mansurov added that they would try to prevent a raid. "There are others here who will make this decision. But if we hear something about a storm, the other parents and I will come over to you and let them blow us all up together."[39]

Putin had finally authorized his Chechnya adviser, Aslambek Aslakhanov, to go to Beslan, and as the plane lifted off from a Moscow airport, many in the command center hoped he was bringing something concrete from the president that would change the dynamics. They got back on the phone with Zakayev, the Chechen emissary in London, and talked about him coming to negotiate; just give them two hours to get things arranged, they told him.[40] In the meantime, authorities finally came to an agreement with the hostage-takers to remove the bodies of the men killed on the first day. They had been lying on the ground for forty-eight hours baking in the late-summer sun.

Four men dressed in uniforms of the Ministry of Emergency Situations pulled up in a truck outside the school at 1 p.m. They approached a window, where a hostage-taker gave them orders, then disappeared around the side of the school, found the body of a guerrilla killed in the opening moments of the siege, and carried him inside. Hefting an assault rifle, another terrorist in brown civilian pants and camouflage shirt emerged from the school to monitor them. The rescue workers leaned down to pick up the first body of a civilian.[41]

Suddenly a giant clap of thunder split the air. Then another, even louder, just seconds later. Then came the shooting.

No one knew what was happening. Inside the gym, a bomb had exploded, followed by a second, more powerful blast. Scores of children and adults were killed instantly. Pieces of the roof began falling on the survivors. "I felt my whole chest burst," said Alik Tsagolov. "The whole floor was covered by bodies."[42] Lydia Tsaliyeva was knocked unconscious, her legs shredded by shrapnel. Kazbek Dzaragasov couldn't find his sister, the one he had returned to the school for. Three of Raya Tsolmayova's five children were already dead; Madina, the twelve-year-old, opened her eyes after the explosions to a macabre scene—smoke, flying flesh, a woman with no legs screaming, people stepping on each other to flee. Madina started calling her sisters and brother but only found one.

"Madina, it's me, Lyuba," her younger sister cried out.

Lyuba looked like minced meat, all burned, her legs shot through. Madina could see her sister's bones sticking out of the flesh. "Lyuba, is that you?"

"Yes, it's me."

"Let's go."

"No, I just want to sleep."

Madina put her arms around Lyuba and began dragging her along the floor as she crawled toward the weight room.[43]

Other children jumped out the shattered windows and ran for their lives. Their captors began shooting at them, hitting some in the back. Neighbor Kazbek Torchinov watched in horror as two little boys scrambled in the direction of his house and one of them suddenly pitched forward to the ground, evidently gunned down.[44] Outside the school, many local men who had been standing vigil with guns retrieved from their homes had long since penetrated the porous security cordon; now, they began firing, too. The soldiers nearby had orders not to shoot and for a few minutes they held back, unsure what was happening. The Alpha commando squad was not even in place; as the battle began, they raced over toward the school so fast that many did not take time to put on their flak vests, a mistake that would prove fatal for several. Some commandos threw their bodies over the fleeing children to protect them and were killed by gunfire from the building; others were shot in the back by local men firing at the school. The rescue workers who had come to retrieve the bodies dove for their vehicle, but three of the four were shot down and the fourth injured.

For a few minutes, both sides tried to stop the situation from spiraling out of control. One of the hostage-takers frantically called the government's command center insisting they were not blowing up the building while the Russians insisted they had not launched a raid. But it was too late. Eventually, the Interior Ministry's heavily armed OMON troops, the equivalent of an American SWAT team, began opening fire as well.

"We didn't get any orders," one of the soldiers told us later. "When they started shooting at the children ... we started supporting them. We were aiming for the snipers on the roof but we didn't aim for the windows. We didn't fire at the building." The presence of so many hostages made it difficult to mount an effective assault. "We had orders not to shoot at the bottom of the building," another of the OMON soldiers said. "We were confused. We didn't know when to shoot." The armed civilians only made the situation worse, he added. "They were just getting in the way. There were so many of them. They were so aggressive, it was impossible to push them aside." In effect, a third soldier added, "We had to fight on two fronts."[45]

In the gym, the terrorists ordered the surviving hostages to move to the hall if they wanted to live. Those who couldn't get up were shot.[46]

From a block away, we could hear such an intense cacophony of gunfire and explosions it was clear a bloodbath was under way. Even the most intense battles we had witnessed as correspondents in Iraq or Afghanistan paled by comparison. Armored personnel carriers sped along the roads toward the school, with special forces soldiers in bandannas jumping off, carrying Kalashnikov assault rifles and heavy machine guns. Dozens of ambulances followed. Helicopters hovered overhead. Within minutes, we could see local men carrying half-naked children in their arms—fathers and uncles and brothers who had raced right into the school yard, in the midst of the battle with bullets flying everywhere, to save their kids.

Suddenly, a giant cloud of smoke emerged from the school. What was left of the gym roof had collapsed. A barefoot boy wearing only pants and looking about ten years old staggered past us. He had been blown out of the window by the initial explosion. "Many, many dead," he muttered. "Many dead children."

Even as the gun battle raged on, a makeshift evacuation began. Not nearly enough ambulances were on hand, so every man in town, it seemed, drove his own car to the scene. They screeched up, jumped out, and threw open the back door. "Here, here!" they yelled. Other men carried out blackened and bruised bodies of children and deposited them into the closest car, whereupon the driver would burst off toward the hospital at top speed. One little girl, completely naked, looked dead. A man lay her down on the grass, sobbing as he tried to revive her. A woman covered in burns was set down on a stretcher in front of us for a moment. "Water, water," she whispered. We found a bottle of water for her and she gulped it down. A young girl on a stretcher told a local police officer, "They're killing us and they're blowing everything up." From time to time, the shooting would grow closer and the would-be rescuers, and journalists, would scatter and run a block away, only to wait for it to die down and edge back again.

Four dead bodies were laid out on the grass in front of us, covered by white sheets stained with blood. They were children, the yellowed foot of one of them sticking out from beneath the sheet. A fifth body was brought out, that of an older woman, and was rolled off a stretcher unceremoniously onto the ground next to the corpses of the children. Eventually parents started approaching, peeking under each of the sheets to see if the dead children were theirs. "Are there dead children?" called out one red-haired woman looking for her twelve-year-old nephew. "Where are the dead children?"

Inside the school, Alik Tsagolov and scores of hostages were huddled in the cafeteria. Gunfire and explosions erupted all around them. A young man in street clothes with short hair and stubble on his chin approached the gym teacher and sank down next to him. He seemed wobbly. Tsagolov realized that the man was not a hostage, but one of the terrorists. He did not give his name, but he was Nur-Pashi Kulayev, a twenty-four-year-old from a village in Chechnya who had served in the Russian army.

"If they take us alive, can you confirm that I had no weapon?" Kulayev pleaded with Tsagolov. "They made me do this. They took my whole family and promised to shoot them down."

"How can I know that?" Tsagolov replied.

"See? I have no weapon. I didn't kill anybody."

Tsagolov could hardly vouch for the man's behavior over the last three days. "I'll say that at the moment I saw you, you had no weapon."

Their other captors were nowhere to be seen at the moment. Tsagolov began trying to evacuate some of the children, ordering them to jump out the first-floor window and run. Several made it. "Then a little boy, seven or eight years old, was standing there ready to jump and one of the terrorists shot him and killed him," Tsagolov said. "The bullet probably went through his heart. The blood was pulsing out."

Tsagolov turned to Kulayev, the scared terrorist. "Tell your guys to stop shooting!" the gym teacher ordered.

Kulayev tried, but the gunman cut him off. "Shut up or we'll shoot you, too," he shouted.

Several loud explosions erupted and the room grew dark with clouds of smoke. Tanks were firing at the school. Tsagolov realized they could be killed by their own troops. By then, the other gunman had disappeared, so Tsagolov turned again to Kulayev.

"Get up and look out the window," he ordered.

"They'll kill me," Kulayev protested.

"You're a sinner. At least clean up some of your sins."

Kulayev peeked out the window and announced, "They're special forces."

"You go out first and if they don't kill you, the rest will follow," Tsagolov said.

"I don't want to leave."

"You don't have a choice."

Tsagolov grabbed Kulayev and forced him to the window. Kulayev jumped, shouting, "I didn't kill anybody!"

Within a few moments, three Russian commandos appeared in the window. One of them covered the hostages with his body and ordered them to get out of the building. Tsagolov helped the children jump, then leapt himself.[47]

It had taken four hours for the Alpha special forces to make their way into the building; once there, they found a deadly maze of barricades, booby traps, and other obstacles. A sniper and machine gunner awaited them on the first floor. Shooting and explosions continued well into the night. Of the thirty-two terrorists, according to official accounts, thirty were killed. One of the two survivors was being led away from the school by Russian troops when a mob of Beslan residents spotted him, shoved the soldiers out of the way, and tore the guerrilla to death on the street. The other survivor was Kulayev, who would later be put on state television to give a well-rehearsed version of how the operation had come to pass under the leadership of Shamil Basayev.[48]

Alik Tsagolov lived, but he had lost track of his sister-in-law and her two children. He later discovered that all three had died. So, too, did Fatima Tsgayeva, who had given her baby to negotiator Ruslan Aushev and then gone back into the school on the second day of the siege to stay with her other two children. Her body was found battered and lifeless; her daughter Kristina was burned to death. Kazbek Dzaragasov, who had escaped on the first day only to turn around for his sister, lost her in the confusion but later found her in the hospital, alive. Lydia Tsaliyeva, the principal who was knocked out by the first explosions, came to and was carried out of the building. Taimuraz Mansurov, the parliament speaker, found his two children at the hospital, injured but alive.

Madina, the twelve-year-old daughter of Raya Tsolmayova and Taimuraz Totiyev, dragged her wounded sister to the weight room and tried to care for her there. Madina grabbed a wooden board, used lipstick to write on it, "Don't shoot, children are here," and held it up to the window. Russian troops broke the window and climbed inside. "Don't take me, take Lyuba," Madina shouted. The soldiers passed Lyuba, then Madina, out the window. But Lyuba's injuries were too severe. She died at the hospital. So did two of their cousins; a third lost his eye. Of the eight children who had left the Totiyev brothers' combined household two days earlier, only two would make it home.[49]

VLADIMIR PUTIN remained cloistered at the Kremlin, publicly silent through the battle. As children died and the school crumbled in what was clearly the worst terrorist attack in the world since September 11, Russia's president did nothing to reassure his nation or share in the public horror. None of the officials in the command center in Beslan publicly recalled Putin playing any role whatsoever in what happened that day. Not until the middle of the night, after it became clear the battle was finally over, did Putin emerge. He got on a presidential jet, flew to Vladikavkaz, the regional capital, and made a predawn visit to the hospital. "All of Russia grieves with you," he said.[50] He was gone again before the town even woke up and realized he had ever been there.

Putin's public performance was typical of his reaction to major crises— long silence followed by a brief, heavily staged appearance shown over and over on television, a pattern of official deception by his government, and finally a lengthy if overdue presidential speech filled with tough talk about hunting down the perpetrators even if it required more trade-offs of Russia's already fragile freedoms. The government had lied from the beginning about the number of hostages, angering both the terrorists and the relatives. It continued to spin out falsehoods as the siege came to a bloody end. Authorities showed footage on state television of the corpses of what they said were ten Arabs and an African among the hostage-takers to make it seem as if they were tied to Al Qaeda instead of Chechnya, even though hostages did not see any Arabs or Africans. And the state almost surely covered up the real death toll.

When the first bombs exploded, CNN and the BBC immediately went to live coverage from Beslan, but Russia's state television networks, controlled by the Kremlin, did not cut into regular programming for an hour, leaving viewers watching a comedy film called *A Lady with a Parrot* on Channel One and *In Search of Adventures,* a Discovery Channel–type program featuring a man's travels to exotic world locales, on the Rossiya channel. Neither network aired a news report on the battle until 2 p.m. By 2:06 p.m., Channel One had dropped the newscast in favor of episode sixty-one of *Women in Love,* a Brazilian soap opera. Ekho Moskvy radio, the last truly independently run broadcaster in Russia, had to resort to watching CNN to tell listeners what was happening.

Even when the state channels were reporting the battle, they presented it with a ludicrous spin. "According to the latest information, the fighting in the school is over," the anchor on Rossiya intoned at one point while gunfire was still blazing at the scene. "There are no dead or wounded there. . . . We can't give more exact figures of the injured—er, the precise figure of how many hostages were freed." NTV, Russia's first independent and most professional news network until it was taken over by a state-controlled company in 2001 at the direction of Putin's Kremlin, was broadcasting an update from Beslan when the battle began, but mentioned nothing of the explosions and gunfire and eventually turned to sports. When it returned later in the afternoon, it continued to censor itself. At one point, a correspondent on the scene reported that he had heard police radios indicating many injured and dead were in the school. The anchor interrupted him. "We have to stop," he scolded. "We cannot broadcast this information. It is unconfirmed." By evening, Rossiya was showing a military documentary series called *On My Honor,* in which heroic Russian soldiers battle evil Chechen bandits. Channel One showed Bruce Willis fighting terrorists in *Die Hard.*[51]

Even the print press, which had been relatively unscathed by Putin's media clampdown, came under pressure. Raf Shakirov, the editor of *Izvestiya,* one of the biggest and most reputable of Moscow's myriad newspapers, had turned over the full front and back pages of his Saturday edition to giant photographs of parents clutching bloodied children; he was immediately fired by the paper's oligarch owners after the Kremlin complained. Authorities tried to minimize the scale of the massacre, and distrust of the state had grown so pervasive in Beslan that many suspected the real death toll was higher than the official body count of 330, even without evidence.[52] The government also gave conflicting numbers of hostage-takers and whether some got away. They initially said they took three terrorists alive, then two, then just one—Nur-Pashi Kulayev. Even as the authorities were claiming that none of the terrorists got away, we ran into a squadron of special forces sweeping through a Beslan neighborhood searching for an escaped *shakhidka.* They ordered our Russian assistant to take off her sweater so they could see if she had bruises, as the woman they were searching for reportedly did.

When Putin finally did speak out, he addressed none of this. In a nationally televised speech a day and a half after the end of the siege, he condemned the attack as "unprecedented in its inhumanity and cruelty," perpetrated by "international terror directed against Russia," and promised unspecified measures "to create a new system of coordinating the forces" that fight terrorism. "In general," he said, "we need to admit that we did not fully understand the complexity and the dangers of the processes at work in our own country and in the world. In any case, we proved unable to react adequately. We showed ourselves to be weak. And the weak get beaten."

For Putin, that was the cardinal sin—appearing weak. More revealing still was his diagnosis of this weakness, a national ailment that he blamed on the end of the Soviet Union. "Russia has lived through many tragic events and terrible ordeals over the course of its history. Today we live in a time that follows the collapse of a vast and great state, a state that, unfortunately, proved unable to survive in a rapidly changing world." In the new Russia, he added, "We all hoped for change, change for the better. But many of the changes that took place in our lives found us unprepared. Why? We are living at a time of an economy in transition, of a political system that does not yet correspond to the state and level of our society's development. We are living through a time when internal conflicts and interethnic divisions that were once firmly suppressed by the ruling ideology have now flared up. We stopped paying the required attention to defense and security issues and we allowed corruption to undermine our judicial and law enforcement system."[53] Never once did the word *Chechnya* pass his lips.

In all of this, the only crack in the veil of official disinformation came the next night on Rossiya television. The state channel aired gruesome footage from the siege that it had censored at the time, then acknowledged that the state had lied about the number of hostages who were being held. "At such moments," presenter Sergei Brilyov declared on the air, "society needs the truth." But it was only part of an effort to inoculate Putin from public outrage. The lie was undeniable by this point, so the broadcast pinned responsibility on the bureaucracy and security establishment. The network did not touch on any of the other lies, only the one that could no longer plausibly be defended. Then, the station put Kremlin political consultant Gleb Pavlovsky on the air to claim the president himself was upset at the deception. "Lies, which really acted in the terrorists' favor, did not suit him at all," Pavlovsky said.[54] A Kremlin aide later told us privately, and bluntly, that truth was simply not the highest priority.[55]

Putin was busy nursing his anger and frustration in the solitude of the Kremlin. The night after the Rossiya broadcast, he invited a group of visiting Western scholars and journalists to his dacha outside Moscow, then spent three and a half hours talking with them about Beslan, Chechnya, and Russia. He rejected the idea of a parliamentary investigation as nothing more than "a political show" that would "not be very productive." Instead he focused blame on Boris Yeltsin and on the West. The war in Chechnya was due to "weak leaders" of the 1990s and mistakes that "I would not have made," he told the visitors, conveniently ignoring his own role in starting the second Chechen war in 1999.

His attack on the West was more hard-edged. He lashed out at those who had tried to pressure him to find a political settlement to the war, comparing it to negotiating with Al Qaeda. "Why don't you meet Osama bin Laden, invite him to Brussels or to the White House, engage in talks, ask him what he wants and give it to him so he leaves you in peace? You find it possible to set some limits in your dealings with these bastards, so why should we talk to people who are child killers?" He quoted from what he presented as surveillance of the terrorists talking over a radio during the siege. "One asks, 'What's happening? I hear noise.' And the other says, 'It's okay, I'm in the middle of shooting some kids. There's nothing to do.' They were bored, so they shot kids. What kind of freedom fighters are these?"

It was a straw man, of course. The West had long ago lost any sense of romance about the Chechen guerrillas, and no one in any position of authority called them freedom fighters. But once again, Putin turned back to the collapse of the Soviet Union as the source of his troubles. The West wanted to keep Russia down. "It's a replay of the mentality of the Cold War," he said. "Certain people want Russia focused on its internal problems. They pull the strings so that Russia won't raise its head." He gestured with his hands as if he were yanking the strings of a marionette. "I've seen it with my own eyes. We're seeing partners in the antiterror coalition having a difficult dilemma. They might want to pull the strings without transgressing the point at which it goes against their own interests."[56]

For more than a week, he offered little more—no plans for reform, no details about what had happened. Back in Moscow, his aides took over a demonstration in support of the people of Beslan organized by a popular radio station and turned it into a Putin pep rally on Red Square, complete with premade signs: "Putin We Are with You." And then he unveiled his plan for fighting terrorism in Russia: a further rollback of democracy. He announced that he would eliminate the direct election of governors and appoint them himself. And he would also get rid of the election of individual members of the State Duma and have all seats filled by party leaders based on voting proportions from a party-list ballot. He took a planned power-grab he had been quietly preparing for months and presented it as the response to Beslan. It would promote "unity of the country" and create a "single chain of command," he said, but did not explain how eliminating elections in the future would prevent terrorism today.[57]

A prominent democratic politician told us it amounted to "the beginning of a constitutional coup d'état" and a "step toward dictatorship."[58] And the West reacted with shock, seeing it as a regression toward the days of Soviet tyranny.

But the only people who were surprised were those who had not been paying attention to the previous five years in Putin's Russia.

Project Putin

Nobody knew he would be president. But all the boys and girls knew that Volodya Putin was a genuine friend and someone you can rely on. Then he became a grown-up, studied a lot, and worked. He helped good people and very much disliked bad people. He often traveled and was away from home for a long time—that was the kind of work he had. His friends, his wife and daughters, missed him. Vladimir always came back because he loved his home, his family, and his friends very much. And he is still not afraid of anything. He flies in fighter planes, skis down mountains, and goes where there is fighting to stop wars. And all the other presidents of other countries meet him and respect him very much. And they show this on television and write about it in the newspapers. Then he had so many friends—the entire country of Russia—and they elected him president. Now everyone says: "Russia, Putin, Unity!"[1]

—ST. PETERSBURG SCHOOL TEXTBOOK

VLADIMIR PUTIN WAS accustomed to cover stories. In sixteen years as a KGB officer, he had masqueraded as a translator, a diplomat, and a university administrator. He told his future wife when he met her that he was a police officer. And so when it came to assuming a new role in that troubled summer of 1999, Putin was ready.

No one knew much about the man anointed as the next president of Russia, and that was the way his Kremlin designers wanted it. Onto the empty tableau was painted the idealized image of a leader for the new Russia, a sober modernizer who would rescue a hobbled nation and restore its historic greatness. By the time schoolchildren in his native St. Petersburg showed up for classes a year later, Putin had vaulted from nobody to virtual tsar, the subject of a hagiographic portrait included in a new school textbook paid for by a Kremlin-manufactured political party called Unity that had not even existed a year earlier. The real Putin, of course, bore only scant resemblance to the cover story. Far from stopping wars, as the children were instructed, Putin's first act in office was to start one.

But if it was a cover story, it was one that Russia was eager to embrace. After nearly a decade of post-Soviet dislocation, Russians desperately awaited a new leader who would put the 1990s behind them. They had watched as the favored few ripped off state assets in rigged auctions, while the working masses lost their life savings in an economic crash. They had seen the pseudodemocracy introduced after the collapse of the Soviet Union corrupted by those with power, while political differences were resolved with tank fire in the streets of Moscow. They had suffered through the embarrassments of an ailing, intoxicated president who disappeared for weeks at a stretch, while his government failed to pay wages and frittered away billions of dollars of international aid. Rather than as the chosen successor to Boris Yeltsin, they came to see Vladimir Putin as the antidote to Boris Yeltsin. Just as the coterie of tycoons and advisers surrounding Yeltsin wanted them to.

The emergence of the new tsar spawned a cult of personality. Soon after his surprise selection as prime minister and Yeltsin's heir apparent, the myth of Vladimir Putin was being spun across the nation. His photograph was dutifully mounted in government offices. A memorial was erected in the Pskov region to mark Putin's path during a recent tour, dubbed "A Walk Along the Places Visited by President Vladimir Putin in Izborsk," complete with plaques at a waterfall he stopped to admire and a square where he tasted a freshly salted cucumber. It was to be only the beginning of the slavish testimonials. Eventually there would be Putin roads and schools, a Putin chocolate sculpture, Putin T-shirts, Putin calendars, Putin Easter eggs, Putin toothpicks, even a new variety of tomato named after Putin. A pop song called "I Want a Man like Putin," devised by an enterprising state public relations official named Nikolai Gastello, would soar to the top of the Russian charts, featuring the lyrical lament of a young woman swooning over the decidedly unmagnetic president:

> And now I want a man like Putin,
> A man like Putin, full of energy.
> A man like Putin, who doesn't drink.
> A man like Putin, who won't hurt me.
> A man like Putin, who won't leave me.[2]

It did not take much for Putin to genuinely impress a country fed up with Yeltsin. Sobriety alone became a major element of Putin's appeal, in contrast to his frequently drunken predecessor; one poll found that 40 percent of Russians said the quality they admired most in the new president was that he was sober.[3] Where past Russian leaders were sometimes bombastic, buffoonish, or fossilized, Putin seemed young and vigorous, cool and detached.

He was hardly a dominating figure in any room, a relatively short man at five foot nine, rail thin with a retreating hairline, hard eyes, and a strained, joyless smile. In keeping with his KGB training, he had a skill for listening and taking on the persona desired by his interlocutors. But Putin was not a born president. He commanded no mass following, articulated no grand vision for his country, had never been elected to public office. At the time of his elevation to prime minister, polls recorded his popularity rating at just 2 percent. He was the creation of one of the most extraordinary political projects in history; Project Putin, as some of those in the Kremlin came to call the effort they were enlisted to run. The oligarchs and operatives around Yeltsin virtually invented Putin, using their command over state television to concoct his image and tear down rivals. They viewed him as a loyalist they could control, only to discover how wrong they were. The project had a life of its own.

Vladimir Vladimirovich Putin was born in the northern city of Leningrad on October 7, 1952, the year before Stalin's death, to a family—and a city—marked by the long shadow of the Nazi siege and the equally formidable legacy of a state shaped by the tyrannical whims of one man. Putin's grandfather, Spiridon, had been a cook for Lenin's family after the Bolshevik revolution and was later transferred to one of Stalin's dachas, where he worked for many years. The nature of the relationship between Spiridon Putin and Stalin remains unknown. "Few people who spent much time around Stalin came through unscathed," Putin once acknowledged, "but my grandfather was one of them."[4] Exactly why, he said he did not know, but it would speak to the survival skills that the grandson would inherit and demonstrate throughout his unlikely political rise.

The proximity to power did not protect the family during World War II, a cataclysmic event in Leningrad, besieged by the Germans for an epic nine hundred days in a blockade that left hundreds of thousands dead. Putin's father, Vladimir Spiridonovich, served at the front, assigned to a demolition battalion of the NKVD, the forerunner of the KGB. Once deposited into German-held territory in Estonia to blow up a munitions dump, Vladimir Spiridonovich's unit became trapped by the Nazis and he barely managed to escape by hiding underwater in a swamp breathing through a hollow reed. Later, he was nearly killed by a German grenade during a battle at Nevsky

Pyatachok, where eight hundred Russian soldiers were dying every day; his legs were shredded by shrapnel. Putin's mother, Maria, trapped inside the city, was so stricken by hunger that she fell into a comatose state and was taken for dead. The senior Vladimir's injuries would ultimately save his wife, since he received food rations from the military hospital and passed them on to Maria. But it was not enough to save their sons; one died shortly after birth, the other died of diphtheria.[5]

By the time their third and final son came along seven years after the war, plans for reconstruction of the city remained unfulfilled. The Germans had wiped out almost everything—including 526 schools, 101 museums, 840 factories, 71 bridges, and the homes of 716,000 Leningraders—and the Soviets were still rebuilding throughout Putin's youth.[6] His was not the Leningrad of gilt palaces, the Hermitage museum, and proud poets, but a working-class city of deprivation. Vladimir Spiridonovich had gotten a job as a toolmaker in a train car factory despite the lifelong limp from battle wounds in one of his legs and eventually became secretary of the factory's Communist Party cell. Maria cleaned buildings as a janitor, made night deliveries for a bakery, and washed test tubes in a laboratory. She was forty-one years old when she had Vladimir Vladimirovich—nicknamed alternately Vovka or Volodya—as a late-life replacement for the sons they had lost. The family shared a fifth-floor communal apartment provided by the factory, occupying a single room themselves and sharing the kitchen with a family of three and a middle-aged couple. The apartment had neither shower nor hot water; the toilet was jammed against the landing and the staircases were pocked with gaps. Vovka and his parents went to public bathhouses to wash themselves. At home, they dodged the "hordes of rats in the front entryway," as Putin vividly recalled. Once, he cornered a particularly large rodent, which then turned fiercely on the boy and chased him down the hall.[7]

Putin's father was a hard man, silent and severe, not given to expressing affection for his son. "Vladimir Spiridonovich was tough," recalled Vera Gurevich, the boy's favorite schoolteacher. "He used to say that it was the only way to bring up a boy. Just watching them, it was hard to say whether they loved each other or not, whether they understood each other or not. . . . He was a very reserved person, not demonstrative at all, keeping everything inside. Volodya took after his father in this."[8] Sergei Roldugin, a longtime friend and godfather of one of Putin's daughters, recalled that Putin and his father argued a lot. "He was a man of *staraya zakalka*," Roldugin said, a phrase that Russians translate as "a man of the old stamp," a harsh, old-fashioned figure. "Vladimir Spiridonovich was of a tough breed. He always worked at a plant.

He could be a prototype for old Soviet movies, an example for others. For people like him, things were either black or white. He thought that a man must make a man's decisions."[9]

By most accounts, including his own, young Vladimir Putin was a foul-mouthed juvenile delinquent. He hung out with the local troublemakers, got into fights, barely bothered with his schoolwork. The Pioneers, the main Soviet youth group, in which membership was obligatory for all but the worst students, would not accept him at first. Once he and his friends got on a train and left the city in the middle of winter without telling his parents; his father beat him with a belt when he got home. Gurevich met him when he was eleven. Everyone told her he was a "hooligan," she recalled. "He had to test everything on his own skin, as we say in Russia, both good and bad things. I saw who he was hanging around with—kids from the neighborhood who were much older than he was. They were smoking, spitting. They had contests like who would spit the farthest or who could make up a more ingenious dirty word. And Vladimir was among them." He took offense easily and fought back eagerly. "He would never be anybody's serf. His way would be to snarl back, even at an older boy, and get a slap. But he would go after his offender, grab hold of him, and fight. . . . He always fought back—kicking, biting, anything."[10] Putin also used the word *hooligan* to describe himself as a child. "I really was a bad boy," he recalled.[11]

Something changed in the sixth grade. He had gotten just threes on a five-point grading scale the year before, and Gurevich lectured him about growing up. "I feel ashamed for you," she recalled telling him. "Are you going to remain a mediocrity your whole life?"[12] Gurevich set up a German class and pushed Vovka to enroll; he found he had a facility for the language. He took up sports—first boxing, then, after his nose was broken, sambo, a form of judo, and then judo itself. Putin, small and wiry, proved a natural. He later credited it with changing his life. "It was sports that dragged me off the streets."[13]

But it was books and movies that propelled him to the KGB. He was captivated by Soviet spy stories, especially the classic *The Sword and the Shield,* a nearly six-hour, black-and-white serial that came out in 1968, depicting a heroic Soviet agent working undercover in Nazi Germany. The quiet hero, Yogan Vais, won the trust of his superiors while he secretly betrayed them. And so the son of an NKVD veteran and grandson of Stalin's cook resolved to join the secret police. In ninth grade, according to the public version he gave later, the spindly teenager showed up at the local KGB directorate and inquired how he could sign up. An indulgent officer explained that he would first have to serve in the army or receive higher education such as law school. And, he added, the KGB did not take volunteers; if the KGB wanted him, it would come and find him.

VLADIMIR PUTIN took the advice to heart, steering his way to Leningrad State University law school in hopes of attracting the KGB's attention. He succeeded. Recruited in his final year, he idealized the spy service as the embodiment of the Soviet state rather than an instrument of repression. He disregarded the secret police's role in Stalin's Great Terror, its function as the conveyor belt for millions of innocent Russians condemned to the gulag. "I didn't think about the purges," he said later. "My notion of the KGB came from romantic spy stories. I was a pure and utterly successful product of Soviet patriotic education." Indeed, he soon became a weapon against those who dared stand against the Soviet state. He recalled almost with perverse pride how the KGB broke up demonstrations by dissidents. "They would think up some act of protest and then invite diplomats and reporters in order to attract the attention of the international community. What could we do? We couldn't disperse them because we had no orders to do so. So we would organize our own laying of the wreaths at exactly the same place where the reporters were supposed to gather. We would call in the regional party committee and the trade unions, and the police would rope everything off. Then we'd show up with a brass band. We would lay down our wreaths. The journalists and the diplomats would stand and watch for a while, yawn a couple of times, and go home."[14]

Putin's path through the KGB started in 1975 but remains largely shrouded in secrecy. What is known suggests a rather modest career at best. He studied at KGB schools in Leningrad and Moscow. His instructor at the Red Banner Institute was distinctly unimpressed. "I wrote about several negative characteristics in his evaluation," the instructor recalled. "It seemed to me that he was somewhat withdrawn and uncommunicative."[15] The official version holds that Putin served most of his time in Service Number 1 in Leningrad, a second-tier office responsible for monitoring foreigners in the city, but others suspect he might have been assigned, like his close friend Viktor Cherkesov, to the notorious Fifth Directorate, established to persecute dissidents. "The details of his biography are just not known," said historian Nikita Petrov, an expert on the Soviet special services. "We don't know anything about the work he did in Leningrad."[16]

The high-water mark of his career evidently was an assignment as a case officer in the Soviet client state of East Germany, although even then it's not

clear whether Putin was promoted to the prestigious foreign intelligence service or merely seconded there on temporary assignment. Of 450 KGB spies in
East Germany in those days, 400 of them were based in East Berlin. Not
Putin. Arriving in the second-tier post of Dresden in August 1985, he
reported for duty to a gray, two-story villa at Number Four Angelikstrasse on
a hill overlooking the Elbe River and across the street from the district office
of the Stasi, the East German intelligence agency. Putin's official cover was
deputy director of the House of German-Soviet Friendship, but his assignment was to recruit potential agents. He was, according to former KGB general Oleg Kalugin, "a nobody."[17]

One of the only testimonials from someone with firsthand knowledge
came from Vladimir Usoltsev, who worked alongside Putin at the KGB office
in Dresden. As Usoltsev remembered it, Putin was a competent but unspec-
tacular officer who ingratiated himself with his superiors and gave the
impression of "a true Communist." At times, Usoltsev recalled Putin expressing outrage at examples of lawlessness he saw in the deteriorating Soviet system or concluding that the war in Afghanistan was "utterly senseless and
criminal." But Putin was hardly a reformer, even if he occasionally showed
sympathy for the budding capitalists back home arrested for currency trading. "No matter how sorry Volodya felt for those *valutchiki* and other victims
of the Soviet justice system, he wanted to live for his own pleasure, without
stuffing his head with unnecessary worries," Usoltsev said. "He liked to see the
world, to have fun, to have a glass of beer. All his *dissidentstvo* was reduced to
one phrase: 'When socialism was not developed well enough, one could buy
sausage in the shops.'"[18]

Putin had almost married a girlfriend in college, then left her at the altar.
In Leningrad, he had met a young flight attendant named Lyudmila, who initially considered him plain and dull but married him anyway. They had a
daughter in Leningrad and then a second in Dresden. Life in East Germany
with his growing family was easy and the stocks of food in the stores more
plentiful than back home. Putin regularly ordered kegs of beer and put on
twenty-five pounds. "He didn't look like a man who had highly ambitious
plans for the future," Usoltsev said. "He was just an ordinary toiler and con-
formist who put up with the system."[19]

The system, though, began disappearing while Putin was in Germany. In
1989, as the Berlin Wall fell and the Soviet Union lost its grip on its Eastern
European satellites, the people of Dresden were in the streets as well, and Putin
began burning documents in his office, shoving so many papers into the fur-
nace that it burst. The crowd stormed the Stasi headquarters, then turned to

the KGB office not far away. Putin took an automatic pistol from one of the security guards and went outside to face the mob. Pointedly cocking the gun, he warned that he would open fire on anyone who tried to scale the fence. The crowd demanded to know who he was. A translator, he told them.

Back inside, Putin tried to obtain instructions on what to do. "We cannot do anything without orders from Moscow," he was told. "And Moscow is silent."[20]

Moscow is silent. That phrase would stick with Putin for years to come. It was a betrayal of Russia's agents in the field. It was the collapse of state power, the end of empire, and he deeply resented it.

Putin was given one last mission in Dresden: to recruit a spy ring to continue reporting back to Moscow even in the newly unifying Germany. Putin chose veteran Stasi operatives but proved a poor judge of character. One member of the ring went to German intelligence eleven months after Putin left for Russia and confessed all. The Germans eventually rounded up the rest of Putin's fifteen agents.[21] Putin was recalled to Leningrad in January 1990, bringing with him a twenty-year-old washing machine given to him by his German neighbors and a sinking realization that his career with the KGB, and maybe the KGB itself, was almost over.

THE COUNTRY that Vladimir Putin returned to was hardly the same one he had left five years earlier. The perestroika reforms of Mikhail Gorbachev had flowered into a movement that was transforming the Soviet Union. The KGB faced the prospect of losing its grip over society; the dissidents it was set up to persecute now had their own seats in parliament. The sword and the shield no longer ruled unchallenged.

Putin found himself at a personal turning point as well. Embittered by Moscow's silence as East Germany fell, Putin later claimed he had begun entertaining second thoughts about his mission in life. At the very least, he had come to understand he had no real future in the organization. He had risen to lieutenant colonel in the KGB and would never make general, so he began thinking about other job opportunities. For a while, he contemplated becoming a taxi driver. Instead, he returned to his alma mater, Leningrad State University, and obtained a job as an assistant to the rector. Putin was still in the service of the KGB, operating undercover, assigned to keep an eye on the university students and professors. Through a friend, he got in touch with his old law professor Anatoly Sobchak, a tall, charismatic speaker who at the time was head of Leningrad's city council and one of the country's most prominent liberal reformers.

Whether the KGB ordered him to infiltrate Sobchak's inner circle remains unknown. But when Sobchak asked him to come to work as an assistant, Putin disclosed his KGB affiliation. "Screw it," Sobchak said, and hired him anyway.[22] "I was struck by the fact that I didn't even ask him about that but he himself brought it up, saying, 'It might tarnish your reputation as a democrat,'" Sobchak told his wife, Lyudmila Narusova, that night.[23] Putin then went to his KGB superiors, according to his account, and offered to resign in order to take the job. The KGB officials saw no reason for him to quit and let him remain in "active reserves." Putin went to work making himself essential to Sobchak, who was on his way to becoming the first elected mayor of Leningrad. The move earned further disapproval from Putin's stern father. "He didn't quite like the new democratic changes," recalled Putin's friend Sergei Roldugin.[24]

Putin's past, though, would not let him go so easily. Putin's secret service colleagues approached him and asked him to forge Sobchak's name to some documents; he said he refused. Word of his secret affiliation filtered through to local politicians who opposed Sobchak and tried to use it against the mayor. Putin claims this was when he finally decided to end his KGB service. He wrote a resignation letter, then contacted Leningrad filmmaker Igor Shadkhan and asked him to make a television documentary in which Putin would disclose publicly for the first time his secret service affiliation. That way, no one could use it against him, Putin explained. "I must admit it alarmed me," Shadkhan told us much later, "because my attitude to intelligence, which was part of the KGB, was not a simple one, and I had just come from shooting a film about the gulag." But Shadkhan was intrigued and taped the interview. Even as he outed himself, Putin offered no apologies for his past. "He never had any regrets about working in the KGB," Shadkhan said. Later, Shadkhan invited Putin to his home and introduced him to a friend, who asked what the former spy thought of a memoir by a Soviet intelligence officer who had defected to the West. "Without thinking, Putin answered my friend, 'I don't read books written by traitors of the motherland.'"[25]

In fact, Putin was still officially a KGB agent. For reasons that have never been explained, Putin's resignation letter was not accepted, and he remained a secret service officer until August 1991, when KGB director Vladimir Kryuchkov helped orchestrate a hard-line coup against Gorbachev. Sobchak rallied behind Boris Yeltsin and flew home to Leningrad to organize resistance to the Communists. Putin decided to throw in his lot with Sobchak. He wrote another resignation letter to the KGB, raced to the airport with armed security guards to meet Sobchak's plane, and sped the mayor back into the city. With Putin's aid, Sobchak marshaled tens of thousands of supporters into the streets of Leningrad.

Did Putin side with the democrats out of genuine conviction or because he sensed that they were likely to win? Was it the act of a man throwing off a lifetime of Soviet training or that of the ultimate survivor? Putin has spoken of his decision with ambivalence. "It tore my life apart," he once said of the coup. "Up until that time, I didn't really understand the transformation that was going on in Russia. When I had come home from the GDR [the German Democratic Republic, as East Germany was known], it was clear to me that something was happening. But during the days of the coup, all the ideals, all the goals that I had had when I went to work for the KGB, collapsed."[26]

Putin spent the next five years at Sobchak's side, moving up to deputy mayor of the city that was renamed St. Petersburg a month after the coup. "He was Sobchak's right hand," said Valery Musin, a former law professor who later worked for Putin. "Mr. Sobchak didn't take any serious decisions without Mr. Putin's input."[27] It was a corrupt municipal government, one that failed to realize Sobchak's vision of a revitalized city of canals and showcase for the new Russia. Putin himself got caught up in a scandal over food contracts. His office signed deals giving favored companies licenses to export $92 million worth of oil products, timber, metal, and other products in exchange for an equal amount of imported food; Putin personally signed one contract for petroleum products worth $32 million. But the food never materialized. A city council committee led by local lawmaker Marina Salye recommended Putin's dismissal for "incompetence bordering on lack of conscientiousness" and "unprecedented negligence and irresponsibility in providing the investigating commission with documents."[28]

Putin kept his job. All manner of scams and schemes, kickbacks and payoffs, had become the norm in many parts of Russia as the state economy suddenly morphed into a free-for-all variant on free markets. The failures of the Sobchak-Putin government were evident enough to the electorate, which turned the mayor out of office in 1996 in favor of Vladimir Yakovlev, a former Sobchak deputy who had turned on his ex-boss. Yakovlev invited Putin to stay on. But Putin, who had called Yakovlev a "Judas" during the campaign, refused. Loyalty mattered to Putin. "It's better to be hanged for loyalty," he said, explaining his decision, "than for betrayal."[29]

PUTIN'S POLITICAL savior was a boisterous operator named Pavel Borodin, Russia's answer to a Chicago patronage chief. Borodin was head of the Kremlin's property department, a seemingly obscure fiefdom he had turned into a mini-empire. Not only was he in charge of the Kremlin facilities, a historic complex of tsarist churches and palaces surrounded by that famous brick wall adjacent to Red Square, he also controlled state property throughout Russia and in eighty-five other countries. The real estate that fell under his purview was worth tens of billions of dollars, if not more, and he commanded a workforce of 150,000 employees. Under Yeltsin, Borodin became a key dispenser of political favors for the Family, as the crowd around the president had come to be known. He masterminded a renovation of the Kremlin palaces that would prove stunning not only for its gilded excess but also for its spectacular corruption. In the end, he spent $300 million on the restoration, reconstructing seven-thousand-pound chandeliers in one hall, laying thirty-two different types of wood for the floor in another, and lacing the entire complex with gold. "Versailles isn't as nice," he boasted as he took us on a private tour one day.[30]

When Sobchak lost reelection, Borodin took it upon himself to arrange for Putin to be hired as Kremlin deputy chief of staff. According to Borodin, the two had first become acquainted when his daughter got sick while at school in St. Petersburg, and he had found Putin when calling the mayor's office from Moscow looking for someone to help. Putin obliged and Borodin never forgot the favor. But the return favor fell through after Anatoly Chubais took charge as Yeltsin's new chief of staff. Chubais, a tall, red-haired reformer who had orchestrated the largest sell-off of state assets in world history, eliminated the position of deputy chief of staff that Borodin wanted to offer Putin. So Borodin hired Putin into his own office to help untangle the messy legal issues surrounding former Soviet property around the world. It was yet another backwater, the Dresden of Russian politics, but the unemployed Putin had little choice. Much later, many Russians would wonder whether Borodin was acting at the behest of others seeking to recruit Putin, but he swore not. "Nobody ever asked me for Putin," he told us.[31]

Putin did not remain exiled in Borodin's property shop for long. After barely half a year, Chubais was replaced by Valentin Yumashev and Putin finally got the deputy chief of staff job. From there, Putin's career took off. Yeltsin claimed to have been struck by Putin's cool, reserved demeanor, although others remembered Putin as a silent presence at Kremlin meetings in that era. "He was always quiet, just sitting in a corner," Kremlin pollster Aleksandr Oslon recalled.[32] "Unlike other deputies, who were always trying to lay out their visions of Russia and the world, Putin did not try to strike up conversations with me," Yeltsin recalled in his memoirs. "Rather, it seemed that Putin tried to remove any sort of personal element from our contact. . . . At first Putin's coolness even made me cautious, but then I understood that it was ingrained in his nature."[33]

Putin took advantage of his new position to help his old patron. Back in St. Petersburg, Anatoly Sobchak had come under investigation by federal prosecutors for corruption. He fell ill under questioning in October 1997 and was rushed to a hospital with an apparent heart attack. Three weeks later, Sobchak was secreted out of Russia on a chartered plane bound for Paris, a move many believed was orchestrated by Putin to shield Sobchak from prosecution. Sobchak's wife, Lyudmila Narusova, confirmed to us that Putin was involved in the escape.[34]

After less than a year in the Kremlin, Putin had so impressed the Yeltsin crowd that in July 1998 they promoted him once again, this time to a position he could never have imagined as a midlevel KGB functionary in East Germany less than a decade earlier—director of the KGB's domestic successor, the FSB. Suddenly the lieutenant colonel was in charge of the main secret police apparatus of the Russian state.

Putin, the onetime nobody, quickly settled into the new role of a somebody in a city where the luxuries of power were increasingly available. One day in December 1998, he invited an attractive young reporter from the Kremlin press pool to lunch at Izumi, one of the first sushi restaurants to appear in landlocked Moscow. Yelena Tregubova showed up to find Putin alone in the dining room, the rest of the restaurant cleared out for the new chief of the secret police. When she sought to talk business, he cut her off and urged her to drink some saki.

"Lenochka," Putin said, using her nickname, "why do you keep talking about politics and only politics? Wouldn't you rather have a drink?"

Tregubova was not sure whether Putin was trying to recruit her or seduce her. But she got a glimpse of an apparatchik who proved adept at working the system—and working people. "He is of a quite average Soviet education, of an average intellect," she would later write. "But he is very, very adaptable. And sometimes with a kind of street kid's . . . charm." She ultimately concluded that Putin was "simply a brilliant 'reflector,' that, like a mirror, he copied the person he was with, to compel them to believe that he was just like them, 'one of theirs.' . . . For a very short moment, Putin manages with frightening accuracy to copy the expression, the turn of the neck, the thrust of the chin, and even the facial features of his counterpart, and is literally mimicking him. Moreover, he is doing this so cleverly that his counterpart apparently doesn't know it, but just feels wonderful." At the end of lunch, neither Putin nor Tregubova paid the breathtaking tab, leaving it to the FSB.[35]

The other main attribute Putin demonstrated during this rapid rise in Moscow was loyalty to the president who had appointed him. When the country's prosecutor general, Yuri Skuratov, began nosing around in the Family's dirty laundry—including Borodin's pricy renovation of the Kremlin, an investigation that bolstered the governors in the upper house of parliament who were trying to impeach Yeltsin—the Yeltsin circle began looking for ways to shut him down. One night in March 1999, state television aired a grainy video in which a naked man who looked like Skuratov cavorted in bed with two naked women described as prostitutes. The video, which had all the hallmarks of *kompromat*, or compromising material, from the FSB, caused a sensation in Moscow. Skuratov cried foul, but Putin publicly vouched for the video, deeming it "authentic," a move that undercut the prosecutor and fatally wounded him politically. Putin met with Skuratov along with Yeltsin to pressure the defiant prosecutor to step down. Just as he had protected Anatoly Sobchak from prosecutors, Putin had once again accomplished his mission of protecting a benefactor.

Probably no other single moment was as important in Putin's rise. Within weeks, Yeltsin rewarded him by adding the post of Kremlin Security Council chief to his FSB title, despite Putin's inexperience in foreign affairs, and the coterie in the Kremlin began whispering that perhaps Putin would be a successor they could trust. Yeltsin, plagued by health problems and increasingly willing to use the levers of power to save himself from his numerous enemies, was preoccupied at the moment with the apparent threat from his own prime minister, Yevgeny Primakov.

A jowly, thick-spectacled throwback to the Soviet era, when he was the last foreign intelligence chief before the collapse of the old regime, Primakov had been forced on Yeltsin by the Communist-dominated parliament the previous fall, but Yeltsin's advisers suspected Primakov was plotting against them. He had openly targeted one of the most prominent members of the Family, the oligarch Boris Berezovsky, a former mathematician who had emerged from the privatization of the 1990s as one of Russia's wealthiest men and its foremost political intriguer. Berezovsky pulled many of the strings at Yeltsin's Kremlin. The investigation of his dealings sponsored by Primakov represented a direct challenge to the established powers. Eventually, advisers convinced Yeltsin to fire Primakov in May 1999 and replace him with the more malleable interior minister, Sergei Stepashin. Yeltsin would later claim that he had already decided by this point to groom Putin as his successor but wanted to hold back putting him in the prime minister's post for fear of making him a target. "It was too early to put Putin in," Yeltsin wrote in his memoirs. "Someone else had to fill the gap. I needed someone to serve as a decoy."[36]

Whether that was the case or not, the innermost Kremlin circle began hearing Putin's name by that summer. One of the few who heard the whispers was Igor Malashenko, one of the founders of NTV, Russia's first independent national television network, who had thrown in with Yeltsin during the 1996 election campaign and had become his campaign manager. Malashenko did not know Putin and decided to find out more about the putative heir apparent. He called Pyotr Aven, a former trade minister who was now one of Russia's leading bankers and a Putin acquaintance, and Aven agreed to set up a casual meal at his country dacha, a spectacular estate complete with its own tennis courts once owned by the officially favored Soviet-era writer Aleksei Tolstoy. Putin, Aven, Malashenko, and Aven's wife relaxed over dinner one night in June, but Malashenko gleaned little about the man who might be the next president.

"I just failed miserably," he recalled later. "After three and a half hours of talking, I knew about Putin as little as I did before. He was a very shallow personality."

One moment, though, opened a small window. Malashenko's wife arrived late and seemed flustered by a phone call from their daughter, who was in London returning to her private school and had not been met by the academy's private car. The girl, Malashenko's wife reported, did not want to simply take a London taxi and was still waiting.

"Our daughter is a strange girl," she sighed. "I would certainly take a taxi instead of waiting at the airport so long."

Suddenly, Putin interjected, "Listen, your daughter is correct and you are not."

Malashenko's wife was slightly irritated. "Why do you say that?"

"You could never be confident it's really a cab," Putin answered.

"But it's a London cab," she protested.

"You don't understand," Putin said. "It doesn't matter."

To Russia's chief spy, anything, even a classic black British taxi, seemed suspicious. "My wife was stunned," Malashenko later recalled, "because here was a guy sitting in front of her who really thought her daughter could be kidnapped in London by a London cab. She thought it tells volumes about Mr. Putin and his mentality."

Not long afterward, Malashenko was summoned to the home of Valentin Yumashev, Yeltsin's close aide. "He asked me directly to support Putin as successor to Boris Yeltsin." It was late at night and Malashenko was a little stunned.

"How can you trust him?" he asked.

"He didn't give up Sobchak," Yumashev answered. "He won't give us up."

Malashenko realized that what Yeltsin's people wanted more than any-thing in a successor was a guarantee that they would be protected, so that a future prosecutor like Yuri Skuratov could not come after them. Putin, they figured, would be there for them. "They were so impressed in how he acted with Sobchak, they thought he was a person to be trusted," Malashenko said.

Malashenko thought about it overnight, then went back to see Yumashev the next day. "Listen," Malashenko told him, "I don't know much about Putin, but I know about him one fundamental thing—he's KGB and KGB can't be trusted. So I can't do it."[37]

Boris Berezovsky had no such qualms about Putin's KGB past. Bere-zovsky, short, balding, and full of manic energy, was impressed by Putin. Berezovsky had first met him in 1991, also introduced by Pyotr Aven. Putin was then a top aide to Sobchak in Leningrad, and Berezovsky had a business venture for which he needed assistance. "He helped me," Berezovsky recalled much later when we went to see him at his sprawling compound outside London. "And what really was absolutely surprising for me was that he was the first one who didn't ask for a bribe." Berezovsky tried to slip Putin money anyway, but he refused. A friendship of sorts developed. Berezovsky took Putin with him skiing in Switzerland in the 1990s. And in February 1999, when Yevgeny Primakov was pursuing Berezovsky, a time when being seen with the oligarch could be hazardous for those working in the government, Putin showed up at a birthday party for Berezovsky's wife. "I absolutely do not care what Primakov thinks of me," Putin told Berezovsky that night. "I think this is the right thing to do right now." The gesture made a powerful impression on Berezovsky. Years later, Berezovsky told us that Valentin Yuma-shev was the first to come up with Putin's name as a successor to Yeltsin, but the oligarch was certainly quick to endorse the notion and help propel it to reality. "Yumashev and those guys, they thought one thing that was clear about Putin was that he was loyal," Berezovsky said later. "They could count on him. He had taken on Skuratov."[38]

By August, Yumashev and Berezovsky decided it was time. The Decem-ber parliamentary elections were approaching, and Primakov was busy preparing his own new political coalition along with Moscow's powerful mayor, Yuri Luzhkov, and a sizable group of regional governors. Sergei Stepashin, only three months in the prime minister's post, seemed incapable of salvaging the situation. They were ready to bring in Putin.

The would-be successor was out of Moscow at the time on vacation in the

French resort of Biarritz. As Berezovsky recalled it, "Yumashev called me and said, 'Boris, you know, Yeltsin wants to discuss [the prime ministership] with Putin. Can you fly to Biarritz and meet Putin and discuss this with him?' And I took a plane and flew to Biarritz. And there I met Putin. He was with his family, his wife and his daughters. Very modest, absolutely simple apartment for the family. We spent the whole day together. I talked with him about it. And he said at last, 'Okay, I am prepared to discuss it with Yeltsin. I will return.'" It was a strange day. Putin was being handed the keys to the Kremlin, yet seemed to hesitate. "He didn't want to," Berezovsky said. "He wasn't sure he was capable of doing that."[39]

On his return to Moscow, Yeltsin offered Putin the prime ministership and told him he would lead a new party in parliamentary elections in just four months. Putin hesitated again. "I don't like election campaigns, I really don't," he told Yeltsin, a consummate campaigner who still relished baby-kissing and other attributes of the democratic system he had introduced to Russia. "I don't know how to run them and I don't like them."

Yeltsin told him that someone else would actually run it and asked him if he was prepared to accept the assignment.

"I will work wherever you assign me," Putin said dutifully.

"And in the very highest post?" Yeltsin asked. Meaning the presidency itself.

Putin paused again. "I had not thought about that. I don't know if I am prepared for that."

"Think about it. I have faith in you."[40]

After Putin left, Yeltsin summoned Stepashin and told him of his plans. Stepashin was crushed. Soon word reached Anatoly Chubais, the perennial power player in Moscow who had been the mastermind of Russia's privatization program and had briefly blocked Putin's first job in Moscow. Once again, Chubais tried to stop Putin's rise, ostensibly because he believed Putin unprepared, but perhaps secretly out of anxiety about handing over power to a KGB agent. Chubais went to see Putin and tried to talk him out of taking the appointment. Putin said he felt he had to accept. Chubais then went to the inner circle in the Family—Yumashev, Aleksandr Voloshin, and Yeltsin's influential daughter, Tatyana Dyachenko. But it was too late.

At eight o'clock in the morning of Sunday, August 8, 1999, Yeltsin summoned Putin, Stepashin, and a few other top officials to his official dacha, known as Gorki-9. The president told Stepashin that he had signed the decree firing him and making Putin his fifth prime minister in two years. It would be announced the following day.

Stepashin refused to concede. "I will not authorize that decree," he stammered.

Nikolai Aksyonenko, a deputy prime minister, interjected, "Stop it, Sergei Vadimovich!"

Putin then stepped in to ease the way for Stepashin. "Nikolai Yemelya-novich. It's hard enough for Stepashin. Let's not make it worse."

Stepashin had no real choice. "All right," Stepashin said. "I'll sign the decree. Out of respect for you, Boris Nikolayevich."[41]

FROM THE moment he took over, Vladimir Putin became a wartime prime minister. The day before the meeting with Yeltsin and Stepashin, Chechen separatists led by the ruthless guerrilla commander Shamil Basayev had staged a raid into villages in neighboring Dagestan for the ostensible purpose of joining the two republics together into a single, independent Islamic state. Federal troops responded with helicopter gunship attacks. The rebels responded by mortaring the Russian airfield.

Putin affected a tough-guy pose and vowed no mercy for the Chechen guerrillas. Yeltsin had already fought one war to prevent Chechnya from splitting off from Russia, a bloody affair that ended in 1996 after two years with federal troops in retreat and a shaky cease-fire agreement that granted the breakaway republic de facto independence. Now the tenuous peace had been shattered and the two sides headed toward another war. With Yeltsin's permission, Putin dispatched troops to the region. This time, he promised, it would be different. No surrender, no bloody morass. The conflict, Putin asserted defiantly, "will be resolved within a week and a half or two."[42]

The claim would prove wildly optimistic, if not downright naive. Within weeks, Russian troops were engaged in a full-scale war in Chechnya again. Then apartment buildings began blowing up. Over a little more than a week, four bombs in Moscow and the southern part of the country demolished massive residential buildings, killing some three hundred civilians, injuring hundreds more, and shattering Russia's illusion of security. As authorities pinned blame on the Chechens, the same public that had wearied of the first war and pressured Yeltsin to pull out now angrily cried for vengeance.

Putin, virtually unknown just weeks earlier and ridiculed as the chosen successor of an anemic, wildly unpopular president, sure to face the same fate as Yeltsin's previous prime ministers, suddenly had a mandate. His steely response to the bombings proved to be just what Russians wanted, down to the earthy prison jargon Putin used when speaking of his Chechen foes. "We will pursue the terrorists everywhere," Putin vowed in late September. "If it's in the airport, then in the airport. You'll forgive me, but if we catch them in the toilet, we'll wipe them out in the outhouse."[43]

The wave of patriotism, or at least ethnic hatred of Chechens, that accompanied the war played right into the hands of Putin's patrons in the Kremlin. In fact, the plan for an invasion of Chechnya had secretly been drawn up five months before the raid into Dagestan with the knowledge of then FSB director Putin, according to Stepashin.[44] Some Chechen leaders, such as Akhmed Zakayev, who served as deputy prime minister in the quasi-independent government of Aslan Maskhadov, would later become convinced that Basayev and the others who had launched the incursion into Dagestan were duped into it by Putin's FSB, seeking a pretext to launch the invasion they had already planned.[45]

What's more, evidence surfaced suggesting that the authorities themselves, rather than Chechens, may have been behind the apartment bombings. Just after nine o'clock the night of September 22, 1999, a passerby noticed two men and a woman unloading bags from the trunk of a white car and carrying them into the basement of an apartment building in Ryazan, a town about 120 miles southeast of Moscow. The witness called police, who arrived to find three large bags of powder and a homemade detonator set for 5:30 a.m. Local law enforcement experts who tested the substance determined it was hexogen, a white crystalline powder that was also used in the four previous apartment bombings. Within forty-eight hours, local authorities had intercepted a phone call leading them to what they thought was a hideout of the would-be bombers, while back in Moscow, Interior Minister Vladimir Rushailo, the country's chief law enforcement officer, told parliament that an explosion had been prevented in Ryazan.

Then, just a half hour later, Nikolai Patrushev, a Putin friend from the Leningrad KGB who had succeeded him as director of the FSB, announced that the powder was really sugar and that the whole thing had been a civil defense exercise. The FSB claimed that the finding of hexogen was just the mistake of a bomb expert whose hands had been tainted. They later blew up the "sugar," effectively preventing any further tests. Around Russia and particularly in Ryazan, many people came to believe that it was a botched operation by the FSB itself to bomb a building and blame it on the Chechens. If so, it would be hard to imagine that Putin, the former FSB chief, did not know, at least after the fact. But no definitive proof ever emerged.[46]

Whatever the truth, Putin soared in popularity on the wave of fear that accompanied the bombings. Recognizing the changing political environment, the Yeltsin team quickly began building its election strategy around Putin.

First up were elections for the State Duma, the lower house of parliament, in December. The Duma was currently dominated by Communists, and now a new coalition called Fatherland–All Russia, spliced together by Yevgeny Primakov and Moscow's mayor Yuri Luzhkov, appeared likely to soak up the rest of the vote. A few days after Putin's appointment, Kremlin leaders held a strategy session at the dacha of Yeltsin chief of staff Aleksandr Voloshin. Among those present were Valentin Yumashev, Tatyana Dyachenko, Boris Berezovsky, his partner Roman Abramovich, and Vladislav Surkov, a crafty political strategist seconded to the Kremlin by oil tycoon Mikhail Khodorkovsky. Berezovsky presented a plan to create a new political party for the Duma elections, one adopting the Russian bear as its symbol. To come up with the acronym MEDVED, which means bear, he thought up the name MEzhregionalnoye DVizheniye EDinstvo, which means Interregional Unity Movement. Eventually, it would become simply Unity. But the others at the dacha were skeptical. Yeltsin was so deeply despised by the public, they figured there was no chance. Only Abramovich stood up for Berezovsky and suggested they had nothing to lose by trying. Putin remained silent. "He just sat," Berezovsky said later.[47]

Berezovsky was a wheeler-dealer who had financial interests in everything from Aeroflot, the national airline, to Sibneft, one of the leading oil companies, to Avtovaz, the major carmaker. But his key asset was Channel One, the country's best-known television network, also called ORT. The state still owned 51 percent of the network, but Berezovsky had the other 49 percent and the right to manage it. To Berezovsky, television was a tool and he knew just who should wield it. He telephoned Sergei Dorenko, a prominent television anchor with a taste for investigative news, an instinct for the jugular, and little interest in journalistic impartiality.

"We want to fight," Berezovsky told Dorenko on the phone. "We want to create a new movement." Would he help?

Dorenko thought it was madness. Clearly Primakov and Luzhkov were on track to win the Duma elections, and one of them would then win the presidential election. It was too late to fight them. "Everything you said is shit," Dorenko told Berezovsky. "We lost, and you personally will be hung in Red Square among the first five executed. I don't see any chance."

Berezovsky told Dorenko if he was going to be so defeatist, then he could just stay out of the initiative.

Dorenko backed down. "Borya," he said, using a nickname for Berezovsky, "we'll hang, but we'll stage a Cossack incursion one last time."[48]

With Dorenko now in the anchor chair, Channel One became a blunt instrument hammering away at Primakov and Luzhkov, night after night, week after week. Dorenko aired at great length details about surgery Primakov had had, suggesting that he was too old to be elected. Luzhkov was linked to the murder of an American businessman, Paul Tatum. Dorenko put on the air a friend of Tatum's saying the dying man had fingered Luzhkov as his killer.[49] On the other side were Igor Malashenko and Vladimir Gusinsky, whose NTV became the vehicle for building up Primakov and Luzhkov, though not nearly as effectively as Dorenko and Channel One were tearing them down. "In essence," recalled Valery Fyodorov, a young political operative working in the Unity headquarters, "Dorenko turned Primakov from one of the most popular politicians into a person like Yeltsin—old, sick and ineffective."[50]

It worked faster than Putin's political team could even have imagined. As poll numbers plummeted for Primakov and Luzhkov, Putin's rating was going up as much as four or five points a week by the end of September. With such popularity, the organizers of the new Unity party wanted to latch on to the new prime minister. "I was trying to convince everyone that Unity didn't need any ideology, it didn't need any program," Fyodorov said. "It only needed one thing—to become Putin's team."[51]

For weeks, Putin resisted endorsing the party before finally agreeing to a meeting with the official party leader, Sergei Shoigu, in front of television cameras. "It was very difficult to persuade him to support Unity," said Kseniya Ponomaryova, the head of Channel One, who was dispatched over to the party election headquarters to work as deputy campaign manager for what she called Project Putin. Just as he resisted the Unity endorsement, and never officially joined the party, Putin remained unreceptive to proposals that he campaign personally, comparing the process to the undignified selling of Snickers or Tampax. "He did not want too many rallies," Ponomaryova recalled. "He did not and does not like meeting people and shaking hands. He absolutely lacks empathy. Maybe in his head, I don't know, he is sympathetic. But he is absolutely unable to show it. If you see him going to hospitals or meeting with orphan kids, they feel it. The kids don't like Putin." Ponomaryova saw a simple reason behind this. "Putin had a very cold and domineering father," she said. "People who knew him when he was a boy say his father never ever told him one good thing."[52] Putin's father died just a few days after his son's appointment as prime minister.

Putin's advisers had to teach him how to walk, what to wear, how to speak, how to appear on television. "He was a fast learner," said Igor Shabdurasulov, who worked on the campaign and later served as Putin's deputy chief of staff. But with the power of the state behind him, personal campaign skills only mattered so much. "We managed to use the resources of the federal authorities—mass media and so on," Shabdurasulov told us. "I'm not defending the ethics of that process. There were many things that today might not look all that pretty. But politics is a dirty business."[53]

Putin's handlers began cutting deals to take advantage of his growing popularity. They made a secret pact with Gennady Seleznyov, a Communist leader, promising support for his bid for governor of the Moscow region; if he failed in that race, the Kremlin team promised it would support making him speaker of the State Duma. In return, Seleznyov would make sure the Communists became, if not outright allies, at least partners with Unity in the next parliament; the two parties would split committee chairmanships and other power posts.

On the other side of the ideological spectrum, many of the free-market democrats who had been instrumental in enacting the reforms of the 1990s, including Anatoly Chubais, former prime ministers Yegor Gaidar and Sergei Kiriyenko, former deputy prime minister Boris Nemtsov, and Duma deputy Irina Khakamada, put together their own Western-oriented party called the Union of Right Forces. Chubais and his allies had sided with Putin on his handling of Chechnya, even though many of their party's core constituents abhorred the war; the decision was critical to winning the prime minister's help in the Duma elections. Lengthy negotiations between Chubais and Aleksandr Voloshin, representing the Kremlin, finally resulted in a televised meeting between Chubais and Putin. The Union of Right Forces leaders handed Putin a large encyclopedia-sized book of reform proposals; the simple picture of him appearing with them proved enough to vault the new party past the 5 percent minimum threshold required for representation in the Duma. The reformers felt they had made a "pragmatic" deal, Khakamada recalled later. "We used the administrative resources of the authorities so that we could be in the establishment."[54]

But the main Kremlin vehicle remained Unity. With Putin and Unity now linked, the presidential and parliamentary campaigns merged into a single headquarters in October. And in a bad omen for Boris Berezovsky, his campaign team fell into conflict with Voloshin's and was largely ousted from decision making. Putin still had no group of his own, just two as-yet-unknown aides he had summoned from St. Petersburg, young lawyers Dmitri Kozak and Dmitri Medvedev. "There was an inner struggle inside Unity," Fyodorov confided later. "The team brought in by Berezovsky lasted maybe a month and had to leave the headquarters."[55] The exact nature of the dispute remains cloudy, but it seemed to have its roots in the simple question of control—who would really be in charge.

The Duma elections on December 19 proved stunningly successful for Unity, which garnered 23 percent of the vote, just shy of the long-dominant Communists at 24 percent. A party that did not exist a few months earlier had suddenly been transformed into the party of power. With its secret deal with the Communists, Unity could exercise control in the next Duma. The Fatherland–All Russia party of Primakov and Luzhkov that had appeared set to sweep the elections just months earlier garnered only 13 percent.

Now it came time for Putin himself. Still a skeptic about campaigns and everything to do with them, Putin had reluctantly started changing his mind after the Duma elections. That fall, he hadn't believed it when Kremlin pollster Aleksandr Oslon showed him polls indicating that Unity's rating had doubled after his endorsement. It was just "deceiving," he told Oslon, some intrigue to raise the party's rating. Now he started to believe. "Putin finally began to understand he was a serious contender," Oslon recalled.[56]

With the end of the year approaching, Yeltsin decided to step down early. Always a lover of the grand gesture, he became enraptured with the notion of going out on New Year's Eve at the close of the millennium. The approaching Duma elections seemed to prove that Putin was ready. Five days before the vote, Yeltsin met with Putin at the presidential dacha and told him of his plan to step down on December 31, making the prime minister acting president until new elections. Putin initially demurred.

"I'm not ready for that decision, Boris Nikolayevich," Putin said, according to separate accounts by both men. "You see, Boris Nikolayevich, it's a rather difficult destiny."

Yeltsin insisted. "I want to step down this year, Vladimir Vladimirovich," he said. "This year. That's very important. The new century must begin with a new political era, the era of Putin."[57]

Putin relented. But there was one more order of business for the Yeltsin circle. They made a secret deal with Putin, according to several former Kremlin insiders—if given power, Putin agreed to prevent any prosecution or other retribution against Yeltsin and the Family. He would protect them the way he had protected Anatoly Sobchak. "It really was very hard, getting Putin into the job—one of the hardest things we ever pulled off," Tatyana Dyachenko, Yeltsin's influential daughter, later told U.S. deputy secretary of state Strobe Talbott.[58]

On New Year's Eve, 1999, Yeltsin met with Putin one last time as president and handed him the four-inch-thick Samsonite case with the codes for launching Russia's nuclear arsenal. They had lunch and watched Yeltsin's pretaped resignation speech on national television, which shocked the country, the rest of the world, and even Putin's wife, Lyudmila, who had been kept clueless by her husband and who spent the rest of the day crying. Yeltsin, his successor, and his ministers had a champagne toast, and then Yeltsin took his leave. Turning to Putin, he said, "Take care of Russia."[59]

Putin's first real act in office was to sign a decree granting Yeltsin and his family immunity from prosecution. Then that night, New Year's Eve, the biggest holiday on the Russian calendar, he traveled to Chechnya to visit the troops.

THE ACTING president settled into his new office with a bank of telephones in the northwest corner of the second floor of the Kremlin overlooking Red Square, just down the hall from Stalin's old living quarters. From the beginning, Putin approached his new job with a certain cynical realpolitik. When Secretary of State Madeleine Albright arrived in Moscow in January 2000, becoming the first senior U.S. official to meet Putin after his ascension, Putin greeted her at the Kremlin. Then he turned to the television cameras. "The U.S. is conducting a policy of pressure against us in Chechnya," he intoned sternly. Only after dismissing the reporters did he turn back to Albright. "I said that so your domestic critics will not attack you for being soft," he told her. Even at that inaugural meeting he linked the Chechnya war to extremist influence from the radical Taliban regime in Afghanistan. "Do not try to squeeze Russia out of this region or you will end up with another Iran or Afghanistan," he warned. Then, in a subtle reference to Albright's childhood growing up in Europe threatened by Nazis, he added, "Instead of another Munich, we are fighting them now before they grow stronger. And we will smash them." Albright suggested a political settlement. Putin scoffed. There was no one to negotiate with, he replied. "The legitimate leaders are petrified; the rest are thugs and murderers."[60]

Russians appreciated this perceived toughness. Unlike the first conflict in Chechnya, Putin's war remained popular at home amid the residual outrage over the apartment bombings. Putin and his team decided to capitalize on the opportunity. With Yeltsin's early resignation, the next presidential election was moved up to March 26, 2000. By now, Putin had emerged as an unstoppable force. When Yevgeny Primakov, once the front-runner, explored a campaign, he solicited a memo from political consultant Vyacheslav Nikonov. "I wrote it requires a lot of money—if you don't have a lot of money, forget it," Nikonov told us later. Primakov passed.[61] Gennady Zyuganov, the leader of the Communist Party who had nearly toppled Yeltsin in the 1996 presidential election, decided to run, as did Grigory Yavlinsky, the leader of the democratic party Yabloko, who opposed the latest campaign in Chechnya. But it was clear they need not have bothered, given the outcome of the Duma election. "After that," said Igor Shabdurasulov, the Putin aide, "the presidential election was a mere formality."[62]

Putin played the part of commander in chief, even flying into Chechnya in the copilot seat of an Su-27 jet midcampaign. Boris Berezovsky's Channel One lavished coverage of Putin's every move. "His campaign was the war in Chechnya," Nikonov said. "He seemed like a tough guy, capable of doing things, and definitely he was, compared to his predecessor. He won by comparison. He wasn't drunk, which was so unusual. He was young, doing things, moving, meeting people. It was all unusual for a leader. He could walk and talk."[63] To the hardheaded young political operatives who ran his campaign, Putin was just another Yeltsin-era commodity to be packaged and sold, a brand that started out with excellent favorables. "It was clear we were selling a decisive, young, sober-talking defender, progressively minded," recalled Marina Litvinovich, an aide to the Kremlin's outside consultant Gleb Pavlovsky.[64] Nor did Putin's KGB past hurt him. In fact, it was seen as an asset. "Putin was a *chekist*," said campaign aide Valery Fyodorov, using the word derived from the Cheka, the first Soviet secret police. "And by then he had managed to exploit the legend that our services were still one of the only effective, uncorrupted elements of Soviet and post-Soviet society."[65]

Now the former KGB officer who had grown up watching spy movies had catapulted to the highest echelons of power. According to the official count, he collected 53 percent of the vote in an election marred by widespread fraud and manipulation, easily outpacing Zyuganov with 29 percent, Yavlinsky with 6 percent, and a field of lesser-known challengers.[66] Barely half a year after it was conceived, the Yeltsin team's Project Putin had succeeded. Or had it? They had protected Yeltsin, but had they protected his legacy? At his inauguration on May 7, 2000, Putin dutifully vowed to "preserve and develop democracy," yet a starkly different signal came from his guest list, which included not only Yeltsin but also Vladimir Kryuchkov—the same former KGB director who had orchestrated the 1991 coup intended to preserve the Soviet Union, the same coup that Yeltsin had made history by defeating. The new president had evidently learned much from the success of Project Putin—how elections were farces to be rigged, how television was there to be manipulated, how war was good politics, how oligarchs thought they owned the Kremlin. The formula for his own rise to power would shape Putin's presidency, and Russia, for years to come.

At forty-seven years old, Putin had far surpassed his disapproving father's expectations. And he had even surpassed his childhood spy hero, Yogan Vais from *The Sword and the Shield*. "My ambition," Vais says in the film, "is to have as few people as possible to order me around, and to have the right to command as many as possible." It was an ambition that clearly stuck with the grandson of Stalin's cook. After he became president, Putin was asked what he liked about being in the Kremlin. "In the Kremlin, I have a different position," he answered. "Nobody controls me here. I control everybody myself."[67]

A few months later, Putin gave a speech at a closed-door ceremony at the Lubyanka headquarters of the old KGB. The occasion was a Stalin-inaugurated holiday known as Day of the Chekist, marking the anniversary of the founding of the Soviet secret police. Gathered there to listen to Putin were about three hundred generals from the FSB and KGB, and it became a celebration of the rise of one of their own.

"Instruction number one for obtaining full power has been completed," Putin announced to the generals.

The few civilians in the hall thought it was a joke.

Only later, one told us, would they realize how serious he was.[68]

Time of the Patriots

"Are you gangsters?"
"No, we are Russians!"
—FROM THE FILM, *BRAT 2*

I N THE FRENETIC MOSCOW of the early 1990s, Mikhail Kozyrev and his friends had plied their dates with amaretto, the latest novelty liqueur from the West. They had snacked on Snickers and frequented video cafés that played bootleg copies of Sylvester Stallone movies. If it was imported, it was hip. At the time, Kozyrev simply embraced the party that engulfed the once-gray city. An aspiring doctor who had decided to make a career in the trendier realm of rock music, Kozyrev reveled in the novelty of it all. "Most of the nineties . . . was a party and don't look at the bill. All kinds of weird monsters were created. Fake and plastic monsters," he recalled, years later, with a shudder. "The average was worse than the world's average, and the bad was worse than the world's bad. It was 'Achy Breaky Heart' multiplied by a hundred, as disgusting as it gets."[1]

By the eve of the Putin era, amaretto was a sickly sweet memory for Moscow's in crowd, and Kozyrev's world had changed again. In the clubs, party kids took to wearing "USSR" T-shirts and crowding in dank basement rooms that lovingly, if sarcastically, re-created the somnolescent era of Leonid Brezhnev. Retro night at the hippest St. Petersburg dives featured Soviet dissident ballads. On television, Soviet classic movies played in a nearly endless loop, with earnest Young Pioneers and grim Cold War–vintage apartment-block settings attracting both disenfranchised pensioners and sleek young intellectuals. During commercial breaks, Russian bears sold beer, and kerchiefed babushkas starred in cutting-edge music videos. The most successful new brand in Putin's Russia, it turned out, was the Soviet Union—retooled and updated for the Internet era.

There was even a word that summed up this cultural shift back after a decade or more of worshiping the West; if it was *nashe*—Russian for "ours"—it was in favor again. This was the river current that Kremlin pollster Aleksandr Oslon had told the president to swim with, the powerful tide that Project Putin had been tailored to fit. And in the realm of popular culture, Kozyrev identified the moment earlier than most. "It was very uncool to be Russian in the beginning of the nineties," he recalled. "Every newspaper and television show was obsessed with showing how bad this country is and how hopeless we are and how good life is in the West. Now it's cool to be Russian again."

Ersatz Spice Girls and would-be Madonnas would no longer do for Russia in this new era, Kozyrev decided. Instead, his next project would take the nascent Soviet chic and market it, capturing the resurgent nationalism and capitalizing on it with the most cutting-edge techniques imported from the now out-of-favor West. He would promote Russian rock for the Russians, and his new radio network would play nothing but homegrown music. The name he and his partners chose for the station was the one word that kept coming up everywhere. They would call it simply Nashe.

BY THE TIME Vladimir Putin joined the battle, it had long been fashionable to say that Russia was suffering from an identity crisis. A humbled former superpower that was neither the prospering capitalist democracy of its perestroika dreams nor the powerful empire of its past propaganda, the new Russia had no intention of settling for a place in the world as Upper Volta with nukes.

Even Boris Yeltsin, the president who had destroyed the Soviet Union, recognized this. Just days after the 1996 reelection campaign he won by scaring Russians about the prospect of a return to Communist dictatorship, the ailing leader took time out to publicly bemoan the lack of a new national identity to replace Soviet ideology. "In Russian history of the twentieth century, there were various periods—monarchism, totalitarianism, perestroika, and finally a democratic path of development," Yeltsin said. "Each stage had its ideology. We have none." He ordered up a commission to produce a new "national idea." The commission just as promptly disappeared, its recommendations never made public.[2] The old imperial slogan "Orthodoxy, Autocracy, Nationhood" hardly fit the times; Yeltsin had personally done his part to kill off the Communist vision of the "bright shining future." In 1998, parliament was so divided on the question of what should constitute the new Russia's identity it failed to muster the two-thirds vote necessary to approve a new flag and national anthem.[3]

Putin determined to do something about it. Seemingly eager to roll back all things Yeltsin, the new leader ordered a return of the Soviet anthem, with lyrics slightly modified for the post-Soviet era. No longer would Russia have to suffer the indignity of watching its athletes stand silent on the Olympic medals podium, as they had that summer of 2000 in Sydney, winners from a country that couldn't even agree on the words to a song. While Yeltsin had periodically threatened to finally bury Lenin's embalmed body still on display in Red Square, Putin decided to leave it alone. And he reinstated the Soviet red flag for the army—while endorsing the double-headed eagle of the Romanov tsars as the national symbol. This was a president who refused to be ashamed anymore; it was okay, he told Russians in an unusual televised address from the Kremlin, to boast about the Soviet Union again as well as the empire that preceded it. "Was there nothing but Stalin's prison camps and repression?" he asked. "What about the achievements of Soviet science, of the spectacular space flight of cosmonaut Yuri Gagarin, of the art and music of cultural heroes like the composer Dmitri Shostakovich?" It was time, he said, to be proud again.[4]

Such words represented what Russians wanted to hear from Putin. As a country, Russia was tired of being what sociologist Masha Volkenshtein called "the brand that lost its identity." Her firm, Validata, specialized in advising Western corporate giants like Procter & Gamble and Coca-Cola on how to compete in the evolving Russian market. In one survey, they tried to identify what characterized countries as brands. Russia's "brand essence," they found, could be summed up in one word: pride. But it was the pride of a wounded and humiliated former power, one with no present-day heroes and few historical ones. Russians had latched on to brand "icons," such as homemade vodka, black bread, the Kalashnikov automatic rifle, and Gagarin, the first man in space, but it was the lack of identity that troubled survey respondents most. "Russia is looking to completely reinvent their brand identity," Validata concluded. "Until a new identity is created, Russia is 'stuck' with an image of poverty, alcoholism, and Mafia—an image they are very unhappy with . . . leading them to latch onto 'old' assets such as 'Victory in WWII.' Despite this, Russians still view their country positively, especially the bond between people in their country."

In other words, nationalism mixed with Soviet-era symbolism was the perfect balm to the collective bruised ego. Soothing reminders of past glory would sell in a society disappointed with the results of upheaval and mired in intractable conflicts about what course the country should take. Whether the marketplace was politics or pop culture, "people were lost, and they started to look back," Volkenshtein said. "Being in a miserable humiliating position . . . [means] needing a big stable of memories and identification with the past."[5] For some, the past meant the perceived stability of the Soviet Union of the 1970s, for others the "Great Russia" of the nineteenth-century tsars. Putin, with his praise for Aleksandr Pushkin and Fyodor Dostoyevsky and his open admiration of Soviet achievements, offered a strange mix of the two, something just bizarre enough to count for many Russians as *nashe*.

Indeed, the idea of *nashe* (or *nash, nasha,* or *nashi,* depending on usage) was one of the most resonant Soviet concepts to be resurrected for the new era. *Nashe* had been Russian shorthand as far back as nineteenth-century literature for "one of ours," serving as a convenient way of separating the world into friends and enemies. In Soviet times, the word took on a political cast, evolving into a potent, and pithy, way of separating suspicious characters from the mass of good, right-thinking Soviet citizens. "*Nash* began to denote 'ideologically right,' 'true to Soviet ideology,'" according to Moscow linguistics scholar Irina Levontina, a positive meaning that it carried into the troubles of the 1990s.[6]

For a brief moment as the empire collapsed, the liberal intelligentsia that had set itself in opposition to the Soviet Union thought they, too, could now compete to define what constituted *nashe* in the new Russia. Natalya Ivanova, a prominent literary critic and deputy editor of the well-known *Znamya* journal, remembered vividly her teenage daughter returning from the barricades at the Russian White House during the August 1991 coup, where she had gone to take the demonstrators food and cigarettes. "She came back and said now she understands how part of the earth can become *nashe,*" Ivanova recalled. "We had this feeling that *nashe* was winning, that in front of the White House the regime was being changed and freedom was coming."

But the rise of Putin and his brand of nationalism had convinced Ivanova that theirs was a battle lost. Once, she had imagined a definition of *nashe* that would include the best of the Russian past, its literary giants, its legendary composers, the intrinsic beauty of the traditional wooden village homes known as *izba*. But she believed that those who could have made that happen had either left the country or chosen to get rich, opting for "mine" over "ours." Instead, the label was appropriated by the nationalists, the Soviet-era apparatchiks who had never been displaced from their bureaucratic posts, and the nouveaux riches who still carried Soviet definitions of the good life in their heads. Putin was the obvious political by-product.

Ivanova's book, *Nowstalgia,* surveyed the cultural scene and found that in every area—television, theater, the movies—the direction they were moving was "back to the USSR." She concluded that Soviet propaganda, with its skillful use of "mankind's wonderful and humane ideals—unselfish friendship, pure relationship to love, value of labor in contrast to idleness, special attitude to the motherland, respect for the elders, and so on," had become the most successful type of modern public relations. "After Yeltsin, they began to introduce the ideology of what we now call *nashe*," she told us. "Gradually, this mixed with anti-Americanism, xenophobia, chauvinism. Now this idea of *nashe* permeates everything from choosing food in supermarkets to advertising."[7]

No one was more *nashe* than film director Eldar Ryazanov, whose fables about the Soviet everyman and his humble attempts to strike a blow for individuality had livened up life in the stagnant Soviet Union of the 1970s. His most popular movie, *Ironiya Sudby* (Irony of Fate), hilariously lampooned the depressing sameness of the Soviet city when a drunken young doctor, celebrating New Year's Eve with his friends, is mistakenly bundled onto a plane for Leningrad. He gets in a taxi, gives the driver his Moscow address, and is promptly delivered to that address in Leningrad, which looks so similar to his that he doesn't even notice the difference. His key even works in the lock. In the Soviet context, Ryazanov's films counted as quiet dissidence because of their humanity and subtle digs at the system. "Back then, that was a challenge to society, not a political opposition but a human one," Ryazanov recalled, "when people were trying to see something tender, human, in a desperate and cruel time."

His films experienced an unlikely second life in the post-Soviet era. And now they had a different meaning, showing a positive side to Soviet life, when money didn't matter, close relationships were the priority, and there was just one national ice hockey team to cheer for. "There is an instinctive resistance to an alien culture," Ryazanov told us over coffee at the Film Union in Moscow. Back in the 1990s, he said, "people were lost in this mass of cheap Western films. Anatole France said, 'Excess is harmful in everything, even in virtue.' So young people began to turn away. They began to turn back to us."[8]

WITH RUSSIANS longing for something of their own—whether that something was the comfort of their Soviet past, a new creation born of the novelties of the 1990s, or some hybrid of the two—Mikhail Kozyrev thought he knew what to give them, at least the younger, hipper ones who cared to listen. "By '98, there was a strong reaction against anything fake, anything Western," said Kozyrev, who went by the nickname Misha. "A backlash."

It was also the moment of unlikely opportunity for Kozyrev and many other Russian entrepreneurs. As the 1998 economic crisis sent the ruble into free fall and foreign investors scrambling for the next plane to London,

Kozyrev was hired by Russian oligarch Boris Berezovsky and Western media tycoon Rupert Murdoch to work on an idea for a new radio network. They tested three different formats with focus groups—two dominated by Western rock music, a third devoted solely to Russian songs. The Russian version won. In surveys, respondents kept using the word *nashe*. Said Koyzrev, "They wanted to listen to 'our' music, the music of 'our' generation. Every sentence had the word *nashe* in it."

Nashe the radio station launched on December 14, 1998, and rose quickly to become the country's leading rock powerhouse. As Putin came to office the next summer, Kozyrev was being called "the most influential person" in the Russian music industry by the trade press, a tastemaker who could turn new artists into stars and almost single-handedly created a demand for modern Russian rock beyond the underground clubs or the awful commercialized pop of the 1990s. Rarely mentioned publicly was Nashe's foreign backing from Murdoch or its links to the controversial Berezovsky, who helped orchestrate the Russian president's unlikely rise to power and had become an intimate of the press baron's.

Soon new competitors emerged to copy Nashe's formula. Less than two years into Putin's tenure, five major radio networks in the top ten had all-Russian formats, from the market leader, Russian Radio, to Radio Retro. The appeal was often less than subtle as listeners were urged to tune in to the sounds of their socialist youth; Russian Radio, for example, advertised itself all over Moscow on billboards as "Our Motherland USSR." Russia's leading radio-market analyst called what was happening on the airwaves "the time of the patriots."[9]

For Kozyrev, the pitch to nostalgia was obvious. His station specifically aimed itself at young men, between twenty and thirty, who grew up on Soviet underground groups of the 1980s like Kozyrev, and who were most receptive to the new patriotism he was promoting. "When we were young, the trees were taller. It's all about being young," he said. "As children we had the notion of the simplicity of the world. Our ice hockey team versus Canada. It's Brezhnev versus Reagan. It's always black and white. We know now who's the enemy, and for ten years we didn't know."

A fast-talking thirtysomething, Kozyrev seemed an unlikely prophet of Russian rock nationalism. The child of a family of liberal Russian intellectuals in the Ural Mountains, he had headed to the United States in the early years after the Soviet collapse planning to become a doctor. Derailed by a failing score on his U.S. medical boards, Kozyrev ended up as a Russian teaching assistant at Pomona College in California, where he acquired a fluency in the finer points of American rock and a love for FM radio. He hosted a radio show on campus and listened incessantly to KROQ in Los Angeles to master the nuances of the drive-time playlist. In 1994, he came back to Moscow and was promptly hired to work on an early commercial radio station project. "I told him I have no clue how to run a commercial radio station," Kozyrev recalled of that first job interview. "Whatever you know will be more than anyone here," the head of the station told him. Kozyrev got the job as program director of Radio Maximum.[10]

Even years after his return, Kozyrev retained a very American sensibility. He spoke admiringly of Steven Spielberg and Ernest Hemingway and was as likely to refer to *The Simpsons* as to Aleksandr Solzhenitsyn when trying to explain the bizarreness of Russian political life. In music, his genius was the ability to marry the slick techniques of advanced consumer culture learned in the United States with the rough-edged reality of the Soviet protest rock born in the underground of the 1980s perestroika years, when semilegal groups like Alisa turned a new generation against the Soviet state in bootleg tapes that were passed around from hand to hand and called *magnitizdat,* in homage to the forbidden literature known as *samizdat.*

To do so, Kozyrev had to be fluent in both cultures. And for himself, he understood *nashe* to be what set the Russian experience apart from the imports. "Unfortunately," he said, "throughout Russian literature and Russian music the great dilemma of man versus circumstances is completely opposite to American culture. In American culture that lonely and wasted housewife will get a chopper and cut Freddy's head off. In Russia, man is always conquered by circumstances. Circumstances is always stronger. We know that."

In a way, Kozyrev was a prototype of the Putin-era trendsetter in Moscow. Middlemen like him, immersed in the latest that global culture had to offer, became skilled interpreters, reimagining the Soviet past through the lens of the internationalist present. And the same was true in almost every business that hoped to make its mark in Russia. "The most successful products today are local ones created by Western companies and promoted using Western techniques but aimed at Russian patriotism," Aleksandr Gromov, managing director of the Moscow office of the international ad agency Saatchi & Saatchi, told us. "They are talking to Russians speaking their language—but using all the tricks of Western marketing."[11]

AS A MATTER of marketing, the craze for *nashe* went national after the 1998 Russian economic crash, a ruble devaluation that made many imported goods inaccessibly expensive for Russians and caused Western firms to lose as much as two-thirds of their market share, much of it irretrievably. Many prominent global companies didn't even stay to fight, retreating in haste from the Russia they had entered so confidently just a few years earlier. Just up the block from our apartment on one of Moscow's central avenues, one of the city's flagship Pizza Hut outlets abruptly disappeared. The new pizza shop that took its place seemed to gloat over its ignominious exit. In a name defying all logic except the political prevailing wind, it was called Nasha Pizza. And it was very popular.

For those foreign companies that remained, a new discretion ruled. Where once they had found it easy to sell anything with English on the package, they now took pains to obscure their ownership of Russian brands. In the Western-style supermarkets that were springing up around the capital, the trademark onion domes of Russian churches decorated labels for chocolate bars and dumplings. Russian Style, far from being an oxymoron, became a cigarette brand made by a Western tobacco firm just for the Russian market.

Professionals called the process Russification. At a time when globalization meant more of the same around the world, Russia seemed to be defying the trend by turning inward again. Marketing surveys confirmed the dramatic turnabout. Before 1998, according to the firm Comcon, only 48 percent of Russians said they preferred to buy domestic goods when considering quality and not just price. By 1999, that figure was 90 percent.[12] Price had a lot to do with the Russian rout—average incomes hovered under $100 a month at the start of the Putin era and rose to the still-modest level of $200 a month by the end of his first term in office. But the change also tapped into something deeper. In a place where consumer choice was still a novelty, where a dozen years earlier a hunk of generic cheese indifferently wrapped in plain brown paper marked a successful day of shopping, the rejection of foreign goods spoke to Russia's broader uneasiness with its own evolving capitalism and the West that exported it.

British American Tobacco was perhaps the first to capitalize on the idea in its advertising. When it launched its Yava Gold cigarettes just before the 1998 crisis, the spots used to promote them were a prototype for the new patriotism—semihumorously, semiseriously showing a Russian bear in a "retaliatory strike" on the Empire State Building. Like the many imitators that followed, it was revenge on the triumphant post–Cold War West. That those same Western capitalists were often reaping the profits was usually left unsaid.

A homegrown company, Wimm-Bill-Dann, offered perhaps the most widely recognized example of how firms accommodated themselves to the shift in post-Soviet consumer culture. Back in the early 1990s, the new company created a best-selling juice brand with a cryptic and, to a Russian ear, completely Western-sounding name, J7.[13] Reflecting the changed times, Wimm-Bill-Dann by the Putin era had made the politic decision to choose only Russian names for its products. By then, it was the country's largest dairy and juice company, and its more recent line was called, in Russian, Little House in the Country.

Eager to compete with Wimm-Bill-Dann, the international dairy firm Danone invested millions of dollars in local plants and embraced the buy-Russian hook, even marketing its own brand of "Classic Russian" kefir, a sour, yogurtlike drink that is a Russian staple. "Made in Russia" was stamped prominently on its bottle, but Danone's kefir cost more than its competitors' and didn't taste classic enough for the purists. "The 'Made in Russia' label is an affirmation we belong here," said the company's local marketing director, Mark Putt. But he acknowledged, as we spoke in his office at the famous Soviet-era Bolshevik Biscuit Company factory that was the first state firm sold off in the post-Soviet privatization period, "Danone will never be the leaders in kefir. It's a very traditional Russian thing."[14]

On the other side of Moscow from the Bolshevik factory, the cash-strapped teachers of School Number 1280 offered us a private after-school seminar in the psychology of buying Russian, and it was a refrain we were to hear across Russia in the coming years. For them, it was all about identity—a realization that while they were now free to choose Coca-Cola and McDonald's, they really preferred the strong black tea and omnipresent sausages of their Soviet past. "I try to avoid foreign products," said Tamara Filatova over an afternoon snack of homemade wine and sweet Russian cake. Her colleague Yelena Pavlovskaya grimaced when offered a Pepsi, as fellow teacher Svetlana Yevlash threw in, "Our products are better than foreign ones." Like the others, Filatova recalled her first infatuation with Western goods, going to the supermarket "like it was a museum." But she laughed about her one and only time trying a Snickers ("too sweet") and drew the line at just about anything foreign for her home, even resisting her friends' pleas to try a German-made toothpaste.

Later, on a trip to the market together, she put only one imported product in her modest basket—a $1.45 can of cat food. And that only because there was no domestic alternative her cat would eat. Pointing to a carton of Wimm-Bill-Dann's yogurt, Filatova said she chose it over Danone's version. "It tastes better," she said. "It's *nashe*."[15]

■ ■ ■

AT THEIR BEST, the musicians Misha Kozyrev unleashed on the new Russia had an edge missing from the cheery imitative pop of the Yeltsin years. The first star to rise on Nashe's airwaves was Zemfira, a tousle-haired balladeer from the internal Muslim republic of Bashkortostan who used just one name and whose mournful anthem "AIDS" became a sensation. Bleak and nihilistic, it seemed more about life in modern Russia than just about the disease: "You have AIDS. It means we are going to die. We'll take medicine in the hospital. We will not think about tomorrow."[16]

The better sort of new Russian music, Kozyrev said, succeeded because it questioned Russia's ambivalent reality. "Pop will always tell you everything's fine, okay, it's cool. Rock will tell you it's not cool," he said, especially relevant for a country trying to figure out where it was at after a decade of change. "We had an incredible ten-year acid trip, and now we're back and reality's harsh and maybe harsher than before."

But in appropriating the *nashe* label for the music he so ceaselessly promoted, Kozyrev was also flirting with Russia's demons of racial hatred, mindless chauvinism, and subservience to dictatorship—and he knew it. "To me, there is a clear distinction between patriotism, which is good, and nationalism, which is not," he said. The distinction was often lost in the lyrics and offstage pronouncements of the musicians who grew famous on his airwaves, and Kozyrev was regularly accused in the press of pandering to all sorts of ethnic animosity. His annual outdoor rock festival, Nashestviye, drew more than one hundred thousand young music fans to a field outside Moscow each August—and, once, ultranationalist politician Vladimir Zhirinovsky, famous for his racist rants and determined to commandeer a captive audience of cheering Russia-for-the-Russians youth. Kozyrev refused him the stage.

But Kozyrev also owed one of his biggest early successes to a film that critics, even those who liked it, called an ode to xenophobic homicide. He had teamed up with the producers of the wildly popular film *Brat* (or Brother) to put together the sound track for its sequel. The first *Brat* starred young heartthrob Sergei Bodrov Jr. as hit man Danila, who learned to kill in Chechnya and couldn't stop once he returned to civilian life. *Brat 2,* released in 2000, sent the Russian killer to Chicago for an anti-American fable in which the Russians at last triumphed. The baby-faced hero Danila was filled with hate for blacks, the police, and Ukrainians in addition to his American targets and managed to shoot his victims in between reciting a patriotic child's rhyme about "my motherland."

"Are you gangsters?" the revenge-bent characters are asked by a puzzled Chicagoan in the film's most often-quoted scene.

"No, we are Russians!" replies the bald Russian prostitute Danila has just rescued from her black pimp in a blaze of gunfire.

The movie turned out to be even more successful than the first one—and the Kozyrev-produced music became the sound track for a new generation in a more assertive time. "There's a deeply embedded idea about this country—it's illogical, it's screwed up, but it's special," Kozyrev said of the film's appeal. For many, Danila the hit man was equated with Putin, the new tough-talking president. The newspaper *Komsomolskaya Pravda,* the country's most popular, youth-oriented tabloid, even advertised itself using both their images. "Putin is *nash* president, Danila is *nash* brother, *KP* is *nasha* newspaper," said its billboards around Moscow.[17]

Bodrov, the film's star, who was later to die in a freak avalanche while shooting another movie, saw himself as a social commentator. "I said, 'Let's love *nasha* motherland only for the fact that it is *nasha,*'" he told a symposium. The movies, he said, were for "people who have been humiliated, injured, or broken. It's a kind of therapy, oxygen which people need." As for the raw violence and hatred the movies seemed to promote, Bodrov said it was inevitable in a Russia without real laws or morals. "*Brat* is a kind of primeval state. There is still no law. There is still primeval chaos all around. And then one of these people rises and says, 'This is how it's going to be: we will protect the women, the fire, defend *nashi,* and kill the enemy.' These are the first words of the law when there is still no law."[18]

MISHA KOZYREV was no innocent. For most Russians, he knew, the name Nashe on his radio station would inevitably conjure up the one man who had done more than anyone else to ensure that the word entered the political lexicon on the eve of the Soviet Union's breakup.

Nashe as a political slogan had been the brainchild of Aleksandr Nevzorov, a wildly popular investigative journalist from St. Petersburg whose Gorbachev-era television show, *600 Seconds,* chronicled the indignities visited on ordinary people by the decaying socialist state. Nevzorov's heroes were dispossessed pensioners and abused orphans, and his show was an invitation to act against the corruption of the Communist bureaucracy. Dissidents who dreamed of a Western-style democracy loved it, but so, too, did disaffected conservatives who wanted to resurrect Russia as a great power. Everybody watched. "It is the voice of the people's hatred—hatred of everything that is going on," Nevzorov explained to an interviewer at the time.[19]

In January 1991, when the Kremlin ordered tanks into Soviet Lithuania to suppress independence demonstrations and paramilitary OMON police troops killed fourteen people defending the television tower, Nevzorov showed up to make a documentary. And many of his loyal viewers were in for a shock. Instead of praising fellow resisters to Soviet power, Nevzorov's film called the Lithuanian demonstrators "fanatics" and hailed the troops who fired on unarmed civilians for "defending our motherland." Cradling a rifle in his arms, Nevzorov was shown against the backdrop of the Vilnius television tower as dramatic music by Richard Wagner played. Soviet tanks were arrayed around him in a display of imperial power, and written on their sides was a simple new slogan: "Nashi." Nevzorov adopted the name for his documentary.

Nashi turned out to be a powerful rallying cry. In the fall of 1991, just weeks after the failure of the hard-line coup against Gorbachev signaled the beginning of the end for the Soviet state, Nevzorov addressed a crowd in St. Petersburg and called on them to join a new movement. Its goal was the preservation of Russia as an empire pulled back together from the disintegrating fragments of the Soviet Union, and its role model was Peter the Great as well as Lenin. The movement was to be called Nashi.

"Nashi," Nevzorov explained, "is a circle of people—let it be enormous, colossal, multimillion—to whom one is related by common language, blood, and motherland. All the people who consider everything happening today a deep personal tragedy can be called Nashi."[20] Nevzorov's political movement turned out to be too early for its time; democracy and the Western route of liberal economic reforms for Russia were at least temporarily in ascendance. But his popularization of *nashi* endured in the language, earning Nevzorov credit for its subsequent wide usage in the definitive dictionary of twentieth-century Russian.[21]

By the time Misha Kozyrev was ready to name his radio station Nashe, the name was indelibly associated with Nevzorov's particular brand of imperialist chauvinism. Several times, Kozyrev argued heatedly about it with Boris Berezovsky, his financial benefactor. "We weren't sure whether we should dare to use it," Kozyrev recalled, "or whether it had been completely destroyed by Nevzorov." The idea of using Nashe as the station's name had been Kozyrev's, but the guilty liberal in him knew that Nevzorov had "made a major negative impact on this country."

Cautionary tales were not long in coming. An early warning was the evolution of the popular punk band Civil Defense and the increasingly hate-filled views emanating from its front man, Yegor Letov. In the 1980s, the band was banned by the Soviet leadership, and its songs were anthems of the youth underground, filled with racy expletives and ringing condemnations of Stalinism and latter-day socialism. Letov was even falsely accused of insanity and sent to a mental hospital in 1984—a common KGB technique for dealing with troublesome dissidents. In "Everything Is Going According to the Plan," he lampooned the hollowness and absurdity of Soviet central planning to great effect, and the song was his biggest hit: "Everything will be fine under Communism, everything will be okay, just have to wait, everything will be free and nobody will have to die." But in his post-Soviet incarnation, he had joined forces with the radical National Bolshevik Party, using his popularity on the wider punk scene to tout the group's neo-fascist views. Some, but not all, of their songs were banned by Nashe.[22] Many were about as subtle as the anthem by another punk rocker, "Kill the Yankees," which was a hit at Moscow underground clubs in 2000: "Burn the shop with the American shit! Advertise the hard-currency store with a brick. Blow up with a grenade their pretty Chevrolet. Scrawl the word *penis* on their sales logo! Kill the Yankees! Kill the Yankees and all who love the Yankees!"[23]

The band Alisa was to pose an even more difficult test for Nashe's founder. In the 1980s, Kozyrev had simply worshiped them—their music, their outrageous, in-your-face snubs of Soviet authority. Led by Konstantin Kinchev since 1984, the Leningrad-based group had been accused in the Soviet press of advocating fascism, urging young people to evade service in Afghanistan, and general subversiveness. Their most famous song, "My Generation," circulated in the millions and rallied youth against the state.[24] "It really caused people to stand up and question Communism," Kozyrev said. At the time, he saw Kinchev as a rock hero on the order of U2's Bono, "brutal, honest, blunt-talking, no compromise."

But Kinchev traced a depressingly familiar arc—from standing with Yeltsin and the defenders of the White House during the abortive 1991 coup to embracing Russian orthodoxy and Russia-first politics in the mid-1990s to outright xenophobia by the late 1990s. In 2000, he released the hit album *Solntsevorot*. It had a swastika on the cover. Kozyrev refused to play it on his radio station.

A couple years later, Kozyrev turned on state television one morning and saw Kinchev playing a concert on board a Russian military ship, a flag in the backdrop. "And he sings, 'There are enemies all around us, there are different *orda*—Tatars—dark, evil forces, trying to conquer us but we should stand strong because it's a Slavic blood that runs in our veins.' . . . I listen to this sad, pathetic nationalist song and I wished I would have a time machine to go back to 1987, and I would catch him behind the scenes and say, 'This is what you will do fifteen years from now.' I think this guy would not live through the morning. I think he would cut his veins."

As disillusioning as it was to see his teenage idols turn into preachers of racial superiority, banning a few obviously racist songs was not the hard part for Kozyrev. What was harder was accepting that there might have been broader implications to the wave of national assertiveness he had so successfully ridden after Nashe's launch.

"You are flirting with Russian nationalism, or at least riding the wave," an interviewer challenged him in 2002.

"The idea behind the radio station is not to say that *nashe* is the best and everything else stinks," a defensive Kozyrev replied. "The idea is to show that after a decade of self-deprecation, *nashe* can also be very good. And there are things to be proud of here."

But in the end, he feared, his definition of *nashe* had not won out. On the final episode of a television talk show he regularly appeared on, which Kozyrev described as "sort of a *Crossfire* of music," the guests were members of a punk band that had grown famous in the Yeltsin period for a song bragging that "I could be a better president than Yeltsin." The host noted that he hadn't heard them play the song substituting Putin's name since the new president had taken charge, to which the band leader replied that he supported Putin in standing up to the arrogant Americans. Kozyrev remembered it clearly. "He was saying, 'I can say fuck the president, but I'm on his side. I think they flooded our country with McDonald's, and I think it takes away our national identity.' The crowd cheers. I took the microphone and I said, 'I confess I go to McDonald's, like 95 percent of those here who are just ashamed to admit it.' I said, 'How quickly you have learned to hate Americans, and how long will it take you to understand what our country does in Chechnya? You know how to think, but you don't want to.'" Dead silence greeted his speech.

His radio station, after its fast early ascent, struggled to maintain a place in the top ten as new competitors appeared that copied his all-Russian format but were even less refined in their musical tastes. Kozyrev's original backer, Boris Berezovsky, after falling out with the man he helped install in the Kremlin, also thought it politically wise to sell out his stake in Nashe to Rupert Murdoch.

Kozyrev had made a few stars like Zemfira, but had never persuaded a mass audience to embrace his brand of socially conscious, politically liberal rock—indeed, he had stood by and watched as the first Russian group to make it big in the West turned out to be Tatu, a faux lesbian pop duo who pranced around in schoolgirl miniskirts and were just as famous for French-kissing on Jay Leno's show as for any of their lyrics.

One afternoon at a café named for the French cognac Courvoisier ("My friend convinced the company to let him use their brand name," Kozyrev told us over carrot juice and an omelet), he seemed tired of the struggle for Nashe's identity. In the Putin era, Kozyrev now thought, *nashe* was something darker than it had once seemed. "I hope that everyone who listens to Nashe knows why," he said. "I don't want to reach the conclusion that this sheep-minded mentality is printed in our mind. I hope not."

Unlike the old-style dissidents who had never really attempted to fight since the Soviet collapse, Kozyrev had tried to stake his claim to *nashe*. He had tried to sell his young listeners on Chechen rock bands with a social con-science who sang about the forgotten war down south and to embrace the global culture that no longer had to be smuggled surreptitiously across Russia's border. He had played Ukrainian rock as well as Russian on his station, until giving that up, too, in frustration, and loved to give visitors tours of the radio station he had built with the most sophisticated technology "between here and London," as he couldn't help but brag. But *nashe,* he said sadly that afternoon, had not been defined by him. "It turned out to be narrowing and closing," he reflected, "rather than the open-mindedness I hoped for."

He then posed the question that seemed so obvious we were almost afraid to ask it ourselves: "Would I dare to call it Nashe today?" he asked. "I wouldn't. It's too dangerous."

The Takeover Will Be Televised

We prefer to rot in hell.
—Yevgeny Kiselyov

Andrei Norkin slipped on his jacket and settled into the anchor chair. It was eight in the morning on April 14, 2001, time for the morning news show on NTV. His lead story? The Kremlin takeover of NTV itself. Six minutes into the broadcast, the plug was pulled. The picture on television sets across the nation abruptly dissolved into a multicolored test pattern.

The Kremlin had taken Russia's only independent national television network off the air after months of denying it planned to do any such thing. The president who had come into office impressed that he could now "control everybody" in the Kremlin had taken the next step, trying to extend the reach of his control to those outside it as well. NTV had proven to be a choice target, the most potent political instrument in the country not already in state hands. Vladimir Putin had seen what television was capable of doing during his own rise to power, when it effectively created his presidency and destroyed his opponents. He would not allow it to destroy him.

For Norkin and the other journalists at NTV, the takeover that morning was the culmination of a yearlong battle for survival. While its founders had at times used it to advance their own political agenda, NTV had also made a mark as the first national television outlet ever to operate in Russia outside the authority of the state, the first to regularly report what the government did not want it to report. In a country accustomed to stolid Soviet anchors reading heavily censored reports on the fall harvest, NTV had been a powerful awakening. In its seven years of broadcasting, it had exposed corrupt figures, forced authorities to respond to societal problems, and brought the war in Chechnya unvarnished into the living rooms of everyday Russians. It had come the closest to establishing a Western-style level of professionalism. "NTV was a pioneer," Norkin told us later. "On that NTV, for the first time, not only anchors became honest but correspondents. We had live reports from places. For the first time, people could see good foreign-made films, political talk shows." He sighed. "It couldn't go on forever."[1]

Tall with thick glasses that gave him a slightly nebbish look, Norkin was an unlikely revolutionary. He had started out his career during the final days of the Soviet Union as a game-day announcer at a sports stadium, where his only small insurrection against the stilted system was trying to mimic the flamboyant style of American sportscasters while calling soccer and hockey games ("You sort of prolong your vowels"). When the stadium was transformed into a large flea market and he was left making sales announcements ("Tights are available in kiosk number four"), Norkin left to try his hand at radio, joining an FM station funded partly by Americans just two months after the failed August 1991 coup. After five years playing deejay and reading short news updates, he moved to NTV as the host of a morning program.

Like many of his colleagues, he was determined to fight for what they had built. When Gazprom, a state-controlled company chaired by a Putin aide, orchestrated a boardroom takeover ousting NTV's founders on financial pretexts, Norkin and the others barricaded themselves inside the station's headquarters at the Ostankino television tower in northern Moscow, airing an around-the-clock protest. A few thousand Moscow intellectuals rallied to support them outside in the cold, but the bulk of Russian society remained indifferent. For eleven days, they held out, until a squadron of burly security men descended on Ostankino in the middle of the night and seized the offices. Turning to their contingency plan, Norkin and the others marched out of the NTV offices and set themselves up in a borrowed studio across the street, where they tapped into a pirated feed on the network's frequency and began broadcasting their drama to the rest of the nation. But the state team found the link just minutes after Norkin went on the air and severed it.

Back at NTV headquarters, a few journalists stayed behind, uninterested in crusades or hoping to reach an accommodation with the new owners. One of them was Olga Belova, a young correspondent with piercing gray-blue eyes who was tapped to go on the air as an anchor by the new management. When she led into the 4 p.m. newscast just hours after the takeover, the difference was obvious. She opened with the new state-installed general director speaking uninterrupted for several long minutes as he cast events in his own terms. Belova then went to a reformist member of parliament who criticized the move, but finished with two top political leaders who characterized it as nothing more than a business dispute. None of her colleagues who quit en masse was shown speaking on air.

This traumatic moment had divided the NTV family. As soon as she left

the set, we found Belova in the newsroom, huddled in a corner with her producer, taking deep drags on a cigarette and quietly crying.

"My nerves are no longer steady," she told us. "People who you considered
not so much friends but more or less colleagues tell you things to your face,
several things that were very hard—" She left the thought hanging.[2]

We ran into Norkin, standing in a stairwell across the street. He ended up
finishing the thought for her. "Now friends have found themselves on different sides," he said. "For me, it's hard to imagine how I could meet with those
people."[3]

THE SHOWDOWN at Ostankino had been building ever since Igor Malashenko had refused to help the Kremlin install Vladimir Putin as the next
Russian president in the summer of 1999, saying he could not trust a KGB
man. Malashenko had been one of the original architects of NTV. In 1993,
he was a top executive at the state-owned Channel One, the nation's most-
watched station, when one of his journalists came to him with an idea.
Yevgeny Kiselyov, a former Persian-language instructor for the KGB who
became captivated with the possibilities of journalism during glasnost, was
anchoring a Sunday-night news analysis program called *Itogi* (Results), but
every week he still needed to report to authorities what he planned to say on
the air. Kiselyov was bristling at the strictures, and so he and Malashenko
came up with the idea of privatizing *Itogi* by forming their own independent
production company that would sell the program to the state network. To get
independent funding, they figured the man to see was Vladimir Gusinsky.

Born just five days before Putin in 1952, Gusinsky was one of the most
prominent of the so-called oligarchs who had emerged from the wreckage of
the Soviet system to build private fortunes. A Jewish former theater director
whose grandfather was shot during the Stalinist purges, Gusinsky had over
the years driven a taxi, worked as a street merchant, and plotted ways to get
ahead in the new capitalist system. One venture led to another until finally
he was able to put together a bank in 1989. He named it Most after the signs
on the ubiquitous automatic teller machines that had impressed him during
a visit to Washington. His breakthrough moment, though, was befriending
Moscow's strong-willed and powerful mayor, Yuri Luzhkov, who steered tens
of millions of dollars in city money through Most Bank accounts and even let
Gusinsky set up his headquarters in city hall.[4]

By the time Malashenko and Kiselyov came to see him, Gusinsky had
already caught the media bug. He was financing Ekho Moskvy, the country's
first independent radio station, made famous for its broadcasts during the

1991 coup, and he had helped start a newspaper, *Sevodnya* (Today). Short with a roundish face and expressive manner, Gusinsky fairly brimmed with an infectious energy, "a kind of electrical power," as Grigory Kritchevsky, who later became NTV's news director, put it.[5] Gusinsky enjoyed the theatrical- ity of media—and also understood it could be a powerful weapon in his many business and political battles. So when Kiselyov and Malashenko pro- posed a weekly television program, Gusinsky stunned them by thinking big- ger. "Look, why should we be making one program?" he asked. "Let's make a channel."[6]

Thus was born NTV. After relentless lobbying, Gusinsky's people per- suaded Boris Yeltsin to sign a decree in January 1994 giving them the license to a seldom-watched channel. The new network went on the air with Kiselyov, Tatyana Mitkova, and a few other state-television alumni in a quickly assem- bled studio painted gray because they considered it avant-garde. Their broad- cast was considered avant-garde as well. When Yeltsin launched the first war in Chechnya in December 1994, state-television channels featured dry, uninfor- mative briefings by military officers, while NTV dispatched its inexperienced twentysomething correspondents to live virtually full-time in Chechnya and beam back graphic frontline pictures that shocked Russians, who had never seen war played out on their television screens before. Kiselyov offered unstint- ing analysis of Russian abuses and setbacks in Chechnya each Sunday on *Itogi*, becoming the country's best-known journalist, a familiar face with his trade- mark mustache, thick brown hair, and penetrating eyes.

The brave coverage nearly got NTV shut down on more than one occa- sion, and Kiselyov several times ordered a tactical retreat to keep the Krem- lin from pulling the plug. At one point during the war, Gusinsky left the country for six months, fearing retribution. But Gusinsky got back into Yeltsin's good graces by signing up for his 1996 reelection campaign, detailing Malashenko to run the president's advertising effort at the same time he was overseeing NTV. Like the rest of the Russian media, the network's coverage reflected an open tilt, its adulatory portrayal of Yeltsin a stark contrast to its denigration of Communist challenger Gennady Zyuganov. The NTV crew rationalized its pro-Yeltsin advocacy by concluding that the return of the Communists would mean the end of free press. "There was a feeling that Yeltsin must win," recalled Alim Yusupov, the correspondent assigned to improve the president's terrible public image. "I understood he was not the best of presidents, that what he did was not perfect. But there was the feeling of danger, that if Zyuganov came to power, things would be extremely bad."[7]

But in agreeing to be used to support Yeltsin, Gusinsky and the others inadvertently sealed their own fate. Soon after Yeltsin won reelection, Gusinsky was rewarded with hundreds of millions of dollars for his Media-Most empire from the state-controlled energy monopoly, Gazprom, in exchange for 30 percent of NTV stock. Unsatisfied, Gusinsky demanded more payback in the form of a stake in the massive state telecommunications company, Svyazinvest, a cash cow eyed by several of the oligarchs. But Anatoly Chubais, the deputy prime minister who had presided over a long string of rigged auctions, chose this moment to insist on a fair contest, and Gusinsky lost out to another oligarch whose bid was put together by a hustling Russian-American banker named Boris Jordan in an auction run by Chubais's lieutenant Alfred Kokh. Furious, Gusinsky lashed out, launching what would become known as the Information War. A media scandal fanned by NTV revealed that Chubais and Kokh had received $90,000 and $100,000 respectively in book contracts from a publisher owned by the winner of the Svyazinvest auction. "Gusinsky told me point-blank that he would put me in jail, that police were on their way to arrest me, and he was saying all this with a smirk on his face," Kokh recalled later.[8] Kokh did not go to jail, but lost his job and endured two years of investigation.

The NTV journalists understood they were being used. "When journalists reported these events, they were told what accent they were supposed to emphasize," Tatyana Mitkova, one of the original anchors, told us later. "It became obvious to us that it was the end of independent journalism at NTV—at least the way we thought of ourselves."[9] Kiselyov acknowledged that he regularly had to try to fend off Gusinsky's agenda, sometimes unsuccessfully. "Of course he expected returns for his investment, political returns," Kiselyov told us. "We understood that." In hindsight, Kiselyov said he came to regret the political manipulation. "Later we started to understand we should have distanced ourselves. But we were still fresh from the battles." And the attacks on Chubais and Kokh? "Yes, probably we were not right. Yes, we should have probably distanced ourselves from that. We probably should have realized this was an orchestrated thing."[10]

The Information War did not end Gusinsky's relationship with the Kremlin. A year later, after the 1998 economic crash, Gusinsky received a bailout from Gazprom in the form of $261.5 million in loans—in effect, a state subsidy as a reward for past service. But the Kremlin wanted its political returns as well. As it geared up for the next election, it expected the same sort of political subservience it had enjoyed in 1996. Kiselyov had a meeting one day in early 1999 with Kremlin officials who told him they wanted NTV to commit to supporting Yeltsin's chosen successor—whoever it would be.

"Join us or rot in hell," Kiselyov recalled a Kremlin official telling him. Kiselyov refused, saying, "We prefer to rot in hell."[11]

Gusinsky only exacerbated the schism by ordering NTV to carry critical reports of the second war in Chechnya after Vladimir Putin came to power, while openly promoting Yevgeny Primakov and Yuri Luzhkov. The price of defiance became clear just four days after Putin's inauguration as president in May 2000 when masked, gun-toting tax police arrived at Media-Most offices and ransacked the place. Within a few weeks, Gusinsky was summoned to the prosecutor's office for questioning, only to be arrested once he showed up and thrown in jail for alleged financial misappropriation. The blatantly political nature of the case was amply demonstrated when Putin's press minister, Mikhail Lesin, offered Gusinsky a deal straight out of a bad Mafia movie: give up NTV in exchange for freedom. After three days behind bars, Gusinsky agreed and was released. On July 20, he signed a formal document agreeing to turn over his Media-Most company to Gazprom explicitly in exchange for the end of the case against him, a document that Lesin signed as well, as if a press minister should be deciding criminal prosecutions. The prosecutor promptly lifted travel restrictions against Gusinsky, who immediately raced to the airport, boarded a plane, and left Russia for good.

VLADIMIR PUTIN was obsessed with television. Each night he would bring home videocassettes of that day's news to watch how he was covered, then return to the Kremlin the next morning with his judgments. "He watches himself on television, he goes through everything," a top aide told us. And so it wasn't enough to drive Vladimir Gusinsky out of the country. Putin was determined to oversee all of the country's major broadcast outfits. No one understood better than Putin just how powerful television could be in the new Russia and that he who controls it controls the country. "He came to power through television, and that's why to have an [independent] channel that covers sixty-five percent of Russia, that creates a danger," the aide said.[12]

In his first few months in power, Putin had made moves that convinced some that he might really be a reformer who would finish what Boris Yeltsin had started. He had named Yeltsin's pro-market finance minister Mikhail Kasyanov as prime minister, a signal, it seemed, that he was serious about reinventing Russia in a Western mold. Broad-shouldered, with an easy smile, Kasyanov was a career economist in his early forties, respected in the West as a formidable international-debt negotiator and seen as a reliable promoter of capitalism—so much so that some had questioned whether he was profiting personally on the side. With Kasyanov as his partner, Putin moved quickly to clean up Russia's notorious finances, weaning the government off its addiction to foreign loans and even building up budget surpluses. By summer, he had instituted a new 13 percent flat tax in hopes of convincing Russians, almost none of whom paid taxes in full, to emerge from the shadow economy, declare their income, and pay their fair share. He then moved to advance new land codes to allow property to be bought and sold for the first time since the Bolsheviks, a new labor code recognizing private employment and allowing businesses the right to fire workers, and new reforms to overhaul the famously corrupt and inefficient state electricity and natural gas monopolies. Kasyanov and other liberals took heart in the flurry of action, seeing Putin as the implementer of Yeltsin's vision.

But Putin had a different vision in mind. After all the political unruliness of Yeltsin's 1990s, Putin had decided to institute discipline in Russian society in the form of a new system he called "the vertical of power"—a single chain of command with himself at the top. A system of vertical power abhors competing power centers, whether parliament, the media, regional governors, courts, opposition parties, or nongovernmental organizations, and Putin wasted little time setting in motion an unspoken years-long plan to systematically eliminate any rival concentrations of influence. Besides Gusinsky's NTV, his first targets were the governors of the eighty-nine regions that composed the Russian Federation, a motley collection of willful regional barons who had taken seriously Yeltsin's offer following the collapse of the Soviet system to "take as much sovereignty as you can swallow."[13] Many openly defied Moscow, refusing to send tax receipts to the federal government or flouting inconvenient federal laws. Putin's solution to a legitimate problem was to crush the governors. First he proposed kicking them out of the upper house of parliament, the Federation Council, which had led the fight against Yeltsin's attempts to dismiss the hostile prosecutor Yuri Skuratov a year before. And then Putin decided to install seven new presidential envoys, or supergovernors as some called them, to supervise the governors, and to give himself the power to fire those regional leaders who got out of line. Five of the seven supergovernors were generals, *siloviki* from the KGB and military like the president they served. Putin resolved that Moscow would never be silent again.

To Boris Berezovsky, the oil-and-metals magnate who had helped elect Putin, the moves were disturbing. Big businessmen, who often exercised de facto control over the regional governments where their main factories or oil wells were located, had found the old system useful. And Berezovsky's sense of ownership over Putin seemed to know no bounds. Shortly after the presidential election, according to his confidant Sergei Dorenko, Berezovsky told Putin that he would be just a temporary figure, that a permanent new president would be picked in 2004. Dorenko was shocked at the effrontery. "How were you telling him these things?" he asked Berezovsky afterward. "Did you bend on your knees?" Berezovsky said of course not. "Borya," Dorenko responded, "do you realize that Volodya does not exist anymore? There is the emperor's throne. Today you sentenced yourself."[14] Berezovsky later told us he did not recall telling Putin he would be a temporary figure, but did suggest to the new president he would create a loyal opposition party to fill the void left by the Kremlin's destroyed rivals. It could be a leftist party or a rightist party, Berezovsky said. "It doesn't matter which kind of opposition it will be," he remembered telling Putin. "The most important thing is that opposition should be."[15]

Putin disagreed, just as he disagreed with Berezovsky's criticism of the Chechnya war. Soon Putin stopped returning Berezovsky's calls or replying to his letters. Frustrated at being shut out, Berezovsky decided to sink Putin's plan to restructure the Federation Council. When he heard that the Kremlin was paying State Duma deputies $5,000 apiece in bribes to vote for the changes, Berezovsky, who had once unsuccessfully tried to bribe Putin years before in St. Petersburg, decided to outbid the Kremlin. "I spread this information through deputies that I will pay seven thousand dollars" to those who voted against the Putin legislation, he told us. Furious, Putin summoned Berezovsky to the Kremlin.

"Boris, do you really start to fight against me?" Putin demanded, according to Berezovsky.

"No, I fight against the law which you proposed," Berezovsky answered.

"But I was told that you promised to pay seven thousand dollars to each parliament member from the Unity party not to vote for that," Putin complained.

"But you were the one who started it!" Berezovsky said.

"But we are the state!" Putin retorted.[16]

It's impossible to verify Berezovsky's admittedly biased account, although even Kremlin loyalists agree that Putin has always taken offense when the state's actions are questioned. And many Putin advisers have acknowledged that votes in parliament were regularly bought by all sides in legislative battles; it was just how business was done in Moscow.

Putin took a similarly aggressive approach to the broader oligarchy that had emerged during Yeltsin's time and helped put him in office. Overnight billionaires like Berezovsky and Gusinsky, having made their money through shady deals in the 1990s, were enormously unpopular in Russia, and Putin had made a point of denouncing them during his campaign. Under his presidency, he promised, "There will be no such oligarchs as a class."[17] At the time, the oligarchs did not take the threat too seriously. They knew it was just good politics, and besides, they still considered Putin a creature of the Yeltsin Family, which was virtually a wholly owned subsidiary of the oligarchs.

But Gusinsky's arrest was just the warning shot. Suddenly, law enforcement agencies were nosing around many of the tycoons. Prosecutors threatened to reverse the privatization of Vladimir Potanin's Norilsk Nickel metals giant, while tax authorities began investigating Berezovsky's Avtovaz carmaker and Vagit Alekperov's Lukoil energy giant. "The security services think they hear the old music playing," mused Pyotr Aven, the banker who had first introduced Berezovsky and Putin.[18] Berezovsky grew increasingly distant from the president he had helped install. In a period of a few weeks in the spring and summer of 2000, he issued a letter criticizing Putin's plans to rein in regional governors, announced he would form his own political party to counter an increasingly "authoritarian" presidency, and finally quit his seat in the State Duma to protest what he called "a deliberate campaign aimed at destroying independent big business." Berezovsky proposed a general amnesty for the privatization era. "Everyone who hasn't been asleep for the past ten years has willingly or unwillingly broken the law," he said.[19]

Now that Putin had their attention, he called in the oligarchs to lay down the new law—his law. Boris Nemtsov, the former deputy prime minister who now led the reformist Union of Right Forces, organized a meeting at the Kremlin with twenty-one leading business tycoons. Late in the afternoon of July 28, 2000, the moguls settled into seats around an outsize conference table in the ornate Catherine's Hall, unsure what to expect. Gathered there were Potanin, oil magnate Mikhail Khodorkovsky, aluminum king Oleg Deripaska, and the other cardinals of Russian capitalism. Three of the oligarchs Nemtsov had put on his proposed list were not invited by the Kremlin: Gusinsky, Berezovsky, and Roman Abramovich. Gusinsky had left the country a few days before, never to return, and Berezovsky was increasingly on the outs. Abramovich, on the other hand, remained such a Kremlin favorite that his peers figured he did not need to be invited since he retained his own private channels to the president.

Putin set the tone from the beginning of the meeting, giving a nod to the power of the oligarchs before making clear that it was over. "I want to draw your attention to the fact that you built this state yourself to a great degree through the political or semipolitical structures under your control," he told the gathered business leaders. "So there is no point in blaming the reflection in the mirror. So let us get down to the point and be open and do what is necessary to do to make our relationship in this field civilized and transparent."[20] Just like that, the world was different. Putin was in charge, he was saying, and the oligarchs had no one to blame but themselves since they had been responsible for his rise. Over the next two hours and forty minutes, Putin reassured them that they could keep the spoils of the 1990s privatizations—if they kept their hands off the government. "There was such a statement, a message: 'You stay out of politics and I will not revise the results of privatization,'" Oleg Kiselyov, one of the oligarchs at the meeting, told us later.[21] Anyone who violated those terms, Putin made clear, would pay the price. The businessmen were suitably chastened. "Today's meeting draws a line under ten years of the initial accumulation of capital," Nemtsov reported to the media afterward. "The era of the oligarchs is over."[22]

IT DIDN'T TAKE long for Putin to face the first real crisis of his presidency, an experience that would scar both him and the country for years to come. Just three months after Putin's inauguration, the Russian navy staged an elaborate military exercise in the Barents Sea to demonstrate Russia's continuing relevance in the world. Yet instead, it cost the country one of its most sophisticated nuclear submarines and an ocean of credibility.

Commissioned in 1994, the *Kursk* was one of the most fearsome weapons in the modern world, an Oscar II–class submarine designated K-141 that stretched the length of one and a half football fields and towered five stories tall. Designed to destroy U.S. aircraft carriers, the *Kursk* left port in August 2000 armed with eighteen torpedoes and twenty-three SS-N-19 Granit cruise missiles. But something went terribly wrong with one of the torpedoes. At 11:28 a.m. on August 12, an explosion ripped through the bow of the boat, followed by a second, more powerful blast two minutes and fifteen seconds later that registered 3.5 on the Richter scale at monitoring stations as far away as Africa and Alaska. Many in the crew of 118 were instantly killed. As the boat plunged to the soft mud and sand at the bottom of the sea 354 feet below the surface, the survivors fled to the rear compartment. By the time it was sealed off, just twenty-three men were left to huddle there in the dark and cold, praying for a miracle. "It doesn't look as if we have any chance. Ten to 20 percent," Captain-Lieutenant Dmitri Kolesnikov scratched out in a note to his wife. "We will hope that at least someone will read this. . . . There's no need to despair."[23]

Aboard the cruiser *Peter the Great*, Admiral Vyacheslav Popov, commander of the Northern Fleet, was informed that explosions had been detected
near the *Kursk*, but did nothing for nearly twelve hours as he waited for the
next scheduled radio communication. Putin flew that day to the resort town
of Sochi for vacation. By his account, he knew nothing until the next morning when the defense minister called. Instead of rushing back to Moscow or
to the Northern Fleet base near Murmansk, Putin remained in Sochi jet-
skiing with his family. And officials continued to reveal nothing to the public except for a statement by Popov calling the exercises "a great success."
When the government finally acknowledged two days after the fact that the
Kursk had sunk, it issued a string of lies, blaming "a malfunction" and saying
the fleet was in radio contact with the crew and supplying it with oxygen and
water through tubes.

There were more excuses and new deceptions as the days wore on. Dropping the radio contact claim, the navy said it was communicating with the
crew by knocking on the hull, but added that storms, strong currents, a damaged hatch, and the sharp angle of the boat were frustrating rescue efforts. A
headline blaring across the front of the popular tabloid *Moskovsky Komsomolets* reflected national frustration: "Damn You, Do Something." Asserting
that the *Kursk* may have been struck by a foreign submarine, Moscow
deflected every offer of outside assistance until President Bill Clinton called
Putin and personally pleaded for the Russians to accept.[24]

Watching television from his vacation, Putin grew increasingly livid at the
skeptical coverage. Vladimir Gusinsky's NTV aired tough reports about
the government's failure to handle the situation, Putin's public silence, and
the navy's numerous lies. Boris Berezovsky's Channel One approached the
story more gingerly at first, but its tone shifted after Berezovsky tried calling
Putin to advise him to return to Moscow and had his calls go unreturned. "All
right," Berezovsky told anchor Sergei Dorenko, "there are no restrictions
about coverage of the issue. . . . Do what you want." Unshackled, the Channel One journalists aired interviews with wives of *Kursk* sailors distraught at
the way the situation was being handled. That set off Putin, who called personally to rail at the report and accuse the journalists of faking it. "You hired
two whores for a hundred in order to push me down," Dorenko remembered
Putin saying. Dorenko was taken aback. "They were officers' widows," he said,
"but Putin was convinced that the truth, the reality, did not actually exist. He
only believes in [political] technologies."[25]

The public anger boiled over at a meeting between relatives of the crew
and military officers six days after the submarine sank. Nadezhda Tylik, a

spiky-blonde-haired mother of a twenty-four-year-old sailor, shouted at the assembled brass, "Swines! What did I bring up my son for? You are sitting there getting fat but we haven't got anything. My husband was in the navy for twenty-five years. What for? And now my son is buried down there. I will never forgive you. Take off your epaulets and shoot yourselves now!" At that point, a female medic approached from behind and injected a sedative into Tylik through her coat, then when her legs buckled, carried her out of the room, an action captured on tape and broadcast on Berezovsky's and Gusinsky's channels, further fueling outrage at a government that would drug its own people to keep them quiet.[26]

When British and Norwegian divers finally reached the *Kursk,* they realized the Russians had lied about everything—there had been no storms, no strong currents, no damaged hatch, and no steep angle. Western listening devices had never detected any knocking on the hull. Norwegian rear admiral Einar Skorgen contacted Popov and demanded proper information or he would abort the operation. "I was really furious," he said afterward. "The Russians at times gave us such bad data and such disinformation that it began to put the lives of the Norwegian divers in danger."[27] When the divers accessed the submarine's rear compartment on August 20, it had already flooded and no one was left alive.

Through all of this Putin had remained silent in Sochi, returning to Moscow only a week after the submarine sank. Three days later he flew north to meet victims' relatives in an officers' hall. "My heart hurts, but yours hurt even more," he told them. He went on to say the Russians had done everything they could and accepted international help as soon as it was offered.

Fuming relatives shouted him down, saying they knew from television that foreign governments had offered help earlier.

"Television?" Putin exclaimed. "They're lying. Lying. Lying."

He then launched an attack on the oligarchs. "There are people in television who bawl more than anyone today and who over the past ten years have destroyed that same army and navy where people are dying today. And here they are today leading the support for the army. . . . They have been stealing money to their hearts' content over the last few years and now they are buying everyone and everything."

Asked why the Russians had to rely on foreigners for help, Putin blamed the decrepit condition of the military. "So far as these rescue means are concerned, they broke down," he told the relatives. "There's not a damn thing left. There's not a damn thing left in the country. It's as simple as that."[28]

The next day, back at the Kremlin, he expanded his message for a national television audience. "I still feel a total sense of responsibility and sense of guilt for this tragedy," Putin said. Then he opened up on his critics. In an obvious reference to Berezovsky and Gusinsky, he said, "It would be better for them to sell their villas on the Mediterranean coast of France or Spain. Only then would they explain why all this property is registered in dummy names and in the names of juridical companies. We would then ask them where the money came from."[29]

That spelled the end of Berezovsky and Gusinsky in Russia. Gusinsky, who had fled abroad after being released from jail a month earlier, renounced the agreement to give up NTV, noting that it had been signed under duress. After the *Kursk* incident, prosecutors reopened their case against him, and Gazprom launched a drive to take over the network by leveraging its credits and minority stock holdings. As for Berezovsky, he went to the Kremlin for a meeting with Putin to discuss the president's complaints about *Kursk* coverage, only to find Aleksandr Voloshin, the president's chief of staff and political enforcer, waiting for him instead.

Voloshin had a blunt message: Berezovsky had to give up his management and ownership interests in Channel One. "You should return the shares or you will follow Gusinsky to jail," Voloshin told him bluntly, according to Berezovsky.[30]

Berezovsky bristled and refused to talk about it with him, demanding to see Putin instead.

The next day he returned and met with Putin and Voloshin. Putin was no less blunt. "I want to run ORT," the president told the oligarch, using Channel One's initials. "I personally am going to run ORT."

"Listen, Volod, this is ridiculous, at a minimum," Berezovsky claimed to have said. It was an extraordinary idea, the president personally taking over a television network. "Do you know what you are talking about? In fact, you want to control all the mass media in Russia—yourself!"[31]

Berezovsky recounted that Voloshin had threatened him with Gusinsky's fate if he resisted and challenged Putin on that. "Is it your idea or his idea to put me in jail?" he asked. As Berezovsky recalled it, Putin made clear he shared Voloshin's sentiment.

Berezovsky understood that it was over. Putin was no longer under his sway and had determined to break away from his onetime patron. Fighting him, the oligarch realized, was pointless. "After that, they opened a case against me and I left for France," he told us later.[32] Like Gusinsky, Berezovsky would never return to Russia for fear of politically motivated prosecution. Berezovsky sold his share in Channel One to his estranged partner, Roman

Abramovich, who later transferred it back to the state. The Kremlin installed friendly management, and the days of semi-independence at Channel One abruptly ended.

Putin never did seem to understand that the outrage over his handling of the *Kursk* was not a political plot by Gusinsky and Berezovsky. A couple weeks after the submarine accident, he visited the United States and appeared on CNN's *Larry King Live*.

"What happened with the submarine?" King asked.

"It sank," Putin said coldly.[33]

WHILE PUTIN was turning on his oligarch patron, he remained loyal to the man who had first brought him to Moscow. Pavel Borodin, the Kremlin property chief who had hired Putin, was arrested in January 2001 at a New York airport as he arrived on his way to an inauguration event organized by supporters of incoming president George W. Bush. The U.S. authorities were acting on an international arrest warrant issued on behalf of Swiss investigators looking into the shady Kremlin renovation projects involving the Swiss firm Mabetex. By now, Borodin had been removed from the property job and given the largely ceremonial position of secretary of the largely symbolic union of Russia and the former Soviet republic of Belarus. But the Swiss were not ready to give up on his activities in his previous post. Borodin, they charged, had pocketed $25 million for himself in kickbacks stemming from the Kremlin renovation.

Putin came to Borodin's rescue. After the Americans extradited Borodin to Switzerland, Putin put up $3 million in Russian government money to bail him out. Borodin returned to Russia, escaping the Swiss, who a year later convicted him in absentia of money laundering. Borodin considered Putin's help payback for getting him the Kremlin job in the first place. "When he found himself in trouble, I helped him," Borodin told us. "When I was in trouble, he helped me. The score between us is one to one. I don't like to either win or lose."[34]

Putin was not so forgiving of the crew at NTV. Even with Vladimir Gusinsky out of the country, the Kremlin remained determined to seize the network—and make a point to the other oligarchs. "This is how I see it," Putin told French journalists who asked him about his relationship with the tycoons. "The state holds a club, which it uses only once. And the blow connects with the head. We have not used the club yet. We have only shown it and the gesture sufficed to get everyone's attention. If we get angry, however, we will use the club without hesitation."[35] Authorities began using the club. They threw Gusinsky's chief financial officer in prison, raided Media-Most offices more than thirty-five times, seized one and a half tons of documents, froze all activity by Gusinsky's bank, convened hearings to liquidate the company, and even summoned anchor Tatyana Mitkova for questioning about loans from the company to buy an apartment. In theory, prosecutors were investigating Gusinsky for defrauding Gazprom by not repaying the energy company's loans, even though some were not yet even due; at the same time Gazprom was moving to seize Media-Most and the television network, citing the same justification. Many Westerners were willing to believe that it was just a dispute over money or to conclude that Gusinsky had it coming since he had played politics himself, but the financial issues were a smoke screen. "This was politically motivated pressure on the old forces," acknowledged Gleb Pavlovsky, the Kremlin political consultant.[36]

To the journalists working at the network, there were no illusions. Whatever they thought of Gusinsky, having the state take over all national television was not a step toward democracy. When Mitkova was interrogated by prosecutors, her colleagues accompanied her, and talk-show host Svetlana Sorokina spoke directly into a camera appealing to Putin to put a stop to the campaign against NTV. "We are not oligarchs, nor members of the board of directors," Sorokina said.[37] A few hours later, her telephone rang and she found Putin on the other end. He invited the journalists to meet at the Kremlin. Some at the station thought this might be their salvation. Russians historically have believed in the *dobry tsar,* the benign autocrat who if he only knew of all the atrocities committed in his name would surely put a stop to them. "We believed that somewhere up there in the Kremlin we would be forgiven," Mitkova said later.[38]

But Yevgeny Kiselyov held out no such hope. He had grown increasingly defiant and fatalistic. We went to see him that weekend to ask what he would tell Putin. As he sat in his conference room, he laid out three cellular telephones in front of him; he constantly switched phones, he said, to keep ahead of the authorities, who were surely tapping into any line they discovered him on. The meeting with Putin, he fretted, would only turn out to be a political trap to make the president look as if he cared about freedom of speech and to distance himself from the campaign against NTV.[39]

Kiselyov was right. Putin welcomed Kiselyov, Mitkova, Sorokina, and a half dozen other NTV journalists into the wood-paneled, green-hued Kremlin library and told them he sympathized with their plight. For more than three hours, he took notes as he listened to their grievances and said he did not want to see the NTV team changed. But then he asserted that he had no control over the prosecutors. "There is nothing I can do," he told them with a straight face. "I'm glad to help. I will try. But they do not obey me."[40] Never mind that he seemed particularly well versed on all the details of the charges against Gusinsky—and that just prior to the session with the journalists he had met with Prosecutor General Vladimir Ustinov.

The pressure was taking its toll. Back at NTV, Mitkova and others proposed that they negotiate a compromise that would, in effect, toss Gusinsky overboard as long as the journalists could remain independent. Kiselyov rejected the idea. Mitkova decided he was a kamikaze waging a political crusade and resigned in protest, along with talk-show host Leonid Parfyonov. "The journalists were made hostages," she told us later. "That's what made me quit, because I did not want to participate in it."[41]

Through all of this, NTV paid little deference to the new power bearing down on it. Most cutting of all on its airwaves was the weekly puppet program, *Kukly*, in which the country's best political satirist, Viktor Shenderovich, produced wicked send-ups of the latest news in the form of allegories and literary takeoffs. Russia's major political figures of the day were depicted by puppets with wildly exaggerated features. The portrayals were never flattering. Putin professed not to be bothered by it, but privately insiders said he grew incensed. One episode of *Kukly* that particularly aroused his wrath showed an ugly dwarf encountering a kind witch who runs a magic comb through his hair, and suddenly everyone starts to see him as beautiful, even though he has not changed at all. The dwarf was Putin and the witch was Berezovsky. Most of Moscow laughed uproariously. Not in the Kremlin. Shenderovich was told by an insider that he had finally crossed a line and "the Kremlin would never forgive us." Soon after, he told us, "our leadership had a meeting with one of the bosses at the Kremlin, and at that meeting they came up with concrete conditions and terms—if we agreed, they would stop all criminal cases against Gusinsky and economic cases against the company. There were three conditions—change the information policy on Chechnya, stop all investigation of corruption in the Kremlin and the Family, and third, remove the first face from *Kukly*." The "first face" being Putin's.

Shenderovich didn't take the warning as seriously as it was meant. "Here our caution went away. We decided to make a program based on the Bible, and the first face in accordance with the Bible was invisible. We were talking about the Ten Commandments, and Putin was depicted as a burning bush or a storm or thunder, and the Ten Commandments were like 'Don't kill anyone except people of Caucasus nationality,' 'Don't steal anything except federal property,' 'Don't create idols except the president, Vladimir Putin.'

Technically we observed the conditions because we removed the Putin puppet. But that didn't make us any more loved."[42]

The rifts from the Information War also came back to haunt Gusinsky
when Gazprom found the perfect man to lead its campaign against NTV—
Alfred Kokh, the same privatization chief who had been targeted by Gusinsky
after the Svyazinvest auction. Kokh orchestrated a boardroom takeover and,
to be the new general director of NTV, brought in his old friend and vacation partner Boris Jordan, the same banker who had put together the Svyazinvest bid that had beaten Gusinsky. As they completed their seizure of NTV,
Irina Khakamada and other democratic politicians in the Union of Right
Forces who wanted to protest were ordered to keep silent by Anatoly Chubais,
the same former deputy prime minister who had also clashed with Gusinsky
over the telecommunications auction.

Boris Jordan was, in many ways, the perfect choice for the Kremlin to take
over NTV. As an American, he could tout his fealty to democracy and free
speech and provide political cover for Putin with the West. As a Russian-
speaking descendant of the old prerevolutionary aristocracy, he could portray himself as a returning favorite son. The thirty-four-year-old financial
whiz kid with the buoyant personality and receding hairline made his debut
as NTV's new general director at a news conference after Kokh's boardroom
coup. He pledged not to storm into the station. "I will not enter the building
under police guard," he vowed that day.[43] Barely a week later, he entered the
NTV building after sending a squad of private security officers in the dead
of night to seize control from anchor Andrei Norkin and his colleagues.

As he settled into the conference room that had been Yevgeny Kiselyov's
until that morning, Jordan insisted to us that he was no Kremlin hatchet
man. "I've never been to the Kremlin under Putin except to go to concerts,"
he said. Yet he conceded that the hostile takeover struck a negative chord
abroad. "Sure, it looks different in the West. But one has to get away from the
sensationalism and go to the facts. . . . Did I have to do that? Yes, I had to do
that. That's the realism of doing business in Russia."[44]

Jordan had no experience running a news organization but plenty in the
realism of doing business in Russia. Born in New York and raised speaking
Russian in a fiercely anticommunist home, Jordan arrived in Russia in 1992,
just months after the fall of the Soviet Union, "a cherub twenty-six-year-old,"
as he put it, there to open an office for Credit Suisse First Boston. Jordan later
advised the Yeltsin government on how to privatize state enterprises and
helped organize the first sale of a government-owned factory, the Bolshevik
Biscuit Company. He also played the other side and eventually formed his

own investment bank. But Jordan did not get rich without making people angry. Twice his visa was yanked in retaliation by rivals with allies in the government. He was accused of stripping companies of prime assets and playing fast and loose in the anything-goes Russian market of the 1990s. Gennady Seleznyov, the Communist speaker of the State Duma, called Jordan "a cheating businessman" who "would sell you your own boots three times more expensive."[45] Jealous griping or sour grapes, Jordan said. Either way, Jordan claimed he would preserve NTV as an independent news operation, with the help of Tatyana Mitkova, Leonid Parfyonov, Olga Belova, and another prominent Russian journalist, Savik Shuster, recruited from U.S.-funded Radio Liberty. "What I want people to judge us by," Jordan said, "is what we build here."[46]

YEVGENY KISELYOV was in Spain consulting with the self-exiled Vladimir Gusinsky when Boris Jordan's security team stormed NTV. Kiselyov immediately hopped on a plane back to Moscow and arrived in the early evening to find hundreds of forlorn journalists awaiting him. As we watched from a corner of the jammed room, Kiselyov told the ousted team that he had found a new home for them at another, smaller station that they could build into a new independent network. TV-6, primarily owned by Boris Berezovsky, had offered to make Kiselyov its general director and to accept his team.

But the Kremlin was determined to destroy or seize all remnants of Gusinsky's empire. In the seventy-two hours after the NTV takeover, Gazprom closed Gusinsky's newspaper, *Sevodnya,* and fired the entire editorial staff of his newsmagazine, *Itogi,* which was published in conjunction with its American partner, *Newsweek.* The new TV-6 lasted just nine months. Press Minister Mikhail Lesin, the same man who had pressured the imprisoned Gusinsky to sign away his property, had offered Kiselyov a deal in which he could stay on the air if he cut ties with Berezovsky, but the anchor refused. So the Kremlin-friendly Lukoil energy company's pension fund, a minority shareholder in TV-6, got a court to liquidate the station by citing a law that had already been repealed, and Lesin then pulled the network off the air at midnight one night. When Kiselyov and his team reorganized as yet another television network, this time called TVS, it fared no better. Putin had signed off on the venture because some friendly businessmen were involved in the ownership. "He thought he could somehow control the situation," a senior Russian official told us, "but the oligarchs were much smarter than he thought and they arranged things to be independent, so he decided to stop it."[47] Mikhail Kasyanov privately argued with Putin to keep TVS on the air, but the president ignored his prime minister and then bypassed him by directly ordering Lesin to yank the network's license and turn over the channel to an all-sports network.

The message to the rest of the media was clear. Putin did not like criticism and would not tolerate powerful television channels in anything but loyal hands. "We taught them something," another high-ranking Kremlin aide told us. "We gave a shake to them."[48] Putin later installed Aleksandr Zdanovich, an FSB general and longtime spokesman for the secret service, as deputy director of the company that ran Rossiya television. Each Friday, the Kremlin summoned the directors of the major television networks and gave them marching orders for the week—what topics were acceptable, which ones were off-limits. The Kremlin's expectations were clear. Once when a group of Western correspondents was invited to interview Putin at his dacha, Kremlin press secretary Aleksandr Gromov told our U.S. television colleagues that they should not ask about Chechnya during the part of the session that would be taped for broadcast; they ignored him and asked anyway, but most Russians did not have that option.[49] Eventually, it got to the point that Russian journalists did not need any direct instructions. Just as in Soviet days, they instinctively recognized what would be dangerous territory and veered away. The Kremlin press pool, the only journalists who ever got in the same room with Putin regularly, was stocked with docile reporters who understood they were not to ask tough questions and were there simply to take dictation of Putin's words.

Unlike television, the print press remained relatively lively in Moscow, featuring a wide spectrum of outlets ranging from serious business newspapers to crusading scandal sheets to crime-blotter tabloids. Some continued to write brave and hard-hitting reports about the government, investigating the cover-up of the *Kursk* disaster or Russian military abuses in Chechnya. The Kremlin evinced little interest in what they wrote, knowing that most Russians got their news from television anyway. "The president has a very clear idea: let them print whatever they want, nobody reads it," a senior official recalled.[50]

Russian journalism had yet to develop strong traditions of professionalism. Many in the Russian media were accustomed to serving one agenda or another. Business tycoons often used their media outlets as weapons in feuds with competitors, and those without their own media organizations could rent one; for a price, they bought articles, a practice called *zakazukha*. A few weeks before Boris Jordan seized NTV, a public-relations-firm hoax made the point. It sent out an "article" about the "grand opening" of a new electronics store to twenty-one Moscow newspapers, offering money to editors for printing it as if it were news written by one of their reporters. Thirteen of the twenty-one accepted and ran the "article," often under bogus bylines, in exchange for payments ranging from $135 to $2,000. The supposed electronics store was actually nothing more than a garbage-strewn lot.[51]

The Russian public understood this and to a large degree discounted a lot of what they read and heard in the media on the assumption that it served someone's interest. Raised in an era when every word spoken on television was controlled by Soviet censors, many Russians had yet to come to expect genuinely independent sources of information or to appreciate the ones they did have. As NTV was being swallowed up by Gazprom on behalf of the Kremlin, a poll by the Public Opinion Foundation found that 57 percent of Russians supported censorship of the media.[52] While the intelligentsia was outraged at the loss of NTV, the vast majority of the public was not, so long as they continued to get foreign movies and other high-quality entertainment they had come to expect from the channel. At the height of the battle for NTV, a crowd of perhaps twenty thousand supporters rallied in Pushkin Square. By coincidence, around the same time, more than one hundred thousand people protested in the much smaller Czech Republic against the appointment of a new state television director they considered insufficiently independent.

The contrast was not lost on the NTV journalists. They came to understand that by compromising their independence in 1996, even for the worthy cause of preventing a Communist comeback, they had sold their integrity. If the Kremlin under Boris Yeltsin could expect the media to serve his interests, it should have come as no surprise that the Kremlin under Vladimir Putin would expect the media to serve his interests as well. Putin's attitude was clear. In discussing the state's relationship with the media shortly before his ascension to the presidency, Putin had quoted a European film: "A real man should always try, and a decent woman should always resist."[53] Vladimir Gusinsky realized that he had not resisted back in the 1996 campaign, and so the Kremlin had kept trying. "Gusinsky admitted that it was his fault," Viktor Shenderovich, the NTV satirist, told us much later. "He comprehended that and acknowledged that. Gusinsky played by the rules of the game. He was appointing and removing ministers. He was buying [State Duma] deputies. Only a lazy person or a poor person didn't do that. He used his television business as a tool of pushing his business interests. You know, history is not made of clean hands."

Putin was a product of the Cold War, the showdown between democracy and tyranny, and he owed his presidency to the power of television. "It's important to understand Putin's character," said Shenderovich. "He's a creature of the system. He was brought up in this clash of two systems. He didn't know anything about personal ethics. It's all about the conflict—you're either with us or against us. . . . The war against NTV was especially important for them. First of all, they wanted to eliminate a source of independent information, and secondly they wanted everyone to learn the lesson, to show everyone the new rules of the game. During the NTV era, Putin was very upset about international opinion. That's why a lot of effort was spent on PR, on bribing journalists, or threatening them, blackmail and direct threats. Because after they destroyed NTV, there was no one left who would become a critic. All of society was demoralized—I mean that part of society that understood what was going on. The majority of people didn't feel freedom of speech to be necessary. The majority thinks this is the privilege of the intelligentsia. . . . That's why the authorities were able to win."[54]

Just an Ordinary Crime

I envy those who don't have blood on their hands.
—SHAMIL BASAYEV

THE ROAR OF THE ARMORED personnel carrier rumbling up to his house and the telltale sounds of soldiers removing the safeties from their assault rifles roused Visa Kungayev from his sleep on the couch. The Russians were outside and he assumed they were coming for him.

It was just after midnight on the night of March 26, 2000, and the rest of Russia was absorbed by election night returns confirming the success of the Kremlin's Project Putin. The popularity of his war in Chechnya had boosted the unknown Vladimir Putin to the presidency; now, at the very moment of his election, Putin's war had arrived at the brick threshold of house number 7 on Zarechni Lane in the village of Tangi-Chu.

The village at the foot of the mountains, not far from the trading town of Urus-Martan, had endured three days of constant Russian bombardment the previous December, sending most residents fleeing and leaving a path of destruction. Now, the entire settlement of three thousand was living under an 8 p.m. curfew, surrounded by Russian troops who said they were there to search for Chechen rebels. The electricity was out and none of the houses had a telephone; one had been installed for the entire village just a few days before the presidential election and would be removed again afterward. Sometimes there was running water and sometimes not—in any case, never hot. With no heat, the villagers stocked up on firewood each winter, but after this latest round of conflict had erupted they dared not venture into the nearby forests because of land mines and began burning apple trees and wood fences, even chairs and tables.

Visa Kungayev had every reason to fear. A late-night visit by soldiers in Chechnya usually meant one thing—the seizure of any men in the house. Sometimes the men were later released after a beating or small bribe to their captors, but more often they were tortured, killed, or disappeared. That was already an active verb in Chechnya, as in *to disappear* someone. Visa Kungayev seized his only chance to escape, fleeing out the back door and through a fence to his brother's house next door.

His five children were still in the house when the soldiers burst in waving their rifles. Loud music blared from their armored personnel carrier, masking the children's screams. However, the soldiers had come not for Kungayev but for one of his daughters. First they set their sights on twelve-year-old Khava, until the man in charge spotted the oldest, Elza, five days past her eighteenth birthday. Known to her family as Kheda, she was shy, preferring to play with dolls instead of other children when she was younger and staying away from wedding parties now that she was older, afraid of missteps that would draw punishment from Allah. On her birthday, her parents had given her a ring that she put under her pillow for safekeeping.

Minutes after the soldiers arrived, Visa Kungayev's brother snuck over to the house. As Adlan Kungayev entered through the back door, he heard noises coming from the girls' room to his left. He rushed in, pushing aside a soldier just inside the door. He saw two other soldiers and his brother's five children huddling together in the corner.

"Who are you?" demanded the commander of the soldiers.

Adlan saw a thick man with cropped hair and hard eyes wearing the uniform of a Russian officer. Adlan knew the face. This was the colonel who led the tank regiment stationed just outside town. Only the day before, Adlan had seen the man beating up the head of the village. "He had three stars on his epaulet," Adlan recalled later. "I recognized him immediately." Adlan figured the soldiers were there to rob the house. "I'm the brother," he said. "What do you need here? If you need food, I can give it to you."

The colonel slammed the butt of his gun into Adlan.

"You're so proud," the colonel mocked, and turned the gun around to point it at Adlan's stomach and push him out into the hallway. "Get out."

Adlan noticed another soldier at the back door. The soldier hissed a warning. "Get out of here. He'll kill you." Adlan fled.

Inside, the colonel ordered his men to seize Elza, but she tried to get away, running around the bed several times until she tripped at his feet. The colonel grabbed a blanket, wrapped her in it, and carried her out of the house.[1]

The colonel was Yuri Budanov, a veteran tank commander who had terrorized the village for weeks. Budanov would later tell investigators that he had been searching for a female sniper who had been shooting at his troops, and that informants had identified Elza Kungayeva's house as a shelter for Chechen guerrillas. But that was not the impression other soldiers had when they saw Budanov arrive back at their camp. As Budanov's men dragged Elza into his quarters, a tent set up on the flatbed of a Zil-131 truck, one witness turned to a senior officer and asked what was happening. "The commander brought a girl again," the officer replied.[2]

For two hours, Budanov and Elza were alone in his tent. Budanov later claimed that he was questioning her about her rebel ties and that she insulted him, threatened to kill his family, and lunged for his gun. Yet Elza could hardly speak Russian, relatives said later, and was incapable of such elaborate conversation in what was to her a foreign language.

Sometime after 3 a.m., Budanov emerged from the tent. Inside, Elza was dead. She had been beaten, stripped naked, and strangled.

Budanov ordered his soldiers to retrieve her battered corpse and bury it in the nearby woods. The autopsy photographs would later show her face brutally pummeled, bruises covering every inch. The initial examination would also determine that she had been raped and sodomized.[3]

By morning, word reached the Russian commander of the western tank forces that a young Chechen woman was missing. General Valery Gerasimov called Budanov and two other colonels in the area and ordered them to find and return her. Later that day he traveled to Budanov's base to check on the case. Budanov lied. "He said he knew nothing about the abduction and the situation in the unit was normal," Gerasimov would later testify.

In the village, scores of people had gathered to demand answers about the missing young woman. Gerasimov went to talk with Visa Kungayev and found angry crowds. "I promised him to find the criminals and asked him to tell the people to disperse and go home. He did that." Visa's brother Adlan, who had seen Budanov take Elza but did not know his name, described the colonel to Gerasimov. "At first . . . I didn't believe that," the general said. Then he returned to the base to find Budanov.

Confronted by the general, Budanov pulled out his pistol in an apparent attempt to resist arrest, but shot himself in the foot by mistake. Gerasimov instructed his officers to disarm and detain Budanov. Then several of Budanov's men rushed to the scene and aimed their rifles at the general. After a few tense moments of mutiny, Budanov ordered the men to stand down.[4]

THE FATAL confrontation in the tent between Yuri Budanov and Elza Kungayeva that night would soon come to symbolize the brutality of a war with few if any rules. And what would happen next would test Russia's commitment to justice and explore the depths of hatred that had gotten the country to that point in the first place. That it all started on the day Vladimir Putin was elected would transform the case into a symbol of Putin's war.

But the murder of Elza Kungayeva could trace its origins back to long before either she or her killer was born. From Peter the Great's first failed attempt in 1722, Russia had never fully succeeded in conquering the querulous territory his soldiers called Chechnya after the name of one of the early towns they encountered. A rugged land in the Caucasus Mountains on the southern periphery of the Russian empire, Chechnya was home to a fiercely independent, clannish society that resented outsiders. The initial Russian forays into the Caucasus in the eighteenth century met unyielding resistance. A young student of Islam who called himself Sheikh Mansour led a *ghazavat*, or holy war, to drive the invaders out and destroyed an entire Russian brigade in 1785, drawing even more *murids*, or faithful, to his cause. The Russians sent a pitiless officer, General Aleksei Yermolov, to pacify the region, and in 1818 he built a fortress in the foothills he dubbed Grozny—which means "terrible" in Russian—and then lived up to the name. Rampaging through the countryside, his forces burned down villages and committed widespread atrocities. "I will never rest until not a single Chechen remains alive," Yermolov was quoted as saying.

It only inspired a more stubborn insurgency. A young preacher named Imam Shamil rallied an army of Muslim guerrilla fighters against the Christian colonizers in the 1830s and spent the next twenty-five years tearing at the foundations of Russian rule with stunning success. Not until 1859 did the Russians finally put an end to his rebellion by capturing his son and forcing Shamil himself to surrender. The tsar made peace with Shamil, bringing him to St. Petersburg and giving him a cushy exile there. But Shamil would go down in history as Chechnya's most iconic leader, a hero for thousands of his countrymen to emulate in the wars to come.

After the Bolshevik revolution of 1917, many Chechens took up arms again, joining the Reds in the ensuing civil war in an effort to destroy the monarchy forever and win back their independence. Unfortunately for them, they took too seriously Bolshevik promises of self-determination for oppressed nationalities. In 1924, Lenin created an autonomous republic for the Chechens that also included their ethnic cousins, the Ingush, but residents eventually came to learn that Moscow's tyranny had not abated with the fall of the Romanovs.

By the advent of World War II, Chechens were considered suspect enough in their loyalties that Stalin declared them all Nazi collaborators and deported the entire population. Known as the Vysl to Chechens, Operation Chechevitsa (a play on the word for Chechens that also means "lentils" in Russian) was unleashed the night of February 23, 1944. Russian troops spread through the republic, herding people onto trains bound for the inhospitable steppes of Kazakhstan with the help of American Studebakers provided by the United States under the Lend-Lease Act. The boxcars were so crowded that people had to stand the entire trip. At least a quarter of them never made it to Kazakhstan, succumbing to cold, hunger, or disease; the dead bodies remained trapped aboard the boxcars with the survivors through the long journey. Six days after it began, secret police chief Lavrenty Beria reported to Stalin that 478,479 people had been deported, including 91,250 Ingush.[5] Those who survived their hardscrabble exile, and many tens of thousands did not, were allowed to return only in 1957, four years after Stalin's death.

Their latest campaign against the Russians started along with the collapse of the Soviet Union in 1991, when Chechnya tried to join the rush for the door and declared its independence from the Russian Federation. Dzhokhar Dudayev, a major general in the Soviet army and an Afghan war veteran, returned to head the liberation movement, an unlikely leader of a religiously inspired effort who did not at first even know that Muslims pray five times a day. But while Boris Yeltsin allowed much of the old empire to slip away, he drew the line at Chechnya and dispatched troops in 1994 to bring the defiant local government back in line.

Thus began the first of two ruinous wars fought in Chechnya over the last decade over an oil-rich piece of land no bigger than New Jersey, wars that would devastate the republic, kill an estimated one hundred thousand people, further humble one of the world's great powers, and compromise the moral standing of an international community that stood by and did nothing to stop the slaughter. The overconfident Russians carpet-bombed Grozny and flooded the territory with troops, only to be humiliated by determined bands of irregulars just as they had been in Afghanistan a decade before. They succeeded in killing Dudayev with a guided missile that homed in on his satellite telephone in April 1996, but within months were forced to retreat from the region, agreeing to a tenuous cease-fire that gave Chechnya de facto autonomy and formally postponed any final decisions on its status for five years. Vladimir Putin would later call the deal brokered by Boris Yeltsin's negotiators a "national humiliation," a view that would shape his own Chechen policy, with scorched-earth consequences.

Aslan Maskhadov, a former Soviet artillery officer who had become a top commander in the war, won election as president of Chechnya after the peace talks, but lost control over the republic as it degenerated into a cesspool of banditry, kidnapping, and corruption. Among those challenging

Maskhadov's grip on power was Shamil Basayev, a radical young field commander who first came to Moscow's attention when he hijacked a Russian plane in Turkey in 1991 and earned international notoriety four years later when he took an entire hospital and a thousand patients, doctors, and nurses hostage in the town of Budyonnovsk, near Chechnya. Basayev lost the presidential election to Maskhadov and briefly tried to reinvent himself as Maskhadov's prime minister. Once an admirer of the Marxist guerrilla Che Guevara, he now supposedly had ties to Osama bin Laden and led Chechnya's radical Islamic faction along with a mysterious Arab militant named Khattab, who had fought alongside bin Laden in Afghanistan as a teenager. In August 1999, Basayev launched the incursion into Dagestan that triggered the second war and Putin's rise to power, telling one of his last visitors before the raid, "I envy those who don't have blood on their hands."[6]

YURI BUDANOV had dreamed of a military career even as a boy. Growing up in the Ukrainian industrial city of Donetsk, he applied to a military college to train as an officer but failed the entrance exam, so he joined the army as a simple soldier. Eventually his service convinced his commanders to send him to a tank institute in Kharkov. When the Soviet Union collapsed, he was stationed in what became the country of Belarus and refused to stay, securing a transfer to the Lake Baikal region in Siberia. He fought in the first war in Chechnya, coming away with the medals and scars to prove it.

As commander of the 160th tank regiment, Budanov helped storm Chechnya in 1999 when Putin launched the new ground offensive. He seemed to relish the bloodshed. In one memorable scene, NTV filmed him on January 9, 2000, bragging about his exchanges of artillery fire with the rebels. In celebration of Orthodox Christmas a few days earlier, he had even launched a barrage for the cameras from his post near the village of Duba-Yurt, already decimated by Russian artillery. "We will send them a present now," Budanov exclaimed. "Fire! Go! Merry Christmas!"[7] On January 13, his men set up a checkpoint there, at the mouth of the Argun Gorge, and announced they would permit refugees to go back up into the mountains to retrieve their belongings. Four men riding in trucks were detained at the checkpoint that day, and witnesses later said Budanov personally took them away. They were never seen alive again.

On February 6, the same day Russian forces were capturing Grozny, fellow troops entered Duba-Yurt, then emptied of all residents, and burned down the entire village. Ten days later, on February 16, Budanov's regiment was redeployed outside Tangi-Chu. Shortly afterward, the corpses of three of the men who had disappeared at the Duba-Yurt checkpoint were discovered in a grave near town, their noses, ears, and tongues cut off and their bodies riddled with bullet holes. The investigation went nowhere; Budanov was promoted from lieutenant colonel to full colonel.[8]

By that point, Budanov was growing increasingly volatile. During a home leave in Siberia, he snapped when he found a cut on his toddler daughter's hand and she told him her brother had caused it. Budanov burst into his son's room, grabbed the boy, and prepared to throw him out the fourth-floor window until his wife stopped him. "Yuri, this is your son!" she cried. Budanov then cut short his leave and returned to Chechnya.

He later told his psychologists that during the home leave he had run into the wife of a fellow officer who had been killed, decapitated, and left to hang from a tree. As the woman gave him warm clothes to pass along to her husband, Budanov could not bring himself to tell her that he was dead. "What was I supposed to tell his wife?" a lawyer later quoted Budanov as asking. "That her husband was hanging from a tree without his head and without his penis?"[9]

In Tangi-Chu, Budanov's forces had surrounded the village, barring anyone from entering or leaving. On March 25, 2000, the day before the presidential election, the head of the village, Shamsudi Dzhambulatov, heard that a Russian colonel and his troops were there conducting a *zachistka,* one of the Russian military's infamous cleansing operations. "They were very cruel," Dzhambulatov told us later. "They were harassing women, killing dogs, scaring people by shooting at them." Dzhambulatov tracked down two FSB officers he knew, and the three headed off together to confront the colonel. They found Budanov wearing rubber boots, a wool mask, and a surly attitude. Angry at being challenged, Budanov ordered his soldiers to strip the FSB officers of their weapons. "He disarmed both of them and started to beat them," recalled Dzhambulatov. "The soldiers tied them up. Then he harassed them with his questions: 'Who are you? Why are you here?' They nodded toward me and he came rushing over to me like a bull charging a red cape." Budanov demanded to know if Dzhambulatov had brought the FSB officers. "He grabbed me by the shirt. When he started to twist my shirt, I grabbed him, too."

Villagers started gathering, aghast as Budanov's men began hitting their elder. Among those watching was Adlan Kungayev, Elza's uncle, who would recognize the colonel's face as he took away the young woman barely twenty-four hours later. "They were beating me with gun butts and smashed my face," said Dzhambulatov. "They took my own belt and tied me to the fence.

They started to search my pockets, looking for weapons." Instead, they found documents identifying him as head of the local administration. Budanov changed course, but warned the elder that any attempt to cross his troops would be answered with a bloodbath reminiscent of the one in a village that had been savaged by artillery and air strikes the month before. "He said, 'Let's be friends. If you don't, I'm going to create a second Komsomolskoye here,'" Dzhambulatov said.[10]

The next day was the election and villagers streamed to the polling place as Russia voted Putin into the presidency. Budanov and his troops took much of the day off. It was also his daughter's second birthday. To celebrate, he gathered some of his colleagues for a boozy lunch, toasting the little girl. His lawyers would later say Budanov had six shots of vodka, not enough to last in his system late into the night, but others insisted he remained drunk throughout the evening. After the party, Budanov's top deputy ordered Senior Lieutenant Roman Bagreyev to fire an artillery battery at the village to show off the unit's readiness; Bagreyev balked at using fragmentation shells against civilian targets, sending the colonel into a fury. Budanov and his deputy pummeled the lieutenant, punching and kicking him to the ground, then tied his hands and feet, threw him into an open pit, and ordered chlorine poured over him. For good measure, Budanov's deputy then urinated on Bagreyev and left him in the pit overnight.

About midnight, Budanov set off in search of a young woman. He ordered three other soldiers to join him and they roared down the road to Tangi-Chu.

THE MURDER of Elza Kungayeva set off tremors as far away as the Kremlin. Nothing made Vladimir Putin angrier than criticism about his conduct of the war in Chechnya, even the mild, almost ritualistic complaints issuing from an otherwise disinterested U.S. government; it was the one topic guaranteed to make the frosty former agent lose his cool and the source of the few public gaffes Putin would ever make over his presidency. The first time we met him, for a three-hour interview in the wood-paneled Kremlin Library, the president calmly held forth over even the most divisive topics, impressing us and other American correspondents with command of details like the average velocity of a ballistic missile and even joking that his KGB training was good preparation for "working with people." But when we turned the subject to Chechnya, Putin's tone abruptly changed. "When it comes to Chechnya, I am getting tired of repeating these things again and again," he told us hotly. "It would appear that it takes a real dumb person not to understand."[11]

And from the first, the Kremlin had understood that an officer gone berserk on the day Putin was elected president would only confirm the evidence compiled by human rights investigators and foreign journalists that Russia was brutalizing a civilian population in the name of fighting separatism. No matter how commonplace Yuri Budanov's crimes were by that point, Russia had yet to hold anyone to account. And so, with international human rights groups issuing report after report, the Kremlin finally decided to make an example of this one tank commander in hopes of getting the West off its back.

By the time Budanov killed Elza Kungayeva, the Russians had driven Chechen rebels from the main cities, but they had not followed even the minimal conventions of war set out in Geneva a half century earlier. In the first two weeks of December 1999, troops led by Budanov's commander, General Vladimir Shamanov, rampaged through the village of Alkhan-Yurt—a once-prosperous settlement with a prewar population of nine thousand west of Grozny—killing at least seventeen civilians. After taking control of the village on December 1, the soldiers conducted a *zachistka*, sweeping through town, looting homes, and shooting anyone who got in the way. Among those killed was a woman over one hundred years old, her chest raked by automatic rifle fire. Three other women died when soldiers tossed a grenade into the basement where they were hiding. A sixty-three-year-old man begged soldiers for his life, pleading, "I'm an old man, don't shoot"—whereupon they opened fire and then burned his body using a gas canister. Another man later found his son's headless body. When villagers approached Shamanov to complain, he threatened to shoot them.[12]

Two other massacres quickly followed. Near the end of December, Russian troops in the Staropromyslovsky section of Grozny launched a month-long killing spree that left at least fifty civilians dead. By early February, Russian troops succeeded in recapturing Grozny by providing an escape route for Chechen rebels—one laced with land mines. The rebels marched into a killing field and Shamil Basayev lost a foot in an explosion. Days later, Russian soldiers stormed through Aldi on the southwestern outskirts of Grozny, gunning down civilians, burning homes, killing livestock, stealing everything in sight, even pulling the gold teeth out of the bodies of their victims. In the end at least sixty-two people died. Corpses lined the streets. "We were told to kill everybody," one soldier explained to a woman he spared.[13] The Kremlin looked the other way. A brief investigation of Alkhan-Yurt went nowhere, and Shamanov was soon given a medal. Shamanov was the kind of officer Moscow needed, brash and ruthless, so harsh that even his wife called him a "fascist" for the way he raised his son.[14] "Russia cannot afford to toss aside such generals as Vladimir Shamanov," Putin said.[15]

Russian journalists who tried to investigate such atrocities independently were targeted themselves. Andrei Babitsky, a correspondent for the U.S.-funded Radio Liberty who had been one of the few to report from behind Chechen rebel lines, was arrested by Russian forces in mid-January and then supposedly traded to Chechen fighters for five Russian prisoners; his long disappearance caused an international stir but made no impression on Putin, who declared him "a traitor" who was "working directly for the enemy."[16] Anna Politkovskaya, a crusading reporter for *Novaya Gazeta* newspaper, was detained as well for more than a day in February by Russian soldiers who beat her, threatened her with rape, and conducted a mock execution. "You're a militant!" one of them yelled at her. "You came here to look at the pits! Slut! Bitch!" When she was finally released, a lieutenant colonel told her, "If it were up to me, I'd shoot you."[17]

The pits were not to be looked at but to be feared. Just as Yuri Budanov threw his balky artillery officer in a pit and left him there, Russian soldiers imprisoned Chechens in the ground, where they were kept cold and hungry for hours or days at a time. Those who survived the pits were often sent to so-called filtration camps, where Russian forces ostensibly sifted through the masses of refugees in search of rebel fighters. Masked guards regularly beat detainees with their fists, feet, and rubber truncheons, sprayed tear gas into their cells, broke their teeth, and raped both men and women. Babitsky was among those sent to the most infamous of the camps at Chernokozovo, north of the Terek River, and later disclosed what happened there to the outside world. He dismissed his own beatings, consisting of several dozen blows from a club, as merely "routine light registration" compared to the excruciating torture most of the detainees endured. "Everything we read about Stalin's concentration camps, everything we know about German concentration camps, can be found there," he said on Radio Liberty after his release.[18]

Putin never addressed the abuses. Instead, he claimed that the war was virtually over. "We'll be able to sum up the final results of the operation shortly," he said on February 22.[19] It was a claim he would make every few months for the next four years, regardless of the continued bloodshed in Chechnya.

The Budanov case a month later suggested quite powerfully how wrong he was. But it also gave the Kremlin a chance to prosecute a high-profile human rights case. The military moved quickly to charge Budanov with rape and murder. Anatoly Kvashnin, chief of the military general staff, then pronounced him guilty during a televised meeting with Putin. The president himself remained silent on the case, as he would for the next several years. But Kvashnin told Putin in no uncertain terms that Budanov had "humiliated" the Chechen woman, denouncing the colonel's behavior as "barbaric and disgraceful."

The autopsy report left little doubt about that. The examination by a military forensics laboratory found black-and-blue marks all over Elza's face, neck, and body, strangulation marks on her neck, and severe damage to a "plethora of internal organs" that appeared to be the result of repeated blows by a heavy object. The experts reported finding injuries to her hymen and rectum along with bleeding proving "those injuries were inflicted approximately one hour before death."[20]

The Kremlin held Budanov out as an example of Russian justice. "Yes, Budanov has committed a grave crime," Putin aide Sergei Yastrzhembsky told a news conference a couple weeks after the murder. "The perpetrator has been arrested and we hope he will be prosecuted to the full extent of the law."[21] But the official outrage would not last long. On the same day Yastrzhembsky was waxing indignant, the military moved to drop the allegations of rape, announcing that, despite the autopsy report, Elza Kungayeva was not sexually assaulted while she was alive but violated after she died. Private Aleksandr Yegorov, one of the soldiers Budanov assigned to bury the young woman, eventually took the blame, claiming he defiled her lifeless body with the handle of a spade. He was charged along with the two other soldiers on the burial detail; all three were immediately given amnesty and released. The reason for this sudden shift in stories was obvious: in Chechen society, rape was seen as the most heinous of crimes.

By the time Budanov finally arrived for the beginning of his trial in February 2001 at the military courthouse in Rostov-on-Don, the headquarters for the military in southern Russia, the political dynamics had turned completely in his favor. Instead of representing the terror of Tangi-Chu, he had become in the public eye a Russian martyr to foreign pressure. As he was taken into the courthouse, dozens of nationalists dressed in combat fatigues and armbands with emblems that resembled swastikas demonstrated outside, the women throwing flowers at him and the men shaking their fists in anger at the Chechens who had come to attend the trial. Public sympathy was decisively with Budanov; 50 percent of those surveyed at the trial's outset wanted Budanov released, compared with just 19 percent who felt otherwise.[22] General Vladimir Shamanov, the colonel's former commander, blamed the prosecution of Budanov on "ideological intervention by Western countries" and praised him as "an asset to Russia."[23] Shamanov showed up in court with his Hero of Russia medal pinned to his navy blue suit and shook Budanov's hand through the metal cage where defendants are kept in Russian courtrooms. Even the newly appointed defense minister, Sergei Ivanov, Putin's close confidant, called Budanov a "respected officer" and expressed compassion for him. "I do feel sorry for him as a human being," he told a group of Russian editors. "If you like, Budanov is a victim both of the circumstances and imperfect legislation."[24]

The military command sensed the shifting winds. But although they had made the rape charge go away, the authorities could not just dismiss the case. Budanov had admitted killing Elza Kungayeva. His only defense was that he suspected she was a sniper and strangled her in a blind rage. But he had trouble providing corroborating evidence. He claimed that two Chechen informants had pointed out her house as the home of a female sniper, but one of the supposed informants told authorities he did not remember telling Budanov that and the other could not be located. Budanov insisted he had been given a photograph of the ostensible sniper and it showed Elza Kungayeva, but no such picture was ever found.

Seeking a way out, authorities turned to an old reliable for the Russian state. They shuffled Yuri Budanov off to Serbsky.

BEHIND THE high white wall, across the leafy side street from ordinary Moscow balconies filled with ordinary Moscow laundry, Yuri Budanov awaited a verdict. The question was not whether he had killed Elza Kungayeva. The question for the psychiatrists at the Serbsky Institute for Social and Forensic Psychiatry was whether he was mentally responsible for his actions.

Just as the drunken rampage of a Russian colonel had become a referendum on the war in Chechnya, the case was also developing into a painful reminder of psychiatry's shameful past in the Soviet Union. In the same wards where Budanov was kept for months, dissidents had been dazed with powerful psychotropic drugs, subjected to fake diagnoses, and forced to sit through inquisitions on their sanity with the outcome predetermined by the KGB. Serbsky had been not so much an institution for mental health as an instrument for the state's repression of its own people. By the time Budanov was sent there, a decade after the disappearance of the Soviet Union that had created it, Serbsky was still working as a virtual arm of the state, and many of its top officials were the same ones who had condemned people to the asylum for the mental illness of daring to oppose the Soviet regime.

The head of the commission assigned to examine Budanov in that summer of 2001 was Tamara Pechernikova, the same doctor who once condemned poet Natalya Gorbanevskaya for daring to protest the Soviet invasion of Czechoslovakia in 1968. The second Serbsky commission to look into Budanov's mental health would initially include Georgy Morozov, the institute's former director, who had sat on many of the committees that declared prominent dissidents insane during the 1970s and 1980s. "Practically nothing has changed," Yuri Savenko, head of the Independent Psychiatrists Association of Russia, told us. "They are the same people and they do not want to apologize for their actions in the past."[25]

Ever since its founding in 1921, Serbsky had played a unique role in Soviet psychiatry, handling the most difficult and politically sensitive cases. By the 1960s, Serbsky had become famous for pioneering a new diagnosis it called "slow-developing schizophrenia." Signs of this supposed illness: "stubbornness and inflexibility of convictions" and "reformist delusions." In other words, anyone who resisted Soviet power. Among Serbsky's best-known patients was General Pyotr Grigorenko, who turned against the Soviet regime after the invasion of Czechoslovakia and became immortalized in Report 59/S in November 1969. The general, the doctors wrote in an evaluation later smuggled out of the Soviet Union, "was unshakably convinced of the rightness of his actions." More broadly, "his psychological condition was characterized by reformist ideas," and he seemed to have a peculiarly un-Soviet view of his ability to influence the totalitarian state. "He considered it necessary to react to any events which he considered unjust, although they had no relation to him." In his prison diary, Grigorenko recounted his time at Serbsky. "Of course, if it is only a person who bows submissively before any arbitrary act of the bureaucrats who is considered a normal Soviet person," he wrote, "then I am 'abnormal.' I am not capable of such submissiveness, no matter how or how much I may be beaten up."[26] The man who headed the commission that put him away was Georgy Morozov.

When we tried to peek behind the high white wall more than a decade after the fall of the Soviet Union, we found an institution still shrouded in secrecy and self-justification. For a month, the director, Tatyana Dmitriyeva, refused to see us, insisting that the Russian Ministry of Health had to approve such a meeting, even though the ministry said there was no such requirement. When she did finally agree to sit down, she seemed the picture of the post-Soviet apparatchik, a middle-aged woman wearing expensive new clothes but old attitudes. She had little patience for the gray areas of Serbsky's past. Essentially, she said, the dissidents *were* crazy by Soviet standards since only a madman would risk his life by defying the state. "There were social standards, norms of behavior," she explained. "When a person walked away from these norms, any person would point and say he's insane." In such a system, she added, "only an insane person could protest what was going on in the country."[27]

Officially, political cases at Russia's mental hospitals ended in 1988, when the last dissidents were released from Serbsky, but political cases still came its way. Alina Vitukhnovskaya, a young poet with a flair for controversy, ran afoul of the FSB in 1994 and was charged with drug possession. After six months in jail, she was taken to Serbsky. "I was thinking it can't be true, such things can't still be happening in Moscow," she told us. Arriving at Serbsky, "I was terrified. I knew what they did to political dissidents, their history of cooperating with the KGB." The first evaluation concluded she was not crazy, and she was eventually released by a court. Two years later, she was arrested again on the same drug possession charge, along with a new allegation that she was "acting with the purpose of trying to destroy the secret service of Russia." Again she was sent to Serbsky. "When I was brought to Serbsky for the second time, I was hysterical," she recalled. "I was convinced that the decision was already made and I could not do anything about it."[28]

By the time Yuri Budanov arrived at its gates, it was clear Serbsky was once again serving as an instrument of state power.

FOR VLADIMIR Putin, Chechnya had developed into the trap from which he could not escape. The easy, two-week war he had promised after becoming prime minister in 1999 had instead turned into an endless struggle that haunted his presidency. From the moment he had vowed to "wipe them out in the outhouse," Putin had decided that force was the only option for resolving the conflict, ignoring any other potential alternatives. At every turning point, he took the same route. He toyed with negotiations with separatist leaders, only to abandon them. He agreed to crack down on human rights abuses, only to not follow through. He promised genuine democratic institutions in Chechnya, only to rig two elections there to install his handpicked viceroys. "This is my approach, and I'm not going to change it," he told reporters at a news conference two years into the conflict.[29]

From the start, some Russian politicians and academics urged him to find a peaceful solution through talks, but Putin would only talk with Chechens already loyal to him. "I had this conversation with him many, many times," Grigory Yavlinsky, leader of the Yabloko party, told us. "He would say that he has his own strategy. He would say, 'We are for negotiations.' I was saying, 'It's necessary to negotiate with the people who are your enemies, not your own puppets.'"[30] In February 2000, just weeks before Yuri Budanov would kill Elza Kungayeva, Putin gave some thought to softening his approach. He visited leading Chechnya specialists at the Russian Academy of Sciences. Scholar Sergei Arutyunov talked for more than an hour about the region, advising Putin to moderate his rhetoric about Islam and consider granting Chechnya significant autonomy within the Russian Federation. "Putin was quite attentive," Arutyunov said. "It seemed that in March and April he followed some of our recommendations. But then everything returned to its normal circles."[31]

By the time the Budanov trial began in early 2001, the public had tired of the war and the Kremlin appeared to be laying the political groundwork for a long fight, comparing Chechnya to decades-long conflicts such as in Northern Ireland. "It would be naive to forecast the finish of this situation in some foreseeable future," Sergei Yastrzhembsky, Putin's aide, told us over lunch one day. "There is no medicine for quick treatment of this crisis."[32] But the public was turning against the war, with support less than half the 70 percent it had been when Putin had first launched the conflict in 1999. Nearly 60 percent now wanted Putin to enter peace talks.[33]

He would not hear of it. Then later that year, the September 11 terrorist attacks on the United States suddenly redefined the world. Putin wasted little time casting his fight with the Chechens as part of the broader global war on radical Islamic terrorism. In Washington, the Bush administration was ready to rethink its outlook on Chechnya and was eager to eliminate the restive republic as a terrorist haven. Putin took advantage of the moment to demand that the separatists lay down their arms and cut any ties to Al Qaeda. At the same time, under American pressure, he quietly opened the door for the first time to negotiations with Aslan Maskhadov, the Chechen president-turned-rebel commander. Within the Chechen leadership, a debate erupted. Maskhadov did not trust Putin and initially refused. But Akhmed Zakayev, Maskhadov's chief deputy, argued that Putin wanted them to turn him down so he could pin the blame on the Chechens. "It was important to announce our readiness for such a meeting," Zakayev told us. "Otherwise, we were losing the political battle, because in the eyes of the whole world, Putin, a man who wanted peace, would be on top, and we, who did not want peace, would find ourselves on the bottom."

Ultimately, a meeting was set. Zakayev flew to Moscow's Sheremetyevo Airport on November 18 with a Turkish envoy as guarantor of his safety and sat down in an airport VIP lounge with General Viktor Kazantsev, Putin's presidential envoy for southern Russia. Zakayev presented a peace plan—

declare a cease-fire, halt the *zachistka* cleansing operations, and establish a bilateral commission to negotiate the future of Chechnya while turning temporary governance over to a Kremlin representative. If genuine, the proposal would have satisfied Putin's main demand that Chechnya remain under Moscow's control. Zakayev pressed Kazantsev for a signal. He recalled asking, "'What do you think? Are we going to have another meeting?' I needed to know his personal reaction and opinion about our proposals. And he said, 'It's ninety-nine percent certain that we will continue our dialogue and the war will end. But it's one percent unclear. Because it is Putin who must make the final decision.' That's how our meeting ended. And of course after that we had no other meetings."[34]

YURI BUDANOV was not ready to give up his war either. As Putin's Kremlin flirted with peace talks, the colonel was back in court spending his days lashing out at the Chechens who had come to see him brought to justice. He took a particular dislike to one of the lawyers for Elza Kungayeva's family.

"We can have a new exchange of opinions," Abdulla Khamzayev, the attorney, told Budanov during a session at the beginning of July 2002.

"I will only talk to you with a Kalashnikov rifle in my hand!" Budanov snapped back.[35]

By then, the trial had entered its seventeenth month. The prosecutor in the case, Colonel Sergei Nazarov, had all but adopted Budanov's version of events, declaring there had been no kidnapping, much less rape, and that the colonel's real crime was simply abusing his authority in handling a suspected sniper himself rather than turning her over to investigators. "The prosecutor was acting as another defense attorney for Budanov," recalled Stanislav Markelov, who also represented the Kungayeva family. And Budanov had an ace in the hole—he had come back from Serbsky with a finding that he had suffered shell shock and therefore was temporarily insane at the time of the murder.

But as July opened, the political currents suddenly shifted yet again. The day before the verdict was to be read, the Russian military abruptly fired Nazarov and replaced him with another prosecutor. The next day the judge decided not to issue his verdict and sent Budanov back to Serbsky for yet another psychiatric examination.

The day after he arrived at Serbsky, the extent of the authorities' manipulation of the case became clear. A reporter for the Russian tabloid *Moskovsky Komsomolets* tracked down Aleksandr Yegorov, the army private who had taken the fall for supposedly violating Elza Kungayeva's dead body. As the reporter secretly videotaped their conversation, Yegorov disclosed that he had lied to protect Budanov at the instruction of the authorities.

"The prosecutor told me from the beginning that I would be amnestied," he said.

"And why did they want this deal?" the reporter asked.

"Why? Budanov is commander of the regiment. He must be good. They want to justify him, make him look good."[36]

Budanov's new review at Serbsky again found him insane at the time of the murder, but a couple of experts on the panel dissented. On New Year's Eve at the end of 2002, the military court in Rostov-on-Don accepted the majority view and found him not guilty. Budanov was not in court at the time, nor was Elza Kungayeva's family. A supporter of the renegade colonel, though, rejoiced, yelling, "Freedom!"[37]

Not yet. The case now was complicating Putin's attempt to resolve the war in Chechnya on his own terms. Just as the trial was wrapping up, some prominent Chechen leaders had approached the Kremlin with a plan to introduce self-governance to the region. Local representatives would be elected in villages and towns, then gather to write a new constitution. The plan, they argued, would deprive Maskhadov's resistance of its legitimacy. "They listened to me very well," Shamil Beno, one of the Chechen leaders, told us after meeting with Putin aides at the Kremlin.[38] But if they listened, they did not hear. Putin soon announced his own unilateral political settlement. The Kremlin would draft its own constitution for Chechnya, then hold a referendum on it in the spring and a presidential election in the fall to ratify Putin's handpicked administrator, Akhmad Kadyrov, as the Chechen leader. The idea was to turn over the conflict to loyal Chechens, a concept some called "Chechenization," much as the Americans pursued the "Vietnamization" of their own quagmire war a generation earlier.

Putin did not want to have to sell the Chechens on his plan amid anger over soft-shoe treatment of Budanov. Even Kadyrov, the Putin loyalist running the region for the Kremlin, professed outrage at the direction the Budanov case was headed and called for his public execution. "We will not be able to restore order until everyone is held responsible for their conduct, regardless of rank or post," Kadyrov said at a news conference in Grozny.[39]

At the end of February 2003, just days before the constitutional referendum in Chechnya, the Russian Supreme Court rejected Budanov's insanity finding and overturned the acquittal. The case went back to Rostov-on-Don for another trial. This time, Budanov, recognizing the writing on the wall, stuffed cotton in his ears and read books in his cage. Five months later the military court, now relying on the psychiatric judgment of the dissenters on the Serbsky panel, convicted Budanov of kidnapping and murder, sentencing him to ten years in a maximum-security prison. *Rossiskaya Gazeta,* the official government newspaper, headlined the verdict, "The War Is to Blame, Yet Budanov Is Convicted."[40]

But Putin aide Sergei Yastrzhembsky voiced the relief felt in the Kremlin as he hailed the decision. "It has incalculable significance for the Chechen republic because the outcome of the case was awaited with particular impatience there," Yastrzhembsky said. "There is no doubt," he added, "that the international reaction will be positive."[41]

IF VLADIMIR Putin hoped the resolution of the Yuri Budanov case would change anything, he had miscalculated. The trial had twisted in so many directions in response to the political moods that by the end few took it seriously. While Budanov was led off in handcuffs to pay for the murder of an eighteen-year-old woman on the day of Putin's election, many others had been left free to maraud through Chechnya unhindered. More mass graves turned up, more *zachistki* were conducted, more civilians were snatched in the middle of the night never to turn up again. Even by the government's own unpublished estimate, more than eleven hundred civilians were murdered in Chechnya in 2002, a number that was almost certainly an underestimation.[42] When the military responded to complaints by issuing what it called Order 80, requiring troops conducting house-to-house sweep operations to identify themselves to homeowners and allow local officials to accompany them, it quickly became observed mainly in the breach.[43]

The Russians claimed to control the territory but still retreated into the safety of their bases at night when guerrillas, foreign Islamic militants, and thugs roamed virtually at will. The Chechen resistance still ambushed troops and staged periodic raids on high-profile targets. And most ominous of all, they had turned increasingly to suicide bombings and other terrorist strikes against civilian targets from southern Russia to faraway Moscow.

Corruption, double-dealing, and mistrust hobbled every effort to end the conflict. For many on both sides, Chechnya had developed into a virtual business, a black market bazaar of gunrunning, kidnapping, looting, oil smuggling, and other scams that meant it was in their interest to keep the war going. To prod hundreds of thousands of refugees to return to Chechnya and prove that the republic had returned to normal, Putin promised compensation for destroyed homes. But the three hundred thousand rubles (just more than $10,000) was hardly enough to rebuild a house, and many refugees told us they were either refused the compensation or forced to turn over 50 percent or more in kickbacks to the officials in charge. Moscow had earmarked 3.5 billion rubles a year ($120 million) for the reconstruction of Chechnya, a fraction of the $1.5 billion to $4 billion that General Gennady Troshev, a former commander of the forces there, estimated was needed. And much of what Putin did send to Chechnya was stolen by corrupt officials. A Russian audit in 2004 estimated that 25 percent of the Chechen budget was illicitly diverted; all told, the audit found, some 5 billion rubles ($172 million) targeted for restoration of the broken republic had been rerouted over three years.[44] In early 2004, Putin appointed an anticorruption commission headed by Prime Minister Mikhail Kasyanov, but it met only once and was never heard from again.

Once a teeming capital of four hundred thousand residents, Grozny remained a shattered city, a collection of craters and collapsed buildings much like Kabul or Sarajevo. With little help from the government, residents had tried to rebuild some of it on their own, putting up a store here, a beauty salon there. Minutka Square, where Russians and Chechens fought some of their most pitched battles, was now lined with trucks of bricks for construction work. But it was more Russian *pokazukha*—to walk along the street in Grozny and look at the storefronts at eye level might give the illusion of a real city, but a simple glance upward at the rest of the hollowed-out buildings quickly dispelled that fantasy.

Putin did nothing to seriously change that situation and instead focused his anger not on lying, thieving subordinates but on Western critics who dared suggest a political solution to the conflict or question Russian atrocities. At a news conference in Brussels after rejecting European entreaties to sign a joint declaration on Chechnya that mentioned human rights, an angry Putin essentially threatened to mutilate a French reporter's penis for asking about Russian tactics that endangered Chechen civilians. The Chechen rebels, Putin told the reporter testily, were Islamic extremists who wanted to kill non-Muslims. "If you are prepared to become a radical Muslim and undergo circumcision, I invite you to Moscow," the president continued. "I suggest that you have an operation so that nothing grows out of you again."[45] The stunned interpreter did not translate the remarks; only later did the European Union officials standing next to Putin learn what he had said.

Putin's attitude toward human rights abuses in Chechnya trickled down to the troops. Even if he gave lip service from time to time to satisfy the West, the men in the field understood that the trial of Yuri Budanov was the exception and there would in fact be no accountability for any manner of violence visited upon civilians no matter how barbaric. Only a handful of other soldiers were ever brought up on charges for abuses in Chechnya. And the other side used Budanov to justify its own atrocities against civilians. "We cannot hunt down every Budanov," Shamil Basayev said on a Chechen Web site, "but we can punish the people who give their blessing to all these crimes. We watch TV and see how all these policemen are sent here, how they say goodbye to their wives, sisters, and mothers. We will bring our acts of vengeance to the cities and villages they come from."[46]

For Elza Kungayeva's family, the three-year ordeal that followed her murder proved a searing lesson in war and justice in Putin's Russia. "We thought Russians and Chechens were one nation," Rosa Kungayeva, Elza's mother, told us later. "We made no distinction. We thought we were citizens of the Russian Federation and that Russian laws would protect us. But at the trial in Rostov-on-Don, we had to face a lot of awful things. What happened at the trial, what happened all around it, it all smacked of nationalism. We were insulted, we were threatened."[47] The family fled to one of the many refugee camps in neighboring Ingushetia, where hundreds of thousands of displaced Chechens were living in crowded tents on rations that sometimes included only one helping of meat a year. The Russians, sensitive to the image of so many homeless families afraid of the war that the Kremlin had repeatedly declared over, spent enormous energy trying to close the camps, often by crudely intimidating refugees. In August 2003, the Kungayev family moved to Norway.

Budanov was shipped off to a prison in the region of Ulyanovsk, a rural area that had given birth to Vladimir Lenin and by then had a new governor elected with the help of the Kremlin—General Vladimir Shamanov. From his new position, Budanov's friend and former commander would continue to champion the convicted colonel's cause. During a table-thumping performance for us in his office one day, Shamanov railed about how the colonel had been made a scapegoat by a Kremlin eager to pander to the West. "Budanov came in handy," Shamanov said. "From the very beginning they made a political case out of it, made a big deal out of it and developed a negative attitude toward the officer corps of the Russian armed forces." Budanov only killed Kungayeva to protect himself from a sniper who was reaching for a gun, Shamanov insisted. "I don't think we can look at a person who was at war in the context of civilian life. The conditions there are different. It's a war! And he became a victim of this war."

We turned to Shamanov's own victims and asked about the massacre at Alkhan-Yurt.

"Fairy tales," he scoffed.

What about the Human Rights Watch report documenting seventeen deaths?

"This is not true," he said. "You can invent anything. It happened after the events in Grozny. The bodies could have been brought from Grozny."

So human rights investigators dragged corpses from the battle of Grozny, deposited them in Alkhan-Yurt, and fabricated a slaughter to impugn Russian troops?

"There were numerous cases like this one in both campaigns," Shamanov insisted. "When people try to raise funds and to draw attention to their groups, they use anything."[48]

We visited another of Budanov's champions in Rostov-on-Don after the trial and found him equally adamant. Aleksei Dulimov, an old-school Soviet lawyer who took on Budanov's defense midway through the proceedings, portrayed his client as a persecuted war hero. "From my point of view, the victim is Budanov," he said when we sat down in a hotel coffee shop. "His only mistake was that he was a soldier in that war and was so focused on the idea of fighting the enemy." Dulimov recounted how Budanov had had to bring his dead soldiers back to their families in Siberia. Suddenly the lawyer paused for a moment as he struggled against tears, then got up from the table to recover his composure. When Dulimov returned, he brought up the Chechens who had insisted on prosecuting Budanov over Elza Kungayeva's death. "They created such trouble out of her," he said dismissively. "Just one girl died. Just one girl died. They created such national trouble."[49]

Tears for the killer, disdain for the victim. For Russia, the Budanov case had become a test of attitudes toward the war in Chechnya. "In America, there was the case involving Calley. Here we had the Budanov case," said Stanislav Markelov, the articulate young lawyer who had worked for Elza Kungayeva's family. In Russia, the Budanov case had exposed the common cruelties of the war in Chechnya, but did not fuel opposition to the conflict in the way that Lieutenant William Calley's My Lai massacre had spurred protests against the Vietnam War. Instead, it served mainly to rally the nation behind its own military regardless of its excesses and to further polarize two peoples against each other. Markelov found the situation so poisoned that it was hard to focus simply on the case at hand. Eventually, he wound up clashing with the prosecutors, his fellow attorney, and human rights groups, all of whom he felt were pursuing agendas that went beyond finding justice for the death of one eighteen-year-old woman. When it came to the Russian and Chechen sides, he said, "Their attitudes sort of merged. They had the same attitudes. We had to withstand two things—on the one hand, the attitude of the Russian *siloviki* who were actually protecting their corporate interests and the right to get away with anything in Chechnya, and on the other hand, the Chechen residents for whom the court was another vehicle for fighting the war. For them, it was the continuation of the war, but without Kalashnikovs.

"Budanov indeed was sacrificed," he went on, "but you could say the whole process ended in practically nothing because eventually they failed to discover the origin of such crimes—why were such crimes committed in the first place? The ones who were satisfied were the ones who wanted personal revenge against Budanov . . . but that's the wrong approach to this case because without discovering the origin of such crimes this particular case became just an ordinary crime."[50]

Soul Mates

We will be great friends. Tell him that.
— CONDOLEEZZA RICE

ON SUNDAY, SEPTEMBER 9, 2001, Vladimir Putin placed an urgent call to the White House. He had a dire warning to deliver to President George Bush. The fabled leader of the antigovernment resistance movement in Afghanistan, Ahmed Shah Massoud, had just been blown up by two Arab suicide bombers posing as journalists. The Afghans were still publicly denying that he was dead, but the Russians knew the truth. And, Putin told Bush, Russian intelligence had concluded that the move against Massoud signaled something larger might be afoot.

To most Americans, Massoud was an unknown figure, and the guerrilla war he was waging in Afghanistan was just another of the world's unfathomable conflicts that seemed to have little bearing on their lives. Not to the Russians. They were intimately familiar with Afghanistan after the disastrous decade-long Soviet war that exposed the military impotence of the Cold War superpower. Massoud had been instrumental in beating the vaunted Soviet army in the 1980s; the legendary guerrilla leader known as the Lion of the Panjshir had fended off nine consecutive Russian thrusts into his native valley north of Kabul. In the last several years, however, the Russians had forged an alliance of convenience with Massoud and his ragtag coalition of militias against the new government of Afghanistan, led by the radical Taliban movement with the support of Osama bin Laden's Al Qaeda organization. Moscow was convinced that bin Laden's terrorist training camps were churning out foot soldiers for the war against Russian forces in Chechnya and was busy shipping arms, supplies, and money to Massoud's Northern Alliance in hopes of shutting off the pipeline.

Putin called Bush that day to express his concern about the larger implications of Massoud's assassination. "I told him I had a foreboding that something was about to happen, something long in preparation," Putin recalled.[1] But the Russians came away worried that Bush had not really understood the warning, feeling that "he did not fully grasp the seriousness of the issue," as former prime minister Yevgeny Primakov later put it.[2]

Barely two days later, everything became clear when hijacked airplanes smashed into the World Trade Center and the Pentagon in the United States, part of a carefully orchestrated operation presaged by the murder of Massoud. In killing him, Al Qaeda had eliminated its most dangerous enemy in their home base and the most formidable ally a vengeful United States could have wanted in seeking retribution inside Afghanistan. Putin was at the Kremlin when the first plane hit just before 5 p.m. Moscow time and learned of the attacks on the United States from the media. The Russian president summoned his top aides to a conference where they flipped on the television and watched in horror as the Twin Towers collapsed. The normally cool Putin was as shaken as everyone else. "He took it very close to heart," Sergei Prikhodko, his chief foreign policy adviser, told us later.[3]

Putin turned to Defense Minister Sergei Ivanov. "What can we do to help them now? What do they need now?"

Ivanov noted that the Russian military just the day before had started exercises in the northern Pacific Ocean, simulating a Cold War–style nuclear conflict with the United States.

Putin ordered him to call them off. "The president said the exercises must be canceled so that they wouldn't distract the U.S. forces," Prikhodko said. "He said the Americans had a lot of problems as it was; they didn't need more problems to distract them from the most important things."[4]

Then Putin picked up the phone himself and called Bush, becoming the first world leader to reach out to the American president at this moment of extraordinary crisis. At first, he could not get hold of Bush, who was flying around his country from one undisclosed location to another, so national security adviser Condoleezza Rice took the call. Bush later called back himself. "I didn't allow myself to say, 'We did warn you about this,'" Putin recalled. "No, it wasn't the moment. I frequently talked about the threat in Afghanistan. I said it's not only a threat to us because the training camps there are sending terrorists to Chechnya. It threatened the whole world."[5]

Like other signals of an impending Al Qaeda attack in the weeks and months before September 11, American officials said later that the Russian warnings were not tangible enough to pursue. "Generally the information the Russians provided was pretty broad, not specific—light-years away from being actionable," recalled U.S. ambassador Alexander R. Vershbow. "And so, yes, they had raised some warnings in the months preceding about a potential move, particularly by Al Qaeda, but very nonspecific as to what, where, and when."[6]

But as lower Manhattan and the Pentagon were smoldering, Putin seized the moment. The attack on the United States was, in his rendering, analogous to the sort of terrorism that had struck Russia in the last few years, the American equivalent of the 1999 apartment bombings in Moscow and southern Russia. Now perhaps the rest of the world would understand the threat from radical Islam that he had been talking about for the last two years whenever the West criticized his war in Chechnya. In short order, Putin summoned the television cameras to address the Russian nation, a striking departure for a Kremlin that usually took hours if not days to respond to even the most major of news events. "This is a blatant challenge to humanity," he said. "Russia has firsthand knowledge of what terrorism is. Better than anyone else, we understand the feelings of the American people."[7]

How much Putin's response reflected genuine human empathy rather than strategic calculation remains unclear. But Putin's words had captured the broad sentiment across the country. For the moment, at least, tension between the two former Cold War adversaries had vanished. Russian television preempted all programming to carry CNN's international feed live and uninterrupted. No translation was even needed. The pictures said everything. We found people in the streets in Moscow overwhelmed with emotion at the chilling images of destruction in New York. "I've been there," cried Anna Kuchumova, a student who pulled out her photographs of the World Trade Center from a 1995 visit. "I couldn't believe my eyes. It's inhumane to do something like this."[8]

Putin recognized the tragedy as an opportunity to profoundly refashion relations with the United States. He immediately offered to share intelligence information with Washington. If the Americans were going to retaliate against Osama bin Laden and his Taliban hosts, the Russians could offer them a tutorial in Afghanistan, having documented its topography, climate, and fierce spirit through painful experience in the 1980s. But how much further was Putin willing to go? To launch military operations in Afghanistan, the Americans would need military bases around Afghanistan—and that meant former Soviet Central Asia.

THE RELATIONSHIP between Vladimir Putin and George Bush had started off rocky before either of them had gotten into office. As the Texas governor began building his campaign for the White House virtually unschooled in foreign affairs, he submitted to the tutelage of Condoleezza Rice, a former aide to his father and provost of Stanford University. A Soviet specialist by training, Rice had taken a decidedly skeptical view of Boris Yeltsin ever since their first personal meeting, when he was just a Communist functionary, had left her with the impression of a crude boor unable to resist the bottle. Bill Clinton's long and lusty embrace of Yeltsin only confirmed to her that U.S. policy toward Russia had been off track in the 1990s. As she and her foreign policy team drafted the first major foreign policy speech of Bush's campaign, Yeltsin and his new prime minister, Putin, were just launching the second war in Chechnya. It was a ripe avenue for attack on the incumbent Democrats.

"Even as we support Russian reform, we cannot excuse Russian brutality," Bush said in his address at the Ronald Reagan Library in California in November 1999. "When the Russian government attacks civilians, killing women and children, leaving orphans and refugees, it can no longer expect aid from international lending institutions. The Russian government will discover that it cannot build a stable and unified nation on the ruins of human rights; that it cannot learn the lessons of democracy from the textbook of tyranny. We want to cooperate with Russia on its concern with terrorism. But that is impossible unless Moscow operates with civilized self-restraint. Just as we do not want Russia to descend in cruelty, we do not want it to return to imperialism."[9] Rice expanded on the new Bush doctrine toward Russia in a television interview nine days later. "The international community has to speak out against what is really a quite brutal campaign against innocent women and children in Chechnya," she said. "No one denies that Chechnya is a part of the Russian Federation, but I think the Russians have gone beyond the pale and I think that the international community can only speak out, and I also agree that international financial assistance needs to be at risk."[10] In an article in *Foreign Affairs* a couple months later, she added that the Clinton administration had engaged in "happy talk" that papered over the ugly reality in Russia. By transforming the Clinton-Yeltsin friendship into a substitute for genuine relations between nations, she wrote, support for democracy "became support for Yeltsin," while "the looting of the country's assets by powerful people either went unnoticed or was ignored."[11]

It was a powerful indictment and neither Clinton nor Vice President Al Gore, who had been assigned to manage Russia relations, ever successfully rebutted it. By the time the new Bush team arrived in Washington, it was ready to take a harder line with Yeltsin's successor. Many Bush advisers came to power with views shaped by Cold War assumptions. In a private memo written in January 2001, newly installed defense secretary Donald H. Rumsfeld articulated potential threats that should guide U.S. foreign and military policy during the Bush presidency and listed the theoretical adversaries he had in mind. Along with the future "axis of evil" states of Iran, Iraq, and North Korea, Rumsfeld included Russia, ignoring a decade of post-Soviet friendship and billions of dollars in U.S. and international aid.[12] Vice President Dick Cheney seemed particularly wary of a Russian president produced by the Soviet secret police, privately telling people that every time he saw Putin, "I think KGB, KGB, KGB."

The new administration was eager as well to do the opposite of whatever its predecessor had done. "The baseline was anything the Clinton administration had done was suspect, if not out-and-out wrong," said a senior Pentagon official held over in the new Bush administration. "On the political level for Russia, it was the personalization of the relationship between Clinton and Yeltsin. The White House thought, 'That was a personal relationship with a drunk, and that's not how we're going to do business.'"[13] Instead of agreeing to a quick meeting with Putin, Bush decided to put off their first summit, while the main vehicle for talks in the past, the Gore-Chernomyrdin commission, established by the vice president and then Russian prime minister Viktor Chernomyrdin, was scrapped. "It was just talk, talk, talk," John R. Bolton, the new undersecretary of state for arms control, said of the disbanded commission.[14] A veteran of the Reagan administration who took a skeptical view of international organizations and arms control treaties, Bolton would become a key interlocutor with the Russians for Bush.

The spy scandal surrounding the capture of Robert P. Hanssen, the longtime Moscow mole inside the FBI, further soured the atmosphere and prompted a round of diplomatic reprisals the scale of which had not been seen in fifteen years. In March 2001, Washington expelled fifty Russian diplomats and Moscow retaliated by kicking out fifty Americans. Russian television showed grainy surveillance video of an American military attaché supposedly recruiting a spy. A twenty-four-year-old American Fulbright scholar was arrested at a nightclub in the southern Russia city of Voronezh for holding a matchbook filled with marijuana and then publicly branded a spy-in-training because he spoke Russian so well and showed an inordinate interest in "strategic facilities" by picnicking in a park near a power station. Just a few months earlier, U.S. businessman Edmond Pope had been tried on espionage charges, the first American convicted of spying in Russia in forty years. In a Cuban restaurant in Moscow the weekend that the diplomat expulsions were announced, we found ourselves under assault by a drunken FSB agent with a gun on his holster and a desire to punch out Americans. If the Cold War was back, he wanted to be in on the ground floor. "Fuck George Bush," he muttered as he demanded a fight.

All this frustrated Putin. He and his closest advisers had been eager for a Republican administration, no more enamored of the Clinton crowd than the Bush team was. Putin had met with Clinton several times in the waning days of the Democratic administration, and the two shared a mutual mistrust. "Clinton felt patronized," his deputy secretary of state, Strobe Talbott, wrote about one unproductive meeting. "Clinton knew a brush-off when he saw one." After another session produced nothing but talk, Clinton told Talbott, "I got the feeling he was treading water. Putin's obviously holding back for a president whose time in this job will overlap more with his own."[15] For his part, Putin found Clinton off-putting, even condescending. "Clinton had a bad reputation among some people in Moscow," Mikhail Margelov, chairman of the International Affairs Committee in the Federation Council, the upper house of parliament, and a Putin adviser, told us. "It was a general problem with the Clinton administration, especially at the end. It sounded very didactic when it came to Russia." Moreover, he said, "Putin felt that Russia was betrayed by the U.S. and that's why the approach was very cautious."[16]

All along, Putin had counted on a Bush victory in 2000. "The first person who told us that Bush would be president was his father," recalled Sergei Prikhodko, the Kremlin's foreign policy chief and an influential player in Putin's inner circle. The senior Bush had been in Moscow for an investment conference back even before the Republican nomination battle. "He was dining with President Yeltsin and he said to Yeltsin, 'I know who is going to be the future president—my son.' And we took it very seriously."[17] Seriously enough that Putin began courting his future counterpart. He had his political party, Unity, send a delegation including Margelov to the Republican National Convention in Philadelphia, where they worked to cement ties with Condoleezza Rice and the rest of the Bush kitchen cabinet; five months later, another delegation went to the inauguration, where they partied late into the night at the black-tie ball held at Washington's Union Station. Even as she was condemning Russian brutality on television, Rice tried to pass along a secret message to Putin. "We will be great friends," Rice told one Russian foreign policy adviser. "Tell him that."[18]

But now it was months later, and the Bush team refused to get down to business. Not only had no get-acquainted meeting been scheduled between the two presidents, Putin's advisers could not even get the new administration in the White House to talk about when that might happen. "When Mr. Bush came to office, we had tremendous difficulties," a senior Russian official told us later. "Continuity was lost for several months. Everything was broken."[19]

Kremlin frustration turned to aggravation as the Bush agenda on Russia became clear. The only issue that the new American government wanted to discuss with the Russians was Bush's missile defense program, a scaled-down version of Ronald Reagan's Strategic Defense Initiative, or Star Wars, which was no more popular in Moscow than it had been two decades earlier. No matter how many times Bush administration officials insisted that missile defense was aimed at defending the United States from rogue nations such as North Korea, the Russians persisted in seeing it as a means of negating the only geopolitical card they had left, the nuclear arsenal still capable of destroying America with the push of a button. Rebuffed by Washington, Putin spent much of the spring of 2001 traveling to world capitals rallying international opposition to Bush's plans to gut or abandon the Anti-Ballistic Missile Treaty of 1972.

Bolton, the brash Cold Warrior who led the discussions with Moscow, finally decided he had to force the Russians to understand that Bush would not be swayed. At a meeting at a guesthouse in Moscow with fifteen Russians on one side of the table and fifteen Americans on the other, Bolton made clear that Bush would jettison the treaty whether Putin liked it or not. "You think this is a permanent treaty with a six-month withdrawal clause, and we see it as a six-month treaty renewable daily," he told the shocked Russians. As Bolton later recounted the moment to us over coffee, he smiled. "Half of my own side's jaws dropped, too. But we were trying to get their attention."[20]

He had it. But the friction proved neither deep nor permanent. The Russians did not want to scrap the ABM treaty. Neither were they eager to let the tit-for-tat diplomatic expulsions poison the waters. "We just reciprocated to show we wouldn't be pushovers," a senior Russian official confided to us much later.[21] "No one was taking that scandal seriously," added Margelov. "It was like a bad joke."[22] Foreign Minister Igor Ivanov was sent to Secretary of State Colin L. Powell with a message: the Russians didn't want the episode to get in the way. "We made it clear," Ivanov told us. "I discussed it with Colin Powell, that this was not our choice, and if the United States would go on this way, we would be forced to respond adequately to these actions." But, he told Powell, the Russians would prefer dialogue. In the end, the peace overture worked; at last, Bush agreed to a summit. "Powell immediately gave a positive reaction to our proposal, and after that we made a decision to hold an unofficial meeting of our presidents," Ivanov said.[23]

They had lost nearly half a year, but by the time Putin and Bush got together for that first meeting in June 2001 just outside Ljubljana, Slovenia, both sides were ready to get down to business. "Clearly they were prepared, both of them, they were eager to form a chemistry," said Sergei Karaganov, chairman of the Council on Foreign and Defense Policy, a Moscow group with close ties to the Kremlin.[24] When Putin walked into the gold-draped room at the sixteenth-century castle where they met, he showed he had done his homework by mentioning one of Bush's sports. "I *did* play rugby," Bush replied. "*Very* good briefing."[25] As the two sat down with just their national security advisers and translators, Bush recalled his own briefing. "I said, 'Let me say something about what caught my attention, Mr. President, was that your mother gave you a cross which you had blessed in Israel, the Holy Land,'" Bush recalled later. "And he said, 'It's true.' I said that amazed me, that here you were a Communist, KGB operative, and yet you were willing to wear a cross. 'That speaks volumes to me, Mr. President. May I call you Vladimir?'"[26]

Putin instantly sensed that Bush judged other people, even other world leaders, in part through the lens of his own strong Christian faith. Putin gave little public evidence of being so personally devout himself—he did not actually wear the cross to Slovenia.[27] But his KGB training served him well as he seized on this apparent point of commonality to build a bond. He told Bush the story of how his dacha had once burned to the ground and the only thing he recovered from the ashes was that cross. Bush nodded approvingly: "I said, 'Well, that's the story of the cross as far as I'm concerned. Things are meant to be.'"[28]

For Putin, that was all there was to be said on the subject, and he quickly turned to more urgent matters, like the crushing burden of old Soviet debt. For Bush, though, the moment evidently left a deep impression. He immediately invited Putin to visit him at his Texas ranch later in the year. Emerging from the private talks in Slovenia, Bush practically gushed about his new friend Vladimir. "I think I made progress getting him to trust me," he told aide Karen Hughes.[29] Later, he met reporters and declared, "I was able to get a sense of his soul," calling Putin "an honest, straightforward man."[30] He was even more buoyant with a European leader, privately describing Putin as "one cool dude."[31]

Putin does not gush. But he, too, seemed moderately upbeat afterward. The next day he told Russian lawmaker Dmitri Rogozin that he was impressed with Bush's plainspokenness. "When we were flying, I asked him point-blank about his impression of Bush," Rogozin told us later. "Putin said he thought Bush was a lively politician and a man who loved his children and family. . . . And the most important thing he noted about Bush was that he was not a snob."[32] Putin told Mikhail Margelov that Slovenia was a good start. "We have bones," Putin said. "We have to put meat on these bones."[33]

Two days later, we were invited to meet with Putin along with a few other correspondents, his first meeting with the American press at the Kremlin since taking office. In keeping with what we would learn to be his habit, we were kept waiting nearly four hours before he finally joined us in the Kremlin library. In person, Putin came across as distant and calculating—and also well briefed. While Bush had praised his soul, Putin drily described the American president as "a nice person to talk to." Still, he signaled the beginning of a new relationship, telling us that Russia and the United States were starting with "a clean sheet of paper" and that he and Bush had forged "a very high level of trust." He even held out the prospect of a deal on missile defense.[34]

As for the cross, Putin would remember Bush's fascination with it. He brought it with him a few weeks later to Italy, to show the American president when they met at the Genoa summit of the Group of Eight (G-8), the major industrialized nations.

THE FAST friendship Bush found that day in the Slovenian castle would only grow with Putin's gestures following September 11. Bush seemed to believe that he had found a true partner, someone he could do business with, and that the terrorist attacks had opened a historic window to transform U.S.-Russian relations.

The first test would be Russia's response to American requests to deploy troops to the former Soviet republics in Central Asia, a region that would be vital to any assault on Afghanistan. While the newly independent nations of the area no longer formally answered to Moscow, in reality Russia still played the dominant role there and could pose a major problem if the United States tried to go in without the Kremlin's blessing. The notion of American troops in former Soviet territory was explosive among Russian traditionalists in the armed forces who had spent most of their careers drawing up war plans to battle the U.S. military, war games they had continued to play as recently as September 11. And the first instinct was to say no to Washington.

Inside the government, the leader of the opposition to Americans in Central Asia was Sergei Ivanov, the defense minister and Putin's closest friend in the cabinet. A former KGB general who had served overseas as a spy, Ivanov was a sophisticated, English-speaking figure—and also the most powerful of the hard-line *siloviki* faction. "I see absolutely no basis for even hypothetical suppositions about the possibility of NATO military operations on the ter-

ritory of Central Asian nations," he told reporters just three days after the terrorist attacks.[35]

His comments sent U.S. officials into a scramble. They thought Putin was
on board, yet he seemed to be wavering. He dispatched his national security
adviser, Vladimir Rushailo, to Central Asia to instruct regional leaders to hold
off making any commitments. Tajikistan's president Emomali Rakhmonov
had initially told Americans that he would allow his country to be used in a
military operation against the Taliban, then backed off after Rushailo told
him to rethink his position.[36] Condoleezza Rice tried to reason with Sergei
Ivanov by telephone. She had gotten to know him when he was Putin's
national security adviser and, in a break with protocol, had kept up contact
even after he moved to the Defense Ministry, much to the aggravation of
Donald Rumsfeld, his official counterpart. "She had fallen in love with Sergei
Ivanov," a senior administration official recalled. "It used to really hack off
Rumsfeld, and I think that's one reason why they have no personal relationship." Rice believed it was useless to deal with Rushailo, her ostensible interlocutor, or Igor Ivanov, the foreign minister, since neither really had Putin's
ear. "That was Condi's argument—Igor is a bureaucrat, he does what he's
told. You need to get to the one who's telling him what to do," the official
said.[37]

The same day Ivanov ruled out any cooperation by Central Asian nations,
we flew down to the Uzbek capital of Tashkent, where we found the government eager to jump into the U.S.-led coalition despite Russian resistance. In
the last few years, an extremist group called the Islamic Movement of Uzbekistan, or IMU, had staged terrorist attacks aimed at toppling the government
of President Islam Karimov, the republic's last Communist boss during
Soviet times who had slid into his new role after independence in 1991. Karimov enforced an autocratic secular rule and had grown determined to break
the IMU after it had tried to kill him by setting off bombs in central Tashkent
as he rode by in a limousine in 1999. With the IMU operating out of the safe
haven of neighboring Afghanistan and slowly integrating itself into Al Qaeda,
Karimov had managed to find common ground with the CIA nearly two
years before the World Trade Center fell. Langley had decided to secretly
train a counterterrorism strike force commanded by the Uzbek military with
the hope that it would launch operations into Afghanistan and perhaps even
capture Osama bin Laden or his top lieutenants. As part of their top-secret
partnership, Karimov also allowed the CIA to use Uzbek air bases for helicopter operations and Predator spy plane reconnaissance missions over Taliban territory.[38] By the time Bush was seeking allies in the wake of the

September 11 attacks, Karimov saw it as his chance to get rid of a dangerous nemesis once and for all. "We're prepared to discuss any issue that would be conducive to eliminating terrorism in our region," the foreign minister, Abdulaziz Kamilov, told us shortly after we landed in Tashkent.[39]

With Washington-Moscow telephone calls getting nowhere, the Bush team decided to bypass Russia and loaded John Bolton aboard a Gulfstream jet for Tashkent. For a day and a half, he met in secret at a guesthouse with Kamilov and other top Uzbek officials and discovered that they were unmoved by the Russian resistance. "They couldn't have cared less," Bolton recalled. Soon he was ushered in to meet with President Karimov. "I'm all prepared for how hard it will be and he said, 'Why aren't you asking for a permanent base?'"[40]

Karimov had good reason to court the United States: he knew a new alliance with Washington would buy him relief from international criticism of his abysmal human rights record. More than seven thousand political prisoners were held in Karimov's jails, often beaten, choked, raped, and electrocuted, many for no greater crime than wearing a beard as a sign of Muslim faith or circulating religious leaflets. Karimov had locked up so many observant Muslims that he had to build the instantly notorious Jaslyk prison camp in the desert, where temperatures climbed to 120 degrees in summer as inmates were left to roast in the daytime sun.[41]

As we moved about the dusty capital that fall, we found many people too afraid to talk openly about the regime. One of the few who would was Mikhail Ardzinov, who ran an independent human rights group despite brutal government pressure. We sat down with him in a cramped Tashkent apartment nearly overwhelmed by piles of ancient papers. Two years earlier, Uzbek police had burst into the apartment and beaten him. Ardzinov excused himself to retrieve the bloodstained shirt he had been wearing that day and handed us photographs of the wounds on his face. His telephone was still bugged and his movements still tracked by the Uzbek secret service. "They have promised us that America will not sell out human rights to get Karimov's friendship," he told us. "But we know that the tone will change now."[42]

Back in Moscow, Putin was facing pressure from the military establishment, which interpreted the impending American war on terrorism as part of a broader conspiracy to extend U.S. influence at the expense of Russia's strategic position. "You Americans want to start these small wars and conquer every country one by one," Major General Makhmut Gareyev told us in a Defense Ministry conference room where we met one day.[43] Under Yeltsin,

Colonel General Leonid Ivashov had probably been Russia's most prominent anti-American hawk. He so frustrated his U.S. interlocutors with vituperative rants that they began referring to Ivashov as Evil-shoff, and some suspected he was secretly among the generals behind the unauthorized Russian seizure of the Pristina airport in Kosovo that had triggered a tense standoff with NATO forces in 1999.[44] But Putin had cashiered Ivashov a couple months earlier and stopped listening to him. "We were constantly voicing our point of view," Ivashov told us later. "We brought our conclusions to the presidential administration and the government. But Putin's people are very self-confident. They think they know more than we do."[45]

PUTIN SLIPPED off to Sochi to consider his next move. For days, he and his top security advisers debated the Central Asian question, though it was never clear whose voice really mattered. In office for nearly two years by now, Putin had still created no disciplined decision-making structure on foreign policy; otherwise, Sergei Ivanov would never have made such a categorical statement before the real decision was reached. "Most things are ad hoc–ish," said Sergei Karaganov, the foreign policy adviser. In this case, he added, "It was a mess. It was clear people were thinking what to do and it wasn't a very easy decision."[46]

Ivanov continued to represent the hard-liners. "That was his natural reaction," said Aleksei Arbatov, a parliamentary leader on defense matters. "But then Putin said, 'Come on, how can we say no?'"[47] Pushing Putin in this direction was Sergei Prikhodko, the pragmatic Kremlin foreign policy chief, who thought Russia should aid the Americans in whatever way it could short of putting boots on the ground itself. Prikhodko, a burly career diplomat who had insinuated himself into Putin's inner circle, was not so much pro-American as pro-internationalist and saw this as a signal opportunity to firmly anchor Russia in the world community. He also knew that allowing the United States to topple the Taliban and oust Al Qaeda from Afghanistan would benefit Moscow because it could eliminate the threat of Islamic radicalism on Russia's southern frontier. "What was done in Afghanistan was not only in the interests of America but also in the interests of Russia," he told us later in his office overlooking the gilded spires of the Kremlin cathedrals.[48]

Frustrated at the lack of a clear response from Moscow, Colin Powell asked Bush to call Putin. By then, the Russian had decided. "We are going to support you in the war on terror," Putin told Bush on September 22, according to the White House transcript of the forty-two-minute conversation. Putin promised to allow the U.S. military to fly through Russian airspace, though only for humanitarian purposes, a definition that would later prove conveniently elastic. "We can't put any Russian troops on the ground in Afghanistan. That makes no sense for you or for us," Putin said, alluding to Russia's traumatic history there. "But we are prepared to provide search and rescue if you have downed pilots in northern Afghanistan." Bush thanked Putin and asked him to tell the Central Asian leaders that it would be okay to permit U.S. forces into their countries. "I am prepared," Putin said, "to tell the heads of governments of the Central Asian states that we have good relations with that we have no objection to a U.S. role in Central Asia as long as it has the object of fighting the war on terror and is temporary."[49]

Putin got ready to make his decision public. On Monday evening, September 24, he summoned to the Kremlin the leaders of the various parties in parliament, including his own Unity party, the Communists, and the two pro-Western parties, headed by Grigory Yavlinsky and Boris Nemtsov. Putin told them he was about to announce his response to the U.S. requests for help against Afghanistan and asked for their views. "Everybody except Yavlinsky and Nemtsov said they would take a middle-of-the-road policy. Only the two of them spoke for full support," recalled Vladimir Lukin, a leading Yabloko deputy and a former Russian ambassador to the United States. The rest opposed standing by Washington. Putin listened as the discussion went around the room. Finally he announced his decision. "He said he would support the United States," said Lukin. "And then in keeping with our Byzantine traditions, everybody spoke for a second time and said they supported his decision."[50]

Within hours, Putin went on national television to enlist Russia in the U.S.-led coalition. He vowed stepped-up military aid to the Northern Alliance in Afghanistan and made clear that Russia would have no objection to U.S. bases in Central Asia. "Other deeper forms of cooperation between Russia and participants in the antiterrorist operation are possible," Putin said. "The depth and character of this cooperation will directly depend on the general level and quality of our relations with these countries and on mutual understanding in the sphere of fighting international terrorism."[51]

However dense, Putin's words seemed clear: If the United States returned the favor, Russia would continue to cooperate. Putin said there would be no "haggling" over terms of Russia's support, but his advisers quietly tallied up a list of trade-offs they hoped to gain for their assistance: Additional foreign investment. Repeal of the Jackson-Vanik trade restrictions, enacted during the Cold War. Restructuring or forgiveness of billions of dollars in old Soviet debt. Some sort of accommodation over the ABM treaty and missile defense.

Accelerated entry into the World Trade Organization. A delay or cancellation of planned NATO expansion into the former Soviet republics along the Baltic Sea. Perhaps even NATO membership for Russia itself. More broadly, Russia wanted integration with the West. And Putin himself was eager for leeway to prosecute his war in Chechnya without second-guessing from outsiders. Maybe now, he figured, the Americans would see that the Chechen conflict was really just another front in the war on terrorism.

FOR SEVERAL weeks, a certain headiness governed the new relations between Russia and the West. European and American policymakers began looking at Putin as a genuine Westernizer in the tradition of Peter the Great, whose portrait he had hung in his office in St. Petersburg all those years ago. British prime minister Tony Blair proposed a new cooperative structure between NATO and Russia. And Putin, in the spirit of the moment, decided to push for a resolution to the missile defense dispute.

A month after the September 11 attacks, Putin met with Bush on the sidelines of an Asian-Pacific summit in Shanghai and surprised the American delegation with a secret proposal to liberalize the ABM treaty's restrictions in exchange for an agreement to keep the pact in place for at least another twelve to twenty-four months. Under the proposed deal, the Americans could continue to test their potential missile system as long as they didn't go any further toward development and deployment.[52] Putin was trying to buy time. He figured the Americans would discover that such a system was technologically, financially, or politically infeasible and therefore the threat to the ABM treaty would dissipate on its own. At the very least it would head off any imminent confrontation over the issue at a moment the two countries seemed to be drawing closer. Neither president publicly disclosed the discussion afterward, but Bush was interested and ordered aides to pursue it. "After Shanghai we were quite sure" there would be an agreement, Alexander Vershbow told us much later. "The president made quite clear he wanted to work out a deal if we could as the bridge to the future."[53]

But the hawks in Bush's Defense Department were aghast and moved to kill the idea. In early November, just days before Putin was to visit Washington and the Bush ranch in Texas, the U.S. side invited top Russian officials to New York to hear a secret briefing on the scope of testing the Pentagon had in mind for the next year or two. Rumsfeld sent J. D. Crouch, an assistant defense secretary, who put on what a senior U.S. diplomat later called a "maximalist view of the testing program," including every conceivable type of testing that might be done. The Russians were outraged. "They believe the DOD threw in everything but the kitchen sink to make it impossible for the Russians to say yes," the diplomat told us.[54] Or as a senior Russian official in the room later recalled, "They told us, 'We will violate everything sooner or later, we will violate everything.' We sat tight and tried to keep our cool, but some of us broke."[55]

By the time Putin arrived in Washington later that month, the chances of a deal had collapsed. Instead, the two presidents announced they would each unilaterally slim down their nuclear arsenals, bringing the number of strategic nuclear warheads from the 3,500 allowed under the second Strategic Arms Reduction Treaty (START II) to between 1,700 and 2,200. Having failed to come to a deal on missile defense, Bush privately told Putin that he would withdraw from the ABM treaty by the end of the year. "We were disappointed, those of us who knew how close we were," said the senior Russian official. "It wasn't a feeling of crisis. It was a feeling that we had failed."[56]

Putin then headed to the Crawford ranch, where the presidents and their advisers shucked the uniforms of their capitals for blue jeans and sweaters, huddling inside against the late-autumn chill and howling rain. Condoleezza Rice played piano while Bush and Igor Ivanov, the Russian foreign minister, chatted in Spanish, unsettling nervous aides who could not understand them. As lightning crackled outside, the two presidents traded toasts. "We are seeing a historic change in relationship between Russia and the United States," Bush said. "Usually you only invite friends to your home, and I feel that is the case here." Putin reciprocated. "I've never been to the home of another world leader, and it's hugely symbolic to me and my country that it's the home of the president of the United States."[57]

Bush and Putin the next day made a remarkable joint appearance before a local high school audience, where they joshed good-naturedly with each other; Putin was looser than he ever was in Moscow. The personal relationship was growing. Before leaving for his U.S. trip, Putin had told Dmitri Rogozin, the legislator, that the trust developing between Russia and the United States as they shared highly sensitive intelligence data rivaled that between Washington and London during World War II. In this formulation, Bush was FDR to Putin's Churchill. "It spoke of a very deep mutual understanding between him and Bush," Rogozin told us much later.[58] Mikhail Margelov sensed the same sort of attitude on Putin's part. "Putin feels that Bush is together with him in the war," he said. "It's like brothers in arms or something like that."[59] For Bush's part, he had signaled his personal affection for the Russian leader by privately assigning him the nickname "Pootie-Poot."[60]

The two leaders were developing a rhythm with each other that translated into a comfortable dialogue. "Putin does a lot of the talking," Vershbow, the American ambassador, told us once. "He's got this encyclopedic mind and tends to speak in long, detailed paragraphs, and Bush responds in a more staccato fashion. But there is a clear bond between them. I think they both see each other as having a similar view of the world, compared to those Europeans who tend to keep their heads in the sand about a lot of the global threats of the day and are very introverted with their own problems. Bush and Putin both see the world as a dangerous place that can't be treated with benign neglect, that we have to act to change the conditions for the better and remove the threats or reduce the threats. On that level, they have a certain bond."[61]

COLIN POWELL showed up at the Kremlin a few weeks later with a piece of paper in hand. It was the statement that the United States planned to issue formally withdrawing from the ABM treaty. Powell wanted to show it to Putin and hoped to coordinate the Russian response in "one news cycle," Vershbow said later, "so the world could see this wasn't a crisis." Putin agreed and ordered his own government's statement shared with the Americans.[62] Each side would go through the Kabuki dance of public disagreement without allowing it to develop into real conflict. "We could have played it differently, a sense of crisis, but it would have undermined other things that we wanted to do," the Russian official explained.[63]

Putin's more pressing goal was to craft a legally binding treaty codifying the cuts in the strategic nuclear arms stockpiles that the two sides had announced in Washington. Bush didn't want a treaty. As he saw it, a treaty meant months and years of arduous negotiations in Geneva over throw weights and technicalities producing a dictionary-size document that could make only a lawyer happy. Cheney and Rumsfeld strongly opposed it as well. If the Russians were friends, they reasoned, why did they need a treaty? Eventually, though, Bush caved and agreed to a treaty as long as it was short and signed during an upcoming summit in Russia in May 2002. "He made the decision that we would do this because Putin needed it," Vershbow said. "It was basically quid pro quo for Putin's cooperative approach. We would do this to make it as easy for him back home."[64]

Yet May arrived with no treaty. For months, the hard-liners on both sides haggled over the wording. Rumsfeld flooded other administration officials with nearly a dozen classified memos objecting to various elements. The summit was just weeks away and it looked as if the two presidents would have nothing to sign. "We were really at loggerheads," John Bolton recounted later. "The May summit was approaching, time was short, and we didn't know what we were going to do."[65] The two sides were stuck on two main points—counting rules and an escape clause. The Americans wanted to count only actual warheads deployed, while the Russians wanted to preserve the practice of past arms control treaties, which had always counted the number of potential warheads each missile was capable of carrying. The American negotiators also wanted to allow either side to violate treaty limits with forty-five days' notice and an explanation without voiding the pact altogether, a provision they privately called "the China clause," in case Beijing started a strategic arms race. "We said, 'No way, no way,'" the senior Russian official recounted.[66]

Finally, the Russians summoned Bolton back to Moscow. It had not gone unnoticed that Sergei Ivanov, the defense minister and Putin's friend, was handling the negotiations rather than Igor Ivanov, the foreign minister. As Bolton walked in, Sergei Ivanov handed him a new draft treaty. "Somebody named Ivanov ought to give you this," the Russian joked. The draft was vastly pared down and simpler; more important, it accepted the American counting rules. Bolton took it home and reported back. Bush agreed to drop the China clause.[67]

Just days before Bush arrived in Moscow, they finished the document. As treaties go, it was not much. At 475 words, it was the shortest in the history of U.S.-Russian arms control and less than a third as long as the story about its signing in the next day's *Washington Post*. It committed both sides to reducing their arsenals to between 1,700 and 2,200 by the end of 2012, but neither outlined intermediate deadlines nor committed them to observing the limits after that date. It also allowed the countries simply to put the warheads in storage rather than destroy them. In effect, then, either nation could simply stash a thousand warheads in a warehouse for a single day, December 31, 2012, then pull them out again the next day and still meet the terms of the treaty.

But as the two presidents sat at a table in the Kremlin's St. Andrew's Hall and put their pens to the Treaty of Moscow on May 24, 2002, they focused on the spirit of the agreement. "This treaty liquidates the Cold War legacy of nuclear hostility between our countries," Bush said, conveniently ignoring that the Cold War had ended a decade earlier. Putin called it "a very good sign as regards the relationship between our two countries."[68]

Bush said nothing about the war in Chechnya, nothing about the textbook of tyranny. The campaign rhetoric was long since forgotten; Putin's agenda had become the American agenda. Before leaving St. Petersburg, Rice gave an interview in which she fairly beamed about the new relationship. "It's historic, the end of the Cold War, the end of the transition, but also, really, three hundred years of European history in which Russia may finally be finding its rightful place in Europe," she said. Instead of threats to cut off international financial assistance, there was talk of new cooperation in the war on terror. "Russia has been one of our best allies in terms of intelligence sharing, in terms of support for American operations that have taken place out of Central Asia, part of the former Soviet Union. In terms of general support, diplomatically, this has been an extremely important relationship to us, really one of our most, and it is confirmation that there is a new basis for a cooperative security relationship with Russia."[69]

It was, for better or worse, quite a lot of happy talk.

Boomtown

There always has to be something new.
—KSENIYA SOBCHAK

AT 4 P.M., SVETLANA Kochetkova and Dmitri Komarov were ogling the flat-screen television and gallery-quality art in the sleek apartment of one of Moscow's best-known political operatives. A half an hour later and a few buildings away, they watched as a housewife made cabbage-stuffed dumplings for dinner and explained that her communal apartment had no hot water. The two university students, part of an army of more than five hundred thousand that fanned out across Russia in October 2002 to conduct the country's first census of the post-Soviet era, were learning just what a city of extremes the new Moscow had become. As they trekked through a cold fall rain, they marveled over the sharp contrasts to be found in the space of a few blocks—from wealthy New Russians without college degrees to college professors in crumbling tenements. In one building, they found a room full of unemployed drunks on the first floor, and an apartment of well-heeled Australian diplomats several flights up. They poked around a squalid old wooden house filled with illegal Uzbek immigrants, then turned the corner into a courtyard of parked Mercedes.[1]

In 1989, the last census had offered a final snapshot of the Soviet empire on the eve of its collapse. Then as now, Moscow was the showcase city, a magnet for all those who could manage to obtain permission to live there. But in most other respects, the Russian capital in the Putin era was a place both transformed and transforming, a megalopolis with 10 million–plus residents, impossible traffic, insane real estate prices, twenty-five-cent subway rides, rioting skinheads, and street-corner kiosks that now sold sushi in addition to sausage. This new Moscow was a place of parallel worlds that rarely intersected, where the Soviet Union lived on next door to the international jet set, and those who vacationed at the dacha jostled for parking spaces with skiers just returned from Davos. It was also a political capital that cared little about politics, where rallies seemed like a quaint relic of a more earnest time, the relentless war down south was easily forgotten amid boomtown reveries, and building a new life seemed more important than what was happening in the Kremlin.

Eventually, Moscow during Putin's presidency would come to boast thirty-three billionaire residents, more than any other city in the world, including New York, though as much as one-fifth of the population lived below the poverty line and middle class meant a relatively modest $500 a month.[2] The neon lights of casinos and the jarring inequity of babushkas rooting around in the trash were no longer novelties a decade into the city's capitalist era, but what was astonishing was Moscow's continuing capacity for change as Putin stability flooded the capital with money. One year, dozens of American-style cafés with names like Coffee Mania emerged within the space of a few months—and everyone realized there simply hadn't been any before. The next season, it was modern twenty-four-hour drugstores. The next, shoe shops. Malls, the massive suburban kind with parking lots as big as the forests they replaced, had hardly existed in Moscow when we arrived. Soon, they ringed the city. In the capital's aggressive tabloids, there were fewer headlines about gangland-style killings of bandit capitalists and more about racist pogroms targeting the traders from the Caucasus who thronged the city's open-air markets.

Armed with clipboards and plastic security whistles, Kotchetkova and Komarov were assigned to record scenes from this unfinished Russian transition. Both were fourth-year students at the neighborhood's prestigious linguistics university, and they were told by school officials that service was voluntary in the sense that if they chose to participate, they wouldn't be expelled. For a month's work, each earned fifteen hundred rubles, a little over $50. Their tutorial took place in Moscow's fast-changing Ostozhenka neighborhood, a historic haunt of the city's intelligentsia filling up with newly rich Russians eager to live near the city center.

At 3 Ostozhenka Street, the hallways were dark and musty despite the glamorous Art Nouveau facade, with that only-in-Russia entryway smell of mold and cigarettes and unwashed bodies and stale alcohol that seemed to be the same whether the residents were millionaires or pensioners. After a long negotiation through a closed door, the students went from the dim corridor into an apartment straight out of *Architectural Digest*. Sitting at the smoked-glass dining-room table, Komarov learned he was in the home of Marat Gelman, a self-declared "spin doctor" often employed on the Kremlin's political projects. Gelman had just been hired in the run-up to the 2003 elections to take charge of the political message on state-run Channel One, the most-watched news network in the country. "I'm afraid of people who are not real people coming into our house," Gelman's wife, Yulia, told the students. "And I'm afraid the information will be sold all over Moscow, where everything is for sale."

A short walk away, Nadezhda Litvina was more welcoming. On the fourth floor of a collapsing building that had started life as a workers' dormitory, she interrupted dinner preparations to describe twenty years in a communal apartment shared with two other families without a shower, bath, hot water, or central heating. Soon, the developers would almost certainly come after their decrepit refuge, but Litvina was determined to stay on in Ostozhenka as long as she could, reluctant to move out to the city's soulless new suburban ghettos even if living conditions were better there. She understood why her better-heeled neighbors were reluctant to cooperate with the students. "After all, they have something to lose," she said. "We have nothing."

WHEN WE ARRIVED in Moscow at the start of the Putin presidency, we thought we knew what to expect—a city-state far removed from the rest of Russia, richer but harsher, too, with over-the-top New Russians and nuclear-scientists-turned-gypsy-cab-drivers. And this we found. What we didn't anticipate was the palpable sense of movement, the energy of a city being reinvented while at the same time never quite leaving behind the relics of the Soviet past.

We moved into the *Washington Post* apartment in the same dreary Brezhnev-era compound where foreigners were once walled away from the rest of Moscow. Each summer, the hot water was still turned off for a month—as it was all over Moscow—for unspecified "maintenance" that few believed actually occurred. For some, life in the compound had changed little. These wary expatriates shopped only at the Finnish supermarket, whose arrival had been one of the great joys of the 1990s, and ate out only at the authentic American diner that had been imported to Moscow down to the vinyl in the booths and the frozen bagels on the menu. Outside the compound's guarded gate, one small kiosk sold flowers, another offered bottled beer, candy, loaves of bread that went stale as soon as you cut into them, and cigarettes that never cost more than a dollar a pack. On the way to the nearby subway station was an unlit park overgrown with weeds and populated by tiny Russian babies swathed in layers of clothing no matter what the season and their babushka minders. Each morning and each evening, the eight-lane avenue in front of the complex, known as Kutuzovsky Prospekt in honor of the Russian general Mikhail Kutuzov, who drove out Napoleon's invaders, ground to an eerily silent halt as President Putin's blue-light-flashing motorcade swept past. The resulting traffic jam—known as a *probka*, or "cork"—was horrendous.

As Moscow rapidly revived itself following the 1998 financial crash, we grew accustomed to living in a neighborhood in flux. First to arrive was a new Porsche dealership right outside our gate, and the attendant menacing guards. That, and a new sushi restaurant in a glorified kiosk that charged astronomical prices for California rolls and attracted the bulletproof-Mercedes crowd, made us fear that in fact the gangland 1990s were not entirely a thing of the past. The late-night shooting of two mob leaders—one Azeri, one Chechen—who had reportedly called a summit meeting at the sushi place did little to dispel such fears.

But we also saw signs of the once-mythic middle class. Across the street, a new Italian restaurant opened with not only the obligatory oligarch-priced dining room but a separate café that served authentic thin-crust pizzas and espresso to an enthusiastic crowd of neighborhood families. Next door, a Soviet-style toy store closed, and after a lengthy renovation, a huge cosmetics superstore appeared, part of a Russian-owned chain called Arbat Prestige that tapped into the Moscow woman's psyche with its gleaming ranks of beautifully packaged lipsticks and mascaras and face creams at all price levels. In a city where women spent an astonishing 12 percent of their paychecks on cosmetics but where until recently the shopping choices had been limited to high-end luxury stores or open-air market stalls rife with fakes, Arbat Prestige was immediately busy. "It's a sip of oxygen for people in conditions of this dirty and exhausting city," the chain's founder, Vladimir Nekrasov, told us of the "little joys" he peddled.[3]

Not all changes were for the better. One morning, the flower kiosk was gone, with nothing remaining but a pile of wood and a hole in the ground. The minimarket kiosk soon followed. Then a phalanx of city workers moved in, repaving the broad sidewalk and landscaping where our little stores had been. This, we came to realize, was part of Mayor Yuri Luzhkov's grand plan for Moscow. A post-Soviet Rudolph Giuliani with a New Deal Democrat's love of giant public works projects, Luzhkov had already taken aim at street bums, dirty cars, and store owners who failed to decorate their windows for Christmas. Now, he had decreed the era of kiosk capitalism over in Moscow, to be replaced by real stores like those in other world capitals. This was progress with an exclamation point, and where could be a better place to start than Kutuzovsky Prospekt, so Putin each day could see for himself evidence of the city's beautification? One boulevard over, of course, the ramshackle kiosks remained, but Putin never traveled there.

Ours was just a tiny corner of boomtown Moscow, a city truly in the "fever of the present tense," as Andrei Sakharov's American biographer marveled,[4] propelled ahead by the country's rapidly accumulating oil revenues and the rise of a service sector in a place almost comically resistant to customer service. Moscow had long dominated in national wealth, a tendency exaggerated after the collapse of the Soviet Union when newly born companies, no matter what remote part of Siberia they extracted their mineral riches from, headquartered themselves in the city. But that, it turned out, had been just a prelude to the real Moscow decade at the beginning of the twenty-first century. In the first post-Soviet years, Moscow had an estimated 8.6 million population—5.8 percent of the overall. But even as Russians died off at alarming rates and the country experienced its most serious demographic crisis since World War II, the capital continued to add more people. By 2002, the official population was counted at 10.4 million by the census takers—up to 7.2 percent of Russia's rapidly shrinking total of 144 million people.[5]

Moscow was getting richer at a similarly disproportionate rate. By the Putin years, it was producing 25 percent of the gross domestic product (up from 13 percent in the late 1990s) and receiving 42 percent of all foreign investment in the country (foreign investment itself had nearly tripled, to $13.9 billion in 2003).[6] Average income was 40 percent higher in Moscow than the Russian standard, and nearly 30 percent of the entire country's retail sales took place in the capital.[7] If regular Muscovites benefited from the roaring economy, the city's rich collected breathtaking dividends from it—Russia's wealthiest man, oil tycoon Mikhail Khodorkovsky, saw his net worth rise along with the stock market from $2.4 billion in 2001 to more than $15 billion two years later.[8]

At times, Moscow's relentless building boom, the constant search for the next novelty, and the mysterious sources of income fueling all this development drew comparisons to the previous gilded age, which ended spectacularly with the ruble crash of 1998. This time, the bubble was made of oil, and analysts often wondered what would happen if the price per barrel sank back below $20. Even the boomtown leader worried about Russia's new identity as a petrostate. "The economic growth of recent years has sufficed merely to prevent us from falling even farther behind other countries," Putin lectured at his 2002 state of the nation address.[9] "This place reminds me of Houston," Robert Dudley, the American president of TNK-BP, Russia's third-largest oil company, worried to us over lunch at Oblomov, one of the myriad new restaurants selling ersatz prerevolutionary charm and $20 beef Stroganoff. "When the price of oil falls, the whole city could fall apart."[10]

But that doomsday scenario overlooked one of the most striking changes of Moscow in the Putin era: the advent of a middle class financially able to participate in the newly arriving mass consumer culture. Until recently, consumerism had remained a luxury for the much ridiculed handful of rich New Russians. Since 2000, the temptations that had flooded the city were aimed at a broad swath of the population in addition to the wealthy few. In 2002 alone, eighteen new malls opened in Moscow, most of them modern trading centers for the middle class anchored by supermarkets and multiplex theaters and new chain restaurants like Shesh-Besh, which catered to the everyday city dweller with affordable shish kebabs and salad bars. When Putin came to office, there weren't more than a handful of such places; with the 2002 boom, Moscow boasted fifty-five modern malls. By 2005, the city would have 21 million square feet of mall space, up from barely 2 million in 1999.[11] Since the precrisis year of 1997, the number of cars on Moscow roads had quadrupled to 3 million, and there were increasing numbers of midpriced foreign brands, not just the old smoke-belching Soviet Zhigulis and Ladas.[12]

Many dated the inauguration of serious shopping for the city's middle class to March 22, 2000, four days before Putin's election, when forty thousand Muscovites battled gridlocked traffic in the grim suburb of Khimki to make it to the opening of Russia's first IKEA. At the time, the city's Ring Road was seen as an impenetrable commercial barrier beyond which retailers would not go, and Muscovites remained trapped in a home-shopping wasteland where nothing existed between the high-end world of Italian leather and the omnipresent bottom of cheap Russian-made furniture still seemingly churned out according to the decrees of long-vanished Soviet central planners. The Swedish furniture giant bet $100 million on its 325,000-square-foot complex, and coming less than two years after the ruble crash had all but destroyed the Russian economy, no one knew what to make of IKEA founder Ingvar Kamprad's opening-day boast: "We're not coming just to sell home furnishings. We're bringing a certain kind of lifestyle."[13]

Success was by no means assured. After the Soviet collapse, those who managed to make money spent it on once-forbidden luxuries like new cars or foreign travel rather than their apartments. As late as IKEA's opening in 2000, market research found that home furnishings ranked sixth on the list of things Russian consumers most wanted to spend money on, and even those who bought stylish clothes or traveled to Paris on vacation were likely to live in an apartment with little furniture or filled with relics of the Soviet past. But the answer to Kamprad's bravado came within hours, as customers trudged through fields of slushy late-winter snow or sat in the three-mile traffic backup then waited for hours more at checkout lines to make their purchases.

Suddenly, it seemed, everyone was redecorating in Moscow, and one could find little totems of IKEA everywhere, from the place mats at the chic new café near the Kremlin to the identical couches that soon graced several of our friends' homes. Imitators lined the road to IKEA, advertising deals on Romanian living room sets and Polish patio furniture. Glossy new shelter magazines, do-it-yourself television decorating shows, city-center home boutiques, and suburban superstores followed. Nesting was officially in. "The business of home beautification is booming," said pollster Aleksei Levinson. After several years in the city, IKEA commissioned a survey by Moscow State University. Home furnishings had shot up from sixth to first on the spending priority list—before new cars, vacations, and even education spending.[14]

"We got a very standard image of what living space was supposed to look like as a result of seven decades of the Soviet regime," said Natalya Maltseva, the host of a popular new television show on NTV called *Apartment Question.* The name was a play on a famous quote from author Mikhail Bulgakov's once-banned *The Master and Margarita,* in which he observed that people in Moscow in the 1930s had been ruined by "apartment questions," such as how many square feet of living space they were entitled to. Each week Maltseva and her staff sorted through hundreds of letters, with gloomy pictures attached, from Muscovites desperate to redecorate their Soviet-vintage apartments. They picked one flat to redo in a two- or three-day whirlwind. Bright colors, clever space-saving solutions, and adorable knickknacks—all now available in Moscow—appeared overnight. The emotional high point came at the end of each Saturday show, when the astonished family returned home. Since going on the air at the start of the 2002 season, Maltseva had been surprised to find "what a huge number of people still live life inside these Soviet stereotypes" and how eager they were finally to change. "Now everything connected with the home is a priority for people," she told us when we visited her on the set one day between takes redecorating a kindergarten. "Even those with a small amount of money spend it on their homes."[15]

Still, the new consumerism was a tenuous thing in a city where even a steady monthly income was often not enough to overcome the ingrained fear of a crisis tomorrow. When we made the mistake once of talking to our friend Svetlana about "middle-class people like you," she sternly chided us. "There is no such thing as the middle class in Russia," she declared. No matter the evidence to the contrary, the nicely renovated apartment she lived in just off the

New Arbat, the trips to Western Europe and the United States and resorts in Turkey and Egypt, the stylish clothes she always wore, and the evenings at the theater. Without security, Svetlana would never call herself middle class. "And we will never have security," she insisted.

But the changes in the city had a measurable impact on how people like Svetlana lived, and the numbers showed that Muscovites were eager spenders now that the malls had opened. With 70 percent of Russians still refusing to save money in banks and expenses like rent, taxes, and transportation far lower than elsewhere in Europe, analysts figured that Muscovites had as much as 80 percent of their income left for other spending compared with just 45 percent in the West. The city, in other words, had millions of potential consumers ready to start consuming even with monthly pay that seemed no better than poverty level. One investment bank found that the threshold for the Moscow consumer takeoff was an average wage of just $150 a month, a benchmark crossed in 2001.[16] And nobody believed the monthly income numbers were really correct anyway; one of the enduring mysteries of the city was how everyone managed to spend so much while supposedly making so little. "Objectively, there aren't enough real characteristics of a middle class. If we take income, it doesn't exist at all," sociologist Olga Vendina told us. "But the Moscow middle class does exist. They don't save; they invest in a way of life, and it is the way of life of the middle class."[17]

Perhaps as important as take-home pay was the process that a sage engineer we ran into at a do-it-yourself home store called "perestroika of the mind," new thinking that seeped so imperceptibly into Muscovites' lives that they themselves often couldn't say when it had started seeming normal for office drivers to take vacations in Egypt and for babushkas to take their grandchildren to the mall on a snowy afternoon. At such a time, politics seemed increasingly beside the point.

WHEN IT FIRST became a neighborhood, in the Moscow of Ivan the Terrible in the sixteenth century, Ostozhenka was a rural outpost, named after the haystacks that lined the banks of the Moscow River. The tsar gave tracts of land there to members of his feared *oprichnina,* the original Russian secret police, whose violent rampages and fierce loyalty to their sadistic leader helped earn Ivan his enduring nickname. Much later, after the tsars had decamped to their northern capital in St. Petersburg, Ostozhenka filled up with the mansions of rich merchants and aristocratic families. Its quiet lanes served as temporary residence for writers Aleksandr Pushkin and Ivan Turgenev, and Tsar Nicholas I built the massive gold-domed Cathedral of Christ the Savior right at the start of Ostozhenka Street to celebrate Napoleon's defeat. Avant-garde artists and writers flocked to the neighborhood in the years before the revolution. At one point, modern dance pioneer Isadora Duncan, having moved there with the Russian poet Sergei Yesenin, organized a school of free dance at their Ostozhenka apartment.

In Soviet times, the grand Art Nouveau mansions became run-down offices, the noble eighteenth-century palaces turned into scientific institutes with long names. Other impressive buildings morphed into threadbare communal apartments. Stalin famously destroyed the Cathedral of Christ the Savior, intending to build in its place a skyscraper that would dwarf the Empire State Building, only to discover too late that the soil would not support such an edifice. Left with a gaping hole in the ground, a chagrined Nikita Khrushchev years later ordered up a massive outdoor swimming pool, the world's largest. Ostozhenka Street was renamed Metro Builders' Street, in honor of the city's first underground line, which ran directly under the avenue as it headed toward the redbrick walls of the Kremlin less than a mile away. But the neighborhood also retained its small-town charm and reputation as a hangout for the intelligentsia. Anna Akhmatova, the poet who would later become the conscience of a traumatized nation with her forbidden verse in memory of Stalin's victims, lived there during the revolutionary turmoil and wrote about it in "Third Zachatievsky," a poem named for the side street she lived on. Her close friend Nadezhda Mandelshtam, whose legendary poet husband, Osip, died after being sent to the gulag for secretly reciting a couplet comparing the Soviet dictator to a hunchback, survived for years as an instructor at the linguistics university on Ostozhenka Street. The area retained its historic feel even during the post–World War II building boom because the Communist central planners shifted development out to the edge of Moscow, preferring to produce ranks of identical concrete apartment towers far from the city center and leaving Ostozhenka's old buildings in a state of what could only be described as beautiful rot.[18]

Now Ostozhenka was called the Golden Mile, and its real estate prices were among the highest in a city where high-end apartments went for some of the most astronomical sums in the world. It was not uncommon for developers to charge as much as $12,000 a square yard for space in the new "elite housing" that had crowded out the communal flats—up from $2,000 when Putin came to office.[19] The old Ostozhenka of Akhmatova and Turgenev, of prerevolutionary mansions and ancient wood-frame houses, had all but disappeared in the short time since the evaporation of the Soviet Union. Holdouts like Nadezhda Litvina, the communal apartment dweller encountered by the young census takers, were an increasing rarity, not expected to last the decade in the neighborhood. "It was a village in the center of Moscow—we all loved it," architecture critic Nikolai Malinin told us. "Unfortunately, there's no way out. The only thing we can do is shed tears for the old Moscow. It's too profitable to stop what's happening."[20]

All across Moscow, the fevered pace of architectural change was greater than at any time since the 1930s, when Stalin set out to reshape the sleepy former capital of the early tsars into the showplace of proletarian ambition and thought nothing of knocking down thousands of buildings to do so. This time, it was money and the market, not dictatorial designs, that drove the process, helped along by Yuri Luzhkov's city hall. Aleksei Komech, the director of the Institute of Art Studies and one of the mayor's fiercest public opponents, believed that as many as four hundred buildings—including sixty listed architectural monuments supposedly protected by national law—had been demolished on Luzhkov's watch.[21]

Dozens of cultural leaders appealed to Putin to stop the "criminal" destruction, but to no avail. The president was resolutely silent in public on all matters concerning the city run by his onetime political rival. "The region of Ostozhenka has disappeared, the face of the Moscow embankments has been ruined," the petitioners wrote. "Commercial profit cannot excuse the systematic destruction of our own history, culture, and national identity."[22] Luzhkov simply scoffed at them. His vision for the city emphasized the ersatz over the real, an aesthetic reflected most pointedly in the grandly rebuilt Cathedral of Christ the Savior on the corner of Ostozhenka Street.

Many of the vanished buildings were landmarks so central to the city's sense of itself that Muscovites simply considered them untouchable—until they, too, disappeared under the wrecker's ball. The Soviet-era Moskva Hotel, directly abutting Red Square and across the street from the State Duma, went up in a cloud of dust in the summer of 2004, leaving a gaping hole for the tourists. The mayor promised to rebuild the hotel with luxury improvements and underground parking; it, too, had been on the federal protection list. Also gone were the famous Art Nouveau department store Voyentorg and the historic mansion of the aristocratic Rimsky-Korsakov.[23] "It's barbaric," Komech told us in his proudly shabby office in a mansion once owned by Russia's noble Golitsyn family. "The silhouette of the city is disappearing just as fast as under Stalin."[24]

Many of the new buildings that rose faster than seemingly possible to reorder the city's historic contours had a distinctive Putin-era cast. The Moscow developers of the 1990s had built great towers of glass, hoisted dizzying neon signs along once-gray avenues, and invested millions of dollars in shimmering new buildings whose main architectural style was best described as late Las Vegas. Anything Soviet was out, and anything that smacked of Western-style modernism, no matter how tacky, was in. But in Putin's Moscow, political slogans of stability and restoration of Soviet-era symbols were mirrored in the changing landscape. Architects called the design concept of the moment neo-Stalinism, in homage to the style decreed by Stalin, who had reshaped Moscow after World War II by building seven imposing skyscrapers and a host of shorter cousins to emphasize the grandeur of the victorious Soviet state.

"After Yeltsin," Malinin reflected, "after all the putsches and the crises and the default of '98, naturally there appeared a certain reaction, and everybody wanted stability and order and old songs. It's clear it was not by accident, and these buildings fit those sentiments. Society wants stability and order, and society has a certain memory that there was order and stability, and this architecture gives people a certain illusion that it brings stability back."[25]

Dozens of new buildings evoking Stalin-style stability appeared and just as quickly sold out. One was Triumph Palace, a massive tower rising just off Leningradsky Prospekt, marketed as the long-planned but never built eighth Stalin skyscraper. The building's luxurious accoutrements included an in-house fitness center, underground parking, and direct Internet hookups for the capitalist era, but its design was copied directly from the workshops of socialism. With a spire thrust 866 feet into the air, Triumph Palace was planned to be the tallest residential building in Europe. A year before its 2004 completion, its 960 apartments had all been snapped up for an average $450,000 each.[26] The new buildings, architecture writer Yevgenia Mikulina told us, played off buyers' "subconscious connection with wanting to be great and glorious and respectable."[27] Or, as a headline in a journal devoted to the new phenomenon put it sarcastically, "Under Stalin, we had order."[28]

But the buildings, many of which were conceived soon after Putin's rise to power in late 1999 and began opening a few years later, were not only an echo of the changed political climate. More subtly, they reflected uniquely Russian notions of what constitutes status. In terms of Moscow addresses, the seven Stalinist skyscrapers—known simply as Stalinkas—were considered the height of unattainable luxury, with solid construction, relatively lavish materials, high ceilings, classical details, and prime locations. The country's best architects designed them; Stalin personally approved key details of their construction. Reminiscent of the Art Deco skyscrapers of New York, they also boast Gothic towers and spires ordered by the Soviet leader. Early on, they were compared to wedding cakes—and the nickname stuck. Only the best-connected Muscovites linked to the Communist Party elite could ever hope to obtain an apartment in one of three Stalinkas devoted to residential space; no amount of money could secure one. Actress Lidiya Smirnova recalled that she actually fainted when she saw how nice her new apartment was—a flat she managed to get only after personally appealing to Stalin's feared security chief, Lavrenty Beria. That much of the labor was done by Stalin's prisoners never seemed to detract from the buildings' reputation.[29]

Even decades after they were built, the Stalin-era buildings maintained their aura of exclusivity. "For many years, the ultimate dream of every Soviet person was to live in a Stalinist skyscraper," said Mikulina, the critic.[30] The new buildings in the Stalin style explicitly appealed to consumers who had the money to buy what could previously not be bought at any price—and with modern conveniences that the decaying and poorly maintained originals could not offer. To many, that was just like the deal that Putin offered them in politics—the Soviet Union, updated and without the bad parts.

In Ostozhenka, the reinvention of Moscow had taken on its own ineluctable logic. Historic buildings came down to satisfy the demand for the new and improved, as Moscow developers offered up complexes like the one called simply New Ostozhenka, on Zachatievsky Lane, where Anna Akhmatova had once lived. A standard tactic was the addition that overwhelmed the historic original, an especially favored route in Ostozhenka, with its preponderance of distinguished older buildings.

Urban legends grew up around the few who chose to resist, however futilely. In Ostozhenka, neighborhood groups celebrated the tale of Ivan Boldovsky, who refused to vacate the office he had purchased when developers got a court to invalidate his contract. Boldovsky locked himself inside rather than leave. And for twenty-four days, he stayed on, resisting attack by water hose and undeterred by the iron bars the construction company installed to lock him in his cage. His wife and daughter passed him food and a cell phone through the bars. On day twenty-five, he reluctantly left his office, and the rest of the building was pulled down.[31]

Alla Vlasova headed a neighborhood group called Ostozhenka trying to fight off the developers; in 1996, she said, the group had members in thirty-seven apartment houses, which was down to seventeen buildings by 2002, the rest having been evicted or seen their buildings torn down. "The number of people who live here is catastrophically dwindling," she said. "For years, old buildings are not repaired. Then they are announced to be dangerous for living and put up for reconstruction. . . . If the authorities do not feel our resistance, it will be the end."[32]

While the relentless force of their dollars had forever altered the neighborhood, Marat Gelman and the other wealthy residents who now bid up the prices in Ostozhenka had done so precisely because the area offered the charm so often missing in the modern Moscow megalopolis. They came, Gelman reflected over tea in his living room on Ostozhenka Street, because of a "feeling that this is a secret center of Moscow," a hidden spot of beauty that had been "preserved practically as a village" thanks to the benign neglect of the Soviet urban planners. His own apartment, with its straight-on view of the golden cathedral dome, exposed brick walls painted white, and whimsical touches like a Yoda doll peering down on the living room, would not be out of place in any hip urban neighborhood anywhere in the world. He had bought it just before the boom, for $1,200 a square yard, in an Art Nouveau masterpiece of a building, and he loved to tell the legend of the early-twentieth-century builder, who supposedly gave up drinking when he started the place and commemorated his decision by placing a cupola in the shape of an overturned wineglass on top of the building.

Until recently, three families had lived together in Gelman's apartment, and even now some of his neighbors remained, pensioners hanging on to their corners of communal flats. "When we came here, Ostozhenka was not yet the Golden Mile," Gelman said. Now that it was, he planned to move on, out to the prestigious suburb of Zhukovka, where he was building a house with a big lawn for his toddler daughter and there were no communal apartments at all. Gated communities for the rich were all the rage there, the next stage in the Moscow evolution.[33]

FOR A TIME after the Soviet collapse, Ostozhenka's most prominent corner was taken up by a shoe store. Then it became the briefly trendy bistro Tren-Mos. Finally, it came into its own as Vanil, a sleek restaurant marrying French and Asian fusion cuisine with picture windows looking out on the rebuilt Cathedral of Christ the Savior directly across the street. Its handsome waiters never blanched at offering $25-a-glass wine without mentioning the price, and at times the ranks of Mercedes SUVs were so stacked up outside that they took over a full lane of traffic.

This being Moscow, there was the obligatory sushi on the menu along with truffle-tinged guinea hen. And this being a restaurant opened by Arkady Novikov, the fashionable crowd embraced the place in the certainty that Novikov's imprimatur guaranteed it was cool. "Arkady Novikov is the master.

Any place that carries his signature is the most fashionable," said Kseniya Sobchak, the twentysomething daughter of Putin's late St. Petersburg patron, Anatoly Sobchak.[34] An international partyer dubbed by the glossy magazines Russia's first "it girl," Sobchak had grown up a Petersburger but reinvented herself as a Muscovite in love with the possibilities of Putin's capital.

Novikov, a Soviet cooking-school graduate once rejected for a job at Moscow's first McDonald's, was by now the undisputed restaurant king of the reborn city, his growing empire of places to eat an encyclopedia of Moscow food chic. There was a little bit of everything in the Novikov portfolio—highbrow ethnic at eye-popping prices, tsarist hunt country, jet-set generic. Some, like the chain of Yolki Palki bistros he had started in the 1990s and the Kish-Mesh restaurants offering Central Asian kebabs that had opened in the first years of the new decade, were midpriced spots aimed at the emerging middle class. But he was most famous for his upscale restaurants like Vanil, the ones with the restless rich searching for novelty and willing to pay $100 or more a person to find it. Moscow by this time was indeed a city of endless new entertainments for its growing class of the well-off, with perhaps one hundred thousand truly wealthy residents and more than 2.5 million who earned the European average. The gilded crowd no longer had to fly to London and Paris for their amusements; they could get Prada and Armani at home and even, starting in 2002, pick up a Bentley on an impulse.[35] For food, Novikov was their restaurateur of choice.

Kseniya Sobchak said Novikov had flourished by knowing his over-monied audience. "Arkady understands better than I do that in Moscow a restaurant can't be fashionable for a long time—there always has to be something new," she told us one afternoon in between takes on the set of the new reality television show she was hosting. By day an international relations student, by night a self-proclaimed member of the jet set who said she'd be at Cannes right then if it weren't for her television show, Sobchak saw Novikov's restaurants as part of the rapid upgrading of her adopted city. "So many nice places are opening, like every month, new buildings, new houses, new restaurants, renovations of the museums. . . . It's not only about spending money. Here the people for so many years were stuck in a situation where they couldn't surround their life with such beautiful objects. Now they take revenge for the Soviet Union."[36]

The unassuming Novikov didn't look like the food guru of the oligarchs when we met for lunch one day at one of his latest, Café Gallery. He wore a plain T-shirt, not the pricy Italian-label clothes of his customers. His cell phone was the only office he had, and his only assistants were the waiters who took care of him when he ordered a simple spring minestrone for lunch. But he had embraced his mission of selling good taste to the city's fledgling capitalists, and he said that by the Putin era, Moscow's *slivki obshchestva*— literally "cream of society"—had finally learned how to eat and drink well. "They've been to the best restaurants in the world by now. They know the difference now between good mozzarella and bad, and even between good mozzarella and very good." Novikov had grown along with them.[37]

Fine dining in Moscow had still been an oxymoron when Novikov had opened his first restaurant in the early 1990s. Food was a practical matter, dining out a frustrating exercise in what was available, which usually came down to mayonnaise-laden salads, overfried cutlets of indeterminate origin, and side dishes heavy on the sour cream. For the newly rich, though, opulent palaces had sprung up, places that were all about what Novikov called "The Show"—Silver Age, where the gimmick was a nightly auction of a long-stemmed red rose in which the going price usually topped $1,000, or Maxim's, where managers fondly recounted stories like the one about a $20,000 tab run up by Mayor Luzhkov and his friends and paid on the spot in cash.[38]

But Novikov had a different idea. He would sell good taste to those still learning how to spend their money. "They didn't know there was a difference between Pepsi and Coke," he recalled, or, in some cases, even "how to use a knife and fork properly." Like his clients, Novikov did not start out with a yearning for truffles and brandy. He grew up Soviet poor in a Moscow apartment so small there was no room for a bicycle even if his family could have afforded one. His mother, a kindergarten teacher, was a good cook in the Russian tradition, but mostly that meant doing well with what was available. They ate fried meat and fried potatoes, and kasha—buckwheat porridge— when there was no meat, which was often. In the late 1970s, Novikov's dream was to become a chef at a Soviet embassy, a glimpse at the forbidden world just as alluring to him as the idea of cooking. He signed up as a member of the Communist Party. "In principle," he reflected, "I even believed."

In 1992, Novikov borrowed $50,000 from a friend and scored his first hit with Sirena, a seafood place with a massive aquarium beneath the see-through floor. In the beginning, Novikov was not immune to the lures of The Show. Indeed, most of his early successes were variations on it, gaudy theme spots such as Beloye Solntse Pustini, or White Sun of the Desert, with a Central Asian decor based on a popular Soviet-era film of the same name, shimmying Russian girls with flat stomachs dressed as improbable belly dancers, live cockfights, and an overflowing buffet of Uzbek delicacies. But by Putin's time, an outbreak of good taste had overcome his customers, who spent as much as ever but professed to do it more discreetly. "There is no show now," Novikov said. "The time is all but past."[39]

Simple food was their new mantra, dieting and yoga were their new hobbies. At home, this meant abandoning the gold-encrusted furniture for the clean lines of a $10,000 Armani Casa dining table whose only ornamentation was the wood itself. In the clubs, it meant the arrival of oxygen bars and VIP chill-out rooms.[40] A craze for sushi inaugurated the minimalist era among the Moscow elite as the millennium arrived; soon, raw fish would become a staple of nearly every ambitious restaurant menu in the city, regardless of whether the rest of the dishes were Mediterranean or Russian or Chinese. At first, Novikov resisted the sushi mania. But eventually, he owned three Japanese restaurants, and sushi turned up at his other places as well.

The city's restaurant explosion was happening at a frenetic pace and Moscow was now the scene of more hot restaurant openings than perhaps anywhere else in Europe: a French chef who came to town bragging of plans (as yet unrealized) to acquire the city's first Michelin star, a Culinary Institute of America graduate who brought Brooklyn-style shabby cool and real New York–style pizzas to the city's first real foodie mecca. Not a week went by without a sleek new spot opening—experts couldn't say for sure but estimated that thirty to forty restaurants were starting up each month.[41] Novikov embraced expansion more fervently than most. Over lunch, he said he couldn't even remember how many restaurants he had opened in the previous year. "Maybe ten, maybe more," he said. "I'm not counting really." Each restaurant cost at least $1 million, an extravagant sum in Russia, and Novikov brought in London interior designers and Italian chefs and French partners to make them happen.[42] For Vanil, he had teamed up with a family of famous Russian film stars. "Novikov is a brand already," said restaurant critic Svetlana Kesoyan. "Each new restaurant of Novikov's is an event."[43]

Often, the dining experience at such places, Novikov said, was entirely secondary to the *tysovka* experience, *tysovka* being the Russian equivalent of a happening. "Good food is just a plus," Novikov admitted.[44] But Kesoyan, restaurant critic for the magazine *Afisha*, said that while Novikov was famous for being fashionable, she liked his restaurants because they were centers of innovation. Novikov, she said, was among the first to understand that "the time of the Disneyland restaurants is over in Moscow."[45]

At Vanil one Saturday afternoon, over a glass of freshly squeezed carrot juice and a bowl of spartan soup, Yelena Myasnikova reflected on the new city whose style she had done as much as anyone to invent, or at least to chronicle. Myasnikova, a former language professor, had become one of the editors of the Russian-language edition of *Cosmopolitan* a decade earlier, at a time when ten easy ways to a better orgasm and earnest pieces on how to dress for seduction seemed like Western fairy tales. Back then, its only competitors were *Krestyanka* (or Peasant Woman) and *Rabotnitsa* (Working Woman). "We didn't try to adopt the Russian reality of dirty streets and long lines," Myasnikova recalled, just imported the recipes for sexy hair, makeup, and fashion. "They didn't want to face their life today, they wanted to see the possibilities of another life tomorrow."

But in recent years as Moscow's possibilities had expanded, the fairy tale had become a how-to manual. *Cosmopolitan* was now far and away Russia's most successful magazine, three times bigger than its closest competitor, and already the best-selling *Cosmo* edition in the world aside from the American original. Its readers were not those who frequented Novikov's restaurants, but they were, disproportionately, Muscovites, and they were everywhere in the capital, always fully made up and invariably teetering on high heels no matter how high the snow was piled on the sidewalks. Putin-era stability and utter indifference to politics were the perfect complements to what Myasnikova called "our very egocentric formula," and the magazine had more than doubled in size as international companies, mostly of the cosmetics and fashion variety, raced to advertise to *Cosmo*'s Russian audience of big-spending, never-saving young women.

"The *Cosmo* reader doesn't want to know about politics, nationalism, terrorism, anything gloomy," she said, and in that, too, the *Cosmo* girls were the perfect reflection of the booming city. "The time is much more pragmatic. People here work, people make money, people sleep, people travel. They don't have time to sit around the kitchen table talking anymore."[46]

Fifty-seven Hours in Moscow

I need to know: How will I recognize you in heaven?
—Yaroslav Fadeyev

At first it seemed like part of the show. The second act of the musical *Nord-Ost* had just opened, and a troupe of actors in olive-drab World War II uniforms had just tap-danced its way across the stage. They were singing about the derring-do of Soviet pilots, the thrill of the narrow escape. No one thought much of the masked man dressed in camouflage and toting an assault rifle entering from stage left. Even after he let loose a burst from his Kalashnikov into the air, some theatergoers still considered it part of the performance.

Not Irina Fadeyeva. While the rest of the audience at the theater on Dubrovka Street waited with anticipation for the next song, she gripped her fifteen-year-old son, Yaroslav, sitting next to her in the theater's eleventh row. This wasn't right, she thought. "What is it? What is it?" she whispered to her sister, Viktoria Kruglikova.

Her sister was not worried, thinking maybe it was an official raid, the police for some reason seeking someone in the audience. "Ira, calm down," Kruglikova whispered back. "They'll check our passports and that's it. It's going to be a routine check."[1]

Suddenly, armed men were everywhere, onstage, in the aisles, at the exits. People in the audience gasped, some ran for the doors, but Fadeyeva, Kruglikova, and most of the others sat paralyzed with shock. It was a frigid, drizzly October evening in the heart of Moscow, just three miles from the Kremlin, and dozens of heavily armed terrorists had somehow infiltrated the theater and in a matter of moments taken more than nine hundred people captive. "Everyone put your hands behind your head!" one of the men in camouflage shouted. They were from Chechnya, the guerrillas declared, and the audience members were now their hostages. Their demands were simple: Russia had to end the war in Chechnya, otherwise the theater would be blown up and everyone in it would die. "If they don't start moving troops out of Chechnya by tomorrow," shouted the leader, "we're going to begin shooting you!"

Then Kruglikova and the others noticed the women. Some had been sitting at strategic points in the audience and took this moment to stand up, others then entered from the corridors, nineteen in all, each of them wearing a black *hijab,* the head scarf that marked them as followers of Islam, and a belt packed with explosives, the weapon that marked them as potential suicide bombers. Some of the male guerrillas attached a Chechen flag to the stage curtain, while others mounted one on a balcony. Others hung a black banner that said in Arabic, "There Is No God but Allah and Mohammed Is His Prophet" and "Victory or Death." More shots were fired above the audience's heads. And then came the sound that would haunt many of the hostages for weeks and months to come, the distinctive sound of duct tape being unreeled as the terrorists hurriedly attached explosives to columns around the hall, turning the theater into a giant bomb waiting to be set off.

"They fired several salvos above our heads," Kruglikova recalled later. "It had a paralyzing effect. They said, 'Keep calm and you'll be alive. Our demands are to the president.'" Sitting at the end of the row near an emergency exit, she toyed with the idea of making a break for it. But her daughter, Nastya, was hysterical. "She began to shout, 'Mother, are they going to kill us?' Of course I tried to calm her down. She was in shock. She kept repeating, 'I want to live. I don't want to be killed. Mother, hide me.' She was trying to hide. And she is the kind of person who attracts attention."[2] Others did try to get away. The entire orchestra retreated from the pit into the orchestra room and switched off the lights, only to discover the window was locked with a heavy padlock. Within minutes, the Chechens chased them down, pounding on the door. "We've closed all the exits!" one of them shouted. "If you don't come out, we'll toss a few grenades in there and shoot the lot of you! Come out!" Defeated, the musicians opened the door and joined the hundreds of others as hostages in the main hall.[3]

Georgy Vasiliyev may have been the only one outside the theater hall to run toward it. The creator of *Nord-Ost,* Vasiliyev had worked for years to bring genuine Russian musical theater to Moscow and was upstairs in a sound studio when the stage manager called to report gunshots in the theater. Vasiliyev dashed downstairs and pushed his way into the hall just before the guerrillas sealed the doors shut. He had no time to think. "I had to get into the hall in time," he explained later with a rueful smile, "so that I wouldn't feel ashamed afterward. I wouldn't be able to survive if I had failed to get into the hall."[4]

A young entrepreneur who spent the 1990s transporting Western capitalism to Russia in the form of a futures market and cellular telephones, Vasiliyev
had dreamed up the idea of bringing musical theater to Moscow during a trip
to New York, where he saw *Les Misérables* on Broadway. His attempt to buy the
rights to *Les Misérables* failed, and so he decided to develop a homegrown
Russian production, something that would be *nashe*. He derived his story
from Veniamin Kaverin's book *Two Captains,* an epic tale of romance and
betrayal that plays out across the mile markers of modern Russian history,
from the Bolshevik revolution to the siege of Leningrad. He would call it
Nord-Ost, or North-east, and make it a celebration of the Russian spirit.
"*Nord-Ost* was a sort of protest against tarnishing our history, against not
believing in your own strength, against all this pervasive, depressing, ugly stuff
in the mass media," he said. "*Nord-Ost* is the opposite. It's a romantic story
about a family. It's a story that elevates us and our history. It's a story that
enables us to look at our history not as the history of class struggle, wars, and
repressions, but a history of people and personal achievements."[5]

It took three years to turn it into reality as Vasiliyev struggled against the
prejudices of Russia's theater community, which considered the concept the
thespian version of McDonald's. Vasiliyev had to create a school to teach actors
how to perform in a musical and had to convert a spacious, dilapidated auditorium at an old state-owned ball-bearing factory on Moscow's Dubrovka
Street into a modern theater suitable for elaborate special effects, including a
mock airplane that would land onstage in the show's most dramatic moment.
All told, he spent $4 million, by far the most expensive theater project in Rus-
sian history. His billboards were all over town, but no one was sure Muscovites
would pay the $15 ticket price, an extraordinary expense in Russia. Vasiliyev
reassured his financial backers with a psychological-marketing study showing that rising incomes and evolving sensibilities meant that 30 percent of
Moscow's population fit the profile audience, enough people to keep the show
running for years.

Viktoria Larina had been one of those new middle-class Muscovites he
had in mind. She had come to the theater that night on a whim with office
colleagues, while her husband, Sasha Chekushkin, was busy elsewhere. Now
that whim looked as if it would cost her her life. She watched in horror as the
Chechens placed a massive bomb in the seat in front of her. "I was in a
panic—why here? Why in the center of Moscow? When you see on television
that terrorists have captured someone somewhere, that's one thing. And now
here I am."[6]

Movsar Barayev, the young guerrilla who was leading the terrorists, was ready to announce his arrival to the outside world. "You have a chance to let your relatives and your government know that you are hostages," he told the audience. All around the hall, people pulled out their cellular telephones and hurriedly pressed the numbers of their loved ones. With hundreds of outgoing calls all in one confined space, the circuits quickly jammed and not everyone got through. Viktoria Larina could not reach her husband, so she sent him a text message through the phone.

At 9:13 p.m., across town, the screen on Sasha Chekushkin's black Nokia cell phone flashed: "This is not a joke. We are hostages. There are Chechens all around."[7]

THEY HAD been scouting theaters for weeks. Just as Georgy Vasiliyev had done a marketing survey, so, too, had the Chechens. First they looked at a showing of the American musical *42nd Street* before dropping it because they wanted to target Russians, not foreigners. Eventually, they settled on the 323rd performance of *Nord-Ost* because it had become a symbol of that same Moscow prosperity Vasiliyev catered to. The hostage crisis on Dubrokva Street represented a daring strike not only against Vladimir Putin's capital but against the Russian middle class itself, the same people who had energetically been remaking boomtown Moscow even while averting their eyes from the horrors inflicted in their names in the far-distant mountains of Chechnya. "You are responsible," one of the hostage-takers told the musical's stage manager, Anatoly Glazychev, during the long, tense hours to come inside the theater. "It's your indifference."[8]

The leader, Movsar Barayev, was a baby-faced, cold-eyed twenty-five-year-old killer with just a bit of stubble on his face, a black wool beret on his head, and a Kalashnikov assault rifle with notches on the butt in his hands. For years, Barayev had been fighting in Chechnya under the tutelage of his uncle Arbi, one of the most ruthless rebel commanders and mastermind of an infamous 1998 kidnapping and decapitation of four technicians from a British telecommunications company working in Chechnya. Russian troops had finally caught up to Arbi Barayev and killed him in June. Just ten days before the theater siege, they had claimed to have killed Movsar as well in a series of artillery and air strikes, liquidating a man they called "the notorious leader of a terrorist group"—only to discover how wrong they were.[9] Barayev's chief lieutenant in the theater seizure was a shadowy, volatile figure with a goatee who went by the name Abu Bakr; authorities insisted he was an Arab, one more piece of proof of the Chechens' links to international terrorist groups, but the Russians who would talk with him over the next three days were certain he was Chechen or perhaps half-Chechen because he spoke the language fluently. They answered to the most fiercesome Chechen commander of all, Shamil Basayev, the man who had led the raid into Dagestan that triggered Putin's war in 1999 and had grown more fanatical by the year. From some unknown headquarters, he had sent his lethal squadron to the capital. And as they stalked through the building, his twenty-two male terrorists, mostly in black masks and guerrilla uniforms, seemed restless, anxious, angry. "I swear by God," Movsar Barayev said in a video released just after the theater was seized, "we are more keen on dying than you are keen on living."[10]

The Chechen women were quieter but no less desperate. Many had lost husbands, brothers, or sons in the war and were there to take revenge, or perhaps to end their own suffering in as spectacular a way as possible. The emergence of such "black widows" was a frightening new development in an old conflict that had not generally seen suicide bombings before. Among them reportedly was Zura Barayeva, Movsar's aunt and Arbi's widow, ready to press a detonator to bring the building down. And there were two young sisters, Fatima and Khadzhad Ganiyeva, from a family in the tiny Chechen village of Assinovskaya. Two of their brothers had died in the war, and a missing sister was presumed dead. Four months before the theater raid, Russian soldiers had arrived at the family home and taken away Fatima, twenty-three, another brother, and another sister. Khadzhad, then fourteen, screamed at them bitterly, "Are you really brave when you take away girls?" Only when her mother jumped in was Khadzhad spared. The three captive children were taken away to a shed; the brother was beaten until he passed out, then revived with a bucket of water over his head so he could be hit some more. The girls had metal wires attached to their fingers and were tortured with electric current. After three days, their father secured their release by paying $1,000 in ransom, but the girls were never the same. "We are now in shame, they held us for three days, we can't live like this anymore," their mother recalled them saying when they came back. By saying they were in shame, the young women were probably indicating they were raped, as so many Chechen women had been. Fatima and Khadzhad left home a month before the theater seizure, telling their parents they were going to visit relatives. Their brother, Rustam, a twenty-one-year-old fighter for Shamil Basayev, had recruited them to join a suicide attack on Moscow. Russian authorities later claimed Rustam sold his own sisters for $1,500 apiece for the kamikaze mission.[11]

In the theater, the hostages found their captors surprisingly faithful to Islamic tenets, even refusing cigarettes. It occurred to Georgy Vasiliyev, the musical's producer, that the women were "hostages like us." Unlike the gun-men, who might be able to escape, the women in their suicide belts had no way out. They ate and drank sparingly. "Do as we do and prepare yourselves to die," one of the women told him. Vasiliyev decided to get close to her, hop-ing against hope that maybe he could do something. "I thought I'd try to sit closer to the main bomb and get to know the woman in charge of the deto-nator. Who knows? Perhaps at the critical moment I could push her hand away or rip out the wires. We talked about a lot of things, about the role of women in Islam, about art. She admitted reluctantly that she had enjoyed the show. And she knew I was the coauthor. Oddly enough, she needed to share her impressions of the show." The woman seemed to warm to Vasiliyev and offered him the only solace she could give at that moment. "She wrote an Arabic phrase on a scrap of paper and told me to say it aloud at the moment of my death. If I recited it, then I'd be accepted into paradise as a Muslim. It read, 'La illah ila allah.' 'There is no god but Allah.'"[12]

Others began to talk with the women as well. Viktoria Kruglikova and Irina Fadeyeva, the sisters who had brought their children to the theater on the spur of the moment, recognized the Chechen woman who positioned herself near them. Kruglikova had seen the woman during intermission when she seemed to be staring at their children from across the buffet. "I just saw a look full of hatred. And I was standing and looking her in the eye, sort of daring her," Kruglikova recalled. "I wish I hadn't been such a fool. We ought to have understood and gotten away." Now the same woman was standing next to her with a grenade in one hand and a pistol in the other. The Chechen woman's palms were sweaty, and as she pressed the hand with the grenade against Nastya's thigh, Kruglikova tried to push it away. "She told us, 'Don't be afraid. If something happens, I'll shoot you first so that you won't suffer,'" Kruglikova said. "Strange as it may seem, it had a very good effect on my daughter. She calmed down. She relaxed and even began to laugh. 'Hey, Mom, there won't be any pain.' As for me, I felt really scared after that."

They soon learned the Chechen woman's name was Asya. "She looked at Irina and said, 'Here is your son, sitting next to you, and my son is in Chech-nya. It's easier for you.'" She went on to lecture them about the horrors of Chechnya. "Look, you feel scared now. That's the way we live every day. We are unable to get through to your government. That's why we took you, to get the message across to them. The only thing we want is that our children won't be killed. And we don't want your soldiers to be killed by their own either. You just don't know how scary it is there now, in Chechnya. And you do nothing here. You are happy here and just keep on living."[13]

Fadeyeva was hardly comforted, nor was her son, Yaroslav. As the night turned to dawn, he began to despair.

"Mama," Yaroslav said plaintively, "no one's going to save us. I don't think I'll make it out of here. I need to know: How will I recognize you in heaven?"

Tears in her eyes, Irina squeezed his hand and pulled him close. "Son, you won't need to. I've got your hand and I'm not letting go. We'll be there together."[14]

AT THE KREMLIN, Vladimir Putin found himself confronted with the most serious crisis of his presidency. Suddenly his war had struck home, a line had been crossed. Never before had guerrillas invaded the heart of Moscow in such a daring operation 850 miles away from the battlefield. Now the Kremlin faced an entirely new conflict, one that would only escalate from this point on.

As Putin weighed his options, none was appealing and some were flatly out of the question. He would never withdraw troops from Chechnya. Putin had watched how the previous government had bungled the situation when Shamil Basayev had taken the hospital hostage in the city of Budyonnovsk near Chechnya in 1995, bargaining with him on live television, literally begging him to let the patients go, and sacrificing all honor in Putin's view by allowing the terrorist leader safe passage out of town. Putin would never follow suit. Negotiations were fine tactically, but in the end they would only be a way of buying time for Russian troops to get into position. And so that first night he decided to storm the building as soon as his special forces could prepare. Whatever the risk, Putin concluded, he had to respond with force. His own second-in-command, Prime Minister Mikhail Kasyanov, disagreed with the decision; Kasyanov felt storming the theater could be a disaster and told Putin so the night the siege began. Putin responded by sending him to Mexico the next morning to represent Russia at an international conference, safely out of the way while Russian commandos began preparing an assault. The young boy who had learned on the street growing up to punch rather than talk, who had vowed never to be anyone else's serf, simply could not accept negotiations now. "Putin doesn't like to have discussions," said one senior Russian official. "You shouldn't demonstrate weakness to people. He was always saying, 'As soon as people see you're weak, they will beat you immediately and you will lose.' That's why he does all he does to demonstrate he is strong."[15]

Since the early hours of the siege, Russia's most elite commandos had been preparing to raid the Dubrovka Street theater in what they were calling Operation Thunderstorm. The Alpha forces had penetrated a gay nightclub located elsewhere in the sprawling building, establishing it as a sort of beachhead, then planted listening devices throughout the rest of the building. After mapping the layout and determining where each of the guerrillas and suicide bombers was stationed, the Alpha team replicated it all at the Meridian Theater Center on Kaluzhskaya Road in Moscow so they could practice storming the hall.

The real theater remained tense. Just after four o'clock that Thursday morning, a woman in high heels somehow slipped past the cordon of police outside and marched into the theater. Guerrillas and hostages stared at Olga Romanova, twenty-six, dumbfounded as she strode into the hall and began berating the terrorists impatiently.

"Just look how you've gone and scared everyone!" she exclaimed. "What's all this going on?" She confronted Barayev. "You and your goddamned fasting and praying!" she yelled. Then, turning to the audience, she asked, "Why are you just sitting here? Why are you scared of them?"

"Shoot her!" one of the Chechens yelled from the balcony.

"Okay," she said defiantly, "get on with it."

The guerrillas led her out an exit, and seconds later four shots rang out.[16]

SANDY BOOKER's path to the Dubrovka Street theater that night had started on the Internet eight months earlier when he had posted a personal ad seeking "a Russian wife." He had never been to Russia, didn't speak the language, but from his home in Oklahoma he had been convinced that a Russian wife might be better than his failed experiences with American women. "What I would like to find in you: age 38–48, physically active, not striving after a career or business," he wrote in his ad. Svetlana Gubareva logged on to a computer in Kazakhstan and saw the message on a site called Missing Hearts. She wrote back in Russian, but he didn't understand, so she cracked open dictionaries and translated her messages into English. "I am a cheerful, kind-hearted, and honest woman," she wrote. "I enjoy housework. I have two higher education degrees, and I work at a factory."

Booker, who had worked seventeen of his forty-nine years at General Motors building and repairing robot equipment, jumped into the virtual relationship enthusiastically. Sometimes they sent multiple e-mails a day. He knew nothing of Kazakhstan and she no more about Oklahoma; he explained that Oklahoma was famous for a terrorist act in 1995. He picked up a few Russian words and eagerly spliced his messages with them, hoping she would be pleased. She struggled to compose notes in English, a language she was not really comfortable speaking.

At one point, she told him she was struggling at work. "Are you okay?" he wrote. "Or do I have to fly out tomorrow and kidnap you and bring you here to my home? I would enjoy saving a woman in distress. In America every man wants to become a hero. And I'm no exception. I think it must come from our movies."

"I'd certainly like to be rescued in my distress by a hero," she wrote back. "It's the dream of every woman!" In a later message, she added, "Our acquaintance is like a fairy tale. And I do want the fairy tale to have a happy ending."[17]

For a while, it seemed that it might. After four months of correspondence, he met her in Moscow, where they spent a week along with her thirteen-year-old daughter, Sasha. On the last day of the visit, he proposed. As they flew back home in separate directions, they began making plans for the day they would reunite as husband and wife.

But the fairy tale took a different path, one that led them to the Dubrovka Street theater that chilly night four months later. Booker, Gubareva, and Sasha had gone to the theater to celebrate their impending move to America together, yet now sat just two rows behind a massive bomb. Gubareva tried not to look at it. A Chechen woman holding a pistol, detonator, and matches stared. "The woman noticed my panic and told me, 'Don't think that you'll escape or that you'll be hit more than the others. The explosion is going to be so strong it will be enough to destroy three such rooms.' Strange as it might seem, her words calmed me down."[18]

Booker and Gubareva were not the only ones in the theater who were at a turning point in their lives. At twenty-seven, Viktoria Larina already had a daughter and a divorce certificate from a first marriage and had been trying to start a new life with her second. She worked at the state antimonopoly ministry and liked to spice her life up by dying her hair a bright red; her new husband, Sasha Chekushkin, already balding at thirty-eight, favored black T-shirts and played in a rock band called Autumn. Neither had paid attention to Chechnya, figuring there must be a good reason for the war. "If you look at history, why did Stalin send them to Siberia?" Chekushkin would ask later, confusing the destination of Stalin's 1944 deportation to Kazakhstan. "Maybe he knew they bring only bad things and misfortune."[19]

Unable to reach her husband on the phone from the theater, Larina kept up a steady series of text transmissions to him over the ensuing hours, messages at once plaintive and despairing, loving and remorseful.

"Please get me out of here," she pleaded. "Do something."

Her husband stood just a few hundred yards away, having rushed to the theater in the frigid autumn rain, held back behind a police line. As the hours dragged on, she sounded more and more fatalistic. She tapped out a short message telling Chekushkin she was sorry for everything she had ever done wrong.

"Come on," he typed back. "Don't panic. We will still have babies."

She wasn't convinced. "Please forgive me for all the fights. I love you. I love you all."

Her husband tried weak humor. "What do you mean, 'all'?"[20]

As THE SECOND day of the crisis dawned, authorities opened up the nearby culinary school where Viktoria Kruglikova worked so relatives could gather, yet they provided little more than plastic cups of hot tea. Finally, on the school's decrepit basketball court, with televisions blaring in the background, tearstained relatives crowded a State Duma member, begging for scraps of information.

"We need to hear the truth."

"Where is our government?"

In her fur-trimmed coat and bright lipstick, Aleksandra Buratayeva, a member of Putin's political party, offered reassurance. Authorities were trying to get out children, she told them, and ruled out a raid on the building. "There won't be a storm," she promised. "We are not even thinking about it."[21]

It was either ignorance or deception. Even as she spoke, commandos were inching their way through the crawl spaces of the theater. But the authorities were playing for time, sending in intermediaries to negotiate a peaceful settlement they never expected to materialize. Anna Politkovskaya, the *Novaya Gazeta* journalist who had made her name in Chechnya, was in Los Angeles on a lecture tour when the militants first rushed into the theater. She received a phone call from her office in Moscow telling her what was going on and informing her that the hostage-takers were demanding that she come to talk with them. Then she heard from her son. "Mom, Ilya is there!" he told her, referring to a friend who played in the orchestra. "What should we do? Can you help him? Talk with the Chechens! Please, Mom!"[22]

Putin aide Sergei Yastrzhembsky was getting hold of other possible negotiators as well. He called leaders of the liberal democratic parties who had been critical of the Kremlin's handling of the Chechen war on the theory that the terrorists might be more willing to talk with them. One of those he reached was Irina Khakamada, a leader of the Union of Right Forces and Russia's most famous female politician. Fashion-model tall and thin, with stylish spiky hair and an all-black wardrobe, the chain-smoking Khakamada cut a rare glamorous figure in the dour Russian political world of flabby Soviet apparatchiks. She loved to pose for magazine covers and served as her party's most frequent television spokesperson. She also had a sharp mind and a sharper tongue, neither of which she hid. When Yastrzhembsky called, he seemed unusually uncertain. "He said the situation is difficult," she recalled later, and so she agreed to go inside.

She was met in the lobby by Abu Bakr, the number-two terrorist, who told her Movsar Barayev was asleep and unable to see her. Three of the rebels in eyesight were wearing masks; Abu Bakr and another were not. "I had the impression that they were not suicide terrorists but unschooled, unsophisticated rebels, military trained, but without wild-eyed fanaticism," she said. "Their demands were contradictory, unclear, always changing. But they were not set to blow up everything and kill everybody." Khakamada promised to take their demands to Putin and headed to the Kremlin, where she met with the president's powerful chief of staff, Aleksandr Voloshin. From what she could tell, Voloshin hadn't figured out the best way to handle the situation. While Putin was determined to storm, Voloshin and the men around him were still looking for ways out. "He was of two minds," she recalled. "That's why he was listening carefully to my opinion. But he was very annoyed that I talked with the media." Khakamada recommended against storming the building. "I couldn't imagine how to organize a storm and save people if these women could just push a button and blow things up."[23]

Other intermediaries went in as well, including representatives of the Red Cross, the pediatrician Leonid Roshal, antiwar Duma leader Grigory Yavlinsky, and famed crooner Iosif Kobzon, known as Russia's Frank Sinatra both for his singing style and alleged Mafia ties. A few journalists got in as well, including our friend Mark Franchetti of the *Sunday Times* of London, and a crew from NTV. But the hostage-takers were in no mood to negotiate. "Our task was to come here and take hostages," Barayev told Franchetti. "We have done that. Now we have no plans to leave with the hostages. We don't care. Our aim is not to stay alive. It is to force Russian troops out of Chechnya. We are not terrorists. If we were, we would have demanded millions of dollars and a plane to escape."[24]

After flying halfway around the world, Anna Politkovskaya headed immediately to the government command post. Authorities briefed her and she gathered food and juice to take into the theater, but as she got up to go, an FSB agent abruptly blocked her. "He drew his gun and said, 'No,'" she said. Sergei Yastrzhembsky came to her rescue. "No," he said, "she's going." Inside the theater, Politkovskaya found Abu Bakr, who again said Barayev was sleeping and unable to meet. To Politkovskaya, Abu Bakr and his compatriots were nothing new. She had met his type many times in Chechnya. "He was a typical rebel, strongly built, angry, typical ideology. I've heard his ideology before. If you tell them, 'Please let out the teenagers,' they say, 'They're not teenagers when you do *zachistki*, you don't call our kids teenagers, why should I now give you your teenagers?' And to be quite frank, I didn't know what to say. I knew he was quite right." Yet demands, she knew, would get them nowhere with this Kremlin. "I said, 'Look, you are doomed. This is doomed to failure. There is no sense to it. There will only be victims.' And he said they did not expect to survive." She asked him what would happen if Putin actually did pull out the troops. He answered, "We stay. We're preparing to die and we're going to die." But like Khakamada a day earlier, she heard bluff in their voices. "I'm absolutely certain that some of them wanted to survive. . . . They were not people to play games. They were people of war. But still I had a feeling that they were not exactly visualizing that moment. They were sure at the last moment their demands would be met."[25]

One last set of negotiators arrived in the evening, this group led by former prime minister Yevgeny Primakov. The discussion quickly "took an exceptionally harsh tone," he recalled later. Primakov made the point that the Chechens had succeeded in calling attention to their cause, a victory that would be erased by killing the hostages.

"Attracting attention is just the first step," Barayev snapped. "At noon tomorrow, I will start shooting hostages and continue until you withdraw all troops from Chechnya."

Barayev was in no mood to listen more.

"Get out!" he shouted. "We're finished talking!"[26]

INSIDE THE theater, the situation turned grimmer. Day slipped into night, which slipped into day again, without food or drink. The terrorists broke into the theater's snack bars and passed out chocolate, but there was hardly enough to sustain nine hundred hostages. After two young women escaped by throwing themselves out the third-floor bathroom window, dodging gunfire as they scrambled to safety, the Chechens stopped allowing the hostages to use the toilets and forced them to urinate and defecate in the orchestra pit instead, women on the left, men on the right. They waited in a long line, one after the other stepping gingerly into the well to avoid soiling their shoes.

As the hours wore on, it had become increasingly clear to Georgy Vasiliyev that a final confrontation was imminent. "Something had to happen—either they were going to release everybody or demonstrate their resolution. Something had to happen. That's why the tension was growing." His mind wandered and he began imagining how it would play out. He had always wondered how so many people could go so passively to their deaths in Nazi concentration camps guarded by only a few armed men, and now he understood; their will had been broken, there was nothing to do but wait to be killed. "The issue that concerned most people was how they were going to pick people. Would it be every second person? This idiotic thought kept running through my mind: How were they going to pick people to be shot? By age? Sex? Nationality? It was such a barbaric thing, I couldn't let myself think about it. So I thought about the technique of it. That's what really got me."[27]

Viktoria Larina quietly began panicking all over again.

"I am very afraid," she messaged her husband's phone. "They are shooting at us."

"At least pretend that you are not afraid," Chekushkin wrote back, unsure what else to say.

"Are we going to die?" she asked. "We have mines next to our legs. They are praying. Maybe they are getting ready for something."

She begged her husband to tell the authorities not to raid the theater. Unlike Irina Khakamada and Anna Politkovskaya, she was convinced her captors wanted to die as martyrs in battle. "They're all kamikaze. They will kill us. We are not going to survive."[28]

Finally, a phone call came from the Russian authorities about 11 p.m. General Viktor Kazantsev, Putin's envoy to the southern region that includes Chechnya and the man who had met with the Chechen representative for abortive peace talks in 2001, was flying to Moscow and would come to the theater to talk with the guerrillas at 10 a.m. the next day. Movsar Barayev announced the "good news" to the hostages and assured them they could now go to sleep. "Everything is going to be okay," he told them. "We are not going to kill you if you are quiet."[29]

But then a young hostage named Pavel Zakharov suddenly snapped. Around 1 a.m., he tried to hit one of the guerrillas with a bottle and began running. A Chechen fired but missed and hit two other hostages instead, one bullet slicing through the back of a man's head, emerging from his left eye, and another ripping into the belly of a woman. The Chechens panicked at the mistake, certain that it would be used against them as a pretext for retaliation. "The terrorists were very scared," Viktoria Kruglikova recalled. "They kept saying, 'It's not us. You saw we are not to blame. We saved you. Had he reached the door, he could have blown up the whole building.' Their fear was sincere when they saw the blood."[30]

■ ■ ■

THE FINAL, chilling text message from his wife flashed across Sasha Chekushkin's telephone before daybreak that Saturday morning. "They have started this raid. Good-bye."[31]

Movsar Barayev had proved dramatically mistaken. Viktor Kazantsev would never show up to negotiate with him. It was all a ploy. The Kremlin had wanted the Chechens lulled into complacency when it sprang its trap. Just hours after the phone call to Barayev, Russian agents began hauling in containers with a never-before-used chemical, an aerosolized version of the anesthetic fentanyl. The containers were jury-rigged into the ventilation ducts and the air-conditioning was then turned on. Although the chemical was theoretically invisible and odorless, the Chechens and their captives realized what was happening; some saw a mist or haze, others detected a sweetish smell. Barayev leapt onto the stage and began shouting that the ventilation system had to be shut down, then jumped into the audience looking for an electrician. Some of the hostages covered their faces or their children's faces with wet cloths; others were on their mobile phones describing what was happening live on Ekho Moskvy radio.

"Our security forces have started something," panicked hostage Anna Andrianova cried out into her telephone. "I think they don't want us to leave the theater alive and thus end the situation."

"Anya," the radio announcer said, "can you explain what kind of gas it is? . . . Can you see it or feel it?"

"I don't know. We can see and feel it and we're all breathing into pieces of rags. Our people have started something."

Shots could be heard over her telephone.

"Oh, God!" she screamed.

"Can you hear us?" she asked a moment later.

"Yes," the announcer said.

"Any second now we're going to get blown to hell!"

And then the line went dead.[32]

The commandos, each wearing a gas mask and a white armband, raced into the hall about 5:30 a.m. Some of the Chechens pulled on masks of their own and started smashing windows in a desperate bid to clear the air, but the Russians opened fire. Barayev sought refuge in a small office on the first floor, but commandos cut him down with a grenade and a blaze of gunfire. "The lead we sent at him tore his body away," one commando said afterward. Some Alpha agents had been assigned specific Chechens to kill, and they carried out their assignments with ruthless efficiency. All the female suicide bombers were finished off with a single bullet to the head even if they had already passed out. "Do you think we should have woken them up and called for an honest battle?" the commando asked sarcastically.[33] "I understand it sounds cruel," said another, "but when a person is wearing two kilos of plastic explosives, you see no other way to disarm her."[34]

Within fifteen or twenty minutes, the shooting was over and Russian sappers scurried about the hall trying to disarm the explosives taped to columns. Throughout the theater, the dominant sound was, eerily, an extraordinary chorus of snoring from some nine hundred unconscious people passed out from the effects of the Russian chemical spray. But the Russian authorities had not prepared for what would happen next. In theory it sounded so easy—just put everyone to sleep. But any anesthetic, and fentanyl in particular, must be measured against the individual it's used on; that's why any surgery includes an anesthesiologist monitoring the patient throughout the operation. A dose that would put a healthy young man to sleep can easily kill children, older people, or those with weaker constitutions. The commandos had no way to calibrate the power of the spray for the hostages. In fact, to make the plan work, they had no choice but to use a powerful enough concentration to take out strong, young, battle-hardened guerrillas hopped up on adrenaline and martyrdom regardless of its effects on weakened hostages.

Unsure what to do, the Alpha commandos and other police officers began picking up the unconscious bodies of the hostages and hauling them out of the building into the damp early-morning air. Medical personnel were nowhere to be found initially. "At first no one was even helping us," an Alpha fighter recalled afterward. "We simply did not know what to do with the people." The rescue workers didn't show up for precious long minutes. "It was they who were late. Everyone we carried out from the building was alive." Some of the regular army soldiers sent into the building were told that the hostages were dead, leaving them without any sense of urgency to get them to medical help. And some of the Russian law enforcement agents were too busy helping themselves to help anyone else. "We actually beat up one policeman," the Alpha commando said. "He had come up to a prostrate woman, picked up her bag, pulled out a wallet, and put it in his pocket. Suddenly, he saw her coming around and he gave her a kick in the face with all his strength. We roughed him up. Somebody yelled, 'Kill him! We'll write him off as a combat loss.'"[35]

Watching from across the street, we could see bodies being stacked outside the theater as if just so much cordwood. Finally around 7 a.m. the first of dozens of ambulances raced up to the theater and rescue workers began carting off the hostages in a stream of vehicles in and out. Without enough ambulances to handle the mass casualties, authorities commandeered buses and began piling bodies on board, not bothering to take care in how they were positioned. Many were still unconscious or dying, choking on their own tongues or vomit. Through the windows we could see the few who had regained consciousness struggling to sit up, their faces pale and sickly, their eyes hollowed and in shock. "I felt someone carrying me," Viktoria Larina later said. "I think it was an OMON guy. I opened my eyes and everything was swimming. I didn't understand anything. He said to me, 'Keep breathing, girl, keep breathing.' I wanted to tell him, 'I can't breathe,' but I couldn't. Then I passed out again. . . . I came to in the hospital. I wanted to shout, 'I'm here! I'm alive!' But I couldn't say anything. No sound came out of my mouth."[36]

Viktoria Kruglikova's husband, who worked in secret services himself, managed to get through the police perimeter and rushed into the theater looking for his family. For three days he had been waiting outside; now that the climax had come, he knew enough about how Russian law enforcement organizations worked not to leave it to someone else to find his family. Scouring the theater, littered with broken glass and spent ammunition and prone bodies, he saw that all the faces of the hostages looked alike, bluish with distorted features and strangely bared teeth. He thought they might all be dead. Finally he came across his wife's limp body. She was wheezing and moaning. Their daughter was there as well but unmoving, so he picked up his wife, carried her outside, and put her in an ambulance. Then he ran back inside for their daughter. When he found her again, she was lying beneath a pile of other bodies that had been stacked on top of her in the moments he had been gone. He frantically pulled them off her.

As he hovered over what he thought was his daughter's dead body, a man he took to be a doctor ran through the room.

"Why are you standing like that?" the man demanded.

"This is my daughter and she's dead," he answered.

But the man shouted that he was wrong. "They're all alive." The man threw him a tube and told him to use it to help the girl breathe, then ran off to try to help others.[37]

In fact, virtually no one had been told what to do. Medics and rescue workers showed up at the scene with the hundreds of bodies without being informed what chemical had been used, without being given instructions for how to revive people before they succumbed to the effects of the spray. Even the well-meaning almost certainly caused the deaths of some people simply by carrying them with their heads tilted back or placing them on the ground faceup, leaving their tongues to swell and clog air passages. Piling bodies on top of each other surely led to the deaths of many hostages. Doctors kept in the dark about the fentanyl-like drug were left to guess what they were dealing with. Had they been told, some said later, the casualty count could have been kept low. The key was immediate attention at the scene. "If people were intubated and helped to breathe with artificial ventilation while still in the vehicles being brought to the hospitals, almost everyone would have survived," one senior doctor who treated many hostages told us a few days after the end of the siege. "Everyone brought to my hospital alive is still alive."[38]

Instead, 130 hostages would needlessly die. Sandy Booker, the American, died after scrawling out a farewell message on his forearm to his daughter back in Oklahoma. His Russian fiancée, Svetlana Gubareva, also lost her teenage daughter, Sasha. Viktoria Kruglikova's husband, after finding her and their daughter, went back into the theater and came upon his sister-in-law, Irina Fadeyeva, her face deathly white rather than blue, and her clothing seemingly splattered with blood. But no matter where he searched, her son Yaroslav was nowhere to be found. Fadeyeva later woke up in a hospital lying on the floor in a hallway stark naked. A tiny icon she normally kept in her bra was pressed in her hand. She struggled to her feet without realizing she had no clothes on until someone gave her a blanket to cover herself. For many months afterward, she and her family would wonder why she had been stripped while others had not been; perhaps, they suspected, it meant Yaroslav had actually been shot by the Russian commandos and his blood had stained her clothes, which they removed to eliminate the evidence.[39]

Russia's leaders were too busy congratulating themselves to look into such mysteries. They had headed off the explosion of the building and rescued the vast majority of the hostages, and that seemed enough. Putin went on television and offered a valedictory over "the armed scum," as he put it. "We achieved the nearly impossible, saving hundreds and hundreds of people," he said. "We proved that Russia cannot be forced to its knees." In a rare moment of regret, he added a brief apology to the families of those who did not survive. "We could not save everyone. Forgive us."[40]

While Putin hailed his own unbending response to terrorists, he virtually ignored their victims. Relatives of the hostages such as Sasha Chekushkin were left to wander from hospital to hospital in search of loved ones, with little or no help from authorities. Hospital officials ordered the iron gates around their buildings locked to keep them out. Chekushkin found his wife, Viktoria Larina, alive, but many people discovered that family members had died only by going to the morgue and scanning the corpses until they found one they recognized.

After getting out of the hospital, Irina Fadeyeva finally tracked down Yaroslav, laid out in a city vault, waiting for identification and burial. It seemed to her that there was a small hole in his forehead, possibly a bullet wound, but the autopsy called it a deeply caved cut. Either way, he was gone. She stroked the cold face of the son who wanted to know how to find her in heaven.

"Now I've found you," she told him. "Just wait there. I'm on my way."

She slipped out the back of the morgue unseen by anyone, flagged down a passing car, and asked the driver to take her to a bridge over the Moscow River. She had no money, so she yanked off her wedding ring and gave it to the driver for payment. After he dropped her off, Fadeyeva peered over the railing of the bridge at the freezing river below. Winter was already gripping Moscow, but she barely noticed the chill. Yaroslav was dead. She had nothing left. Summoning her courage, she threw herself over the railing into the icy water far below.

But somehow the fall did not kill her and passersby pulled her out. She did not succeed in joining Yaroslav. "I didn't even catch a cold," she said later, ruefully.[41]

THE REST OF the world dispatched congratulatory telegrams and phone calls to Putin. Never mind that the Russians refused for days to identify the chemical they had pumped into the theater, relenting only after foreign scientists figured it out for themselves, and even then keeping the actual formula a state secret. Never mind that the postraid rescue mission had been so badly botched by secrecy and mismanagement that it cost nearly all of the 130 lives that were lost. Never mind that the knockout spray did not work immediately, meaning that the guerrillas had precious seconds, even minutes, to set off their explosives had they decided to. It fell to the U.S. ambassador, Alexander Vershbow, a longtime career professional diplomat with an inconvenient streak of integrity, to say the obvious. "It's clear that perhaps with a little more information at least a few more of the hostages would have survived," he told reporters in a briefing three days after the raid.[42] For his candor, according to another U.S. official, Vershbow would later privately be chided by the State Department, which had chosen to support Putin through the episode regardless of the less savory aspects.

Any domestic critics were quickly silenced as well. Toxicologists were barred from testing the bodies of the victims to find out the exact formula of the chemical used. Doctors who treated the survivors were ordered not to talk with the press. Under "cause of death," officials listed things like "terrorist act" or "preexisting condition" on the death certificates of the slain hostages. Irina Fadeyeva's son would have a simple dash put in that space on his death certificate. And in case the facts weren't damning enough, some of the Russian commandos planted syringes and a bottle of liquor around Movsar Barayev's body to make it look as if the Islamic radical had been drugged and drunk.

During the fifty-seven-hour siege, the government clamped down on the media. The local channel Moskovia TV was taken off the air just two minutes before its 6 p.m. newscast on the day before the raid and not allowed back on for fifteen hours. NTV was barred from airing its interview with Barayev. Even the state-owned *Rossiskaya Gazeta* newspaper was reprimanded by the Press Ministry for publishing a photo of two doctors removing the body of a dead hostage from the theater.

The siege would prove to be another moment of truth for NTV, already seized from its previous owners and under the command of management installed by state-controlled Gazprom. In the eighteen months since Russian-American financier Boris Jordan had taken over, NTV had become somewhat tamer, somewhat more respectful of Putin and the state, but still more independent in tone than the state-owned channels. Jordan had vowed to maintain NTV's integrity, and he had done more to live up to that pledge than anyone had expected, much to the Kremlin's chagrin. In the days after he took over, his new masters had pushed him to complete the job of destroying NTV founder Vladimir Gusinsky. "They came to me and said, 'Okay, now you've got to finish him off,' and I said, 'No, we're going to play it my way,'" Jordan told us.[43] Instead of more confrontation, he slowly bought Gusinsky out of his remaining NTV shares. He also turned around the network's poor finances and wiped out nearly $1 billion in debt. He targeted a younger audience and brought in Russian-dubbed versions of *Sex and the City* and *The Sopranos*. Along the way, however, he also broke away from the monopoly control over television advertising held by Video International, a firm linked to the press minister, Mikhail Lesin. Jordan was walking a dangerous line. Every day, he later said, someone from the Kremlin or elsewhere in power would call to complain about something on the air. "He used to say, 'Be more careful, be more careful, take it easy, you're getting me in trouble,'" anchor Tatyana Mitkova said later. But at the same time, she said, "He also wanted to take risks."[44]

The theater siege made clear the limits of Putin's patience with his new television network. When the Kremlin released video footage with no sound showing Putin meeting with advisers during the siege, Leonid Parfyonov, host of NTV's popular Sunday newsmagazine *Namedni*, hired a lip-reader to determine that the president was talking about raiding the theater. Another host, Savik Shuster, invited the parents of hostages onto his talk show, *Svoboda Slova* (Freedom of Speech), to air their pleas for a peaceful resolution of the siege and an end to the Chechen war. The Kremlin was livid.

The night before the raid, Lesin called Jordan. "He said, 'When you shut your signal off at two a.m., I'd like you not to come back on until I call you,'" Jordan told us later. "I told him, 'Well, we have a schedule, we come back on the air at six a.m.' 'Well, there's a national security reason for you not to do it.' He didn't tell me I couldn't, but I agreed to it." By 3 a.m., a weary Jordan finally went home for a few hours, leaving Shuster in charge with the instruction to stay off the air. Then at 5:45 a.m., as the raid was beginning, the phone rang at Jordan's house. "I got a call from a yelling minister of press. 'You guys are on the air! This is bullshit!'" It seemed that Shuster had gone to get coffee, and while he was away, troops began entering the theater and a young correspondent at the scene went on the air to report that something was happening. Jordan called the station and yanked the plug until 6:10 a.m. "The whole thing really upset Putin," Jordan said. "He was really under a lot of pressure at that time, and he felt that it could have foiled the storming if people saw it on the screen and he's right."[45] Although Putin accused NTV of airing live pictures of commandos moving into position a few minutes before the raid was launched, that was not true. No pictures went out until after the raid began. And the lip-reading segment as well did not air until after the raid was over. But the details didn't matter to Putin. Within three months, Jordan was fired.

The handling of the theater siege had again laid bare the persistent preeminence of the state over individuals in Russia, the government's disregard for the lives of its own people, and its penchant for secrecy. After the crisis was over, Boris Nemtsov, the Union of Right Forces leader, proposed that the State Duma investigate the incident to find out what had gone wrong, only to have the Kremlin squelch the idea and ensure that no comprehensive independent probe would ever be conducted. Clearly furious, Putin publicly accused politicians of scoring "PR on blood"—a clear reference to Nemtsov—and hosted his main rival for leadership among the democrats, Yabloko's Grigory Yavlinsky, at the Kremlin in a televised meeting to thank him for not exploiting the drama politically.

Nemtsov's Union of Right Forces conducted its own brief inquiry anyway into the rescue response at the end of the siege, concluding that more than half of the dead hostages lost their lives not because of the chemicals but because of the failure to provide them immediate medical care. "That's why they died," Nemtsov told us later. "It was a disaster." But when Nemtsov went to the Kremlin more than a month later to give Putin his findings and recommend changes in the emergency response system and an investigation of the officials in charge of it, he found a cold response. Ultimately the report was buried. "The Kremlin did nothing—nothing," Nemtsov told us afterward. "They said, 'You know these victims are [dead] and we can't save them now.'"[46]

Putin could silence Nemtsov, but he could not turn off the war he had started. On the tape that NTV was barred from showing until after the siege was a young female suicide bomber, who vowed blood vengeance for the death of her brother and other Chechens. "We have children, too, old folks and women who are dying," she said. "Even if we all die here, it won't be over. There are many of us. It will continue."[47]

That would certainly prove true. The theater siege signaled a decisive turning point in the Chechen war, the radicalization of a movement that would begin to adopt attributes of the Palestinian intifada against Israel and further link it to the worldwide Islamic struggle. Chechens, who had only rarely embraced suicide bombing as a tactic before *Nord-Ost,* turned it into their major weapon afterward, having seen that it was the only way to get Russia's attention. Over the two years starting with the Dubrovka Street theater siege, about a thousand people would die in terrorist incidents in Russia, more than in Israel or virtually any other country in the world in that period. Every month seemed to bring another deadly explosion—eighty killed when a vehicle packed with explosives rammed into a Grozny government building, fifty-nine killed when a truck smashed into another government complex in northern Chechnya, eighteen killed when a lone woman blew herself up next to a bus ferrying soldiers, seventeen killed when two women detonated explosive belts at a Moscow rock concert, forty-six killed when a bomb ripped through a commuter train in southern Russia, forty killed when a similar bomb shredded a subway car in the Moscow metro. At times, the attackers got chillingly close to the centers of power. Just two days after parliamentary elections in December 2003, a woman on a main street in Moscow stopped to ask directions to the State Duma building, then exploded moments later, presumably prematurely. She was barely a hundred yards from the Duma and the Kremlin.

Most of the suicide bombers were women, many apparently, like the *Nord-Ost* women's brigade, the widows and orphans of slain Chechen guerrillas. The surviving twenty-year-old sister of Fatima and Khadzhad

Ganiyeva, both killed in the theater, went into hiding because her brother Rustam now wanted to strap her with explosives and send her out on a fatal mission as well. "It's considered a great achievement for Wahhabite men," said another woman allegedly recruited as a suicide bomber by Rustam. Zarema Muzhakhoyeva, twenty-three, agreed to go along after despairing because of family troubles that had resulted in her child being taken away from her. Rustam's compatriots sent her to Moscow, where a Chechen guerrilla prepared her for a suicide bombing attack along Tverskaya Ulitsa, the capital's most fashionable boulevard. "He gave me a black *hijab*, which almost completely covered the face, and ordered me to put on a black dress with long sleeves and high collar to cover the neck," she later told a Russian reporter. "He gave me a piece of paper with the text of what was supposed to be my last address to the people. I vaguely remember the text. It said something like 'My day has come and tomorrow I'll go against the unfaithful in the name of Allah, for the sake of you and me, for the sake of peace.'" She was videotaped reading the statement. "I wanted my relatives . . . to see my address so that they would know that I died and washed my shame off, that I'm a good girl, a grown-up, that I wouldn't bother them anymore."[48] But by the time she was dropped off in front of a café on Tverskaya, she had changed her mind. Rather than set off the bag of explosives she carried, she acted nervously until the restaurant security guards stopped her and called police. Still, an FSB demolitions expert sent to defuse the bomb died when it detonated in his face.

The echoes of the hostage crisis reverberated far beyond the shopping malls of the capital—in the bloodied faces of bewildered Central Asian laborers rounded up in mass detentions and told to leave Russia because they wore beards, in the mosques along the Volga River raided by zealous police who seized the Koran as proof of terrorist intentions, in the mobs of skinheads regularly rampaging through markets determined to kill "blacks" like the Chechens. Inside Chechnya, too, Russian soldiers quickly fanned out to take their revenge after the theater siege. Troops arrived at the Assinovskaya house of Fatima and Khadzhad Ganiyeva and without notice blew it into rubble. Their parents were spared only because they were watching television at a neighbor's home at the time.[49] Toxic hate, intolerance, corruption, indifference to human life—in Putin's Russia, these were the legacies of the war in Chechnya that became clearer than ever when the chemical spray dissipated in the theater on Dubrovka Street.

"It seemed to me in the first months after *Nord-Ost* that many people, judging by the mail I received, began to think the government's policy was wrong on Chechnya—'We understand that you were right,'" Anna Politkovskaya, the journalist who tried to play intermediary, recalled later. "But it lasted only a half year. Then it went away. . . . I think things are back where they were." Sitting at her desk at *Novaya Gazeta,* she picked through the piles of paper and held up a clipping of a story she had recently written about another tragedy in Chechnya. Someone had cut it out of the newspaper and sent it back to her in the mail, scrawling on it, "Stick it up your ass," and, "Your dollars come from the CIA and [billionaire financier George] Soros. You will pay for it."

"People are dying and this is what I get every day," she said. It was willful ignorance. With so many atrocities committed in their name in Chechnya, the Russian people received virtually no information about what was really happening there, "and the message from this," she said, holding up another letter, "is 'I don't want to know.' People don't want to hear it."[50]

Sick Man of Europe

If you don't stop it now, it'll destroy the country.
—STEVEN L. SOLNICK

I N HIS MIND, Andrei Artyomenko can pinpoint the day he became infected. He was twenty-one years old, a junkie in the Siberian city of Irkutsk. He looked the part, too, a wraith of just 128 pounds in perpetually dirty clothes. His mother wouldn't let him come home because he kept stealing from her to pay for his habit. His friend that day had some heroin and the two retreated into the darkened stairwell of a nine-story apartment building. "It was a Sunday and the drugstores were closed," Artyomenko recalled. "He had just one syringe. He warned me. He said, 'I'm not sure, but I think I got bombed'"—meaning infected. "I ignored that. I said, 'I don't care, I'll burn the needle with a lighter.'" Artyomenko sighed at the recollection. "Of course it's crazy," he reflected. "All I could think about was the needle. I had to have it."[1]

That spring of 1999 would introduce HIV into Russia's bloodstream as well. It was the spring of The Explosion, as it came to be called in Irkutsk, when the remote Siberian outpost suddenly was no longer so cut off from the rest of the world. An industrial city with a river still frozen as late as May each year, Irkutsk sat on the crossroads between Europe and Asia, a major transit hub for the wave of drugs produced in Afghanistan to the southwest. Until that spring, youngsters in Irkutsk had used opium cooked over a stove that they called *chernyashka*, "black stuff," but the advent of liquid heroin in vials made needle-sharing the new fad. Teenagers would take some of their own blood and mix it with heroin so that five or six of them were effectively trading the virus all at once. One day a student from a technical school checked into a hospital for unrelated reasons and tested positive for HIV. Concerned medical officials then began testing other students, only to discover that quite a few of them had also been infected. Other schools were tested and the extent of the epidemic began to dawn on a panicked Irkutsk. A region that started 1999 with barely a hundred known cases of HIV infection suddenly erupted; by 2004, it would officially register more than seventeen thousand, still just a fraction of the real number but enough to make it proportionately the most infected region in all of Russia.[2] "The school was just a symptom, the first sign that the infection had crawled into Irkutsk," said Aleksei Trutnev, who tested positive at the beginning of 1999, only the 130th person determined to have the virus in Irkutsk. Like others, he knew his registration number by heart.[3]

Russia's long isolation under the Communists had sheltered it from the sort of AIDS outbreak that had afflicted the United States, Europe, and Africa in the 1980s. But the arrival of heroin in mass quantities changed the picture. Within just a few years, a country that had virtually no AIDS problem found itself with the fastest-growing HIV infection rate in the world. As Vladimir Putin took office, just a few thousand people had tested positive in Russia, according to official statistics; by 2004, the number of Russians registered with HIV had jumped to 290,000 and was still rapidly rising. Because official numbers always understate the real problem, most experts estimated that 1 million had actually been infected, more than in the United States with twice the population and a much longer history with the disease. In Russia, the infection had reached 1 percent of the adult population, a proportion the World Health Organization considered the tipping point of epidemic.[4]

The AIDS toll in Russia was unique. Nowhere else in the world had AIDS afflicted a major nation that was already dying out. In recent years, the death rate in Russia had soared far beyond the birth rate, leaving the population to plummet faster than in any other industrialized nation. In the first dozen years after the fall of the Soviet Union, Russia's population fell by 4.5 million people to 144 million, a plunge unmatched in peacetime since Stalin's purges and famine in the 1930s. For every 100 children born in Russia, 171 people died.[5] Russians drank more, smoked more, and committed suicide more than practically any other people. They suffered from some of the world's highest rates of heart disease, accidental death, tuberculosis, hepatitis, and syphilis. Some forty-one thousand Russians died each year from alcohol poisoning, compared to maybe four hundred in the United States.[6] The average life span for a Russian man fell to fifty-eight, below that of Bangladesh and even war-torn Bosnia.[7] The consequences for Russian nationhood were nothing short of staggering. Under one projection by the Russian government, the country's population would fall from 144 million to 102 million by 2050, and under the most pessimistic forecast to just 77 million.[8] "If the current tendency continues, the survival of the nation will be threatened," Putin told parliament in his first year in office. "We really do face the threat of becoming an enfeebled nation. Today the demographic situation is one of the most alarming that the country has."[9]

As AIDS enters into the equation, the situation will only worsen. For the first few years of Putin's tenure, relatively few Russians died from the disease because it was still in its early stages, but it began to break out into the mainstream population through sexual transmission. In coming years Russians will begin dying off in accelerating numbers. By 2010, according to the most optimistic scenario developed by the World Bank, 250,000 Russians will be dying every year from AIDS; in the worst case, the bank projected 650,000 annual deaths, more than the cumulative death toll in the United States after two decades. And it will kill young men and women in childbearing years, the backbone of Russia's dwindling workforce and the only hope for replenishing the population. In economic terms, the World Bank estimated that AIDS could sap $70 billion out of the Russian gross national product by 2020.[10] "It's going to affect labor productivity, it's going to affect family formation, it's going to affect reproductive health," said Murray Feshbach, of the Woodrow Wilson International Center for Scholars, the preeminent expert on Russian demographic patterns. "The totality of all this is I think potentially devastating for the society, economy, and social stability."[11]

Despite Putin's alarm over the country's demographics, neither he nor his government seemed all that concerned by the threat of AIDS. As the epidemic reached crisis proportions, the Russian Health Ministry still had just five people working on the issue, and the federal government was spending not quite $1 million a year on prevention. Putin mentioned AIDS only once in a major speech, and then only in passing in a single sentence that listed it along with other major health issues confronting Russia. His government supplied antiretroviral drugs to fewer than two thousand Russians infected with HIV in 2004, despite estimates that as many as fifty thousand people needed them; unlike other countries, Russia had done nothing to negotiate lower prices for the drugs, which cost $6,000 to $12,000 a year per patient, compared to $1,000 in many other countries.

Seeming to ignore the crisis as a matter of national pride, the Russian government turned down international aid, preferring to portray itself as a donor to the Global Fund for AIDS, Tuberculosis and Malaria rather than a recipient. Instead, the fund awarded $88 million to a consortium of private groups working in Russia, one of the only times it had bypassed the host nation.[12] As Vadim Pokrovsky, director of Russia's Federal Center for AIDS Prevention and Treatment, lamented, "There's a lot of concern about the situation in Russia voiced abroad; the concern is much greater than that expressed by our own public and our own government."[13] To Russia's detriment. "If you don't stop it now, it'll destroy the country," said Steven L. Solnick, director of the Moscow office of the Ford Foundation, which in 2003 began dispensing grant money to help fight AIDS in Russia. "Russia should be one of the success stories because you have universal literacy, because you have a pharmaceutical industry, because you have a television in every home. There's no reason millions of Russians should die of this disease, and yet it looks extremely likely that millions of Russians will die of this disease."[14]

ONE OF THE first places they will die will be Irkutsk, a city in the middle of nowhere with a powerful hold on the Russian imagination. First built in the mid–seventeenth century as a tsarist fort on the Angara River, Irkutsk grew into one of the capitals of Siberia, a "thoroughly refined" town, as Anton Chekhov put it, despite its frontier location. A fire that ravaged much of the city in 1879 did nothing to discourage residents from rebuilding the classic Siberian wooden houses that even today form the heart of the city's identity. "You have only to enter their formation, to take the first steps down a narrow street warm with the warmth of its own life, before you very quickly lose your sense of time and end up in a wonderful, fairy-tale world, the one from the famous tale in which a magical power casts a spell and puts everyone to sleep for a hundred years, making everything all around inviolable," writer Valentin Rasputin once rhapsodized about his hometown.[15]

Although now a city of six hundred thousand, the modern Irkutsk was a traditional, even simple place where the bars had names like Good Beer and religious icons were sold in sidewalk kiosks. As the Putin era opened, young men like Andrei Artyomenko found themselves lost in the new world around them. His father was an alcoholic thrown out of the house by his mother when Andrei was just two; her next husband held his booze but not his temper until he, too, was evicted. "I wouldn't say it was an especially warm atmosphere at home," Artyomenko told us years later over dinner. The stepfather stayed seven years. "He would beat me for coming home late. That was my happy childhood." At fourteen, Artyomenko was smoking, drinking, and using pills. Within a few years, he found *chernyashka* and the transactional friends who came with it. "I understand they were just lost souls like me." Then it was liquid heroin. "AIDS came with it."

By the time his mother forced him to get help, it was too late; he had spent one too many hazy days in that darkened stairwell. Her intervention, though, did save him from the drugs. Artyomenko met Igor Vankon, who had arrived in Irkutsk in 1998 to set up the region's first drug rehabilitation clinic.

Vankon made him get the HIV test that forced him to confront the consequences of his drug days. For a month, Artyomenko could not bring himself to tell his family about his positive test result; when he did, they made him use separate cups and plates and towels. At the same time, the rest of Irkutsk was waking up to what had happened. "People were stunned and frightened," he recalled. "The tension between sick people and drug addicts and the rest of society really escalated."[16]

The rush of outside cultural influences brought on by Russia's opening to the rest of the world had overwhelmed many of Irkutsk's young men. For some, American movies such as *Pulp Fiction* became a twisted bible for how to lead their own lives. As a twenty-one-year-old, Yevgeny Sherbakov idealized the film's dark blend of violence and drugs. "I was bringing it to life," he recalled much later. "I considered myself cool. Later on, when I started selling my clothes off my body, I realized it wasn't fun at all." By that time, he was already a heroin junkie with HIV.[17] Unfamiliar with the new disease, some assumed it meant prompt death and took it as license for more self-destruction. "I didn't know anything about HIV, absolutely nothing," said Aleksei Trutnev. "I thought at best I had two years. So what did I do? I increased my dose and used even more often." Eventually, he emerged from his heroin haze. "In two years, I realized that nothing is changing. I'm not dying. I need to live."[18]

Authorities in Irkutsk, as in the rest of Russia, remained in their own haze at least as long. With few resources to fight the new disease and little sympathy for its victims, the government figured they would just die off and the problem would go away. When Igor Vankon and other activists went to a senior Irkutsk medical official in 2000 and argued for treatment and prevention programs, they were rebuffed. "She just opened her arms and said, 'Sorry, we're not doing anything but diagnosis,'" Vankon told us. "When they offered her a harm-reduction program, she said, 'No, we don't need it.'"[19]

Eventually, a government AIDS center opened in a remote cluster of unmarked buildings on a hill on the outskirts of the city where visitors were left to puzzle out its location by hunting for a series of directions chalked in white on the brick walls. In 2002, authorities began a needle-exchange program. The next year, with American funding, the local chapter of the Red Cross opened its own AIDS center on Lenin Avenue right in the middle of town. But it remained a constant battle. One day in 2004, while we were in Irkutsk, the Red Cross received a letter from drug enforcement authorities ordering them to halt the needle-exchange program immediately because it represented "open propaganda of drugs."[20] The letter came just as the Kremlin was reforming Russia's drug laws to decriminalize possession of small amounts of drugs, a move hailed by activists as a way to encourage users to get treatment or at least clean syringes. It was just one of many conflicting signals to this most marginalized group.

"Drug addicts have isolated themselves from healthy society, and healthy society isolated itself from the drug addicts," Boris Tsvetkov, director of the Irkutsk AIDS center, told us. The needle exchange particularly inflamed passions. "The idea that people had was that healthy people don't have enough syringes and you're going to give them to drug addicts? They didn't understand that in helping drug addicts stay healthy we help ourselves."[21] Predictably enough, it did not take long for the disease to break out of the drug community into the rest of the population. According to official numbers, nearly 30 percent of new cases in Irkutsk stemmed from sexual transmission compared to just half of one percent initially. And still the state was doing little to treat these patients to head off the wave of death that would otherwise inevitably follow. Just sixteen children and three adults were receiving antiretroviral treatment in Irkutsk in 2004, a fraction of what outside experts estimated was necessary. Andrei Artyomenko took no medication, relying instead on cold showers and yoga. Tsvetkov insisted that everyone who needed it was receiving the medication but acknowledged that the shortage of treatment was about to explode. "The problem is going to stay," he said. "The more time passes from the beginning of the disease, the more people are going to need the treatment. It's going to be very big money."[22]

As the disease spread through Irkutsk, nothing had changed the underlying problems, the sense of hopelessness in the confusing new Russia. Every day, Andrei Artyomenko still went home to his apartment in the Energetika village on the outskirts of Irkutsk where he saw young men who looked the way he used to, huddling with their needles on the street, disappearing into the shallow solace of drugs. "Life is so empty here," he said. "I look around and I see all these young people using drugs and I know why they do it. They're afraid of living. They don't know where they're going. Each person needs love. And people don't love themselves."[23]

IN RUSSIA, the original drug of choice was vodka. Even today, many Russians ascribe medicinal, almost supernatural powers to the national drink. Parents soak cotton balls in vodka and dab them on children to bring down a fever or ease an earache. Vodka with pepper is prescribed for an adult's cold, vodka with salt for an upset stomach. Some nuclear scientists even drank to protect themselves from radiation.

As Russian historians tell it, alcohol helped define the emerging state more than a millennium ago. When Prince Vladimir chose the official religion in the year 988, he picked Orthodox Christianity, so the story goes, because it would allow followers to drink every day, not just on holidays. Ever since, drink has unraveled the strategies of generals and thwarted the will of tsars. The Russian army forfeited a battle against the Tatars in 1373 because they were so drunk by the time the enemy showed up that they couldn't fight. The inebriated Russians were ingloriously thrown into the nearby river, which became known as the Reka Piyanaya, the Drunk River. Vodka itself showed up about five hundred years ago, named for the diminutive for the Russian word for water. Repeated attempts to control, regulate, or tax it led only to frustration. The prohibition endorsed by Lenin eventually gave way to the daily hundred-gram allotment provided to soldiers by Stalin during World War II. Mikhail Gorbachev's ill-fated antialcohol campaign in the 1980s contributed to his fall from grace in the public eye.

By one estimate, the typical Russian in the Putin era drank five gallons of vodka a year. Since vodka once opened in Russia is almost always finished, bottles produced for the domestic market came with a tear-off top rather than a screw cap that could be replaced. At street kiosks, a bottle can be had for just a couple of bucks. In recent years, beer has joined vodka as a Russian national drink, tripling in consumption over six years and even overtaking vodka in total sales by 2003.[24] Yet it did not replace vodka; it only served as a new gateway into alcohol use. To Russians, beer was only a soft drink. We saw teenagers walking down the street every day with open bottles as if they were soda. A short-lived attempt to classify beer as an alcoholic beverage was quickly quashed by the liquor lobby. And Putin himself vetoed a bill in early 2005 restricting public beer consumption.

According to some estimates, as many as 8 million Russian men were alcoholics as well as 2 million women; another five hundred thousand children under fifteen suffered from alcohol dependence.[25] The number of Russians who died of alcohol poisoning every year had doubled since the breakup of the Soviet Union. One of them was Aleksandr Nakonechny, who won an all-you-can-drink Vodka Marathon contest sponsored by a store in the southwestern town of Volgodonsk by downing three one-pint mugs of vodka in quick succession, then dropped dead before he could claim the prize—ten bottles of vodka.[26] Alcohol abuse contributed to heart trouble, traffic accidents, suicide, and other serious conditions that brought life to an early end for many Russian men. Each year some seventeen thousand Russians drowned, nearly all of them drunk—a proportional rate six or seven times as high as for Americans.[27] In Moscow alone, about twenty-four hundred people fell, jumped, or were pushed out of windows every year, roughly six or seven every day; about three-quarters of them died and nearly all of them were drunk at the time.[28]

Other than alcohol, the most popular drug in Russia remained tobacco. Even as the West steadily kicked the habit, some 70 percent of Russian men still lit up, more than anywhere else in Europe; so did a third of Russian women. A pack of cheap Russian cigarettes went for forty cents, and even American brands like Marlboro cost no more than a dollar. Until the last few months of our tour in Russia, restaurants had not discovered the virtues of no-smoking sections. Aeroflot did not ban smoking aboard all Russian flights until long after we arrived in Moscow; even then, many Russian passengers at first simply ignored the rule. It took its toll. As many as seven hundred people died of tobacco-related conditions every day.[29] A Russian man was two to three times as likely to die from heart disease as an American, and the rate increased by 10 percent in the first two years of Putin's tenure.[30]

That still only told part of the story of Russia's multifaceted health crisis. Tuberculosis spawned a full-fledged epidemic, tripling in incidence during the 1990s. The government now recorded some 130,000 new cases of TB annually, with nearly 30,000 people dying from the disease each year, about thirty times as many as in the United States proportionately. The syphilis rate was four hundred times the rate in Western Europe.[31] Violent death also reached crisis level in Russia. Men under sixty-five were four times as likely to die from injury or poisoning as in neighboring Finland, which had the worst rate in the European Union.[32] Some fifty-seven thousand Russians killed themselves every year, a 50 percent increase over the past decade.[33] Aside from tiny neighboring Lithuania, Russia had the highest suicide rate among men in the world.[34]

Even those who didn't drink, smoke, or do drugs were likely to find themselves contaminated by the environment around them. As many as twenty-two thousand Russians died each year from the solid particulates in the air; pollution was blamed for high miscarriage rates in some locations. At the end of the Soviet Union, 3 million smokestacks were spread around the country, only half with pollution abatement equipment, and only a third of those worked. While many of those factories later closed, the commitment to clean air had hardly risen. A drive through Moscow's jammed streets with the windows open would choke a healthy driver, surrounded by thousands of cars running on leaded gasoline without antismog equipment. Outside the capital, the country's booming oil business managed to spill the equivalent of twenty-five *Exxon Valdez* accidents each month.[35] As Putin was coming into office, the state environmental agency estimated that 15 percent of Russian territory was "ecologically unfavorable," invariably the territory occupied by the population.[36] None of this made it to Putin's priority list. One of his first acts as president was to disband the state environmental agency.

RUSSIANS TURNED to a health care system singularly ill-equipped to cope with their myriad ailments—and often seemingly uninterested in trying. The hostages who emerged gasping for breath from the chemical injected into the Moscow theater on Dubrovka Street that night in October 2002 discovered that firsthand. Hundreds of them reported lingering health problems— pounding headaches, memory loss, heart trouble, liver damage, respiratory problems, temporary hearing loss, and signs of persistent post-traumatic stress such as nightmares, fear of public places, and deep depression. But the state had pronounced their problems over. It arranged for compensation amounting to $9,500 for each family of a hostage who died, and $2,700 for each hostage who survived. It sent some children to sanitariums for a rest and put some adults on disability worth about $70 a month. And that was it. The government never revealed the contents of the chemical it had exposed them to. It did not study their continuing reactions to it, much less organize any kind of comprehensive follow-up care. And it simply dismissed their health problems as nothing more than preexisting conditions or even figments of their imagination.

When we went to see Nikolai Lyubimov, an articulate seventy-year-old with a salt-and-pepper goatee, it was clear his partial paralysis was neither a figment of his imagination nor something he had been afflicted with before. "I was a healthy person," he said, hunched over in his tiny bedroom just a short way from the theater where he had worked as a security guard for a decade. "I went to work. The Chechens captured me, scared me, intimidated me. But I was poisoned not by them. I became disabled and lost my health not because of them. I was poisoned by our Russian authorities." When the commandos seized the theater, he succumbed to the chemicals, slipped into a deep coma, and was mistaken for dead. Afterward, he would swear he could hear a doctor standing over his body say, "He's gone. Let's take him to the morgue." He regained consciousness. But now he suffered from arrhythmia, ischemia, and partial paralysis on his left side. As we sat and talked, he poked himself on the left side of his face over and over. Nothing, not even a flinch. His left hand dangled at his side. No sensation there either. "It feels like wood," he told us as he tapped on it. "Wood." Some doctors told him it was simply a consequence of lying on his left side too long; others offered no diagnosis at all. Each day was an exercise in frustration as he waited in lines up to four hours long at the grim neighborhood Polyclinic 37 just to see a doctor selected at random. When he would come back the next day, the wait would be the same, the doctor different. "It's just a madhouse," he told us. "There were sign-up folders for different doctors, but when I come, they're all filled up a week in advance. They try to throw you out. You have to show them a certificate. But the treatment is not real, it's just to get the certificate extended. I'm still worried about my arm. No one helps. I get no therapy for it. They don't know themselves what they're treating me for. It's a conveyor belt. They might not even remember me. . . . If I go to the polyclinic and there's some bullshit and I get angry, they say to me, 'What, are you the only one? We have other hostages.'"

Lyubimov was surviving on a pension of seventeen hundred rubles a month, less than $60, but was paying at least that much for medicine. One day he heard a city official on the radio promising help. "So I called on the phone and I said, 'I'm in dire straits. The medicines are expensive and I can't afford to buy them.'" He later received a letter from the city in response: "They had no instructions from above and none of their charity could be extended at all." The day we visited, Lyubimov had just received his official certificate confirming his disability status. It had taken four months to get, and all it meant was that he could now apply for yet another certificate that would in turn entitle him to an additional $16 a month from the state. The certificate would in theory allow him to receive free medicine as well, but at least half the drugs he was taking were not on the approved list. "Now in practically all dealings, not just with the health system, I hit a wall of resistance and indifference," he sighed.[37]

The main Moscow institution assigned to deal with the *Nord-Ost* victims was Hospital 13, a series of run-down buildings with eleven hundred beds built in 1940 on a triangular campus not far from the theater. In the immediate aftermath of the commando raid, Hospital 13 treated 359 hostages in an emergency ward designed for 50. Months later we went to see hospital officials to ask why so many of their patients were still sick, but found denial and disinterest. "With the majority of ex-hostages, we don't see any medical consequences," insisted head doctor Leonid Aronov. "As a rule, we deal with chronic situations, which most former hostages had before the event." A few patients' problems "might be connected" to the theater siege, he allowed, but even those he attributed not to the government's chemicals but to the long hours the hostages went with little sleep, food, or water.[38]

Aronov said he sent out seven hundred letters inviting former hostages back for follow-up care, an offer taken up by more than half. But some of the hostages told us that turned out to be little more than a bureaucratic exercise. Antonina Titova, forty-six, who suffered from memory loss, pain in her right side, and nightmares after the theater siege, went back to Hospital 13 after receiving Aronov's letter and was asked only about what illnesses she had before the hostage crisis that could be causing her problems now. No allowance was made for the possibility that the chemicals could have been responsible. And even at that, the doctor seemed uninterested in the answers. "She said it was a formality, to check it off the list," Titova told us.[39]

Hospital 13 hardly stood out in Russia's dilapidated health care system. One out of every ten Russian hospitals was built before World War I, and one in five had no running water. Most were desperately short of medicine, supplies, and even syringes. Some went years without any new equipment; some begged hand-me-downs from foreign institutes. At another Moscow hospital, doctors did not use latex gloves in surgery because there were not enough to go around. They had no CAT scanner, only worn-out ventilators, a blood-gas analyzer that broke down regularly, and a manual pump that they relied on to suction fluid out of patients when the central vacuum system gave out, as it often did.[40]

The first hospital we ever visited in Russia was the top medical facility for the country's air force officers on the outskirts of Moscow. We went there to interview Dennis Tito, an American multimillionaire who had bought a seat on a Russian rocket for a joyride to the International Space Station for $20 million, making him the world's first paying space tourist. Tito was suffering from a mild ailment at the time and was being treated at the most elite military hospital in the capital. Yet when we arrived, we found a nearly pitch-dark lobby, broken elevators, and grungy walls. Even the hospital sheets were ratty, fraying, and gray from too many patients over too many years—a sharp comedown for Tito, who lived in a thirty-thousand-square-foot hilltop mansion with an eight-car garage back in Los Angeles.[41]

The rich, of course, had more options outside the government health care system. Pricey private hospitals with modern equipment and cutting-edge treatment had sprung up in Moscow in recent years. But even the elite found themselves victimized by a corrupt and uncaring system. One day we went to see Yevgeny Kiselyov, then the general director of NTV television. He walked in late and his secretary kept popping her head in to interrupt him with another call. He would excuse himself, talk with someone intensely, come back in for a few minutes, and then the whole cycle would repeat itself.

When he finally did sit down long enough to talk, he was distracted, his eyes watery with emotion. We figured he was stressed by his ongoing political battle with the Kremlin, but he told us he was upset because one of his best friends from school had had a stroke and the hospital wouldn't give him a bed since he was only going to die anyway. As that sank in, he took another call from someone he hoped could help. "Hello, this is Yevgeny Kiselyov, general director of NTV," he introduced himself. "Maybe you know me from television." Here was one of Russia's most famous men, the equivalent of Tom Brokaw or Dan Rather, using every bit of pull he had just to get a dying friend into a hospital. In the end, we later learned, his friend died the next day.[42]

In theory, the Russian constitution required the state to provide free, basic medical care for every Russian, but government funding had fallen by one-third since Soviet times, and in reality even minimal care depended on under-the-table payments and privately obtained medicine. One study showed that state financing actually covered only one-third of health care costs, with the rest picked up by patients.[43] For a country with so many medical crises, Russia spent just 5 percent of its gross national product on health care, barely a third of what the United States devoted and less than even El Salvador or Lebanon.[44] If indifference kept domestic spending low, pride kept international assistance down; the Russian Health Ministry initially rejected a $150 million World Bank grant to fight AIDS and tuberculosis in 2001 as unnecessary, just as it would later turn down a chance to obtain money from the Global AIDS Fund. Left on their own, doctors typically earned just $200 a month and often relied on patients to slip them money just to get by. Although the state was supposed to provide drugs such as insulin, some two hundred thousand diabetes patients weren't able to get it; at least twenty thousand cancer patients died each year because they couldn't afford the right medicine.[45]

Many Russians did not even realize just how poor the care they were receiving was, leaving them ill-equipped to push for better treatment. Our friend Volodya had a history of heart trouble. One day he went to a Moscow hospital, where they determined that he had a blood clot in his leg; left untreated, it could migrate to his heart and kill him. The doctors dealt with the clot but then left him to lie in a sweltering room without air-conditioning at the height of summer along with six other patients so they could give him antibiotics intravenously instead of with pills. That was the extent of his aftercare. Volodya seemed satisfied until we called a clinic for foreigners and asked them what they would do; the doctors rattled off a long list of tests they would conduct and medications they would prescribe. Only when we read the list to him and asked if his Russian doctors had done any of those things did it dawn on him that he should be demanding better care.

Another friend, Irina, knew better than to take anything on faith when her husband, Boris, broke various bones in a fall. After he was taken to a hospital, she herself set about buying all the medicine he would need, then secured the blood he might need for the subsequent surgery and slipped money to the hospital nurse to make sure to look after him. Even then, it was not enough. After Boris had two simultaneous operations to repair the extensive damage, the doctors failed to give him the proper painkillers. Boris was left to scream in agony for more than an hour. The hospital did not have morphine. This experience was typical. One study found that 30 percent of families seeking medical help from outpatient clinics and 50 percent of those going to hospitals ended up having to pay money *na leva*, on the side, for services they were supposed to receive for free.[46]

In an emergency, even money couldn't help. Paul Klebnikov, an American investigative journalist who had made his share of enemies through years of muckraking reports on the shady side of Russian business, was gunned down on the streets of Moscow in a mob-style contract hit in July 2004, just months after launching the Russian-language edition of *Forbes* magazine. As he lay on the asphalt dying of four bullet wounds, he begged for oxygen, but the ambulance that showed up had none. When the medics loaded him aboard and reached the hospital, they found the gate locked and waited a precious minute or two for someone to open it. Then as they wheeled him to an operating room, the hospital elevator broke down. It took at least ten minutes for a repairman to arrive. When the elevator doors finally slid open, Klebnikov was dead.[47]

TATYANA YAKOVLEVA was among those trying to change that. A pediatrician in Ivanovo, the poorest region in central Russia, Yakovleva discovered how a rigid system refused to help itself when she became head doctor at her hospital. "I wanted to stimulate doctors. I wanted to create incentives. I wanted doctors to be materially rewarded—you can give them awards, but it doesn't do any good if they can't buy bread," she recalled. "I wanted to use my funds to help my doctors and I was rejected. I was told, 'This isn't an approved use of funds.'" Russia's health system remained the Soviet health system, down to never-overturned regulations and rules still handed down from the Moscow center. If she saved money in one department, the money went back to the government; she could not use it to handle demands in another area. "I had all these linens and bedding and sheets, but I needed diagnostic equipment for cardiac disease. I didn't have money to buy that, but I had plenty of sheets. I asked if I could use the money from linen to buy diagnostic equipment and I was told no. That's the old Soviet state."

Yakovleva decided to run for the State Duma, won a seat in 1999, and was reelected four years later. She was more a collaborationist than a radical reformer, joining Putin's political party and toeing the Kremlin line. Yet even when this Putin loyalist made halting efforts to change the system, the government proved uninterested. As chairwoman of a health care committee, Yakovleva wanted to eliminate wage arrears for doctors, give hospitals more spending flexibility, introduce merit pay for medical professionals, and cut down on the glut of unnecessary hospitals. She tried to develop a system in which the state paid for basic treatment—not just claimed that it did—while allowing patients to pay for extras, such as foreign pharmaceuticals instead of Russian drugs. She also tried to find ways to encourage more private health insurance. "We have to change the system," she said. "We want doctors to be paid for quality. If you don't have many patients, you get paid less. If you have many patients, you get paid more. . . . If the state is telling the people that it pays for health care, then it should pay, not the way it is now." But she found the Kremlin more obsessed about rebuilding the country's economy. "I keep trying to convince our Russian officials that the health issue is important, not just the economy."[48]

Putin's Kremlin never bothered to advocate genuine health care reform. Instead, the president seemed to believe he could cheerlead the birthrate up to solve the demographic crisis while bolstering the population by luring more Russians home from former Soviet republics. Asked once how he would increase the birthrate, he pointed to his consolidation of power. "The main thing is there should be political, economic stability, well-considered decisions for the development of the state's economy," he said.[49] When the number of births rose for the first time in many years, he trumpeted the news in his New Year's Eve midnight address to the nation as Russia ushered in 2004. "One particularly pleasing fact is that more new Russian citizens were born this year in comparison with last year," he said. "This is a good sign. It means that people in our country are looking forward to the future with confidence."[50]

Such hopeful talk seemed to defy reality. By 2004, virtually all the Russians living in newly created independent countries who planned to return had long since done so. Just four thousand more people moved to Russia in the first quarter of the year than left. And while Putin was right that women were beginning to have more babies, it was hardly enough to yank the country out of its population tailspin. The number of births per woman inched up from 1.17 in 1999 as Putin took office to 1.32 in 2002—still considerably shy of the 2.33 that demographers believed was necessary simply to ensure population replacement.[51]

In the meantime, Putin ignored the health care system as Russians kept dying at alarming rates. The job of health minister had turned over about a dozen times since the fall of the Soviet Union, and the system resisted modernization. Russia was still too enamored of long hospital stays for ills that could be better treated with outpatient care, too overloaded with specialists and too short on general practitioners. Yet many doctors refused to change, stubbornly romanticizing the Soviet past as if it were a golden period for Russian medicine. "Our health care system used to be one of the best," huffed Leonid Roshal, the pediatrician famous for going into the Dubrovka Street theater during the *Nord-Ost* siege and later to Beslan for the school hostage crisis. "I don't see why it should be overhauled to suit Western standards."[52] Doctors who had spent much time abroad, though, knew better than most how far behind the Russian system had slipped. Rinat Akchurin, one of Moscow's most celebrated heart surgeons, had treated Boris Yeltsin alongside American specialists and seen U.S. hospitals firsthand. Their technology and equipment far outmatched anything the Russian hospitals had. "The only challenge for Russian medicine is to create a system for good care and good service, which did not exist in Soviet times and is still very weak now," said Akchurin. "Today, we're slowly moving toward freedom of choice for each patient. We don't need just to transform free-of-charge medicine to private sector, which is impossible, one hundred percent impossible, in this country. But we'd like to have everyone have the kind of quality of care they get in Switzerland, Germany, and the United States."[53]

THE CONSEQUENCES of Putin's failure to address the situation loomed large. Russia's health care crisis posed dramatic geopolitical risks. How could he rebuild his military if many young Russian men continued to be rejected from the draft for health reasons and the number of eligible recruits, healthy or not, was projected to plunge in coming years? How could he rebuild his economy if the working-age generation was dying off from AIDS? How could he hold on to the largest landmass in the world if one-third of his population were to disappear in the next few decades?

The future threat of broad instability due to Russia's demographic decline was already on display in the Far East, the sprawling, largely empty outpost of empire along the Pacific Rim just north of a burgeoning China. On the

Russian side of the border was a seemingly endless expanse of land rich in resources and light on population, occupied by a mere 7 million Russians and fewer with each passing year due to the country's high death rate and out-migration from the region. On the Chinese side was a bursting-at-the-seams society desperate for breathing space and raw materials to feed its modern-izing economy, with 77 million people living just in the three provinces bor-dering their northern neighbor. The imbalance seemed precarious. "We have the psychological sense that it's dangerous for us," Sergei Drozdov, head of passport and visa services in the Far East capital city of Khabarovsk, told us. "The Russian population is declining. Nature doesn't tolerate a vacuum. When there's a full bottle there and it's empty here, at some point the bottle will burst and spill over to here."[54]

Russia had secured the Far East from China in the mid-nineteenth cen-tury after hundreds of years of expansion and in 1860 claimed control of the port city of Haishenwei and renamed it Vladivostok. The Chinese had long resented the land grab. Mao Tse-tung and Deng Xiaoping were both quoted as saying the Russians took too much territory, and Mao reportedly even said Vladivostok and Khabarovsk should by right be Chinese. Soon after he took office, Putin visited the region and warned of social cataclysm if nothing was done to regenerate the Far East. "If we don't take concrete actions," he said, "the future local population will speak Japanese, Chinese, or Korean."[55]

When we visited Khabarovsk, we found Chinese already spilling over the border. At least two hundred thousand were by then living in the Far East, according to the most conservative estimate, up from virtually none at the end of the Soviet Union, and some estimated that the number could be as high as eight hundred thousand or 1 million. Many more Chinese stayed in the Far East for long stretches without officially making it their home. At first, that was fine with the Russians. The Chinese migrants were a welcome flow of low-wage labor. But in the Putin years, they had begun putting down roots and starting their own businesses. The Russians who had once hired them were now often employees of the Chinese. Nine Chinese restaurants, two Chinese hotels, and three hundred other Chinese businesses had opened in Khabarovsk, while ferryboats carried shuttle traders across the Amur River each day with packs of cheap Chinese consumer goods from the other side of the border. "Everyone understands perfectly well that we have a demo-graphic shortfall and it needs to be filled from somewhere," said Maksim Tarasov, a deputy to the region's economic minister.[56]

At Khabarovsk's busy outdoor market, Chinese merchants hawked plastic sandals, compact disc players, and leopard-print bikinis in between games of mah-jongg. Outside the market we found a group of grizzled Russian men playing cards and grousing, gypsy-cab drivers waiting for customers, men who had once had it better: a former engineer, a former teacher, several former military men. They were trading complaints about the Asian threat. A man named Sergei glared bitterly at a Chinese man with a fancy foreign car. "They'll take over and invade our country without weapons," he grumbled. "Eventually, they will kill us." A Russian woman named Lyudmila lugging a couple sacks of Chinese goods out of the market came up looking for a ride. "They're behaving as masters of the land," she complained about the Chinese. Khabarovsk's days as a Russian city, she figured, were numbered. "Why did we warm up the place for them? They're building their economy on us." Slava, a former Soviet navy sailor, said Russia should take action to save itself. "They have to be kicked out because Russian Ivans should work this land." Otherwise, he added, "soon we're going to be refugees."[57]

The future of the demographic crisis could also be found in a cold, sterile orphanage in Irkutsk, where forty-eight children ranging from newborns to toddlers were housed, all born to HIV-positive mothers in the last few years. An AIDS–baby boom was emerging in Irkutsk and the rest of Russia for which the country had done little to prepare. In the Irkutsk orphanage, five or six children slept in bunks in each room, only a third of them receiving the antiretroviral cocktail. Nastya Cherkashena was one of them. Four years old and wearing a red dress with a blue bow in her hair the day we stopped by, she was curious but said nothing. Her eyes were heavy with fatigue. A couple rooms down was Edik Zolotavin, just about to turn eight years old. He stared without comprehension from his bed, his eyes wide and his mouth hanging open. Rosa Varnakova, the head of the department, pulled back the sheet to reveal an emaciated child the size of a boy barely half his age, his arms and legs just sticks. He was the oldest child with AIDS in her wing and seemed far gone. He was fed only pureed food. His heart and kidneys were so badly damaged that the staff did not expect him to live long. "I think God needs to decide," Varnakova said grimly.[58]

Russia was having a hard time waking up to such challenges. Better to stash away a few dozen HIV-infected children in a hard-to-find institution than address the fact that inevitably many more thousands like them were on the way. Putin's government resented the implication that it was not doing enough even as it did so little. One day we went to see Aleksandr Goliusov, who headed the tiny AIDS section at the Russian Health Ministry in Moscow. Even before we had asked the question, he launched into a twenty-minute rant disputing the notion that Russia had shirked its duty to confront AIDS.

Russia's problems with AIDS had been exaggerated, he insisted. Putin had attacked the issue aggressively, he maintained. The government had earmarked plenty of money for the disease, he asserted, and after its initial resistance had finally decided to apply for grants from the Global AIDS Fund. "We can talk about whether we do things right or wrong, but we do all we can," he said. "Of course, I'm not saying that things are perfect here and that everything is good and great. But I'm so tired of all the hysteria about Russia."

The prickly diatribe finally ran its course. As he calmed down, his tone changed. Quietly he acknowledged that Russia faced a "huge problem" in the next few years and that he did not have enough funding to deal with it. Within three years, he conceded, tens of thousands of people would be dying each year, and Russia's pharmaceutical industry was not doing anything to develop affordable drugs to stem the lethal tide because "in their eyes it's not worth it."

He sighed as he considered the looming disaster.

"It's breathing down our neck," he said.

"Death's breath," his assistant added.[59]

Runaway Army

My son was happy just to have bread.
—NATASHA YAROSLAVTSEVA

ILYA CRIED QUIETLY, head in hands to cover his eighteen-year-old angst. Ruslan stared impassively, nodding from time to time in agreement. Sasha simply seemed angry as he pulled up his sweatpants to reveal the glaring red scars on his legs, pointed to the injury on his head, and described the kidney pains that never quite went away. Tired of abuse from fellow soldiers and fearing more, the three young conscripts had run away from their military fire brigade in Russia's Far North and traveled thousands of miles to where they now sat, after a week as fugitives, in the dingy basement of a comfortably anonymous apartment building in the southern Russian city of Volgograd.[1]

Usually, the runaways came in a trickle of scared pairs or unhappy threesomes, a shadow army of teenage deserters whose existence the Russian military often preferred to ignore. But just a few days before Ilya, Ruslan, and Sasha had showed up one September morning in 2002, a group of fifty-four conscripts had crammed into the same Volgograd basement to pour out their stories to the local activist group Mother's Right. They were still in uniform, exhausted, and starving after walking a day and a night from the firing range where they were stationed. They complained their senior officer had severely beaten five soldiers for several hours as they looked on—and threatened to attack the rest of them. It was the largest mass desertion ever to become public in Russia.

And it was particularly embarrassing for a city that saw its very existence as a testament to Russian military glory. In World War II, when Volgograd was called Stalingrad, more than 750,000 Soviet soldiers were killed or wounded defending the city in the bloodiest battle of the war. Today, Volgograd is still very much a military town straddling the broad expanse of the Volga River, its garrisons serving as the rear for the troops massed farther south near the Chechen war zone. But otherwise times have changed. "There is no more Russian army to speak of," lamented Vyacheslav Kommisarov, a regional parliamentary leader, on hearing of the mass desertion. "Osama bin Laden could put on our uniform and march from the Far East to Moscow and nobody would notice him."

We went to Volgograd a few days after the mass walkout in search of Russia's secret underground of deserters and what this dramatic if hidden protest could tell us about the country's massive anachronism of an army, which remained even well into the Putin era the most visibly unreconstructed Soviet institution in Russian life. Tatyana Zazulenko, the impassioned founder of Mother's Right, explained how it worked in between counseling the beleaguered trio of Ilya, Ruslan, and Sasha. The Russian military, she told us, remained an army of conscripts, differing from the Soviet Red Army only in that it was smaller, far more corrupt, and with no empire to patrol. "The Russian army *is* the Soviet army," as a veteran of Soviet military intelligence put it to us.[2] Its involuntary eighteen-year-old recruits accounted for 75 percent of the force, most of them desperately poor and uneducated young men from the provinces. For two years, they served in conditions that could only be described as horrific—inadequate food and medical care, violent hazing, the constant threat of being sent to fight in Chechnya. In many cases, they were put to work as slave labor—building a general's country house, for instance, or even rented out to a local factory. They were paid one hundred rubles—about $3—a month.

Each year, Zazulenko found herself fielding pleas for help from one thousand or more conscripts and their parents at Mother's Right, the local branch of the national soldiers' rights movement sustained by mothers desperate to help their sons avoid Chechnya or the more routine violence rained on conscripts in their barracks. In Volgograd, nearly 80 percent of her cases involved desertions. These were Russia's most vulnerable young men; the wealthy or smart either earned university deferments or bought them. Many conscripts were sick or physically handicapped and should never have been accepted into the army in the first place. Nearly all complained to Zazulenko about the notorious Russian practice of physical and psychological humiliation by longer-serving soldiers, known as *dedovshchina*.[3]

For years, Zazulenko had been hearing complaints in particular about the abuses at the 20th Motorized Rifle Division, stationed nearby at the Prudboy firing range, legendary for the harsh treatment meted out there. Several years back, an officer punished two recruits by throwing them in an underground pit; one died when the wooden planks covering the hole caved in.[4] Still, she said, "even I was surprised" when the crowd of deserters crammed into her office after 7 p.m. on a Monday night. She had just received a call from one of the soldiers, asking, "Can you help us punish an officer who beats soldiers?" Flippantly, she had replied, "No problem," and told him to come to the office. "He said, 'There are many of us,' but I thought he meant three or four, the usual number." Only when she heard the tramp of dozens of boots on her stairs did she realize this was a different sort of desertion entirely.

The exhausted men asked for milk and bread to eat. Neighbors poured out of the apartments upstairs bearing cookies, fruit, and cigarettes as their tale spread. Eventually, it was decided the soldiers—all fifty-four of them—would spend the night, then turn themselves in to the military prosecutor in the morning. Instead, military officials, finally tipped off to the runaways, who had left their post two days earlier, raided the office, taking all the soldiers away. Zazulenko found out in a 2 a.m. phone call.

By the time the news got out the next morning, the military was spinning the story hard, claiming falsely that the soldiers had been picked up while marching to the prosecutor's office.[5] "It was an attempt to save face," Zazulenko said.

Just then, our discussion was interrupted by a phone call.

On the line was a panicky railroad station employee. She was harboring a young runaway, and she was afraid he would fall into the military's hands. Zazulenko dispatched an assistant to pick up this latest deserter.

When he got to the office an hour later, Andrei was a slim eighteen-year-old in a T-shirt. He said he and a friend had run away from their unit in Astrakhan, more than 250 miles south of Volgograd, about a week earlier. The pair had simply climbed over a fence, then walked for three days with no food or money. Eventually, they were picked up by a truck driver, who took them as far as Volgograd. A conscript from the Stavropol region, he had only been in the army a few months. Almost right away, a fellow conscript was beaten in front of Andrei, his head cracked open by a wooden chair. Then, a lieutenant ordered Andrei and his friend to come up with a bribe of ten thousand rubles—more than $330. The lieutenant kicked them and threatened more beatings to come.

Andrei ended up at the Volgograd railway station. When he asked a young woman working there to help him call home, she called Mother's Right instead. By later that day, Andrei had called his father and was waiting to be picked up. But the surprise was who his father was—a top military counterintelligence officer. "I think he'll understand why I did it," Andrei said.

In the meantime, though, the ordeal was just beginning for Zazulenko's earlier troika of runaways: Ilya, Sasha, and Ruslan. Ruslan had been dragged

away in handcuffs from the Volgograd post office, where he was using a public telephone to try to contact his mother. Sasha's tearful mom, Valentina, had
been standing by his side, and she went rushing back to Mother's Right seeking advice on what to do next.

She had hidden the other two boys. "What shall we do?" Valentina cried.
"If they are sent back to their unit, they will be killed."

THE VOLGOGRAD mass desertion came at a moment of renewed political
urgency over the long-running debate about how to reform Russia's crumbled military. Vladimir Putin, it seemed, might finally do something about a
problem that had both infuriated Russians and stymied their leaders for well
more than a decade.

The collapse of the once-mighty Soviet army was a disaster that had been
unfolding in Russia since the twilight of the 1980s, and by Putin's presidency
the military had long since collapsed from a 5-million-man force guarding a
vast empire to a 1.1-million-man shadow of its former self. Nuclear warheads
long past their expiration dates decayed in rotting silos, the linchpins for
wildly outdated yet still operative war plans that called for fighting a massive
nuclear-armed confrontation with NATO in Europe. The military talked of
preparing to meet the challenges of the twenty-first century—terrorism, local
conflicts, high-tech information war—but this was hollow rhetoric from an
establishment still organized around the dubious notion of waging World
War III.

For years already, politicians had agreed—at least in principle, as Russia's
elite so loved to say—that the only way to transform the outdated army
would be to end conscription and remake the military into a smaller, profes-
sionalized force. But nothing ever seemed to happen. Three times since 1992
sweeping military reform plans had been enacted and just as promptly disappeared. Boris Yeltsin campaigned for reelection in 1996 on a pledge to
overhaul the military and even signed a decree vowing a transition to an all-
volunteer force starting in 2000. No one was surprised when 2000 came and
went without any change at all.[6] Putin arrived in office more interested in
exercising the military's might in Chechnya than in taking on its reform-
resistant leadership, and he initially made little mention of how he would
address the problem.

But Putin soured on his generals almost right from the start. Chechnya
served as a daily reminder of the military's inability to achieve a decisive victory. Putin had been lied to by the uniformed brass not only about the situation in Chechnya but also about the tragic sinking of the *Kursk* back in 2000,

and he had seemed angry and mystified why an army of more than 1 million men had been forced to send untrained eighteen-year-old conscripts to die in the North Caucasus when fighting had erupted there at the beginning of his rule. "We had to have young men fighting on the front line who had been drafted just a few months before," Putin told a television interviewer in one uncharacteristic outburst. "Why did that happen? Surely not because we lived so well but because we had no one to fight there. And yet there are 1.3 million men in our army."[7]

The president was embarrassed yet again when a grossly overloaded Mi-26 transport helicopter crashed outside Chechnya in August 2002, killing 118 aboard despite military regulations barring it from carrying passengers. Although hit by a rebel's shoulder-fired missile, the helicopter survived to land; the massive loss of life resulted mostly from disabled cargo-hold doors that trapped people on the helicopter as it burned in a minefield. Once again, military officials initially chose to lie rather than admit their role in the catastrophe. A furious Putin blamed "failure by officials to carry out their duties adequately"—responsibility, he noted pointedly, that started "from the top leaders."[8]

Putin was now regularly proclaiming himself a convert to military reform. The previous November, Putin had unexpectedly signed a decree ordering the military to begin making the transition to an all-volunteer force in 2004—a process that was to be finished with a conscript-free army by 2010.[9] In his annual state of the nation address in April 2002, he had called military reform "a clear priority" for the first time in public, promised fast and "substantial" reduction in the amount of time conscripts would have to serve in the transition period, and ordered the military establishment to get it done quickly. "We can't drag our feet on the reform," he said.[10]

As a matter of politics, by the fall of 2002 Putin finally seemed impressed by the incessant lobbying campaign run by the Western-oriented liberals in the Union of Right Forces and the Yabloko party. Public opinion, fueled by fears about sons being forced to serve in Chechnya and a seemingly endless succession of headline-grabbing abuses against conscripts, had long since turned decisively against the military. According to one survey by the Public Opinion Foundation, 49 percent of Russians had a negative view of the military's performance while just 19 percent had a positive view. Focus groups conducted by the All-Russia Center for the Study of Public Opinion found that the profession of "soldier" was considered one of the least prestigious in the country, and focus group participants called the current system of conscription "slave labor."[11]

To the reformers who set out to persuade Putin, there was a crucial reason for taking bold action to dismantle the Soviet-style military. Although divided on what new plan to follow, they were united in believing that the current military was the army of an authoritarian state, where individuals were merely instruments of the government subject to involuntary servitude. The new Russia, they fervently believed, needed a democratic-style army in order to create a democratic society. "It's not a coincidence," said military analyst Aleksandr Golts, "that all dictatorships have conscript armies."[12]

Immediately after Putin's election, the Union of Right Forces, which had vaulted into parliament on the back of its quasi-endorsement from the new Kremlin leader, had developed a reform plan to present to the president and decided to publicly agitate for it as loudly as possible. Working through the economics institute run by Yegor Gaidar—the onetime Yeltsin prime minister whose name was indelibly associated with the painful price liberalization of 1992 called "shock therapy" by Russians—the party produced a detailed program. From the start, it was meant to be a compromise, a "practical, serious" plan with a real chance of passage, as Gaidar put it.[13] Instead of eliminating the draft altogether, the plan called for reducing mandatory conscription to six months of training and professionalizing all branches of the military at the same time. To attract high-caliber recruits, salaries would be set well above the Russian average. To attract support from the change-resistant military, they emphasized the pragmatism of their plan as a way for the army to survive the impending demographic crash. Experts figured that by 2007, the number of potential conscripts would plunge as a result of Russia's catastrophic drop-off in births starting in the late Soviet period.[14]

As controversial as the plan was the public way in which the party decided to push it. Gaidar preferred to work behind the scenes, as he had in advocating the 13 percent flat income tax that became a key reform of Putin's first year in office. No fingerprints, he was sure, would be a better way to take on the military. In the party councils, he urged caution. "You should not be too public about the fact that it's your proposal," he warned.[15]

But inside the party he was challenged by Boris Nemtsov, the party's telegenic leader in the State Duma. A young physicist who had first come to national attention as the reformist governor of Nizhny Novgorod, the curly-haired politician with a natural gift for glad-handing had been elevated by Boris Yeltsin to deputy prime minister and had once seemed on track to claim the mantle of Yeltsin's successor. Even now, he was perhaps the most prominent of Russia's liberal politicians, and he was sure that military reform would prove a populist hit for a party usually identified with its handful of wealthy capitalist backers. In going up against the generals, they would have to fight publicly, he argued at the party's internal meetings, or else have "zero chances of prevailing."[16]

In late 2001, Gaidar and Nemtsov forwarded the proposal directly to the president. Putin seemed impressed and ordered the generals, who had assumed the president's official silence on military reform meant he wasn't interested, to cooperate with the political reformers. Nemtsov was granted an audience with Defense Minister Sergei Ivanov, and Gaidar with the army's powerful chief of staff, General Anatoly Kvashnin, a Yeltsin holdover who had risen to the top job despite commanding the disastrous invasion of Grozny during the first Chechen war. Putin also gave Nemtsov and Gaidar seats at the table for government meetings on how to accomplish the change.[17]

By September 2002, there was a palpable sense that reform might really be happening. In Moscow, the day after the Volgograd desertion became public, the Russian parliament opened its first day back in session with a closed-door briefing from Ivanov on the army's desperate situation. Ivanov was Putin's close friend, his fellow KGB spy and latter-day political confidant, placed in the key post at the Defense Ministry in the spring of 2001 after the president had tired of an embarrassing public feud between the previous minister and Kvashnin, whose institutional prerogatives made him more powerful than even the minister. At the Duma, Ivanov warned the deputies about the "crisis of conscription," with the military only able to drum up some 10 percent of the draftees it needed. And those who did show up, he said, were often in such poor physical condition that they needed months of supplementary nutrition to get into shape.[18]

Ivanov also announced the long-anticipated beginning that September of the military's experiment with its first all-volunteer division in the western Russia city of Pskov. In an effort to buy time, the military had convinced Putin that it was necessary to test out the concept of professionalization with one division before deciding how to proceed further. Now, the fate of reform would hinge on what happened with the 76th Airborne Division. And it soon became clear that the unit was meant to be a showcase not of reform, but of the obstacles to it. In Pskov, officials said they could not find enough volunteers to make the experiment work. Military leaders complained about the unit's prohibitive cost, and within days of the experiment's official start a top official decreed the effort "on the verge of failure."

"They are building a Potemkin village in Pskov. They want to find arguments against reform," Nemtsov told us at the time. "They want to show the president that it will be impossible financially to transform the army." The military brass, he said, was falsely claiming that it would cost $100 million just to reorganize the Pskov division. The total, he said, was vastly inflated by including the cost of building new apartments for all those who signed contracts. In housing-deficient Russia, he pointed out, that would prove to be an impossibly expensive folly. Not only that, but volunteers in Pskov were being offered salaries below the average wage level, hardly a way to lure them to a potentially deadly job. "The Russian generals are like generals the world over. They don't want to lose their cheap labor force," Nemtsov said.[19]

Coming in the midst of the political debate on military reform, the mass desertion in Volgograd seemed like a worst-case scenario for the embattled generals, highlighting their morale problem with an event of such scale it was impossible to ignore or cover up. "It's like a slap in the face for the entire officer corps," one high-ranking military officer in Volgograd told us.[20] By one estimate, the incident was just one of at least twenty-four large-scale desertions in 2002. Even official statistics that human rights groups believed were significantly understated acknowledged 2,270 cases of soldiers escaping their units just in the first half of the year.[21] Military officials were especially furious at the groups of soldiers' mothers that gave the young runaways shelter and made their escapes impossible to cover up. "Who sponsors them? How do they survive?" Ivanov demanded to know of the passionate mothers' organizations.[22] The men in epaulets seemed on the defensive. The liberal politicians were confident. Gaidar called that fall "the high point of the hopes."[23]

NOT THAT long before the scared young conscripts deserted in Volgograd, Natasha Yaroslavtseva's son, Sasha, hanged himself. He was twenty-one and just back from the war in Chechnya. Back to Sochi, the famous and run-down Soviet-era resort on the Black Sea, to the same hundred-square-foot basement apartment where he had grown up. Where there were no jobs for young veterans like him, and where, as elsewhere in Russia, the right thing to say about the long-running conflict in Chechnya was often nothing at all. He, too, had been a conscript, but he had served his two years and come home changed. "People are afraid to talk to me about it," said Yaroslavtseva as she prepared to mark a year without the son who had been her only companion. "When they come back, people like my Sasha, nobody needs them anymore."[24]

His unnoted death was one of many suicides that would never show up in the official statistics as a casualty of Russia's war in Chechnya. In Sochi, there were other consequences of the conflict, too, that were rarely a matter of public concern, like the violent drunken rages of Pavel Brazhnikov, who drove a car that picked up corpses in Chechnya and now threatened his paralyzed father with a knife. Or the homelessness of Leonid Pensakov, a veteran who now slept in a shack on Sochi's famed black-pebbled beach.

Outside Chechnya, the legacy of nearly a decade of on-again, off-again war remained a largely taboo subject, one about which the majority of Russians "don't want to know and don't want to try to understand," as Lev Gudkov, a Moscow pollster, told us.[25] To human rights groups, opposition politicians, and the small minority of Russians who had personally suffered as a result of the war, that indifference was an attempt to ignore the damaging consequences of Chechnya on the rest of Russian society. The ripple effects of "Chechen syndrome," they believed, were far broader than the thousands dead, ranging from the psychological trauma on veterans to more acceptance of brutality in society, increased skepticism about government, and heightened ethnic conflict.

Corruption, already rampant in Russia, was also exacerbated. Desperate parents paid large sums to exempt their sons from the draft now that it was a wartime conscription again. "How much does it cost?" asked one parent in a typical Internet chat. By the next day, he had received back detailed price lists: for full exemption from the draft, $6,000; for one year's draft-dodging, $1,500; and for service in a cushy, safe Moscow unit, $3,000.[26] In the provinces, prices could be much cheaper. Many draft-evasion specialists even advertised, with little fear of arrest. Some arranged fake marriages or bogus psychological exams—including certificates attesting that the would-be draftee was gay—or dubious student exemptions from universities with no official certification. Overall, the market for bribes to get out of the draft was estimated at billions of dollars annually and would remain a growth business as long as young soldiers like Sasha were sent to Chechnya despite military rules barring new conscripts from serving in combat zones.[27]

Nowhere was Chechen syndrome more apparent than inside the military itself. Cases of hazing, killings, suicides, acts of insubordination, and thefts grew each year. Far more such violations were registered in the North Caucasus military district—Chechnya and the surrounding region—than elsewhere in Russia. And few doubted that Chechnya had profoundly influenced statistics across the board for the worse. "When the majority of us have been there [to Chechnya] and seen things, we understand it has a negative impact on people. Each person who goes there sees his task just to survive, get out, and return to Tyumen or wherever," Arkady Baskayev, a State Duma deputy who had served as commandant of Grozny in the first Chechen war, told us.[28]

A chilling internal report from the chief military prosecutor, Aleksandr

Savenkov, to Defense Minister Ivanov offered page after page of statistics proving it was more dangerous with each passing year for young men inside the army. Day-to-day living conditions in the military were so deplorable that Savenkov wrote, "A very high rate and alarming dynamics of accidents which led to death or mutilation of servicemen are more proof of poor performance of their duties by military officials, their negligence and failure to provide for safe conditions of military service, as well as of numerous violations of people's rights to life and health." In 2002 and 2003, the report said, the army suffered more than two thousand "noncombat losses," meaning deaths. Some four thousand soldiers suffered from reported acts of hazing or beatings in 2002, a number that had shot up to more than six thousand by 2003. Abusive officers forced their men to drink ten bottles of vodka in a sitting, then watched as one died of alcohol poisoning. A young conscript was beaten and tortured with electricity until his spleen ruptured. Rebellious or vengeful soldiers routinely took up arms in self-defense against colleagues or officers. Cases of murder, premeditated assault, and driving men to suicide were all up in each of the last few years. And these were just the examples that found their way to the military prosecutor's office.[29]

The mothers at home in Sochi left to deal with their brutalized sons needed no official report to show them the consequences of military service. "The state took these children and threw them into this bloody war and sent our children back with broken psychologies, and nobody wants to do anything about it," said Natalya Serdyukova, who saw two sons drafted and sent off to two successive wars in Chechnya. "I was very naive. When my first son was sent to Chechnya, I believed very much that if women of all Russia grabbed hands together, regardless of social status, and we expressed our protest, it could have been stopped. It didn't happen because everybody is concerned only with themselves. I told them, 'Today it's my problem, but tomorrow it will be yours.' But the only ones who heard were those whose children were in the army."

Sochi, with its honky-tonk beachfront boardwalk and an uncomfortable proximity both to Chechnya and the civil-war-torn region of Georgia known as Abkhazia, was like the rest of Russia in its indifference to the conflict. Many residents told us they were convinced that Chechnya simply diverted money and attention from the country's more pressing economic problems. Putin was a regular visitor each August, but in his presidency Sochi attracted half or fewer of the 4 million tourists who had come to sun themselves on its rock-strewn beaches in Soviet times. Package tours to Turkey or Egypt were cheaper for Russians and despite a few new hotels and garish casinos, signs of deterioration were everywhere in the city of more than four hundred thousand year-round residents—from the once-famous flowers that no longer lined its boulevards to the massive concrete tower built as a relaxation center for the proletariat that sat abandoned on the city's outskirts. "It's like heaven and earth, the difference between now and what this place was before," said Lydia Vlasenko, a retired nurse who had lived in Sochi since just after World War II. "It's all slowly falling apart," echoed Aleksandr Zvyagin, a member of the Sochi city council. "In the next ten to fifteen years, we'll not see anything in Sochi when it comes to development, and I'm an optimist."

Natasha Yaroslavtseva was one of the ones who paid attention to the Chechen war's consequences, but only after it was too late for her son, Sasha. At first, she recalled, she was like all the other mothers in Sochi—she prayed for her son to be sent anywhere other than Chechnya. At first, she believed the cheery letters home. Only when Sasha landed in the hospital with what he said was the flu did Yaroslavtseva became suspicious. "He wrote to me, 'Mom, in the hospital everything is all right. We have enough bread and the tea is hot.' For me, it was a shock to see that my son was happy just to have bread."

Then came worse news. Her son had been attached to the border troops guarding the mountainous divide between Chechnya and the neighboring Russian republic of Dagestan. When Chechen rebels launched the incursion into Dagestan in 1999 that helped precipitate the current round of conflict, Sasha was in an area with heavy fighting. He and his fellow soldiers had no barracks, just an earthen trench known as a *zemlyanka* they dug themselves. At one point, he complained of skin problems and she asked why he was not receiving treatment. "He said, 'Mom, there are no sick people here, just living and dead.'"

By the time Sasha returned to Sochi early in 2002, Yaroslavtseva said, he was unrecognizable. "Even his eyes were crazy, senseless," she recalled, pulling out a small black-and-white, grim-faced picture of Sasha when he had come home. He couldn't sleep, had nightmares, couldn't find work. After six months, he gave up trying to adjust and talked only of death. Once, he tried to slit his wrists at a birthday party. When Yaroslavtseva summoned the ambulance, the woman on the other end of the phone line knew immediately. "The first question she asked was 'Did he go to the war in Chechnya? They're all like that.'" From then on, "he was always walking around saying, 'I don't want to live. For what? I will get drunk, buy a motorcycle, and smash myself into the wall.'"

Shortly after 6 a.m. on June 28, 2002, he succeeded in killing himself. All he said before he hanged himself in his bedroom was "Okay, Mom, I'm going now."

Before, Yaroslavtseva and her son were believers in the hopes brought by Putin. They voted for the president and thought he would bring change. A divorced single mother who had brought up Sasha in their tiny basement apartment, Yaroslavtseva worked two jobs—one washing dishes in a restaurant, the other at a sewage-system pumping station. They were never in favor of the war in Chechnya, but it never occurred to them to do anything against it either. They had neither the inclination nor the money to try to bribe Sasha's way out of his military service. But now her son was dead after serving in a war no one wanted to talk about, and Yaroslavtseva had come to see the difference between herself and her neighbors. "I finally understand that we are not needed by anybody," she said. "In Russia, people don't believe they can change anything themselves. But now I know we need to change the system completely."

THE SYSTEM, however, was fighting back. "You can't reform everything endlessly," Sergei Ivanov complained to reporters. "Combat readiness can't be achieved by constant changes."[30] At the same time Putin was talking openly and regularly of the need for major restructuring, Ivanov had embraced the generals' view. From now on, even the word *reform* would be suspect to the minister of defense.

In Pskov in the fall of 2002, the experiment produced the expected dismal results. The military's cost estimates for professionalizing just this one division had gone up so rapidly it was almost comic—from 500 million rubles to 1 billion rubles to 2 billion rubles to almost 2.5 billion rubles now that the exercise with the 76th Airborne Division was actually under way.[31] When Boris Nemtsov and Eduard Vorobyov, a member of parliament from the same party and a retired general who had quit the military rather than lead troops in the first Chechen war, tried to inspect the volunteer soldiers in Pskov at the end of September, the handful they encountered had been ordered not to talk to them. Not even Vorobyov, resplendent in full military uniform, could persuade them.[32] Anatoly Kvashnin, the chief of the general staff, visited a couple days later. The division was behind schedule on everything, he announced. At the rate things were going, he lectured a subordinate in full view of reporters, "after a few days there will be no contract servicemen in the unit." Sure enough, dozens of volunteers got the hint and dropped out in the days after Kvashnin's visit.[33]

Nemtsov took his complaints about Pskov directly to the president and was sure he had made an impression. Putin, he said in late October, "does not want to be taken for a ride. To all appearances, he is sick of the Potemkin villages in Pskov and of falling helicopters in Chechnya.... The Kremlin realizes that military reform must not be entrusted to the generals." Nemtsov was sure he had cut a deal with Putin; he knew he had allies in Prime Minister Mikhail Kasyanov and Finance Minister Aleksei Kudrin. "They have agreed with us," he insisted publicly, "that compulsory service must be for six months, that the pay must be increased."[34]

But now that the fight was on, military hard-liners closed ranks. Even those who had once seemed willing to embrace change now spoke strongly against the reformers who were pushing it—an evolving position best illustrated by Major General Makhmut Gareyev, the head of the Russian Academy of Military Sciences and onetime deputy chief of the Soviet General Staff. At first, Nemtsov and Gaidar had actively courted Gareyev's support, paying his institute for research on the reform plan and touting him as a contributor to the proposal they sent to Putin.[35] Gareyev had been an early backer of the idea that the Russian military could evolve into a hybrid—part contract, part conscript—and the liberal politicians claimed their idea for draftees to serve just six months came directly from Gareyev's plan. "They were the first to propose this," Gaidar's top military reform specialist told us.[36]

But the general was soon emphasizing the benefits of continued conscription. It made sense that soldiers volunteering to serve in Chechnya, he said, should be paid better. "But Russia is not rich now. We need soldiers to guard things, to check passes. We don't need soldiers for fifteen thousand rubles standing there checking passes, we need soldiers for one hundred rubles," Gareyev told us in a Defense Ministry conference room one afternoon.[37] The Union of Right Forces, he claimed, had modified his proposal to maintain conscription, cutting the proposed length of service to a mere six months. Aleksandr Golts, the military expert who wrote a book, *The Russian Army: 11 Lost Years,* chronicling the reform efforts, said Gareyev had indeed been the "real author" of the plan but then turned on the party as the *siloviki* around Putin did. "Looking at his maneuvers, you can know what people in the Kremlin think," Golts said.[38]

Gareyev now had nothing but bad things to say about the reformers. "Nemtsov and others are doing their best to destroy the Russian army," he said. They "took some of what I said and added something of their own and submitted their idea to the president under Gaidar's signature. For [the party], it was very important that everyone know it was their draft. It was not to help the army but to gain political capital." As far as this general was con-

cerned, the Union of Right Forces was nothing but an American front organization trying to humble Russia. "They cannot think themselves, you made
them think so. . . . It's clear they don't have anything of their own. Why didn't
anyone in Russia trust them or vote for them? Because the Americans barely
do something and they say we should do it the same way."[39]

As the generals regrouped, the reformers were unanimous in concluding
that the Pskov experiment was "designed to fail," as Aleksei Arbatov, Yabloko's
defense expert in parliament, put it.[40] But as was so often the case during
Putin's presidency, the two main factions of the pro-Western democracy
movement reserved their most bitter words for each other. The purists in
Yabloko bitingly attacked their Union of Right Forces rivals for compromis-
ing and agreeing to a military draft of any length. It was an "artificial project,"
Arbatov said, that served only the military's interests and not that of reform.
He warned, presciently, that the military would not stop with the Nemtsov-
Gaidar plan but would use it as a pretext to cancel draft deferments.[41]

For its part, the Union of Right Forces insisted that its fellow democrats
were demagogues uninterested in serious policymaking. "Unlike some of our
opponents," Gaidar told us later, "we had a chance to implement some practical reforms. They had never done that. . . . Until you can put it in a way that
you are making a serious point with authority, you are just making politics."[42]
But independent experts believed that the party's plan was pure politics, a
compromise that contained the seeds of its own defeat. "These six months
made the plan very vulnerable. Any military will tell you it's impossible to
train in six months. On the other hand, they say, 'Okay, if we limit military
service to six months, we have to draft three times more people,'" Golts
recalled. "The military very skillfully used it against them."[43]

On November 21, 2002, a government meeting to adopt a reform plan
convened with both the generals and the liberal reformers present. Sergei
Ivanov spoke first, then Anatoly Kvashnin, then Boris Nemtsov. But the president had already made up his mind; he had met with Ivanov in the Kremlin
the day before the meeting, and it was clear the military establishment would
have its way. There would be no end date set for conscription. There would be
no talk of a radically shortened six-month service, as Nemtsov and Gaidar
proposed, just a vague promise to reduce the term substantially. And the generals were already rallying for their next cause—if conscripts were to serve for
less than two years, then more of them would be needed, they argued. Deferments would have to be canceled, more young men would have to serve.[44]

Technically, the reform process was not over; as a next step, Prime Minister Mikhail Kasyanov would appoint a working group to examine how to

carry out the gradual professionalization of the military. But the reformist politicians feared they were headed toward defeat. "We were relatively close to winning the battle" up to that point, Gaidar recalled later, "but we lost." He was told by contacts close to the Kremlin that the decision had been made not to hand his party a political victory. "Publicity," he felt, was a reason for the failure.[45] Nemtsov, who had just weeks before been confidently predicting victory, emerged from the government meeting trying hard to put a positive spin on it. But then a correspondent mentioned Putin's meeting with Ivanov. "The president is trying to support everyone who comes to his office," Nemtsov said bitterly.[46]

Politics is rarely subtle in Russia. Five days later, Putin signed a new decree. From now on, he ordered, the Communist red star, retired with the collapse of the Soviet Union, would once again adorn the banners, flags, and uniforms of the Russian army. "The star is sacred for all servicemen," Ivanov told a televised meeting of top generals as the decision was announced. "Our fathers and grandfathers went to battle with the star."[47]

VITALY TSYMBAL knew he was outnumbered. After all, the government's newly created working group on military reform consisted of several dozen generals and colonels, a handful of numbers-crunching officials from other ministries, one colleague from Gaidar's institute, and him. Eduard Vorobyov, the retired general who now belonged to the Gaidar-Nemtsov faction in the State Duma, was their lone ally in epaulets. Tsymbal, a mild-mannered former colonel who had once researched ways to build better missiles for the Soviet Union, had spent the last decade at Gaidar's Institute for the Economy in Transition, running mathematical models to figure out how to reform the Russian military without crippling the Russian budget.[48]

The reformist politicians had known their cause was doomed as soon as they had heard who Mikhail Kasyanov had appointed; Nemtsov had confronted the prime minister about it. It was a "commission of reactionaries," Nemtsov complained to Kasyanov. Where are the representatives of civil society, the experts, the soldiers' mothers, and the public figures? he demanded to know. "It's necessary to compromise," Kasyanov told him.[49]

Left to face the generals, Tsymbal was unprepared for the vitriol as he listened to rants about the political opportunism of Gaidar and Nemtsov. Once, on a break, one of the brass issued what sounded like a threat to Tsymbal, telling him he would surely have a heart attack if he continued to press the reform point. They told him his mathematical models were nonsense meant only to "mislead the society." This went on several times a month through the

winter and spring of 2003 as the working group junketed all over Russia, flying on military planes to "inspect" regional headquarters in all of the country's six military districts, being feted at long-winded military banquets.

Often, Tsymbal would point out that his economics institute was the only
representative of the Russian people present. "They said this problem concerns military organizations, not citizens. Citizens only perform their duty
when they join. It's up to the military organizations to decide how to implement things," he recalled. "As a military man and retired colonel, I heard a lot
from them that I was betraying the interests of the collective."[50]

Vorobyov came in for similar lectures and soon grew weary of hearing
complaints that Nemtsov didn't know the difference between a commander
and a higher-ranking commandant. Like Tsymbal, he understood from the
commission meetings that the generals didn't accept even the basic principle of military reform, instead taking it as a "populist idea" being exploited
to secure votes. In the end, he concluded that virtually all the commission
members were "cautious or hostile in their approach to the concept itself."[51]

In April 2003, the military scored its formal victory when Kasyanov
chaired another government meeting on the reform plan. Instead of six
months of service for draftees, the official plan stipulated service "up to a
year." All-volunteer units would be mandated only for the small part of the
military that had been designated "units of permanent readiness" in an effort
to keep some part of the army well-equipped and ready for action despite the
post-Soviet budget cuts. But even then, the goal would be to accomplish the
transition by 2008. Conscription remained sacrosanct. The political reformers had envisioned the whole exercise as a way of transitioning the Russian
army away from the draft. But their involvement had now totally backfired.
Putin publicly announced that conscription was and would always be the
basis for the Russian army.[52]

The decision made, Russian leaders were not inclined to be generous to
the liberals. Putin had one last private session with Nemtsov. "I will publicly
say I support you," the president told him.[53] And soon after, in a meeting with
students, Putin did just that, praising the Union of Right Forces reform plan.
"This party," he said, "has done not a little in order to prepare the concept of
reforming the army." Despite their arguments with the General Staff, he also
praised the liberal politicians for sharing the "common goal of making our
army smaller in number, cheaper for the state, but more efficient." But the
remarks were deleted when the talk was shown on state television that
evening.[54] And the two never met again on military reform, indeed, never
spoke about the topic again in any forum. "He had a choice—Ivanov, his

friend, his fellow KGBer, or Nemtsov," the liberal politician said later. "Putin chose to bury military reform together with Ivanov."[55]

Inside the military, those who had beat back reform were even less inclined to forgive political meddlers like Nemtsov. On paper, it seemed a great win for Anatoly Kvashnin, the chief of the General Staff. Despite Putin's clear reservations, he had persuaded the president to back the military and successfully sold the notion that the goal of reform was not to end the draft but to get the military through the demographic crisis years when there wouldn't be enough eighteen-year-olds available to fill the quota. With the economy floating on oil revenues, he had secured several consecutive years of military budget increases, reversing the constant cutbacks of the Yeltsin years. And he had Putin's promise not to shrink the already much reduced military any more.

But Kvashnin was still angry. For four hours in late 2003, he held forth in his office on military matters to two leaders of the Kremlin-connected Council on Defense and Foreign Policy. And Putin's initial flirtation with the politicians from the Union of Right Forces still rankled. "Kvashnin complained, 'I had to talk to Nemtsov and Gaidar about it,'" recalled Vitaly Shlykov, a former military intelligence officer and one of Kvashnin's guests that day. "He was angry that President Putin forced them to consider that seriously." From the start, Kvashnin made clear to his visitors, he had determined to crush the liberals' reform plan and the commander in chief's obvious interest in it. "The military would never accept it," he told them, "because it would ruin what's left of the army."[56]

On October 2, 2003, Sergei Ivanov offered his own postscript to the fight. "Radical transformation within the framework of military reforms has been completed," he announced. Reform was over. Victory had been accomplished.

Never mind that reform had not in fact started, even the military's modest variant on it. Never mind that each spring and each fall, close to two hundred thousand young Russian men would still be rounded up for their mandatory two years. It was one of those moments when the Soviet Union seemed never to have disappeared, so alive was its idea of proclaiming the impossible accomplished in the face of a contrary reality. In Ivanov's statement echoed many predecessors—it was the Politburo's announcement that "developed socialism" had been attained and the ghost of every overfulfilled Soviet five-year plan. "The positive results that have been achieved," Ivanov said confidently, "make it possible to switch from measures to ensure the survival of the armed forces to comprehensive military development."[57]

What Sort of Allies?

Vladimir, you're wrong.
—GEORGE W. BUSH

B Y THE TIME YEVGENY Primakov's car wound its way through the grove of tall, thin birch trees and up to the presidential dacha outside Moscow, it was already one o'clock in the morning on a clear winter night. For late February, it was unseasonably warm, about twenty-eight degrees, a thaw as Russians were calling it. As soon as Vladimir Putin had summoned him, Primakov had thrown on a coat and tie and raced to the secluded state residence. The president greeted him in casual clothes and ushered him into the elegant two-story, columned mansion in Novo-Ogaryovo.

The official compound at Novo-Ogaryovo was actually a series of spacious residences clustered together on a patch of woodland west of the capital, one a converted country church, another a stately old home once used by a Politburo member. The estate was built in the 1950s for Soviet prime minister Georgy Malenkov, but construction lasted longer than he did and he never moved in. Nikita Khrushchev used it for distinguished guests. Mikhail Gorbachev gathered leaders of the Soviet republics there in 1991 to begin forging a new treaty intended to save the Soviet Union. After that, it fell into disuse until Putin picked it for his official residence in 2000 and had it renovated for his wife and two daughters. Despite the formal setting, Putin called it his country dacha.

As he sat up late that winter night in early 2003, Putin was brooding about the looming war in Iraq. Despite Putin's opposition, George Bush seemed determined to launch an invasion to dislodge Saddam Hussein. Tens of thousands of American troops were mobilizing in Kuwait and elsewhere in the Middle East to assault a country that had long been an ally of Moscow's. While Putin could tolerate U.S. troops in Afghanistan fighting a mutual enemy, an American occupation of Iraq would not only destabilize the region and further enhance Washington's hegemony in the world at Moscow's expense, it would also jeopardize enormous Russian economic interests, particularly in the oil industry. Russian business leaders had been pressing Putin to stop Bush, but every effort to head things off through diplomacy at the United Nations or on the telephone had gotten him nowhere. So now Putin was enlisting Primakov, his onetime political rival, for a surprise last-ditch effort to prevent war.

Putin had a secret mission for him that night: go to Baghdad and tell Saddam Hussein to resign. "He asked me to fly there immediately and deliver his oral message to Saddam personally," Primakov recalled. "He wanted me to talk to Saddam privately, one-on-one, to make it easier for Saddam to make a decision to retire."[1]

Primakov was the logical choice. A gravel-voiced model of the old-school Soviet diplomat, Primakov had served as head of Russia's foreign intelligence service, foreign minister, and eventually prime minister. For much of the post-Soviet period, he had been the face of Russian resistance to American dominance in the world, frequently preaching the need for a "multipolar" order versus a "unipolar" world. As the United States and the rest of NATO prepared to go to war with Serb forces in Kosovo in 1999, Primakov, then prime minister, jetted toward Washington in hopes of blocking a military operation. When he learned halfway over the Atlantic Ocean that orders had been given to launch the bombing strikes, he abruptly ordered his airplane to turn around and head home in protest. Primakov had also been Gorbachev's special envoy during the Persian Gulf War of 1991, often speaking out in defense of Hussein against the American-led coalition, once even meeting with the Iraqi leader during a bombing strike on Baghdad. For the rest of the decade, as the United Nations struggled to disarm Iraq, Primakov regularly backed Baghdad's positions, much to the frustration of the U.S. administration and the weapons inspectors. Richard Butler, the head of the U.N. weapons inspections team, later asserted that Primakov was even paid off by the Iraqis, a charge the Russian heatedly denied.[2]

Putin knew Primakov was the most friendly Russian face he could send to see the Iraqi leader, who modeled himself after Stalin and reportedly kept a picture of the Soviet dictator in his office. Primakov was, after all, "the person Saddam knows better than anyone else from the outside world," as Moscow security expert Aleksandr Pikayev put it.[3] If Primakov told him to go, maybe Hussein would realize his time in office had to come to an end.

Primakov agreed. "I was sure it was the right idea and I didn't object," he said. "The only thing I told Putin was I really doubted Saddam would agree."

By morning, he was on a government plane to Baghdad.

It was warm when he landed. The ancient city was bustling, traffic moving on the streets, people shopping in the souk and praying in the mosque; it did not look like a place on the edge of war. Primakov was met at the airport by a high-ranking Iraqi official, who offered to take him somewhere to freshen up, but Primakov demanded to see Hussein immediately. He was driven to a guesthouse to wait, then offered dinner. He demurred again. Then the Iraqis asked him to meet with Tariq Aziz, the deputy prime minister. Primakov refused, knowing that Aziz would only grill him on his mission and tip off Hussein first.

Then ninety minutes after landing, Primakov was taken to one of Hussein's many palaces and ushered in. He had not seen the Iraqi leader since the Gulf War, when he was taken to three different palaces before being allowed to meet with Hussein; this time they went straight to him. It was about 10 p.m. Hussein was decked out in a military uniform, as he was increasingly in the days leading up to war. He seemed inordinately calm and unruffled, like the capital around him. Primakov thought he might not really understand what was happening. "I want to talk with you privately," he told the Iraqi. Hussein dismissed Aziz and the two sat down with just an interpreter Primakov had brought from Russia.

"I think you should take care of the future of Iraq and its people," Primakov began. "That is why I'm asking you to pay very close attention to the proposal that Putin has made. Putin's message was, 'I think for the sake of your people, for the sake of your country, you should retire from the presidency and make an appeal to the parliament to have democratic elections in order to avoid any chaos.'" Primakov didn't say it directly, but he hinted that Hussein could remain in the Baath Party and in Iraq; by speaking with him privately, Primakov hoped to keep Putin's message a secret so that if Hussein went along with the idea, he could save face by appearing to step down on his own initiative rather than under pressure from Moscow.

As Primakov spoke, Hussein took notes, jotting down everything his visitor said. Primakov took that as a sign that he might agree. "I got some hope," he recalled later.

But it was false hope. Hussein asked Primakov to repeat his pitch in front of Aziz. Primakov agreed and Hussein's retinue was summoned. After Primakov repeated his message, Hussein lashed out.

"Russia has turned into a shadow of the United States," Hussein growled at Primakov. Exhuming decade-old resentments, Hussein accused Primakov of betraying him during the Gulf War, asserting that the Russian had promised there would be no U.S. ground operation if he would remove troops from Kuwait. Primakov remembered it differently, recalling that Hus-

Boris Yeltsin *(right)* made Vladimir Putin his handpicked successor after advisers concluded the onetime KGB spy would protect their interests. Putin was no baby-kisser, but he did don military uniforms *(below),* and he even flew to Chechnya to win votes in 2000. *(Photos by Ilya Pitalev/*Kommersant.*)* Tycoon Boris Berezovsky *(below right)* helped bring Putin to power with a secret plot called Project Putin but later fell out with the new president and fled to Britain. *(Photo by Pavel Kassin/*Kommersant.*)*

Tatyana Shalimova *(above)* was one of our early guides to the new Russia, showing us the divide between her life in fast-changing Moscow and her backwater hometown of Mokshan. *(Photo by Paul Miller.)* Mikhail Kozyrev *(below left)* started Nashe Radio to promote Russian rock but struggled with the nationalist wave he rode to success. *(Photo by Sergei Mikheyev/Kommersant.)* Boomtown Moscow *(below right)* boasted more billionaires than anywhere else in the world. *(Photo by Aleksei Kudenko/Kommersant.)*

George W. Bush *(above left)* embraced Vladimir Putin as a friend after the Russian told him a story of a cross his mother once gave him. But after looking into Putin's soul during their first meeting, Bush would later discover that his friend was no democratic reformer. *(Photo by Dmitri Azarov/Kommersant.)*
One of Putin's first targets was the independent NTV network, whose anchor Yevgeny Kiselyov and his team of journalists *(below)* fought a losing battle to stave off a state takeover. *(Photo by Pavel Smertin/Kommersant.)*

The war in Chechnya claimed many lives, including eighteen-year-old Elza Kungayeva, who was murdered by a Russian colonel the day Vladimir Putin was elected and whose family *(above)* waged a bitter campaign for justice. *(Photo by Sergei Veniavsky/Kommersant.)* The war struck Moscow when guerrillas seized a theater showing the musical *Nord-Ost* *(below left, photo by Valery Melnikov/Kommersant).* After Prime Minister Mikhail Kasyanov argued with Putin *(below right)* over plans to raid the theater, Putin sent him to Mexico to be out of the way. *(Photo by Dmitri Azarov/Kommersant.)*

The *Siloviki:* The former military and secret-police officers known as the men of power rose to new heights under Putin, including a trio of KGB veterans, Defense Minister Sergei Ivanov *(above, photo by Dmitri Azarov/*Kommersant*)*, presidential envoy Viktor Cherkesov *(above right, photo by Yevgeny Pavlenko/*Kommersant*)*, and Kremlin deputy chief of staff Igor Sechin *(right, photo by Dmitri Azarov/*Kommersant*)*. Ivanov positioned himself as a successor to Putin, while Cherkesov rebuilt a giant state police force and Sechin maneuvered to take over the country's biggest oil company.

The Opposition: Irina Khakamada *(above)*, a Western-oriented democrat, ran a doomed campaign against Putin for reelection in 2004. *(Photo by Susan Glasser.)* Her colleague, Boris Nemtsov *(below left)*, fought to reform the military and investigate *Nord-Ost* but was blocked by Putin's Kremlin. *(Photo by Dmitri Lebedev/*Kommersant.*)* Sergei Glazyev *(below right)*, a disaffected Communist, created a new nationalist party with Kremlin blessing only to be crushed when he tried to go independent. *(Photo by Dmitri Lekay/*Kommersant.*)*

Oil magnate Mikhail Khodorkovsky *(right)*, Russia's richest man, defied Vladimir Putin's monopoly on power and wound up in prison as the Kremlin dismantled and effectively renationalized his Yukos Oil Company. *(Photo by Dmitri Lebedev/*Kommersant.*)* Tanya Levina *(below)* and her Moscow high school history class struggled to understand the changes in their country, with Tanya concluding that Lenin had been right after all. *(Photo by Yulia Solovyova.)*

Chechen rebels and their allies shocked the world with the seizure of School Number 1 in the southern Russian town of Beslan, which left hundreds of children and their parents and teachers dead. The burned-out school building became a shrine for Russians, who trooped through and left behind tokens to mourn the tragedy.
*(Photo above by Valery Melnikov/*Kommersant. *Photo right by Peter Baker.)*

sein had promised to withdraw his forces and have Aziz make a public statement, only to not follow through.

At that point, Hussein dropped the argument. "Then he just put his hand
on my shoulder and left," Primakov recalled.

Aziz looked at Primakov and said, "Ten years will pass and you will
understand who was right—our dear president or you."

Primakov headed immediately for the airport. He had been on the
ground only four hours but his mission was a failure. Clearly, Hussein would
not step aside and Russia would not be able to head off the war. Not trusting
the telephones at the Russian embassy in Baghdad, Primakov waited until he
had flown through the night back to Moscow to call Putin to report on his
talks. "It was like you and I expected," he told the president. "He said no;
unfortunately, he didn't accept our proposal." Later that day Primakov went
to the Kremlin to give Putin a fuller debriefing. "He was not surprised," Primakov said of the president. "But I felt he was satisfied that Russia had done
everything it could."[4]

BUSH'S DETERMINATION to invade Iraq was proving to be a decisive test of
the new relationship he and Putin had struck. Since the end of the Cold War,
the Russians had resisted American assertion of power in the world but
proved impotent to stop it. The interventions in Bosnia and Kosovo had particularly infuriated the anti-American forces inside Russia. But Iraq held even
more strategic interest for Russia and was more than Putin could take for the
sake of the relationship. Russia's interest in Iraq reached back decades to
when the Soviet Union was cultivating client states in the Arab world and
happily accepted Saddam Hussein as he built the former British protectorate
into a regional power. Over the years, thousands of Soviet specialists had
worked in Iraq, and Moscow had sold Baghdad considerable weaponry for
which it had never been paid, leaving an $8 billion debt that the Kremlin still
hoped to collect. As both countries worked to rebuild from their separate
upheavals during the 1990s, they drew even closer economically. By the final
years of Hussein's rule, Russia had emerged as Iraq's largest trading partner
under the U.N. oil-for-food program, purchasing 40 percent of Baghdad's
permitted oil exports and selling Hussein's government more food, medicine,
and oil-industry equipment than any other country since the program's start
in 1996.

Every day, Russian companies drilled or shipped as much Iraqi oil as
allowed under U.N. auspices and dreamed of the time they could do more.
Iraq was so lucrative for Russian firms that everyone from engineering com-

panies to machinery manufacturers to politicians wanted in. Vnukovo Airlines, whose main task was ferrying passengers across the vast Russian countryside, established its own trading firm to get a share of the Iraqi oil business. Even the Russian Ministry of Emergency Situations, the agency responsible for responding to floods and forest fires, had gotten into the game by setting up a subsidiary to trade Iraqi crude. "Almost all Russian companies work with us," Hussein's ambassador to Russia, Abbas Khalaf, boasted to us one day in the run-up to the war.[5]

But the real money for Russia in Iraq was still in the ground. With the world's second-richest oil deposits, Iraq was ripe for prospecting, and the Russians were eager to claim the prize. "Everyone is dreaming of projects there," said Yuri Shafranik, chairman of a small Russian oil company and head of a committee promoting Russian-Iraqi economic cooperation.[6] The biggest long-term development deal was a $20 billion agreement granting Lukoil, then Russia's largest oil producer, rights to lead a consortium developing part of the massive West Qurna field in southern Iraq. Another part of West Qurna was allocated to a partnership of three other Russian firms, Tatneft, Rosneft, and Zarubezhneft, all owned by the state. Slavneft, another state-controlled company, had a contract to develop the Luhais field in southern Iraq, while a subsidiary of Gazprom, the state-controlled natural gas monopoly, had agreed to develop a gas field. The booming business continued right up until the war, as we found when we went to visit executives at Zarubezhneft not long before the U.S. invasion. Undeterred, they were busy organizing a convoy of trucks carrying oil-drilling equipment across the border from Syria into Iraq with plans to begin drilling some forty-five wells in the dusty frontier around Kirkuk.

Along the way, much of the money was ending up in Hussein's pocket. Iraq was charging a premium of twenty cents to fifty cents per barrel of crude sold through the oil-for-food program, which added up to billions of dollars, most of it effectively illegal kickbacks to the government. A later investigation would find that starting in 2000 Iraqi ministries forced foreign companies to deposit 10 percent of the value of any contract into secret bank accounts in Jordan and Lebanon in violation of U.N. sanctions. Russian firms were willing to pay. Emercom, the company founded by the Russian emergency ministry, for instance, began picking up oil business from Iraq even as the United States was trying to put the screws to the Baghdad government. U.N. officials believed that two contracts signed by Emercom were worth $1.8 million in illegal kickbacks to Hussein; the company insisted it had complied with U.N. rules and denied paying bribes without directly disputing that it had paid surcharges. Overall, investigators concluded that Hussein made as much as $11 billion in illegal income in his final years in office.[7]

Money was also finding its way into key Russian pockets. Some Russian politicians openly advocated for Hussein in Moscow, none more so than Vladimir Zhirinovsky, the flamboyant ultranationalist deputy speaker of the State Duma, who unabashedly boasted of his relationship with his "good friend" Hussein and regularly led delegations of Russian business-men to Baghdad to arrange lucrative deals. Many considered Zhirinovsky to be Hussein's personal ambassador in Moscow, a "bought-and-paid-for agent," according to U.S. scholar Ariel Cohen.[8] When we went to see Zhiri-novsky at his smoky parliamentary office in the summer of 2002 to ask him about this, he did little to dispute it, denying only that the Iraqis gave him money "directly" but acknowledging that he had asked them for cash.[9] Zhirinovsky's deputy, Aleksei Mitrofanov, told us they received money from Russian companies that got contracts in Iraq thanks to Zhirinovsky's help.[10] One executive at Transneft, the state-owned pipeline company, called Zhirinovsky "the locomotive who wanted to open doors for us at all the ministries" in Baghdad.[11] He was hardly the only one. After the war, investigators would discover that Saddam Hussein had given secret oil vouchers permitting the recipients to sell Iraqi crude to nearly fifty Russian individuals and organizations. Not only did secret vouchers go to Russian oil firms such as Lukoil and state-owned Rosneft, Zarubezhneft, and Tat-neft, but also to the Russian Communist Party, Zhirinovsky's party, and even Putin's Unity party. The son of Russia's ambassador got several secret vouchers, according to documents, as did the Russian Foreign Ministry and the Russian presidential office itself. Aleksandr Voloshin, Putin's chief of staff, was listed as receiving a voucher.[12]

So as Putin contemplated how to respond to the U.S. threats against Iraq, the calculation was complicated: Would he sacrifice a fruitful relationship with an old ally, no matter how unsavory, that provided tangible economic benefits to Russia for an uncertain and so far unprofitable budding partner-ship with the most powerful country in the world? In the months following the signing of the Treaty of Moscow cutting nuclear arsenals, Russians had come to resent what they saw as the one-sided relationship with Washington. It seemed all give and no take. Russia had surrendered Central Asia, rolled over on the ABM treaty and NATO expansion, closed its Soviet-era military bases in Lourdes, Cuba, and Cam Ranh Bay, Vietnam, and offered intelli-gence help in Afghanistan. For what? Putin's most important priority was rebuilding his economy, and Bush had done nothing to help him with that.

The early dreams of quick accession to the World Trade Organization or a new wave of American investment in Russia or even repeal of the Jackson-Vanik trade restrictions had evaporated by the fall of 2002 as Bush was going before the U.N. General Assembly seeking an international coalition against Iraq. Instead, all Russia had gotten, as many saw it, were increased tariffs against Russian steel and loads of cheap imported U.S. chicken drumsticks that Russians derisively called "Bush legs."

The frustration was palpable. Voloshin, the generally closemouthed Kremlin chief of staff, finally erupted one day during a private meeting with British journalists. "What sort of allies are we?" he asked scornfully. "Russia undertook lots of steps for the USA. We closed our radar stations in Cuba, offered intelligence and communications with the Northern Alliance to help bring victory in Afghanistan. What was the response? The USA tried to push Russia out of Afghanistan and oust members of [President Hamid] Karzai's government who supported us. It has fought against Russia's interests in the [former Soviet Union], encouraging Radio Liberty to broadcast in Ukrainian. It is really aimed at weakening Russia's position. Jackson-Vanik has not been rescinded twelve years after the collapse of the USSR. It's a political signal that we are not good partners. We are glad-handing and there are no real tangible steps being taken toward us."[13]

Russian officials voiced their discontent in meetings with American counterparts as well. "There was definitely a lot of heartburn that the relationship is all give and no get," the State Department's John Bolton later recalled. He thought there was some merit to the Russian grievances. His own administration had done virtually nothing to follow through on its pledge to convince Congress to lift Jackson-Vanik. "Every time it came up, it never happened," he told us. On Capitol Hill, he said, Colin Powell seemed to focus on the department's budget to the exclusion of other issues. "A lot of the other things haven't engaged his attention. If you really want it done, one could think it could be done." But Bolton also believed the Russians were trying to trade in on some moves that were not so much concessions as financial necessities; Moscow needed to close overseas bases anyway because it could no longer afford them. "It's the retreat from empire, the retreat from Soviet days. That was inevitable once the Soviet Union collapsed."[14]

To some Russians, the attitude emanating from Washington was a familiar case of imperial hubris. Even liberals used to defending the United States in Russian circles were "so disenchanted with America, they sound anti-American," as Aleksei Arbatov, the State Duma deputy, told us. Moscow security specialist Aleksandr Golts began calling American leaders the "Busheviks." Sergei Prikhodko, Putin's foreign policy adviser, said the Kremlin couldn't help but draw parallels between the Bush administration and the strict ideologues who once ran the Soviet Union. "The Bolsheviks had a very contagious ideology, because their slogan—'he who is not with us is against us'—was adopted by our friends and colleagues in Washington," he told us one day in the Kremlin. "That was Lenin's favorite slogan. But he ended badly."[15]

THE RIFT began opening even at the very moment the two sides were celebrating their new relationship with the Treaty of Moscow in May 2002. During a private meeting between the two presidents, sparks flew over trade. Bush had imposed a steel tariff for domestic political reasons, and in retaliation Putin had cut off import of American chicken drumsticks. Now Putin was confronting Bush about the supposed poor quality of the poultry sent to Russia.

"I know you have separate plants for chickens for America and chickens for Russia," Putin told Bush.

Bush was flabbergasted. "Vladimir, you're wrong."

But Putin would hear none of it. "My people have told me this is true."[16]

Bush took it as a sign that Putin's KGB advisers were feeding him deliberate disinformation to poison the relationship. But Putin appeared to really believe that Americans kept good chickens to themselves and sold bad chickens to Russians. In the run-up to war, Putin increasingly reverted to such Cold War thinking and began reaching out to Iraq, North Korea, and Iran—all, of course, members of Bush's "axis of evil." In July 2002, Prime Minister Mikhail Kasyanov signed a plan for increasing nuclear cooperation with Tehran, a touchy issue with Washington. Under the plan, Russia would build five more civilian nuclear reactors over the next decade on top of a facility at Bushehr that was already riling the Americans. The plan was leaked on a Friday afternoon. When Condoleezza Rice read about it in the Saturday newspaper, she erupted in anger and picked up the phone to call her counterpart in Moscow. The Russians started backpedaling; it was only a draft, they insisted to her, conveniently ignoring that Kasyanov had signed it. Evidently some in the Russian government were pushing the plan but had not told others, including Atomic Energy Minister Aleksandr Rumyantsev. Bush instructed Energy Secretary Spencer Abraham and John Bolton, the undersecretary of state, who were already scheduled to fly to Moscow, to demand explanations and make his displeasure known. The Americans raised what one later called "a real big stink," and Abraham pointedly canceled a news conference with Rumyantsev.[17]

A few weeks later, Russia tweaked Washington again by inviting North Korea's Stalinist leader, Kim Jong Il, to visit. The reclusive Kim rarely ventured out of his hermit kingdom, but the year before had embarked on an odd railroad trip across the breadth of Russia to Moscow aboard a lavish train stuffed with gourmet food, liquor, and women. Now he was coming back to the Russian Far East, as Putin continued to woo the eccentric North Korean. Then one day in August, we went to visit the Iraqi ambassador in Moscow, and he told us that Russia and Iraq had crafted a new $40 billion economic agreement that would spell out cooperation in oil, electrical energy, chemical products, irrigation, railroad construction, and other transportation projects. The timing was hardly a coincidence. The message from Saddam Hussein was simple: you have more to gain by standing with us than abandoning us. Or as the ambassador, Abbas Khalaf, a former translator for Hussein, told us, "Russia was, is, and will be our main partner."[18] Once again, the Americans were taken by surprise and exasperated with Putin.

The rift illustrated a fundamental American misunderstanding about Putin. Bush had come to think of him as a friend, a fellow Christian, a compatriot on the battlefield against terrorism. But Putin's priorities were not the same as America's. He understood the limits of Russian military might— Chechnya, if nothing else, had taught him that—and took a more realistic view of Russia's role on the geopolitical stage. Rather than building a new army to flex his muscles abroad, Putin believed that the key to restoring Russia as a great power was economic. He had started his tenure noting that it would take fifteen years to catch up to Portugal economically, and three years later he vowed to double the Russian gross national product by 2010. Putin demonstrated a neo-imperial streak, throwing his weight around in former Soviet republics, but typically used economic rather than military pressure to keep neighbors in line, such as cutting off natural gas to Georgia or Belarus when their leadership irritated him. Focused on the need to rebuild, Putin put less priority on world affairs that did not directly concern him. "We are all concentrated on our internal issues," said his informal adviser Mikhail Margelov, the senator. "The main goal of our foreign policy is to create friendly or at least neutral [relations] . . . to give us a chance to concentrate on our economic problems."[19]

So as Putin assessed the international map that summer, he saw little new investment coming from the United States, not even symbolic repeal of Jackson-Vanik or an official Commerce Department designation that Russia now had a market economy. Russian pride led the government to kick out the Peace Corps even as Russia was flirting again with Iraq, Iran, and North Korea. Thanks to oil and nuclear contracts, Iran and Iraq represented important trading partners. Money was at stake and Putin wasn't going to simply abandon those old friends for another visit to Bush's ranch.

At the same time, Putin did not plan to break with Bush to save Saddam Hussein either. If the United States went ahead with the war, Putin had decided to express his reservations but not to expend any political capital to stop it. The last thing he wanted was to be another Boris Yeltsin, railing against the U.S. operations in Yugoslavia, inflaming anti-American sentiment at home while revealing his inherent weakness abroad. "The reaction was harder and more emotional" during the Yugoslav wars, Sergei Prikhodko, the Kremlin foreign policy chief, later told us. "Today our attitudes are more pragmatic. We want to preserve the positive trends that interest us. In both cases, we objected to imposing political will for the sake of some dubious goals. But if we are doing it as partners, we must preserve partnership relations." And Putin told Bush this. "We said that we were not going to take advantage of their mistake and fan anti-American sentiments or in any other propaganda way," Prikhodko said. "We just told them it's a mistake."[20]

The Kremlin squelched Russian initiatives that it viewed as unhelpful. Yuri Shafranik, head of the Russian-Iraqi cooperation committee, chairman of the board of Soyuzneftegaz, a state-owned oil firm, and himself a recipient of Iraq's secret vouchers, organized a delegation of senior Russian political and business leaders for a trip to Baghdad in early 2003. But the Kremlin pressured participants to back out. "At the last minute they decided not to fly, and the reason was the Kremlin hadn't shaped its attitude in a firm way yet," Shafranik told us later. "The arguments were 'Don't go against America.' What does that mean? These arguments were weak. We were talking about Russia's interests."[21] Putin himself likewise extinguished an effort by Boris Nemtsov, the Union of Right Forces leader, to forge a U.S.-Russian deal to replace Hussein with Tariq Aziz. "I talked about it with Putin—that plan could be the plan of Russia," Nemtsov recalled. "Tariq Aziz could work for both of us. Putin said the Americans never would agree to that. It would be just a fantasy."[22]

Yet if Putin was for the moment looking to avoid a deep split with Bush, he still did not take kindly to efforts to push him into backing Washington's war with Iraq. Mikhail Khodorkovsky, the oil magnate who had no substantial economic interests of his own in Hussein's Iraq, urged the Kremlin to side actively with the United States. "If there were sufficient political will,"

Khodorkovsky told us at the time, "if there were consortia formed before all of this happened between American and Russian companies . . . they would have a good chance to have positive results."[23]

THE AMERICANS were relentlessly moving to war. Russia had leaned on Saddam Hussein to accept new U.N. weapons inspections and signed on to a new Security Council resolution warning Iraq to come clean on any hidden arms program. In a fit of pique, Hussein's government then canceled Lukoil's contract to develop the West Qurna oil fields, a self-defeating move for Baghdad that only eliminated the most compelling economic incentive Russia had for sticking by the current Iraqi regime. It soon became clear that the inspections would do nothing to deter Bush. Putin sent his foreign minister, Igor Ivanov, to New York for the February 5 Security Council session where Colin Powell would unveil U.S. evidence of Iraqi duplicity and clandestine weapons of mass destruction. Ivanov decided the substance of Powell's presentation was meaningless. "It became clear to us that the United States had already made the decision to launch a military operation," Ivanov told us during a later interview at the Kremlin. Ivanov confronted Powell. "I told him why these arguments seemed unpersuasive to me." Powell didn't answer. Ivanov took that to mean his American counterpart agreed but could not speak against policy imposed from above. "From that moment on," Ivanov told us, "our task moved into a new stage—to reduce the possible damage from the war and to move on to a political settlement as soon as possible."[24]

Publicly, Putin was still keeping his cards close to his vest. The day after Powell's presentation, the Russian president spoke by telephone with President Jacques Chirac of France and arranged to come see him. A few days later, he left Moscow, stopping first in Berlin to consult with Chancellor Gerhard Schröder, who put heavy pressure on Putin to join him and Chirac in vocally opposing the war. Schröder "begged him to support the European position," Sergei Karaganov, the foreign policy analyst who advised the Kremlin, recalled later. "He said, 'Vladimir, if you are a friend, help.'" Putin then flew on to Paris, where Chirac arranged for a welcome perhaps unseen for any Russian leader since Tsar Aleksandr I's triumphant visit following the defeat of Napoleon. "The president laid out unbelievable hospitality," Karaganov said. "I mean, they closed half of Paris and laid out carpets on the streets." Chirac personally greeted Putin at Orly airport and led him in a motorcade down the Champs-Élysées, lined with French and Russian flags, for a ceremony at the Arc de Triomphe. The Franco-German seduction was working on Putin. "Gradually, under the positive and negative pressure, he moved a lot closer to the European position," Karaganov said. "He started off closer to the Chinese position—no, but a quiet no. But then he was really wooed by his European friends. It was unbelievable. He started to repeat things we hadn't said in two or three years, about a multipolar world and all that. The position was, is, and will be we don't want to confront the United States over this. But we were dragged into it by the Europeans."[25]

That visit marked the turning point for Putin. In an interview with French television before leaving for Paris, he had said, "There is only one task for the international community to accomplish in Iraq—to make sure that Baghdad has no weapons of mass destruction or to find that it has and make Iraq eliminate those weapons. In this connection, we share the position of our American partners, which is that we must do everything for Iraq to cooperate with the U.N. inspectors in full measure."[26] But just days later, on February 10, he was in Paris joining a tripartite declaration with the French and Germans opposing the use of force. "Russia is against the war," Putin said flatly at Chirac's side.[27] The next day, in an interview with another French television network, he called the impending war a "grave error," used the word *multipolar*, and aligned himself with France rather than sharing the position of his American partners. "The positions of France and Russia are practically identical, or very close," he said. He hinted that he would use his Security Council veto along with France to stop a war. "If today a proposition was made that we felt would lead to an unreasonable use of force, we would act with France or alone."[28]

Chirac pressed his advantage, even passing along what the Russians considered disinformation. As the days ticked off toward war, Chirac met with a visiting high-ranking Russian official and insisted he forward intelligence directly to Putin. "Chirac said . . . he knew for sure about Bush's secret plan to divide Iraq into four states, and he wanted him to carry this to Putin immediately," a well-connected Russian official told us.[29]

GEORGE BUSH and his advisers had convinced themselves that Putin would eventually support the United States in Iraq, at least privately if not publicly. Now, the increasing solidarity among Paris, Berlin, and Moscow, the so-called *non-nein-nyet* alliance, caught the Americans off guard. Only when Putin began ratcheting up the rhetoric did they come to realize they had misjudged him. "We ultimately thought the Russians would come along," one senior Bush administration official who was closely involved in the matter told us later. The Bush team hoped to crack the European opposition. "Fundamental to our strategy was that one of them would cave," the senior official said. "We thought it would be the Russians. . . . The fact that the Russians stayed with them surprised us. That may have come from overestimating the personal relationship."[30] That an American government would be counting on Russia to side with it against traditional U.S. allies like France and Germany spoke to the dramatic changes in Washington's relations with the outside world. It also spoke, as the senior Bush administration official suggested, to the Americans' faulty understanding of the Russian president. "The U.S. analysis at the beginning was that Russia at crucial moments would probably abstain rather than directly oppose the U.S. on key resolutions," Alexander Vershbow, the U.S. ambassador, said later. "But then as French and German opposition hardened and the dynamics were different, I think Putin calculated there was no gain for him in terms of Russian public opinion and in terms of being softer than America's traditional allies. He was drawn into a more opposition position by the Germans and the French rather than leading the pack."[31]

As they came to understand they would not have Moscow's support, the Americans grew angrier. Fueling the irritation were fresh U.S. intelligence reports showing that a Russian arms manufacturer, Avia Conversia, was selling Iraq equipment designed to jam global positioning satellite technology, potentially interfering with U.S. precision bombs. The reports had first surfaced in the fall, and the Russians had flatly denied them. Now, with the war just days away, Condoleezza Rice came to Moscow and confronted Sergei Ivanov, the defense minister, on the matter in person. Ivanov again insisted to her that it was not true. Rice pressed him, even uncharacteristically raising her voice; GPS jammers were a direct threat to U.S. military forces, she said. "It was not a happy conversation," Vershbow recalled later. "They tried to dismiss it. They said we read the information wrong. We stood by the evidence and we had other information that these things were even being used by that point. It was not a satisfactory response." In the end, the GPS jammers proved no help to the Iraqis, but U.S. forces occupying the country after Hussein fell did find proof that the Russian company had been shipping the jammers through the Iraqi embassy in Moscow, including a crate with a fresh Russian label. Either Ivanov and the other Russians were lying or they were complicit in allowing their technology to be shipped out without their knowledge. "It was a pretty sour note," Vershbow said.[32]

In fact, the Russians were secretly shipping Iraq far more in weaponry in the weeks running up to the war than the Americans realized, weaponry that could have been used against U.S. forces. Russia had long been Iraq's preeminent arms supplier, so much so that Iraqi embassy personnel in Moscow for the previous two years had been arranging weekly charter flights filled with smuggled illicit goods through Damascus to Baghdad, including not just the GPS jammers but also radar jammers, night-vision devices, and small missile components. In January and February 2003, even as U.S. troops were gathering in the dusty Kuwaiti desert in preparation for their invasion, Russia's state-owned arms exporter, Rosoboroneksport, received two delegations from Iraq and offered to sell Igla-S shoulder-fired rockets, Kornet antitank missiles, SA-11 and SA-15 air defense systems, and T-90 tanks, investigators later discovered. In the end, the Iraqis secretly signed four contracts with the Russians, who to cover their tracks demanded that the arms be shipped through a third country with false end-user certificates, documents the Iraqis promptly obtained from Syria.[33]

Even if not directly authorized by the Kremlin, none of this could reasonably have escaped the attention of Putin or his secret service coterie. But the Russian president still wanted to prevent a U.S. invasion. A couple weeks after the failure of Yevgeny Primakov's mission, he sent another message to Baghdad through State Duma speaker Gennady Seleznyov, the longtime Communist who had recently quit the party in protest of its moribund leadership and was trying to rally the old left behind himself without much success. Seleznyov strongly opposed the U.S. conflict with Iraq and wanted to show solidarity with Hussein. When he went to see Putin at the Kremlin before flying to Baghdad, he found the Russian president irritated at Bush's obstinance. "He was frustrated with America sticking to this one line," Seleznyov told us later. Putin instructed him to tell Hussein that Russia had done everything it could and would not support the war.

Seleznyov arrived in Baghdad on March 9 and soon was ushered into one of Hussein's palaces to meet with the Iraqi dictator. For three hours, they talked over tea and strong cigars, taking a break only once during Muslim prayer time. Seleznyov passed along Putin's message. "He promised that Russia at the Security Council would not support a resolution that would contain the word *attack*," Seleznyov recounted to us.

Hussein railed defiantly against the Americans. "It's not me they want," he told Seleznyov. "They want my country, which is rich with oil." Hussein promised a relentless battle. "Every bush, every stone, every child, will fight the aggressors," Hussein said. He also used his visitor to get out his message once again that he would not leave Baghdad. "I will die here," he told Seleznyov. "If the country dies, I will die here."[34]

Seleznyov obligingly emerged from the meeting parroting Hussein's line. "Iraq will fight to the last child," he told Russian journalists, predicting the Americans "will have their teeth broken in Iraq."[35]

■ ■ ■

JUST AS PUTIN was the first to call Bush after the planes struck the Twin Towers, so, too, was he quick to pick up the phone after the first bombs fell on Baghdad. For months he had been part of the European troika opposing the war. But now that it had started, he made a point of reaching out to Bush.

"This is going to be awfully difficult for you," the Russian told Bush on the morning of March 24, hours after the war began. "I feel bad for you. I feel bad."

"Why?" Bush asked.

"Because there's going to be enormous human suffering."

"No," Bush insisted, "we've got a good plan. But thank you for your concern."

Putin had been through this himself. He had leveled Grozny, carpet-bombed civilians, and left a path of destruction throughout Chechnya. He assumed Bush would do the same to Baghdad, as the Russian generals were telling him. He did not understand that the American military ethos was to avoid the sort of indiscriminate devastation wrought by the Russian armed forces. But in any case he was sending a personal signal to Bush that no matter what their differences on policy, he was there for the American president. "It was a genuine call," Bush later recalled to Bob Woodward. "It wasn't a told-you-so. It was a friendship call. And I appreciated it. . . . That's the only call I got along those lines, by the way."[36]

With the war under way, Putin kept quiet for a while. He offered no running commentary on the troubles the U.S. forces initially ran into with Hussein's militias, and the Kremlin pressured the State Duma to shelve a resolution condemning the U.S. war. As American forces approached Baghdad, Russian ambassador Vladimir Titorenko fled for the Syrian border in an eight-car convoy carrying twenty-three diplomats and journalists on April 6, only to come under fire from U.S. troops, who apparently mistook it for an Iraqi military caravan despite the small Russian flag flying on his vehicle. The first shot whizzed right past the ambassador as his driver yelled at him to get down; the driver was shot twice in the stomach and four others were injured as well. Even then, Putin said nothing. Instead, he met with Condoleezza Rice for an hour the next day at the Kremlin to begin talking about how to repair relations with Washington once the war ended. There was significant work to be done; enough mistrust had developed that some Americans initially suspected that the Russian embassy in Baghdad was sheltering Saddam Hussein in the immediate hours after his regime fell on April 9. But Rice had by this point begun articulating the formula that would govern U.S.

policy toward its European adversaries in the postwar period: "Punish France, ignore Germany, and forgive Russia."[37]

That suited Putin. The Iraq war was a distraction for him, not something worth rupturing his new relations with the United States over. He had always been more cold-eyed in his view of Bush, so he may have harbored less personal bitterness than the Americans over their schism. He found a perfect venue to settle the disagreement. In just a month, he planned to host a global soiree in his hometown of St. Petersburg, celebrating the three hundredth anniversary of the city founded by Peter the Great to serve as Russia's "window to the West." Putin had invested a great deal of capital in the celebration. This was going to be his moment of international glory, when the young Leningrad street hooligan would emerge as the proud successor to Peter the Great, rebuilding his broken city and country. Putin had steered $1.3 billion from the federal budget to fix up St. Petersburg's crumbling exterior and raised $300 million more to reconstruct the sprawling, thousand-room Konstantinovsky Palace to host dozens of world leaders. Peter the Great had laid the first stone for the palace in 1720 but never finished it; during World War II, the Nazis had looted and devastated it. Now in careful symbolism, Putin would complete what Peter had not, a castle with its own canals, pier, and helicopter pad, his personal contribution to a Russia on the rise again.

It was mostly for show. Off the main drags, little of the reconstruction money found its way to helping the city's 5 million residents and much of it disappeared into private hands, "simply hidden in the bushes," as Russia's chief auditor later put it.[38] As foreign leaders began landing at the St. Petersburg airport, police rounded up homeless people and ordered workers out of the city center. And just as Grigory Potemkin had erected facades of thriving villages along the travel route of his lover, Catherine the Great, to fool her into thinking the country was making more progress than it was, authorities erected a high green fence along the highway leading out to Konstantinovsky Palace—quickly nicknamed the Putinstrasse—so visiting dignitaries would not see the blighted villages where ordinary Russians still lived.

But following Rice's formula, Bush was there to forgive. Putin had made it easier by ordering parliament to finish ratifying the Treaty of Moscow arms control agreement four days before Bush's visit so they could sign the ratification documents and make a performance of collaboration after the ballet and fireworks at Peter the Great's summer palace. Once again, Bush was clapping "Vladimir" on the back, calling him "my good friend," and inviting him to Camp David in the fall. "We will show the world," Bush pledged, "that friends can disagree, move beyond disagreement, and work in a very constructive way to maintain the peace." He even promised again to work to repeal Jackson-Vanik; Putin couldn't help smirking at that but said nothing. Instead, he called Bush a "good friend" and even reassured the American that Moscow would help stop Iran from building nuclear weapons. "The positions of Russia and the United States on the issue," Putin said, "are much closer than they seem."[39]

By the time they met at Camp David four months later, the quarrel seemed forgotten altogether. Bush was jovial again in Putin's company and, in answer to a reporter's question, offered him a virtual endorsement heading into the Russian election season. He made no reference to the destruction of political opposition, the virtual elimination of independent broadcast media, or the routine abduction, torture, and killing of civilians in Chechnya. To the dismay of his advisers, he ad-libbed a rosy portrait of a country far different from the one Putin had actually built. "I respect President Putin's vision for Russia," Bush told reporters on that early autumn day in September 2003, "a country at peace within its borders, with its neighbors, a country in which democracy and freedom and rule of law thrive."[40]

Dictatorship of the Law

The romantic stage was over.
—SERGEI PASHIN

T HE FIRST TIME THE JURY came back with its verdict, the judge told
them they hadn't done it right. They had forgotten to rule on one of the
charges and made a mess trying to alter the language of one of the others. The
judge sent them out to try again.

A few minutes later, the jury came back. The judge looked at their decision, shook his head, and pronounced it incomplete again. He sent them back
a second time.

And then a third.

And a fourth.

And a fifth.

The rueful jury foreman shrugged his apologies. "It's the first time," he
called out. "The first blini is always messed up."[1]

It was the first jury trial in Moscow since the Bolshevik revolution, a mile-
stone in the long-delayed effort to overhaul a judicial system still hardwired
by Soviet mentality. For more than eight decades until the murder trial of
Igor Bortnikov in the summer of 2003, Russians charged with a crime in
Moscow were brought shackled into cramped courtrooms where judges,
aided during Communist times by party hacks known as people's assessors,
invariably convicted them—that is, if the defendants received even that much
due process. In the years since the fall of Communism, power in courts in
Moscow and most of the rest of the country had remained in the hands of
judges, who were still finding defendants guilty 99.6 percent of the time when
Vladimir Putin ascended to the Kremlin. The right to a jury of one's peers, a
cornerstone of Western justice, had been enshrined in the new Russian constitution in 1993, but it took an epic ten years to put it into practice in the
aging headquarters of the Moscow City Court. Even then, it was a work in
progress.

The introduction of a more democratic jurisprudence, along with such unfamiliar notions as a defendant's presumption of innocence and a prose-cutor's burden of proof, was intended to help instill a measure of credibility to a system in which the Russian people had no faith. Weighted against the accused, plagued by payoffs, Russian justice offered scant hope to those caught in its grip. From the moment a Russian first encountered the system in the form of a militia officer on the street, justice often had little to do with the process. Slipshod investigations targeted people based on little evidence. Torture was a common form of extracting confessions. Bribes could set the guilty free and convict the innocent. The civil court system was no better. Ordinary Russians aggrieved by neighbors, employers, businesses, or government agencies had little recourse to legal compensation, while tycoons simply shopped around until they found a judge for the right price. Courts obligingly knocked government opponents off election ballots on flimsy technicalities.

Reformers knew that Russia would never build true democracy without the rule of law; it was fundamental to reinventing the country that had first introduced the world to show trials. But the antediluvian system had resisted their attempts to transform it in the 1990s. Prosecutors and judges guarded their prerogatives zealously, and those who wanted to rein them in found themselves frustrated by Boris Yeltsin's political impotence. It fell to Putin to salvage their reformation project. A lawyer by training, Putin had come to office vowing to build a genuinely independent judiciary. Judicial reform was central to Putin's claim to being a modernizer, proof of his commitment to Western-style government. Yet from the beginning, he showed a curious understanding of the concept. "Democracy," he wrote in a message to voters before his election, "is a dictatorship of law and not of those whose official duty it is to enforce the law."[2]

Over eight sweltering summer days in Courtroom 331, a retired air force officer, a pipe fitter, an unemployed cook, a few homemakers, several pensioners, and an engineer-turned-astrologer would struggle with what it meant to be jurors in the new Russia. Moscow's first jury trial in their lifetime presented a case study in the challenges of converting an authoritarian culture into a genuine civil society. "For a person who's never been involved in a court before, of course it's very difficult," the sixty-one-year-old foreman, Aleksandr Abramov, conceded later. "There were some bumps. . . . This court reform, this participation of jurors, it seems to me, needs to be perfected."

The jurors were not the only ones still figuring out their new roles. Under the new system, the judge was supposed to be a neutral arbiter, not an adjunct to the prosecution as in the past. But Judge Pyotr Shtunder, a lanky veteran of the Russian bench with droopy eyes and a droopy mustache, could not help interjecting repeatedly just as judges always did in the old system. When the defendant's attorneys objected to the jury being read a witness statement the defense had never been shown, Shtunder dismissed their concern. "That's your problem," he told them brusquely. When they dared to question the identification of their client by the victim's father, the judge cut them off. "Stop this," Shtunder ordered. "To doubt the investigation is illegal." When the defense attorney continued, Shtunder jumped in again. Turning to the jurors, he instructed, "Accept the evidence that we have as legal and true and evaluate it."

Even the defense team struggled with alien concepts. In the new Russian system, conviction required a simple majority of twelve jurors. When we mentioned during a break that juries in the United States must rule unanimously to hand down a guilty verdict, defense attorney Vladimir Zherebenkov seemed astonished and instinctively translated that into the Russian context.

"Then," he exclaimed, "you only have to buy one!"

SERGEI PASHIN had never met Igor Bortnikov, but the opening of his trial in Moscow represented the culmination of a dozen years of Pashin's work. Probably no other single person had done more to promote the revival of jury trials in Russia than Pashin. Yet he took little satisfaction in that. In fact, by the time the Bortnikov trial opened, Pashin considered himself defeated. "The forces of reaction," he sighed to us that day, "have won."[3]

Tall and beefy with a boyish face and short-cropped hair, Pashin had been the founding father of judicial reform in Russia before turning thirty years old. His family, like most others, had experienced Soviet-style justice during Stalin's era. His grandfather, assigned to collect money from families for postwar reconstruction in 1947, took pity on women with many children and allowed them to pay less. He was charged with sabotage and sentenced to ten years in the gulag; he died of starvation in a camp in 1951. His grandson decided to study the law in hopes of changing it. At Moscow State University law school in the 1980s, Pashin was drilled in the particulars of the same system that had condemned his grandfather, a system designed to perpetuate Russia's historical dominance of the state over the individual. *The Marxist-Leninist General Theory of the State and Law* taught that the concept of "rules over the state and over the political authority, binding and limiting it, is by its nature a disguise for class dictatorship."[4] Pashin was instructed in the evils of Western jurisprudence in courses such as "The Reactionary Substance of the Bourgeois Criminal Process," all the while dreaming of bringing the bourgeois process to his homeland.

When Yeltsin was elected president of Russia in 1991, Pashin joined his team of young reformers. At age twenty-nine, Pashin helped write the Russian parliament's "Concept of Judicial Reform," passed in October 1991, a landmark document setting out a vision for a radically different system guaranteeing individual rights and a fair and independent judiciary. He simultaneously authored a new law creating the first Constitutional Court in Russian history. The next year, Pashin and allies such as Sergei Vitsin, a former police general, helped found arbitrage courts to hear business disputes and secured passage of a law formally guaranteeing independence for judges. Mikhail Gorbachev had first floated the idea of reviving jury trials, but it was never written into law until Pashin tried in 1993. Parliament approved the move that July, and the right to a jury trial was enshrined later that year in Yeltsin's new constitution. By the end of the year, Pashin was in a courtroom in the provincial city of Saratov on the Volga River, watching Russia's first jury trial since 1917, conducted by a judge who had prepared in part by watching reruns of the American soap opera *Santa Barbara*.[5]

The process resembled the American system but was drawn from Russia's own history. The first jury trials in Russia were introduced by Tsar Aleksandr II as part of his Great Reforms in 1864, three years after he freed the serfs and put in place the first building blocks of a freer society. For the next half century, jury trials flourished in Russia, although not always without controversy. When the government staged a mass trial of revolutionaries in St. Petersburg in 1877, fully 153 of the 193 defendants were acquitted, and many of those convicted were given light sentences. An angry Aleksandr increased some of the sentences and sent some of the acquitted into exile anyway. The next year, a jury found revolutionary Vera Zasulich not guilty of shooting and injuring the autocratic governor of St. Petersburg, touching off a frenzy of cheers in the courtroom. The government, in response, decreed that all cases of rebellion and assassination would from then on be tried by military courts.[6] Still, the tsar did not get rid of jury trials for other crimes, and they remained the standard until Lenin abolished them.

Pashin was excited to see his ideas coming to fruition and took a job as head of a judicial reform department under Yeltsin. "The main thing I wanted to do was create an independent judicial authority," he said. "That was the romantic period of court reform." But the romance quickly faded. To get his jury-trial bill through parliament over the objections of the prosecutor general, who denounced it as a "foreign" concept, Pashin and the other reformers had had to limit it to just nine of Russia's eighty-nine regions, excluding Moscow and other population centers. The hope was it would catch on and spread quickly. It did not. Russia ratified the European Convention of Human Rights in 1995, committing it to a fair, independent, and impartial judiciary without ever taking the necessary steps to make that a reality. The country was still operating with the criminal procedures code written under Nikita Khrushchev in the 1960s. When Yeltsin offered an updated version curbing the power of prosecutors and forcing judges to be dispassionate referees instead of advocates for the state, parliament passed it on preliminary first reading in 1997, then put it in a drawer untouched for the rest of Yeltsin's term. "Yeltsin signed all the orders I prepared," Pashin recalled. But it did not matter. "All my efforts met a wall. The bureaucratic system just reconstructed itself."[7]

Eventually, Pashin's mandate disappeared. His office was eliminated and he found himself without a job. "My work started to irritate my bosses. The romantic stage was over. It was time to work as a rubber stamp."[8] He took an appointment as a judge on the Moscow City Court. The system, he discovered, was as bad as ever. Police could stop anyone on the street without cause. Judges moved suspects through trials like a conveyer belt, earning the court the nickname MosGorStamp, or Moscow City Stamp. Prosecutors did not even bother to show up for many trials, confident the judges would convict anyway. If the cases were too weak, judges simply sent them back for more investigation until the prosecutors got it right. Suspects would sit in prisons rife with tuberculosis for years while evidence was collected against them. Torture was still so routine that police devised new terms for the most popular techniques—putting a gas mask on a suspect's face and making him breathe tear gas was called an elephant, cuffing him to a metal bed with an electrical current running through it was called a crucifixion.[9] Once confessions were secured, sentences were meted out disproportionate to the supposed crimes. A fifteen-year-old boy was sentenced to three and a half years in prison for stealing two hamsters from a pet shop. A mother of three was sent away for four years for stealing twelve cabbages. In a courthouse cafeteria one day, Pashin ran into a fellow judge agonizing over what to do in a murder trial. The prosecutor had withdrawn the accusation, and the judge was balking at freeing the suspect just because he had been exonerated. "I've been a judge for seventeen years and I've never given a single acquittal," she exclaimed in horror. She eventually came up with a solution: she would order a new trial and instruct the government to send her a different prosecutor.[10]

"If judges start expressing some sort of mercy, they're immediately put in their place," Pashin said. "An innocent verdict is considered to be a wreck in your career." The chief judges called judges on the carpet for handing out acquittals. "They'll say, 'Your colleagues never give acquittals and you do. Why?'"[11] Eventually, judges who went against the grain were relegated to minor cases or dismissed altogether. Pashin was fired in 1998 but fought the move and convinced the Supreme Court to reinstate him. In 2000, he was fired again, this time for criticizing another judge's mishandling of a case. Again Pashin fought the move and won reinstatement in 2001, but he decided enough was enough and declined to reassume his seat on the bench. As Putin was taking over the Kremlin, complaints against judges had tripled, and 70 percent of Russians in polls felt judicial reform was needed all over again.[12] Pashin decided to take on the fight from the outside.

THE FIRST thing the jurors noticed was the cage. It was impossible to miss, occupying practically a quarter of the courtroom, iron bars floor to ceiling with metal mesh on the lower half. Sitting inside the cage was Igor Bortnikov, a twenty-five-year-old former soldier and onetime drug user accused of killing a man for his Mercedes. If the jury box was new, the cage was not. Never mind the innocent-until-proven-guilty presumption formally built into Russian law. The cage in Russian courtrooms had for years sent an unmistakable signal about suspects penned like animals. "The environment was a shock—that cage, a person in a cage," Vera Navrotskaya, an unemployed fifty-five-year-old bookkeeper chosen as a juror in Bortnikov's trial, told us. "At first, you think if he's sitting in the cage, he must be guilty."

Wearing glasses, close-cropped hair, and a black T-shirt emblazoned in English "Diesel Special Equipment," Bortnikov sat calmly in the cage, his hands folded in his lap, his dull eyes betraying a hint of boredom in the proceedings even though he faced twenty years in prison. As the trial opened, the newly selected jurors avoided looking at him. Under the new system that had finally made it to Moscow ten years after it was officially adopted in law, defendants in the most serious cases could choose a jury or a judge. Bortnikov gambled that he would be better off with ordinary Russians. "When there's only one judge, he has his own personal opinion and he's always bought and paid for to give a larger sentence," Bortnikov told us later when we reached him in jail on a contraband mobile telephone he kept hidden in a hollowed-out space in the heel of his shoe. "I wanted more people to participate. It would be harder to pay each of them."

The jury impaneled to hear case number 2–184–1/03 was selected from voter lists, but the pool became skewed when fourteen working-age men simply refused to participate. "They just walked away," said Vladimir Zherebenkov, the defense attorney. In the end, out of forty-five candidates, the court chose eight women and four men with an average age of fifty-five years old; only two reported being employed. Jurors would be paid $3 a day for their service. On paper, their duty seemed clear. They took an oath "not to acquit the guilty and not to convict the innocent." But few in the room imagined it would be that simple. The selection particularly worried the victim's family, which no longer had the certainty of conviction it would have had under the old system. "What kind of verdict will we get?" Viktor Shopenkov, the victim's father, fretted during a break. "We can't even know."

Andrei Shopenkov, twenty-six, was strangled with a rope the evening of October 4, 2001. Bortnikov and three friends had been talking to the Shopenkovs about buying their used Mercedes sedan for nearly $9,000. Prosecutors alleged that the young men never really intended to pay for the car and went to meet Andrei Shopenkov planning all along to kill him. In the Russian system, the victim's father was entitled to participate in the trial, given a seat at the prosecution table and the right to question witnesses and address the jury. Yet Viktor Shopenkov bristled at the restraints on what he could tell them, including what he called a confession by Bortnikov. "He told me how he killed my son," Shopenkov told us in the corridor. "I asked him at a private meeting, 'How could you choke a man by the throat so he couldn't survive?' And he said, 'You have to know how to do it. . . . You have to learn how to beat someone without leaving any marks.'"

The trial would be run by Pyotr Shtunder, who had spent twenty-two years on the bench, first in the Soviet Union and then Russia. He sat in the front of the small courtroom wearing a tie, but no jacket or robe. His court secretary recorded the proceedings in longhand. The prosecutor was Lieutenant Colonel Boris Loktionov who, like other state attorneys wore a military-style blue uniform with two stars on his shoulder. His sleeves neatly rolled up, Loktionov started the trial by reading aloud the voluminous binders of evidence he had collected. For hours, he droned on in a relentless monotone, just reading the official case file, also handwritten, sometimes stroking his shaved head or tight mustache. Many jurors looked bored or sleepy. With no air-conditioning, the courtroom grew stuffy in the midsummer heat. Finally, a juror fainted and the judge called a break.

As he retreated from the courtroom, Loktionov contemplated the difference between presenting cases to judges and juries. He dutifully endorsed the concept of a jury trial, but made clear he did not really care for the unpredictability. In the case of one defendant in the provinces, Loktionov recalled,

"They thought he was innocent, and as soon as he went free, he murdered and raped a woman. If they had been more serious and attentive, they could have avoided that tragedy."

VLADIMIR PUTIN assigned Dmitri Kozak to finish what Sergei Pashin and his fellow reformers could not. A lawyer from St. Petersburg, Kozak had started out in the Leningrad prosecutor's office in the final days of the Soviet Union, then became a lawyer for the city council in the new democratic era, aggressively jousting with the mayor's office on behalf of the legislators. Finally, Mayor Anatoly Sobchak neutralized Kozak by hiring him as chief lawyer in city hall, where he met Putin. Eventually, Kozak followed Putin to Moscow. Putin originally decided to make Kozak the country's new prosecutor general and even informed members of parliament that he would submit the nomination. But that night, Aleksandr Voloshin, the holdover Kremlin chief of staff, reportedly went to see Putin and persuaded him to drop Kozak in favor of Vladimir Ustinov, who had proven his loyalty in filling the sensitive post of prosecutor general in an acting capacity since shortly after the dismissal of Yuri Skuratov, the investigator who had crossed the Yeltsin-era Family.[13] Kozak's consolation prize was an office in the Kremlin as Putin's deputy chief of staff, and he quickly became one of the president's most trusted lieutenants, "the eyes of the tsar," as some called him. Kozak would end up with the mission of translating Putin's "dictatorship of the law" into reality.

A forty-two-year-old chain-smoker with blow-dried hair, Kozak quoted Leo Tolstoy and Anton Chekhov and talked in eloquent terms about the need to establish a fair and independent system of justice. A "liberal patriot," he termed himself.[14] He seemed to understand that simply subordinating the judiciary to the whims of the authorities left no protection for those out of power. "If we create a monster in the shape of the state today," he said in those early days, "we very much run the risk of being destroyed by it, too."[15]

Yet he worked in a Kremlin that proved from the beginning that it would manipulate the courts to achieve its ends. The assault on NTV was a classic example. Its owner, Vladimir Gusinsky, was arrested and held in prison for days without seeing a judge, in contradiction to the Russian constitution, only to be released after a cabinet minister forced him to sign away his company. Ustinov's masked men later raided NTV's company headquarters without a warrant just two days after network anchor Yevgeny Kiselyov had reported a scandal involving the prosecutor. NTV had disclosed that Ustinov received a plush apartment worth hundreds of thousands of dollars from

Kremlin property chief Pavel Borodin before dropping a corruption investigation against Borodin. The most blatant example came the day before the Kremlin's allies staged a boardroom coup seizing formal control from Gusinsky. Having been rebuffed at every turn by Moscow courts sympathetic to the state, Kiselyov had secretly found a judge in the Volga River city of Saratov to issue an order blocking the shareholders meeting where Gusinsky was to be toppled. But while Kiselyov was in the car driving back to Moscow, the Saratov judge mysteriously changed his mind and overruled his own order. The judge then disappeared for days. When he finally turned up, he explained his reversal by claiming the NTV side had failed to pay a filing fee of eight rubles, or twenty-five cents.[16] That was too much even for some in the government's camp. Anatoly Blinov, the legal counsel for Gazprom-Media, the state-controlled entity maneuvering to take over Gusinsky's business, quit the next day in protest of the court shenanigans and went on NTV to declare that the network's takeover "is being achieved by such methods that it looks to me that the profession of lawyer soon will become unnecessary."[17]

While all this was going on, Kozak was supposed to be inventing a legal system that would never allow such things to happen. In December 2000, Kozak put together a commission to draft a new criminal procedure code. In January 2001, the Kremlin sent a bill to the State Duma stripping prosecutors of their unilateral power to arrest suspects or conduct searches without obtaining court warrants first—a practice already banned by the Russian constitution in 1993 and a Constitutional Court ruling in 1999, both of which had been completely ignored. Yet critics managed to overwhelm the proposal so quickly that Putin pulled it within hours. Kozak later acknowledged that it had not been well thought out, saying it was rushed to the Duma "very fast without checking" how to implement it.[18] With Kozak in retreat, the hard-line faction of *siloviki* competing for Putin's ear in the Kremlin pressed their advantage. The next month, they secured new regulations allowing the FSB to pursue anonymous tips, a Soviet-era practice from the days when Russians were encouraged to spy on each other that had been banned in 1988 during perestroika.

Kozak went back to the drawing board. He mapped out radical changes in the balance of power in the judiciary system. Prosecutors would need court warrants to conduct searches or to hold suspects longer than forty-eight hours. Jury trials would finally be expanded beyond the few provincial courts that had adopted them in the 1990s to Moscow and the rest of the country. Prosecutors would be required to show up for trials and would no longer be allowed to go back and investigate further when their cases did not add up.

Defendants would no longer face double jeopardy except in rare circumstances. Judges would be required to explain in writing whenever they barred a witness or piece of evidence. To fight corruption, judges would have their monthly salaries increased fivefold, from six thousand rubles to thirty thousand rubles ($207 to $1,034), while losing their immunity from criminal prosecution. New judges would also face a three-year probation period at the start of their judicial career and a mandatory retirement age of sixty-five at the end. A new judicial governing board, including outsiders, would control selections, dismissals, and budgets. As a matter of philosophy, judges would no longer be considered de facto members of the prosecution but, in theory at least, neutral overseers of an adversarial process between prosecutors and defense attorneys.

Every step along the way, though, Kozak ran into virulent opposition from the man who had beat him out for the job of prosecutor general, Vladimir Ustinov. The two met at least once a week for a year, with Ustinov resisting virtually every proposed change in the system. "He thought our country was not ready for such a high level of freedom," Kozak recalled later. Kozak said he would reply "that if you *don't* give this freedom, the country would not be ready even in a hundred years."[19] Instead, Ustinov went public with his attacks. "Many civilized countries have given up on jury trials," he told a Russian newspaper. "It's outdated."[20] Prosecutors were not the only ones to defy Kozak. Judges had little interest in surrendering immunity and introducing outsiders to judicial governance. "People considered themselves almost gods," Kozak said of the judges. "And any legislative mechanism that stipulated that judges should be accountable and responsible for what they are doing even before each other, they considered it insulting to them." Kozak decided it was his job "to bring the judges back down to earth."[21]

The judges considered Kozak's reforms dangerous and unnecessary. "I don't think anything needs to be changed in terms of the status of judges," Yuri Sidorenko, the chairman of the Russian Judicial Collegium, the governing body for judges, and Kozak's main foe, told us later. "I'm not going to say that everything is ideal here. I'm just saying that what has been done recently over the last twelve years was done in the interest of a strong independent court. But to reform judges, one needs time." Sitting in his office in the newly built headquarters for Russia's top courts, the three-decade veteran of the Russian bench was slow to criticize justice under the Soviet system. "They tried to judge judges who judged dissidents in that era," he said. "But they followed the law at that time. Let society blame itself first." Sidorenko was unpersuaded when Kozak took him to Strasbourg, France, to meet with jurists from France and Germany, saying, "I think we are ahead of these countries. In this sense, they can't be an example for us."[22]

Still, the judges' complaints raised serious questions about whether the Kremlin was trying to reform the system or simply take control over it. The new judicial board Kozak envisioned would include representatives appointed by the president, the Justice Ministry, and the prosecutor general as well as judges, and the elimination of judicial immunity could subject judges to more pressure from the state rather than less. At the same time, liberals studying Kozak's plans did not trust a Kremlin run by a career KGB officer to design a genuinely fair system.

Pashin and his old ally Sergei Vitsin, a retired general from the Soviet Interior Ministry who had become a reformer, were also unhappy with Kozak's proposals, particularly the provisions making judges susceptible to outside influence. The new judicial board, they felt, should be stocked with ordinary Russians, not Kremlin stooges. Still smarting from his own battles on the Moscow City Court, Pashin was particularly incensed that chief judges would still wield so much power and that judges would still rely on the state for apartments in the city, dachas in the country, personal cars, and special passes to elite health clinics or vacation resorts. But Pashin and Vitsin split on their approach. Vitsin stayed on a presidential advisory council, while Pashin lobbed rhetorical blasts from the outside and condemned the whole process as neo-Soviet. "This code is a half-measure," Vitsin would later concede. "I see the disadvantages from the other side. It doesn't conform to the idea of a rule-of-law state. It doesn't conform to the ideas of European legislation. But the majority, on the other hand, considered it too liberal. It was only because of Dmitri Nikolaevich Kozak that we were able to adopt this code."[23]

Kozak ended up cutting deals in some cases and getting overruled by Putin in others. He backed off some changes and agreed to delay other features. Jury trials would apply only to the most serious crimes—espionage, rape, bribery, and murder, and even then only to first-degree murder. Prosecutors would still be allowed to use evidence from anonymous witnesses and introduce written statements from witnesses who failed to appear during trial, negating the opportunity to cross-examine them. After the heads of the top Russian courts took their objections directly to Putin, the president dropped the plans for a new judicial governing board and measures that would allow judges to be removed in select circumstances. Kozak reeled at the defeat. "Many were surprised that the clash was so open and fierce," Sidorenko recalled.[24] The Duma passed the final compromise on November 22, 2001.

Putin soon demonstrated that he saw no further need to temper the system with mercy. Viktor Ivanov, a top presidential aide and fellow KGB veteran, who was considered one of the leaders of the *siloviki* in the Kremlin, decided to eliminate the Presidential Pardon Committee, another panel on which Sergei Vitsin served. While Yeltsin had freed fifty-seven thousand prisoners on the committee's recommendations during his presidency, including twelve thousand in his last year, Putin had pardoned just twenty. Putin signed the order abolishing the committee altogether in late December, just a month after the passage of the watered-down judicial reform package.[25]

Although he had enacted more than three thousand amendments to the criminal code, Kozak realized he had fallen short. Pashin's critique burned, but Kozak knew it was legitimate. "It's partially fair," Kozak conceded, "and we understand it ourselves and I repeat it's the result of political compromise." Kozak particularly agreed with Pashin's point about the unbridled power of the chief judges. "As for other things mentioned by Pashin, we know most of them and most of them are real. But it is always easier to criticize than to do something." The more time passed, though, the clearer it became that the judiciary remained unreformed and thoroughly corrupt, no matter what it said on paper. "I don't think that anything has radically changed," Kozak told us. "There have been no radical changes from the point of view of fighting corruption."[26]

Pashin studied the Kozak reforms and saw high-sounding principles not backed up in reality. The system Putin had built was based not on the rule of law but the rule of the state. It was a system Putin and the *siloviki* could still manipulate for their own purposes. "On paper, everything seems to be better," Pashin said. But in fact, "it's become even worse." When his grandfather was sent to the gulag a half century earlier, a Soviet tribunal sped through 970 cases a day. "Now at least they hear the case. But the result would be the same."[27]

"Do you know that your friend is being accused of committing murder? Why did you accuse Bortnikov of murdering the victim?"

"I never accused Bortnikov. I never said he killed him."

Standing at the witness lectern in that summer of 2003 was Aleksandr Vanbin, twenty years old and one of the defendant's friends. Vanbin had already been convicted of robbery in connection with Andrei Shopenkov's death and had given prosecutors a statement identifying Bortnikov as the killer. Now as the defense questioned him, Vanbin tried to take it back.

Boris Loktionov, the prosecutor, jumped up in disgust and read the jury the young man's original statement. The witness listened impassively, sneaking glimpses of his friend in the cage. Asked about the statement, Vanbin insisted it was a lie that investigators had forced him to sign.

"They told me that my wife, who was pregnant at that time, would be giving birth on a bunk in jail and not on a hospital bed," he told the jury. "I testified the way they wanted me to in order to protect my relatives and loved ones. And myself."

The judge did not hide his skepticism. "You survived," he said sarcastically. "Here you are, well and sound."

A few days after Vanbin changed his story, so did another friend, Viktor Bagin, nineteen years old, also already convicted of robbery and sentenced to ten years for the crime. At the witness lectern, Bagin not only tried to exonerate Bortnikov, but even took the blame himself, saying he was the one who choked the victim.

"Did you kill him?" the judge asked in disbelief.

"Yes," he answered. "I killed him unintentionally."

When it came time for Bortnikov to speak in his own defense, he, too, shifted his version of events, disavowing a statement he made to authorities after his arrest. Speaking from his cage, Bortnikov told the jury that he had been present the night of the murder and acknowledged getting into a fight with the victim. But he said he left before the man was killed. "I wasn't there," Bortnikov testified.

When he complained that authorities had pressured him into implicating himself, Judge Shtunder and the prosecutor dismissed his complaints.

Bortnikov, who had remained stoic through long days of proceedings, finally erupted with emotion. "As if you don't know how everything's done here, how money is given so that everybody gets framed," he snapped at the prosecutor.

Then, turning to the judge, he started, "And you, Your Honor—"

Shtunder cut him off.

The next day, the court convened for closing arguments. Loktionov appealed to the jurors to ignore the conflicts in testimony and stand with the state, just as judges always had. "When you go to the jury room, you are building your own house there. Put glass in the windows, stones in the wall, parquet. You become judges there. Use your life experience. Prove to the Moscow City Court that you are not worse than the judge, that jurors can also figure things out and make a fair decision." He added, "This is a historic day for you. You have justice in your hands. Jails full of convicted criminals are waiting for your decision today to see if it's possible to fool a jury or not."

The defense, by contrast, insisted the evidence was too weak to convict their client, nothing but testimony by accomplices with major discrepancies. "Do not condemn if you have doubts," Yevgeny Zhigarev, one of Bortnikov's attorneys, told the jury. "Don't commit this sin. You will be living with your decision your whole lives."

But once again the defense ran afoul of the judge when Zhigarev tried to press the argument that the only evidence against the defendant was coerced confessions. "The prosecutor presented us testimony that was obtained during the investigation when the accomplices were under investigation in jail," Zhigarev said. "If there is a hell, dear jurors, it's in our prisons."

Shtunder interrupted, "I consider this pressure on the jurors."

"Your Honor," Zhigarev countered, "I was just trying to describe reality."

"Don't argue with the judge," Shtunder scolded.

Zhigarev turned back to the jurors and tried again. "Suspects go for any agreement with investigators."

Shtunder stopped him again and told the jurors to ignore the attorney. "Who promised what under what pressure—don't believe these facts," the judge instructed the jury. "All testimony was obtained within the legal framework. All attempts to convince you otherwise, please consider to be pressure on you."

Finally it was the defendant's turn. He spoke softly from inside his cage, reading carefully from handwritten notes. "I believe in God," he said. "I didn't kill and I didn't rob. . . . My fateful mistake was to be present at the scene of the crime. It seems that my fate is to go through this hellish test. One thing I want to ask you—while you make your decision, believe your heart."

As MOSCOW opened its first jury trial in that summer of 2003, a group of everyday Russians led by an aging teacher named Tatyana Karpova was presenting another challenge to the legacy of the Soviet legal system: Would the courts now hold someone responsible for a dangerous product, an airplane crash, workplace harassment, or even government negligence? If Putin's judicial reform was to mean anything at all, it would have to build a court system that was empowered to hold the state itself accountable, even Putin's Kremlin. If the judges were to be genuinely independent, they would have to have the freedom to stand up to society's most powerful institution. Tatyana Karpova was going to find out if that was the case.

Karpova had lost her son, Aleksandr, in the hostage siege at the Dubrovka Street theater the previous fall, and breaking with the Russian tradition of stoic suffering, she had decided to demand the government own up to its tragic mistake. Aleksandr, called Sasha by his family and friends, had been a thirty-one-year-old lyricist for the Russian production of the musical *Chicago* and had gone to *Nord-Ost* that night to check out the crosstown competition. He died from the chemical pumped into the theater to knock out the Chechen guerrillas. No matter how much she tried, Sasha's mother could not accept that he was gone, and her cluttered flat on the eastern outskirts of Moscow was a shrine to him. The front hallway was plastered with flyers advertising his public appearances, including Irish folk music performances under the playful name O'Karpov. The glass cabinets in the cozy living room were covered with his pictures and handbills from *Chicago*. In the aftermath of his death, she had received a letter of condolence from the U.S. ambassador, Alexander Vershbow, but none from Putin or any other Russian official. Now she was determined to make them pay attention. "Putin and the representatives of his government didn't know that we, all of us, are very strong people," she told us that summer. "We don't close our mouths."[28]

Karpova sought out relatives of other victims from the theater siege. The government would not give her a list of the survivors, so she and her new partners compiled their own and formed an association of terrorism victims. Karpova and her new allies interviewed long lists of lawyers before finding Igor Trunov to take their case. Then forty-one years old, favoring a buzz cut and black suits, Trunov ran a small law firm with his wife. He agreed to represent Karpova and the others for free "because I think something should be done, not just talk about it in the kitchen, not just suffer and complain."[29] He quickly concluded, though, that he could not win a negligence suit against the state, especially given the way it had clamped down on information about the theater siege in the name of state security, so he found another provision in Russian law obliging the government to provide "moral compensation" to victims of terrorism and began blitzing the courts with scores of claims asking for $1 million for each plaintiff. Such a strategy would not force the government to admit, or even examine, its own culpability in what had happened, but would not let it simply brush aside the matter as usual.

The state did its best anyway. With the help of friendly businesses, authorities had paid out small sums to the victims already and figured that was plenty in a city where average wages at the time hovered around $500 a month.[30] "This is the biggest financial support ever provided," insisted Olga Gracheva, the Moscow city official who dispensed the compensation. Gracheva saw no need for the government to admit mistakes in handling the siege. "What kind of mistakes were there? . . . I don't have anything on my conscience and no regrets."[31]

Judge Marina Gorbacheva ran through the claims one after the other as
if she were running a factory. She refused to let Trunov call supporting witnesses or present evidence. She gaveled the teary-eyed mothers and widows
silent when they went on too long describing their hardships. "She got tired
of it," Zoya Chernetsova, a former Afghan war nurse whose son had died in
the theater, told us after her own testimony. "It would have been more human
to tell us, 'Don't testify, it's already been decided.'"[32]

When Trunov broached the idea of a settlement before one hearing we
attended, the government side barely answered.

"Unfortunately, we're not authorized to do that," said one of the state's
lawyers, a prim young woman in a pinstripe suit who did not seem to consider this unfortunate at all.

"Will you leave us your phone number so we can talk about it later?"

The woman smiled. "No."[33]

More than a year of litigation would not get the *Nord-Ost* families much
further. In the end, the Russian courts ordered additional compensation only
for those who had lost a breadwinner in the family—meaning that only
underage children, widows, and elderly pensioners would get anything, about
20 percent of the victims. Those who did get compensation were awarded
anywhere from $10 to $500 a month. Tatyana Karpova won 615 rubles a
month, about $21, for her dead son. "The government," she concluded, "eval-
uated the life of our children as the price of a puppy dog."[34]

IT DID NOT take a high-profile lawsuit to test the limits of judicial reform as
Putin's first term came to an end. It took only a drive down the streets of
Moscow. For years, traffic police known as GAI (pronounced *guy-EE*) had
terrorized motorists, empowered to pull anyone over at random with the
flick of their white batons.[35] No matter how law-abiding the driver, the *gaishniki*, as they were called, always managed to find a violation, real or imagined.
While crazy Zhiguli drivers careened past at breakneck speed, ignoring lane
markers, zipping in and out of traffic, the *gaishniki* would scold their chosen
prey for an incorrect date on one of the many documents required to be kept
in the glove compartment. Then they would extract the normal bribe, often
just fifty or one hundred rubles ($1.70 or $3.40). This was such a regular
occurrence that we were once pulled over three times in a single twenty-four-
hour period while showing around visitors from the United States. Putin's
promises to reform the justice system inevitably proved incapable of tackling
this petty everyday corruption. The husband of a Russian friend made the
mistake of refusing to pay $100 demanded by a particularly greedy *gaishnik*

and insisted on being taken to the police station instead. In the end, he was forced to pay a $200 bribe to the station commander.

More than 80 percent of Russians surveyed during the Putin era considered police corrupt, and 25 percent of them considered themselves victims of police abuse, a number that shocked only because it seemed so low.[36] Evidently most people did not believe the extraction of money by *gaishniki* constituted police abuse since we had never met a single Russian who had not been shaken down. So in 2003, as Igor Bortnikov was going on trial and Tatyana Karpova was suing the state, human rights activists Natalya Taubina and Pavel Chikov started the Public Verdict Foundation to empower ordinary people to resist official mistreatment. "We're trying to compete with the state monopoly and destroy it," Chikov told us.[37] But they found the people they wanted to help were as much of a problem as those they wanted to rein in. "They don't believe that it's possible to defend their rights through courts. The police are corrupted and it's easier to give money instead of defending their rights," Taubina said. She sighed. "It's a Soviet mentality. The system had and still has huge power and can do whatever it wants." The Putin reforms, she said, had added up to little. "I'm not optimistic about how it's discussed and what the state is trying to do." If anything, she said, "it's getting worse and worse."[38]

The advent of nationwide jury trials was supposed to start changing that. But the early experience revealed the weaknesses in the system just as Sergei Pashin had feared. Just 8 percent of cases went to juries, and those that went to judges held no more suspense than in Soviet days. In two Moscow district courts, not a single defendant was acquitted in 2003. In the regional court in the southern territory of Krasnodar, no one had been acquitted in ten years. Judges who defied the trend found themselves out, just as Pashin had.[39] Even jury trials, with a 15 percent acquittal rate, proved easily manipulated. A few months after the Igor Bortnikov trial in Moscow, another court in the Siberian city of Krasnoyarsk heard the case of a Russian space scientist accused of spying for China, part of the spate of spy cases brought by the FSB under Putin. Valentin Danilov, a physics professor who spent nineteen months in prison awaiting trial, denied that he had agreed to sell secret satellite technology to the Chinese. It was the first espionage case ever to go to a jury in post-Soviet Russia, and the panel found Danilov not guilty. But the Russian Supreme Court overturned the acquittal on the grounds that the defense lawyers had put "pressure" on the jury by referring to documents that were not entered into evidence. In fact, such results were not uncommon. In the United States, a not-guilty verdict is the end of the game because of the prohibition against double jeopardy. In Russia, prosecutors could and regularly did appeal acquittals with great success. The Russian Supreme Court overruled 32 percent of jury acquittals it considered in 2002.[40] In at least two instances, according to experts, a defendant won acquittal three times and three times the Supreme Court rejected the decisions and ordered new trials. "If they want a conviction, they'll just keep redoing it until they get the verdict they like," said Stephen C. Thaman, a law professor at St. Louis University who spent years studying Russia's troubled jury trial experiment.[41]

International courts during Putin's tenure turned in their own negative verdicts on Russian justice, with judges or government officials in Spain, Greece, Britain, Denmark, and the United States rejecting politically driven extradition requests from Moscow.[42] By joining the European Convention on Human Rights, Russia had accepted the jurisdiction of the European Court of Human Rights, and Russians were beating a path to Strasbourg to lodge their complaints. By the time Igor Bortnikov was going on trial, about 13,600 cases from Russia had been filed in Strasbourg, more than from any other country.[43] Among the petitioners was Tatyana Glazkova, herself a former Russian judge; Glazkova was fired after complaining about alleged manipulation of cases by the chief judge of her court.[44] Vladimir Gusinsky, the ousted owner of NTV, also went to Strasbourg and eventually won. The European court ruled that the state's actions against Gusinsky "insistently suggest that the applicant's prosecution was used to intimidate him" into giving up his media empire. Still, the court did not restore his holdings, concluding instead that the symbolic victory of its ruling and $106,000 in legal fees were enough.[45]

Tatyana Karpova, Zoya Chernetsova, and the other *Nord-Ost* families decided to take their grievances to the European court as well. "The court system in Russia as such doesn't exist at all," Karpova told us. "The courts aren't an independent institution. They're completely under the control of our government. . . . We have to go to the end and prove there are guilty ones for what happened and hold them accountable."[46]

THE YELLING in the jury room during deliberations over the fate of Igor Bortnikov reached such a crescendo that we could hear it clearly out in the corridor. "You interrupted me again!" a man's voice cried out. "You don't let me finish!"

Under Russian rules, the jury had no more than three hours to deliberate. From the moment they entered the room, Lyubov Pavlyuk was determined to keep her fellow jurors from upholding the murder charge. A fifty-six-year-old homemaker with pulled-back hair, watery eyes, and a sharp tongue, Pavlyuk argued it would be wrong to pin the murder solely on Bortnikov when his friends had obviously participated as well. For three hours, she waged a loud and aggressive campaign for acquittal, often butting heads with the foreman.[47]

"She didn't let anybody talk," Larisa Baidina, a thirty-six-year-old unemployed cook with dyed-red hair, told us afterward. "She was yelling, and if anybody disagreed, she screamed and said, 'You don't get it.'" But Baidina and others ultimately agreed with Pavlyuk's point to a degree. "Nobody said they were satisfied with the evidence, that he did it, he was guilty."

Pavlyuk pushed until the panel concluded that the defendant assaulted the victim but was not necessarily the killer. "Some of these people were so convinced," she said later. "It was so hard to change their minds."

Out in the corridor at the time, the defendant's mother, grandmother, and girlfriend huddled on benches. "I'm shaking all over my body," said Tamara Bortnikova, forty-six years old, who had raised her son alone after divorcing and admitted struggling with his teenage drug use. We asked why he initially signed a statement implicating himself. She simply shook her head in disgust. "Because he's a fool." She worried that the jurors would not believe that he had signed under pressure. "I wish they were younger," she sighed. "I looked at them and thought how old they are."

At 8 p.m. on the eighth day of the trial, the jury returned to the courtroom with its answer. Bortnikov studied their faces intently. Most refused to look at him, but one juror winked at the defense attorneys. It would take nearly two more hours for the jury, sent back repeatedly to the back room, to figure out how to express its will properly. Russian jurors were charged with making not just a simple choice of guilty or innocent but with deciding whether certain key elements of the case had been proven. The judge had given them six questions to answer, some of them spelled out over multiple single-spaced pages. Finally, the jury voted nine to three to convict Bortnikov of assault but not murder.

The next day, the prosecution asked for a twenty-year sentence on the theory that the facts as determined by the jury still amounted to attempted murder. But Shtunder rejected that argument, giving Bortnikov ten years instead. The prosecutor and the victim's father left the courtroom vowing to appeal. Bortnikov smiled just a bit as the guards put handcuffs on him to lead him back to jail. "Only my attorneys' skills and the fact that I had a jury saved me," he told us later from jail on the contraband mobile phone. "If it had been like it was before, with just one judge, nobody would have listened to me or my attorneys." One of his lawyers, Vladimir Zherebenkov, thought the verdict would send a message of hope for the system. "Now the number of people asking for jury trials will grow," he predicted. "People will start to believe." That's just what the prosecutor was afraid of. "Jury trials are practically all over Russia now," said Loktionov. "We just can't get away from them."

The jurors returned home to digest the experience. None of them had ever held such responsibility before, and it had been both empowering and nerve-racking. "There was a little bit of fear—not fear, but worry—about making the wrong decision," said Vera Navrotskaya, the bookkeeper. "It was constant work for your soul, your mind, and your heart." After so many years of being shut out of the system, it felt good finally to play a part. In the end, they expressed a bit of the Russian public's deep distrust of its government. "The fact is that the doubts were really powerful," said Tatyana Yegorova, thirty-five, who started the deliberations as an advocate for conviction. "People have been skeptical for a long time. That's the history of our country. Otherwise you don't survive. To live your life in doubt is hard, but to trust all the time is hopelessly naive."

Back in the USSR

The most prepared people decided to take charge.
—VLADIMIR SHAPGAYEV

WHEN WE FIRST MET Viktor Cherkesov, he was ensconced in the splendor of a newly restored St. Petersburg palace, overlooking the fast-flowing spring flood in the Neva River.[1] Until just a few months earlier, the palace—said to be the last one built by the doomed Romanov princes before the 1917 revolution—had been one of the city's marriage registration bureaus, a favorite of St. Petersburg brides because of its prime waterfront location just across the river from the Hermitage Museum, and because it was the only one in the city where marriages involving foreigners could be registered. Now it was Cherkesov's headquarters, and the brides, despite a public outcry, had to go elsewhere for their marriage papers. In the spring of 2001 Cherkesov was the just-appointed presidential envoy for northwest Russia, one of the new supergovernors sent to impose the Kremlin's will on recalcitrant regional barons. He was also a longtime KGB colleague of Vladimir Putin's.

In the waning days of the Soviet Union, Cherkesov had been one of the last of the Leningrad dissident hunters, a KGB investigator in the department's infamous Fifth Directorate who was still tracking down wrong-thinking artists and jailing them at the same time that Mikhail Gorbachev's glasnost was making such political persecutions obsolete. Among former dissidents, it was still an article of faith that Cherkesov was the last KGB agent to successfully launch a case for "anti-Soviet activities."[2] He later went on to head the St. Petersburg regional office of the FSB, where his men initiated a controversial spy case against environmentalist Aleksandr Nikitin, who had blown the whistle on Russian nuclear pollution of the Barents Sea. When Putin was named FSB director in 1998, Cherkesov moved to Moscow with him as his top deputy. He became known for setting up a new system requiring Internet providers to allow agents access to private e-mail accounts.

By the advent of Putin's presidency, Cherkesov was an obvious choice to help lead Putin's campaign to make the country's eighty-nine regions once again bow to the federal center. And he quickly settled in to his new role as a presidential envoy, becoming a political player in St. Petersburg with more than enough clout to commandeer Wedding Palace Number 3—and the resources to renovate it in record time. On the day we met, Cherkesov had come to his office from the opening of an exhibit at the Russian State Archives dedicated to the history of the governors-general who had ruled large swaths of Russian territory as the "eyes and ears of the tsar" from the age of Peter the Great up until the revolution. He was openly contemplating the historical comparison. In Russia, he told us, "Through all times, there is a need to have supreme state control over the activity of local bureaucrats."[3]

Like many of Putin's inner circle, Cherkesov was a believer not only in "supreme state control" but also in the Soviet-era KGB methods used to obtain it. To those who knew him, he projected utter confidence in the secret police, convinced they were "like the Masons, given tasks by God," as a senior Russian official put it.[4] Cherkesov was also defiantly unapologetic about his role in suppressing freedom of speech and his relentless pursuit of independent-minded intellectuals during the late Soviet era. "In the KGB, I was not torturing people, I was not executing people, I was not deceiving, and I was not breaking the law," Cherkesov told us. "So I am not aware of anything I did that would have made me ashamed of my service." And he thought it was not only Putin's right, but his duty, to fill the senior posts of the Russian government with veterans of the Soviet secret police. Why, he demanded to know derisively, should Putin give jobs to "feminists and environmentalists" when the security of the country was at stake? These were, he lectured us, "tense times."[5]

Cherkesov was the prototype of the Putin-era appointee, the first of many KGB agents we would meet who had evolved over time into post-Soviet power brokers. Eventually, Kremlin watchers would realize that the rise of such *siloviki* had been a central aspect of Putin's presidency, a conscious project to remake the Russian elite in the president's image. By the close of his first term in office, veterans of the secret services and the military had come to constitute 25 percent of the country's senior officials, up from 11 percent under Boris Yeltsin and just 3 percent under Mikhail Gorbachev, according to the Russian Academy of Sciences' Institute of Sociology.[6] Like Putin, many still proudly called themselves chekists. "There are no former chekists," Putin once told a questioner on a television call-in show, and indeed experts pointed out that a KGB officer almost never really left—he was either on assignment or part of the agency's so-called active reserves.[7]

"There is a snowball effect caused by the clan structure of power in Russia. Putin, for example, brings ten FSB agents with him to power, and each of them brings ten more, and so on and so on," said Olga Kryshtanovskaya, the sociologist who conducted the Academy of Sciences studies. "It's a brotherhood of chekists." Her research showed how quickly the process had worked since Putin had come to power. When Putin created seven presidential envoys to oversee the Russian regions, five came from military or secret service backgrounds, as did 70 percent of the fifteen hundred staff members each of them eventually hired. Putin named his friend and fellow former KGB spy Sergei Ivanov to head his Security Council, then shifted him over in 2001 to run the huge Defense Ministry. Putin's eventual choice to head the equally unwieldy Interior Ministry was another KGB alumnus and general from the FSB, Rashid Nurgaliyev. Deputies at the press, transportation, foreign affairs, and economic development ministries were also from the special services; overall, 35 percent of the deputy ministers named during Putin's tenure were *siloviki*, according to Kryshtanovskaya's data. Hundreds more were named to less public postings in the government. FSB generals came to power with Kremlin support as elected governors in the regions of Ingushetia, Smolensk, and Voronezh. In the two houses of parliament, as many as thirty deputies and senators from the special services formed a powerful caucus. Inside the Kremlin, KGB veterans controlled access to the president's schedule, his information department, and his security council. Many of these appointees were not only from the secret services but were also the president's fellow Leningraders, like Putin's choice for FSB chief, Nikolai Patrushev. Together, they formed a clan of sorts from Russia's northern capital that Moscow wags dubbed the Northern Alliance, in reference to the Afghan guerrilla force of the same name.[8]

Putin had turned out to be a faithful believer in one of the most oft-quoted bromides of the Soviet era, Joseph Stalin's declaration that "the cadres decide everything."[9] In placing his cadre of former KGB agents strategically throughout the government, Putin aimed to create a core group of loyalists who would challenge the rule of the corrupted bureaucrats that he believed had taken hold in the Yeltsin era. He also hoped to restore the formerly tarnished prestige and status of the KGB, and despite the millions of victims of the agency's excesses still living in Russia, Putin as president rarely missed a chance to promote the latter-day mythology of the KGB as a proud, professional Soviet elite.

The Putin cadre did not yet have the power to decide everything, as the saying would have it. But when we first encountered his presidential envoys to the regions, they were busy trying to undo the effects of the Yeltsin revolution, systematically forcing regional governors and legislatures to overturn thousands of local laws in conflict with federal ones, taking back control over regional branches of federal ministries—such as the prosecutors and the national police—that had in effect been privatized by local power brokers, firing hundreds of officials and setting themselves up as rival political forces to the entrenched regional powers. In some places they cut deals; in others, they simply moved to put Putin's stamp on the place, regardless of the local authorities.[10] "They may be clenching their teeth," Putin's friend Cherkesov told us, "but they are submitting."[11]

As in St. Petersburg, the new presidential envoys often used methods gleaned from the Soviet past. "These guys are coming to power everywhere," observed Nikolai Petrov, an expert on Russian politics at the Carnegie Moscow Center. "They bring with them the mentality and the methods they think are appropriate, and these methods are a continuation of old Soviet KGB techniques," such as consolidating control over the media and using material from secret files to compromise rivals. "They have abnormal resources. That's why they're so dangerous."[12]

Several years later, we met Cherkesov again in Moscow. The presidential envoys were by now established powers in their regions, tax revenues once more flowed through the Moscow center. Yeltsin's 1992 exhortation to the regions to take "all the sovereignty you can swallow" now seemed like a quaint anachronism. Governors had learned to accommodate the demands of their new overseers or face the Kremlin's wrath at election time. Except for marginalized Communists or the remnants of the Soviet-era dissidents, few now directly challenged the rule of the generals under Putin. Inside the Kremlin, the president's fellow chekists were ascendant and on the offensive against the remnants of the Yeltsin-era elite. Yet when the subject turned to the power of the *siloviki* under Putin, Cherkesov was typically understated. So much, he said, had been written about their influence that an unshakable impression had taken hold in the eyes of the public: "We are like some kind of demigods," Cherkesov said wryly of the reputation that had attached itself to Putin's KGB cadre, "doing something that will either save Russia or badly damage it."[13]

To ALL EXCEPT the most alarmist of dissidents, such renewed power in the hands of the KGB would have been unthinkable a dozen years earlier. Sergei Grigoryants was the alarmist exception. A gaunt man who pursued official malfeasance with a persistence that infuriated his targets, Grigoryants had made exposing the misdeeds of the KGB his personal mission for decades. He had survived Soviet jails and exile—twice—and the tragic death of his son in the early 1990s, a never-solved killing he blamed on the agency. After the collapse of the Soviet Union and the official dissolution of the KGB, Grigoryants had a brief moment of cooperation with the new Yeltsin establishment. He brought together current and former spies, KGB dissident-hunters, and the intelligentsia they had so recently persecuted for an unprecedented conference in Moscow's Parliamentary Center. It was 1993, and soon enough after the Soviet fall that emotions on the conference's subject, "The KGB: Yesterday, Today, and Tomorrow," still ran high. Radio stations broadcast live from the meetings, and the auditorium was filled to capacity. The discussion was so heated that Grigoryants had to cancel the breaks. "The myth about the omnipotent KGB has been destroyed," declared Vadim Bakatin, the last head of the Soviet KGB, in his speech.[14]

The KGB had officially been dismantled at the time of the demise of the Soviet Union in December 1991, not long after its leaders had helped organize the failed August coup against Gorbachev. A Russian Security Ministry had taken its place, while many of its core functions—such as the border guard service, foreign intelligence, electronic surveillance, and Kremlin security—had been broken off into newly constituted separate agencies. Its budget was slashed, and those who could scrambled to find new jobs.[15] Most of the democrats advising Yeltsin believed they had successfully crushed the hold of the KGB on Russian public life, even without any legal process or truth commission to hold the agents of the Soviet police state accountable. The archives were opening up, the dark secrets of the past tumbling out. They paid little attention to the unprecedented exodus of the KGB's cadres into public life and business and the upper reaches of the rest of the vast Russian bureaucracy. Or to the hundreds of thousands of KGB agents still serving in one branch or another of the far-flung security services.

The present danger seemed elsewhere, in the rise of hard-line Russian nationalists like Vladimir Zhirinovsky, whose misnamed Liberal Democratic Party would vault into parliament through elections later that year. "It was very fashionable then to talk about the threat of fascism," Grigoryants recalled. "I took the floor and said of course the threat of fascism is very important, but I would suggest paying attention to the organization which exerted very strong influence on the intelligentsia, the KGB. The hall just froze in fright. In ninety-three people didn't say such things from the stage."[16]

He was not the only one to make the point. Vadim Bakatin flatly told the conference-goers that they were deluding themselves if they believed the KGB he had once directed was dead. "The myth about the KGB collapsed, it is for sure, but the KGB has survived," he said. "It is possible to find out that they are among the few institutions which managed to protect themselves against the revolutionary drive intended to dissolve all similar structures and instead attained the path of evolution rather than revolution. They have never lost control."[17] Over the next few years, as his conferences became a post-Soviet tradition, Grigoryants would continue to sound the warning. "We kept saying how the influence of the special services of Russia is growing," he recalled. "Nobody wanted to listen."[18]

Yeltsin and his aides reshuffled the former KGB bureaucracy several more times. After 1993, when his confrontation with the Communist-dominated parliament led briefly to armed standoff, the president renamed the security ministry the Federal Counterintelligence Service and took steps to bring it even more directly under the Kremlin's control—into his fist, as the Russian saying had it. Reformers debated among themselves the proper role and functions for the post-Soviet secret services, but in the midst of Yeltsin's epic political struggles and a seemingly endless series of economic crises, the debate never engaged the broader public. Bakatin had cautioned back at that first conference on the KGB that real reform would never take place unless Russia itself became a democracy, a remote prospect at a time when Yeltsin was turning to force to solve his impasse with the recalcitrant legislature, then rewrote the constitution after he had emerged victorious. "In order to have democratic special services," Bakatin had said, "it is necessary at least to have democracy."[19]

By 1995, the agency had morphed again, into its current form as the Federal Security Service, or FSB. It was the sixth name for the ministry in just four years.[20] The ministry reported directly to the president, as did the other "power ministries," and had regained still more of the KGB's former functions. "A special service far more powerful than the now-defunct KGB has been created under the law," warned one of the Moscow liberal tabloids.[21]

But again the debate remained confined to a small circle of KGB watchers, many of whom had already concluded by 1996 that the political stage had been set for Russians to endorse the return of a Soviet-style law-and-order man and the security services to match. "It is wrong to depict the KGB's successor organization as an impotent, shattered bureaucracy," U.S. scholar Amy Knight wrote that year. "The political climate itself has worked in favor of a strong security service." In a Russia beset by a "weak and unstable" economy, "epidemic" crime, and internal political struggles, "people yearn for the rigid law and order of the past." And a president born of the KGB, she made clear, was unlikely ever to foster Russia's nascent democracy. It was, she concluded, simply "incompatible with a security apparatus wielding the power and influence that it still holds in Russia."[22]

THE ASCENSION of Vladimir Putin marked the second time in two decades that a KGB man had run Russia, and as his first term unfolded, many compared what was happening inside the government with the brief reign of former Soviet KGB chief Yuri Andropov in the 1980s. Under both men, the secret services set themselves up in opposition to what they considered a corrupt bureaucracy, while moving to silence critical voices outside the government. Putin almost self-consciously seemed to take Andropov as his model and posthumous mentor, making a pilgrimage to lay flowers on Andropov's grave not long before becoming president and restoring the plaque to Andropov at the former KGB headquarters on Lubyanka Square. By 2004, Andropov had become the first Soviet leader to be honored with a new monument in the post-Soviet era when a taxpayer-funded memorial went up in the northern border region of Karelia. The vogue for Andropov was such that members of Putin's chekist cadre hung calendars with his image over their desks ("Any country needs myths," said one ex-agent of his Andropov office decor), and newspapers were full of earnest commentary about how the Soviet Union might have been saved if only Andropov had not died months into his tenure as general secretary.[23]

"Putin is the inheritor of Andropov," said Gennady Gudkov, a KGB major who founded a large security company selling the services of former spies like himself before launching a career in politics as a leader of a Kremlin-linked party in parliament. Gudkov described a "brotherhood" of Putin subordinates who believed they had a monopoly on upholding the integrity of the Russian state—and the opportunity with Putin to put their plans into action after what they perceived as the indignities of the Yeltsin era. "The *siloviki* have the mentality of state service. They're used to discipline, they're more organized, they're more precise, more concrete in fulfilling their tasks," Gudkov told us. They were also convinced they belonged to a special fraternity along with the president. "Officers of the special services had access to secret information, giving people who belong to this caste a feeling of deeper knowledge of life. For them, it's much easier to agree with each other. They speak the same language, they understand the real reason standing behind events. This is the secret of their *kooperativnost,* like a Masonic lodge."[24]

We were to hear variants on Gudkov's fraternity-of-like-minded-men from nearly all the KGB veterans we spoke with, as we spent hours with more than a dozen onetime agents trying to understand what made Putin's

KGB-tinged elite different from the Yeltsin cadre of economic reformers, ex-dissidents, and onetime party bosses. Many of the former officers—now in top executive positions, or working as governors, legislators, and senior government appointees—believed, as KGB-spy-turned-billionaire-banker Aleksandr Lebedev told us in his skyscraper office, that to be one of the *siloviki* in Russia was to hold "a noble job in a noble country."[25] They were not ideologues, unless fervent belief in the greatness of Russia counted as an ideology. Instead, they bragged of their superior education, as if the KGB had been not the enforcers of the police state but a club of Harvard graduates embarking on careers in public service. Many mentioned the KGB's effort to instill a sense of professionalism in its recruits, a striking exception in a society whose language does not include a word for "efficiency." And nearly all of them insisted that the KGB's pride of place came from its uniqueness as an institution allowed to tell—or at least know—the truth about the decline and decay of the late Soviet era.

"It was Soviet foreign intelligence which pushed ahead perestroika more than Mr. Gorbachev himself. That was the only institution which was allowed to report to the Politburo about reality," Lebedev said, elaborating a version of history we were to hear many times from other KGB veterans as he recalled his days as a spy in London during the late Cold War years, when he reported on Britain from his cover as a midlevel trade official. "You could have been punished. But at least you could say that it was not your opinion, but the opinion of a foreign expert or foreign government. Sometimes you could use that trick. Sometimes you could report truthful information by [presenting arguments] about whether it is good or bad for the country to move troops into Afghanistan or that private property is more efficient for the economy than the Soviet model. . . . The Soviet sources, except for intelligence, were trying to report to the Politburo what they wanted to hear."[26]

Many onetime KGB agents like Andrei Przhezdomsky were given to repeating the line, almost certainly apocryphal, attributed to the late dissident leader Andrei Sakharov. Despite his long exile in Gorky and years of hounding by the KGB, Sakharov supposedly paid the KGB the compliment of calling it "the least corrupted" institution of Soviet society. Przhezdomsky briefly worked in the Kremlin under Yeltsin, became deputy head of the KGB-style tax police, and had under Putin started a new foundation to monitor elections that insiders believed was backed by the Kremlin. He claimed to have been outraged by what he saw in government in the 1990s. "An adventurer or a scammer or a person with a criminal background" could never have risen under the Soviet system. So, of course, the *siloviki* had to take charge again. "At the current point of our country's development," he insisted, "these people are required in power."[27]

In many ways, their descriptions did not vary that greatly from the portrait of the latter-day KGB offered by independent scholars, who also concluded that Putin's choice to rely on his fellow police-state spies was a natural outgrowth of the KGB's unique role in the Soviet Union. Nikita Petrov had spent his career as a historian for the human rights group Memorial trying to understand how the Soviet secret services operated. He had come to believe, just as Gennady Gudkov and the other agents themselves did, that Putin's KGB cadre was inevitable for a president who came from a closed institution that stressed loyalty to the state and the brotherhood over any ideology. "The explanation is the nature of the Soviet KGB—its clan aspects, its closedness. It's a mafiosi organization from which it is impossible to leave. A person stays forever because he is a 'made' man," Petrov told us. After years of poring through agents' memoirs and party archives, he had come to understand that chekists did constitute "a hidden opposition to the party" in the late Soviet era not because they were liberal reformers but because they were statists who understood the system's dangerous weakness. "They said we are servants of the state and separated themselves from party ideology."

By the Putin era, their ascendancy was in some ways even more unchecked than in Soviet times, when the KGB at least nominally served the Communist Party. Now, Petrov noted, "It's an organization that no longer needs to resort to tricks of the Soviet type, when everything had to be masked behind talk about service to the party, to the world revolutionary process. In a way, it's easier because they no longer need this. Now they've stripped ideology out, and their new ideological version is service to the state. They consider the interests of the people only when they do not conflict with the interests of the state." Putin inevitably promoted others with the KGB stamp, Petrov had concluded. "They recognize each other by methods, from life, how he talks to you, how he looks you in the eye, what he says in conversation. It makes a permanent imprint on his way of life, and that's why there is the restoration of all Soviet methods . . . to use hidden levers to achieve your goals, never to tell openly what you really want, not to show interest—all the methods which employees of the secret services use."[28]

For Sergei Grigoryants, Putin's presidency became a time of watching his Cassandra-like predictions come true. He had spent years listening as KGB men bragged of their special fraternity. "You could call it Nietzschean," he told us one afternoon, in his apartment stuffed with family antiques and musty paintings that had improbably survived the Soviet era. "They consider themselves to be supermen. They say it was only they who understood what happened in the Soviet Union, and the world. They thought they could control it."

In late November 2002, Grigoryants scheduled his annual conference on the KGB. The theme would be straightforward: "Participation of the Russian Secret Services in Governing the Country." It had been years since top officials of the FSB or its sister agency, the Foreign Intelligence Service, participated in his gatherings. But now even former KGB operatives who had willingly shown up in the past refused to come. Vadim Bakatin, the headliner back at the first conference nearly a decade earlier, told Grigoryants that he had nothing new to say. Liberal reformers, too, started to bow out, including Aleksei Arbatov, the Yabloko party defense expert who had promised to speak on Andropov. When it came time for tickets to be handed out, Grigoryants found that many had simply been thrown away rather than distributed.

Left to preach to an audience of the converted, Grigoryants gave an angry talk entitled "Generals and Stool Pigeons Changed Places." It was to be the last conference he would be able to hold on the KGB, and "almost nobody noticed it," Grigoryants recalled. "Everybody understood what kind of country we lived in now."[29]

"I DON'T FEEL ashamed for any minute of it," Georgy Poltavchenko was telling us about his time in the KGB.[30] Another of Putin's seven presidential envoys to the regions, Poltavchenko, like Viktor Cherkesov, was an unrepentant veteran of the KGB, in his case after a career spent largely in counterintelligence. The president had placed him in charge of central Russia—superrich Moscow and the poverty-entangled regions that surrounded it, where paradoxically the geographic blessing of living close to the flourishing capital and the border with the West had not translated into the expected higher living standards. Instead, once-thriving industrial areas like the textile mills of Ivanovo or the black-earth farming belt around Voronezh had simply seen their economies implode, with nothing to replace them, while the environs of Moscow dealt with the opposite crises of unregulated runaway growth, forests clear-cut in the dead of night for housing developments, and an influx of migrant workers from all over the former Soviet Union. In Putin's Russia, there could be no bigger policy task than taking on the challenges of the country's most populated region, its economic, political, and spiritual center.

But Poltavchenko was, like the president he served, first and foremost a law-and-order man schooled in KGB techniques. "All my professional skills come from my service there," he told us. During his time as head of the St. Petersburg branch of the tax police under Yeltsin, the agency had become one of the most feared, and politicized, tools of the new Russia.[31]

Now, Poltavchenko framed his role in terms of securing loyalty to the Moscow center. Unlike Yeltsin's formula urging the regions to take initiative away from the capital, Poltavchenko told us, "Nowadays, the slogan is 'Unite for the common idea—the formation of a stable society, and effective social and economic development of the state built on the basis of this stability.'"[32] That was it. No democracy, no free market. Just stability. And stability, he said, was a perfectly appropriate job for a KGB general, which is why Putin had turned to so many. In practice, the rule of the generals like Poltavchenko would emphasize hard-hitting politics, and his stamp was soon felt on the region in systematic attacks on independent power centers—whether contrarian-minded governors he sought to oust or regional media that were shut down when their editorial lines did not square with the new order. Poltavchenko first dabbled in electoral politics in Voronezh, a rough-edged agricultural area south of Moscow where the local FSB early on in Putin's tenure charged a young American exchange student with drug possession and implied he was a spy. Just months into his tenure, Poltavchenko backed another KGB veteran, Vladimir Kulakov, for governor. Kulakov, once tasked with spying on foreign students at Voronezh's state university, won, beating out the Communist incumbent. Later, his chief political rival, the mayor of Voronezh, resigned under threat of prison by Kulakov's FSB colleagues and dropped plans to run against him.[33]

But nowhere were Poltavchenko's tactics better on display than in the western border region of Smolensk, a historic crossroads 250 miles to the west of Moscow where Russians had battled a succession of Polish, French, and German invaders over the centuries. Although it straddled the main highway connecting the country to Western Europe, Smolensk had become a byword for the failings of the 1990s, gripped by a wave of organized crime attracted by the region's large diamond-cutting factory and vodka distilleries in addition to its prime geographic location. Poltavchenko and his team blamed the mess on the Communist governor, Aleksandr Prokhorov, and launched a campaign to oust him from office in the 2002 elections. Their candidate was another member of the brotherhood, FSB major general Viktor Maslov.[34]

In Soviet times, Maslov told us, he had hunted down "security risks" at Smolensk's nuclear power plant and otherwise searched out the enemy within, right down to the very end of the party dictatorship. He then spent years in the FSB chasing the gangland-style murderers who plagued the post-Soviet city until rising to head the FSB's regional office for Smolensk. He liked to call himself and men like him "soldiers of the tsar." And he was often given to expressing frustration about the overly democratic processes now in effect in Russian courts. Crime, he told us in an interview, would be much more efficiently prosecuted if only criminals could be held accountable as they were in 1937—at the height of Stalin's Great Terror, when the secret services sent millions to death or the gulag. Only after our stunned silence did Maslov move to correct himself. Of course, he added, "this is not acceptable" in the new Russia.

Maslov campaigned in 2002 using the argument that he had to run against the governor to stop the corruption that fueled the city's crime wave. Maslov used his secret service experience as a selling point, citing his access to information, his education, and his ability to manage people. He pledged "progressive" economic reforms. Poltavchenko openly backed him, eager to add another person to the "team of like-minded people" he told us he was building in central Russia.[35]

Maslov's Communist rivals tried to scare the public about the prospect of a KGB-led government. Leaflets were pasted up one night all over town not long before the election, posing "ten questions to General Maslov." They demanded to know why Maslov did not mention his FSB position in campaign materials, why his employees were under the "direct patronage" of criminal groups they were supposed to be catching, and whether he knew enough about the economy. Most pointedly, the leaflets raised the specter of the Stalinist repressions. Why, they asked, did Maslov believe "it would be good to arrange a new 1937"?[36]

Behind the scenes, Maslov was using his law-enforcement position against his political foes. In March 2002, a month after he registered as a candidate, his regional FSB secretly went to court for permission to eavesdrop on the phone calls of his incumbent opponent, Prokhorov, and the governor's first deputy, Anatoly Makarenko. The tap became publicly known only months later when the chief regional prosecutor confirmed it to a local newspaper.[37] Three days before the May election, Makarenko was riding in his car with his young daughter when gunfire hit the vehicle and killed the driver. The deputy governor immediately blamed the attack on Maslov.

But Maslov won the election with 40 percent to Prokhorov's 34 percent, and he quickly moved to put the secret service's stamp on Smolensk. He purged the regional administration's ranks, installed fellow KGB men in key departments, reined in the region's media, and declared war on Smolensk's reputation as a crime center. He brought in public relations specialists from Moscow recommended by the Kremlin. He also exacted revenge on his political rivals. In the year following the election, the former deputy governor, Makarenko, spent months in an FSB detention center on corruption charges, and the former governor, Prokhorov, was charged in another case investigated by Maslov's men. Both were later convicted.[38]

"We had to close the doors of this office to representatives of all criminal groups," Maslov told us in the governor's office, a grand if sparsely decorated affair with the obligatory Putin portrait over his desk. Until then, he said, Smolensk's economic recovery couldn't begin. "Before, people were afraid of going to Smolensk." Maslov went out of his way to cultivate a new, civilian image, down to the blue pinstripe suit he wore instead of his general's uniform and his smooth patter about attracting foreign investment. But in the governor's headquarters, not far from the city's famous hilltop cathedral and its supposedly miracle-working icon, the atmosphere was tinged with Soviet-era suspicions. The new deputy governor refused to meet with us but took time to chase us down as we waited at an elevator to berate us for going unescorted to an interview with one of Maslov's KGB lieutenants. "Foreigners are not allowed," he bellowed, although his own armed guards had let us in.

Maslov moved quickly to consolidate power by bringing in more fellow chekists to the regional administration. While none of his deputy governors was from the secret services, he acknowledged he had hired "people I can trust" from the FSB and put them in other key posts. "I left the security organs to follow my general. Many did," Viktor Khrol, head of the property department and a sixteen-year veteran of the KGB and FSB, told us. "He needed support from his own people who he could trust. We followed our general the same way people who worked with Putin followed him."[39]

The local media soon felt the change. Several editors were forced out, the newspaper backed by the previous governor was closed down, and a new one, *Smolenskaya Gazeta,* opened. One month, it printed thirty-two photographs of the governor in a single issue. "Any criticism about the ruling team was forbidden," said Pavel Filipenko, who resigned as editor of the regional edition of the popular national weekly newspaper *Argumenty i Fakty.* "They just forbade us to write anything bad about the governor. Ironically, under the Communists led by Prokhorov, we had much more freedom of speech."[40]

A year into Maslov's rule, many in Smolensk told us they were still puzzling over what it meant to have a secret service man in charge. "It's not going to lead to anything good," said Aleksandr Shilkin, an activist in the reformist Yabloko party. Even on fighting crime, he said, Maslov hadn't met expectations.[41] But to Maslov's backers, his election and the rise of fellow chekists like Putin elsewhere was an understandable response to post-Soviet turmoil. "I would never have thought that a chekist would become leader of a region," said Vladimir Shapgayev, a KGB counterintelligence veteran who ran a private security firm in Smolensk. "But with such serious changes, the government faced the problem of who is going to run the country. After such a cataclysm, the most prepared people decided to take charge to lead us out of a crisis."[42]

STANISLAV LEKAREV stuck out his hand with a mannered smile. "Call me Stanley," he said in a decent facsimile of an upper-crust English accent. It was impossible not to notice the tweed blazer and old-school tie he wore in the height of the Moscow summer. Twice, he had served as a KGB spy posted to the Soviet diplomatic mission in London; eventually, he went back to Moscow to serve in counterintelligence, overseeing Western turncoats such as the legendary Kim Philby as well as the more routine KGB drudgery of spying on foreign correspondents in even their most intimate moments. He loved to name-drop about the American reporters he had cultivated back in the early 1980s from his cover at the Foreign Ministry and reminisce about how he would impress them with views that seemed to correspond uncannily with their own—because he had secretly listened to their wiretapped apartments before meeting them. He also played the piano, "kissed the hands of the ladies," and embraced the part of a world-savvy gentleman in a place where there weren't many. "They liked me," he said, "because I knew a lot and I was good in conversation."

In Soviet terms, he was the elite, the urbane personification of what the Smolensk KGB-agent-turned-security-boss termed "the most prepared people." Today, Lekarev was also one of the few former KGB veterans still in Russia openly critical of Putin. Lekarev had been a protégé of former KGB general Oleg Kalugin, now in self-imposed exile in the United States and a biting critic of the Russian president. Putin's team of fellow KGB veterans from St. Petersburg was "very weak," Lekarev told us, composed of provincial outsiders to the strictly Moscow-centric hierarchy of the Soviet secret service. "The KGB officers from Petersburg have no experience. Moscow never gave them the chance to get experience. Moscow is the top of the mountain," he said. As for Putin, his KGB résumé seemed to a member of the agency privileged like Lekarev to be proof of an undistinguished career. "Putin is from the [East German] intelligence department, where the worst and weakest were collected," he said flatly.

But Lekarev, who lectured and wrote about the history of the Russian secret services, said he was sure that Putin's goal was to "re-create the former KGB, one hundred percent," and in many ways he saw the president succeeding in the methodical way that was the hallmark of the KGB training under Yuri Andropov. "They will try to re-create the former image of the KGB, they will use this inertia of respect for the KGB that exists," he said. "But it won't really be the KGB, because the people working there will have just three to five years' experience, and I had thirty to thirty-five years' experience and they will have teachers not like me. . . . Everybody who is now leading departments were the worst and weakest pupils of mine, and I'm in sorrow because I am still a patriot. . . . The special services are degraded."[43]

Few KGB veterans were so blunt, at least in public, during Putin's tenure. But the signs of the KGB restoration that Lekarev warned of were increasingly visible. In 2003, the FSB at the president's behest reacquired control over the border troops and government electronic surveillance—two key areas it had lost in the modest reforms of the Yeltsin era. Under Putin, the agency's budget went up each year, outpacing growth for other government ministries and eventually tripling its pre-Putin levels.[44] It was a sign of their ascendance that some former agents, such as Gennady Gudkov, complained that the chekist president should be doing even more. "Officers expected the special services to benefit," Gudkov told us, "but this is what Putin did not do. Part of their expectations never came true," although even hard-line critics allowed that Putin had done more than any figure of the post-Soviet era to bring the prestige back to a demoralized, discredited agency.[45]

For some of the KGB's cheerleaders in Russian public life, outright triumphalism was in the air. "For many years our activities were mixed with dirt. And morally it was very unpleasant and very unfair. We served our country and tried to do it honestly, and we cannot be held responsible for what was happening in the thirties. Putin has eliminated those constant public accusations," Igor Goloshchapov, a onetime major in the elite KGB Vympel unit, told us.[46] Vladimir Zhirinovsky, the radical ultranationalist whose rise in Russian politics had long been rumored to have been boosted by the KGB at the time of the Soviet collapse, drank vodka and gloated to reporters one day at the grave of St. Petersburg liberal reformer Galina Starovoitova, slain on her doorstep in 1998 in a long-unsolved political assassination. "She was fighting against the KGB, and where is she now?" Zhirinovsky said. "As for the KGB, it was, it is, and it will be."[47]

Increasingly, those few who spoke out against the renewed influence of the special services found themselves talking about the return of fear they thought had vanished along with the agency that enforced it. "There's a broad spectrum of fear, and it's a new thing; it's just appeared in Putin's time," said Lev Ponomaryov, a Soviet-era dissident who now led the activist group For Human Rights. "It would be wrong to say Soviet times have come back already, because I'm one of the fiercest critics and here I am in Moscow talking to you. But it's the tendency of those times coming back." Or, as Konstantin Remchukov, a liberal politician close to big business, told us, "People have a genetic memory of those years. They're scared to death."[48]

A series of dubious spy cases initiated and vigorously prosecuted by the FSB was the first signal, going back to Putin's friend Viktor Cherkesov and his decision in the 1990s to pursue environmentalist Aleksandr Nikitin. Nikitin, a former naval officer, worked for the Norwegian environmental group Bellona and was accused of spying in 1996, beginning a legal odyssey that only ended with his acquittal in 2000. In May 1998, the FSB arrested physicist Valentin Danilov, director of a research institute at Krasnoyarsk State University, and accused him of giving the Chinese classified information. He claimed he had only passed along open-source material from scientific journals and the like and even won acquittal at a jury trial. The FSB responded by demanding a retrial on questionable procedural grounds, and a more pliant jury that included a KGB officer convicted him. And then there was the case of Igor Sutyagin, a young researcher at the Institute of USA and Canada Studies. He was accused of spying for allegedly passing classified materials on weapons systems to U.S. agents. Like Danilov, he claimed to have worked on a routine research contract, gathering public materials on the Internet and from academic publications. First arrested in 1999, he languished in jail and went through two court trials before the FSB secured a conviction and a fifteen-year sentence in 2004.[49]

To scholars like our friend Sergei Ivanov, such signals were unmistakable. Ivanov, a Byzantine historian, recalled an incident with a Swiss graduate student who contacted him and asked to be accredited by Ivanov's institute so he could do research in the Russian archives. Ivanov's boss rejected the idea, telling Ivanov, "He could be a spy." Later, FSB agents showed up at the institute demanding a list of scholars with foreign contacts. In the 1990s, such an action would have drawn public protest and cries of outrage. But the scholars of the Putin era simply acceded. "This is characteristic of today," Ivanov sighed.[50]

Others who openly challenged the FSB now feared retaliatory tactics straight out of the KGB's old playbook. Apostates came in for especially harsh treatment. Lawyer Mikhail Trepashkin, a former FSB investigator, publicly accused the FSB of playing a role in the 1999 apartment bombings that the government blamed on Chechen rebels. Just before he was supposed to go to court to press his theory, Trepashkin was arrested by police and accused of carrying a gun in his car—a gun he said was planted.[51]

In the internal republic of Ingushetia, the Kremlin-backed rise of FSB general Murat Zyazikov to the presidency of the unstable region next to Chechnya led to fears that the agency could now operate there with deadly impunity. "We have a Bermuda triangle here," a bodyguard for a local prosecutor whispered to us. Another prosecutor, Rashid Ozdoyev, had recently disappeared after pursuing reports that a wave of local kidnappings might have been the work not of criminal gangs but of the FSB itself. Ozdoyev vanished soon after getting off an airplane from Moscow, where he had delivered a fourteen-page report outlining FSB abuses. The agency denied any involvement in his disappearance, but refused to investigate aggressively; Ozdoyev never turned up. "It looks like the special services took him," his friend and fellow prosecutor Mikhail Akhiliyev told us in a hushed conversation in the corridor of their office. "It's absolutely outrageous," added his father, Boris. "The power of the FSB is enormous."[52]

AND THEN there was Viktor Cherkesov's new project. By the close of Putin's first term in office, his friend had left his post as presidential envoy to take command of a newly created army of forty thousand drug fighters—four times more than the U.S. Drug Enforcement Agency. For Cherkesov, the Federal Drug Control Agency was a powerful fiefdom that had taken much of Putin's presidency to assemble. He had first pushed Putin to create the new agency in late 2001, arguing it was necessary not only because of the massive nature of Russia's newfound drug habit but also because of what he told us was "widespread corruption" among those police supposed to be dealing with it.[53] In mid-2003, the agency was unveiled, and it inherited much of the personnel and infrastructure of the feared tax police, ostensibly dismantled after growing criticism of its nearly unchecked powers and armed raids on businesses.

Aleksandr Duka had hardly heard of the new drug agency when the emergency call came into his Bon-Ton Pet Clinic. The amiable Moscow veterinarian did what he always did in such cases: loaded up his medical bag in his car, prepared a syringe full of the anesthetic ketamine, and prepared to operate on an injured dog. But Duka's callers were actually agents working for Cherkesov, and the emergency for which he had been summoned turned out to be an unusual government sting operation. Soon, Duka was facing criminal charges of drug possession for using the only anesthetic widely available in Russia for treating animals; the stiff penalties he faced were Soviet-era holdovers, like the agents doing the arresting. More cases against veterinarians followed, close to two dozen in all. And veterinarians were not the only group targeted by the new agency. Doctors and dentists, vendors of popular T-shirts with marijuana leaves on them, and booksellers who sold tomes on the medical uses of narcotics were also singled out.

Critics soon came to view the Federal Drug Control Agency as the prototypical Putin-era government body, a sort of reincarnated KGB employing Soviet-era tactics to suppress alternate points of view and running symbolic campaigns while failing to tackle the sources of the Russian drug business. Stuffed with officials who had spent their careers in the KGB along with Cherkesov, the agency boasted victories that often amounted to token blows against uncertain threats, such as persuading a court to declare leaflets urging a change in Russian policy illegal pro-drug "advertising" and seeking the closure of clean-needle programs aimed at fighting the country's growing AIDS epidemic among intravenous drug users. "It's classic Russian bureaucracy—to search not where something is lost but where the light is hanging," said Vladimir Pribylovsky, a political analyst who ran the Moscow-based Panorama think tank. "It's easier to fight against books than heroin or terrorists."[54]

When we met at his new headquarters in the redone tax-police building not far from the Kremlin in Moscow's Kitai-Gorod neighborhood, Cherkesov acknowledged certain "mistakes" and "difficulties" as his agency started work, but said they were mostly bad public relations. "Society doesn't always understand what we are doing and why," he said. On the veterinarians, for example, "I believe we did make a mistake, not in the application of the law but in explaining our position to the society." As for book seizures, he allowed that perhaps employees needed to be more "sensitive," but also insisted the agency had targeted only books "that contain obvious propaganda information. What I mean is recipes for drug preparation, description of a person's state of mind on certain drugs as a way of advertising, which forms a desire in the reader to take these drugs."

In Soviet times, closed borders and police-state law enforcement had meant, as Cherkesov put it, that "the drug culture was virtually nonexistent." After the Soviet collapse, borders opened and drugs flooded in from Afghanistan and Central Asia, creating a new generation of drug users, many of whom graduated right to heroin, which led to needle-sharing and AIDS. Existing law-enforcement agencies were ill equipped to target the drug traffickers, and Cherkesov estimated that every tenth crime in the 1990s was drug-related. By 2003, Cherkesov said, the Russian drug business was worth $8 billion annually.[55]

But the drug-control department quickly earned a hard-line reputation under Cherkesov, and not for its tactics against the drug lords or the corrupt officials who helped them. When the Russian government made a rare move toward liberalization in the spring of 2004, increasing amounts of narcotics necessary to prosecute for criminal possession, Cherkesov's agency strenuously opposed the move. Cherkesov's top deputy, a former spokesman for the FSB, accused other parts of the government of acting on orders from the drug mafia in approving the measure.

"The head of the agency must secretly support the legalization of drugs. How else can you explain such idiotism that is going on—the fight with veterinarians, the fight with T-shirts, the fight with books?" said Nikolai Khramov, head of Russia's libertarian-oriented Radical Party. "In society, it just looks foolish." Khramov was arrested outside the agency's headquarters for handing out leaflets urging legalization of marijuana and a change in Russian drug policy. A court later found him guilty of "advertising" drugs and fined him $70. He hoped to make the case a test of free-speech guarantees and force the issue all the way to Russia's Constitutional Court.[56] "It goes in line with declining democracy in Russia," Aleksandr Petrov, a researcher at Human Rights Watch, said of Khramov's arrest. "I can't imagine you would be arrested like that five or six years ago. Now it looks like something normal under Putin."[57]

Khramov was not the only one to complain that the agency's agenda was cracking down on political dissent rather than drugs. Booksellers across the country had agents turn up bearing orders to confiscate books such as *Marijuana, Forbidden Medicine,* a book about the medical uses of marijuana first published in the United States by Yale University Press, and *Storming Heaven: LSD and the American Dream,* a social history about experiments with the hallucinogen. At the agency's behest, courts in the provincial cities of Ulyanovsk and Yekaterinburg fined bookstores for selling them. "It's an obvious attempt at censorship. It's in the same field as the government closing down TV channels," said Aleksandr Kasyanenko, a senior editor at Ultra Kultura publishing house, which published the books. "They're trying to create a feeling of fear among those who sell books. They want to convince them they should not sell books that are not approved by them."[58]

But the most attention was reserved for the veterinarian affair, in which about twenty animal doctors were charged by the drug police starting just months after the agency opened in the summer of 2003. Several were acquitted due to what judges said was lack of evidence, a striking outcome in a country where virtually all criminal defendants were still found guilty. Not Duka. He was found guilty even though parliament had already legalized the anesthetic ketamine. "They couldn't think of any civilized method of dealing with veterinarians," he said of the drug agency soon after his conviction. "Instead of trying to establish legal order, they chose this punitive method—but only in cases where there was no threat to society."[59]

On a late May evening in 2003, Putin unexpectedly appeared on Red Square. Earlier in the day, he had hosted Beatles legend Paul McCartney in the Kremlin, treating him to a private tour and reminiscing about his love for the Beatles' forbidden music at the same time he was a teenager pining to become a secret agent for the Soviet state. Their songs, he told McCartney, were "like a breath of fresh air, like a window on the outside world." Putin had not planned to attend McCartney's concert that night in the shadow of Lenin's tomb, but showed up anyway, midway through the show. McCartney had already played the one song everyone was waiting for, to wild cheers. But Putin asked for it again and McCartney obliged.

"Back in the USSR" echoed across the cobblestones for a second time. It was, McCartney told the audience, a request "from a very special person."[60]

Putin was never a president for irony. Unlike the club kids in their bright red "USSR" T-shirts or the collectors of Soviet kitsch at Moscow's weekend flea market, when Putin invoked nostalgia for the Soviet Union, he did so without any sardonic commentary intended. The president who was soon to call the breakup of the Soviet empire "a national tragedy on a colossal scale" saw no contradiction in a youth spent simultaneously listening to bootleg tapes of banned rock music and yearning to become one of the KGB agents who did the banning.

Inside his Kremlin, a similar contradiction now reigned. On paper, the remnants of Yeltsin's team held the most powerful positions; holdovers like chief of staff Aleksandr Voloshin, Prime Minister Mikhail Kasyanov, and political adviser Vladislav Surkov served as Putin's public face, promoting the image of the president as an economic modernizer fully committed to a capitalist future for Russia and wedded to the liberal policies promoted by his aides. But there were increasing signs that an all-out power struggle had erupted inside the presidential administration, with the Yeltsin team more and more unable to fend off the machinations of Putin's cadre of advisers from the secret services. By that summer of 2003, recalled one member of the Family faction, "we got the feeling that something changed for the wrong direction," and when he went to the Kremlin each day, he found the place filled with unfamiliar faces, "a whole floor of former or current KGB" in newly prominent presidential positions.[61]

Chief among the *siloviki* faction were two shadowy presidential deputy chiefs of staff, Viktor Ivanov and Igor Sechin. Ivanov, who had met Putin when they were both working for the KGB in Leningrad, had been the president's close aide since Putin had worked for Mayor Anatoly Sobchak. In the Kremlin, Ivanov's official portfolio grew to include all personnel policy, and he was the one who orchestrated the elimination of the presidential pardon commission. Sechin, in Soviet times a translator of Portuguese stationed in Mozambique and almost certainly a KGB agent, had an even closer relationship with the president; as Putin's chief secretary for more than a decade, Sechin controlled all the paper flow that reached Putin's desk in the Kremlin, making him "one of the most influential people in Russia," as the magazine *Kommersant Vlast* put it.[62] "His main asset is his loyalty," said Valery Pavlov, who had worked with both in Sobchak's office. "He would never allow himself to speak about his own point of view on a decision already taken by Putin."[63] The two Putin advisers worked closely with other representatives of the *siloviki* outside the Kremlin. Sechin, for example, was said to be closely linked to Sergei Ivanov, the increasingly powerful defense minister. Both had entered the KGB after studying in the translation department of Zhdanov State University, earning them the nickname "the Petersburg linguists." And Sechin and Ivanov were reported to have close ties to massive state-controlled natural resources companies such as the oil firm Rosneft and the natural gas monopoly Gazprom, giving them financial heft in the backstairs political machinations.[64]

Eventually, the internal feud would go public to the point that Gleb Pavlovsky, the Kremlin political consultant allied with the Yeltsin-era Family, circulated a report he had prepared for Voloshin warning of a "creeping coup" by the *siloviki* and accusing them of creating a "parallel center of power" inside the presidential administration. When we asked him what had inspired the charge, Pavlovsky accused the president's ascendant advisers from the secret services of trying to block economic reform policies, inspiring attacks against wealthy oligarchs, secretly backing new political parties in advance of the 2003 parliamentary elections, and generally behaving like a "political corporation" in which outsiders were considered "either traitors or thieves." Said Pavlovsky, "They speak the language that Putin understands."[65]

Twilight of the Oligarchs

There are worse things than going to jail.
—MIKHAIL KHODORKOVSKY

THE WARRANT CAUGHT UP with him in the quiet riverfront city of Saratov. Mikhail Khodorkovsky, the forty-year-old former Communist youth activist who had capitalized on the privatization of state assets to build an oil empire, was on a speaking tour through the Volga River region. Between engagements, his lawyer called him with the ominous news: the prosecutor general's office wanted to interview him again. More bad news would come the same day when authorities raided the office of the political consultants working for Yabloko, the democratic party Khodorkovsky had been financing. By the time he got to the hotel that night, a copy of the warrant was waiting on the fax machine. Khodorkovsky was ordered to appear immediately at the prosecutor's office to answer questions as a witness. Only there was a misspelling. Instead of the Russian word *sviditel,* which means "witness," a letter had been dropped and the word was printed as *siditel,* which means "prisoner." Some of the men in the billionaire's entourage laughed nervously at the mistake. Over dinner in the hotel restaurant that night the vodka flowed freely to cover their fears. But Khodorkovsky stopped by their table to gently chastise them. "Why are you drinking?" he asked lightheartedly. "The warrant wasn't sent to you."[1]

A short man with close-cropped, graying hair, an intense stare, rimless glasses, and a penchant for sweaters rather than suits, Mikhail Khodorkovsky hardly fit the mold of the corporate titan with the power and hubris to take on the state itself. For a man who commanded an estimated $15 billion fortune and a giant oil company with more than one hundred thousand workers on its payroll, he was strangely shy. But money had a way of transforming people in the new Russia, and Khodorkovsky had more of it than anyone else. Until his birthday a few months earlier, Khodorkovsky had been the second-richest man in the world under forty.[2]

Now he found himself jousting with Russian prosecutors in a high-stakes confrontation with Vladimir Putin's Kremlin. For months, a showdown had been brewing between Russia's richest man and its most powerful. Already, one of Khodorkovsky's partners had been arrested, and another had been indicted; three others had fled the country. Khodorkovsky himself had been summoned to answer questions once before. The authorities had passed along their advice: leave the country and don't come back. But Khodorkovsky had refused. He felt he had a reliable protector inside the Kremlin—Putin's chief of staff, Aleksandr Voloshin, who had privately promised Khodorkovsky that he would not be arrested. So Khodorkovsky shrugged off the latest missile from the prosecutor's office and instructed his lawyer to tell them that he was away on a business trip and would not be available until the following Monday.

It wasn't so much a business trip as a campaign. Facing the threat from the Kremlin, Khodorkovsky had embarked on an openly political barnstorming tour through the Russian heartland. This was the second of five such trips he had planned. At each stop, his staff had arranged speeches at universities, meetings with local governors and business leaders, and two or three television appearances. He knew this would be seen as a provocation inside the Kremlin but did not care. "When we flew on our first trip, Khodorkovsky asked us, 'How many trips are we going to be allowed to make?'" recalled one of his advisers, Aleksandr Batanov. "My view was three trips. His theory was one trip. The truth was in between."[3]

The night Khodorkovsky received the warrant a heavy snow began to fall, unusual for Saratov in October. The next morning, the city was buried and its airport closed for much of the day. Khodorkovsky and his party would not reach his next stop, Nizhny Novgorod, until evening. Once there, Khodorkovsky had dinner with Sergei Kiriyenko, a former prime minister who now served as one of Putin's presidential envoys, and also gave an interview. "Russia is facing yet another turning point and will have to make a choice between authoritarian capitalism and a variant of European democracy," he declared. "Business should not be driven into the shade and governed by fear."[4] Then he boarded his plane for the red-eye flight to his next stop in Irkutsk, in the frozen Siberian tundra. The rest of his staff headed back to Moscow for the weekend.

As the staff's plane took off into clear skies headed for the capital, Khodorkovsky's own chartered Tu-134 passenger jet was mysteriously held on the runway for two hours. It would turn out that he had had to be delayed long enough for another plane to reach Siberia first—one filled with FSB agents. At 5 a.m. Moscow time the next day, Saturday, October 25, 2003,

Khodorkovsky's jet touched down for refueling at Tolmachevo Airport out-side Novosibirsk, a major transit point across the sprawling Russian coun-tryside. The plane was directed to the airport's farthest parking area, where it was blocked by trucks with their headlights cutting into the darkness on one side and the Tu-204 that had just arrived from Moscow on the other.

Khodorkovsky was asleep in a small cabin when a phalanx of FSB agents in fatigues, flak vests, and masks burst onto the plane waving their automatic rifles. "Guns down!" they shouted. Khodorkovsky's security guards had stored their weapons in the cockpit in accordance with aviation rules. The FSB agents forced Khodorkovsky's men onto the floor.

An agent approached Khodorkovsky. "We have a warrant. Follow us." Khodorkovsky offered no resistance. "Okay," he said, "let's go."[5]

Inside the airport, Khodorkovsky demanded his lawyer but was gruffly told he would not need one. The agents handcuffed the billionaire, shuffled him aboard their plane, and took off into the Siberian sky, winging their way back to Moscow and a prison cell where the man who controlled 2 percent of the world's oil production would be locked up.

MIKHAIL KHODORKOVSKY had nursed ambition from a young age. At five, he decided he wanted to become head of a Soviet factory, and the other small children began calling him Director. Little Misha followed the tradi-tional path for success in Soviet society, enrolling in the Mendeleev Institute of Chemical Technology in Moscow and becoming deputy head of its Kom-somol committee, the Communist youth league that nurtured the next gen-eration of the Soviet elite. But as Khodorkovsky was entering his final year in school, Mikhail Gorbachev came to power and loosened the state's con-trol over business. Eager to explore the new opportunities of perestroika, Khodorkovsky opened a Komsomol student café at the institute, only to see it fail quickly due to poor location. After graduation in 1986, he took advan-tage of the freedom given youth science centers to experiment again with enterprise. With seed money from the Institute of High Temperatures, Khodorkovsky started a series of ventures that quickly turned into large sums of cash. He figured out how to convert paper money used by the Soviet government, called *beznalichnye,* into cash rubles and even hard cur-rency by using Komsomol bank accounts, then used the money to import personal computers at a huge markup. By the end of 1988, he had started his own bank, called Menatep. Khodorkovsky relied on his connections to have the dying Soviet government choose Menatep as the authorized bank for transferring government money to state enterprises; in a time of soaring inflation, he could make huge profits by simply holding on to the cash and using it as free capital before sending it along to its intended destination. "It is possible to find loopholes in every law, and I will use them without an instant of hesitation," he boasted at the time.[6] The would-be factory director had made the transformation from Communist youth leader to free-market capitalist. "If the old Mikhail had met the new one," Khodorkovsky told an interviewer, "he would have shot him."[7]

As Boris Yeltsin began building a new capitalist state, Khodorkovsky recognized earlier than many that the future would be in oil. He positioned himself as an informal adviser to Yeltsin's energy minister in 1992, learning the industry and making connections. Along the way he began buying state businesses—a titanium-magnesium plant, textile mills, glass factories, food-processing plants, a fertilizer company. By the age of thirty, he had emerged as one of the leading tycoons of the new Russia.

In 1995, another of the early moguls, Vladimir Potanin, dreamed up a novel scheme. Since the faltering Yeltsin government desperately needed cash, the state should borrow funds from the emerging oligarchs in exchange for the rights to selected state assets; if the state did not repay the funds, as expected, the businessmen would be entitled to buy the properties outright. It would be called "loans for shares," and Khodorkovsky accompanied Potanin to present it to the cabinet in March 1995. Yeltsin's team accepted the idea, seeing it as a way of divesting the state of its businesses before Communists could make a comeback, while simultaneously investing the emerging business moguls in the coming battle for Yeltsin's reelection.

But when it came time to auction off the shares, the oligarchs did not want genuine competition. Instead, they came to an understanding, carving up the state property among themselves. Khodorkovsky claimed Yukos Oil Company, a firm created three years earlier by combining several Siberian production units and refineries. By then, it had become Russia's second-largest oil producer, and Khodorkovsky had already made inroads with the company management to achieve an easy takeover. He also had another major advantage—he made sure the government picked his Bank Menatep to run the auction. The government set a minimum price of $150 million for a 45 percent stake in Yukos that would be auctioned off under the loans-for-shares program, and an identical $150 million minimum price for another 33 percent that would be sold in an investment auction at the same time. On December 8, 1995, Khodorkovsky's investment firm claimed control of 78 percent of Yukos Oil Company for $309 million, just $9 million above the combined minimum bids.[8]

Khodorkovsky proved to be ruthlessly efficient. The first thing he did was send three hundred security guards to Siberia to take possession of the wells and refineries, then began firing thousands of habitual drunks. For nearly a decade after the purchase of Yukos, he kept a weekly log prepared by his security service of those found drunk on the job and insisted that 90 percent of them be fired. He imposed a discipline that had been missing in the first three years of Yukos's existence, bringing down production costs by two-thirds. He proved a master empire-builder as well. He expanded reserves by buying the state's Eastern Oil Company in 1998 and cut a deal with Boris Berezovsky to merge with Sibneft Oil Company to create a combined giant called Yuksi, which could then bid on Rosneft, the last major oil company still held by the state.

By mid-1998, everything started to unravel. The Yuksi merger fell through, and then the economy collapsed with the ruble devaluation and government loan defaults in August. Businessmen around the country were going under, swept away by the riptide of Yeltsin's failed economic policies. Khodorkovsky moved to protect himself with a viciousness that would make him enemies for life. He defaulted on $236 million in loans from Japanese, German, and British banks, then stiffed them when they wanted to seize the 30 percent stake in Yukos he had pledged as collateral. Eventually, he bluffed them into surrender by raising the prospect of a battle in the notoriously corrupt Russian courts that he would inevitably win. In the end, Khodorkovsky bought back 23.7 percent of the collateral Yukos shares at less than half of what he owed. He adopted a similar no-holds-barred approach to the American investor Kenneth Dart, who owned about 12 percent of each of the three main Yukos subsidiaries. Khodorkovsky cooked up a plan to dilute Dart's holdings by issuing tens of millions of new shares in each of the subsidiaries. Dart fought back, but when the Russian Federal Securities Commission opened an investigation, Khodorkovsky dispatched a lieutenant to file a criminal slander case against the commission's crusading chairman, Dmitri Vasiliev, who gave up and resigned. Dart surrendered as well, letting go of his shares in a settlement.

Khodorkovsky reveled in his power. "If a man is not an oligarch, something is not right with him," he said. "It means for some reason he was unable to become an oligarch. Everyone had the same starting conditions, everyone could have done it. And today they could as well. If a man didn't do it, it means there are some sorts of problems with him."[9] But he also remained remarkably deferential to the power of the state. He told one interviewer during this period that if the prime minister asked him to step down as head of his bank, he would do so at once without hesitation. "That's how Russia is organized," he said. "The state is always the dominant force in the economy."[10]

VLADIMIR PUTIN believed the state should be the dominant force in the economy as well. He and some of the fellow KGB veterans around him, such as aides Viktor Ivanov and Igor Sechin, thought the state had made a colossal mistake surrendering so much of its vital assets during the 1990s, particularly in the oil industry. While other energy powers such as Saudi Arabia and Venezuela kept tight state control over their oil sectors, the government controlled only 4 percent of Russia's.

To reassert his government's dominance over business, Putin had driven out of the country two defiant oligarchs, Vladimir Gusinsky and Boris Berezovsky, and ordered the rest to keep out of politics or face his wrath. Yet Putin had hardly destroyed oligarchs as a class, as he had pledged during the 2000 campaign. If anything, with the exceptions of Berezovsky and Gusinsky, the oligarchy had prospered, particularly well-connected moguls such as Roman Abramovich, Berezovsky's estranged partner, and Oleg Deripaska, the aluminum king married to the daughter of Valentin Yumashev, the Yeltsin aide who had first fingered Putin as a future president. Midway through Putin's first term, eight oligarchic clans had accumulated control of 85 percent of Russia's top sixty-four privately held companies, and the combined sales of the top twelve private companies alone matched the entire annual revenue of the Russian government.[11] Putin permitted the oligarchs to get richer while sometimes swindling minority shareholders and manipulating the pliant court system in battles for control of the country's most precious economic resources. The only difference was it was less rough-and-tumble. "It's as intense as before—there's no big change," said Pyotr Aven, the banker who had first introduced Putin and Berezovsky. It was simply, he said, "less criminal than before."[12] Deripaska agreed. When we went to see him at his Moscow office, he was wearing a black shirt, black sports coat, and blue jeans and looked as if he could be heading out to one of the capital's swinging nightclubs. "It's a legal fight" now, he said. "And it's not bad that in some areas and some industries there is consolidation. It brings stability."[13]

In many ways, it was a good time to be a Russian oligarch, particularly for those who controlled oil companies. After the Soviet Union collapsed, so did the country's oil industry. New owners cared more about siphoning off cash than maintaining old fields or developing new ones. Wells shut down en masse. New technology passed the Russians by. By the 1998 economic crisis, Russia's production had fallen to 6 million barrels a day, barely half of its

Soviet-era high. Foreign oil companies weary of corrupt partners and crooked bureaucrats gave up. "I left thinking that's enough, this place will never be ready," recalled Robert Dudley, a BP Amoco executive who abandoned Moscow in 1997.[14]

But two things happened at once to supercharge a dramatic comeback: the price of oil began climbing and the oligarchs grew up. With more cash coming in each day, the newly minted oil barons, led by Khodorkovsky and Abramovich, realized that the ticket to even greater wealth wasn't just sucking their companies dry and stashing the money offshore. They began reinvesting some of their massive profits into their companies, bringing in new technology, upgrading infrastructure, reviving long-dormant exploration and development, recruiting Western managers, appointing outside directors, and paying dividends. Khodorkovsky did a personal makeover as well, shaving off his mustache and trading in his bulky glasses for fashionable, rimless spectacles.

Soon Russia was pumping 7 million barrels a day, then 8 million and 9 million. Russia caught up with Saudi Arabia as the world's largest oil producer, and while it kept more at home for its own use than the Saudis, it established itself as the world's second-largest exporter. Oil replaced military might, putting Russia back on the map as a major international player. BP returned, and so did Dudley. "It felt very different to me than when I was here in the midnineties," he told us. Dudley came to facilitate an extraordinary deal for BP, which decided to spend $7.5 billion to team up with Russia's Tyumen Oil Company (TNK), controlled by Pyotr Aven and his partner Mikhail Fridman, despite a messy feud between the British and Russian oil firms several years earlier. It was the largest foreign investment in Russian history and produced a new oil giant called TNK-BP, owned fifty-fifty by BP on one side and Fridman, Aven, and their partners on the other.

BP had initially considered buying into Khodorkovsky's Yukos as it overtook Lukoil to become Russia's largest oil producer, making it the most successful private company of the post-Soviet era. The BP team recognized that Khodorkovsky had done all the things that foreigners had demanded the Russians do in terms of reforming corporate governance, opening the company's books, and playing by standard rules. It was the closest thing to a major Western company in Russia. "In many ways," Dudley said, "Yukos was ahead of all the others."[15] BP representatives met with Khodorkovsky and his partner, Platon Lebedev, and outlined a half dozen possible deals. But Khodorkovsky and Lebedev were about to issue an initial public offering for Yukos stock, and a major deal in the midst of that seemed too much of a conflict for the British.

The TNK-BP deal, though, proved it could be done, and Khodorkovsky was intrigued enough to talk with other international majors. To make a deal all the more attractive, he decided to merge with another Russian major first—and found a willing seller in Roman Abramovich. Abramovich's Sibneft was the company that most resembled Yukos, smaller but also pursuing Western-style reforms. But Abramovich, the richest man in Russia other than Khodorkovsky, was growing bored. After watching a soccer game one day, he turned to his associates and announced that he wanted to buy a team, turning boyish fantasy into reality on the back of his multibillion-dollar fortune. His agents began scouting all over Europe for a potential purchase.

The merger with Khodorkovsky's Yukos would free up Abramovich to pursue his new interests. Although the two companies had tried and failed to join forces back in 1998, this time each side had an incentive for making the deal, and they hammered out an agreement with little trouble in April 2003, just ten weeks after the BP deal with TNK. Emerging from the partnership would be YukosSibneft, Russia's first genuine oil major on a scale with the Western giants and the fourth-largest oil producer in the world, worth a combined $35 billion on the Russian market. The company would pump nearly 2.4 million barrels a day, rivaling the oil emirate of Kuwait, and sit on 19 billion barrels of oil and gas reserves, among the world's largest. "This will allow us to create new potential for Russian business," Khodorkovsky declared triumphantly.[16] Putin's government seemed pleased. Prime Minister Mikhail Kasyanov pronounced the new YukosSibneft "a flagship for the Russian economy."[17]

Satisfied, Abramovich went off in search of soccer teams, eventually plunking down $235 million in cash and assumed debt for Britain's storied Chelsea club, soon nicknamed Chelski by the Fleet Street press. But Khodorkovsky was not finished. The Sibneft deal, massive though it was, was meant to be only a precursor to the ultimate triumph, a sale to one of the Western majors. He began talks with ExxonMobil and ChevronTexaco and found plenty of interest. It would be, he figured, the deal of the decade. And it would fit right in with his personal political aspirations.

MONEY NO LONGER drove Mikhail Khodorkovsky quite as much as it once did. He could hardly spend what he had already made. In public, he began talking about retiring at age forty-five in 2007, the year before the end of Vladimir Putin's second and final term under the constitution. In private, Khodorkovsky had devised a far more ambitious master plan.

Khodorkovsky had begun to see his role in historic terms. Thinking back on America's robber-baron era, he figured that he and his oligarch peers were in effect compressing three generations of development into one, evolving at breakneck speed from the early era of cutthroat capitalism toward a modern system in which business leaders played a responsible role in society. His efforts to reinvent himself, and his company, into clean corporate players reflected this thinking. So did his nascent charitable activities in a country where none of the oligarchs had thus far engaged in significant philanthropy. In 2001, Khodorkovsky founded Open Russia, a charitable group modeled after George Soros's Open Society Institute, and began spreading tens of millions of dollars around to various causes. At one point, he met an American nonprofit executive, Clifford Kupchan of the Eurasia Foundation, and began talking to him about how to build a real civil society. He invited Kupchan to join him for a trip to Siberia, and during the long flight, wearing blue jeans and a turtleneck sweater, the billionaire sat down in the aisle of the Yak-40 airplane next to the American's seat to talk for more than an hour about his vision. Khodorkovsky later donated $1 million to Eurasia. "Certainly Khodorkovsky stood out," Kupchan said later. "You got a real sense of a real younger-generation guy. Now whether it was a makeover or not, I don't know. But he wasn't like the old Soviet-style people he was traveling with. The gut question is whether this was kind of a PR offensive by a guy who had good advisers. That's the cynical explanation. The other explanation is he changed. Dirty money becomes clean with time."[18]

During this makeover, we went to see Khodorkovsky in his office, a wood-paneled facsimile of an English club on Moscow's Garden Ring. "Russia may become a normal country in our lifetime. But that's going to take some effort," he told us. "We believe that the key point here is education, and that's why we give money for education in various aspects—teaching kids how to use the Internet, establishing contacts between young people in the UK, U.S., and Russia, training young journalists, et cetera. The aim is very simple: Twenty years have passed. Another twenty or thirty years and we might become a normal country." He acknowledged that he and the other oligarchs had neglected these societal responsibilities up to now. "While we were dealing with problems of crisis management, we did not have time for charity. Today, the situation in industry has changed a great deal. Plus we have gotten older." When we asked if he was doing this to rehabilitate his image, he demurred. "This is more for the soul," he said.[19]

Khodorkovsky set his real plan into motion in April 2002 when he began sitting down with the leaders of political parties in the State Duma and making them offers. He would pour tens of millions of dollars into their party accounts in advance of the December 2003 parliamentary elections. In exchange, he would have their loyalty and put his own people on their party lists for seats in parliament. Every major Russian business funneled cash into political campaigns, and every major Russian tycoon had his own personal legislators. Duma seats were sold almost openly in Russia, even by the supposedly capitalist-hating Communists. One party official told us with no embarrassment that a spot high enough on the Communists' national party list to guarantee a seat in parliament was going for $3 million to $4 million, while a spot on one of the regional party lists could be bought for $1 million.[20]

But what Khodorkovsky had in mind now was different. He was talking about virtually privatizing the two market-oriented parties, Yabloko and the Union of Right Forces, as well as placing sizable numbers of legislators in the Communist Party and Putin's own newly renamed United Russia Party. All told, he hoped to assemble a bloc that would give him sway over the Duma, not just for his personal legislation like any other tycoon, but over a broad array of national policy matters. His advisers told people they aimed to win 130 of the 450 seats outright, then buy up more after the election. The plan grew even more audacious from there. As a half-Jewish oligarch, Khodorkovsky assumed he could never be elected president in famously anti-Semitic Russia. But he told political allies that he hoped to score enough influence in the Duma to rewrite the constitution and transform Russia into a parliamentary government run by a newly empowered prime minister, leaving the president a figurehead. The plan struck many who heard it as absurd, not to mention dangerous. "He was openly going around Moscow saying they would like to buy one-third of the Duma to be able to block an institutional majority," said Pyotr Aven, the banker. "They were absolutely open about that. . . . It was no secret. They behaved as if nothing had changed and Yeltsin was still the president. . . . They didn't understand that life is changing, that it's changed already. You couldn't behave as you behaved under Yeltsin. It's the new reality."[21]

What's more, Khodorkovsky imagined himself in the role of the new premier. "He was speaking openly that he would be prime minister in this system," said another person who had talked about it with Khodorkovsky. Political allies tried to warn him and his advisers not to float such ideas and risk infuriating Putin. "They were going around saying, 'We can do whatever we want,'" this person told us.[22] Sure enough, word got back to Putin. However unlikely the idea, the Kremlin took it seriously. In its view, Khodorkovsky had disobeyed the 2000 no-politics decree not by giving money but by doing it so brazenly as to defy Putin's authority. The unspoken rule was "to do it illegally," Gleb Pavlovsky, the Kremlin political consultant, told us. "All the big companies without exception pay money to political parties, but people do not like to talk out loud about it. Yukos violated this taboo."[23]

Khodorkovsky began pumping so much money into the political parties that he became virtually the sole source of financing for Grigory Yavlinsky's Yabloko. One party source estimated that Khodorkovsky alone was responsible for tens of millions of dollars, more than half the Yabloko budget; others said it was even higher. The Union of Right Forces got millions as well. Even Putin's United Russia got tens of millions of dollars, according to a source close to Khodorkovsky. All told, political leaders estimated that Khodorkovsky steered as much as $100 million to the various parties. He even tried to broker an alliance between Yabloko and the Union of Right Forces that would finally put the country's perpetually feuding democrats under one umbrella, but failed to overcome the long-running animosity between Yavlinsky and Anatoly Chubais, the 1990s privatization chief and Union of Right Forces leader. For all of this, Khodorkovsky thought he had the general approval of Aleksandr Voloshin, Putin's crafty chief of staff. In fact, Khodorkovsky told at least one senior Russian official that Voloshin had even instructed him to help the Communists as well, evidently part of some Voloshin machination to keep his fingers in many power centers.[24]

But in public, Khodorkovsky began acting more defiant of Putin. In February 2003, Putin summoned Khodorkovsky and other oligarchs to the Kremlin for one of their periodic meetings. Instead of the usual polite deference, Khodorkovsky began lecturing the president. "Corruption in the country is spreading," Khodorkovsky told Putin. The tycoon grilled the president about a recent deal in which the state-owned Rosneft oil company had bought the smaller Severnaya Neft firm for $600 million. Khodorkovsky, who had had his eye on Severnaya Neft as well, implied it was a crooked deal, that the price was so excessive that key Kremlin insiders must be lining their pockets. Putin bristled, his cold eyes glaring at the uppity billionaire. Who was Khodorkovsky to complain about anyone else stealing state assets? Putin reminded him that Yukos had secured huge oil reserves from the state for a song. "And the question is how did they obtain them?" Putin asked pointedly.[25]

The other oligarchs at the meeting winced at the confrontation. "There was so much tension and sparks," said Igor Yurgens, vice president of the oligarchs' association, the Russian Union of Industrialists and Entrepreneurs. "It was obvious something went wrong. And the whole thing came loose after that."[26] Some of Khodorkovsky's own partners at Yukos instantly understood the peril. "It was clear to me that we had signed our own death warrants," recalled Aleksei Kondaurov, head of the Yukos-Moscow management company.[27] Even some Putin aides were surprised at the president's outburst. "Putin just exploded," one told us later. "I didn't expect such a reaction. He was just out of control." When the aide asked Putin about the rigged Severnaya Neft deal, "I discovered he knew about this deeply. I wouldn't say he was himself involved, but he had allowed this to happen."[28]

Khodorkovsky did not back down. Increasingly outspoken, he began to sound to the Putin team as if he were dictating his own national policy. He supported the United States in the war in Iraq while Putin opposed it. He sealed a deal with China promising construction of a new pipeline even though pipelines were the exclusive province of the state-owned Transneft company. He pushed the State Duma to eliminate oil production sharing agreements beneficial to his competitors among the foreign oil companies.

Khodorkovsky felt no need to be subtle. At one point during the Duma floor debate on the oil production agreements, a lawmaker speaking for Khodorkovsky's legislation was interrupted midspeech when another legislator passed him a mobile phone. It was Khodorkovsky's team on the line with instructions on what to say. The Duma speaker, Gennady Seleznyov, later told Putin about the episode. "Putin was extremely angry," said a political source allied with Khodorkovsky.[29] In one recounting, Putin called Khodorkovsky to the Kremlin around this time to ask him about another report he had received. Was it true, Putin asked, that Khodorkovsky had met with Communist leader Gennady Zyuganov and offered to support his party? Khodorkovsky denied it. "Putin was furious," a well-connected government official told us later, "because he already had the minutes from the conversation between Khodorkovsky and Zyuganov, and the minutes came not from the FSB but from the Communist Party staff. And when someone lies to the president, it makes it personal."[30] Another top official tried to intercede on Khodorkovsky's behalf and explain that Voloshin had authorized the political financing. No, Putin shot back. "That's Khodorkovsky. It's his game. He wants to buy parliament. I can't allow this." Putin explained that he had known about Khodorkovsky's funding of the two Western-oriented parties and did not object, but drew the line at the Communists.[31]

In the faction-ridden Kremlin, the situation became entwined in the broader struggle. "There is a very serious internal discussion among Putin's elite about the future development of the country," Gleb Pavlovsky told us. Along with him in one camp, the remnants of the Yeltsin-era Family, led by Voloshin and Prime Minister Mikhail Kasyanov, defended the oligarchs, and Khodorkovsky in particular. But the KGB faction, Pavlovsky said, believed "the president must take power beyond the political and business elites."[32]

Igor Sechin and Viktor Ivanov, the leaders of the *siloviki,* soon found a way to voice their sentiments in public. In May 2003, just a month after Khodorkovsky announced his grand YukosSibneft merger, Stanislav Belkovsky, a political consultant with ties to the Kremlin hard-liners, issued a report warning of "a creeping oligarchic coup." Kremlin officials then arranged it so that the first questioner at Putin's annual news conference a month later would ask about the Belkovsky report. Russia, Putin responded, should not "allow individual businesspeople to influence the political life of the country in their own corporate interests." Without naming them, Putin went on to remind everyone what had happened to exiled tycoons Boris Berezovsky and Vladimir Gusinsky. "Those who disagree with this principle," he said, should remember that others had tried and failed. "Some are gone forever and others are far away," he added, adopting a line from Aleksandr Pushkin's *Eugene Onegin* evoking the fate of the Decembrist revolutionaries of 1825.[33]

Khodorkovsky ignored the hint.

MIKHAIL KHODORKOVSKY opened the door to his office and ushered in his guest, U.S. ambassador Alexander Vershbow. It was the beginning of July and Vershbow was interested in talking about expanding U.S.-Russian energy ties. The two met often, but this time Khodorkovsky had other news. There was going to be trouble, he told the diplomat. The authorities were planning to make an arrest.

The next day Russian militia officers showed up at a hospital where his billionaire partner, Platon Lebedev, was being treated for heart trouble and dragged him away in handcuffs. Lebedev was chairman of Group Menatep, the holding company that controlled Yukos, and Khodorkovsky's primary business adviser. Lebedev was charged with fraud stemming from the decade-old privatization of a fertilizer company. When he was brought to Moscow's Basmanny Court for a bail hearing, his attorney, Anton Drel, was locked out of the courtroom, left to bang on the door in vain. The court denied Lebedev bail.

Khodorkovsky responded with a strategy of maximum public confrontation. Instead of quietly negotiating a deal for Lebedev's release, Khodorkovsky made a point of showing up at Vershbow's official residence, Spaso House, the next day for the annual American Fourth of July celebration, where he knew he would find plenty of foreign correspondents. Sure enough, as hundreds of guests milled around the backyard, a cluster of us surrounded Khodorkovsky, who calmly laid the case at Putin's feet. "In my view, this has nothing to do with substantive legal issues, and I hope the leadership of the country will draw the necessary conclusions," he told us.[34] By the end of the day, prosecutors ordered Khodorkovsky himself to show up for questioning.

The next three months became a game of brinkmanship. "We discussed full, unilateral surrender," a Yukos executive said later. "But we decided that it would be dangerous—it would be taken as a sign of weakness by our opponents in the Kremlin."[35] So Yukos went on the attack. The company put up billboards all over the country emblazoned, "We're Together," to link Khodorkovsky with the public. The company's Web site posted a new feature called "Target Yukos!" Khodorkovsky traveled regularly to Washington, figuring that his friends in the international business and political communities would come to his aid. The campaign against him and his team, Khodorkovsky declared, signaled a return to the "stagnant swamp" of Russia's "totalitarian" past.[36]

For its part, the Russian government began targeting more of his partners and businesses. Soon authorities had launched no fewer than eight investigations against Khodorkovsky's team. Regulators began examining company licenses, tax inspectors started looking through the books. Putin also put an end to Khodorkovsky's China pipeline, bypassing Mikhail Kasyanov to order two cabinet ministers to ignore the prime minister's instructions and freeze the project.[37] With parliamentary elections on the horizon, the attack positioned Putin as an enemy of oligarchs, probably the most hated class of people in modern Russia. More than 70 percent of Russians told pollsters that they disliked oligarchs, and political strategists for almost all of the parties competing for State Duma seats were looking for ways to brandish their antioligarch credentials. "We have no other way but to put you on the shooting range because you are the oligarchs and it's the election period," Igor Yurgens, the oligarchs' union vice president, recalled some political consultants telling his group.[38]

But Putin was preparing to head to the United States for a four-day trip, including a Camp David summit with President Bush, and recognizing the sensitivities, the Russians began easing up a bit on Khodorkovsky. A little less than a week before his departure, Putin invited us along with several other American correspondents to his dacha at Novo-Ogaryovo to talk. It was a classic Putin day. We spent three hours waiting in the billiards room, then when he finally summoned us, he launched into a tireless four-hour-and-ten-minute disquisition on every topic we chose to throw at him. He tried to distance himself from the Khodorkovsky affair, acting as if he were no more than a disinterested observer of the prosecutors' actions, powerless to interfere, just as he had done with the NTV journalists two years earlier. "There will be no revisiting privatization results," he assured us. "But if there were breaches of law and the prosecutor general's office investigates some cases, I have no legal right to object to such actions." We tried to probe whether Khodorkovsky's political financing had drawn Putin's wrath, but he deflected the question. "Very often I don't agree with what they say or do, but I am convinced that these forces should be represented on the political stage. And if Yukos finances them—I hope in the framework of the law—fine, go ahead."[39]

The crackdown on Yukos came at a time when other politically independent forces were also under pressure. Putin's government had just purged the country's leading pollster from his state-owned firm and replaced him with a twenty-nine-year-old neophyte whose only qualification was having campaigned for Putin's political party. The Russian Press Ministry had recently shut down TVS, the last refuge of Yevgeny Kiselyov and the old NTV journalists. Putin had also just signed a new law banning "political advocacy" in campaign news coverage, making it essentially illegal to analyze political events in print; even writing that a candidate had failed to deliver on a campaign promise was technically outlawed. We asked Putin about setbacks for democracy. "If by democracy one means the dissolution of the state, then we do not need such democracy," he told us. "Why is democracy needed? To make people's lives better, to make them free. I don't think that there are people in the world who want democracy that would lead to chaos."[40] Putin had reinterpreted the question to fit his view of democracy—a word he defined as "the dissolution of the state" and "chaos."

Khodorkovsky, the reformed robber baron, believed it had fallen to him to take on the mantle of defender of Russia's endangered democracy. Something had happened to the oil tycoon that mystified even friends and advisers. With an almost messianic fervor, he had adopted his new cause to the point where he seemed to be waging a quest for martyrdom. No longer the young man who would give up his bank if the government asked, Khodorkovsky had turned into a quixotic crusader almost eager for prison. In August, a month after Platon Lebedev's arrest, he met his fellow oligarch Mikhail Fridman of TNK-BP for dinner at Justo, another swish new Arkady Novikov restaurant filled with sushi and supermodels. Fridman was flummoxed by Khodorkovsky's plans to "buy democracy," as he put it. "I told him, 'It's dangerous for you and it's dangerous for the country because the situation, from my point of view, was a lose-lose situation. If Putin allowed you to do this, it means that there is no stability. It means that there is chaos. If he doesn't allow you to do this and you act very cruelly, it means the end of civilized relations between business and power. At the end of the day,' I told him, 'Mr. Putin will react decisively.' And it happened." Khodorkovsky professed to be prepared. "He said that he was ready to go to prison. But I told him, 'It's dangerous for us, not only for you. And you are not ready.'"[41]

Khodorkovsky did not listen. Through his charitable foundation, Open Russia, he bought *Moscow News*, a venerable liberal weekly that had fallen on hard times. Founded in 1930 by Joseph Stalin as a propaganda rag for foreigners, *Moscow News* under Mikhail Gorbachev became one of the first newspapers to experiment with the freedom of glasnost and earned such wide popularity that it sold 1 million copies a week, many to eager readers who lined up at 6 a.m. at its Pushkin Square headquarters to buy a copy. Since then it had lost its edge, and Khodorkovsky decided it could be transformed into an important liberal voice again as Russia slid back into authoritarianism. To guarantee that, he hired a journalist who had consistently stood up to Putin, Yevgeny Kiselyov. Khodorkovsky gave Kiselyov free rein, but in a moment of caution advised him not to go out of his way to provoke the president. "Just don't offend Mr. Putin. Don't call him short and stupid. The rest I'm not going to tell you," Khodorkovsky told Kiselyov.[42]

It was not advice that Khodorkovsky would take himself, though. He practically dared Putin to come after him. When he walked into a meeting in St. Petersburg between Russian and American oil executives in late September, another oilman commented on his short haircut. "I'm getting ready for them to throw me in jail," Khodorkovsky half joked. Then he gave a speech calling for liberalization of the Russian oil pipeline system, a monopoly jealously guarded by the state-owned Transneft, which was already fuming about Khodorkovsky's freelance agreements with China. Afterward, Khodorkovsky spotted the head of Transneft at a luncheon and needled him further.

"So," Khodorkovsky asked mischievously, "how did you like my loyal speech?"

The Transneft executive was red-faced with anger. "If that was loyal, I'm a trolley bus," he shouted.

"So where are your headlights?" Khodorkovsky retorted playfully, mimicking headlights by cupping his hands around his eyes.[43]

Khodorkovsky was still advancing his business plans. On October 3, he completed the merger with Sibneft, creating an even more valuable company than originally envisioned, worth $45 billion. The same morning, Khodorkovsky shared a stage with ExxonMobil chief executive Lee R. Raymond at a Moscow economic forum. Khodorkovsky coyly teased the reporters at the forum. "There is no deal," he said, "but when there is a deal, we will make you happy by telling you."[44] At this point, in fact, Aleksei Kondaurov, the Yukos executive, told us later, Khodorkovsky already had a tentative deal in the works with ChevronTexaco—and had cleared it with the Kremlin.[45] Mikhail Kasyanov had given political approval to a deal with the Americans.[46]

That same morning, though, Putin's prosecutors were moving in, driving out to the gated community in the exclusive Moscow suburb of Zhukovka where Khodorkovsky and his top partners lived, raiding a Yukos business center there and even tromping through an orphanage funded by the Yukos team. The prosecutors did not stop there. Agents searched records at the school of Khodorkovsky's twelve-year-old daughter. Khodorkovsky's lawyer's office was searched. The political consulting firm working for Yabloko was raided and documents relating to the upcoming campaign seized. Prosecutors even called a business rival who five years earlier had alleged that Yukos was trying to kill him and ordered him to return to Moscow to swear out a complaint that they had refused to take at the time. On October 11, Khodorkovsky met with a team of lawyers, including several Americans. He seemed resigned to prison. "There are worse things than going to jail," he said.[47]

Khodorkovsky made one last attempt to head it off. He called a longtime adversary, Aleksandr Dobrovinsky, and asked him to contact prosecutors to see if compromise was possible. "If they lay down all their cards, I'll lay down my cards," Khodorkovsky told him. Dobrovinsky was a telling choice for intermediary; for years, he had sued Yukos repeatedly and represented the man who had accused Yukos of trying to murder him. Dobrovinsky had no love for Khodorkovsky. But even he was disturbed by what the prosecutors were doing, seeing it as a patently political case. He agreed to take Khodorkovsky's message to the prosecutors, but was promptly rebuffed. "They were not willing to put down their cards."[48]

On October 19, Anton Drel drove out to Khodorkovsky's home in Zhukovka about midnight. The children were asleep and the oligarch and the lawyer talked deep into the night. "You understand they might arrest you?" Drel asked.

Khodorkovsky nodded. "I have information that they can arrest me," he said, meaning the prosecutors had gotten permission. "And what's more, I've been advised to leave the country."

Drel took that to mean Khodorkovsky had been tipped off by Aleksandr Voloshin, the Kremlin chief of staff. He was already worried it would come to an arrest. "What are the chances?" Drel asked.

"Higher than ever."

"What's the problem, then?" In other words, why was he staying in the country?

Khodorkovsky had left Russia seventeen times since Lebedev's arrest, but always came back. He adopted his newfound mantle of defiant democrat. "I've been making money and doing all this not to leave the country in one day. I want to have real democratic institutions in this country. I can be useful because I have money." He nodded in the direction of the bedrooms where three of his children were sleeping. "I have my children. I don't want them to have to live outside their country."

"But Russian history has completely different examples," Drel said. In Russia, no one beat the Kremlin.

"I don't think a bad fate is inevitable for Russia," Khodorkovsky insisted. Then the oligarch mentioned the children again. "I want my children to live in Russia and I don't want to be ashamed of Russia."

Drel realized his client would not budge. He got up, shook Khodorkovsky's hand, and headed into the night. "Later I thought about this. Why did he tell me this at home without television cameras there? Maybe he really believed it." Even Khodorkovsky's own lawyer could not figure out what to make of a man of nearly endless means choosing prison at home over freedom abroad. How would it serve his children to be taken away from them for ten years? "He's living in a different sphere now," Drel concluded over dinner with us one evening after visiting Khodorkovsky in prison. "Have you ever heard of someone with several billion dollars being told to leave the country and deciding to stay and risk losing everything? It's a really philosophical question. Even for me. I don't understand him. I think it's very good there are people like him. But I wouldn't be able to do this. Would you?"[49]

A week after his nighttime trip to Zhukovka, Drel was woken by a phone call telling him his client had been arrested. He raced to the prosecutor general's office, where Khodorkovsky was taken after the FSB had stormed his plane in Siberia. Drel arrived to find a calm tycoon, certain he would not be held for long. Khodorkovsky handed the lawyer his watch and wallet. "He took his wedding ring off and gave it to me and asked me not to give it to his wife. He said when he comes out, he wants to be wearing the ring. But if he gave it to his wife, that would mean it's over." Drel agreed, but feared his client's optimism. "He didn't understand it until the end that it was going to be a long time."[50]

THE ARREST surprised Khodorkovsky's patrons in the Kremlin. Mikhail Kasyanov, the country's second-highest-ranking official, learned of it through the Russian media. Aleksandr Voloshin, who had reassured Khodorkovsky nothing would happen, was so stunned he marched into Putin's office at the Kremlin and submitted his resignation. They had clearly lost the struggle for power. If Putin wanted the *siloviki* to run the show, then Voloshin had no choice but to leave. Putin asked him to stay and refused to accept the resignation immediately. Voloshin should at least stay until after the parliamentary elections or allow Putin to announce his departure on his own terms in a calmer moment. But the president made no move to undo what had been done. Khodorkovsky had been clapped in handcuffs and would stay that way no matter what Voloshin, Kasyanov, and the Family thought about it.

The arrest provoked a political crisis unlike any seen before or during Putin's tenure. Political leaders across the spectrum condemned the move, from democrat Grigory Yavlinsky to Communist Gennady Zyuganov. When we reached Boris Nemtsov of the Union of Right Forces, he called it a "political contract hit."[51] Anatoly Chubais, the privatization tsar who now headed the country's electricity monopoly, went on Russian television with a rare statement breaking with the Kremlin and calling on Putin to intervene. By the time the markets opened on Monday, investors were dumping Russian holdings, with the main stock index plunging 14 percent in a matter of hours, wiping out $20 billion in market value.[52] Kasyanov and others complained privately that they were courting economic disaster, but Putin would not listen. "He was angry," said one aide who saw him during this period.[53] To stem the losses, Putin publicly disavowed any plans for a wholesale renationalization of private property. "There will be no generalizations, analogies, or precedents, especially related to the results of privatization. That is why I would like to ask for a stop to any speculation or hysterics on this score," he declared in a veiled warning to Kasyanov, "and I also ask the government not to get involved in this discussion." But Putin weighed in firmly on the side of the *siloviki,* defending the arrest as the product of a "democratic and legally well-balanced" judicial system, vowing that there would be "no bargaining on matters related to the activities of law enforcement bodies."[54]

With Putin's public approval, prosecutors eagerly took the next step, impounding more than 40 percent of Yukos stock, the first such large-scale confiscation of property in the post-Soviet era. The market plummeted again. The news reached a group of foreign investment bankers just as they were waiting at the Kremlin's Spassky Gate for a previously scheduled meeting with Putin. As the confused and worried businessmen settled into their chairs, they noticed that Voloshin was conspicuously absent. In his place was a little-known St. Petersburg lawyer named Dmitri Medvedev. For the next two hours, Putin offered soothing words, explaining that the Yukos shares were frozen so the state could recover the alleged losses from Khodorkovsky's crimes—not mentioning that the state had frozen nearly $13 billion in stock as collateral for theoretical damages totaling no more than $1 billion. After the bankers left, just before midnight, the Kremlin put out a statement announcing Voloshin's resignation and Medvedev's appointment to succeed him. Medvedev, not yet forty years old, had worked with the president since they were both aides to St. Petersburg's Mayor Anatoly Sobchak and had in recent years served as both Putin's deputy Kremlin chief of staff and his handpicked overseer of Gazprom, the state-controlled energy monopoly used for such sensitive tasks as taking over NTV.

The stock seizure only increased the aggravation of Voloshin's remaining allies in government. Defying Putin's warning to stay silent, Kasyanov publicly pronounced himself "deeply concerned" about the stock impoundment, calling it "a new phenomenon, the consequences of which are difficult to judge, as this is a new form of influence."[55] Finance Minister Aleksei Kudrin likewise worried aloud that the Yukos case was damaging the Russian economy. Gleb Pavlovsky went even further, taking on directly the president he had helped elect in 2000. "In my view, the president is under the spell of forces I warned him about," Pavlovsky said, referring to the *siloviki*.[56] He added that "the goal of these people is to seize control over the political center of the country" and called Putin's statement that the case was simply a matter for prosecutors "a textbook argument from the Stalin era."[57]

At the White House, national security adviser Condoleezza Rice and other top Russia policymakers read about the growing crisis with alarm. Conservatives such as Senator John McCain (R-Ariz.) and Pentagon adviser Richard Perle began speaking out, even suggesting that Russia be thrown out of the G-8. Alexander Vershbow, the American ambassador, talked publicly of a "widening values gap" between Russia and the United States. For the first time, Bush administration officials who had harbored romantic views of Putin as a consolidator of democracy began having second thoughts. Some of them, such as Rice, had met Khodorkovsky and respected him. Now those within the government who had been waging a long, losing internal struggle to take a more skeptical view of Putin found themselves finally being heard. "They took a guy who a lot of people had met and knew," a top U.S. official in Washington later told us. "From then on, the president started to get it."[58] In Moscow, we asked a senior U.S. diplomat about Bush's Camp David endorsement just a month earlier of Putin's "vision of Russia" as "a country in which democracy and freedom and rule of law thrive." The diplomat smiled. "You'll never hear that again."[59]

But the West was hardly prepared to do anything about Khodorkovsky's arrest. And for that matter, neither were his Russian peers. No one was more threatened than the members of the Russian Union of Industrialists and Entrepreneurs, the oligarchs' union, yet they were torn about whether even to protest. After Khodorkovsky's arrest, eighteen of them gathered in the evening at the union's headquarters. For three hours, they argued about what to do, some of them shouting. Some wanted to cancel an upcoming congress meeting scheduled with Putin; others maintained that Khodorkovsky had dug his own grave. "There was a lot of debate," recalled Igor Yurgens, the union's vice president. "Some hotheads proposed to cancel the congress and to organize it after the election. Then at least it would be clearer to us whether it is a political campaign for the sake of the election or if it's a substantial case." Instead, the union simply abandoned its most prominent member. "Of course the press, especially the liberal press, painted it as complete capitulation of the [union], which probably it was. But it was hell. If we would have acted otherwise, in two or three hours we would be arrested. I would say that's worse than capitulation."[60]

What was to stop the Kremlin from doing to any of them what it had done to Khodorkovsky? What was acceptable under managed democracy? "Nobody explained at that time and nobody explains now what is permitted and what is not," the tycoon Oleg Kiselyov mused one day. "It was not clear. Must I change the policy of the development of my company? Maybe I must close my educational programs? Maybe I must change the policy of my charity programs? This was not clear. It is still not clear. Many businessmen have made a decision to distance themselves as far as possible from public and political life, which is not making society healthier. Maybe what was hiding behind this doctrine was to have presidential power as a rock dominating everything— society, business, other branches of power. And that has actually happened."[61]

And so, just as with Boris Berezovsky and Vladimir Gusinsky before, the other oligarchs were willing to cut Khodorkovsky loose in hopes of saving themselves. "He is a kind of romantic," Mikhail Fridman told us later. "He thought that it's impossible that the richest, most well-known person would go to jail. . . . Khodorkovsky must have believed that he is an exception, a messiah, a kind of person that things will be forgiven." Fridman added, "From my point of view, it's already over because Putin has already decided he must show who is the boss. And the country has this tradition—it's very bloody about that."[62]

Agitation

We are living in a new Russia now.
—VLADISLAV SURKOV

M ARAT GELMAN HAD an assignment from the Kremlin. As the political overseer of state-run Channel One, the operative who had
made his name selling avant-garde art and his own expertise in "black PR"
would be responsible for turning the television network into what he called
"an instrument for elections, the most powerful instrument of all." For the
last four years, Gelman and the Kremlin consultant Gleb Pavlovsky had
bragged of their role in creating a new system of "managed democracy"
under Vladimir Putin. Now, Gelman told anyone who asked, he had a chance
to use the nation's most-watched news network as a laboratory. It would, he
promised, become an "institution of managed democracy" for the 2003
elections.[1]

Looking ahead to the December parliamentary contest, the Kremlin
hoped to use its power over the media to destroy once and for all the Communist Party, which had bedeviled Russia's leadership throughout the 1990s,
and to assemble an unassailable two-thirds majority for its own new creation,
the United Russia party.[2] Of course, the State Duma was already a compliant
body, filled with timeservers happy to sell their allegiance to the popular,
influential president. But Putin's Kremlin hadn't acquired so much power
over the levers of politics in the last few years so as not to use it.

This time, operatives like Pavlovsky and presidential deputy chief of staff
Vladislav Surkov, the Kremlin's top political adviser, would act to crush the
opposition simply because they could. Surkov, a dark-haired operator still in
his thirties, had started as a protégé of oligarch Mikhail Khodorkovsky's in
the 1990s, a public relations whiz who had dreamed of becoming as rich as
the Richard Gere character in *Pretty Woman*.[3] Even now, with Khodorkovsky
imprisoned and his protector Aleksandr Voloshin out as Putin's chief of staff,
Surkov retained the political portfolio in the Kremlin, and he was both
admired and feared by the politicians whose heads he regularly bashed on

behalf of the president. "Surkov was so proud they can do anything they want to do," recalled Sergei Markov, a political consultant who attended Kremlin election-strategy sessions. "He was repeating many times, 'Diminish the role of the Communists. Don't allow them to play any role in parliament.'"[4]

By now, all three major national networks were firmly under Kremlin control, and television would be one of the keys to victory. Under minders like Gelman, the nightly news had already become Soviet-like in its devotion to Putin, unwillingness to mention controversial subjects, and steadfast dullness. For years, the Kremlin had hosted meetings each Friday with the top television directors, as Surkov, Pavlovsky, and others handed out weekly talking points and charted strategy for the networks. To start, the sessions were meant to share information with the television executives about Putin's planned legislation. But over time, the agenda changed to politics. "It turned into an instrument of control," one regular participant told us. "At first, it was how to conduct reforms and at the end how to praise United Russia and trample on the Communists. It was so direct and unsophisticated, like propaganda." At each session, a written agenda was handed out, with the week's expected news topics and recommended approaches for the television networks. "At some point, the list started including the phrase 'recommendation—don't cover.' It was things not to mention, like Chechnya."[5]

Now, in the election season, the idea was to be even blunter with the television weapon. No one attempted to disguise political ties with the Kremlin. Putin's press secretary, Aleksei Gromov, sat on the board of Gelman's Channel One, while the general director of the nightly news program on the Rossiya network openly proclaimed his fealty to the president. "If I were not loyal to Mr. Putin, I would not work here," the director, Vladimir Kulistikov, told a reporter. The general principle was summed up by Rossiya's anchor, Mikhail Antonov: "If there is no obvious breaking news, we start with the president."[6]

Gelman interpreted his marching orders literally. Each edition of the 9 p.m. nightly news on Channel One and each talk show would be guided in the election season by a simple precept, he told us: "To create the image of United Russia and to destroy the Communists."[7]

THE UNITED Russia political party they created had neither a legislative program nor an ideology beyond vague pronouncements about the greatness of the Russian state. Its leaders refused to debate, and its main selling point was that it already ran the country. Its all-things-to-all-people message on campaign posters featured both Soviet dictator Joseph Stalin and Soviet dissident

Aleksandr Solzhenitsyn. Its only campaign slogan proclaimed its reason for existence: "Together with the president!"

Indeed, United Russia by the eve of the 2003 elections existed less as a political party than as a vehicle to promote the image of one man, Vladimir Putin. "United Russia has a very simple message—it's the party of the president," Kremlin pollster Aleksandr Oslon told us during the campaign. "It's just one thing—it's Putin. That factor of Putin is the decisive one."[8] Vyacheslav Nikonov, the political consultant who now worked for United Russia, joked, "They should put a mask of Putin on every candidate. I am always telling them that's the only thing they need."[9]

The Kremlin's main fear as the campaign season began was that it was not aggressive enough in branding Putin's image on the party. At the time, his popularity was more than 70 percent in the polls, but United Russia had started out the fall election season with a modest 20 percent or so, behind the Communists and their seemingly reliable one-quarter of the electorate. Surkov aimed higher. "The whole campaign was built to have forty percent," recalled Sergei Popov, who served as top deputy at the party's election headquarters. "It was all going according to the plan."[10] And the only way to do that was by marketing the party more strongly as the president's.

In September, Putin broke with post-Soviet tradition under which the president had remained technically separate from political parties when he publicly endorsed United Russia "as a sign of gratitude" for its support in parliament. "I won't hide it," the president said in what might seem a lukewarm embrace for another political system but came across as a rousing cheer in Russia's. "Four years ago, I voted for your party. I must say that I don't regret that decision."[11]

Still, it was not enough. Markov presented the Kremlin a content analysis of party leaders' speeches. "They were too shy to use the words *president* and *Vladimir Putin*," he concluded. "Even Boris Nemtsov and Grigory Yavlinsky used the words *Vladimir Putin* and *president* more than United Russia."[12]

Massive, building-size banners appeared around the country featuring Putin's visage and his exhortation on behalf of United Russia: "Together we must make Russia united, strong . . ." In Moscow, the presidential banner stretched across an entire city block—directly facing the State Duma. A television ad campaign was developed for United Russia as well. In a spot that would run right up until the December 7 elections, an old woman was stopped on the street and asked for whom she would vote. "I am for the president," she said, "and that means for United Russia."[13]

Created in December 2001, United Russia was a merger of Unity, the party hastily assembled to back Putin in the 1999 parliamentary elections, and its onetime rival, Fatherland–All Russia, headed by former prime minister Yevgeny Primakov and Moscow's Mayor Yuri Luzhkov. The reborn party enlisted dozens of Russia's most powerful regional chieftains as well as its top federal officials. But it was explicitly a Kremlin project run by the presidential administration. "'We will do the campaign ourselves without United Russia'—that was exactly the message Vladislav Surkov gave to United Russia activists a year and a half before the elections," as Markov recalled it.[14]

United Russia's long-term goal was far more ambitious than 40 percent in the upcoming elections. It was meant to be the beginning of a project to create and institutionalize a ruling party that could hold on to power in the model of the Liberal Democrats who have run Japan since 1945 or the Institutional Revolutionary Party, which governed Mexico for seventy-one years. Other attempts to create what Russians call a "party of power" had failed in recent years, faltering on the unpopularity of Boris Yeltsin and rifts inside the ruling elite. But Putin's aides hoped to translate the exceptional public support for the president into a lasting political institution using the tools of political management they had worked so painstakingly to acquire over the last few years. "This is a project to help rule Russia for decades," said Michael McFaul, a Stanford University scholar and expert on Russian elections. "It's a fusion of the party and the state in a way never possible in the 1990s."[15]

But if the aim was bold, the party was cautious about what it said on the trail, choosing to run an issueless campaign and proud of it. "People just hate all ideologies," Nikonov, the party strategist, told us.[16] United Russia defiantly refused to spell out where it stood on policy questions, and from the start party leaders were banned from taking part in any candidate debates, open forums, or unscripted appearances where they might be pinned down on the party's positions. Interior Minister Boris Gryzlov, the party's titular head, was so disdainful of the idea of debating rival parties he told reporters that participating would be like "a substitute goalkeeper for a street hockey team" forcing his way into a picture with a Soviet hockey legend.[17]

"From the point of view of the West and the U.S., I know it sounds very bad. How can you not participate in debates?" said Martin Shakkum, a United Russia candidate from the Moscow region and one of the few who agreed to speak with us during the campaign. "But consider the level of development of Russian democracy—it's very weak and society is not well prepared for this."[18]

Surveys showed that United Russia attracted voters who seemed united in little more than their preference for the president. Asked why they were backing the party, 37 percent told Oslon's firm they liked its closeness to Putin or its leaders and 21 percent were simply unsure. "For the majority of the population, it's enough for them to see and hear Putin's activity. The economy's growing, order's being enforced, respect from other countries is growing. The GNP [gross national product] is being doubled. Court and army and education and pension reforms are under way. . . . Budget workers' salaries are going up, as are pensions," Oslon said. "What else do you need?"[19]

For that reason, the Kremlin figured any concrete positions the party took would just lose them support. Talking about Putin was the only safe course. "The rest interfered," Gelman told us. "Only Putin unites."[20]

MARAT GELMAN had another commission from the Kremlin. In addition to his day job as political overseer of Channel One, the strategist had also been enlisted to create a new electoral bloc for the December elections. The idea was to take votes away from the Communists, votes that United Russia could never hope to win directly itself. Gelman came up with a catchy name for the project. He would call it Tovarishch, or Comrade.[21]

Soon, he was teaming up with Sergei Glazyev, a bright young Communist economist who had grown increasingly disaffected with the party's course under its old-style leader Gennady Zyuganov, a self-professed Stalin admirer who had grudgingly accepted private property but resisted most other attempts to reinvent the party of Lenin for the age of the Internet. By the spring of 2003, Glazyev had become openly rebellious.

Only at the last minute did the Communists realize what a problem Glazyev's exit could create. Twice that spring, Zyuganov's deputy, Ivan Melnikov, tried to persuade him over Chinese food that working with the Kremlin would backfire even if he managed to cut into the Communist vote. "I said, 'Sergei, they will use you, and when they don't need you anymore, they will reduce you to zero.' He didn't agree. He thought that he would be able to outwit everyone," Melnikov recalled. He also promised Glazyev one of the top three spots on the party's national candidate list that fall.[22]

By May, Glazyev had definitively split with the Communists and given the go-ahead to Gelman's plans to develop a new electoral bloc. They would forge a coalition among the myriad small parties on the fringes of Russian politics, uniting both right-wing patriots who sought the revival of empire and left-wing campaigners who longed for a genuine social democratic party. From the Kremlin's point of view, Pavlovsky recalled, the precise makeup of the coalition didn't matter nearly as much as the idea to create "an acceptable alternative for voters who were leaving the Communists."[23]

Project Comrade was just one of several election-year inventions to emerge with the backing of one faction or another within the Kremlin, most with the goal of undermining the Communists. "There were half a dozen other projects running in the election, all taking the Communist vote," Nikonov said.[24] It was Aleksandr Voloshin's faction, the remnants of the Yeltsin-era Family allied with consultants like Pavlovsky and Gelman, that sponsored Comrade. Duma speaker Gennady Seleznyov, a renegade Communist like Glazyev, had Kremlin blessing for his Russia's Rebirth party, while the head of the upper house of parliament, Putin's St. Petersburg friend Sergei Mironov, started the Party of Life with tacit Kremlin backing as well. The *siloviki* were behind the People's Party, headed by parliamentarian Gennady Raikov and filled with former spies and generals. At first, Raikov had secured Putin's support. "He infected others with his enthusiasm, including the president himself," recalled Gennady Gudkov, the former KGB agent who would later take over the party.[25] But Vladislav Surkov moved to block the party, convincing Putin it could damage United Russia, according to Markov, at which point the money dried up. The Family feared that the "aim of the People's Party was to create an independent political resource for this chekist group," Markov recalled.[26]

It was by no means certain that Glazyev's would be the one out of all these projects to succeed. But in early summer, Putin personally intervened. The president pulled Glazyev aside for a short chat during a Kremlin reception for the anniversary of Russian independence from the Soviet Union on June 12. He proposed that Glazyev join forces with another up-and-comer in the Duma, a popular nationalist deputy named Dmitri Rogozin. "The president himself asked me to do it," Glazyev said. "His [Rogozin's] inclusion in the bloc was initiated by Putin himself." Soon, Glazyev recalled, Rogozin approached him directly to open negotiations about their merger.[27]

Slick and telegenic, Rogozin had made a name for himself in the 1990s by aggressively defending the ethnic Russians stranded outside the country by the collapse of the Soviet empire and now headed the Duma's International Affairs Committee. A Putin loyalist, he had considered joining United Russia earlier in the year, but claimed to have been blackballed for the job of party campaign manager by Mayor Luzhkov. He and Glazyev had been friendly ever since 1993, when they had defended the hard-line Communist-dominated parliament from the tanks brought in by Boris Yeltsin. In 1995 and 1996, they joined a coalition of nationalists who supported former general Aleksandr Lebed in the presidential race against Yeltsin. This time, the Kremlin wanted to team them up if only to ensure that someone reliable was watching over the openly ambitious Glazyev. Rogozin, said Markov, "was nominated by the Kremlin to be Sergei Glazyev's commissar, his controller."[28]

On July 13, Rogozin had his own audience with the president, traveling to the presidential dacha in Novo-Ogaryovo to secure Putin's blessing. As the project had been explained to Rogozin, it was not yet entirely appealing. "The way he understood his political order was to create a bloc that would steal a few percent from the Communists. . . . Basically it was to destroy the Communists and stop short of creating something truly new," recalled Sergei Butin, a longtime aide to Rogozin.[29]

Rogozin demanded more, including Kremlin backing to help the new venture win the 5 percent necessary to secure party representation in the Duma. "When Rogozin met with the president," Butin said, "he told him he didn't want to participate knowing in advance that he would have to lose: 'I'm not prepared to participate unless I have a chance to win.' His objective was not four percent but victory. He wanted to realize his ambitions."[30] Putin gave his blessing; with it would come access to money and heavy promotion on state television. "I got carte blanche," Rogozin told us later.[31]

Other political figures were soon signed up. Third place on the ticket after Glazyev and Rogozin was taken by Valentin Varennikov, a Soviet general who had participated in the failed 1991 coup against Mikhail Gorbachev. Also enlisted were Viktor Gerashchenko, the Soviet holdover head of the Central Bank until recently, and Georgy Shpak, a general who had headed the country's paratroopers. Andrei Saviliyev, Rogozin's sometime speechwriter, represented the extreme nationalists. Vladimir Pribylovsky, an expert on Russian nationalism, called him an "open racist" who had edited a collection called *The Racial Meaning of the Russian Idea.*[32]

The party would campaign on the idea of reuniting the broken-apart Soviet Union. They wanted state control over natural resources, a ban on sales of farmland, establishment of Russian Orthodoxy as a state religion, and the end of oligarchs as a class. They embraced Rogozin's slogan, "Russians must take back Russia for themselves," and planned to offer voters a heady cocktail of Soviet-style social protection, Russian imperialism, and religious and ethnic chauvinism. And they would present it in a polite, made-for-television style, eschewing the buffoonery of ultranationalist Vladimir Zhirinovsky and the leaden anachronisms of Gennady Zyuganov.

Notwithstanding the party's soak-the-rich platform, financing was rounded up from wealthy businessmen—some of whom were placed on the party list as candidates for parliamentary seats. "For many businessmen, it was a commercial project," Pavlovsky told us.[33] Among the financiers, according to several sources, was billionaire Oleg Deripaska, whose control over Russian Aluminum made him one of the biggest of the oligarchs. "Russian Aluminum finances them only because the Kremlin asks them," said Markov.[34]

But as Glazyev and Gelman went about building their coalition, Rogozin was already planning to shift the emphasis toward nationalism and away from socialism. The opportunity came late at night before the party's founding congress in September as the principals met to hammer out last-minute details. Rogozin and others brought up the proposed name—Comrade, they said, just wasn't right, "a lousily concealed plan of failure," as Rogozin would later put it. Well after midnight, they came up with an alternative—Rodina, or Motherland. Glazyev reluctantly went along. Rogozin and his aides saw it as the beginning of their takeover. "After the decision was taken on the name, it was clear that this was a completely different project," Butin said. "The final product was very far removed from the original Glazyev-Gelman concept."[35]

On September 14, the new party was officially born. It started life as an asterisk in the polls.

VLADISLAV SURKOV summoned the would-be Chechen president to the Kremlin that fall. Malik Saidullayev, a prominent businessman who made a fortune in Moscow running a national lottery, had decided to take Vladimir Putin at his word that conditions in his war-torn homeland were "normalizing" and return to run in Chechnya's upcoming presidential election. Putin's political consiglieri had no intention of letting that happen. It would be a test run for the nationwide parliamentary elections to follow just two months later.

Early surveys showed Saidullayev leading the field, far ahead of Putin's handpicked administrator, the former rebel mufti Akhmad Kadyrov, who had been running the ravaged region as the Kremlin's viceroy for three years already. Several other credible contenders had also decided to risk the hazards of campaigning. More than 60 percent of Chechens polled said they would not under any circumstances vote for Kadyrov, whose son led a feared militia blamed for the disappearance and torture of thousands.

When they met in his office, Surkov ordered Saidullayev to drop out of the race. He should quit, Saidullayev remembered being told by Surkov, because "an order had been issued to pull Kadyrov through." Saidullayev refused. The next night, Surkov showed up at the Horse and Hound, the English pub Saidullayev owned in Moscow that served as his unofficial headquarters. Again, Saidullayev refused. The following night, Surkov came to

Saidullayev's office and stayed for three hours, cajoling him to quit. "I was offered various positions, including in business, politics, and the presidential administration," he recalled. "Many different things were offered to me, but I kept refusing."[36]

Rebuffed, the Kremlin decided to kick Saidullayev off the ballot. Four days later, another candidate—in reality an aide in Kadyrov's press office— went to court to invalidate Saidullayev's candidacy, citing incomplete nominating petitions. The court obliged within forty-eight hours, and just like that Saidullayev was out of the race. The same week, the Kremlin lured the other two conceivable threats to Kadyrov out of the running. Khusein Dzhabrailov, another businessman in Moscow's large Chechen diaspora, abruptly dropped out after talking with Surkov. Aslambek Aslakhanov, Chechnya's representative in the State Duma, pulled out after Surkov's boss, Aleksandr Voloshin, summoned him to the Kremlin and offered him a job as the president's top adviser on Chechnya. Aslakhanov told us he had concluded that he could not win anyway faced with Kremlin opposition and decided that at least "now I have the chance to meet with the president anytime I want."[37] The field was clear for Putin's choice.

For Putin, the idea of elections managed by his own aides had become such standard practice that he appeared mystified even to be asked about the systematic elimination of Kadyrov's challengers from the race. "This is more an issue of preelection tactics," he said when one of our American colleagues questioned him about it during a group interview at his dacha. "There is no violation of any legislation, democracy, nothing like this. But this is a matter of tactics employed in the preelection campaign."[38] Outcomes were what mattered, and the goal of the Chechen presidential election, just as with the forthcoming national parliamentary and presidential races, was perceived legitimacy. "People will no longer be able to say, as they sometimes do, that I am Putin's puppet," Kadyrov bragged on election day.[39] When the votes were counted from the October 5 balloting, Kadyrov was credited with more than 80 percent.

Russians had developed an all-purpose phrase to describe such electoral tactics, calling them "administrative resources." The handy catchall was used to cover the entire spectrum of latter-day political abuses—from the heavy-handed Kremlin intimidation seen in the Chechen race, to reliance on the state's army of workers to get out the vote, to governors who received election orders for how many votes they were to deliver as if these were central-planning decrees to be fulfilled. For United Russia, thirty governors were named to head the party candidate lists in their home regions—even though not a single one of them planned on actually taking a seat in parliament. Other bureaucrats and law-enforcement agents were assigned to mobilize the party's vote. Courts were used to an unprecedented degree, with a large number of lawsuits by United Russia candidates challenging opponents' rights to be on the ballot. Promotion of United Russia on television had by now reached such proportions that even Russians raised on Soviet propaganda didn't know what to make of it. "It seems that even when you plug in your iron, you will hear about this party again," joked Vladimir Podoprigora, leader of the small Democratic Power of Russia party.[40]

Typical was Konstantin Titov, governor of the industrial Samara region along the Volga River who had run against Putin in the 2000 presidential election but now promised to deliver 40 percent of his region's vote to United Russia in exchange for what local political sources told us was the Kremlin's backing for Titov to secure a third term. "It turned out we have the same political views," Titov told us. "He's helping me a lot. . . . If the president works this way, I should stand by him."[41]

For many, there was no better example of United Russia's heavy-handed campaign than in Moscow, where powerful Mayor Luzhkov was running for reelection to a third term at the same time he was running on the United Russia list for parliament. In the city's popular chain of Sedmoi Kontinent (Seventh Continent) supermarkets, United Russia bought an "advertising contract" requiring all clerks to wear party baseball caps and buttons, regardless of their personal political views.[42] In Moscow's metro, United Russia ads dominated to the virtual exclusion of all others. More than 2 million city residents received a letter from United Russia urging a vote for the party. The experience of popular incumbent Mikhail Zadornov, from the Yabloko party, was typical. Zadornov found his contracts for billboards and bus shelters mysteriously canceled, his supporters were threatened with losing their state jobs, and his United Russia opponent took him to court to try to kick him off the ballot. "All systems of the state and the Moscow government" are now working for United Russia, Zadornov found.[43]

And yet political consultants discovered that such tactics were acceptable to the pragmatic voters of the Putin era. Week by week through the official "agitation" period—the apt Russian term for campaigning—United Russia's poll ratings grew. Aleksandr Oslon's firm found that the party started at just 17 percent on November 6, hit 20 percent on November 20, 25 percent on November 27, and 28 percent by December 4.[44]

"Political ideologies stopped working. Labels like 'red' and 'white,' 'Communists' and 'right'—all these things do not pass with people anymore," political consultant Yekaterina Yegorova, whose firm was working for forty United Russia candidates, realized as the campaign progressed. "When they vote for the party of power, they understand that most likely they can get something from this candidate and very unlikely from his opponents. . . . So when people vote for United Russia it is not only because of their love for the president. But since this party is attached to the president, they think maybe they could get something out of it. The context has changed. Nobody is scared of the Communist threat anymore, nobody cares about the romantic notions of liberalism."[45]

THE CONTEXT changed again on October 25, the day Vladislav Surkov's former patron, Mikhail Khodorkovsky, was arrested and the government's campaign against Yukos Oil Company went into full swing. It was a big break for the fledgling Motherland party.

The rest of Russia's political elite either spoke out against the arrest or approached it warily, waiting to see what Putin would say. United Russia's top leaders were almost painfully silent, as they would remain for months, even when the financial markets quaked and chief of staff Aleksandr Voloshin resigned in protest. But Dmitri Rogozin and Sergei Glazyev attacked. Not only was the arrest justified, but other suspect privatization deals of the 1990s should also be investigated, they said. Their party, after all, had been founded in opposition to the oligarchs—"our enemy," Rogozin had called Russia's richest men back at the party's founding congress in September, never mind its funding from Oleg Deripaska, the aluminum king.[46] "It's important to have a public opponent, and it's important that it was scary," recalled Marat Gelman, the Motherland operative.[47]

For the democrats, already divided among themselves and financially indebted to Khodorkovsky, the arrest was a disaster. Yabloko lost nearly all of its funding, the Union of Right Forces a significant percentage. Both parties were hovering around the crucial 5 percent barrier in the polls; if they fell below it, they would be out of parliament. Just two days before the arrest, Yabloko's campaign consulting firm was raided and police confiscated the computer hard drives that contained the party's entire campaign plan down to television advertising scripts—a move seemingly intended to taint the party in the public mind as a creature of crooked oligarchs. "It was a signal," as Yavlinsky put it to us, "that Yabloko was supported by people who are thieves."[48]

Still, both parties had no choice but to defend their patron. Anatoly Chubais, the red-haired leader of the Union of Right Forces, had never been close to Khodorkovsky. But he consulted with Boris Nemtsov, the party's parliamentary leader, after Khodorkovsky's arrest. "I talked with Chubais and said there were two opportunities for us—to finish our political careers to protect Khodorkovsky or to continue them and be like prostitutes. So I asked him, 'What is better? To be a prostitute or to be dead?' And we made a decision to be dead."[49] Chubais would issue what became the most stinging public denunciation of the arrest, a demand for Putin personally to explain what was happening. It was aired on Gelman's Channel One, reflecting his close ties to the Kremlin faction of Voloshin, the angered chief of staff who was soon to quit.

Irina Khakamada, the third leader of the party and its most visible television spokesperson, disagreed, but as often was the case inside the faction-ridden Union of Right Forces, she was not asked for her opinion. "Chubais after consultations with Nemtsov announced emotionally that we need to call on the president to enforce order," she recalled. "It was a mistake because Putin hates it when somebody tries to put responsibility on him. It just irritates him."[50]

But it was the Communists who may have suffered in the most surprising ways from the arrest of Russia's richest tycoon. "The presidential administration had a job—to mess up the Communists," Gelman recalled.[51] And it had laid the groundwork for accusations that would now prove brutally effective against the party. Well before Khodorkovsky's arrest, stories had started to appear in the Kremlin-friendly Russian media about the party's supposed flirtation with exiled oligarch Boris Berezovsky. In the midst of the election season, one of Putin's predecessors as FSB chief accused Berezovsky of teaming up with Communists in a "plot against Russia," and more stories appeared detailing the preponderance of oligarch-supported candidates on the Communist parliamentary list. Gennady Zyuganov, the party leader, had played right into the Kremlin's hands by apparently auctioning off seats to the highest business bidders; one of the party's contenders, millionaire Aleksei Kondaurov, was a top Khodorkovsky lieutenant and head of the Yukos management firm.[52]

By now, Zyuganov had realized the danger and he warned publicly that Putin was running a "war of extermination" against his party.[53] But the polls were moving against him. Motherland was starting to find a ready audience in the electorate. It was a made-to-order home, a way station, for those voters who, as Pavlovsky told us, were pro-Putin but antiestablishment, no longer Communists but definitely not believers in the idea that Western-style democracy and market economics represented Russia's future. These were Russia's struggling small businessmen, its angry lower-middle class.

They were people like Anatoly Laptev, a fifty-one-year-old engineer reduced to hawking cheap Chinese-made toys in a tiny store on Moscow's soulless outskirts. A self-described nationalist, monarchist, and nostalgist for the vanished Soviet empire, Laptev was also a discontented salesman who professed willingness to give up commerce altogether if it meant that Russia had found a better, noncapitalist path to restore its past greatness. In short, he was thrilled by Motherland's arrival in Russian politics.

"In the 1990s, they told us that there is Communism and there is democracy, and nothing else in between," Laptev said. "That is not right. It is not a choice between black and white. I've lived under Communists, I've lived under democrats. It doesn't work. Motherland is another way."[54]

CHIC AND formidable in a black astrakhan fur jacket, Irina Khakamada surveyed the sad-eyed crowd at St. Petersburg's Nikolskoye Cemetery. They were there to mourn the city's best-known democratic politician five years after she was gunned down—and there to mourn as well the decline of the democracy that Galina Starovoitova had fought to build. "Galina, we will remember you," Khakamada vowed as she addressed the flower-covered grave. "We will do what we can."

In the troubled annals of recent politics in Russia, Starovoitova was the closest thing to a martyr, her murder destined to remain unsolved, the Western-oriented reform party she had helped found marginalized almost to the point of irrelevance. It was her grave that Vladimir Zhirinovsky, the ultranationalist, drank over as he testified to the perils of crossing the reinvented KGB. For Khakamada, running to fill Starovoitova's long-empty seat in parliament, the campaign was all about taking on the mantle of the slain democrat she called a close friend with whom she shared everything from ideology to fashion tips. "We are here together in her memory," said Khakamada. "Unfortunately, five years have passed and we are getting the impression that we have to start from scratch again." Russians, she said, "have fallen asleep."[55]

In many ways, the 2003 election season had revealed more starkly than ever Russia's disaffection with the democracy that Starovoitova had embraced—problems that the former Soviet dissident foresaw not long before she was shot to death on her doorstep on November 20, 1998, when she said, "The way to freedom turned out to be far harder than we thought."[56] But even she might have been shocked at the democrats' predicament just two weeks before the parliamentary elections. Both Yabloko and the Union of Right Forces faced the prospect of being ousted from the Duma. Privately, party leaders were "scared to death," as one longtime observer put it, but publicly they presented the same divided front that had long compromised their effectiveness. A disturbing number of disillusioned democratic voters were telling pollsters they either planned to vote for United Russia or not vote at all.

Instead of teaming up at a time when they each acknowledged that Russian democracy was under threat, the two parties continued to act as rivals. When Anatoly Chubais publicly proposed a deal in early November, saying it was time for him and Grigory Yavlinsky to get over the "stumbling block" of their personal feud in order to head off "a return to dictatorship," the response was a resounding no. "Nothing but cynicism and hypocrisy," replied Sergei Mitrokhin, a Yavlinsky deputy.[57] Confronted with potential extinction, the two democratic parties then spent the campaign's final days in recriminations over why they couldn't unite. Privately, the negotiations never really had a chance. "My party was never prepared to make any sort of deals with them," Yavlinsky told us later.[58] The nearest they had come had been the previous summer, when Mikhail Khodorkovsky decided to play peacemaker and twice came close enough to have aides write the text of a proposed agreement.[59] But throughout all the public speculation, Yavlinsky and Chubais had never once talked.[60]

Consumed by the internal fight, many party leaders were in denial about the seriousness of their plight. Yekaterina Yegorova, the political consultant, repeatedly talked with Nemtsov, warning him about the danger signs they were picking up in races across the country. "When we told him, 'Boris, you need to conduct this or that campaign, communications program, and so on,'" she recalled, "he said, 'I'm the best PR man in the country!'"[61]

But the ads by Nemtsov's Union of Right Forces were disastrous. On television in the campaign's closing weeks, they showed the party's three top leaders—Chubais, Nemtsov, and Khakamada—in the cocooned luxury of a private jet, talking over Russia's problems from the sanctuary of cream leather seats high above the gritty problems of a troubled, impoverished land. The Russian office of the international ad agency Saatchi & Saatchi had made the spot—"They suggested the stupid film on the plane," Nemtsov told us later, while admitting he had approved it—and it seemed to confirm voter preconceptions about the party as a club for the rich wildly out of touch with Russian reality.[62]

Even in democratic-oriented St. Petersburg, the campaign had so far showcased the failures of the democratic movement that Galina Starovoitova had once led as Khakamada ran against Gennady Seleznyov, the State Duma speaker whose Russia's Rebirth party was yet another of the Kremlin projects to break up the Communist monopoly on left-leaning voters. Khakamada had collided with what her aides called democracy fatigue—"social apathy after ten years of free elections in Russia where the population has not felt any positive changes," as her campaign consultant Sergei Gaidai told us.[63]

In Moscow, Seleznyov was viewed as a deal maker who had chosen close ties to the Kremlin over ideology. The Duma he presided over was considered a haven of vote-buying so endemic that Seleznyov himself told us it was embarrassing to run a place "always perceived as corrupted in the eyes of the public."[64] But in St. Petersburg, his native-son status and the reliable turnout of old-age pensioners who favored his Communist-flavored message were seen as overwhelming political assets.

Which is why Khakamada's campaign had come down to a last-minute rally in hopes of waking the slumbering liberals who honored Starovoitova's memory. "We have to frighten them that if they sleep through the election, the country will go back to the past," Gaidai said.[65] But in the gloom of a St. Petersburg November day, as Starovoitova's family members, political colleagues, and fans from the liberal intelligentsia trekked from event to event in her memory, few were convinced that Khakamada's strategy was working. "I am worried," Olga Starovoitova, Galina's red-eyed sister, whispered to us moments before the graveside service.[66]

SERGEI MARKOV went to the Kremlin with a proposal. With the new chief of staff, Dmitri Medvedev, sitting in on the last-minute campaign-strategy meeting, Markov suggested that the presidential administration make a late effort to head off the public relations nightmare that would surely result if the democrats were kicked out of parliament altogether. He and Gleb Pavlovsky had been going over the polls, and they were sure that it was in Putin's interest to try to help Yabloko keep its toehold in the Duma. "We have managed democracy, yes?" Markov recalled his pitch. "We have control over the media, yes? Isn't it exactly how managed democracy should be used?"

In keeping with how things worked at Putin's Kremlin, Medvedev said neither yes nor no to the idea. But within a couple days, Markov heard that Grigory Yavlinsky and his deputies had been summoned for a televised session with Putin—"a small advertising made by the Kremlin with the president as the main actor." He also heard that the orders had gone out to the television networks. "It was recommended to all TV media," Markov said, "to increase time for Yabloko and to say good words about Yabloko."[67]

Four years earlier, the Kremlin had singled out the Union of Right Forces, not Yabloko, for last-minute electoral help, grateful for its leaders' endorsement of Putin's war in Chechnya. After a televised meeting between Putin and the Union of Right Forces leaders in the 1999 campaign's final days, the party ended up with a higher-than-expected 8.6 percent of the vote, while Yabloko barely squeaked by with 5.9 percent. But Putin had long since soured on the Union of Right Forces, harboring an especially personal dislike of Boris Nemtsov, whom he accused of trying to profit politically by blaming the Kremlin for the bloody end of the Moscow theater siege. Yavlinsky, despite his stinging public rhetoric about Putinism as "capitalism with a Stalinist face," had ironically maintained much closer relations with the president, and so he showed up for his Kremlin photo op with Putin.[68]

Chubais chose a different course for the campaign's final days—an all-out attack on Motherland in hopes of scaring his own voters to the polls. In mid-November, Dmitri Rogozin said, he received a call from Chubais lieutenant Leonid Gozman. "Dmitri, we have invented a weapon against you," Rogozin recalled him saying. "From now on, you are going to be a national socialist."[69]

"These people are Hitler in the 1920s," Gozman later told us with typical bravado.[70]

In the last days before the election, the Kremlin also seemed to worry that its Motherland project was growing too successful and pulled the plug on the extravagant television coverage. Neither Rogozin nor Glazyev got any free airtime on the state-controlled news after November 24. "The administration was letting us be shown on TV as long as they thought we were stealing votes from the Communists. As soon as they realized that we are becoming an independent political force, they got scared," Rogozin told us right after the election.[71]

Despite the last-minute intrigue, the Kremlin had little doubt about the outcome headed into December 7—pollster Aleksandr Oslon was able to tell us with near-exact precision the percentage points that would be received by the winners and losers. In the end, the appeal to support the popular president had worked. For an electorate generally indifferent to politics and still influenced by Soviet-era deference to authority, even United Russia's lack of a program and refusal to debate didn't matter as the election approached. Indeed, one of Oslon's polls found that United Russia was judged to have won the televised debates—without having participated.[72]

"We'll just go and look on the ballot for Putin," said Irina Martinova, a twenty-year-old student who couldn't name United Russia but planned to vote for it nonetheless.

Her friend Olga Glozovskaya nodded. "Most other parties aren't interesting to us," she said. "And besides, it's our duty to vote for the president."[73]

■ ■ ■

PUTIN ATTEMPTED to strike a note of modesty at the end of a campaign that had ceaselessly promoted his United Russia party. "I think my preferences are already known," he said drily as flashbulbs clicked at his polling station.[74] On state television, the election-day clip played over and over, interspersed with charming footage of Putin and his rarely seen wife, Lyudmila, playing with a litter of new puppies born to their dog just that morning.

Putin's prime minister, Mikhail Kasyanov, whose popularity ratings were almost as low as the president's were high, found himself pelted by an egg as he voted, from a protester who shouted, "Your elections are a farce!"[75] Anatoly Chubais was already pretty sure of what the results would bring that night. "Many of our voters do not realize how serious the situation is," he told reporters at midday. "It could really happen that we will wake up in a different country tomorrow."[76]

As United Russia coasted to victory, the only suspense was whether the democrats would be entirely eliminated from parliament. Chubais's Union of Right Forces, officially out of favor with the Kremlin, harbored few illusions. It wasn't even midnight when Yegor Gaidar, the onetime whiz-kid economist prime minister who had masterminded Russia's rapid detox from Communism to capitalism in 1992, looked glumly over the remnants of the party he had helped found. Gaidar recalled the title of his memoir, *Days of Victory, Days of Defeat,* and turned to a visitor. "This is one of those days of defeat," Gaidar told him.[77] A few of the partygoers wondered if total defeat might not be a good thing for a party that had wavered between supporting Putin and calling him a dictator-in-the-making. At least that way, they reasoned, they would really have to go into opposition.

Yavlinsky, soothed by what appeared to be Kremlin pledges of assistance in the final days, still held out hope for his Yabloko party as the night wore on. At 2 a.m., as he rode through Moscow in his car, his mobile phone rang. Putin was on the line. "He called and said, 'Congratulations, you have overcome the five percent barrier. Please send my best regards to your colleagues, and I think we will be cooperating in the future as before,'" Yavlinsky recalled. The Yabloko leader replied that official results did not yet show his party clearing the hurdle. Don't worry, Putin replied, "I know the results in Moscow, St. Pete, and the European part of Russia, and you've overcome five percent."[78]

Over at Gelman's Channel One, Glazyev was preparing to go live on well-known host Vladimir Pozner's election-night talk show to bask in Motherland's strong showing. It was already clear that the party, which had not even existed three months earlier, had easily cleared the 5 percent hurdle to make it into parliament. As Oslon had predicted to us the week before the election, Motherland was the not-so-secret "surprise" of the night.[79] But the orders still stood from the Kremlin not to give Glazyev and his team too much publicity. "I wasn't allowed to appear," he recalled. "Some lady showed up just before the start and ordered Pozner to ban me from the program." Glazyev demanded to know who she was; he was told by people at the station that she received orders "directly from Surkov," Putin's chief political aide.[80]

By morning, the decimation of the democrats was so complete that both parties finished behind "none of the above" in the party-list voting, with just over 4 percent each, despite Putin's reassurance to Yavlinsky. Not a single one of Russia's most prominent democratic leaders won an individual seat in parliament either. Overall, just a handful of democrats were elected—four from Yabloko and three from the Union of Right Forces, compared with forty-eight before the election. Even in Russia's two most liberal cities, Moscow and St. Petersburg, which had benefited the most from the economic reforms of the 1990s, democrats finished a distant third. "It's all our fault," Khakamada, who also lost her race in St. Petersburg, told reporters. "The democrats themselves are to blame."[81]

Otherwise, Oslon's predictions were dead-on accurate. United Russia finished with 37 percent of the party-list vote—just shy of the 40 percent target the governors had been ordered to produce. The humbled Communists had fallen to just 13 percent, roughly half of their total of four years previously and barely ahead of Vladimir Zhirinovsky's misnamed, ultranationalist Liberal Democrats, who took 12 percent for their strongest showing in years. Motherland had the 9 percent Oslon had foreseen for it, meaning that together the two nationalist groups claimed 21 percent of the vote.

In reality, the scale of United Russia's victory was far bigger than the party-list voting indicated. The party had also finished strongly in the balloting for individual districts—winning 100 seats out of the 225 up for grabs—and other pro-Kremlin independents who had not run on the United Russia line would be persuaded to join the party's faction once the Duma met. So even though less than 40 percent of Russia's voters had opted for United Russia, Putin's party would claim 68 percent of the new Duma.

"We are living in a new Russia now," Surkov crowed the next morning. "A new political era is coming, and the parties that have not gotten into the Duma should be calm about it and realize that their historical mission has been completed."[82]

United Russia had managed to pull off Surkov's goal—it now controlled the two-thirds of the Duma necessary to change the constitution. In the future, Putin's already unchallenged hold over parliament would be unassailable. Now, the Kremlin would be able to do whatever it wanted—including possibly getting rid of the limit restricting Putin to two terms in office. To foreign observers, the elections were egregiously flawed, "free but not fair," as the largest independent group, the Organization for Security and Cooperation in Europe, termed it the day after the balloting. In particular, the monitors decried "unequal campaign opportunities" and "clear bias" in the media on behalf of United Russia. News was so tilted, the OSCE found, that 56 percent of all coverage on Marat Gelman's Channel One in November was about Putin or United Russia.[83]

"Politics is finished," Gelman declared.[84] His mission accomplished, Gelman resigned the day after the elections with a flourish, bragging of his success in crushing the Communists and insisting that in Putin's Russia there was no more need for political consultants or even political analysis of any sort on television. "They have other instruments—very effective ones," Gelman said laughingly when we spoke with him at his modernist Moscow flat several months later. "Like tax inspectors and prosecutors." For all of his efforts on Putin's behalf, Gelman had come to recognize the dangers of the one-party rule he had helped establish. The people in the Kremlin, he realized, had unchecked power. "They've got all the instruments at their disposal now," he said, "and it is very dangerous."[85]

Putin's Russia

The time of uncertainty and anxious expectations is past.
—VLADIMIR PUTIN

KATYA KHROMOVA WAS depressed. She cried too readily. She had a hard time sleeping. She worried constantly about what would become of her and her husband, Misha, and their seven-year-old son, Danil. Maybe if she had a bathroom in her tiny two-room apartment. Or if she hadn't seen the neighborhood kids shooting up heroin right outside the crumbling apartment house where they lived. Or if Misha could find a better job. Or if his sister weren't so successful in a city best compared to an industrial disaster area.

"This year I told Misha, 'Enough! I cannot take this anymore,'" Katya recounted to us, tears leaping unsummoned from her delicate brown eyes as she surveyed their minuscule kitchen.

Her ultimatum, of course, had gone unanswered, just another debate in the continuing series of how to change their lives. The Khromovs, college sweethearts who had married at twenty-two, now feared they were trapped before they turned thirty. They never stopped discussing the future—for themselves and their battered city of Ivanovo. In Vladimir Putin's Russia, it was the one question that mattered, and they were afraid to answer it.[1]

Paralyzed by stability, the tenuous stability of the four years of Putin's presidency, they lived on as they had been. Each Sunday, they took Danil to his grandparents' wooden cottage for a weekly bath and a glimpse of their braying cows. Nearly every day, they agonized over whether Misha should find a new job, abandoning the modest security of his government's paycheck for the risky but potentially more lucrative life of a private lawyer.

"Some call it stability," said Misha, "but you could just as easily call it stagnation."

As he said it, it was hard to tell whether he was talking about Russia's situation or his own.

We met Misha and Katya on the eve of the presidential election in the spring of 2004, as Putin headed toward an inevitable victory and the young pair wrestled with whether to vote for the president and took stock of what his four years in power had brought them. Far away from the fawning pro-Putin propaganda on Russia's now entirely state-controlled television, far removed from the neon lights of the Moscow boom, their debate about the president was the one the country might have had—if there had been a public debate at all about an election whose preordained outcome masked a Russia firmly behind Putin yet still deeply uncertain about his policies.

On a trip to Ivanovo, a bumpy four-hour drive northeast from Moscow, we stumbled on the Khromovs through the night cleaning lady at the local newspaper office, who was a moonlighting doctor unable to survive solely on the poverty-level wages offered at the state-run lab where Katya worked as an assistant. While Misha and Katya hesitated about voting for the president, Misha's thriving sister and her husband had no qualms about supporting him, because Putin represented "strength," and they were all about backing the winner. Misha's parents, at home with their cows and their memories of a better life, knew for sure they would not vote for him.

For all of them, the question posed by the election was not whether to choose the already anointed president but the choice he offered them: a return to a more authoritarian Russia in exchange for an end to the upheavals of the 1990s. At home, Misha worried he was trading opportunity for security, just as he fretted that Putin-style order was only a variant on the dead-end past. He was uncertain about the president, and about his own course.

"People like President Putin because he is the one who guarantees a quiet life," Misha told us the first time we met over tea and sweet cakes in their tiny apartment. He just wasn't sure that was enough for him. "There is stability in my job," he added, "but no possibilities."

These were no abstractions. Misha's family was divided between nostalgia for the Soviet past and a hard-edged present where money came to the few who were lucky or tough enough to get it. On one side of town, his parents lived in a dilapidated wooden house, selling milk to survive where they had once lived comfortably. Misha's father, Valery, a physics teacher trusted enough by the Communist Party to work abroad in Algeria, now pitched hay and kept his party card as a valued relic of a different time. On the other edge of Ivanovo, Misha's sister, Lena, lived in a custom-built chalet, debating whether to send her daughter to a Swiss boarding school and filled with plans for the 150-room hotel she had just purchased.

Misha was exasperated by both. He thought his parents were crazy to be raising cows in the middle of Ivanovo. "Cows should be in a village, where there are fields," he said. "But this is a city! Cows should not be where there are trolleybuses." As for his sister, why didn't she just pay their parents to give up the cows? "They would take it if she came and put money on the table," he said.

Katya veered between despair and resignation, powerless to affect events, whether the presidential election she called a game in which ordinary people like her were not welcome or the future of a city where everyone was divided into winners and losers and those like them, hovering precariously between the two. "New times bring new illnesses," she said of the depression that had struck her the previous fall. Then she squared her slight shoulders and headed back down four flights of stairs in the dank hallway that always smelled slightly of cat piss to take Danil to the $2.75-a-month music lessons that let her preserve the illusion of being middle class.

As CAMPAIGNS go, the third presidential election in post-Soviet Russia was off to an inauspicious start. At precisely 8 a.m. on February 12, 2004, the race lurched to an official beginning with the first in a series of televised debates between the candidates, the early hour guaranteed to attract few viewers. Putin boycotted. Instead, breakfast was interrupted for a little-known Communist, a socialist, and a capitalist, who took turns politely answering questions from the audience. Finally, even the moderator was bored.

"Where are the debates between candidates?" he interjected plaintively.

Irina Khakamada, the capitalist with the couture wardrobe, quickly retorted, "Bring Vladimir Putin here, and we will have a debate."[2]

The real campaign began a few hours later, when Putin addressed supporters at Moscow State University. Despite rules forbidding a candidate from receiving unequal airtime, the president's half-hour-long address was carried live and in full on state television. Later, the Central Election Commission obligingly brushed aside complaints on the matter, citing the great public interest in what the president had to say.

Bolstered by an approval rating north of 70 percent, a booming economy, and the decision of virtually all the country's leading politicians to sit out the race, Putin had adopted the campaign strategy that he had won with four years earlier: elusiveness. Not only did he eschew debates, he had no campaign ads on television, no placards plastering the cities, no campaign slogan or policy platform, and no plans to produce any.

His six rivals were a study in obscurity. The Communists, humiliated in the December parliamentary elections, offered up Nikolai Kharitonov, a little-known former collective farmer and colonel in the special services, rather than party leader Gennady Zyuganov, who had almost toppled Yeltsin from the presidency in 1996. Even ultranationalist Vladimir Zhirinovsky, usually first in line for any opportunity that offered him a microphone, declined the race, putting forward his former bodyguard instead. Sergei Mironov, a Putin loyalist from St. Petersburg who headed the Federation Council, or upper chamber of parliament, was running despite being a presidential cheerleader, almost certainly at the behest of the Kremlin to foster the illusion of a genuine democratic competition. Mironov did not even bother to hide his backing for the president. "When a leader goes into battle, he cannot be left without support," he said by way of explaining his candidacy to us.[3]

Sergei Glazyev, the Communist defector who had helped lead the new Motherland party to its surprising success in December, had founded the group with tacit Kremlin aid but broke with his partner, Dmitri Rogozin, and insisted on running against Putin anyway. For much of the race, the young economist was in second place behind the president—with no more than 4 percent in the polls. "Putin's glory is at its zenith right now," Rogozin told us not long before his rift with Glazyev became public and irreconcilable. "Serious politicians are getting ready for the next elections [in 2008] when [Putin] will withdraw from the scene and are not getting involved in this circus."[4]

Khakamada, Russia's best-known female politician, was one of the only serious figures to enter the race. Yet she did not even have the endorsement of her own party. Some of her Union of Right Forces colleagues favored a boycott of the election, while others at least tacitly backed Putin. Spurned by them, she turned to imprisoned oil magnate Mikhail Khodorkovsky's partners for help. Her campaign staff was paid for by Leonid Nevzlin, a Khodorkovsky partner who had fled to Israel to avoid prosecution. "People should learn how to resist," Khakamada told us. "We cannot win, but we have to learn to resist."[5]

But Khakamada found little audience for her accusations about Putin's "Sovietization" of Russia. Indeed, the only candidate aside from the president to receive much attention was Ivan Rybkin, a former speaker of the State Duma now bankrolled by exiled oligarch Boris Berezovsky. As if to prove the election-as-farce theory of current Russian politics, Rybkin disappeared mid-campaign, reemerging days later to declare that he had sneaked off to Ukraine and then decided to remain in hiding there because he feared the Russians might harm him. After fleeing to London, he then recanted his story and spoke of being drugged and kidnapped by mysterious KGB-like agents.[6]

Putin himself gave little hint that February day where he would take Russia in his second term. He never asked for anyone's vote and began his speech by swearing off "self-promotion" and other conventional forms of electioneering. Instead, he lamented the collapse of the Soviet Union in stronger terms than he ever had before publicly, calling it a "national tragedy on a colossal scale." Unlike his campaign rhetoric of four years earlier, he made not even token references to democracy and offered no promises about future economic or political reforms. And he gave voters neither the comfort of a new ideology nor the shared enterprise of a national project.

Instead, he made the case simply for stability. Although he had already been running Russia for more than four years, he emphasized himself once again as the anti-Yeltsin and traced the country's current evils not to seven decades of Communist dictatorship and decay but to the tumultuous liberal experiments of the 1990s. "It seemed at times that the string of upheavals would never end," he said. "Today we feel that the time of uncertainty and anxious expectations is past."[7]

AT 6:30 A.M., Misha Khromov was already awake, ready to head to his office in the blue government building, in the shadow of the massive Lenin quote praising Ivanovo's proletariat for helping give birth to the Bolshevik revolution. Misha commuted by foot and bus because they had no car. "Ivanovo," he said, "is like when they say on the weather forecast that it will be sunny everywhere except for one place where it's raining. Ivanovo is the rainy area."

In Soviet times, everyone knew about Ivanovo, the textile city on the banks of the Uvod River, thanks to the song from the 1981 movie *Honest, Intelligent, Unmarried*. People can still quote it from memory, the one about a man's unrequited love and his threat to go to Ivanovo, "the city of brides," to find a woman grateful for his attentions. Back then, in Misha and Katya's childhood, Ivanovo was called the Red Manchester by the party's propagandists, and its forty-four mills turned out two-thirds of all the cotton fabric in the Soviet Union. It was there they made the suits for Central Committee members and the uniforms for the Soviet army. Thousands of women worked in the mills, many of them imported from Central Asia along with the raw cotton. Men were outnumbered ten to one.

These days, the factories mostly sat idle in the city of 432,000. Some had been converted into malls filled with imported fabrics, which were both cheaper and higher quality than the remaining bolts turned out in Ivanovo. Official figures showed that 63 percent of residents now lived in poverty, the highest total in central Russia. Left behind and aware of it, the region was one of the few still governed by a Communist. "Sooner or later," Katya said of their city, "it will just die."

Misha and Katya came of age amid the empire's collapse. They started university in 1991 during the Soviet breakup. In 1996, they married and Misha began work as a lawyer in the Tax Ministry; in 2002, he was promoted to head the regional legal department. At the age of twenty-nine, Misha had by now been a tax man his whole working life; even his parents called him a born *chinovnik,* a bureaucrat. He saw little but corruption and paper-shuffling at his work. Talk of modernizing the system, he told us, "is like believing you can launch a nuclear missile from a peasant's hut." In court, he faced private lawyers he called "sharks" and quietly wondered whether he could be like them.

The couple had little nostalgia for the past. To Katya, the enforced uni-formity of their Young Pioneer days was a curse she hoped their son, Danil, would never have to bear. But to Misha, the hard times of the last decade were just as problematic. "I don't know what we did, but we got through it," he said. "Russians have always been like lab rats—the harder the conditions, the more desire to live. It's very hard to destroy us, to drown us."

Putin had been to their city just once, during the 2000 election. He had visited the institute where Katya worked and announced he would never stoop to campaign advertising, as if the president of Russia were "a Tampax or a Snickers." Left to divine Putin's intentions, Misha had voted against all candidates in 2000 because "I quickly understood that this was what we were offered to eat and I didn't want to partake of it." Now, he was more sanguine as the new election approached. "At least I know what Putin is," he said, "and I'm not that allergic to him."

They had seen modest changes in the city for the better in Putin's first term, like the appearance of the supermarket around the corner where Katya now shopped and the modern electronics store where they bought a com-puter for Danil on credit. But they had also seen how Ivanovo had lost out, its airport closed, its streets cratered and mostly unlit in the perpetual gloom of the Russian winter. For all of Putin's promises of reform, mortgages to help them buy a better apartment remained more urban legend than reality. Gov-ernment salaries had been raised, but as Misha said, "if my salary went up eleven percent, inflation was twelve percent."

With household income around $450 a month, the couple was doing well by Ivanovo standards.

It just didn't seem that way.

"What we are offered," Misha said wryly on a day off for Defenders of the Fatherland Day, a Putin-era addition to the Russian holiday calendar when many toasts were drunk to the glorious victories of the Soviet army, "is a cer-tain compromise between the bad and the not so bad."

■ ■ ■

IT WAS NOT by accident that Russian voters ended up with such a choice. From the start, Putin's Kremlin aides were determined to control every facet of the president's inexorable march to a second term, down to deciding which token candidates would run against him.

As with all of Putin's political operations, the effort was run by the aggressive young operative Vladislav Surkov, the former Mikhail Khodor- kovsky lieutenant now willing to stay on as the Kremlin set out to destroy his onetime boss. In charge of Putin's campaign headquarters was Dmitri Kozak, the fellow St. Petersburger who had led the early failed drive for judicial reform.

To start, their job was to ensure that neither Gennady Zyuganov nor Vladimir Zhirinovsky, the two potential candidates who could conceivably force Putin into a second-round runoff by holding him under 50 percent, would run. "They were very, very focused. For them it was very important to win in the first round," recalled Sergei Markov, the Kremlin-linked political consultant.[8] Both politicians quickly received the message after the December parliamentary elections. Two days after the balloting, Zhirinovsky had even announced his intention of running against Putin—only to withdraw his candidacy well before the end of the month.[9] Zyuganov also abruptly bowed out. Neither offered much explanation.

With the main obstacles to a first-round victory eliminated, Kremlin aides shifted attention to threats such as Sergei Glazyev, the articulate leftist popular for his oligarch-bashing and pledges to restore the Soviet-era social safety net that Putin seemed intent on dismantling. At first, Surkov sent his messages to Glazyev through Dmitri Rogozin, the Putin loyalist who was leading the Motherland Party along with Glazyev. Rogozin passed them along, warning Glazyev not to run and promoting instead the token candi- dacy of Motherland's Viktor Gerashchenko, the geriatric former Central Bank chief once called "the worst central banker in the world."[10] Rogozin made no effort to disguise his notion that the effort would be symbolic.

But Glazyev was intent on running himself, insisting he was uninterested in endorsing a "farce" with a "candidate who wouldn't pose any threat to Putin whatsoever."[11] Suddenly the party was on the verge of breaking up just weeks after its triumph. Surkov cut out the middleman and started calling Glazyev directly. "The calls from the Kremlin followed saying that I shouldn't run in the election because it's not part of their plan," Glazyev recalled. "Surkov called several times and demanded that I put my plans aside. They wanted the mechanism of managed elections to work."[12]

On December 20, Motherland's Rogozin-dominated political council met and shunned Glazyev, formally endorsing the central banker as its presidential candidate. Glazyev refused to accept the decision, announcing instead his own bid and plan to create a new political movement under the Motherland banner. Rogozin took it as a declaration of war. "He wanted to steal the political brand of 'Motherland,'" recalled a senior Rogozin aide. It was, he said, Glazyev's "fatal mistake."[13] The Kremlin had not succeeded in driving him out of the race, but from that point on, Putin's aides would make common cause with Glazyev's erstwhile allies in trying to destroy his candidacy.

At the same time it was trying to force Glazyev out, the Kremlin was urgently trying to encourage at least one candidate among Russia's feuding, demoralized democrats to run—to ensure that a challenger could be found for the president who would confer a stamp of legitimacy on the race in the West. "It was also important not to make it a farce," recalled Markov. "They wanted to stop a boycott."[14]

Just days after his party was knocked out of parliament, Yabloko leader Grigory Yavlinsky was approached by Putin aides who tried to recruit him to run to give the contest the appearance of a real election. "Some people in the Kremlin asked me to run," he recalled in an interview at Yabloko's spacious new headquarters, paid for a year earlier with Khodorkovsky's now rapidly disappearing money. "I responded, 'No way, I am not going to take part in the play.'"[15]

The Union of Right Forces leader Boris Nemtsov also flirted with the idea, but then claimed that Yavlinsky had spoiled the democrats' chances by refusing to go along with a joint effort. "He was not ready to support me as a united candidate. Of course, he said a hundred times that he was prepared for it, but when we discussed the matter, he said no," Nemtsov said. Others then turned to an articulate young member of parliament, Vladimir Ryzhkov, who had emerged as the leader of the few independents left in the State Duma now that the two established democratic parties were no longer represented. Ryzhkov was intrigued, but told Nemtsov he could not run without support from all the varied democratic factions, and once again Yavlinsky emerged as the main obstacle. In the end, Ryzhkov, too, declined a mission that could end up as political suicide, leaving some like Nemtsov convinced that "Ryzhkov was afraid of pressure, of the Kremlin."[16]

But as always, the intrigue was so thick it seemed that many of the democratic leaders were more interested in plotting ways to inflict further damage on each other than on the president. Khakamada, soon to style herself the "kamikaze" candidate in homage to her father's Japanese ancestry, recalled those December meetings as a tortured set of machinations. "There was always one goal—to put forward a person whose future wouldn't be ruined by it," she told us, "and that's why Nemtsov said no, because he keeps thinking about the future. Well, I told him there won't be any future. Then they proposed Yavlinsky so that he *doesn't* have any future. He figured it out and refused. Then Vladimir Ryzhkov refused, also because he was thinking about the future. I said that I didn't care about the future because there is no future and it has to be built here and now. Everybody disagreed with that. . . . Each one was only thinking about his own future. That's why the democrats lose everything in Russia."[17]

By late December, the democrats were leaning toward a boycott of the race altogether as they tried to regroup from the disastrous elections. Looking toward 2008, Nemtsov even secretly reached out to Putin's prime minister, Mikhail Kasyanov, to see if he would be interested in becoming the party's new leader.[18] At the decisive meeting just before the end of the year in a conference room at Moscow's Marco Polo hotel, however, Khakamada insisted on running. Nemtsov and "shock therapy" architect Yegor Gaidar angrily told her she was crazy, that there was no way they could collect the signatures necessary to put her on the ballot. Many were sure Khakamada had become a candidate at the Kremlin's behest, a lingering suspicion that was mostly put to rest when she published a broadside attacking Putin's handling of the 2002 Moscow theater siege by Chechen terrorists and decided to accept the financial patronage of Leonid Nevzlin, Khodorkovsky's exiled partner. But in the system of managed democracy, it seemed plausible that even the president's harshest critic could actually be acting on his behalf. "The elite," she recalled, "kept trying to figure out whether I was bought by the Kremlin or not."[19]

MISHA KHROMOV's sister, Lena, nibbled on the green grapes and Brie she was serving as hors d'oeuvres on a Tuesday night not long before the election. She had on a T-shirt and sparkly flip-flops that showed off her pedicure. Outside their chalet, her award-winning landscape garden was still covered under a blanket of late-winter snow.

She and her husband, Sergei, were talking about Misha, and what he should do. Lena, thirty-six, said she had offered to help her brother find a private-sector job. "But he was afraid," she said. "He didn't want to lose his stability."

Their own fears were different.

"When we got property," Lena said, "we started to feel very insecure."

"Because when you have property, there is always someone who wants to take it away from you," Sergei added.

The two started as *spekulanty* in the late 1980s, speculators who sold jeans, cosmetics, whatever was available; Lena's Communist parents were appalled. As the Soviet Union broke apart, the young couple opened a network of kiosks. By 1997, they had enough to buy shares in a textile factory and to build their dream house. In 2003, they purchased Lunyovo, a Soviet-era concrete-block "house of rest" on the banks of the Volga River about fifty miles north of Ivanovo and turned their efforts to the hotel business. They predicted a great future in the revival of Russian domestic tourism.

At home, their daughter Leya's room was almost as big as Misha's entire apartment, and Sergei was debating whether to buy a billiards table to fill up the empty expanse on the third floor. They vacationed in Europe and Dubai. For her eighth birthday, Leya received a cell phone. "All the other kids have them," Lena explained before heading back into the gourmet kitchen for the fish and vegetable-studded rice. But theirs was a world without certainty. "In Russia, you can be rich, but you can become a beggar overnight. You can easily end up in prison," she said, shuddering at the thought of Khodorkovsky, jailed since the previous fall.

In their business, Sergei said, "everything is possible" as long as you pay the right bribes and befriend the right officials.

"Putin's 'dictatorship of the law' is just words," added Lena, though she still planned to vote for the president.

The next morning, Sergei, driving a borrowed Soviet-vintage Zhiguli because his Audi was in the shop, headed to the hotel.

At first, he was expansive, running through a list of improvements to the place they had in mind—a water-treatment spa, tennis courts, private villas built in "Russian village" style. But Sergei and Lena were not yet believers in banks and credit cards, and they needed the hotel to make enough money to finance their ambitious plans. And so far, guests were few, even at $15 a night, three meals included. Inspecting the hotel's empty rooms, Sergei waited expectantly for a report on an upcoming holiday weekend. But the bookings were not good. "Only fifty-two," Sergei said, visibly disappointed.

Just then, his cell phone buzzed with news from Lena. The hotel's liquor license was about to expire, and no one had submitted the paperwork to renew it. If they didn't get it immediately, even the modest proceeds from the weekend would evaporate. In Russia, a hotel without a liquor license is no hotel at all.

At first, Lena reported over the mobile phone, the bureaucrats were unresponsive and the new license wouldn't be ready for a month.

"This isn't going to work," Sergei said testily to an aide. "Why didn't you do it before?"

But, as the late-afternoon sun dropped away from the frozen expanse of the Volga, the phone rang again.

"It'll be ready on Friday," Lena said.

"You are such a fixer!" Sergei told her. If there was a price, he didn't mention it.

PUTIN'S FIXERS set out not only to guarantee his victory, but to determine every detail of it—from the size of the turnout and pro-presidential vote they would demand from each governor to the amount of television time allotted to each of the also-rans. The orders were specific, almost comically detailed at times. To "ensure the victory of our candidate with at least 80 percent of the vote," a memo sent out to top government officials in the central Russia region of Mari El demanded a program of talent shows, disco dances, folk art displays, and jamborees aimed at "enforcing a voter turnout close to 75 percent." Every polling station was required to play music to lure voters on election day, and officials had to organize meetings in all government agencies beforehand to ensure participation. Where necessary, state employees should not hesitate to "conduct persuasion work," the memo said.[20] "Our candidate," of course, was Putin.

In managing the race so completely, the Kremlin's main adversary may well have been overconfidence. Just how big, wondered some of the president's political advisers, was too big for a Putin victory? Although the orders went out in some regions demanding more, presidential operatives from the start fixed on a number just over 70 percent. Impressive, but not greedy, went the reasoning. "This time the only problem was not to get too much," Vyacheslav Nikonov, the Kremlin-tied political consultant, recalled. "Seventy-five would be too much. Seventy-two was just right."[21]

Little was left to chance. Early on, for example, NTV announced that it would not air the presidential debates since Putin was not participating. "It was clear that its management did not do it of their own will," Irina Khakamada recalled, "because just before that they talked to us about our participation, how much we'll have to pay for it—because debates on private channels are paid for." For her, it was a "disaster," since NTV, not the stodgier state channels, attracted virtually all the younger, better-off viewers who might conceivably have supported Khakamada.[22]

At times, local zealousness to carry out orders from the center resulted in excesses that were particularly heavy-handed. In the Far East city of Khabarovsk, hospital patients were ordered to vote—or find themselves out of a hospital bed. Others resorted to more positive incentives, such as free movie tickets in Vladivostok and hair-salon coupons in Nakhodka. In the Siberian province of Yakutia, voters who turned out were promised a discount of five hundred rubles ($18) off their utility bill, a savings of up to one-third their monthly payment.[23]

Even the token campaigning attempted by Putin's rivals was often blocked. Glazyev found halls shuttered and lights turned off across the country. Khakamada was barred from meeting with students in Nizhny Novgorod and union members in Moscow.[24] "Ironically, I realized that the top leadership of the Kremlin benefited from my appearance, but the machine was already running by itself," Khakamada said. "They can't manage this machine anymore. It kills everything. It starts self-censorship, self-control. It's the fear that's been accumulating in people's minds for centuries. . . . The authorities—they make one step, and the remaining so-called vertical continues it with thousands of steps."[25]

Whoever gave the order, running against Putin was made to be as difficult as possible. "In the regions they several times wouldn't let us meet with voters, just refused," recalled Khakamada's campaign manager, Marina Litvinovich. "We could not find office space for the headquarters. They just heard the name Khakamada and refused. We were looking for a company to cut the ads. They said they did not want problems with the tax police. Then we received phone threats. . . . They called me and said, 'It's antistate activity. Think well what you are doing. We know where your child is.' Right on my mobile phone."[26]

The president's men were particularly determined to crush Sergei Glazyev, and not only in the election. Vladislav Surkov, Putin's political enforcer, took personal charge of the effort to make an example of the politician who had balked at the Kremlin's rules, meeting individually throughout February and March with the members of Motherland in parliament to organize Glazyev's ouster as the party's official Duma faction leader. Dmitri Rogozin also worked hard against his onetime partner. "This was personal. They thought he promised them not to run," Sergei Markov recalled. "It was the president, not just Surkov."[27] Putin, recalled one of his advisers, "understood that Glazyev started to behave independently. It's not allowed. It's against the rules."[28]

Rogozin's aides whispered of Glazyev's alleged ties to the hated oligarch

Boris Berezovsky, talked of his "Napoleonic complex," and even played on Russia's male chauvinism by telling other parliament members to compare the effectiveness of Rogozin's all-male staff with that of Glazyev's female aides.[29] One of Surkov's Kremlin staffers worked openly out of Rogozin's office. "They tried to intimidate our deputies. Businessmen were promised Khodorkovsky's fate if they didn't comply, bureaucratic careerists were promised jobs, others were promised medals and money for political treason," Glazyev told us.[30] Rogozin was unapologetic about the hardball tactics. "Glazyev could have dedicated himself to party-building," said Rogozin's adviser. "But he chose an independent political game."[31] In the end, control of Motherland's parliamentary faction came down to Sergei Baburin, head of the nationalist People's Will party, part of the Motherland coalition. With Baburin's allegiance secured just weeks before the presidential election, Rogozin won Glazyev's post as party leader, while Baburin scored the party's vice speaker slot, Glazyev's office, and his official car. "I told Glazyev directly—you wrecked the bloc," Baburin said when the move became public.[32] Administrative levers were also deployed against Glazyev—the Justice Ministry decided to grant Rogozin's Russia's Regions party the right to rename itself Motherland, thus blocking Glazyev from using the name. The bureaucrats acted on Rogozin's request in an unheard-of three days.

The message was clear: "The reason they got rid of me is because I didn't play by the rules they were forcing on me," Glazyev told us several months later, sitting in the cramped cubbyhole he now shared with two aides as he fought off a Kremlin-inspired court challenge to strip him of his parliamentary seat. "According to these rules, all politically active people have to report to the presidential administration."[33]

But several weeks out from the election, Putin's three most plausible rivals briefly threatened to defy the Kremlin's script, as aides to Kharitonov, Khakamada, and Glazyev held secret negotiations about dropping out en masse from the increasingly absurd race. "It was a chance to turn the election into a farce. Everybody understood it," recalled Marina Litvinovich, the Khakamada aide.[34] For days, the secret held. Then, Glazyev's campaign manager announced publicly the morning of February 24 that he was thinking of dropping out. Khakamada quickly followed suit. Kharitonov, too, seemed receptive.

It was the only weapon they had left.

VLADIMIR PUTIN summoned his long-serving prime minister, Mikhail Kasyanov, to his office that same afternoon.

"Unfortunately," Putin told him, "I have to fire you."

Even as he spoke, the Kremlin was already releasing the news. Upstaging his challengers, Putin had decided to dismiss Kasyanov and the rest of the cabinet. It was the first such shake-up in the president's four-year tenure. "I have decided today that the government is to resign," Putin declared in the terse public statement. No reasons were given.

Despite the president's overwhelming advantages, Putin's advisers were secretly worried that a mass dropout of candidates would make the race so uninteresting as to reduce turnout below the required 50 percent threshold. If that happened, another round of elections would have to be scheduled, and the Kremlin would have to deal not only with that embarrassment but with the specter of Kasyanov becoming acting president for the month between the end of Putin's first term and the new balloting. It was a remote possibility, but still untenable for a Kremlin that believed no detail of democracy was too small to be managed. "In his mentality," as one senior official told us of Putin, "every risk should be minimized to zero."

Inside the Kremlin, the *siloviki* who had long agitated for Kasyanov's ouster had seized on such fears to convince Putin now was finally the time to fire the prime minister. Kasyanov was the last senior link to the Boris Yeltsin days, and virtually the only member of Putin's government who had offered even token public disagreement when Mikhail Khodorkovsky had been arrested. He had fought Putin in private sometimes as well, opposing the storm on the theater on Dubrovka Street, which would prove so deadly. And now his rivals had effectively poisoned the president against him, warning that Kasyanov was entertaining offers from Boris Nemtsov and others to lead the democratic opposition. "His people took that fact and accelerated it into this great story," recalled the senior official.[35]

Kasyanov was also highly unpopular, associated in the public mind with oligarchs and the shortcomings of the Yeltsin era; firing him would only shore up the president's support in the upcoming election. While Putin's approval rating was stratospheric for a politician, Kasyanov generally registered no more than a 30 percent positive rating in polls and 50 percent negative—a classic case of the Russian penchant to blame the tsar's courtiers, and not the tsar himself, for the government's failings.

Putin had signaled his discontent just two days earlier, clashing with Kasyanov at a closed-door cabinet meeting over the cutoff of gas deliveries to neighboring Belarus until the discussion became so heated Putin abruptly ended the session. But according to an account Kasyanov later gave associates, the prime minister had no sense of his impending ouster until Putin abruptly canceled their daily meeting the morning of Kasyanov's final day. When Putin summoned him that afternoon, the president never even gave a reason for the dismissal. Kasyanov was so stunned he simply assumed Putin meant he would be out of a job when Putin began his expected second term in May. "I mean now," Putin corrected the prime minister.

The decision had been made so hastily that neither Putin nor chief of staff Dmitri Medvedev was aware of the procedure for firing the prime minister— which required Putin to fire the rest of his cabinet as well—until Kasyanov mentioned it. Putin's aides made clear to the ousted prime minister that even the distant prospect of Kasyanov as acting president was enough to force him out. After all, Kasyanov would at least technically gain control over the television airwaves—and with it, the power to determine the election's outcome. Putin remembered all too well how he had been a creature of television back in 1999, and he did not trust Kasyanov with such a powerful instrument. "He understood," the official said, "that television could be switched, just like he did, and everything could be turned in one month."

To the public, Putin's move simply seemed an effort to liven up the nonexistent campaign. For four years, Kasyanov's job had regularly been rumored to be in jeopardy. But somehow when the ax finally fell in the middle of the campaign, it still came as a surprise. "It adds an element of drama," Vyacheslav Nikonov said of the move.[36] In a race whose outcome was already known, the Kremlin had even taken to stage-managing the suspense.

WORK WAS Katya Khromova's refuge, a two-room lab where she spent her days processing blood tests to determine genetic birth defects. They were perpetually short of the expensive Finnish reactives needed to do the tests, and their facility of about a hundred employees had only one telephone line. Salaries were barely above the official poverty level—$100 a month for lab assistants like Katya, $200 for the doctors. The foursome of two doctors and two lab assistants cooked lunch together on the office hot plate—usually porridge, "sometimes sausages, if we can afford it," said Yelena, one of the doctors. Irina, the other doctor, was the one who had taken a second job as a cleaning lady at the local newspaper—for $1.75 a night. The other lab assistant had lost her son, a veteran of the war in Chechnya working as a security guard in Ivanovo, when he was killed in a robbery by men believed to be his fellow veterans of an elite police unit.

All Katya's workmates were older than she was and served as a constant sounding board of advice and counsel. They were intimately familiar with the troubles in her narrow life. "One head is good," Katya said. "Four heads are better." Each of them found herself struggling with the trade-off between stability and opportunity that had come to obsess Misha and Katya at home. Irina could have found a second job in the world of the new capitalist Russia, selling cosmetics as an Avon lady, "but there's no stability. You might waste time and not get anything. But with cleaning floors, you know you will get fifty rubles a day."

They rarely talked about politics, convinced, as Katya said, that in Russia it was not an audience-participation sport. Recently, though, the presidential election had intruded on their daily group therapy. The head of the institute was one of Putin's three designated campaign leaders for the region and had ordered employees to sign petitions to place him on the ballot. None of them particularly liked Putin; all of them signed. This was the sort of Soviet-era command-driven politics that all except for young Katya still readily remembered.

"Sure, we have stability," Irina said. "Everything's bad and stable."

"At least if we fall down, we don't have far to fall," Yelena joked.

Katya left the room to change into street clothes for the long afternoon of trudging through icy streets with Danil. Complaints aside, the others said they would vote for the president. Even fears of Putin's authoritarian leanings would not deter them. The Russian ballot offered them the option of voting "against all" candidates, but there seemed no point.

"If we vote against all, then what?" Yelena said. "It's definitely not going to be better."

"I'm not afraid of anything or anyone," Irina added. "We've already lived through so many things—we're on the edge already. What could dictatorship do to us?"

"In any case," Yelena said, "it won't be dictatorship like Stalin."

OFFICIALLY, PUTIN'S campaign-season visit to the Siberian capital of Krasnoyarsk was still a state secret when the police showed up to talk to Sergei Zhabinsky. All over the city his party of Western-oriented reformers had plastered signs and billboards with a simple slogan: "Time to Change Power!"

Local authorities were not amused. It didn't matter that the posters were meant to influence the upcoming mayoral contest and not the presidential election. Or that there was no visible campaign in Krasnoyarsk or anywhere else in Russia against the president. Or even that he faced a handful of opponents who between them commanded barely 10 percent support in the latest polls.

"Imagine that Putin goes by and sees this," a police officer told Zhabin-sky. "He would not understand."[37]

By the time the president roared into Krasnoyarsk two weeks before the election, the signs remained in place along his motorcade route. But a slogan that might possibly have been misconstrued as attacking the president was as close to an electoral threat as Putin faced in the Siberian heartland. Relieved of the need to solicit votes, Putin's noncampaign arrived in Krasno-yarsk determined to project the image of a noncandidate attending his non-political business. It was, said Kremlin aide Svetlana Shportenko, just a "normal working trip" to one of Russia's richest regions, a vast area of mines and forests the size of France but occupied by just 3 million people.[38] There would be no rallies for Putin on his visit, and certainly no dancing like Boris Yeltsin's memorably drunken jig back in 1996. "We don't have to campaign," a senior Kremlin official traveling with Putin told us bluntly.[39]

Instead, Putin's election season boiled down to carefully scripted trips like the one to Krasnoyarsk. At one photo op, he stood on the deck of a submarine praising the sailors taking part in what was billed as the largest Russian mil-itary exercise of the post-Soviet era. It later turned out that planned missile tests had been aborted at the last minute while Putin was on board in an embarrassing reminder of the abysmal state of the Russian nuclear arsenal. But state television never mentioned the miscue; in Putin's Russia, that was as good as if it had never happened.[40] Immediately before landing in Krasno-yarsk, Putin had spent a perfunctory six hours or so on the ground in the Far East city of Khabarovsk, where he cut a ceremonial ribbon meant to open the decades-delayed Chita-Khabarovsk highway, the final link in Russia's first cross-country road across steppe and tundra and ten time zones. The fawn-ing television media did not bother to report that the highway, a longtime dream of Soviet leaders, was not actually complete, with entire sections still unpaved at the time of Putin's dour-faced appearance.[41]

For this Krasnoyarsk trip, the Kremlin had taken the unusual step of invit-ing foreign journalists along—for the first and only time of our four years as Moscow correspondents—but then never allowed any of us into the same room as Putin and insisted that we watch his events instead on live video feeds. Some reporters spent five days waiting for the president to turn up for a visit that lasted less than twenty-four hours, marooned in the cockroach-infested hotel where Kremlin officials insisted they stay, because Putin's aides refused to reveal the timing of the presidential visit. During his day on the ground, the president met only with prescreened audiences of local university students, regional governors, and educational leaders and took no questions from the news media. He kissed no babies, gave no autographs—his pen froze in the Siberian frost—and asked for no one's vote.

Just days after Putin fired Mikhail Kasyanov and the rest of the cabinet in the biggest shake-up of his four years in office, no one bothered to ask the president about it. When we asked one of the members of the carefully selected pool of Russian reporters who traveled with Putin why journalists were so hesitant, she simply laughed. Not only would they never think of asking an unapproved question, she said, but Kremlin aides did not even bother to spin the compliant reporters or tell them what points Putin hoped to emphasize. "The president speaks for himself," she told us in the drafty gym where we were kept for hours. "We are not supposed to need clarification of his words."

The only time the word *elections* publicly crossed Putin's lips during the entire visit was as a joke. When a student worried that "idiots" might gain control of state-owned forests, the president laughingly cut her off. "Please don't point at me," he implored. "I still have elections ahead."[42]

In the tiny nearby hamlet of Ovsyanka, where Putin paid his respects at the grave of the writer Viktor Astafyev, crews came in to clear up the snow-clogged streets lined with picturesque wooden cottages, and Astafyev's house-museum was scrubbed clean. But several villagers, accustomed to pilgrimages from Mikhail Gorbachev and Boris Yeltsin, were not impressed with Putin's imperial style. Yeltsin the populist had walked their streets glad-handing and met with residents to talk over problems. Putin had no such plans. And besides, villagers pointed out, all the visits by Kremlin entourages to their famous writer over the years had never resulted in positive changes for a village where there was still no indoor plumbing and babushkas hauled water home in plastic buckets in the cold of the Siberian winter.

Then again, even many disgruntled Putin critics planned to vote for the president, saying they were convinced that, as homemaker Nina Yomshina put it, "What choice do we have with just one contender? The others are not real."[43] When we spoke with her, Yomshina was waiting to hand a personal complaint to the president at his campaign's public reception room in the Krasnoyarsk House of Teachers. Seven hundred supplicants like Yomshina had arrived since the center had opened in early February—the only public evidence that Putin's campaign existed in Krasnoyarsk. Most came, an aide said, not because of the election, but to pass along their pleas for pension increases, better apartments, and the like.

Would-be political opponents in Krasnoyarsk, as in the rest of Russia, were divided among themselves, resigned to Putin's victory in a system they considered so rigged they were not sure how or whether to participate in it. "We are as far from democracy as from the moon here," said Vladislav Yurchik, leader of the Krasnoyarsk Communists and a member of the State Duma. "My personal inclination is not to take part in this farce."[44]

The region's Western-style liberals, led by Sergei Zhabinsky, were in similar disarray. The local head of both Yabloko and the Union of Right Forces, Zhabinsky had defied the national parties and endorsed Irina Khakamada, but he had no funds for ads, leaflets, banners, or any other campaigning. His real hope was that Khakamada would follow through on her threat to drop out of the race. That way, he told us wistfully, "I could vote against all and express my protest against this whole campaign."[45]

On the Friday of Putin's perfunctory stop in Krasnoyarsk, that threatened boycott still seemed like a real possibility out in the regions, even though back in Moscow political operatives knew that the secret negotiations had already collapsed. The Communists suspected Sergei Glazyev too much to broker a deal with him. Khakamada's campaign manager was sure the Kremlin had bought off the Communists by promising them second place. Already, their standard-bearer, Nikolai Kharitonov, was receiving noticeably more airtime on the state channels—and would soon surpass Glazyev in the polls despite a campaign whose most memorable act was a commercial featuring a talking dog.

By Monday, no one was paying attention to the also-rans anyway. The Kremlin that day unexpectedly announced Putin's choice for his new prime minister, an obscure former tax police chief named Mikhail Fradkov. A fifty-three-year-old career bureaucrat with a résumé that suggested a KGB background, Fradkov was not openly allied with either of the feuding Kremlin factions and commanded no political constituency of his own. At the time, he was serving as Russia's envoy to the European Union and was so little known that in the week of speculation following Putin's firing of Kasyanov not a single media outlet had even mentioned his name as a possible successor. In keeping with his cryptic campaign-season performance, Putin offered little explanation for Fradkov's selection, describing him simply as "a good, strong administrator" who "has thorough experience in fighting corruption."[46]

Fradkov himself said nothing at all publicly on learning of his nomination. But one clue did turn up—a single reference to Fradkov as a future Putin prime minister more than two years earlier on a Kremlin-linked Internet news site. "Kasyanov's Successor Found," said the dispatch from the same people who had accurately foreshadowed the Kremlin's future campaign against Mikhail Khodorkovsky.[47] At the time, no one had even noticed their plug for Fradkov, who was touted as a favorite of the St. Petersburg hard-liners in the Kremlin when he had worked at the start of Putin's presidency as the deputy secretary of the Security Council. His boss and patron was reported to be none other than Putin's close adviser and fellow KGB veteran Sergei Ivanov.

MISHA KHROMOV finished work at the tax office late, delayed by the inspectors in town from Moscow to audit their operations. They would stay for a month and expected to be entertained with vodka-soaked banquets and weekend outings.

He headed to his parents, to the cottage where the picturesque green trim on the outside gave way to the chaos of a farmyard where there wasn't meant to be one.

Valery and Albina had had their moment of decision a decade ago, as their Soviet safety net crumbled. "We either had to work hard on our own or find dishonest ways of making money," Valery recalled. So they bought a cow.

With the milk, they made butter, sour cream, and a Russian variant of cottage cheese called *tvorog*. Albina kept track of the accounts on her abacus. Each dairy cow—they now had two—brought in an extra $140 a month on top of their meager pensions. "This is not a life," she said. "This is a fight for survival," Valery added.

They knew what their children thought about the cows. But as they described it, their farm animals in the city had become a form of protest against the breakup of the Soviet state, a state that Valery still mourned despite the fact that his wife's father had been imprisoned in the gulag. "They told us to get rid of the cows," Albina recalled of her disapproving children. "But then Dad said, 'Will you give us as much money as the cow?'"

Now it was Misha's turn to figure out what to do. His father thought that someday, if only Putin would deliver on his promises, if only the rule of law would take hold in the corrupted judicial system and the gangland business world, Misha might flourish outside the government. "This is not his limit," Valery told us that night.

Misha listened intently. But he was less sure, undecided to the end about the president and about his own next step in life. He told his father that Putin was not offering that kind of reformed country yet but something more modest.

"It's like a deal with Putin: he gives us the opportunity to work and we give him our votes," Misha said. "It's the chance to stand up from the mud. Only when we stand up from the mud, then we will see."

On March 14, 2004, a sunny day that held with it the promise of spring even in muddy Ivanovo, Katya refused to go to the polls. She was so indifferent by this point she had no idea whether Misha would even bother to vote and never spoke with him about the election again. After all the anxious deliberations of the last few weeks, Misha had reluctantly concluded that he could not accept the terms of the president's deal. Putin had not earned his vote and so he cast no ballot. "Nothing is getting better in this country," he decided. "But at least, I sometimes think, it could have been worse." Either way, he resolved to let the inevitable take place without him.

Several months later, he quit his job as a government tax man. He would risk it in the private sector for the first time in his three decades, trying out a new career as a lawyer for one of the new textile holding companies that had been born out of the remnants of Ivanovo's decrepit factories and anachronistic fabric mills. The job kept him long hours away from home and did not pay as much more as he had hoped.

But no matter. Now, Misha, too, would be one of the sharks he had admired and feared for so long.

THE HISTORIC Manezh exhibition hall in the shadow of the Kremlin was burning, the bright orange flames leaping toward Vladimir Putin as he celebrated inside the Kremlin. Not long after the polls had closed on election night, as the scale of Putin's long-awaited victory became clear, a fire broke out consuming the eighteenth-century landmark at Russia's most famous address, an unscripted, and decidedly unwelcome, news event, and an ominous portent in a country that still took its deadly omens seriously.

As the Manezh burned, Putin made a late-night visit to his campaign headquarters across the river from the Kremlin. Wearing a black turtleneck and flanked by aide Dmitri Kozak, he summoned a small group of reporters after 1 a.m. to give his victory speech. The president either ignored or dismissed concerns that he had disdained the electoral process by refusing to participate in the campaign. Yet he also spoke of democracy—a word that rarely crossed his lips otherwise—and made the sort of promises he had not before and would never repeat again. "Democratic gains," he vowed, would be "guaranteed and safeguarded." Asked by a reporter what his top priority would be in his second term, Putin replied unhesitatingly, "Above all, the strengthening of democratic institutions."[48]

The next morning, election officials announced that Putin had collected just over 71 percent of the vote—nearly exactly what memos like the one circulated to top officials in the region of Mari El had ordered. Communist

Nikolai Kharitonov received his designated 14 percent for a second-place finish, while the thoroughly marginalized Sergei Glazyev and Irina Khakamada
each ended up with about 4 percent. In some regions, zealous local authorities had produced astronomical totals in favor of the president—a whopping
92 percent for Putin in war-torn Chechnya and an even more impressive 98
percent in neighboring Ingushetia under the stewardship of former FSB general and Kremlin protégé Murat Zyazikov. In Ivanovo, with its Communist
governor and a population close enough to the booming capital to know just
how far behind they had fallen, Putin still fared well, polling 67 percent of
the vote. Although few doubted the president's victory reflected the will of
Russian voters given their choices, reliable reports of fraud surfaced, from the
mysterious election-day disappearance of a million registered voters from the
national total announced in the parliamentary elections just a few months
earlier to obvious vote tampering in individual precincts.[49]

Even with his election victory in hand, Putin still gave few hints about
what he would do next. But he made clear that he felt free to disregard public opinion, no matter how assiduously his fixers had spent the last few
months shaping it. "We often say that so-called unpopular decisions are
needed," he said at a televised meeting with his new cabinet the day after the
balloting. "Our decisions don't have to be popular. They must meet the country's needs."[50]

Some, like Marat Gelman, the political consultant who had been dispatched to oversee state-run Channel One during the parliamentary campaign, were certain that the Kremlin would now turn its attention to the only
powers left that could still conceivably challenge the president—regional
governors. "A purge of the governors will come this fall," he told us. "In 2004,
local authorities will become part of the vertical of power."[51] Other advisers
claimed, perhaps wishfully so, that the president would now push forward a
variety of long-delayed liberal economic reform initiatives, such as revamp-
ing the banking system, natural gas and electricity monopolies, tax code,
health care, education, pensions, and the housing system. "The plans are
rather ambitious," Mikhail Margelov, a member of the upper house of parliament and Putin adviser, told us that Monday. "This will be the second
major wave of reform."[52]

But Putin himself made no such commitments. And when he was inau-
gurated to his second term two months later in a Kremlin ceremony that married tsarist splendor with Soviet-era symbols like the national anthem revived
by Putin, the president returned to the vague pronouncements that had gotten him reelected in the first place. "Transformations in the country"—he

never said what sort—would continue. Russia under his watch, he vowed, would be a "fundamentally better" country. He alluded only vaguely to Chechnya, and not by name, as a battle long since completed to preserve Russia's "territorial integrity" and spoke in ominous terms of the unwelcome influence of foreign-financed human rights groups in the country.[53]

Four years earlier, a largely untested and unknown Putin had pledged to "preserve and develop democracy" in his first inaugural address. This time, he never even mentioned the word.

Scam of the Year

For 1,500 years, the government has been blaming us just for living in Russia.
—ALEKSANDR MARKUS

ALEKSANDR MARKUS SHOOK his head as he looked at the two identical boxes of men's underwear. This was his business now, and he had learned all too well the difference between briefs that would sell and those that would not—like the two Russian-made models he was scrutinizing in his storeroom. "Too expensive," he said. "Badly packaged." And he shrugged. Surely, the subject was "banal," he said, repeating a word he used at least a dozen times a day, "but I have to eat."

Once, Markus studied advanced physics and was recruited to work at a top-secret Soviet nuclear research facility. Now he was a reluctant underwear salesman, a capitalist who never meant to be one in a country still uneasy about market forces unleashed with the fall of Communism. "I'd give it up tomorrow—with pleasure," he told us when we went to visit him in the once-closed city of Nizhny Novgorod. "Business for business's sake never attracted me." But in the carnivorous world of Russian capitalism as Markus had experienced it in the fifteen years after the fall of the Soviet Union, the banality of his current life represented a victory of sorts, his tentative stability a product of the relative calm reigning in Russia under Vladimir Putin. "Before it was senseless to have property because you could lose it all," he said. "Now there are some rules that sometimes even the authorities obey." His trade-off mirrored Russia's: a free hand for the president and utter indifference to the Kremlin intrigues that made the summer of 2004 a season of uncertainty about the future of Russian commerce as Putin took on the country's richest man and the world wondered how far he would go in clamping down on private enterprise.

Markus's faith in the system, any system, had long since disappeared along the raucous, violent, twisting path that had led him to the quiet life of a trafficker in bras and bathing suits. Indeed, his was a career that traced the arc of Russian capitalism to the ambivalent present. In the 1980s, he had embraced the free market and flirted with dissidence. In the 1990s, he had learned the hard way about what he sardonically called in heavily accented English "Russian business"—armed mafiosi who seized his first store, crooked insiders who bankrupted the bank he worked with, Western companies that promised better but whose products were not what they seemed. Only now, thanks to Polish panties and Turkish socks and the Putin era's comparative prosperity, had Markus found a measure of economic security for the first time in his tumultuous life. At age thirty-eight, Sasha, as his friends and family called him, had built a modest chain of six stores in his industrial city on the Volga River. He employed fifty people, supported three children, and played computer games in the office because the work was not very challenging for a man who had planned to be a physicist. "At last," he said, "I'm bored."

There were few idealists left in Russia among those who had, like Markus, experienced the rise of capitalism firsthand, and no slogans to rally him to any cause beyond that of making do in a system he believed was dominated by equally odious clans: "parasite" bureaucrats and greedy oligarchs like imprisoned oil tycoon Mikhail Khodorkovsky. Khodorkovsky had made his last public appearance before his arrest in Nizhny Novgorod the previous October, and he had warned businessmen like Markus of the fight to come. "Business should not be driven into the shade and governed by fear," Khodorkovsky had said.[1]

But Markus had left behind the age of fear in the dislocations of the 1990s. No cause, and certainly not that of a jailed oligarch, could inspire him now. He had long since given up on the democrats he had once believed in and who now made him "feel like puking because they are just like everyone else." And although he was wary of the president he had voted for but did not really like, he was ready to accept a more authoritarian system as the price of a more predictable life. "I gave up being afraid," he said. "At least they managed to significantly reduce the number of bandits in this country."

Yet it would be a mistake to think of him as a believer in the promises of Putin's Russia. As we drove through Nizhny Novgorod's cratered streets that summer, Markus nodded at a gleaming new mall anchored by a Turkish superstore, the city's first. This was his own turning point. "We haven't yet faced these giants. That's why we can live," he said. But soon enough, he believed he would have to expand his business to match the outside competition or else risk failure yet again. In expanding, though, Markus feared becoming exactly what he disdained—a capitalist like Khodorkovsky, making money by "stepping on the bones of my neighbors," and vulnerable to the state that for now largely ignored him because he was too small.

So Markus remained a skeptic as Khodorkovsky's fate unfolded in a Moscow courtroom that summer, his skepticism earned at the barrel of a gun. "Rich experience in this country," he said, "tells me real stability will be achieved only after death." And he wasn't really joking.[2]

THE STABILITY in Mikhail Khodorkovsky's life now came in the form of twenty-three hours a day in a cramped prison cell with two other inmates who were almost certainly reporting his every whisper back to authorities. The other hour each day he was allowed to exercise in the squalid yard. The oil tycoon's confidence that he would be released soon after his arrest had proved as naive as his assumption that he could take on the Kremlin and win. Having already sanctioned the arrest of Russia's richest man and ridden out the initial waves of international outrage and investor panic, Putin saw no additional political cost in keeping Khodorkovsky in jail. He knew foreign investors would soon write off Khodorkovsky because the profits to be made in Russia were just too great. "People will forget in six months that Khodorkovsky is still sitting in jail," William F. Browder, the biggest American investor in Moscow, told us the day after the arrest.[3]

Khodorkovsky was put in a seventy-five-square-foot cell on the fifth floor of the famously overcrowded Matrosskaya Tishina (or Sailor's Silence) prison in Moscow, the same detention facility where the hard-line Communist coup plotters who tried to bring down Mikhail Gorbachev in 1991 had been locked up. Shivering against the cold, he wore a track suit or jeans and a woolen sweater. He survived on fish soup supplemented with chocolate brought by his lawyers. And in his absence, his business dreams began to fade. Within weeks of his arrest, his erstwhile merger partner, Roman Abramovich, went to the Kremlin and met with Putin, then abruptly pulled the plug on the YukosSibneft mega-deal.

As Khodorkovsky and his lawyers began to scour through the charges against him, they found an indictment stitched together from the remnants of closed cases. The prosecutors had revived an old dispute over the 1994 privatization of a fertilizer company called Apatit, a dispute that the government had already settled in civil court with the blessing of the same prosecutors now reversing themselves to make a criminal case out of it. In many ways, the Apatit sale could be a case study in all that had gone wrong with the Russian privatizations of the 1990s. As outlined in the authorities' documents, Apatit was a tale of a manipulated auction, deceptive accounting, broken obligations, sham transactions, and meaningless court rulings. In the end, according to prosecutors, Khodorkovsky and his team ended up with a 20 percent share of a large company for just $225,000 instead of the $283 million they had agreed to pay. But even in their rendering, Apatit was just that—a classic example of the many privatizations that were rigged, par for the course in an era of bandit capitalism. "This is a very typical case," said Boris Kuznetsov, a prominent Moscow attorney who was not involved. "Even if there were mistakes during this privatization, they are the same mistakes that were made during the privatizations of dozens if not hundreds of companies. I know many such companies, and nobody's looking at their cases now because they're loyal to the authorities."[4]

At the time of the stock sale, Apatit was a state-owned company in the far northern city of Murmansk and the largest Russian producer of apatite, or phosphate minerals. Four bidders showed up on July 1, 1994, for the investment tender to win a 20 percent stake in the company, and the high offer of $1 billion was declared the winner. But the winner and the two runners-up then declined to move forward with a purchase, leaving the low bidder, a firm called Volna controlled by Khodorkovsky's Bank Menatep, to claim the shares for just $283 million. According to prosecutors, the three other bidders were sham competitors secretly controlled by Menatep as well; their bid guarantees were all signed by Khodorkovsky's partner, Platon Lebedev, on the same day, June 27, 1994.[5]

Under the terms of the auction, Volna paid only $225,000 to the state, essentially a down payment, but was obligated to invest $283 million in the company in two installments over the next year. Volna did not do so, and when authorities pressed the matter, the firm simply sold the Apatit stock to a series of other companies that prosecutors alleged were also controlled by Menatep. In 1998, a Moscow court invalidated the auction. But since the Apatit shares had already been sold, the state could not reclaim them. Ultimately, the Khodorkovsky team helped build Apatit into a thriving business, which was the point of the investment requirement, and eventually the Russian Federal Property Fund negotiated a $15.5 million penalty to settle the complaints about the auction. A court approved the deal and Volna paid the fine on Christmas Day, 2002. The deal was also signed off on by Prosecutor General Vladimir Ustinov. In an April 28, 2003, letter Ustinov wrote that an investigation into the Apatit case had determined that allegations of antitrust and tax law violations "were unfounded. Therefore, there is no reason for further actions by the Prosecutor General's Office."[6] Just two months later, Ustinov had Platon Lebedev arrested on those "unfounded" charges. Nearly four months after that, he arrested Khodorkovsky as well.

The rest of the prosecution's case charged Khodorkovsky with committing fraud in another privatization in 1995, this time of a fertilizer research institute called NIUIF; embezzling assets by transferring them to fellow oligarch Vladimir Gusinsky; and bilking the state of hundreds of millions of dollars in taxes by employing oil transfer pricing schemes that virtually every major Russian company used to shelter revenue from taxes. He was also accused of obtaining a business consultant's license that allowed him to pay personal taxes at a dramatically reduced rate. Virtually every oligarch avoided taxes in the 1990s, as did the vast majority of Russian citizens, and the murky nature of the law at the time made it easy to do so. But only Khodorkovsky was being prosecuted for it. As even Eric Kraus, an investment analyst and self-proclaimed "Putin apologist" in the fight against Khodorkovsky, put it, "Accusing Russian oligarchs of past tax evasion is like handing out speeding tickets at the Indy 500."[7]

The case seemed suspect enough that Putin felt the need to bring Ustinov to a closed cabinet meeting in February 2004 to describe and justify the charges. Ustinov "was reading for an hour all this bureaucratic stuff, not understanding half of what he was saying," one participant later told us. "He wanted to make everyone think he was guilty."[8] Many in the cabinet did not. But Putin would not yield, even in the face of continuing private arguments with Prime Minister Mikhail Kasyanov. For Putin, it was about respect, and Khodorkovsky had not given it. "For him, it's absolutely important. It's issue number one—respect for him and to understand that he is not weak."[9]

Khodorkovsky's lawyer, Anton Drel, would prepare his defense. But Khodorkovsky soon began to spend the empty hours in prison dwelling on the state of Putin's Russia. He had risked everything and for what? The two democratic parties he had supported were ousted from the State Duma altogether, reformers were on the retreat, autocracy on the rise. Russia was once again becoming, as it had so often been throughout its history, a country of one-man rule. If Khodorkovsky seriously envisioned himself as a champion of democracy resisting the Putin revanche, he had clearly failed. He began voicing his thoughts to his visiting lawyers, and they cobbled together their notes into a letter from prison published in the newspaper *Vedomosti* in March 2004 under the headline "The Crisis of Liberalism in Russia." Coming just after Putin's reelection, the letter was a punch in the jaw to Russia's already dispirited and discredited democratic reformers. Khodorkovsky laid blame for "the capitulation of the liberals" at their own feet, castigating them for their "genetically rooted servility" in the face of power and their eagerness for creature comforts that had led them to abandon principles "for a plate of sturgeon with horseradish." They had squandered the legacy of the revolution that had brought down the Soviet Union. "They thought about the living and working standards for ten percent of the people who were ready for radical change and rejection of state paternalism. But they forgot the other ninety percent. They covered the tragic failures of their policy with lies. They closed their eyes to social reality when they made the sweeping brushes of privatization, ignoring its negative social consequences and coquettishly describing it as painless, honest, and fair." He added, "The time of reckoning has come. The people said a firm and merciless good-bye to official liberals in the 2003 elections."[10]

Khodorkovsky acknowledged that business had as much to do with it. "It was standing side by side with the liberal rulers. We helped them make mistakes and lie. We never admired the authorities, but then we did not contradict them either, so as not to risk our bread and butter." He argued that his oligarchic peers now needed to share more with the people, even through greater taxation of oil companies. And he went so far as to praise Putin himself. "Putin is probably not a liberal or a democrat," Khodorkovsky wrote, "but he is more liberal and more democratic than seventy percent of the population."[11]

Most of the media attention on the letter focused on Khodorkovsky's seeming jailhouse conversion to Putin, interpreting it as a plea for clemency. But his broader point about the crisis of liberalism touched off a provocative round of soul-searching and finger-pointing among the democrats he assailed, the ones who had benefited from his largesse and protested his arrest yet failed to persuade the rest of the country that democracy was necessary for Russian society. Several of the most prominent liberals bristled at Khodorkovsky's critique. "I wish Khodorkovsky repented for his own sins and left my sins to me," huffed Anatoly Chubais, the architect of the 1990s privatizations.[12] Boris Nemtsov, the Union of Right Forces leader who had once cozied up to Putin, now rejected the notion that liberals should succumb to the Kremlin's monopoly on power. "I completely disagree, one hundred percent, with Khodorkovsky's idea. Putin is the adversary," he told us.[13]

Not long afterward, we went to a conference for the tenth anniversary of the Carnegie Moscow Center, the premier think tank in Russia, financed with Western money. Once a storehouse of ideas for the young reformers running Boris Yeltsin's Kremlin, Carnegie by the Putin era had become a "refuge," in the words of director Andrew Kutchins, for liberals forced out of power.[14] At the conference, they debated the reasons for their electoral failure and upbraided Chubais and his adversary, Grigory Yavlinsky, for their petty divisiveness. In the end, it fell to Yavlinsky to sum up the situation. Asked whether Russian democracy was dead or merely dying under Putin, he repeated an old joke about an ambulance driver taking a man to the morgue.

"Why?" the man asked. "I'm not yet dead."

"Well," the driver replied, "we're not yet there."[15]

"I DON'T WANT to spit at the mirror in the morning," Sasha Markus said, arguing good-naturedly with his best friend, Valera Nakaryakov, back in Russia for a visit after emigrating nearly a decade earlier.

Nakaryakov was eager to blame Russia's "wild capitalism" for the many reverses his friend Markus had suffered, a route Nakaryakov had considered for himself and rejected. "I had to make a conscious decision: either work in business here or leave," he said. "I left." Now Nakaryakov was a British citizen, a prominent young space physicist at the University of Warwick who listed fifty-eight scholarly publications on his résumé. He consulted for NASA and the European Space Agency, and his latest findings were the subject of glowing press releases.

Over a beer near the classrooms where they were once inseparable in Nizhny Novgorod, Nakaryakov told his friend he would always see him as an unwilling capitalist.

"You were forced to work in business," he said. "You did it against your will."

Actually, it was politics—Markus's one and only flirtation with it—that had first set him on the path toward the life of an underwear salesman. The year was 1989, and the young physicist was one month short of finishing university. Nizhny Novgorod, at the time still a closed defense-industry city called Gorky, seethed with activists hoping to emulate the nuclear-scientist-turned-dissident Andrei Sakharov, who spent much of the 1980s in exile there. "We were all democrats then," Markus recalled.

But he and Nakaryakov—both of them married already, with young daughters—had prestigious jobs lined up at Arzamas-16, the nearby secret nuclear facility. Markus felt conflicted. By 1989, "everything was falling apart," he recalled. "I wanted to feel like a dissident and help break it down completely." That May Day, he joined protesters at the annual labor parade shouting pro-democracy slogans. The police detained them. "The whole crowd was happy, we were all singing revolutionary songs. Even in jail we were happy," he said.

"Sasha was idealizing them," Nakaryakov told us. "But they were just cynically using fools like us." His friends scrambled to help but couldn't think of anything to do other than shave off Markus's long dissident-style beard, which Nakaryakov's wife did as soon as he was released from jail. Even sympathetic professors could not hush up the scandal. Not only was Markus barred from graduating, but Nakaryakov and other friends lost their promised jobs at Arzamas-16. Markus was uncertain what to do next until a friend "gave me a tip that there's this word called *business*" and introduced him to a group buying computers cheap in Moscow and selling them expensive in Nizhny. Markus became technical director because he "at least had seen a computer before." The money was great. "Any business then was supersuccessful. There were no rules of the game in the new market—or in the new country—and the attitude was 'easy come, easy go.'"

Never a joiner, Markus soon struck out on his own. "I was just learning," he said. "Later I realized it doesn't matter what you trade, as long as you don't trade people, drugs, and weapons." But it was disorienting. He was flush with unaccustomed money and surrounded by risqué new friends from the world of gray commerce. His marriage fell apart in 1991 as the Soviet Union dissolved. "He got into business and that's how he started drowning," his first wife, Anna Marinichenko, told us. "People started getting money they had not seen before; it was a party time. Many Russian men got broken at that time."

By then, Nizhny Novgorod's name had been restored, and city fathers imagined a trading future for the town based on its historic past as the commercial crossroads of the Volga. The new governor was a young physicist named Boris Nemtsov from Markus's university who vowed to make Nizhny a showcase for capitalism. Markus opened a modest general store on Gorky Street. But bandits preyed on owners like him, demanding protection money to serve as the store's *krysha* (roof). Markus slept at home with a new wife and a hunting rifle. One night in 1993, gunmen burst into his apartment and demanded he give them his store. "They put a gun to my wife, so of course I gave them the store," he said.

When he later went begging for his store back, the gangster made him a different offer, asking Markus to work with his bank. He accepted and learned from the inside about so-called banks that proliferated in the 1990s, serving as private money caches and laundering operations for well-connected insiders. Ostensibly, he was there to check on borrowers' collateral. "But it turned out nobody needed it. All these banks gave credit exclusively on the principle of friendship or direct orders from the owners," Markus recalled. In 1995, the bank imploded in what he called an "artificial bankruptcy." He found work at a large agricultural firm selling fruit and immediately hated it. His second wife left him. After the bank disaster, "both the bandits and the police were chasing me," he recalled. The police found him first.

THE TRIAL OF Mikhail Khodorkovsky opened on July 15, 2004, in a tiny chamber at the end of the hall in the Meshchansky Courthouse in northern Moscow. Guarded by a squadron of uniformed officers with automatic rifles, the courtroom was smaller than the office where we had interviewed Khodorkovsky two years earlier. As the proceedings began, Khodorkovsky and Platon Lebedev were brought into the courtroom and escorted into the defendants' cage. Seated on a slightly raised platform were three judges in black robes, all stern women in their late thirties or early forties. At the defense table were more than a half dozen laptop-wielding lawyers. At the state's table was a young prosecutor in his blue uniform with three stars on his shoulder, his hair perfectly in place, and his case already rigged for victory.

The opening day consisted mainly of the prosecutor, Dmitri Shokhin, reading the charges against Khodorkovsky and Lebedev, followed by the two defendants entering not guilty pleas. The whole exercise had the feeling of actors reciting from a script where everyone had already skipped ahead and read the ending. During a break, Khodorkovsky's aging father, Boris, was asked what he thought the outcome would be. "We already know what it will be," he said wearily.[16] For all of the discussion of judicial reform in recent years, trials in Russia still gave the illusion of fairness while blatantly violating due process. Khodorkovsky was ineligible for one of Russia's new jury trials, which were only available in cases of murder or other serious violence, and even after Dmitri Kozak's hard-fought overhaul, judges in Russia still issued guilty verdicts in 99.2 percent of trials.[17] No one in the courtroom, much less Khodorkovsky himself, expected him to be among the 0.8 percent.

By the time his trial began, Khodorkovsky had been held behind bars for nearly nine months even though he had turned in his passport and demonstrated he was no flight risk. The court in Moscow regularly considered, and denied, his petitions for bail, in violation of usual practice for white-collar financial cases. Prosecutors had violated many other standards of due process along the way. They had raided Anton Drel's office and tried to make the lawyer answer questions despite attorney-client privilege. They had conducted searches without warrants. They had arrested Yukos security chief Aleksei Pichugin and injected him with psychotropic drugs, according to his lawyer. And they had all but ignored the deteriorating medical condition of

Platon Lebedev, who was apparently suffering from a liver ailment and showed up for trial pale, weak, and sipping constantly from a yogurt drink he fermented in his prison cell called *prostokvasha*.

Khodorkovsky and Lebedev got their first chance to speak out the next day. Dressed in a black V-neck pullover and blue jeans, his graying hair shorn close, Khodorkovsky looked smaller inside the cage, no longer the untouchable oligarch. He portrayed himself as only the latest victim of repression in a country with a long history of it.

"The demonstration of force indifferent to the law, albeit going through the motions of observing its procedures on the surface, is extremely dangerous for the prospects of development of our country," he said.[18]

Lebedev was blunter. "I've come to realize," he said when his turn came, leaning against the bars for support, "that the state is repressing me for political . . . reasons on charges invented or craftily organized."[19]

The notion of billionaires as latter-day dissidents seemed an odd twist of history. But Khodorkovsky, at least, had come to view himself as a martyr to the cause of civil society and democracy. A couple nights before the trial began, we met for dinner again with Anton Drel, the lawyer whose jailhouse visits to his client meant he spoke with Khodorkovsky more than any other outsider. Drel found a prisoner unbowed, convinced of the righteousness of his cause and envisioning a rather grand role in history. "He's already won. That's my personal opinion," Drel said. "For him, the most important thing is his reputation, and he wants to use the court to prove he's really innocent." The process, Drel added, "is going to show the lack of any future for Russia."[20]

Thin, young, with stylish glasses, impeccable suits and cuff links, and a tiny mobile telephone that rang constantly, Drel had been Khodorkovsky's personal lawyer for three years, practicing civil matters until one day at the beginning of 2003 when the oil magnate told him he thought Drel might have to prove his mettle at criminal law soon. At thirty-five, Drel had gone to law school after his obligatory stint in the army and studied briefly in the United States on a Columbia Law School exchange program. As the case progressed, Drel appeared increasingly weighed down, the bags under his eyes drooping farther down and his already slender frame shedding twenty-five pounds. As we talked that night just before the trial, the phone repeatedly demanded his attention. "I'm ready, I'm ready, of course, I'm ready, I'm ready," he assured one anxious caller.[21]

No matter how ready he was, though, Drel's client knew better than to count on victory. Khodorkovsky, Drel said, was prepared to do the ten years in prison he would receive if found guilty. "This verdict would be unfair," Drel said, "but he's ready to face any decision of the court. He's also a Russian citizen and a realist."[22]

Not satisfied to put Khodorkovsky behind bars, the Kremlin, led by *siloviki* Igor Sechin and Viktor Ivanov, decided to take over his oil conglomerate as well. Just as with the criminal case against Khodorkovsky, the government proceeded with the veneer of legality; rather than simply expropriate the company, it found a seemingly legitimate justification to go after its assets. And just as with the Khodorkovsky privatization charges, the government went back and rewrote history. In the case of Yukos, authorities reopened company tax returns from past years that had already been audited, then reinterpreted a key section of Russian law to rule that tax shelters widely used by Russian companies were no longer legitimate—even though the state's own audit chamber had decreed those tax shelters legal just months earlier. Relying on the new interpretation, authorities slapped Yukos with a $3.4 billion bill for back taxes, penalties, and interest from 2000, then began going through returns from 2001, 2002, and 2003 as well. In the weeks before Khodorkovsky's trial opened, the tax authorities had gotten a court to order Yukos to pay the bill immediately or forfeit its assets. Yukos tried to fend off the attack with a series of settlement offers, only to be ignored. When court marshals arrived at Yukos headquarters to serve the court order, Yukos executives tried to give the marshals the company's shares in Sibneft Oil Company, which by themselves would have been worth enough to satisfy the tax debt. The marshals refused. Khodorkovsky and his partners then offered to give up their own stake in Yukos if it would save the company. The offer met with no reply. And the court then froze various Yukos bank accounts so that even if it wanted to pay the debt, it could not access the cash it did have on hand.

The turmoil surrounding Yukos rippled across world oil markets and helped send international prices to record heights. Yukos pumped 1.7 million barrels a day, by itself 2 percent of the world's oil production, even more than all of Libya. The notion of Russia's largest oil company being seized by the state sent tremors through stock markets and boardrooms from Moscow to London to New York. But the takeover of Yukos was like a slow striptease: each day brought another incremental development sheathed in bureaucratic process, which had the effect of dulling the impact and shrouding the final goal. And at every step, brokers tried to convince themselves and their clients that Putin would never go all the way, constantly redefining the worst-case scenario until finally there was no way to pretend the state was not trying to seize Russia's most successful company. When Khodorkovsky had first been

arrested, the analysts had asserted that it would end with him and not harm
Yukos. Putin himself had provided such false reassurance, saying "the state
should not really seek to destroy" the company.[23] Then when the tax authorities began going after Yukos, the analysts consoled themselves by saying the
state would extract its pound of flesh from the company and that would be it.
But the tax bills began adding up. After demanding $3.4 billion from Yukos
for 2000, the government ordered the company to pay another $3.4 billion
for 2001. The announcements seemed timed to drive the Yukos stock price.
One day saw a leak hinting at a deal, then the next saw another crackdown—
probably the result of insiders deliberately orchestrating events to profit off
quick stock sales.

Five days after Khodorkovsky's trial opened, the state dropped the biggest
bombshell—it announced plans to seize and sell off Yukos's primary production unit, called Yuganskneftegaz, the crown jewel of Khodorkovsky's
empire. By itself, Yuganskneftegaz pumped 1 million barrels of oil a day, 60
percent of the Yukos total and equal to the entire North Slope of Alaska.
Without it, Yukos would be gutted. Yuganskneftegaz held reserves worth $30
billion, according to Yukos, and yet the state was planning to take it away to
satisfy a tax debt less than one-quarter of that. Only at that point did the
international business community begin to wake up to what was happening.
Suddenly a company that had been worth $41.6 billion at its peak just three
months earlier had seen its stock value plummet to $9.6 billion. By late fall,
it would plunge even further, down to $1.7 billion, meaning that 96 percent
of the company's worth had simply disappeared.[24] The decision to dismantle Yukos and sell off its most prized asset shook the confidence even of
Putin's supporters in the investment community who loathed Khodorkovsky
for his past sins. One friend of ours, who had been among the most vocal
Putin backers against Khodorkovsky, turned increasingly glum. The attack
on Yukos appeared to be large-scale theft for the benefit of Putin insiders, not
a legitimate reigning in of out-of-control tycoons. "I've been thinking my
optimism in Putin was misplaced," he confided one night. Then, he quickly
asked us not to quote him by name for fear of repercussions. "Please don't
have me say anything about Putin."[25]

The fear was spreading. Khodorkovsky defenders turned silent, worried
that they could be targeted next. During a television interview as Khodorkovsky's trial was beginning, Arkady Volsky, head of the oligarchs' union, said
it was clear who was behind the attack on Yukos and its shareholders, seemingly a clear reference to the Kremlin *siloviki*. But Volsky said he dared not
identify them. "I'm very scared to name names now, I'm simply scared," he

said. "I have six grandchildren, after all, and I want them to be alive. I'm scared to give you the names of those I can see behind it."[26]

SASHA MARKUS was able to make his own jailhouse stay relatively brief. After a month behind bars, he convinced the authorities that he was just a witness to the failed bank's crimes, not a participant. After he was sprung, he turned for the first time to the world of socks, stockings, and underwear.

Markus set up several small stores, relying on a supplier he found in Moscow that imported cheap Turkish goods. But business wasn't great. In 1997, his partners cut Markus loose and he found himself liable for $10,000 in debt. Threatening envoys arrived, demanding money he didn't have. Markus had no way to pay, and as he said wryly, "They couldn't do anything except kill me, and if they killed me, they wouldn't get anything." At one point, the Moscow firm sent what Markus called their *krysha*, an imposing athlete named Oleg Gavryuchenkov, "to make an impression on me." When we met Gavryuchenkov, he told us he owed his formidable physique to years of water polo, but declined to discuss his first encounter with Markus. Asked what business he had been in back then, he said with a modest smile, "People who had problems trading—we solved these problems."

At first, Markus tried to round up cash by working for a French firm that sold food supplements. After three months he gave up and went to Moscow to pay his debt by working directly for the company. It was the spring of 1998. "I became a slave," he said.

The Russian economy crashed that August. Their business, along with tens of thousands of others, was ruined when the ruble devaluation made the cost of imported goods prohibitively expensive. In the crisis, though, Markus saw opportunity. He had decided that Gavryuchenkov, the beefy enforcer, was a decent sort, and the two took a proposal to management. They would sell the company's stock at the wholesale market on the grounds of Moscow's Luzhniki Stadium. And so that fall, Markus learned what it was to rise at 4 a.m. for a hard day's labor as they off-loaded the remnants of the company. Even after all he'd been through, the brutal laws of the market were a revelation to the lanky would-be physicist. "Luzhniki is a place you can make two thousand or three thousand dollars a day—and lose five thousand or ten thousand dollars," he marveled. "It's not a very human way of life."

By late 1998, Markus had acquired just enough money and Turkish socks to return home and start a new business. The first of what would become his modest chain was a rented corner in a food store. There was room only for one stand of socks. But Markus gave the enterprise a grand name: European

Tricotage. After everything that had come before, selling underwear was hardly the worst thing that had happened to Markus. "It was a pleasure," he said, "to bring a bit of beauty to people."

During the height of the swimsuit season that summer as Mikhail Khodorkovsky went on trial, we accompanied Markus as he inspected Number One, his first store on Freedom Square. Two sales assistants were occupied with customers as he glanced at the neat ranks of T-shirts with names like Nike and Polo, Donna Karan, and Dolce & Gabbana printed conspicuously on them, all fake. "Everybody knows what these are and we don't try to hide it," he said. "Real brands are completely inaccessible to the people who shop in our stores."

For the last five years, Markus's business had grown along with incomes and the perception of stability. Number One had always been his best shop; turnover surpassed $20,000 a month. Gangsters no longer came demanding money. "The last offer from a *krysha* came four years ago. We refused with great pleasure," Markus said. European Tricotage was now a well-known name in Nizhny Novgorod, and he was expanding into wholesale. He had recently made his first foreign business trip to Turkey. Pressured by clients eager to "normalize" business, Markus even opened a company bank account—a huge leap after years of operating on an all-cash basis.

But Markus was still just a member of what the head of the Russian small business association called the "commercial proletariat." He was visibly stressed, a bearded wraith whose clothes flopped off his thin frame. He rarely ate during the day, subsisting on coffee and cigarettes. He owned no car or mobile telephone. His modest apartment, where he lived with his third wife, her ten-year-old daughter, and his twelve-year-old, cost just $300 a month— the first time he had had a home of his own since the mid-1990s. Boris Nemtsov's dream of a capitalist model city on the Volga had long since vanished; Nizhny Novgorod was no longer even in the top ten regions for foreign investment. Salaries hovered around the national average of $200 a month. Markus's sales assistants took home as little as $100 a month.

The smothering hand of the bureaucracy was a constant problem; Markus couldn't stand the bureaucrats, the *chinovniki*. "Mr. Chinovnik is like a parasite on people like me," he said. Usually, he deputized his brother, Maksim, a construction engineer by profession, to handle headaches like the $85 fine they received for having the incorrect time on their cash register. "We got the fine and said, 'We won't pay, you sue us,'" Maksim recalled. "But the tax inspectors said, 'No, you sue us.' To sue your tax inspector, well, it is bad for the future. We understood that."

Sometimes, the demands were so brazen that Markus had to get involved himself. A year and a half earlier, an inspector threatened a fine of five hundred thousand rubles ($17,000) for not keeping the original of a good's bill of origin at the store. "I told him, 'For five hundred thousand rubles I could hire killers and kill the whole tax inspectorate and it would be cheaper!' We agreed on a small fine."

But he was still angry about what it said about the attitude of the state toward its people. "For fifteen hundred years," he said, "the government has been blaming us just for living in Russia."

And yet at times, Markus was cautiously optimistic, contemplating plans to open a warehouse in Moscow and expand his wholesale trade. "We're just starting the process in which people think about tomorrow," he said en route to another of his shops. "For ten years, it was very hard to plan anything. We had such a struggle. But now, I would like to make some forecasts." He saw his small underwear empire as a haven where he could take refuge with a small circle of trusted friends. He had no intention of getting involved in politics or business groups or civic action of any sort. "Like many of my generation, I separated myself from the state long ago, and I'm living in the worlds I like more," he said. "Any person involved in small business builds his own state himself."

THE STATE THAT Mikhail Khodorkovsky had built for himself came crashing down for good the following fall. The trial dragged on for months, dominated by a compendium of details that at times hardly seemed to add up to much. Dmitri Shokhin, the ambitious young prosecutor, spent the first weeks of the trial doing nothing but reading aloud documents from the evidence collected against Khodorkovsky. He did not bother to explain what any of the documents were supposed to mean or why they added up to the crime. He just read. And read. And read. Attorneys drifted off to sleep, friends in the audience put their heads down on the bench in front of them, the judges often stared off blankly and yawned. A guard once dozed off so deeply that his snoring woke everyone else up. Khodorkovsky partner Vasily Shakhnovsky brought his own entertainment. One day, he sat down next to us, powered up a laptop computer, pulled out a small earpiece, and popped in a bootleg DVD copy of Michael Moore's *Fahrenheit 9/11*. As Shokhin began the day's droning, the image of U.S. attorney general John Ashcroft flashed across Shakhnovsky's computer screen.

Such was Russian justice. The emphasis was not on stirring courtroom rhetoric or clever cross-examinations. It was on paperwork, the sheer bulk of it, the more the better, all designed to give the appearance of procedural fairness. In this case, prosecutors had collected 227 binders of documents to prove their case against Khodorkovsky and another 167 binders for Lebedev, filled with random memos and news clippings. Buried in such minutiae, a trial that could help determine the future of Russian capitalism dropped off the Moscow radar screen in the doldrums of late-summer dacha season.

By fall, the prosecution had more or less shown that the auction of the Apatit fertilizer company had been orchestrated to benefit Khodorkovsky's team. Nikolai Olshansky, a witness involved in one of the three shell firms supposedly competing against Khodorkovsky, testified that Bank Menatep controlled his bidding company, which dropped out in favor of the eventual winner. "I think that the sense was that by withdrawing applications from the tender they wanted to reach an offer with the minimal amount of investments," Olshansky told the court.[27] Yet many of the prosecutor's other witnesses only undercut the rest of the case. As Shokhin was trying to prove that Khodorkovsky's teams had failed to make required investments in the fertilizer institute NIUIF after taking it over, he called to the stand the institute's former director, Pyotr Klassin. But Klassin said the institute was far healthier financially than before. "Considering the developments of the last nine years, I can say that the investment program has been overfulfilled many times," he testified.[28] And the next day, when Shokhin called a former tax inspector who had examined Khodorkovsky's returns for the years he was accused of tax evasion, she testified that she did not have any complaints about Khodorkovsky's declarations, which were within the law at the time. "His papers were filled out properly and matched the contracts he provided," Svetlana Kutchinskaya testified.[29]

But the denouement approached. As Russian officials prepared for a fire sale of Yuganskneftegaz, Putin installed his aide Igor Sechin as the new chairman of the state-owned Rosneft oil company, the firm that had crossed swords with Khodorkovsky over the shady sale of an oil field back in 2003. Behind the scenes, Rosneft was lobbying the Kremlin to be given Yuganskneftegaz, a transfer that would overnight transform it into one of Russia's biggest oil companies. But even at a cut rate, Rosneft did not have enough cash in its accounts to pay for Yuganskneftegaz, a firm more than twice as big, and the government clearly did not want to simply hand it over without the appearance of a legitimate process. So the Kremlin deployed the weapon it had used in its last fight against an oligarch: Gazprom. The state-controlled natural gas giant, which had wrested away control of NTV from Vladimir Gusinsky on behalf of the Kremlin in 2001, was now ready to do the same to

Yukos. In September 2004, the government announced that Gazprom would take over Rosneft in a complicated stock swap, allowing the gas company to create its own oil operation. The newly merged firm would be a natural new home for Yuganskneftegaz. And then Putin would have what he had wanted all along: a dominant state energy conglomerate that would control the world's largest natural gas reserves and a huge pool of petroleum as well.

The Sechin plan was serving several goals for Putin: Aside from eliminating Khodorkovsky as a political rival, it was reasserting the Kremlin's control over Russia's booming privatized oil sector. For the first time since the fall of the Soviet Union, the state was effectively taking back more of the economy. Now if Yuganskneftegaz fell into the hands of the government, the state's share of the oil sector would more than double to 18 percent. Putin found other ways to increase control over the energy industry as well. As international oil prices rocketed past $40 a barrel, then $45, then $50, the Kremlin imposed a new taxation scheme in which 90 percent of all oil revenues over $25 a barrel went straight into state coffers. As long as oil prices remained so high, that meant the Russian government was taking in about $200 million extra every day, money it was using in part to boost spending on its decrepit military. The state also annulled a 1993 tender and stripped ExxonMobil of its rights to develop the Sakhalin-3 oil project off the Pacific coast so that it could re-auction the license for more than $1 billion. Even companies that remained private learned that in Putin's Russia they were obligated to demonstrate fealty to the state first and their shareholders second. Lukoil, the largest oil company besides Yukos, transferred $200 million one day to the state treasury without being asked and promised to forgo using even legal tax shelters. "We think the fact that the state is domineering now is good," Leonid Fedun, Lukoil's vice president and part-owner, told us. "Oil is a strategic thing and of course the state should participate . . . [since] oil is the basis for the economy."[30]

The increasing state capitalism, a trend dubbed "people's oil" by the Troika Dialog investment house, was not eliminating oligarchs as a class, as Putin had promised. Instead, it was promoting oligarchic loyalty to Putin. No longer were tycoons financing human rights groups, media organizations, or other nongovernmental groups that might anger the Kremlin; instead they stuck to ventures sure to curry favor with Putin, such as when oil-and-aluminum tycoon Viktor Vekselberg, Russia's third-richest man, bought the late Malcolm Forbes's collection of imperial Fabergé eggs for more than $90 million and brought them back to Russia to be displayed at the Kremlin.

Putin was also creating a whole new generation of oligarchs. Igor Sechin, now serving as head of Rosneft, had no experience in the oil sector. At forty-three years old, he boasted the résumé of a KGB veteran who had adapted to the new system. As the Kremlin deputy chief of staff, Sechin rarely appeared in public and gave no interviews. But he had an inside line to the prosecutors pursuing Khodorkovsky—Sechin's daughter had reportedly married the son of Vladimir Ustinov, the prosecutor general, shortly after the oil tycoon's arrest. As all the pieces fell into place, even some Putin aides came to understand that the Yukos affair was at least partially about enriching a new generation of insiders. "At first, when they started, it seemed there had been some personal conflict between Putin and Khodorkovsky," Vladimir Milov, who was deputy energy minister under Putin until 2002, told us shortly after Sechin's ascension. "Now it seems it may be connected to efforts to redistribute property that was privatized in the nineties."[31]

The state piled new tax bill after tax bill on Yukos until it all added up to $28 billion, more than sixteen times the company's remaining worth. The total taxes claimed for 2001 equaled 100 percent of the company's revenue that year, and the claim for 2002 represented 105 percent of that year's revenues.[32] Finally, on December 19, 2004, the state's property fund sold Yuganskneftegaz for $9.3 billion, even though the government's own valuation of the property conducted by a German firm pegged its worth between $14.7 billion and $17.3 billion.[33] Only one firm bid at the auction, a mystery shell company called Baikal Finance, whose listed address turned out to be a building housing a bar and video store in the provincial town of Tver. Gazprom had planned to bid but lost its international financing when Khodorkovsky's partners filed suit in a U.S. court. So in an absurd charade, the Gazprom representative at the auction sat on his hands while the mysterious Baikal man raised his paddle and outbid himself five times until reaching the price that had evidently been settled on in secret beforehand. Baikal then turned around and sold itself to state-owned Rosneft, which was being swallowed up by Gazprom. The Kremlin had succeeded in effectively stealing Russia's biggest oil company with the same sorts of shell-company manipulation that it had put Khodorkovsky on trial for using in the first place.

Even Putin's chief economics adviser, Andrei Illarionov, could keep silent no longer. A week after the auction, he denounced the renationalization of Yukos. "The sale of the main oil-producing asset of the best Russian oil company . . . and its purchase by Rosneft company, one hundred percent owned by the state, has undoubtedly become the scam of the year," he told a news conference. "When the Yukos case began, everybody was asking what will be the rules of the game. Now it is clear that there are no rules of the game."[34]

Heading into the spring of 2005, the three judges of Moscow's Meshchan-sky Court were poised to find Mikhail Khodorkovsky and Platon Lebedev guilty on all counts and sentence them to ten years in prison. In our last dinner with Anton Drel, the lawyer, we asked again whether Khodorkovsky, the billionaire oil magnate, was genuinely prepared for a decade behind bars. "He says yes," Drel told us. "But not a single normal person could be ready."[35]

MIKHAIL KHODORKOVSKY's attempt to reform and transform himself from bandit capitalist to democratic champion never sold with the Russian public, nor did his self-image as a victim of a power-hungry authoritarian regime. However genuine his conversion, however true his warnings about the dangers of Putin's monopoly on power, the excesses of the oligarchs still resonated through Russian society. The ambivalence about capitalism, and capitalists, proved a powerful force and one that enabled Putin to do anything he wished without public backlash. Better to be subservient to Putin than to the oligarchs.

Sasha Markus talked about it one day with his friend Valera Nakaryakov at the little café near the university in Nizhny Novgorod. The new Russia had not turned out as they wished. The Khodorkovskys of the present, they believed, were still the greater evil than the KGB veterans of the past.

"Originally," Markus said, "my opinion was that we had a choice: either to create a new world or to join a new system. For me, it was more comfortable to be in opposition to both systems—the West and our local system—and to create something new."

"For me," Nakaryakov replied, "it was not so much criticism of the system but criticism of the people—the Komsomol, the party members. . . . Now we can see the same people are standing at the head of our democratic state. Khodorkovsky was . . . Komsomol and then a capitalist. The same person I would never like to have anything to do with."

"It's the same show," Markus interjected.

"If we talk about Khodorkovsky," Nakaryakov continued, "what is happening with him is good. Evil must be punished."

"A different evil."

"Even if the instrument of good is evil as well."

Lenin Was Right After All

They are not really for democracy.
— IRINA SUVOLOKINA

T ANYA LEVINA KNEW the answer. She was absolutely sure of it. Lenin, she said, had been right after all.

It was September 2003, the beginning of their last year in high school for a class of Russian teenagers on the far southeastern edge of Moscow. They were talking about the revolution that had given birth to the Soviet Union, and Tanya was preaching its virtues to her fellow students. "The notion of democratic freedom is alien to Russian society," she argued. Sure, the Bolsheviks had illegally seized power in 1917, but still, even now, knowing what she did about Joseph Stalin and the camps and all that had come later, "It was the best choice for Russia."[1]

Her teacher couldn't have disagreed more. Irina Viktorovna Suvolokina was committed to teaching the truth about Soviet history—its party-led dictatorship, reckless waste of human life, and centrally planned economic folly. Her version would once have landed her in jail. But her greatest challenge now came from her skeptical students, not repressive authorities. She had nine months to change, or at least open, their minds, starting with her most outspoken student. If she could convert Tanya, she figured, the rest of the class would follow.

"It's not the end, it's the beginning," the teacher told us, an optimist in perhaps the way all teachers are optimists each September. "When they finish, they'll all be Republicans and Democrats like in America."

Addressed with Russian politeness as Irina Viktorovna by her students, she knew how daunting a task it would be. Although not one of them was old enough to remember the Soviet Union, which had collapsed when they were toddlers, many heads nodded that day in September when Tanya said the Communist past was more suited to Russia than the capitalist present.

At seventeen, these children of Russia's brief embrace of democracy began their eleventh and final year in high school largely uncertain that this was the right course for their country. Back in the 1990s, it had been an article of faith that this next generation, unencumbered by a Soviet upbringing, would break away decisively from the past. But it had not turned out that way. More free than any generation of Russians had ever been, they just weren't sure they wanted it.

And from the start, Tanya set the tone. The daughter of an officer in the modern successor to the KGB, she liked rap music and Beethoven and planned to study economics—the capitalist kind—at university. She was certain that in fast-changing Moscow she had no choice but to "live for today," and also that "Communism is the better system for Russia."

When Irina Viktorovna divided her students into sections and asked for opinions on the revolution and bloody civil war that had followed, Tanya huddled with one group of girls to pronounce the Bolsheviks a success. "The results were positive," she said. "The Bolsheviks concentrated the entire country in their hands. They had concrete ideas, concrete goals, and concrete plans for the development of this society."

A group of boys disagreed. "Lenin led the country to an extreme," said their leader, Vanya Gogolev. "The extreme was dictatorship."

At the end of their discussion, the teacher handed out a questionnaire. Whose side, she asked, would you have been on in 1917?

After class, she tallied the results: the Bolshevik cause advocated by Tanya won, with ten votes. The short-lived provisional government overthrown by the Bolsheviks got seven votes. Two students voted for the restoration of the tsar. The rest declined to state a position.

"They're not Bolsheviks by conviction," Irina Viktorovna said of her students as the year began, "but they are still for Soviet power."

WE CAME TO Moscow's School Number 775, on the city's anonymous outskirts, looking for a window into the Russian past as seen through the eyes of the country's future. We weren't sure what to expect, but we knew that it was in the classroom where we would find clues as to where Russia might be headed. The students couldn't fail to be caught up in the larger debate facing Russian society as Vladimir Putin spoke of democracy while his critics called him a budding dictator and commentators argued over whether Western-style liberal democracy made sense for a country with a thousand-year tradition of autocratic rule. In Soviet times, the old joke had it that the future was assured; it was the past that was unpredictable. Now, Russia's history seemed up for grabs again—and history class more relevant than ever.

Throughout his presidency, Putin had not only resurrected Soviet symbols like the Stalin-inaugurated national anthem but also actively promoted the idea that the required high school history class should teach patriotism. He praised Stalin for being indelibly associated with the World War II victory, and back in his tenure as head of the FSB, he had famously installed a plaque honoring Feliks Dzerzhinsky, founder of the Soviet secret police, at the notorious headquarters on Lubyanka Square.[2] In the one and only speech of his reelection campaign, he had called the breakup of the Soviet Union a "national tragedy on a colossal scale."

Many of Putin's allies went further, openly seeking to restore tributes to Soviet excess that had been toppled in the short-lived euphoria around the breakup of the Soviet Union. In Moscow, Mayor Yuri Luzhkov proposed putting the massive Dzerzhinsky statue back on the pedestal in front of the KGB building—a statue whose August 27, 1991, fall just after the aborted hard-line coup against Mikhail Gorbachev had served as a symbolic coda to Soviet power.[3] Communist and nationalist legislators lobbied to change Volgograd's name back to Stalingrad, arguing that the city on the Volga River was only famous to the rest of the world because of the World War II bloodletting there. Putin was at least partially convinced, ordering the word *Stalingrad* engraved in place of *Volgograd* on a war memorial next to the Kremlin's walls in 2004 in a decision that marked the first time in more than four decades that Stalin's name would be used in a public monument.[4]

While some aspects of the Soviet past seemed ripe for resurrection under Putin, other controversies that might raise questions about the glories of the Communist state were not officially recognized—an attitude perhaps best summed up by a Russian Foreign Ministry statement in mid-2004. At the time, Poland was engaged in a soul-searching debate about the failure of the 1944 Warsaw uprising against the Nazis, and historians there had turned up compelling evidence that Stalin had made a calculated decision to avoid aiding it. Rather than address those claims, the Russian government chose to respond in classically Soviet fashion: "It is inappropriate and blasphemous toward the memory of those killed to engage in public debates on this issue."[5]

At the same time, the more recent past of the 1990s was undergoing a sharp revision. Although Boris Yeltsin had made him his handpicked successor, Putin often spoke of his mission in terms of overcoming Yeltsin's legacy. The phrase "chaos of the 1990s" became a new conventional wisdom,[6] and public debate no longer centered on the crippling legacy of the Soviet system but on the failures of Yeltsin's young liberal reformers. *Democracy* was now an officially suspect word, removed even from presidential speeches because, as Kremlin consultant Gleb Pavlovsky told us, it was tarnished by association with the 1990s.[7]

Such attitudes were reflected across a broad swath of Russian society as opinion polls of the Putin era registered a close, and growing, connection between ambivalent attitudes toward democracy and continued respect for the Soviet Union. Back in the eighties, at the height of Gorbachev's perestroika and the near-daily revelations about once secret Soviet abuses, only small numbers named Stalin as Russia's most outstanding historical figure. By the Putin presidency, 47 percent believed he had played a positive role in history and 31 percent would want to live under his leadership.[8] When two American social scientists conducted an extensive survey around Russia in 2003, they asked whether respondents would consider voting for Stalin if he were running for president of Russia today. A stunning 26 percent said definitely or probably yes and another 15 percent said they couldn't decide whether "they would vote for a leader who, by all accounts, killed, tortured, enslaved, and imprisoned many millions of his country's citizens." Most surprising, answers from younger Russians under age thirty mirrored the overall results. "The younger generation," concluded the scholars, Sarah E. Mendelson and Theodore P. Gerber, "is somewhat more inclined to value democracy rather than authoritarianism, yet a substantial number—in any case, more than half—are still ambivalent at best in their rejection of Stalin. Overall, optimism that the younger generation of Russians has enthusiastically embraced democracy is clearly misplaced. Assumptions that a younger generation of democrats will simply replace the older generic communists have little basis in reality."[9]

In the classroom, too, the democratic revolution in history teaching was proving to have been short-lived. For the ideologues of Communism, there had been no more important subject than history. "History *was* ideology," recalled Galina Klokova, a diminutive woman who had started as a Stalin-era history teacher and eventually rose to head the institute in charge of the history curriculum during Yeltsin's presidency.[10]

From the 1917 Bolshevik revolution until the early 1930s, history had not existed at all as a required course in school, a casualty of revolutionary upheaval. Communists had thrown out the old tsarist texts but were too busy making new history to teach it. By 1934, having consolidated power, Stalin realized the significance of the subject. He and his Politburo colleagues personally wrote instructions on what should be included in the first national history textbook. In later years, the Supreme Soviet took charge of what could be taught, and every regional committee of the Communist Party had a third secretary in charge of history to make sure no deviations from the official line were tolerated. Party membership was a requirement for teachers in charge of such a sensitive subject.

Until 1988, that is. In one of the most stunning developments of Gorbachev's glasnost policy, the national history exam was simply canceled that year. The history being taught students was a lie, the Soviet authorities suddenly decreed, so they would no longer be tested on it. Bewildered teachers put aside their textbooks and began lecturing to their students from magazines and newspapers that were full of disclosures about the past. Once again, revolution took precedence over history lessons, and it would take several years before a new generation of scholars started writing textbooks suitable for the new Russia.

Under Yeltsin, history was no longer a state priority. The time devoted to the past was cut sharply—many students now had just two or three hours a week—and what they were taught in the required ninth- and eleventh-grade courses on modern Russian history varied widely. In many schools in Russia's far-flung regions, the old Soviet textbook remained in place. By the mid-1990s, though, there were new options for teachers, taking a variety of approaches.

Under Putin, these were joined by a new set of more patriotic books. Echoing the president, many of the new textbooks took the line that the "breakup of the Soviet Union was a tragedy," Klokova told us.[11] She had just undertaken a review of fifteen history textbooks dealing with the twentieth century and found that "many say Soviet times were not as bad as they had been described." Some refused to call Stalin's dictatorship an example of totalitarianism, while others mentioned Stalin's mass arrests and killings but failed to address the system that had produced such horrors. One popular textbook used Soviet propaganda images on its cover—a massive statue of a collective-farm girl, a recruitment poster reading "The Motherland is calling," and the Soyuz-Apollo space docking.[12] "During Putin's presidency, there have been many hints—we are supposed to be proud of our country, so let's try to find in our history these things that unite us all and these pages in our history that are glorious and forget the black pages," Klokova said. "Let's talk about flights to space and electric power stations."[13]

Curious about how this debate would play out in the classroom, we approached several schools in Moscow. A number of them were afraid to grant permission for us to attend history class, insisting on letters from the Ministry of Education that we were assured were impossible to obtain. We found School Number 775 and its director, Elizaveta Chirkova, through a friend of a friend. Hers was an absolutely ordinary school in an absolutely ordinary place, but she dreamed of making it a "model school" on the arid rim of the megalopolis and was herself curious about what we would find in Irina Viktorovna's history class. She came with us to the first class we attended in September and listened, stunned, to Tanya. "This is not what I expected," the director said later.

WHEN IRINA Viktorovna started at School Number 775 back in 1980, in the twilight of the Leonid Brezhnev era, there had been no freewheeling debates among students, no open disagreements with the teacher. She had dutifully recounted the history of Communist Party congresses and Soviet triumphs as decreed in the single national textbook. Discipline was strict. Stalinism was an all but forbidden subject.

"In my classes then, I never pronounced the words 'What do you think?'" she recalled. "You were supposed to learn and then answer exactly the way I told you."

At school now, the teacher found Tanyas in all her history classes, students who she believed were still being raised by "Soviet parents in Soviet homes." This particular group she had known since they were third-graders, and they were all neighborhood kids like her son Dima, who was also in the class.

The neighborhood was Lyublino, a working-class region of iron foundries and oil refineries and railway depots since the Soviet era of rapid urbanization, and her students were just a generation or so removed from the peasant poverty of their grandparents' time. "Village kids," she called them, though they lived on the edge of the massive city. There were no great post-Soviet success stories among their parents, and most households made do with less even than the Moscow average at the time of $600 a month. Nearly all twenty-nine students in her class hoped to major in economics or computers once they went on to university. The girls wore clothes as fashionable as they could afford and flipped through *Cosmopolitan* magazine when they were bored. The boys affected poses of disinterest and blared music from a boom box during class breaks. They all had cell phones.

Tanya lived a short walk from school, in the same three-room apartment where she had lived since she was born; her mother worked at a factory producing medical equipment. Tanya's classmate Lyudmila Kolpakova, known by her nickname, Lusya, was the only child of a truck driver and a nurse from the provinces on Russia's western border. Another classmate, Anton Tretyakov, a perennial cutup with a streak of intellectual curiosity, was the son of a jack-of-all-trades father currently working as a plumbing distributor. Like the rest, Anton planned to go on to university, not least to make sure he didn't end up conscripted into the Russian army. Ever since grade school, these three students had dominated the class, although neither Anton nor Lusya had Tanya's persuasive passion when it came to history.

At forty-five, Irina Viktorovna was the same age as most of their parents, and she had risen to deputy director of School Number 775, with eight hundred students crammed into a decrepit former hospital where no more than five hundred were meant to learn. There were broken windows and ceilings on the verge of collapse. The building was in such bad condition that Moscow authorities had promised it would be the first school in the neighborhood to be renovated. Even as a top administrator, she made only $200 a month. But she believed her job was crucial, preparing students to be citizens of a Russia teetering between democracy and the leftovers of dictatorship. And she thought, too, that this is what the students wanted from her—a chance to debate current questions of Putin's Russia. She planned not to bother them with tests or essays and was the kind of teacher who blamed herself if they were passing notes or dozing off. With only three hours a week to teach them history, she was well aware how hard it would be to help them navigate the political minefields of their collective past.

"For me, the most important thing is that they can find their place in political life, so they know what things are happening in public life," she said as the school year began. "I want history to serve them for the future."

THE CLASS had settled in to a fast-paced discussion of why totalitarianism arose in twentieth-century Europe: social inequality, global economic crisis, the post–World War I political settlement. It was late October, and this was their final session in the decayed old hospital before moving to temporary quarters in a new school even farther out on the city's anonymous frontier.

Then Tanya interjected with the word she often employed when talking about the Soviet Union or Stalin: "Genius." Fascism and Communism, she said, "were systems of genius."

Irina Viktorovna tried not to overreact. "What was so genius about it?" she asked.

"One person managed to restore the country, was able to rule it," Tanya replied, "and that was a new system for the world."

Lusya, Tanya's curly-haired rival for leadership among the girls, interrupted from the front-row seat where she always sat. She considered herself a moderate when compared with Tanya, but also confided after class one day that "if you have complete freedom, there will be chaos."

Lusya said totalitarianism was not a "system of genius." But, she added, authoritarianism was. In an authoritarian state, she insisted, "You can think and say whatever you want," as long as you never directly seek power.

This, Irina Viktorovna thought, was a teaching moment if ever she had seen one. She decided to talk about the forest and the trees.

Trees, she said, are individuals and the forest is made up of the individual trees, and this is democracy. In a totalitarian society, it is the forest that matters and the trees that are an anonymous mass. "Now tell me, please, where you would like to live: in a society where you are a mass or a society where your interests, individual interests, are respected?"

She called for hands to be raised, for all those "who think they would rather live in a society where their interests are respected."

Most, the silent majority, raised their hands.

"And now those who think it is better to live in a society where your interests are lost, ignored, and where you turn into a mass?"

Tanya and Lusya raised their hands.

Irina Viktorovna was still thinking about trees. "You can't chop wood without making chips fly," she said. So, she asked, who wants to be a wood chip? No one volunteered. "Then I do not understand where this wish to be dissolved in the mass is coming from," she said.

Tanya replied, "I personally have not seen an example of the first type of society, and I know examples of the second type."

Said the teacher, "Even if you haven't seen such a society, don't you want to try to create one in your own country, or shall we continue to live like we used to?"

"It will not work out," Tanya said. "If we can do whatever we want, it's going to be a disaster."

Anton was stuck on the trees. That, and how his own need for strict discipline was really a metaphor for a country full of misbehaved kids like himself.

"Have you ever thought that this saying about the trees and the forest is very harmful to states that are not morally or socially ready for it, like Russia, for example?" he asked. "Let's say I just decide that I will not go to class, I just decide as an individual that I do not feel like going and I don't care, but maybe my future depends on this particular class. . . . We won't be able to do anything if some firm hand doesn't take us all and lead us to our goal.

"So I think to speak about democracy in our society, well, it is premature. . . . Our country needs this strong hand to establish order."

"That means repressions," said Irina Viktorovna.

Anton nodded.

"So," said the teacher, "are you ready to become a wood chip?"

"Yes," said Anton, "if it is necessary. If it is for the sake of the people."

FOR IRINA Viktorovna, history class was more about thinking than about facts and dates. The textbook could provide those at home. *Russia and the World* was not the book she would pick; actually, she said, "I don't like it at all." But Moscow school authorities sent it to School Number 775 and paid for it. And besides, she had no one to complain to about its failures.

She knew it was flawed. The devastating famine that had resulted from the Soviet Union's forced collectivization policy and killed an estimated 7 million people in Ukraine and southern Russia in 1932–33 was covered in one paragraph.[14] Even the fact that tens of millions perished in Stalin's labor camps was omitted—because, the book's coauthor said in an interview, he couldn't say for sure whether 15 million or 50 million had died.[15] When it came to the current president, the textbook was outright sycophantic. "Residents of Russia on the whole have positive attitudes toward the policy of the government," the book concluded about Putin. "Many are attracted by the democratic values, openness of society, possibility of free choice, market abundance, and, finally, hope for economic growth and improvement in the quality of life in the future."[16]

Still, the textbook did include facts withheld as recently as the late 1980s. The Nazi-Soviet pact of 1939 was there, as was the American Lend-Lease program that had provided the Soviets with key military aid during World War II—even if it was covered in just a sentence.

Irina Viktorovna was familiar with the explosive power of such information. She refused to avoid lightning-rod subjects like Stalin's gulag or Putin's ongoing war in Chechnya, although she felt pressure to be patriotic. "I wanted to give them the real facts," she said. "I don't think we are diminishing Soviet patriotism to say they were eating American meat."

But with Tanya, even facts failed to persuade. At the start of a November lesson, the class read a letter from a Communist Party activist accusing Stalin of betraying the revolution and destroying the army leadership on the eve of war with Nazi Germany. The teacher had chosen it specifically with Tanya in mind, she told us later, because "it's the evidence of a true believer" in Soviet power.

Still, Tanya refused to agree. "Under Stalin, the army was not in a poor state," she insisted. "It was strong."

She was unhappy with how Stalin had been portrayed, all this emphasis on repressions rather than his achievements in modernizing a backward country. The textbook, she was sure, was not giving "a full reflection of Stalin's policy," as she put it after class, and neither was the teacher.

For once, Dima, the teacher's normally quiet son, took her on. "Stalin destroyed practically all the command staff," he said. "The army was decapitated."

But Tanya would not bend, not even when the teacher noted that all five of the army's top marshals had been executed. "The army was in a great state," the student insisted.

"Come on," Irina Viktorovna said. "The army in a great state surrendered half the territory of the Soviet Union."

For the most part, though, this was a class where facts were assumed and debate was the point. Tanya might say Russia didn't need freedom, but she would have every opportunity to exercise her right to free speech in Irina Viktorovna's classroom. On the question of Stalin's purges, many disagreed with her.

"Stalin's policy was against people," Anton said. "He destroyed a huge number of people, all the smart people, all the people who could have achieved something. Basically, he destroyed the human resources of the country."

But Anton and others in class harbored a nagging sense that maybe Tanya was right and all the horror had been necessary. "Despite the fact that all of this was destructive for our country," he said, "a solid foundation was created at that time, even though it was a bloody foundation. If it had not been for that, there would have been a disaster."

Anton asked what the teacher thought. This almost always happened, and Irina Viktorovna almost always avoided answering, convinced this was a Soviet instinct for self-preservation by the students and that "if I said my opinion, they would all agree with me." But this lesson on Stalin was different. She was sure they did not hear unvarnished accounts of the Soviet dictator at home. Even their own family's stories were kept secret from them, which is why Anton said he thought that his great-grandmother had been "in the repressions, but I'm not sure."

"We should learn all the facts of our history," Irina Viktorovna told her class. "We should learn our history with Stalin and Lenin and Ivan the Terrible and so on, and know who we are and what our history is. . . . If we keep silent about facts from our history it will never bring good results. Why? Because if we don't talk about our mistakes, we will make them again."

As HER STUDENTS debated Stalin's legacy and each other, the type of unvarnished history of the Soviet Union being taught by Irina Viktorovna was under assault in the upper reaches of the Russian government for the first time since the Soviet collapse.

The target was Igor Dolutsky, a soft-spoken historian who, like Irina Viktorovna, taught at a Moscow high school. In the mid-1990s, Dolutsky had written one of the first of the post-Soviet history textbooks to address the previously secret flaws in the Soviet past. His book, *National History, 20th Century,* was now in its seventh edition and was often recognized as a leader in the now-crowded field. It was everything that the textbook used by Irina Viktorovna's students was not—precise in its citations, meticulous in offering an array of viewpoints, and focused on presenting not only unpleasant facts about Soviet history but also in explaining how the abuses were integral parts of the Soviet system designed to shore up the power of the party dictatorship. "Dolutsky is the best one," Galina Klokova told us after conducting her review of the leading history textbooks on the market.[17]

Uncompromising in his democratic politics as well as rigorous in his historical standards, Dolutsky had written a book suitable for citizens of a country determined never to go back to the Soviet past. The problem, of course, was that this was not a settled question in Putin's Russia. Dolutsky's sardonic asides, his snide references to Stalin as the self-proclaimed "Generalissimo," his evident glee in quoting the dissident jokes of the 1970s, and his skewering of the hollow excesses of Soviet propaganda were jarringly out of step with the new political zeitgeist. For the 2003 edition, he decided to update the book with new material about the current president, including quotations from a liberal commentator warning of a "state coup" and liberal politician Grigory Yavlinsky calling Russia under Putin a "police state." Whether deliberately defiant or not, Dolutsky had laid down what amounted to a direct challenge to the Kremlin. When one of his editors saw Dolutsky's additions, she recalled, "I felt sick."[18]

At first, nothing happened, just a disquieting incident in September 2003, when Putin's then chief of staff, Aleksandr Voloshin, and his press minister, Mikhail Lesin, visited an exhibition of textbooks in Moscow. The two officials approached the chief editor of Mnemozina publishing house, and to her delight, they asked for a copy of Dolutsky's history book by name. She gave them the only copy she had, the one on the display stand. At the time, the editor simply believed it was terrific recognition for Dolutsky. Too excited to sleep, she called him that night around 2 a.m. "She said, 'Igor, we are so happy,'" Dolutsky told us later. He knew better. "I said, 'Now we are going to have a huge problem.'"[19]

The problem came without further warning in November when Education Minister Vladimir Filippov declared that Dolutsky's book was being reviewed by an expert council, later announcing ominously that there was no space in Russian classrooms for "pseudoliberalism aimed at distortions of history." The ministry told Russian reporters that the textbook was way out of line in its criticism of Putin. "The textbook elicits contempt, natural contempt for our past and for the Russian people," the ministry's top textbook official said.[20] Dolutsky was speaking about the controversy on the radio station Ekho Moskvy the day the news broke when he learned that Putin himself had weighed in. The president had made a speech to a gathering of Russian historians at which he said that inculcating patriotism was the proper job of a history textbook. Such books should "not be a field for a new political and ideological battle," he said, but should "foster a sense of pride for one's history and one's country."[21] Suddenly, just two weeks before the Russian parliamentary elections, the teaching of history had become a political cause célèbre.

No one at the ministry would tell Dolutsky what exactly was wrong with the book. But his initial impulse was to fight; by inclination, he was still the dissident he had been back in Brezhnev times, when he had had his first brush with the authorities and had been kicked out of the university for publishing a poem in the departmental newspaper with a line stolen from Hamlet: "Something's rotten in our state." He had no compunction about appearing on whatever programs would have him to complain about the campaign launched against his book. In one appearance, he called it an "election-year gift" to Putin—and by the way, he added, he thought Yavlinsky was right about the "police state." He was sure he had rattled the authorities. "They were scared," he said later, "of all this noise I was creating."[22]

But then a contact at the Education Ministry leaked a marked-up copy of Dolutsky's textbook to an editor at his publishing house. They never found out who exactly had highlighted the objectionable passages in the book, but were stunned to see sentences underlined on nearly every page. This was not just a matter of a few critical comments about Putin, it turned out, but a wholesale revision of the Soviet era's history. Here, in paragraph after paragraph, they were seeing what the new policy of patriotic education meant in practice. "The main idea of the criticism is that I'm undermining the true values of the Russian people and imposing liberal values that are not typical for the Russian people," Dolutsky said.[23]

It started on the very first page of the ministry's marked-up copy, where Dolutsky had mentioned the Soviet massacre in the Katyn Forest of as many as fifteen thousand Polish officers during World War II, a tragedy that officials had blamed until recently on the Germans. On page eight, he described the

Soviet "occupation" of the three Baltic countries at the start of World War II that lasted until 1991 and asked students if they understood what attitude Latvians, Lithuanians, and Estonians might have toward Russians as a result. He portrayed Stalin as a willing dupe of Adolf Hitler in passages that were marked, and mentioned that 160,000 Soviets had been shot in the early stages of the war for "panic and cowardice" in another sentence that drew objection. His comments about the key wartime role played by the United States and Britain were highlighted, as was a question to students asking them to ponder why Germans were greeted as liberators in parts of Soviet territory such as western Ukraine. More black marks appeared next to his description of the deportation of the entire Chechen people during the war. When it came to the book's account of mass arrests and killings inside the Soviet Union, entire pages were singled out, among them those noting Stalin's postwar turn toward anti-Semitism.

On page ninety-six, Dolutsky quoted from the official history textbook of the 1980s, according to which the economy of the Soviet Union under Stalin had "developed at a furious pace," while "the standard of living of workers grew," "literary life became lively," and "preconditions were established for the spiritual development of man." Up until the Putin era, he pointed out, many Russians still believed that version of the past. This paragraph was also marked by the ministry. As for more recent history, the anonymous editor objected to a quotation from the well-known Czech author Milan Kundera about the Soviet invasion of his country in 1968, as well as Dolutsky's inclusion of jokes about Leonid Brezhnev and paragraphs explaining how a gerontocracy (average Politburo age in 1976: sixty-seven) had come to rule the Soviet Union. His entire description of the war in Chechnya was marked, as was everything having to do with Putin's unlikely accession to power. On page 254 were the famous quotes about Putin's "police state," duly marked.

And then there were Dolutsky's closing words, on page 259, in which he told students that "what will come next depends on you" and warned that extreme nationalism combined with antidemocratic rule could be the path Russia takes out of the post-Soviet problems that have beset the country.[24]

Uncertain how to respond to the ministry, Dolutsky and his editors combed through previous editions of his textbook. They found that virtually all of the passages now being questioned had been included in the book before—without drawing objection from officials. They sent a letter pointing this out, but it did not matter. In early December, the official word came out: the Education Ministry had decided to yank its required seal of approval from Dolutsky's book, effectively banning its use in the classroom. The decision marked the first time such an act of educational censorship had taken place since the fall of the Soviet Union. Over the following winter, Putin instructed the ministry to go even further and launch a comprehensive review of all 107 history textbooks in use in Russian schools. Many authors feared that this signaled a future return to just one officially authorized version of the Soviet past.

Dolutsky, after all his years of battling the system, told us that he had finally given up. His textbook was no longer officially approved, and his publishers were too scared even to sell the remaining ten thousand copies sitting in their warehouse. His high school students, practical-minded members of the Moscow new rich, had no interest in politics and no real commitment to democracy. "I've been fighting for twenty-five years," he said with weary finality one afternoon, "and I lost."[25]

Irina Viktorovna, stuck with her inadequate textbook and her miserly three hours a week to teach her students complicated lessons about mass murder and socialist utopia, had paid close attention to the controversy. The government's campaign against this textbook, she said, was "a disgrace."

BY JANUARY, Tanya seemed to have softened. The topic was the Cold War and which country was more to blame, the Soviet Union or the United States. Tanya said it was the Soviets' fault. "The policy of the Soviet Union was aggressive," she said.

Why? Irina Viktorovna asked.

"Because this was a totalitarian country, a totalitarian regime," Tanya responded.

Irina Viktorovna thought she had finally gotten through. "Tanya, you have changed your opinion!" said the teacher. "You are blaming Stalin for aggression."

Momentarily confused, Tanya quickly found her bearings again. "No," she said. "I am not blaming Stalin. I am proud of him, because I think it is hard to oppose the entire society, the entire world."

Outside their classroom, it was election season in Russia, and this, too, meant another set of questions Irina Viktorovna could not avoid.

In the December parliamentary elections, she said she had voted for the defeated democrats, along with so few others that both Western-oriented reform parties were knocked out of the State Duma. In the spring, before the March 14 balloting that they all knew in advance that Putin would win, she told the class that she would vote for Irina Khakamada, the presidential critic who did not even have the endorsement of her own reform party.

The students were surprised. "They kept asking me, 'Why do you not like Putin?' I said he does not even pretend to be a democrat," Irina Viktorovna recalled.

A show of hands revealed that most of their parents planned to vote for the president. Many were like Lusya's parents, who told her, "Why should we vote against him when he will win anyway?" They were "like the mass in Russia," Lusya observed. "But at least he's trying to do something."

Anton wasn't sure whom his parents would vote for, but he knew that the president's decision to refrain from campaigning, to refuse debates with his opponents, or to offer an election platform had angered his father. "It's happening like we are cattle," his father told him.

Tanya's parents exercised the option on the Russian ballot to vote "against all" rather than for Putin. She thought that was the right choice. Despite her belief in the Soviet Union, she saw today's Communists as a pale echo of their predecessors, "embarrassing for Russia because they've lost their ideology."

A few weeks after Putin's landslide election win, Irina Viktorovna circled back to the past, returning to the enduring imprint of Soviet life on today's Russia.

"What is conformism?" she asked.

The class was silent. All year, Irina Viktorovna had heard Tanya idealize a Soviet society she had never lived in. Now, for once, Tanya had no ready answer.

So the teacher told them what it had been like to be a Young Pioneer, about parade time when they were lined up in huge ranks, "such a beautiful line of identical white blouses, a line of identical red Pioneer ties and ribbons!"

She told them how it was to stand in that line, about the feeling "that comes up from the very depth of your soul. You feel almost happy that you belong to this huge power.... You have this feeling of security and a feeling of, if not happiness, then something very close to it, because you think that you can rely on this huge power. But what if you do something wrong? They pull you out of this rank, put you in front of the other Pioneers, and start scolding you. All the other kids stare at that one Pioneer in the middle, their eyes saying, 'Shame on you.' Imagine what this one person must feel, being alone face-to-face with this huge mass.... A kid starts crying, ready to promise anything, to do anything only to have a chance to get back to his place in the rank, to blend in and be the same as everybody else. For that, he is ready to give anything away."

For once, the class was spellbound.

She quoted the poet Vladimir Mayakovsky, a Soviet icon of the 1920s and 1930s now known mostly as the name of a subway station in downtown Moscow. He had written glowingly of Soviet society as "a hand of a million fingers, squeezed in one wrist smashing everything. A single one—nonsense, a single one—zero."

She tried to explain what it meant. As an individual in the Soviet dictatorship, "one couldn't be but 'one-millionth fraction of a ton,'" she said, quoting Soviet exile Yevgeny Zamyatin. "Do you understand the difference?"

It was still a hard sell.

The class had started with Tanya insisting that Soviet man was a nobler creature than his post-Soviet counterpart. "He was trying to achieve something, he was building Communism," Tanya had said. But the post-Soviet Russian didn't believe in anything, "just lives day by day, no future, no goals."

It was then that Irina Viktorovna turned to explaining what life was really like in the worker's paradise of Tanya's rendering. She knew where her students' attitudes were coming from.

She had asked for a show of hands. "Where is your social consciousness formed?" Nearly everyone said at home.

So Irina Viktorovna had talked about the archetypal Soviet home, the communal apartment, still not entirely gone even in Moscow, where each family had one room to live in and they all—dozens sometimes—shared a single kitchen and bathroom. In such homes, she had said, knowing that many of these kids' families had once lived in such places, "They reported on each other, gossiped, wrote complaints, persecuted people."

"What is conformism?" she had asked.

And after the silence she had answered for them.

"TANYA'S REALLY changed," Irina Viktorovna said hopefully as sunny late April turned to a blustery May 2004. On the eve of high school graduation, Irina Viktorovna thought that Tanya was listening more and advocating less.

But Tanya pronounced herself unmoved. "Irina Viktorovna tells me I'm not right. I would just say I will only change my mind when I really see I'm not right," Tanya told us one day after class, sitting on the hard bench next to the bathroom with no toilet paper and the window looking out on a gritty field of hastily built new apartment towers in pastel colors so incongruous the kids called them "candies."

She still believed Stalin was "a person of genius," and she still planned to major in economics at the management university. "Putin is not moving Russia ahead," she said. "We're just swimming with the current." Tanya said she had "loved" the chance to speak her mind freely in Irina Viktorovna's class and knew she wouldn't have been able to do so in Stalin's time. "It's a plus," she allowed, "but only a very little one."

As Tanya held firm to her beliefs, Anton and Lusya and many of the others were determined to split the difference, to find an acceptable middle between their classmate and their teacher, "something of democracy, something of authoritarianism," as Lusya put it.

No longer the optimist of September, Irina Viktorovna now said she had a more modest goal in mind, "to move their brains in certain directions." She knew that Tanya believed she hadn't changed, but still thought the lessons had made an impact. "She's not as categorical as she used to be," the teacher said. All year, she had tried to demolish the enduring Soviet myths they had grown up with. All year, she had interjected with subtle points about the responsibility of individuals in a free society and the soul-annihilating quality of life in the Soviet Union.

Just as persistently, Irina Viktorovna's students had insisted on debating what it all meant for today's Russia: Didn't the country really need a "strong hand" at the helm? Wasn't chaos the real consequence of democracy? Was this Russia of theirs a democracy at all, and if so, why did it seem so unfair? These teenagers were fixated on the upheavals of the 1990s as the only history relevant to their daily lives, and if that was what counted as democracy, they rejected it. When the Soviet Union entered their arguments, it was usually as an example of the better life that might have been.

In a way, Irina Viktorovna was glad the students could only idealize Soviet times, that they had never experienced the repressive system themselves. Maybe, she said, her voice trailing off, Russia would embrace freedom in three generations or so, assuming nothing terrible happened.

"They are not really for democracy," she said. "But at least something is going on in their minds."

After Beslan

The Russian mentality needs a baron, a tsar, a president. . . in one word, a boss.
—VALENTINA MATVIYENKO

T HE BODY COUNT FROM Beslan was still rising weeks after the battle ended. Families continued to search the morgues each day, desperate to recognize their own child in the rows of tiny charred corpses yet to be claimed. Chechen warlord Shamil Basayev boasted over the Internet of his role in the seizure of Beslan's School Number 1, while Russian authorities blamed trigger-happy locals as well as Basayev's hardened guerrillas for the horrific massacre. Conspiracy theories ran through the devastated town. When we returned a few weeks after the bloody end to the siege in the fall of 2004, the dreary round of funerals was punctuated by talk of revenge. Some men brandished hunting rifles and muttered threats against the ethnic Ingush and Chechens in the neighboring republic, while others turned to the scapegoat within, blaming the school's seventy-two-year-old principal for somehow not protecting the children. Mostly, Beslan was a place over-whelmed by grief. "In the morning you don't hear the roosters anymore," said Elza Baskayeva, a woman we had befriended while her daughter was among the hostages. "Even the dogs have stopped barking."[1]

In Moscow, Vladimir Putin had just announced his plan to eliminate direct election of governors and independent members of parliament, claim-ing it was an urgent necessity to fight terrorism after Beslan. For years, Putin had disavowed intentions to make such a move—at least six times he had publicly forsworn interest in canceling gubernatorial elections. "Some have even suggested more radical measures than those contained in the submit-ted draft laws, going so far as suggesting that governors should be appointed by the Russian president," Putin had said in 2000 as he first began his cam-paign to centralize power back in the Kremlin. "But I still think that the heads of the regions of the federation must be elected by the people. This procedure has become established, it has become part of our democratic state system."[2]

In fact, the plan put into effect after Beslan had been worked on for months, even years, in the Kremlin, where Putin's former chief of staff, Aleksandr Voloshin, had long promoted the idea. It had been an open secret, as Marat Gelman and others close to the Kremlin told us months before Beslan, that "the governors were next." The slaughter of hundreds of schoolchildren and their parents and teachers became a convenient excuse to execute the plan. By late October, parliament rushed through the end of gubernatorial elections, and governors were stampeding to join the Kremlin-created United Russia to pledge loyalty. By the beginning of 2005, the law was in effect. Russia's last race was for governor of the oil-rich Nenets autonomous region, a contest in which the Kremlin-backed candidate finished third. Such unmanageable outcomes would no longer be risked in Putin's Russia.

Indeed, the final consolidation of power now seemed a foregone conclusion for a president who had taken office five years earlier eager to "control everybody." Putin's pocket parliament, controlled by United Russia and minus both the Western-oriented democratic parties, hesitated even to comment on the Beslan tragedy at first, then approved a commission to look into the school seizure with only Kremlin loyalists as members. Putin's putative rival Mikhail Khodorkovsky languished in jail, his conviction a presumed certainty along with the impending breakup of his Yukos Oil Company. Other oligarchs were cowed into submission or quietly headed out of the country, like Kakha Bendukidze, a civic-minded tycoon who had served on a Kremlin commission tasked with drawing up economic reform proposals for Putin's second term but who concluded the times were so fraught that he would be better off outside Russia. With little fanfare, Bendukidze quit and moved to his native Georgia, where he accepted a post as state minister in charge of reforming the former Soviet republic's troubled economy, giving up charge of a company with twice the budget of his homeland.[3] On television, Putin no longer needed to take home videotapes to study coverage of himself; the unwritten media loyalty code had become so powerful that even journalists who had tried to accommodate themselves to the Kremlin's dictates were now being forced out. Not long before Beslan, the once-independent NTV had brought in a new director from state television, whose first act was to yank the network's one remaining candid forum for political debate, the talk show hosted by Savik Shuster called *Freedom of Speech* (*Svoboda Slova* in Russian). The Kremlin was hardly chagrined by the predictable headlines announcing, as the newspaper *Kommersant* did, "Freedom of Speech Canceled."

After an election campaign where Putin had never needed to make extravagant promises to collect his 71 percent of the vote, the president had

used his mandate to launch the most controversial initiative of his tenure—
a sweeping elimination of the social benefits, like free bus fare for pensioners,
that constituted what remained of the Soviet social safety net, in exchange for
a cash stipend. Parliament passed the wildly unpopular bill with only token
debate. As the measures took effect, Russians accustomed to the cradle-to-
grave care of the state, however frayed since the collapse of Communism, rose
up in protest. Hundreds of thousands of people took to the streets in the first
sign of a genuine grassroots political movement since Putin had taken over.
In Moscow, some of Putin's most vigorous foes among the intelligentsia
found it painfully ironic that the one thing that had finally aroused widespread public outrage was not the rise of authoritarianism but an economic
reform predicated on a philosophy they themselves subscribed to.

Other long-promised reforms to the corruption-ridden police force, the
inadequate banking system, the massively inefficient and theft-riddled electricity and natural gas monopolies, and the overwhelmed and underfunded
health care system had yet to be put forward by the president. And systemic
changes that had been attempted at the beginning of the Putin era had long
since fizzled, expectations tempered by a change-resistant reality. Even
Dmitri Kozak, the Putin aide who had tried to craft a new, more Western-
oriented judicial system, had admitted failure by 2005. "The situation in the
judicial system that remains today bears a catastrophic, threatening character," he reflected publicly. "People are convinced that this system is destroyed
by corruption and it's impossible to find truth there. . . . If people don't
believe in the judicial system, then it's impossible to hope for economic or
political progress."[4]

Inside the Kremlin, Putin's KGB circle now appeared to dominate so thoroughly that latter-day Kremlinologists studying what market analyst Christopher Weafer termed the "New Politburo" believed the power struggle was
now between different factions of the *siloviki*. Among those in the ascendancy
was Putin's KGB confidant from their Leningrad days, drug tsar Viktor
Cherkesov, who had told us back in 2001 about the "need for supreme state
control" over corrupt bureaucrats. In a published manifesto not long after
Beslan under the headline "KGB in Fashion?" Cherkesov exhorted fellow
members of what he called the "chekist community" to unite against the
"antistate and antisocial viruses threatening our society." The revival of the
KGB was no "reason to fear," he concluded, but "absolutely necessary."[5] Sergei
Ivanov, the former KGB spy now running the Defense Ministry, had also
expanded his influence far beyond bullets and conscripts. Ivanov, a potential
candidate to succeed Putin reportedly supported by Igor Sechin, the Putin

aide who had managed to take over most of Yukos, now proclaimed as his goal nothing less than indoctrinating Russians with a new patriotism. "The moronization of the people must be stopped," Ivanov declared before starting a new national television network called Zvezda, or Star, short for *Red Star,* still the name of the ministry's official newspaper. The new Defense Ministry network would make its mission to show what its director called "the hits of the Soviet Union."[6] This despite the fact that the main state-controlled networks had already touched off a wave of patriotic fervor with a revival of films depicting KGB men as heroes saving Russia from Chechen terrorists, Russian oligarchs, Western spies, and sometimes all three in the same episode.

A few final holdovers from the Boris Yeltsin era remained in top government jobs—men like Finance Minister Aleksei Kudrin and Economic Development and Trade Minister German Gref—but only, according to a well-placed Russian official, because they were literally not allowed to leave their posts.[7] Fearful of Kremlin reprisal, they stayed in office as a convenient way for Putin to mollify the West and keep up the pretense of reform abroad, while at home they were forced to take the blame for the mishandled social benefits reform. "I'm ready to be the target, whether it is for this or the lack of toilet paper," Gref said as protests mounted over the revoked benefits.[8]

Mikhail Kasyanov, the prime minister allied with the Western-style reformers who had been fired by Putin on the eve of his reelection, had now become the Kremlin's most prominent critic. Few of the president's intimates had ever spoken out, even after being banished. But Kasyanov began privately making the rounds in Moscow, London, and Washington, telling Putin skeptics that the man he had served for four years had fooled him, that instead of a new-breed democrat Putin was just an old-breed KGB officer imposing his own new order in Russia. Kasyanov then made his public debut at a news conference in February 2005 on the first anniversary of his dismissal and blasted the president in what many took to be his coming out as an opposition leader. Russia, Kasyanov declared, was headed "in the wrong direction." No longer, he added, was there any confusion about the country's course under Putin. "Russia does not support, does not follow, and does not respect any democratic principles."[9] Within hours, state television aired an interview with Kremlin political consultant Gleb Pavlovsky, who called the former prime minister a U.S. puppet, doing the bidding of "American concepts, values, and political tasks."[10] Kasyanov's criticism of the Kremlin was not shown.

One day not long after Beslan, we were summoned to the Kremlin to meet the president's political strategist Vladislav Surkov. The architect of the "managed democracy" elections, Surkov rarely gave interviews or spoke publicly, which added to his mystique. In person, he was so soft-spoken he seemed to be mumbling, and he talked in the colloquial Russian of a street-tough operator. A handful of Russian reporters were around the conference table with us as he explained why democracy was a Western luxury item that Russians weren't ready to buy. He refused to have much of what he said quoted. But Surkov made himself clear that same day in an interview with the Russian tabloid *Komsomolskaya Pravda*. Those who objected to Putin's campaign to take back power were nothing more than a "fifth column" of Russia haters, he said, composed of "false liberals and real Nazis" and sponsored by unnamed nefarious forces in the West. Democrats might claim to "hate Putin's Russia," Surkov said, "but in fact they hate Russia as such."[11]

In his public comments after the school seizure down south, Putin himself had hinted at dark forces in the West pulling strings against Russia. Soon, he would be engaged in Cold War–style shadowboxing with the United States over the presidential elections in neighboring Ukraine. As the campaign heated up in the fall of 2004 to determine whether Ukraine would accept the handpicked successor of scandal-plagued President Leonid Kuchma, Putin decided to export managed democracy next door. Gleb Pavlovsky and his fellow consultants Marat Gelman and Sergei Markov signed on with Prime Minister Viktor Yanukovych's campaign, urging the same recipe of heavy promotion on state-controlled television and use of administrative resources by the local authorities that had worked so well for Project Putin. The Russian president himself flew to Ukraine just days before the balloting in a not-so-subtle endorsement. Opposing the Russians were thousands of youthful activists trained by American-funded organizations and led by Western-oriented economic reformer Viktor Yushchenko, a former prime minister who barely survived a mysterious midcampaign dioxin poisoning. Election-day abuses were so glaring that tens of thousands of Ukrainians spilled into the streets when officials tried to declare Yanukovych the winner. Notwithstanding blatant evidence of fraud, Putin declared through his spokesman that the race was "open and honest," and congratulated Yanukovych.

But Ukrainian democracy turned out to be unmanageable. The street protests became a street revolution as swelling crowds wearing Yushchenko's trademark color of orange refused to accept the flawed results. By December, Yushchenko was president. Back in the Kremlin, Putin was reduced to denouncing the West for trying to create a "system of permanent revolutions" on the Russian frontier.[12]

■ ■ ■

LOOKING AHEAD, Russian politics seemed to come down to just one question: Would Putin leave office in 2008, as the Russian constitution decreed, or would he find a way to hold on to power past his two terms? Putin himself had always denied any intention to remain in the presidency once his eight years were up, but his allies regularly floated the idea of constitutional changes to enable him to do so or, perhaps, of setting up a new system of government in which more powers would be delegated to the prime minister, a post Putin would then assume. The president began playing coy when asked what the future would hold. "I do think about how we will negotiate the landmark of 2008," he said cryptically when asked about it at his year-end news conference in December 2004.[13]

When Putin had first come to office, Russia watchers had wondered whether the unlikely president was sincere when he called himself a democrat. By the end of his first term, Putin had long since abandoned the label, no longer bothering with the fiction of preserving the fragile emerging democracy that Boris Yeltsin had bequeathed to him and promising only to avoid a return to totalitarianism. The new system built by the Kremlin offered what political analyst Lilia Shevtsova aptly called "imitation democracy" without its inconveniences[14]—television with fancy graphics but Kremlin-dictated scripts, elections with multiple candidates yet preordained outcomes, a court system with judges and juries but no justice, a parliament with opposition parties but all created by, subservient to, or wholly owned subsidiaries of the president. But there was little ideology apparent in Putinism beyond the patriotic cheers and the resurrected Soviet symbols. Stability had been Putin's slogan, but even that mantra was in doubt now that the wave of Chechen-related terror attacks had raised serious questions about just how much safer Putin had made things. Among the experts, the debate was no longer about Putin's identity, but about how he would handle his newly consolidated power: Was Russia under Putin a "soft" authoritarian regime or something more menacing?

The eminent Russia historian Richard Pipes sparked an academic furor when he wrote in *Foreign Affairs* of "Russians' flight from freedom" and argued that Putin's policies were merely a reflection of the public's rejection of Western-style democracy. The president was "popular precisely because he has re-installed Russia's traditional model of government: an autocratic state in which citizens are relieved of responsibility for politics and in which imaginary foreign enemies are invoked to forge an artificial unity," Pipes wrote.[15] More and more, this was the argument advanced by Putin himself and his political allies. Russia, they now proclaimed openly, was neither ready for democracy nor historically suited for it. "Everything we built up was right. In our country that's the right thing to do," Aleksandr Voloshin, the Kremlin chief of staff until the Khodorkovsky affair, told colleagues behind closed doors. "The Russian people are not ready for democracy."[16] It fell to Putin's protégé Valentina Matviyenko, a former Communist Party functionary newly installed as governor of his St. Petersburg hometown, to peel back the facade and articulate in public the guiding principle that outsiders had long suspected. "We are not ready for such an experiment," she told a reporter when asked about the idea of establishing a parliamentary democracy in Russia and eliminating the presidency altogether. "The Russian mentality needs a baron, a tsar, a president . . . In one word, a boss."[17]

When Putin and President Bush met for lunch that November in Santiago, Chile, on the sidelines of an international summit, even the American leader came in for a lecture on the uniqueness of Russia and its need to have a "style of government that was consistent with Russian history," as a senior Bush aide described their talk. Bush's advisers in Washington equivocated, with some demanding a review of U.S. policy toward Russia and others continuing to insist on the benefits of the Bush-Putin relationship. Increasingly, official Washington was concluding that Bush had misjudged Putin. Pressure mounted from both right and left on Capitol Hill and K Street to speak out on Putin's clampdown. Freedom House, the U.S.-financed group that monitors worldwide democracy trends, downgraded Russia to "not free" for the first time since 1989. Vice President Cheney privately wondered whether the Americans were being tough enough on Putin and regularly slipped in conversations by referring to Russia as "the Soviet Union." As Bush was preparing to begin his second term, one disillusioned adviser told us that he had always tried to give Putin the "benefit of the doubt," unlike the "democratization people," who had long prodded the president to change his view. "It is always depressing when they are right and those of us who had hoped for better are wrong," he said.[18]

Bush continued to publicly stand by his "good personal relationship" with Putin and in private absolved the man he steadfastly called a friend by blaming the developments on the KGB coterie around the Russian president. Yet by the beginning of 2005, even Bush was no longer able to avoid taking on the situation more directly. He had announced a sweeping new vision in his second inaugural address aimed at confronting tyranny around the globe, and Russia's rollback of democracy had become an early test of whether Bush meant to follow through. On his way to meet Putin in Slovakia in February, he stopped in Western Europe and privately asked one European official if he had been wrong about Putin.[19] Facing reporters after the Slovakia meeting, Bush offered no further testimonials to Putin's vision for democracy, no more generous assessments of the Russian's soul, instead awkwardly urging "Vladimir" to consider the benefits of the rule of law.

For his part, Putin disavowed any aspirations to restore Soviet-style dictatorship, then returned to his favorite theme, the need to preserve Russia from the sort of democracy that had sprung from the Soviet collapse. Even now, he was still fighting the ghost of the Yeltsin era. "Democracy is not anarchy," he cautioned. "It is not the possibility for anyone to rob your own people." Bush pronounced himself reassured. "When he tells you something," Bush said with Putin at his side, "he means it."[20]

Putin was still far from a Soviet-style dictator; whatever his aspirations, the political system was still too weak to allow anyone to exert the sort of control that had not so long ago landed Russians in jail for the jokes they whispered or the friends they kept. And despite the success of Project Putin in returning power to the Kremlin, some saw signs of dangerous instability for the increasingly unaccountable president. As social protests spread across Russia, his approval rating fell to its lowest level since the disastrous sinking of the *Kursk* in his first year in office. Internationally, his prestige suffered after the embarrassing failure to block the Orange Revolution in Ukraine, which was soon followed by the Tulip Revolution in Kyrgyzstan in March 2005. And then there was Chechnya, the unresolved crisis down south that had spilled over to the children of Beslan and now threatened to spread farther.

Putin still held to the course of confrontation he had pursued at every turn in the conflict; there would be no negotiations, no seizing the moment of revulsion at the massacre of innocents. "The weak get beaten," Putin had declared in his post-Beslan address; his own youth on the Leningrad streets had taught him to avoid that. Putin dispatched Dmitri Kozak, the disenchanted would-be judicial reformer, down south as his new presidential envoy, while inside Chechnya troops launched a new cycle of violence. When we visited the ravaged region after Beslan, we found a wave of fear gripping many homes as Russian soldiers began showing up in the middle of the night to take away women on the pretext that they might become *shakhidka* suicide bombers—just as they had come for so many years for the men they called rebels. They came for Khalimat Sadullayeva, the mother of four children, as the family was sleeping before dawn one morning. "This is her," said one of the Russian-speaking men wearing military uniforms. The children started screaming. "Our mama is being taken away! Don't take our mama away!" Weeks later, she remained missing and no one would admit to having taken her into custody. "I never saw a woman taken away before," her stunned father, Khamid Magomadov, told us. "All that time, they never touched women. Now they're starting to take them, too."[21] Beyond Chechnya, neighboring republics saw a new spasm of political assassinations, coordinated guerrilla attacks, and bombings all seemingly designed to underscore the point that Putinism was *pokazukha,* a show of fake stability manufactured for television and swallowed by a viewing audience that was eager to embrace it.

Even Putin himself seemed shocked to encounter a reality different from what he had seen on those endless cheery television reports. Not long after his handpicked leader for Chechnya was killed, the president had staged a flyover of the republic's devastated capital, Grozny. From his helicopter, Putin had not seen the reconstructed city he had expected but the ruins of a place laid waste by Russian carpet bombing and years of urban warfare. A shaken president told his cabinet later that day that he had flown over Grozny. "It looked horrible," he said.[22] But this, too, was no reason to change course. In March 2005, the Russians finally killed separatist leader Aslan Maskhadov by lobbing a grenade into his hideout just a few miles from Grozny. Maskhadov had been the one possible figure to engage in talks with Moscow. With his death, Putin would no longer face calls for a negotiated settlement. There would only be more war.

FOR MANY OF those we encountered over the years of Putin's presidency, the months after Beslan were a time of disillusionment as they weighed the diminished possibilities of a Russia that may or may not have been more stable but was certainly less free. Misha Kozyrev, the music tastemaker who had once hoped to harness the nationalistic tenor of the times in service of Russian rock for the Russians, had had his illusions dispelled by Khodorkovsky's arrest. Beslan had merely confirmed it. But now Kozyrev's original fears about using the loaded word *nashe* for his radio station were proving to be all too accurate. Just as he had worried back in 1998, the political power of the word *ours* had proven ripe for exploitation by the newly assertive Kremlin. Alarmed by the democratic street revolution in neighboring Ukraine and the rise of protests in Russia against Putin's dismantling of the Soviet safety net, a new Komsomol-style youth group was unveiled early in 2005, started by a former Kremlin aide under the patronage of Putin political adviser Vladislav Surkov. These would be the shock troops to prevent any democratic upheaval at home. And the name the Kremlin chose for the project was Nashi.[23] It was now official; there would be an "us" in Putin's Russia and a "them."

A chagrined Kozyrev took to playing on his Nashe Radio one of the era's few protest songs, a ballad of wishful thinking called "I'm Free" by Sergei Shnurov of the group Leningrad. Inspired by Khodorkovsky's arrest, it spoke about the Russia that Kozyrev had thought it possible to create when he had returned from California in the mid-1990s—and also about the long echo of the past in which Russians had for decades believed the only true freedom came, as the song depressingly put it, "behind bars." Now, Kozyrev increasingly believed, it was that past that guided the country's future course.

> *Only when you're swimming against the current*
> *You understand the value of a free opinion.*
> *Links form a chain*
> *Life shrinks into a dot.*
> *Step by step they make your case*
> *Putting effort and heart into it.*
>
> *Here, behind bars*
> *The colonel is the boss.*
> *My freedom is a radio set*
> *I'm free like a bird in the sky.*
> *I'm free, I forget what fear is like.*
>
> *To be different means always to be alone.*
> *You make a choice for yourself—wealth or prison.*
> *Freedom is not given to people easily.*
> *There is neither entry nor exit to it.*
> *Freedom is something I've got inside.*[24]

At least the young and successful of boomtown Moscow like Kozyrev had the choice to opt out of Putin-era politics, retreating as the song would have it into an updated form of what the dissidents in Brezhnev times used to call internal exile. Those who had dabbled more openly in politics did not have that luxury. Irina Khakamada, the stylish, sharp-tongued democrat who had challenged Putin for reelection, set about vainly trying to assemble a new unified democratic opposition movement. Boris Nemtsov, the leader of the Union of Right Forces who had tried to reform the military and investigate the handling of the Moscow theater siege only to be ousted from parliament, saw little hope in that and ended up going to work for Viktor Yushchenko in Ukraine. Putin grew livid at Nemtsov's disloyalty and made a haranguing phone call to register his displeasure. Boris Berezovsky, the oligarch who had helped install Putin, then turned into his most vociferous critic and fled the country, remained in exile in London financing any and every organization that sought to oppose the Kremlin. Yelena Tregubova, the young reporter who had a quasi-romantic Japanese lunch with Vladimir Putin during his rise to power, later went on to write a tell-all book about her experiences covering him. After a small bomb exploded outside her apartment door, she took the hint and left the country. Andrei Norkin, the young NTV anchor who had been yanked off the air midsentence during the state's takeover in 2001, now worked for a Russian television channel that broadcast only outside Russia. In the years after NTV had been taken away, he had grown increasingly despondent. "Back then, I was not scared of anything. I was not afraid of being arrested. Now I have this fear all the time. I'm not going to be coy about it. The country has changed. When the owners of NTV were replaced by force, the main topics in the news were Chechnya and Putin. Now it's arrests, courts, lawyers. It's a different reality. Is it a police state? Maybe not yet. But every day I see that my main news is about the actions of law-enforcement bodies."[25]

For many Russians, though, politics remained little more than a corrupt form of warfare waged between equally unappealing clans. This was a view of the Putin-era battles shared even by many insiders who believed, as a disenchanted senior official put it to us, that the current shake-up was simply a fight for the financial spoils that came with control of the Kremlin. "The ideology is power and redistribution of property," the official said. "Power is a means of keeping property in their hands."[26] We heard this view whenever we asked regular Russians to explain the paradox of a country that embraced Putin but rejected many of his policies, where the public refused to participate in political life and claimed not to want democracy while cherishing rights like the freedom to travel and speak openly that had only been won with the Soviet collapse. These were contradictory times, as Tanya Levina and the other history students had taught us, when a new generation of cellphone addicts could speak confidently about business school degrees one minute while bemoaning the collapse of the Soviet Union the next. Putin remained the politician who could straddle that seemingly unbridgeable divide—a KGB colonel in a modern suit.

As we prepared to leave Moscow at the end of our posting there, the city was still recovering from the collective shock of Beslan. Several years earlier, Tatyana Shalimova had helped introduce us to the paradoxes that would shape our stay in the country, showing us around the new Moscow she inhabited and the far older Russia where her family remained. In many ways, the Putin era had been good to her. She had stability for the first time in her professional life—a job she had kept the entire length of Putin's presidency. And she had a home of her own, a modest apartment in Moscow she had purchased, which was now her haven even if the country around her failed to live up to expectations. "I made it how I like it," she told us proudly.

But Tatyana had just returned from a visit to the town of Mokshan, where she had grown up, where her family and friends had watched the horror of Beslan and believed the lies on television. Even years earlier when we had met, Tatyana had been part of the minority in her skepticism about Putin, telling us she could never support a president from "the organs." Now, over a farewell lunch, she said she felt angry to have been proven right. "I still can't trust anyone from that institution," she said.[27]

ACKNOWLEDGMENTS

This book would not have been possible but for the vision, enthusiasm, and unflagging spirit of Lisa Drew at Scribner, who helped conceptualize and bring it to life. She's a legend in the publishing industry and rightly so. The rest of the family at Scribner, including especially Susan Moldow, Samantha Martin, Erin Cox, and everyone in the talented production and design departments, went out of their way to help make the final product so much better on an exceedingly tight deadline. Our agent and friend, the indomitable Raphael Sagalyn, once again helped transform the first germ of an idea into a full-fledged project, then spent many long months nursing it to reality.

It's become a cliché of authors at the *Washington Post* to thank the top executives and editors, but with good reason. In an era of increasingly superficial journalism and dwindling corporate commitment, the *Post* stands out as a redoubt of serious craft and steadfast dedication to covering the world. Donald E. Graham and Boisfeuillet Jones Jr. are unwavering in their support of the newsroom and book projects such as this. Leonard Downie Jr. and Steve Coll have built and preserved the most remarkable news-gathering operation around. Philip Bennett, then the assistant managing editor for foreign news and now the managing editor, gave us the opportunity to move to Russia and was a terrific editor, mentor, and friend through many adventures. David Hoffman, our predecessor in Moscow and Phil's successor, was a regular source of smart advice. Other editors who have inspired and looked out after us include Mike Abramowitz, Karen DeYoung, Bill Hamilton, Fred Hiatt, Robert G. Kaiser, Maralee Schwartz, Margaret Shapiro, Liz Spayd, and Bob Woodward. On the foreign desk, Ginny Hamill and then John Burgess ably steered our copy into the paper, and the fantastically capable Lou Ann McNeill and Emily Messner made sure we didn't get lost in the shuffle.

Through most of our time in Moscow we were blessed with one of the finest colleagues anyone could have. Sharon LaFraniere helped introduce us to our new home and offered friendship and camaraderie. Every *Post* correspondent who has passed through Moscow for the last fifteen years has also benefited from the guidance of Russia's best journalist, Masha Lipman, who along with her husband, Sergei Ivanov, has generously educated successive generations of neophytes in the mysterious ways of Russia.

Irina Makarova was not only the best of researchers and translators, but a sage adviser and warm companion who helped us understand her Russia and shaped this book on every page. Anna Nemtsova put her own life on hold numerous times to travel with us to the farthest reaches of Moscow's old empire and became a lifelong friend along the way. Natasha Abakumova generously introduced us to her own friends and took us deep inside the Russian family and Russia's next generation. They were part of the best bureau staff of any news organization in Moscow, some of whom have moved on but were all like a second family to us: Volodya Alexandrov, Natalya Alexandrova, Sergei Belyakov, Masha Danilova, Anna Masterova, and Yulia Solovyova. Svetlana Prudnikova and her daughter Nastia could not be warmer guides to their country. And we owe a debt of gratitude to Boris Shekhtman and Natasha Simes for laboring to teach us Russian. *Spacibo bolshoi.*

Moscow is full of the most extraordinary correspondents from news organizations around the world, and we were fortunate to work with, learn from, and compete against them. Two of the best by far are Mark Franchetti of the *Sunday Times* of London and Paul Quinn-Judge of *Time,* who patiently tutored us in the art of foreign correspondence and shared many adventures with us along the way. Andrew Higgins of the *Wall Street Journal* may have been the single smartest observer of Russia in our time there. Other colleagues who gave us their friendship and insights included Anna Badkhen, Christian Caryl, John Daniszewski, Robyn Dixon, Jill Dougherty, David Filipov, Andrew Jack, Drusie Menaker, Kim Murphy, Steven Lee Myers, Natalie Nougayrede, Eileen O'Connor, Liam Pleven, Maura Reynolds, Sabrina Tavernise, Jeanne Whalen, and Michael Wines.

We also discovered a new set of friends in the many enormously talented Russia scholars, including Michael McFaul, Sarah E. Mendelson, Celeste A. Wallander, Murray Feshbach, Toby Gati, Fiona Hill, Clifford Kupchan, Robert Nurick, Margaret Paxson, Lilia Shevtsova, Steven L. Solnick, and Melanne Verveer. The staff at the U.S. embassy also deserves thanks, particularly Ambassador Alexander R. Vershbow and his wife, Lisa, John R. Beyrle, Tom Leary, and Jackie McKennan.

As always, our families were remarkably supportive and endlessly patient no matter how crazy they thought we were. Thanks and much love to Lynn and Steve Glasser; Ted and Martha Baker; Linda and Keith Sinrod; Laura, Jeff, and Jennifer Glasser; Karin Baker and Cindy Wallace; Esther Glasser; Agnita and Alex Schreiber; Dan and Sylvia Baker; and Mal and Inge Gross. Our friends are like family, too, especially Mike Allen, Albert and Staci Bailey, Gary Bass, Rajiv Chandrasekaran, Juliet Eilperin, Jennifer and Ryan Frey, Ed Gargan, Elliott and Heather McLeod Grant, Mike Grunwald, John Harris, Spencer Hsu, Maria Koklanaris, Valerie Mann, Bill and Ellen Morris, Kristin Morse, Ellen Nakashima, Vera Obolonkina, Nicole Rabner, Mike and Caitlin Shear, John Smith, Jonathan Socolow, and Tim Webster.

Most of all, we dedicate this book to Theodore Alexander Baker, who had the great generosity and extraordinary sense of deadline performance to wait to start his entrance in this world until ten minutes after we sent the final chapters to the publisher.

This book is the result of five years of reporting in Russia, starting with our first trip there together in March 2000, continuing throughout our four-year posting as the Moscow Bureau chiefs of the *Washington Post* from January 2001 to November 2004, and concluding with a final trip in March 2005. Much of the material has appeared in different form in the *Post,* but this account is also based on more than two hundred original interviews conducted exclusively for the book. We also benefited greatly from the reporting of our Russian and Western colleagues. A note about style: for the sake of simplicity, in the text and in the following footnotes, we use the terms *we, us,* and *the authors* generally to represent either or both of us.

INTRODUCTION: TATYANA'S RUSSIA

1. Tatyana Shalimova generously agreed to hours of interviews in Moscow and her hometown of Mokshan in July and August of 2001.
2. See for example data collected during the Putin era by U.S. scholars Sarah E. Mendelson and Theodore P. Gerber. Mendelson concluded, "Russia today looks to be composed of roughly one-third democrats, one-third autocrats, and one-third that are ideologically up for grabs—people who do not know if they prefer authoritarian or democratic forms of government." Poll data in Gerber and Mendelson, "Up for Grabs: Russia's Political Trajectory and Stalin's Legacy," November 2003, PONARS policy memo 296.
3. The phrase *managed democracy* was associated from the start with Putin's Kremlin, especially after an influential essay by the commentator Vitaly Tretyakov in *Nezavisimaya Gazeta* titled "Prognosis: Managed Democracy," January 13, 2000. That appears to be the first use of the phrase—in Russian, *upravlayemaya demokratiya*—publicly linked to Putin. Managed democracy, Tretyakov wrote not even two weeks into Putin's presidency, is "better than despotism (dictatorship) and even than authoritarianism, but worse than simple democracy."
4. We traveled to Magnitogorsk with our *Washington Post* colleague Sharon LaFraniere.
5. Voter interviews in Moscow, March 26, 2000.
6. Kseniya Ponomaryova, interview with authors, April 8, 2004.
7. Senior Russian official, interview with authors. This official spoke on condition of anonymity.
8. Gleb Pavlovsky, interview with authors, March 14, 2001.
9. Aleksandr Oslon, interview with authors, September 21, 2004.
10. Yevgeny Yevtushenko's poem "Half Measures" is the epigraph for his book *Fatal*

Half Measures: The Culture of Democracy in the Soviet Union, trans. Antonina W. Bouis (Boston: Little, Brown & Co., 1991). Used by kind permission of the author.

11. Lev Ponomaryov, interview with authors, December 8, 2003.

CHAPTER 1: FIFTY-TWO HOURS IN BESLAN

1. Raya Tsolmayova and her husband, Taimuraz Totiyev, interview with authors, October 8, 2004.
2. Aleksandr (Alik) Tsagolov, interview with authors, October 7, 2004.
3. Lydia Tsaliyeva, interview with authors, October 21, 2004.
4. Tsagolov interview.
5. Kazbek Torchinov, interview with authors, October 8, 2004.
6. Olga Sherbinina, interview with authors, October 9, 2004.
7. Tsagolov interview.
8. Sherbinina interview.
9. Pamela Constable, "Bin Laden Tells Interviewer He Has Nuclear Weapons," *Washington Post,* November 11, 2001, citing an interview by Pakistani journalist Hamid Mir, published in the newspapers *Ausaf* and *Dawn.*
10. Andrew Higgins and Alan Cullison, "The Saga of Dr. Zawahri [*sic*] Helps Illuminate Roots of Al Qaeda's Terrorism," *Wall Street Journal,* July 3, 2002. This is a fascinating account of Zawahiri's journey to Russia, based in large part on an Al Qaeda computer that Higgins and Cullison bought in Kabul in the days after the fall of the Taliban. Russian officials never had a clue that they had had Zawahiri in custody until the *Journal* told them.
11. Final Report of the National Commission on Terrorist Attacks upon the United States, also known as the 9/11 Commission, 165–66 in the version published by Norton.
12. Interfax, September 1, 2004.
13. Taimuraz Mansurov, interview with authors, October 13, 2004.
14. Mikhail Markelov, interview with authors, October 18, 2004.
15. Totiyev interview.
16. Markelov interview.
17. It remains unclear where the terrorists got their weapons, whether they brought them in or had them previously in place. Many people in Beslan believe that they had managed to stash guns and bombs in the school in advance of the raid, basing this on the fact that some of the guerrillas broke into the floorboards in the school library and elsewhere during the siege. This led to a conspiracy theory that the weapons had been secreted away in the school by Chechen construction workers during a renovation over the summer, but in fact the supposed Chechen workers were really the relatives of the school custodian and were ethnic Dagestani. Officials largely discounted the floorboards theory but never bothered to try to stop the rampant rumors, which led to death threats after the siege against the principal, Lydia Tsaliyeva, who was presumed to be culpable for allowing the supposed Chechen construction workers to plant the weapons—even though she had worked at the school for a half century and made it her life's work.

18. Tsagolov interview.

19. Aslan Kutsayev declined to speak with us, but his wife confirmed the details of his experience by telephone, October 13, 2004.

20. Aslambek Aslakhanov, interview with authors, October 26, 2004.

21. Mansurov interview.

22. Tsaliyeva interview. Also Leonid Roshal, interview with authors, September 17, 2004.

23. Roshal interview.

24. Putin speech, Rossiya television, September 2, 2004.

25. Lev Dzugayev, interview with authors, October 14, 2004.

26. Mansurov interview.

27. Akhmed Zakayev, a Maskhadov deputy, told us about the capture of Maskhadov and Basayev relatives. For a good account of that episode, also see Kim Murphy, "During School Siege, Russia Took Captives in Chechnya," *Los Angeles Times*, September 7, 2004.

28. Markelov interview.

29. Kazbek Dzaragasov, interview with authors, September 4, 2004.

30. Tsagolov interview.

31. Sherbinina told us this story and Tsaliyeva later confirmed it.

32. Ruslan Aushev news conference at Interfax, September 28, 2004, as translated and transcribed by Federal News Service; Aushev interview on Ekho Moskvy, October 13, 2004.

33. Various hostages and officials told somewhat different versions of the story, and it was difficult to confirm a single account. In some renditions, the room erupted in applause when the hostages saw Aushev; in others, hostages said they heard no applause. The likeliest variation is that some people near Aushev applauded but that other hostages sitting farther away could not hear it.

34. Tsaliyeva interview.

35. Fatima Tsgayeva's story, well-known around Beslan, was confirmed to us by teachers who organized a committee after the siege and posted information on *http://www.beslan.ru*. It was also confirmed to us by one of her neighbors, Susanna Dudiyeva.

36. Akhmed Zakayev, interview with authors, September 2, 2004. Also confirming this were public statements by Aushev as well as author interviews with Mansurov and others who were in the command center.

37. Tsagolov interview.

38. Tsaliyeva interview.

39. Mansurov interview.

40. Zakayev interview.

41. Torchinov interview, as well as other witness interviews.

42. Tsagolov interview.

43. Tsolmayova recounted for us the story of Madina inside the school. Madina listened in on some of our interview, but was still too upset to describe it herself.

44. Torchinov interview.

45. We interviewed a half dozen OMON troops the day after the siege ended, but they declined to give their names for fear of reprisals by their commanders.

46. Tsagolov interview.

47. Ibid.

48. Kulayev, appearing haggard and scared, said on state television on September 5, 2004, that the guerrillas were told that the goal of their raid was "to unleash a war on the whole of the Caucasus," parroting the line the Kremlin had taken in recent days.

49. Tsolmayova interview.

50. Putin statement on Russian television, September 4, 2004.

51. Our staff closely monitored Russian television during the siege and its aftermath and kept track of what it showed. We later obtained from the stations minute-by-minute breakdowns of the day's broadcasts on Channel One and Rossiya television. In the eleven hours between 1 p.m., when the battle began, and midnight, Rossiya aired six hours and eighteen minutes of entertainment programming, while Channel One stayed with entertainment eight hours and twenty-one minutes. Also see a smart piece on Russian television that discussed its performance during Beslan by Arkady Ostrovsky in the *Financial Times Weekend Magazine*, October 9, 2004.

52. As of a month after the siege, the committee of Beslan teachers had compiled on their own a list of hostages and counted 329 bodies identified and buried by that point and another 76 still missing. The committee organizers said then that they believed the real toll was about 500, but they later dropped those assertions and formally accepted the official number.

53. Putin speech, September 4, 2004. Posted on the official Kremlin Web site, *http://www.kremlin.ru/eng/speeches/2004/09/04/1958_type82912_76332.shtml*.

54. Rossiya television, September 5, 2004.

55. Senior Kremlin aide, interview with authors. This aide spoke on condition of anonymity.

56. Eileen O'Connor, a former Moscow Bureau chief for CNN and now a private-sector consultant, was among the invited guests to the session with Putin on September 6, 2004, and took thirty pages of extensive notes that she generously shared with us.

57. Putin announcement, aired live on Rossiya television, September 13, 2004.

58. Sergei Mitrokhin, interview with authors, September 13, 2004.

CHAPTER 2: PROJECT PUTIN

1. The Putin paean was included in ten thousand textbooks distributed in St. Petersburg schools in September 2000, the brainchild of Viktor Yurakov, an ideologist from the local branch of the pro-Kremlin party Unity. Excerpts of the textbook were printed in the *Washington Post* Outlook section on October 15, 2000, to accompany an article by former Moscow Bureau chief Robert G. Kaiser. Reuters news agency also translated a version that was transmitted on September 29, 2000.

2. Aleksandr Bratersky, *Izvestia,* August 24, 2002. Gastello formed a girl band called Singing Together specifically to perform the song. The name of the band was a takeoff of the youth group formed by the Kremlin called Moving Together.

3. Poll conducted in the summer of 2003 for the International Republican Institute, a U.S.-funded organization that provides political training in Russia and other foreign countries.

4. Vladimir Putin, *First Person: An Astonishingly Frank Self-Portrait by Russia's President,* with Nataliya Gevorkyan, Natalya Timakova, and Andrei Kolesnikov, trans. Catherine A. Fitzpatrick (New York: Public Affairs, 2000), 3. Originally published in Russian as *Ot Pervovo Litsa: Razgovory c Vladimirom Putinim.*

5. Ibid., 3–9.

6. Harrison Salisbury, *The 900 Days: The Siege of Leningrad* (London: Martin Secker & Warburg Limited, 1969. Reprint: Pan Books, 2000), 573–74.

7. Putin, *First Person,* 10.

8. Vera Gurevich, interview with authors, February 27, 2004.

9. Sergei Roldugin, interview with authors, February 27, 2004.

10. Gurevich interview.

11. Putin, *First Person,* 18.

12. Gurevich interview.

13. Putin, *First Person,* 19.

14. Ibid., 41–42, 49–50.

15. Ibid., 55.

16. Nikita Petrov, interview with authors, September 17, 2004.

17. Oleg Kalugin, once the KGB's foreign counterintelligence chief, who spent decades as a spymaster in the United States, left Russia and returned to live in America in the mid-1990s, before Putin's rise to power. After he disparaged Putin's KGB service, Putin angrily branded Kalugin "a traitor." Two years later, Kalugin was tried and convicted in absentia in Moscow on charges of high treason for purportedly disclosing state secrets in a post–Cold War book on the KGB.

18. Vladimir Usoltsev, *Sosluzhivets: Neizvestnye Stranitsy Zhizni Presidenta* (Co-Worker: Unknown Pages from the President's Life) (Moscow: Eksmo, 2004).

19. Ibid.

20. Putin, *First Person,* 79.

21. Mark Franchetti, *Sunday Times* (London), March 19, 2000. Franchetti, reporting out of Frankfurt, interviewed Klaus Zuchold, who told of being recruited by Putin over a period of years before finally signing up with the KGB in January 1990, evidently right before Putin returned to Russia. Zuchold told Franchetti that he turned himself over to German intelligence at the end of the year out of fear that he would be exposed and gave up the names of four former East German police officers who were part of the ring. The Germans eventually followed the trail and busted fifteen Putin spies. Adam Tanner, a Reuters correspondent, filed a similar report out of Berlin on May 26, 2000, based on records from East German special services.

22. Putin, *First Person*, 88.

23. Lyudmila Narusova, interview with authors, February 11, 2004.

24. Roldugin interview.

25. Igor Shadkhan, interview with authors, February 27, 2004.

26. Putin, *First Person*, 94.

27. Valery Musin, interview with authors, February 27, 2004.

28. Marina Salye held a news conference to publicize her allegations of Putin's corruption in spring 2000. Extracts from her news conference were posted on the Web site of the Glasnost Foundation on March 18, 2000, just days before Putin's election, under the title "V. Putin Is the 'President' of the Corrupt Oligarchy." Since then, Salye has disappeared from public view.

29. Narusova interview.

30. Pavel Borodin, interview with authors, February 12, 2004.

31. Ibid.

32. Aleksandr Oslon, interview with authors, September 21, 2004.

33. Boris Yeltsin, *Midnight Diaries* (New York: Public Affairs, 2000), 326.

34. Narusova interview. Sobchak returned to Russia in July 1999 after twenty months in self-imposed exile, evidently now safe from prosecution with Putin as head of the FSB and weeks away from becoming prime minister. Sobchak died the next February, living long enough to see his protégé and protector installed as acting president.

35. Yelena Tregubova, *Baiki Kremlevskovo Diggera* (Tales of a Kremlin Digger) (Moscow: Ad Marginem, 2003).

36. Yeltsin, *Midnight Diaries*, 284.

37. Igor Malashenko, interview with authors, July 15, 2004.

38. Boris Berezovsky, interview with authors, October 20, 2004.

39. Ibid.

40. Yeltsin, *Midnight Diaries*, 330–31.

41. Ibid., 334.

42. ITAR-Tass, August 10, 1999.

43. Putin made the remark during a state visit to Kazakhstan on September 24, 1999, when reporters quizzed him about Russian forces hitting civilian targets. The Russian word Putin used, *mochit*, actually means "to make wet," a street-criminal slang phrase for killing.

44. Sergei Stepashin told *Nezavisimaya Gazeta* in January 2000 that plans for an invasion of Chechnya had been drawn up in March 1999, five months before the Dagestan incursion. The plan called for an attack in August or September and would have gone forward "even if there were no explosions in Moscow," Stepashin told the newspaper. Stepashin also said Putin knew about the planning.

45. Akhmed Zakayev, interview with authors, July 17, 2004.

46. For a fuller exploration of the Ryazan conspiracy theory, see a documentary called *Assassination of Russia* (Charles Gazelle, Transparences Productions, France, 2002). It was based in part on the book *Blowing Up Russia: Terror from Within*, by Yuri Felshtinsky and Alexander Litvinenko (New York: Liberty Press,

2001). Thousands of copies of the book were seized by Russian authorities at the border, and a Moscow theater later canceled a Chechen film festival funded by Putin critic Boris Berezovsky that was to debut the documentary. Mikhail Trepashkin, a lawyer and former FSB investigator, later probed the apartment bombings and concluded they were the work of his former colleagues at the secret services. But he never got to present his findings in court because a few days before a scheduled hearing he was stopped by authorities while driving and arrested for having an illegal gun, a pistol he said was planted. Other charges were later added. He was convicted in May 2004 and sent to prison for four years. Boris Berezovsky has actively promoted the FSB conspiracy theory since going into opposition-exile against Putin, sponsoring the showing of the documentary and promoting Trepashkin's cause through his foundation.

47. Berezovsky interview.
48. Sergei Dorenko, interview with authors, October 18, 2004.
49. Paul Tatum was a partner along with the Moscow city government in the Radisson Slavjanskaya Hotel, the headquarters for many Western businessmen in the early days following the collapse of the Soviet Union. After getting into a dispute with his partners, Tatum was shot dead in front of the hotel on November 3, 1996, a particularly notorious murder that caused waves in two countries but was never solved.
50. Valery Fyodorov, interview with authors, September 21, 2004.
51. Ibid.
52. Kseniya Ponomaryova, interview with authors, April 8, 2004.
53. Igor Shabdurasulov, interview with authors, October 5, 2004.
54. Irina Khakamada, interview with authors, February 12, 2004.
55. Fyodorov interview.
56. Oslon interview.
57. Yeltsin, *Midnight Diaries,* 6. The account in Putin's *First Person,* 204–5, is pretty similar.
58. Strobe Talbott, *The Russia Hand: A Memoir of Presidential Diplomacy* (New York: Random House, 2002), 7.
59. Yeltsin, *Midnight Diaries,* 14.
60. Madeleine Albright, *Madame Secretary* (New York: Talk Miramax, 2003), 438–39.
61. Vyacheslav Nikonov, interview with authors, August 23, 2004.
62. Shabdurasulov interview.
63. Nikonov interview.
64. Marina Litvinovich, interview with authors, September 27, 2004.
65. Fyodorov interview.
66. A monthlong investigation by the *Moscow Times* called the official outcome of the election into question. The *Times,* the capital's English-language daily, found massive fraud in several Russian provinces clearly aimed at vaulting Putin past the 50 percent threshold needed for victory in a first round and concluded, "Putin would not have won outright on March 26 without cheating." At the same

time, the paper agreed that Putin was by far the most popular candidate and would almost certainly have won a runoff against Zyuganov, the runner-up from the first round. So the purpose of the fraud would appear to be either a desire to avoid the embarrassment or inconvenience of having to submit to a second round of voting, or even a more fundamental distrust of democracy and inclination to use whatever means necessary to retain power.

67. Putin, *First Person*, 131.
68. Senior Russian official, interview with authors. This official spoke on condition of anonymity.

CHAPTER 3: TIME OF THE PATRIOTS

1. Quotes throughout are from three extensive interviews, April 13, 2001, November 21, 2003, and September 29, 2004, with Nashe Radio founder Mikhail Kozyrev.
2. Boris Yeltsin spoke on the lack of a "national idea" on July 12, 1996, in a speech later cited by James Rupert, "In Search of the Russian Meaning of Life; Yeltsin Asks Bear of a Question of His Post-Soviet Nation, Wants Answer within a Year," *Washington Post*, August 4, 1996. Rupert also noted that the official state newspaper, *Rossiskaya Gazeta*, even sponsored a reader contest for the best new national idea, offering a $2,000 prize.
3. David Hoffman, "Legislators Fail to Approve Russian National Symbols," *Washington Post*, January 25, 1998.
4. Putin speech, December 4, 2000.
5. Masha Volkenshtein, interview with authors, November 13, 2003. Validata survey "Nations as Brands," April 1, 2003.
6. Irina Levontina, interview with authors. Unpublished memo "Nashe," March 2004. Among examples she cited was the line of a typical Soviet bureaucrat in the popular 1968 movie *Diamond Arm*. Suspicious that the movie's hero has been corrupted by a trip to the "rotten West," a dour caricature of Soviet officialdom spies him getting into a taxi and demands to know where he is headed. The hero insists he's merely off to buy some bread, but the official triumphantly unmasks him. "*Nash* people don't go to the bakery in a taxi!" she says in a rejoinder still widely quoted by Russians today.
7. Natalya Ivanova, interview with authors, November 13, 2003.
8. Eldar Ryazanov, interview with authors, December 1, 2003.
9. Irina Chmovzh, "Time of the Patriots," *Izvestia-Media*, October 29, 2001.
10. See also a profile of Kozyrev by Todd Prince, "Medical Student Meets His Fate on FM Radio," *Moscow Times*, January 28, 2003; an interview with Kozyrev by Ana Uzelac, "Finding a Vibe That's Nashe," *Moscow Times*, February 22, 2002; and a piece by Charles Clover and Anna Ivanova-Galitsina, "Pop Music Goes Back to Its Roots in the USSR," *Financial Times*, March 3, 2001.
11. Aleksandr Gromov, interview with authors, April 2001.
12. Susan B. Glasser, "Patriotism, Selling Like Hotcakes," *Washington Post*, May 9, 2001.

13. J7 sounded foreign to a Russian ear because there is no letter *j* in the Cyrillic alphabet. The closest equivalent is usually transliterated as *zh*.
14. Mark Putt, interview with authors, April 2001.
15. We visited School Number 1280 in spring 2001.
16. Lyrics from Zemfira's songs can be found on her Web site, *http://www.zemfira.ru*.
17. *Komsomolskaya Pravda* advertisement cited by political consultant Andrei Lebedev in *Viza* magazine, March 2004.
18. Bodrov panel discussion in *Iskusstvo Kino* (Art of Film), May 2002.
19. Patricia Patchet-Golubev and Felix Golubev, *Toronto Star,* May 18, 1992.
20. Associated Press, February 16, 1992.
21. Dictionary cited in Levontina memo.
22. Alexander Bratersky, "The Songs of Protest," *Moscow Times,* November 15, 2001.
23. Andrew Higgins, "When Russians Sing 'Kill the Yankees,' What Do They Mean?" *Wall Street Journal,* November 1, 2000. The songwriter told Higgins he didn't mean the violent lyrics literally, whatever his fans might think. But, said Alexander Nepomnyashchy, "It's necessary to kill the values of liberal, post-industrial society."
24. Details about Alisa's history can be found on their Web site, *http://www.alisa.net*.

CHAPTER 4: THE TAKEOVER WILL BE TELEVISED

1. Andrei Norkin, interview with authors, November 5, 2003.
2. Olga Belova, interview with authors, April 14, 2001.
3. Andrei Norkin, interview with authors, April 14, 2001.
4. David Remnick, *Resurrection: The Struggle for a New Russia* (New York: Random House, 1997), 186–89. See also David E. Hoffman, *The Oligarchs: Wealth and Power in the New Russia* (New York: Public Affairs, 2001); and Chrystia Freeland, *Sale of the Century: Russia's Wild Ride from Communism to Capitalism* (New York: Crown Publishers, 2000).
5. Grigory Kritchevsky, interview with authors, November 7, 2003.
6. *Self-Portrait—Ten Years on NTV,* aired on NTV, October 11, 2003.
7. Ibid.
8. Ibid.
9. Tatyana Mitkova, interview with authors, December 18, 2003.
10. Yevgeny Kiselyov, interview with authors, November 26, 2003.
11. Yevgeny Kiselyov, interview with authors, January 27, 2001.
12. Senior aide, interview with authors. This aide spoke on condition of anonymity.
13. Yeltsin used the phrase on August 8, 1990, while visiting Kazan, the ancient capital of the Muslim region of Tatarstan, hoping to prevent republics from breaking away.
14. Sergei Dorenko, interview with authors, October 18, 2004.
15. Boris Berezovsky, interview with authors, October 20, 2004.
16. Ibid.
17. Putin made the comment during an interview with Andrei Bystritsky on Mayak Radio on March 18, 2000, just a week before the election.

18. John Lloyd, "The New Statesman Profile—Vladimir Putin. Liberals fear a Pinochet-style regime, but Russia's new leader is their best hope," *New Statesman,* July 31, 2000.

19. Berezovsky held a news conference on July 17, 2000. Sarah Karush, "Berezovsky Says He's Quitting Duma," *Moscow Times,* July 18, 2000.

20. Sabrina Tavernise, "Putin, Exerting His Authority, Meets with Russia's Oligarchs," *New York Times,* July 29, 2000.

21. Oleg Kiselyov, interview with authors, October 5, 2004.

22. Charles Clover, Fiona Fleck, and Arkady Ostrovsky, "Putin Says There Is to Be No Review of Privatizations," *Financial Times,* July 29, 2000.

23. ITAR-Tass, November 2, 2000.

24. Admiral Vladimir Kuroyedov put the theory of a foreign submarine into play from the beginning of the crisis. "There are signs of a big and serious collision," he said. Russian officials continued to cling to the foreign sub collision theory for many months, long after other nations denied having any boats in the area.

25. Dorenko interview.

26. Peter Truscott, *Kursk: The Gripping True Story of Russia's Worst Submarine Disaster* (London: Simon & Schuster UK, 2002), 84–85.

27. Einar Skorgen to Norwegian newspaper *Nordlandsposten,* as translated by Agence France-Presse, August 24, 2000.

28. Putin's meeting with relatives was taped by Andrei Kolesnikov of *Kommersant Vlast* magazine, and a transcript was subsequently published.

29. Putin gave the interview to Rossiya state television on August 23, 2000, as translated and transcribed by the BBC Worldwide Monitoring service.

30. Berezovsky interview.

31. Hoffman, *Oligarchs,* 488.

32. Berezovsky interview.

33. *Larry King Live,* CNN, September 8, 2000.

34. Pavel Borodin, interview with authors, February 12, 2004.

35. Putin's interview with French journalists Charles Lambroschini and Patrick de Saint-Exupery was translated and reprinted in *Kommersant* newspaper on October 27, 2000.

36. Geoffrey York and Chrystia Freeland, "Putin's Progress," *Globe and Mail,* December 16, 2000.

37. Svetlana Sorokina spoke live on NTV, January 26, 2001.

38. Mitkova interview.

39. Kiselyov interview, January 27, 2001.

40. Putin met with the NTV journalists for three and one-quarter hours on January 29, 2001. Afterward, several of the journalists recounted to us his assertion about not being able to do anything.

41. Mitkova interview.

42. Viktor Shenderovich, interview with authors, November 18, 2003.

43. Boris Jordan, news conference, April 3, 2001.

44. Boris Jordan, interview with authors, April 14, 2001.
45. *Ogonyok,* April 2001.
46. Jordan interview.
47. Senior Russian official, interview with authors. This official spoke on condition of anonymity.
48. High-ranking Kremlin aide, interview with authors. This aide spoke on condition of anonymity.
49. Putin interview with American correspondents at his dacha in Novo-Ogaryovo outside Moscow on September 20, 2003.
50. Senior Russian official interview.
51. Fred Weir, "PR Firm Stings Russia's Media," *Christian Science Monitor,* March 5, 2001.
52. Public Opinion Foundation poll, March 22, 2001. Past polls by the foundation, known by its Russian acronym, FOM, can be found at *http://www.english.fom.ru.*
53. Geoffrey York and Chrystia Freeland, "Vladimir Putin's Secret Dream," *Globe and Mail,* December 14, 2000. Putin was clearly enamored of the line. He used it again nearly four years later in discussing the media with a group of Western academics visiting just after the Beslan siege.
54. Shenderovich interview.

CHAPTER 5: JUST AN ORDINARY CRIME

1. Adlan Kungayev, interview with authors, October 10, 2004. The authors also interviewed Elza Kungayeva's parents, Visa and Rosa, in Norway, where they later fled, as well as three other relatives still living in Tangi-Chu.
2. Anna Politkovskaya, *A Small Corner of Hell: Dispatches from Chechnya,* trans. Alexander Burry and Tatiana Tulchinsky (Chicago and London: University of Chicago Press, 2003), 155–56.
3. Autopsy report obtained by the authors.
4. Said Bitsoyev, "A Country of Diminished Responsibility," *Novye Izvestia,* October 3, 2002.
5. Aleksandr Yakovlev, *A Century of Violence in Soviet Russia* (New Haven & London: Yale University Press, 2002).
6. See an excellent profile of Shamil Basayev by Andrew Higgins, Guy Chazan, and Gregory L. White, "Battlefield Conversion: How Russia's Chechen Quagmire Became Front for Radical Islam—Aligning with Arab Militants Gained Money, Fighters for Rebel Leader Basayev—Swapping 'Che' for Allah," *Wall Street Journal,* September 16, 2004.
7. NTV, as recounted by Maura Reynolds in "Russia Admits to Major Setbacks in Chechnya," *Los Angeles Times,* January 10, 2000. Another version of this appeared in Michael R. Gordon, "Russian Troops in Chechnya Find Little Quiet on the Southern Front," *New York Times,* January 10, 2000.
8. Abdulla Khamzayev, lawyer for Elza Kungayeva's family, described the Duba-Yurt slayings at a news conference on June 3, 2002.
9. Pavel Astakhan, interview with authors, September 29, 2004.

10. Shamsudi Dzhambulatov, interview with authors, October 11, 2004.
11. Putin interview with American correspondents at the Kremlin, June 18, 2001.
12. Open Letter to Prime Minister Vladimir Putin, sent by Human Rights Watch on December 28, 1999.
13. Sharon LaFraniere and Daniel Williams, "Chechnya's Bloodiest Massacre," *Washington Post,* June 2, 2000.
14. Anna Politkovskaya, *A Dirty War: A Russian Reporter in Chechnya* (London: Harvill Press, 2001), 188.
15. Putin interview on Russian television, January 17, 2000, as translated and transcribed by Federal News Service.
16. Putin, *First Person,* 169–74.
17. Politkovskaya, *Small Corner,* 51–53.
18. Andrei Babitsky on Radio Liberty, as quoted by Daniel Williams, "Released Reporter Describes Beatings," *Washington Post,* March 1, 2000.
19. Interfax, February 22, 2001. Putin was speaking with reporters in the southern city of Volgograd.
20. Autopsy report.
21. Sergei Yastrzhembsky, news conference, April 7, 2001
22. Public Opinion Foundation survey, March 14, 2001.
23. Interfax, March 2, 2001.
24. A transcript of Sergei Ivanov's session with five Russian editors was printed in *Izvestia,* May 17, 2001.
25. Yuri Savenko, interview with authors, autumn 2002.
26. Susan B. Glasser, "Psychiatry's Painful Past Resurfaces in Russian Case," *Washington Post,* December 15, 2002.
27. Tatyana Dmitriyeva, interview with authors, autumn 2002.
28. Alina Vitukhnovskaya, interview with authors, autumn 2002.
29. Putin held his first full-fledged news conference at the Kremlin on July 18, 2001, when he bristled at a question about his Chechnya policy.
30. Grigory Yavlinsky, interview with authors, September 10, 2004.
31. Sergei Arutyunov, interview with authors, September 10, 2004.
32. Sergei Yastrzhembsky, interview with authors, June 2001.
33. The survey by the All-Russian Center for the Study of Public Opinion, known by its Russian acronym, VTsIOM, in June 2001 showed that 35 percent of Russians supported the war and 75 percent said the government's policy had shown no results.
34. Akhmed Zakayev, interview with authors, July 17, 2004.
35. "Russian Faces Murder Conviction in Watershed Chechnya Trial," Agence France-Presse, July 2, 2002.
36. The authors viewed the videotape of the interview by the *Moskovsky Komsomolets* reporter.
37. The Budanov supporter was shown shouting on Russian television.
38. Shamil Beno, interview with authors, September 10, 2004.
39. Interfax, May 20, 2002.

40. Lyuba Pronina, "Budanov Jailed for 10 Years in Retrial," *Moscow Times,* July 28, 2003.

41. Ekho Moskvy, July 25, 2003.

42. Human Rights Watch report, April 11, 2003.

43. General Vladimir Moltenskoi, commander of forces in Chechnya, signed Order 80 on March 29, 2002, but within weeks the human rights group Memorial had documented widespread examples of it being ignored in a report issued May 14. Order 80 followed Decree 46, issued in July of the previous year, requiring much the same, particularly that local officials accompany any sweep operations. It, too, was ignored. Human Rights Watch report, April 2002, *http://www.hrvc.net/htmls/reports2.html.*

44. Kazbek Tsuraev and Aslanbek Badilaev, "Chechens Disappointed by War Reparations," International War and Peace Reporting Center, October 2004; Vladimir Mukhin, "The Deceptive Figures of Chechnya," *Nezavisimoe Obozrenie,* August 6, 2004; and "Russian Audit Chamber Details Chechnya Restoration Budget Thefts," *Kommersant,* March 20, 2004.

45. United Press International, November 12, 2002.

46. Basayev interview published on Caucasus Center Web site, according to Shamsudin Mamayev and Maria Kravtsova, "The Boomerangs of Basayev and Kadyrov," *Ekspert,* June 16–22, 2003.

47. Rosa Kungayeva, interview with authors, March 3, 2004.

48. Vladimir Shamanov, interview with authors, September 27, 2004.

49. Aleksei Dulimov, interview with authors, October 15, 2004.

50. Stanislav Markelov, interview with authors, March 4, 2004.

CHAPTER 6: SOUL MATES

1. *Avenging Terror: Dubya's Posse,* Brook Lapping Productions documentary for Britain's Channel Four as well as WGBH/Frontline in Boston and other networks.

2. Yevgeny Primakov, *A World Challenged: Fighting Terrorism in the Twenty-First Century* (Washington: The Nixon Center and Brookings Institution Press, 2004), 76–77.

3. Sergei Prikhodko, interview with authors, May 17, 2004.

4. Ibid. Richard A. Clarke, the White House counterterrorism chief at the time, presented another version of this in his book *Against All Enemies,* in which he took credit for discovering that the Russians were planning to hold exercises and having U.S. officials convince Moscow to call them off.

5. *Avenging Terror.*

6. Alexander Vershbow, interview with authors, May 19, 2004.

7. Putin's speech was shown on all Russian television channels the evening of September 11, 2001.

8. Street interviews by authors, September 11, 2001.

9. George W. Bush at Ronald Reagan Library, November 19, 1999.

10. *This Week,* ABC, November 28, 1999.

11. *Foreign Affairs*, January/February 2000.

12. Ron Suskind, *The Price of Loyalty: George W. Bush, the White House and the Education of Paul O'Neill* (New York: Simon & Schuster, 2004), 77.

13. Senior Pentagon official, interview with authors. The official spoke on condition of anonymity.

14. John Bolton, interview with authors, May 19, 2004.

15. Strobe Talbott, *The Russia Hand: A Memoir of Presidential Diplomacy* (New York: Random House, 2002), 4, 400.

16. Mikhail Margelov, interview with authors, June 3, 2004.

17. Prikhodko interview.

18. Well-placed Russian source, interview with authors. This source spoke on condition of anonymity.

19. Senior Russian official, interview with authors. This official spoke on condition of anonymity.

20. Bolton interview.

21. Senior Russian official, interview.

22. Margelov interview.

23. Igor Ivanov, interview with authors, June 22, 2004.

24. Sergei Karaganov, interview with authors, May 17, 2004.

25. Karen Hughes, *Ten Minutes from Normal* (New York: Viking, 2004), 218–19.

26. Bob Woodward, *Bush at War* (New York: Simon & Schuster, 2002), 119–20.

27. Putin has claimed that his mother secretly baptized him as a boy, but he has made little public demonstration of genuine faith. Asked during an interview with Karen Elliott House and Andrew Higgins of the *Wall Street Journal* whether he is personally religious, Putin gave a circuitous answer: "In every person there should be a moral or spiritual basis. . . . If there is a God, it must be in the heart of a person. Philosophy of religion is very important for a country like Russia, because after the dominant ideology—communist ideology, which essentially took the place of religion in our country—ceased to exist as a state religion, nothing can replace universal human values in a human soul as effectively as religion can. Religion makes a person spiritually richer." Having not answered the question, Putin paused before continuing, "I'd like to leave it at that. I don't want to go into details on this as I consider this to be something very personal. And I don't think that this is a sphere which should be . . . used to some political ends." See House's column in the *Journal* on February 12, 2002. Others find it more plausible that Putin is genuinely religious. Our colleague Paul Starobin spent time with Putin's confessor, Archimandrite Tikhon Shevkunov, and came away convinced that Putin's faith was real. He wrote about this in a provocative and fascinating article in the March 2005 issue of the *Atlantic Monthly*.

28. Woodward, *Bush at War*, 119–20.

29. Hughes, *Ten Minutes*, 218–19.

30. For a full transcript of the news conference in Slovenia, go to the White House Web site, *http://www.whitehouse.gov/news/releases/2001/06/20010618.html*.

31. Jim Hoagland, "Reassessing Putin," *Washington Post,* March 13, 2005.
32. Dmitri Rogozin, interview with authors, May 20, 2004.
33. Margelov interview.
34. Putin interview with American correspondents, June 18, 2001.
35. Sergei Ivanov's statement was aired on Russian television September 14, 2001.
36. Deputy Secretary of State Richard Armitage, interview in *Avenging Terror.*
37. Senior U.S. official, interview with authors. This official spoke on condition of anonymity.
38. The secret Uzbek relationship with the United States was first disclosed in an article by Thomas E. Ricks and Susan B. Glasser in the *Washington Post* on October 14, 2001. More details were later reported in Steve Coll's book *Ghost Wars: The Secret History of the CIA, Afghanistan and Bin Laden, from the Soviet Invasion to September 10, 2001* (New York: Penguin Press, 2004), 456–58, 525–27.
39. Abdulaziz Kamilov, interview with authors, September 16, 2001.
40. Bolton interview.
41. The State Department human rights report on Uzbekistan for 2003, released February 25, 2004, can be found at *http://www.state.gov/g/drl/rls/hrrpt/2003/27873.htm*. The 2004 report, released February 28, 2005, can be found at *http://www.state.gov/g/drl/rls/hrrpt/2004/41717.htm*.
42. Mikhail Ardzinov, interview with authors, September 30, 2001.
43. Makhmut Gareyev, interview with authors, June 28, 2004.
44. Talbott, *Russia Hand,* 345–49.
45. Leonid Ivashov, interview with authors, June 11, 2004.
46. Karaganov interview.
47. Aleksei Arbatov, interview with authors, May 27, 2004.
48. Prikhodko interview.
49. Woodward, *Bush at War,* 117–20.
50. Vladimir Lukin, interview with authors, July 6, 2004.
51. Putin's comments were aired on Russian television on the evening of September 24, 2001.
52. U.S. and Russian sources disclosed the secret discussions at Shanghai to the authors.
53. Alexander Vershbow, interview with authors, 2002.
54. Senior U.S. official, interview with authors. This official spoke on condition of anonymity. J. D. Crouch, who later became ambassador to Romania and then President Bush's deputy national security adviser, told us in an interview on March 30, 2005, that he tried to be as open as possible about the options and how they did not fit in the scope of the ABM treaty.
55. Senior Russian official, interview with authors.
56. Ibid.
57. Hughes, *Ten Minutes,* 284–85.
58. Rogozin interview.
59. Margelov interview.
60. James Carney, "Our New Best Friend?" *Time,* May 27, 2002.

61. Vershbow interview, May 19, 2004.
62. Vershbow interview, 2002.
63. Senior Russian official interview.
64. Vershbow interview, 2002.
65. Bolton interview.
66. Senior Russian official interview.
67. Bolton interview.
68. Federal News Service transcript, May 24, 2002.
69. *Fox News Sunday,* Fox News Channel, May 26, 2002.

CHAPTER 7: BOOMTOWN

1. We spent October 9, 2002, with the census takers in Moscow.
2. *Forbes Russia,* May 2004. According to the magazine, New York City was second with thirty-one billionaires.
3. Vladimir Nekrasov, interview with authors, March 16, 2004. The 12 percent figure comes from the Comcon-Pharma market research firm.
4. Richard Lourie, "The Sophisticated Traveler: Moscow," *New York Times Magazine,* September 29, 2002. Among other works about Russia, Lourie wrote *Sakharov: A Biography* (Hanover, NH: Brandeis University Press, 2002).
5. Despite the census, few believed the official figure of 10.4 million people for Moscow once it was released by the State Statistics Committee. In part, the skepticism was based on the huge inflow of illegal migrants to the city unable to obtain the officially required *propiska* to register there. A holdover from Soviet times, the *propiska* was technically illegal under the Russian constitution of 1993, which guarantees citizens the right to live where they please, but Moscow's Mayor Yuri Luzhkov had repeatedly fought legal attempts to jettison the *propiska,* so the system remained despite its dubious constitutionality. According to a Moscow Migration Board report on April 30, 2003, the city's real population was more like 12.5 million, of whom about 3 million were not official Muscovites. However, sociologist Olga Vendina believed the census numbers were skewed in the opposite direction and that the real population was more like 9.5 million. She noted that Luzhkov had announced the 10 million figure even before the census started and also pointed out that the Moscow police may want to artificially inflate the number of migrants they have to deal with. Olga Vendina, interview with authors, August 16, 2004.
6. Foreign investment: Moscow city government, *http://www.mos.ru.* Moscow's 35 percent share of foreign direct investment comes from Peter Westin, chief economist of Aton Capital brokerage, as cited by ITAR-Tass, June 30, 2004. The 42 percent of all foreign investment figure comes from Standard & Poor's credit rating report for the city of Moscow, June 1, 2004.
7. Mikhail Balyasny, "Study: Half of Economy in 6 Regions," *Moscow Times,* June 29, 2004; and "Russia's Retail Sector: A Chain Reaction," Renaissance Capital, October 6, 2003, 11.
8. *Forbes,* 2004 rankings.

9. Vladimir Putin annual address, April 18, 2002, available at *http://www.kremlin.ru.*

10. Robert Dudley, interview with authors, July 29, 2004. Oblomov is the name of the fictional hero of Ivan Turgenev's novel of the same name, a famously indolent specimen of the mid-nineteenth-century upper classes who never rose before noon and made it a point to set a fine table.

11. "Retail Market Profile," December 9, 2003, Stiles & Riabokobylko Ltd., a property consulting firm, accessed at *http://www.snr-realty.com.* Renaissance report, 24. The report documents the explosive growth in Moscow retail—foreign investments in the sector were $8.4 billion in 2002, more than double the $4 billion of the year before, according to the Moscow city government. Muscovites spent on a par with Europeans, a minimum of $550–650 a month, but still had far fewer shopping opportunities. Overall, the city had 1.8 shops per 1,000 people versus 3.7 in the United States. Renaissance estimated Moscow should grow to 3.5 shops per 1,000, doubling the current number.

12. Douglas M. Birch, "Moscow is drowning in an ocean of traffic," *Baltimore Sun,* July 20, 2004.

13. Kathy Lally, "IKEA's Gleam Meets Russia's Gloom," *Baltimore Sun,* March 23, 2000; and Peter Baker, "Moscow's Mall-ization; Russia's Middle Class Is Breeding a Western-Style Consumer Culture," *Washington Post,* October 18, 2002.

14. Susan B. Glasser, "In Moscow, No More Flat Denial; With Western Exposure, Drab Apartments Get Makeovers," *Washington Post,* June 17, 2003.

15. Ibid.

16. Renaissance report.

17. Vendina interview.

18. Details on historic Ostozhenka come from Kathy Berton Merrill, "Aristocratic Street of 'Purity,'" *Moscow Times,* May 24, 1994; Sergei Sossinsky, "Red Chambers and Naval Glory," *Moscow News,* April 2, 1998; Sergei Sossinsky, "Education, Ignorance, and the Plague," *Moscow News,* April 23, 1998; and Natalya Davydova, "Ostozhenka Will Be First," *Moscow News,* June 21, 1992.

19. Nikolai Malinin, interview with authors, June 9, 2004.

20. Ibid.

21. Aleksei Komech, interview with authors, December 16, 2003.

22. Kevin O'Flynn, "Angry Architects Lobby Putin," *Moscow Times,* April 27, 2004. O'Flynn and other journalists, architects, and historians based in Moscow founded a lobby group dedicated to preserving the city's cultural heritage, called the Moscow Architectural Preservation Society (MAPS), which collected and disseminated information about threatened buildings.

23. A Russian-language Web site, *http://www.moskva.kotory.net* (meaning "Moscow that isn't"), showed buildings that had been destroyed.

24. Komech interview.

25. Malinin interview.

26. Susan B. Glasser, "Buildings Evoking Stalin Era Are All the Rage in Moscow; Retro Look Brings Sense of Order, Hefty Price Tag," *Washington Post,* December 25, 2003.

27. Ibid.
28. Ibid.
29. Ibid.
30. Ibid.
31. Konstantin Mikhailov, "In Whose Interests Is the New Moscow Being Built?" *Rodnaya Gazeta,* August 8, 2003.
32. Ibid.
33. Marat Gelman, interview with authors, August 17, 2004. Until he bought it, three families had lived in Gelman's apartment.
34. Kseniya Sobchak, interview with authors, May 12, 2004.
35. Figures on the number of well-off and wealthy in Moscow come from the Renaissance report. The brokerage house noted that Mercury, the leading luxury-goods retailer in Russia, had estimated sales of $250 million to $300 million in 2002, compared with $60 million to $70 million in 1999, and exclusive rights to sell Prada, Armani, Gucci, Chanel, Dolce & Gabbana, Bulgari, and Fendi in Russia. Mercury also opened the Russian Bentley store. The report notes, "Unlike in many other countries, Russian Bentley usually has a few cars in stock, as Russians, being impulsive buyers, often refuse to wait until the car they picked arrives."
36. Sobchak interview.
37. Arkady Novikov, interview with authors, April 23, 2004.
38. Lee Hockstader, "Puttin' on the Ritz in Russia; New Elite Flaunt Their Wealth in Moscow's Hot Spots," *Washington Post,* August 3, 1995.
39. Novikov interview.
40. One popular new restaurant was called Simple Pleasures, in English. Oxygen bar and other details: Sabrina Tavernise, "Moscow Journal: Waiter, Forget the Boar. I'd Rather Have Oxygen," *New York Times,* September 24, 2002.
41. Oxana Soleil of Restaurant Ratings Moscow, interview with authors, June 2004.
42. Novikov interview.
43. Svetlana Kesoyan, interview with authors, June 2004.
44. Novikov interview.
45. Kesoyan interview.
46. Yelena Myasnikova, interview with authors, March 6, 2004.

CHAPTER 8: FIFTY-SEVEN HOURS IN MOSCOW

1. Viktoria Kruglikova, interview with authors, February 20, 2004.
2. Ibid.
3. Edward Topol, *Roman o Lyubvy i Terrorye* (A Novel about Love and Terror) (Moscow: AST Publishers, 2002).
4. Georgy Vasiliyev, interview with authors, February 11, 2004.
5. Ibid.
6. Viktoria Larina, interview with authors, January 23, 2004.
7. Our colleague Sharon LaFraniere collected the text message traffic between Vik-

toria Larina and her husband, Sasha Chekushkin, for a gripping story, "Couple Clutched Electronic Lifeline," *Washington Post,* October 27, 2002.

8. Anatoly Glazychev, interview with authors, October 27, 2002.
9. Movsar Barayev's supposed death was reported by a number of Russian news agencies, including the state-run RIA Novosti, October 12, 2002.
10. Barayev's video was delivered to Al-Jazeera television.
11. Kim Murphy, "A Cult of Reluctant Killers," *Los Angeles Times,* February 4, 2004.
12. The best broadcast account of the theater siege was a British documentary called *Terror in Moscow.* Producer-director Dan Reed, producer Mark Franchetti. It aired on Britain's Channel 4 on May 12, 2003, and in the United States on HBO on October 23, 2003.
13. Kruglikova interview.
14. *Terror in Moscow.*
15. Senior Russian official, interview with authors. This official spoke on condition of anonymity.
16. Topol, *Roman.* Also see a version written by a former hostage, Vesselin Nedkov, along with coauthor Paul Wilson, called *57 Hours: A Survivor's Account of the Moscow Hostage Drama* (Toronto: Viking Canada, 2003).
17. Topol, *Roman.* Also Svetlana Gubareva, interview with authors, May 26, 2004. She confirmed giving the e-mails to Topol and confirmed the authenticity of his version of them, although she said she otherwise did not approve of Topol's account of her personal story.
18. Gubareva interview.
19. Sasha Chekushkin, interview with authors, January 23, 2004.
20. LaFraniere, "Couple."
21. Although the building was officially closed to journalists, we managed to slip in and watch the unfolding scene.
22. Anna Politkovskaya, *A Small Corner of Hell: Dispatches from Chechnya,* trans. Alexander Burry and Tatiana Tulchinsky (Chicago: University of Chicago Press, 2003), 218.
23. Irina Khakamada, interview with authors, February 12, 2004
24. Mark Franchetti, "Face-to-Face with the Terror Chief," *Sunday Times* (London), October 27, 2002.
25. Anna Politkovskaya, interview with authors, February 10, 2004.
26. Yevgeny Primakov, *A World Challenged: Fighting Terrorism in the Twenty-First Century* (Washington: The Nixon Center and Brookings Institution Press, 2004), 123–25.
27. Vasiliyev interview.
28. LaFraniere, "Couple."
29. *Moskovsky Komsomolets,* October 28, 2002.
30. Kruglikova interview.
31. LaFraniere, "Couple."
32. Transcript of Ekho Moskvy broadcast made by our staff on October 26, 2002.
33. *Argumenty i Fakty,* November 6, 2002.

34. *Moskovsky Komsomolets,* October 26, 2002.
35. *Gazeta,* October 30, 2002.
36. Larina interview.
37. Kruglikova interview.
38. Russian doctor, interview with authors. The doctor spoke on condition that he not be identified.
39. Kruglikova interview.
40. RIA-Novosti, October 26, 2002.
41. *Terror in Moscow.*
42. Alexander Vershbow briefing at Spaso House, the ambassador's official Moscow residence, October 29, 2002.
43. Boris Jordan, interview with authors, November 18, 2003.
44. Tatyana Mitkova, interview with authors, December 18, 2003.
45. Jordan interview.
46. Boris Nemtsov, interview with authors, May 28, 2003.
47. *Terror in Moscow.*
48. *Izvestia,* February 3, 2004.
49. Murphy, "Cult."
50. Politkovskaya interview.

CHAPTER 9: SICK MAN OF EUROPE

1. Andrei Artyomenko, interview with authors, May 5, 2004.
2. Russian Health Ministry.
3. Aleksei Trutnev, interview with authors, May 6, 2004.
4. As of September 2004, the Russian government had formally registered 291,512 people infected with HIV. Most experts consider such numbers a fraction of the actual total of people with the virus. The Federal Center for AIDS Prevention, led by Vadim Pokrovsky, put it at 1 million or more, a number adopted by the U.N. Development Program as a fair estimate. The CIA has suggested the number could be as high as 2 million.
5. When the Soviet Union fell apart at the end of 1991, it left Russia an independent country with 148.7 million people, according to the State Statistics Committee, known as Goskomstat. By the end of 2003, that had fallen to 144.2 million. In 2003, according to Goskomstat, there were 1,360 births per million people compared to 2,161 deaths, a rate of 159 deaths per 100 births. According to statistics for the first two months of 2004, the rate had risen to 171 deaths per 100 births.
6. Murray Feshbach, *Russia's Health and Demographic Crises: Policy Implications and Consequences* (Washington: The Chemical and Biological Arms Control Institute, 2003), 43.
7. According to the World Health Organization, the average life span for a man in Russia fell to fifty-eight, compared to sixty-three in Bangladesh and Guatemala, sixty-eight in Algeria, sixty-nine in Bosnia, and seventy-five in the United States. Russian women, by contrast, live to seventy-two, while American women live to eighty.

8. Goskomstat.
9. Putin speech to the State Duma on July 8, 2000, available on the Kremlin Web site at *http://www.kremlin.ru/eng/speeches/2000/07/08/0000_type70029_70658. shtml.*
10. World Bank.
11. Murray Feshbach, interview with authors, May 16, 2004.
12. Global Fund for AIDS, Tuberculosis and Malaria.
13. Vadim Pokrovsky, news conference, November 24, 2003.
14. Steven L. Solnick, interview with authors, April 29, 2004.
15. Valentin Rasputin, *Siberia, Siberia,* trans. Margaret Winchell and Gerald Mikkelson (Evanston, IL: Northwestern University Press, 1991), 181.
16. Artyomenko interview.
17. Yevgeny Sherbakov, interview with authors, May 6, 2004.
18. Trutnev interview.
19. Igor Vankon, interview with authors, May 5, 2004.
20. Letter from Irkutsk drug authorities obtained by authors.
21. Boris Tsvetkov, interview with authors, May 5, 2004.
22. Ibid.
23. Artyomenko interview.
24. Marketing studies by Business Analitica, a Moscow firm, in 2002 and 2003. The average Russian drank 5 gallons of vodka in 2003, while average beer consumption jumped from 4 gallons in 1996 to 13.5 gallons in 2003. Beer consumption was still below that in the United States, where it was 22.3 gallons per year, but it was more comparable to some European countries. Business Analitica reported that beer sales in Russia accounted for $6.5 billion in 2002 compared to $6.2 billion for vodka, the first time beer had surpassed the national favorite. The growth reflected in part the development of quality homegrown Russian beers for the first time in the country's history, and foreign brewers had rushed in to take advantage as well. Heineken, which was already enjoying 20 percent annual growth in Russia, pumped in 100 million euros starting in 2004 to expand three factories to accommodate another anticipated 50 percent growth in sales.
25. Feshbach, *Russia's Health,* 43.
26. Reports by ITAR-Tass and Agence France-Presse, November 19, 2003. Five other contestants were hospitalized with alcohol poisoning; the store owner was charged with manslaughter.
27. According to the Russian Federal Service for Water Rescues, between 16,000 and 17,700 people died each year from accidental drownings from 1998 to 2002. In 2002, the last full year for which statistics were available, 16,833 drowned in Russia.
28. Nabi Abdullaev, "6 People Fall Daily from City Windows," *Moscow Times,* August 21, 2002.
29. The Russian Association of Public Health produced the statistics on male and female smoking and tobacco-related deaths at a conference on tobacco dependency prevention and treatment, May 31, 2004, as cited by Interfax.

30. Feshbach, *Russia's Health,* 23. The death rate from heart disease in Russia grew to 893.3 per 100,000 by the end of 2001, compared with 267.7 in Belgium, 317.2 in Britain, and 352.3 in the United States. The Russian rate was 9.5 percent higher than it had been at the end of 1999, as Putin took over.

31. Ibid.

32. Nicholas Eberstadt of the American Enterprise Institute, "The Emptying of Russia," *Washington Post,* February 13, 2004.

33. Feshbach, *Russia's Health,* 19, citing Goskomstat (per errata distributed with book).

34. Russia had a suicide rate of 70.6 per 100,000, according to a survey by the World Health Organization using the most up-to-date data as of May 2003, compared to Lithuania's rate of 75.6. Outside the former Soviet Union, no other country came close. The next highest outside the former Soviet Union were Slovenia at 47.3 and Hungary at 47.1. By comparison, the suicide rate was 11.8 in Britain, 20.2 in Germany, 26.1 in France, 36.5 in Japan, and 17.6 in the United States.

35. Feshbach, *Russia's Health,* 51–60.

36. Ibid.

37. Nikolai Lyubimov, interview with authors, June 2003.

38. Leonid Aronov, interview with authors, June 2003.

39. Antonina Titova, interview with authors, June 2003.

40. Michael Wines, "In Russia, the Ill and Infirm Include Health Care Itself," *New York Times,* December 4, 2000.

41. Dennis Tito visit, February 2001.

42. Yevgeny Kiselyov, interview with authors, January 27, 2001.

43. Study by the Independent Institute for Social Policy, a Moscow think tank, and financed by the Moscow Public Science Foundation and the U.S. Agency for International Development (USAID).

44. According to the World Health Organization, Russia spends 5.4 percent of its gross domestic product on health care, compared to 8 percent by El Salvador, 12 percent by Lebanon, and 14 percent by the United States.

45. Wines, "In Russia."

46. Independent Institute for Social Policy study.

47. Aleksandr Gordeyev, interview with authors, July 14, 2004. Gordeyev was editor of the Russian-language edition of *Newsweek* magazine and worked in the same office building with Klebnikov. When he heard Klebnikov had been attacked, Gordeyev ran outside and found his colleague still alive on the street. At Klebnikov's request, Gordeyev tried to get oxygen but was told by the ambulance medics that they were not equipped with it. One of Gordeyev's correspondents accompanied Klebnikov in the ambulance and witnessed the scene at the hospital. Although a medic in the elevator declared Klebnikov dead when the doors were finally opened, a hospital doctor later tried to claim that he had not actually died until he was in the operating room.

48. Tatyana Yakovleva, interview with authors, June 30, 2004.

49. ITAR-Tass, February 12, 2004.

50. Putin New Year's Eve address, December 31, 2003, Kremlin Web site, *http://www. kremlin.ru/eng/speeches/2003/12/31/2355_57960.shtml.*

51. Nicholas Eberstadt, *Public Interest,* Winter 2005.

52. Leonid Roshal, interview with *Sobesednik,* July 21, 2004, as recounted in RIA Novosti's press digest.

53. Rinat Akchurin, interview with authors, July 1, 2004.

54. Sergei Drozdov, interview with authors, July 7, 2003.

55. ITAR-Tass, July 21, 2000.

56. Maksim Tarasov, interview with authors, July 8, 2003.

57. These interviews came from our visit to the Khabarovsk market, July 7, 2003.

58. Rosa Varnakova, interview with authors, May 6, 2004.

59. Aleksandr Goliusov, interview with authors, May 19, 2004.

CHAPTER 10: RUNAWAY ARMY

1. The authors conducted a variety of interviews in Volgograd, September 16 and 17, 2002.

2. Vitaly Shlykov, interview with authors, June 1, 2004.

3. *Dedovshchina* is usually translated as "hazing," but in Russian it has a more complicated set of connotations stemming from the system of abuse inside the military by longer-serving conscripts known as *deds* or "grandfathers." These elders, themselves victims of abuse, repeat the cycle of physical and psychological violence against first-year soldiers. According to several veterans and a history posted on the Web site *http://www.bespredelu-net.ru* (No to Arbitrariness), *dedovshchina* has been a problem since the late 1950s as Stalin-era discipline began to erode, veterans of the prison camps ended up in the military, and the term of conscription was cut from three years to its current two years.

4. See, for example, Daniel Williams, "Russian Conscripts Fear Enemy in Own Ranks," *Washington Post,* December 29, 1998.

5. The incorrect version was put out as fact by the military authorities, who were quoted on Russian newswires as saying the soldiers had gone to seek help from the Volgograd garrison military prosecutor when they were taken into custody.

6. Aleksandr Golts, *Armiya Rossii: 11 Poteryannikh Let* (The Russian Army: 11 Lost Years) (Mocow: Zakharov, 2004), 13. Vitaly Tsymbal, interview with authors, June 10, 2004.

7. Putin interview on Rossiya television, December 25, 2000.

8. Steven Lee Myers, "Putin Dresses Down Military for Crash," *New York Times,* August 23, 2002; and Putin: BBC Worldwide Monitoring service, citing NTV Mir, August 22, 2002.

9. "Putin Reportedly Approves Plan to Abolish Military Draft," *Kommersant,* November 22, 2001.

10. Vladimir Isachenkov, "Putin confirms need for military reform but names no dates," Associated Press, April 18, 2002.

11. Susan B. Glasser, "Deserting Russia's Desperate Army; Tales of Draftee Abuse Expose Failure of Reform Hopes," *Washington Post*, September 20, 2002.

12. Aleksandr Golts, interview with authors, June 1, 2002

13. Yegor Gaidar, interview with authors, July 13, 2004.

14. Details about plan from Tsymbal interview.

15. Gaidar interview.

16. Boris Nemtsov, interview with authors, June 3, 2004.

17. Gaidar and Nemtsov interviews. Golts said in his interview that according to his sources, Finance Minister Aleksei Kudrin got the plan on Putin's desk. Gaidar denied this but acknowledged that Kudrin had been helpful. Nemtsov pointed out that Putin had specifically ordered Ivanov and Kvashnin to meet with the Union of Right Forces politicians.

18. Glasser, "Desperate Army." The claim that only 10 percent of those eligible for the draft served, made repeatedly by Ivanov and other top military officials, has been disputed by independent analysts, who argue it is part of the military establishment's effort to end most draft deferments. In "Draft Board's Fuzzy Math," *Moscow Times*, June 8, 2004, analyst Pavel Felgenhauer wrote, "The 10 percent figure is the result of the Defense Ministry's 'fuzzy math.'" To arrive at that, officials compare the number drafted each year to the total number of men aged eighteen to twenty-seven. Draftees are counted only once, in the year they begin their service. But students are counted as eligible but undrafted each year until they reach twenty-seven. Felgenhauer's sources told him the real figures were very different. From 2000 to 2002, about 30 percent of all eligible men were drafted, while roughly 40 percent were exempted for medical reasons. Of those cleared by the doctors, about 60 percent went on to serve.

19. Glasser, "Desperate Army."

20. Despite the Volgograd military official's view that beating conscripts was behavior unbecoming a Russian officer, serious punishment was never meted out in the Volgograd case to the four officers allegedly involved in the beatings that triggered the mass walkout. One of the four, Major Yevgeny Shiryayev, was tried on March 28, 2003, on charges of exceeding his authority, and sentenced to three years' probation; he continued to serve in his post, according to Mother's Right attorney Sergei Semushin. None of the fifty-four conscripts was prosecuted for leaving his post. Semushin, interview with authors, July 21, 2004.

21. The twenty-four large-scale desertions comes from Golts's book; the 2,270 desertions figure from Glasser, "Desperate Army." See also Fred Weir, "In Russia, an Army of Deserters," *Christian Science Monitor*, September 30, 2002. Weir noted the Defense Ministry broke decades of secrecy on the subject by making that number public.

22. Golts, 9, cites transcript at *http://www.tvs.tv/news*.

23. Gaidar interview.

24. The story of Natasha Yaroslavtseva's son and other veterans comes from interviews in Sochi the weekend of June 13, 2003.

25. Lev Gudkov, interview with authors, June 2003.

26. The Internet chat was at *http://www.no-army.com*, a Web site run by the Committees of Soldiers' Mothers, the best-known soldiers' rights group in Russia.

27. Felgenhauer, "Fuzzy Math." He wrote, "Researchers estimated that parents pay up to $5 billion in bribes annually."

28. Arkady Baskayev, interview with authors, June 4, 2004.

29. Chief Military Prosecutor Aleksandr Savenkov's report for the first quarter of 2004 was obtained from "military sources" and posted on the Russian Web site *http://www.grani.ru* in May 2004. A spokesman at the military prosecutor's office confirmed the report's existence to authors, June 24, 2004, saying it was meant for internal use only and not to be made public.

30. Sergei Ivanov quoted in *Krasnaya Zvezda*, March 30, 2002.

31. Golts interview; and Golts, Russian Army, 98.

32. Nemtsov interview. Also Eduard Vorobyov, interview with authors, June 16, 2004.

33. "Russian General 'Dissatisfied' as He Inspects Pioneering Division," *Izvestia*, October 1, 2002.

34. Boris Nemtsov interview with the news Web site *http://www.gazeta.ru*, October 18, 2002.

35. Nemtsov interview.

36. Tsymbal interview.

37. Makhmut Gareyev, interview with authors, June 28, 2004.

38. Golts interview.

39. Gareyev interview.

40. Aleksei Arbatov, interview with authors, May 27, 2004.

41. Yuri Gavrilov, "Military Conscription for Six Months?" *Moskovsky Komsomolets*, November 22, 2002.

42. Gaidar interview.

43. Golts interview.

44. "Russian Right-Wingers, Military at Odds over Army Reform," *Nezavisimaya Gazeta*, November 22, 2002; and Tsymbal interview.

45. Gaidar interview.

46. Nemtsov quoted on NTV television show *Sevodnya*, November 21, 2002.

47. Vladimir Isachenkov, "Soviet-Era Red Star Gets Rehabilitated," Associated Press, November 26, 2002.

48. Tsymbal interview.

49. Nemtsov interview. The commission was formally called the "interagency working group to evaluate expenditures of transferring the army to a contract basis." It was cochaired by two generals, Vladimir Isakov, deputy minister of defense, and Vladislav Putilin, deputy minister of economy and trade and former head of the Defense Ministry department in charge of the draft. Although this was a public group, the Defense Ministry press service (Igor Kostyshin, July 22, 2004) refused to say how many of the fifty members were generals or even to provide a list of members. The group submitted a report on April 24, 2003.

50. Tsymbal interview.

51. Vorobyov interview.

52. Eric Engleman, "Russian Cabinet Tentatively Approves Plan to Switch Bulk of Military to Volunteer Force," Associated Press, April 23, 2003. At the session, however, Sergei Ivanov said, "Conscription will remain forever."

53. Nemtsov interview.

54. Putin meeting with student winners of competition "My Home, My City, My Country," June 5, 2003. Transcript available at *http://www.kremlin.ru*.

55. Nemtsov interview.

56. Shlykov interview.

57. RIA-Novosti, October 2, 2003.

CHAPTER 11: WHAT SORT OF ALLIES?

1. Yevgeny Primakov, interview with authors, July 9, 2004.

2. Richard Butler, *The Greatest Threat: Iraq, Weapons of Mass Destruction and the Growing Crisis of Global Security* (New York: Public Affairs, 2000), 105–7. Butler, then chairman of the U.N. Special Commission charged with disarming Hussein's Iraq, described meeting Primakov in 1997 and finding him defending Baghdad's interests. Afterward, Butler wrote, "I received reliable intelligence reports concerning Primakov's relationship with the Iraqi regime. The reports indicated that Primakov had been receiving personal payoffs from Iraq. Naturally, I was disturbed by this information, and I questioned my sources intensively. They insisted their facts were rock-solid. They could confirm the details of the payments, the times, the amounts, and the accounts to which they were sent." A year later, Butler wrote, he "was told that fresh evidence further confirmed the accusation." Primakov staunchly denied the allegation. In our interview, he said he'd wanted to sue Butler, but did not because Western courts would have forced him to prove that he did not receive payments and he said he could not prove a negative.

3. Steve Gutterman, Associated Press, February 27, 2003.

4. Primakov interview. Primakov also described the meeting with Hussein in a much briefer form in his book, *A World Challenged*, 91–92.

5. Abbas Khalaf, interview with authors, August 16, 2002.

6. Yuri Shafranik, interview with authors, August 21, 2002.

7. After the war, the U.S. Congress's Government Accountability Office estimated that Iraq had siphoned at least $10 billion from the oil-for-food program by illicitly trading in oil and collecting kickbacks from companies such as the Russian firms that had permission from the United Nations to do business with Baghdad. Chief U.S. weapons inspector Charles A. Duelfer, reporting to the CIA director, later concluded it was $11 billion. His findings in the Comprehensive Report of the Special Adviser to the Director of Central Intelligence on Iraq's Weapons of Mass Destruction detailed an extraordinary web of corruption and kickbacks undercutting U.N. sanctions on Iraq.

8. Ariel Cohen, a research fellow in Russian and Eurasian studies at the Heritage Foundation, used the phrase "Saddam's purse" to describe Zhirinovsky in a

commentary piece published in the *Moscow Times* on August 22, 2002. He did not identify the original source of the allegation in that piece; however, in an article for the *National Review* on May 7, 2002, he attributed the allegation to Vyacheslav Kostikov, a former aide to Boris Yeltsin.

9. Vladimir Zhirinovsky, interview with authors, August 28, 2002.

10. Aleksei Mitrofanov, interview with authors, August 29, 2002.

11. A senior Transneft official, interview with authors. This official spoke on condition of anonymity.

12. Duelfer, "Comprehensive Report," 167–200.

13. Andrew Jack, *Inside Putin's Russia* (London: Granta, 2004), 290. Aleksandr Voloshin gave the briefing to British journalists on June 20, 2003, in advance of a Putin trip to London. The briefing was conducted on condition that he not be identified, and none of the British reporters named him in the resulting stories, including Jack, the Moscow Bureau chief at the time for the *Financial Times*. In his subsequent book, Jack referred to him only as "an extremely senior Kremlin official." However, the Russian newspaper *Vedomosti* outed Voloshin as the senior Kremlin official, and British journalists privately confirmed he was the briefer.

14. John Bolton, interview with authors, May 19, 2004.

15. Sergei Prikhodko, interview with authors, May 17, 2004.

16. Senior U.S. official, interview with authors. This official spoke on condition of anonymity.

17. Another senior U.S. official, interview with authors. This official also spoke on condition of anonymity.

18. Khalaf interview.

19. Mikhail Margelov, interview with authors, May 17, 2004.

20. Prikhodko interview.

21. Yuri Shafranik, interview with authors, June 2, 2004.

22. Boris Nemtsov, interview with authors, June 3, 2004.

23. Mikhail Khodorkovsky, interview with authors, August 22, 2002.

24. Igor Ivanov, interview with authors, June 22, 2004.

25. Sergei Karaganov, interview with authors, May 17, 2004.

26. France-3 television, as transcribed by ITAR-Tass, February 9, 2003.

27. Interfax, February 10, 2003.

28. French TF-1 television, as reported by the Associated Press, February 11, 2003.

29. Senior Russian official, interview with authors. This official spoke on condition of anonymity.

30. Senior Bush administration official, interview with authors. This official spoke on condition of anonymity.

31. Alexander Vershbow, interview with authors, June 22, 2004.

32. Ibid.

33. Duelfer, "Comprehensive Report," 116–19.

34. Gennady Seleznyov, interview with authors, June 10, 2004.

35. Rossiya television, March 10, 2003.

36. Bob Woodward, *Plan of Attack,* 404–05.

37. Condoleezza Rice's formula was first reported by foreign affairs columnist Jim Hoagland of the *Washington Post* in a piece headlined "Three Miscreants," on April 13, 2003.

38. Sergei Stepashin, chairman of the State Audit Chamber, told Rossiya television on February 22, 2003, that 1 billion rubles (about $34 million) earmarked for road construction around St. Petersburg had disappeared and that prosecutors were investigating.

39. See full transcript at the White House Web site, *http://www.whitehouse.gov/ news/releases/2003/09/20030927–2.html.*

40. Ibid.

CHAPTER 12: DICTATORSHIP OF THE LAW

1. The authors attended the trial, which ran from August 4–14, 2003, and interviewed all of the participants during breaks along the way, including the defendant and his family, the victim's family, the prosecutor, defense attorneys, judge, and jurors.

2. Vladimir Putin "open letter" to voters, February 28, 2000.

3. Sergei Pashin, interview with authors, August 5, 2003.

4. *The Marxist-Leninist General Theory of the State and the Law,* as quoted by Mikhail Krasnov in Michael McFaul, Nikolai Petrov, and Andrei Ryabov, *Between Dictatorship and Democracy: Russian Post-Communist Political Reform* (Washington: Carnegie Endowment for International Peace, 2004), 195.

5. Deborah Stead, "The Jury Is Back," *Los Angeles Times Magazine,* April 24, 1994.

6. W. E. Mosse, *Alexander II and the Modernization of Russia* (New York: Collier Books, 1958), 135–36.

7. Sergei Pashin, interview with authors, July 13, 2004.

8. Ibid.

9. Masha Gessen, "A Matter of Justice," *U.S. News & World Report,* November 20, 2000. As Putin's term progressed, new terms were developed. Police who attached electric current to a suspect's earlobe called it *zvanok Putinu,* or "phone call to Putin," according to Russian commentator Yulia Latynina, writing in the *Moscow Times,* August 11, 2004.

10. Pashin interview, July 13, 2004.

11. Ibid.

12. Public Opinion Foundation poll, February 5–6, 2000.

13. Kozak later denied that he was ever chosen, but members of the Federation Council publicly stated that they were informed he would be nominated. Voloshin's role in persuading Putin to drop Kozak in favor of Ustinov in May 2000 was reported at the time by *Sevodnya* newspaper and the Gazeta.ru news Web site.

14. Kozak described himself as a "liberal patriot" in an interview with the newspaper *Vek,* March 24, 2000.

15. Kozak interview with *Kommersant* in 2001, as cited in a *Kommersant* article, November 1, 2003.

16. Sergei Kazovsky, *Noviye Izvestia,* April 5, 2001. Also Alexander Sveshnikov,

reporter for Volga Information Agency, writing in a commentary in the *Moscow Times*, April 13, 2001.

17. Ekho Moskvy, April 5, 2001. Blinov on NTV as reported by Yevgenia Borisova, *Moscow Times*, April 6, 2001.
18. Dmitri Kozak, interview with authors, July 22, 2004.
19. Ibid.
20. *Kommersant,* May 22, 2001.
21. Kozak interview.
22. Yuri Sidorenko, interview with authors, August 6, 2004.
23. Sergei Vitsin, interview with authors, July 26, 2004.
24. Sidorenko interview.
25. Putin's dissatisfaction with the pardon commission was chronicled by Ana Uzelac in the *Moscow Times* on June 1 and August 10, 2001, among other places. The final number of Putin's pardons was put at twenty by Agence France-Presse and twenty-one by the Associated Press on the day he disbanded the commission, December 28, 2001.
26. Kozak interview.
27. Pashin interview, July 13, 2004.
28. Tatyana Karpova, interview with authors, June 11, 2003.
29. Igor Trunov, interview with authors, June 6, 2003.
30. Average monthly income in Moscow in 2002 came to 14,035 rubles, or about $484, according to the Moscow City Statistics Committee. By 2004, it had risen to 18,801 rubles, or about $648. Actual income probably exceeded reported income given Russians' historical propensity not to disclose all earnings to the government.
31. Olga Gracheva, interview with authors, June 2003.
32. Zoya Chernetsova, interview with authors, June 18, 2003.
33. The authors attended a hearing in the *Nord-Ost* cases in Moscow court on June 11, 2003.
34. Tatyana Karpova, interview with authors, July 6, 2004.
35. The GAI was actually the name during Soviet times, standing for Gosavtoinspectsia, or State Vehicle Inspectorate. In 1998, in a much heralded "reform," the name was officially changed to Gosudarstvennaya Inspectsia Bezopasnosti Dorozhnovo Dvizheniya (GIBDD), or State Street Traffic Safety Inspectorate. But no one ever called them that and so Putin tried again in 2004 by renaming it Departament Obespecheniya Bezopasnosti Dorozhnovo Dvizheniya (DOBDD), or Department for Ensuring Traffic Safety.
36. Survey of 2,013 Russians in the country's twelve largest cities, conducted by Yuri Levada's Analytical Center in May 2004, as reported in the *Moscow Times,* May 21, 2004.
37. Pavel Chikov, interview with authors, June 7, 2004.
38. Natalya Taubina, interview with authors, June 7, 2004.
39. Peter Finn, "Fear Rules in Russia's Courtrooms," *Washington Post*, February 27, 2005.

40. Figures on jury acquittal reversals from the Russian Ministry of Justice Web site.
41. Stephen C. Thaman, interview with authors, August 13, 2003.
42. After media mogul Vladimir Gusinsky fled to Spain, Russia demanded he be sent back to Moscow for trial, but a Spanish court rejected the application in April 2001, ruling that the allegations outlined by the Russians would not add up to a crime under Spanish law. Gusinsky was later arrested during a stopover at the Athens airport in August 2003 when Greek authorities found his name in their computers stemming from an old Russian extradition request; the Russians asked the Greeks to send him back to Moscow, but a Greek court in October 2003 came to the same conclusion as had the Spanish judges. Russia also asked Denmark to extradite Chechen resistance leader Akhmed Zakayev when he visited Copenhagen for a conference on Chechnya; the Danes arrested him in late October 2002, just days after the theater siege in Moscow, but the Justice Ministry released him two months later, refusing to send him to Moscow. Zakayev promptly returned to London, where he had been living for nearly a year on the hospitality of actress Vanessa Redgrave. British authorities arrested him in December 2002 on a Russian extradition request but freed him on bail, and in November 2003 a British court rejected extradition. The British Home Office similarly rebuffed Moscow and granted asylum status to oligarch Boris Berezovsky and his associate Yuli Dubov in September 2003. A U.S. federal judge blocked the deportation of Russian millionaire Alex Konanykhin after he was arrested in December 2003 by immigration authorities, who wanted to send him back to Moscow to face Russian embezzlement charges. And an immigration judge in Boston granted political asylum in April 2004 to Ilyas Akhmadov, the foreign minister in the rump Chechen government before Putin's 1999 invasion, finding that if he was returned to Russia, he would surely be "shot without being afforded the opportunity to defend himself in a trial, as has happened to other members of the Chechen government." The Bush administration's Department of Homeland Security appealed but then dropped it in August 2004.
43. Figures provided by telephone by the European Court of Human Rights in July 2003. Charts obtained from the court in writing a year later showed that it had received 5,338 applications from Russia in 2003, more than any of the forty-three other European countries that accepted its jurisdiction. But Russians were not likely to find much satisfaction out of Strasbourg. The European court dismissed the vast majority of Russian complaints out of hand, declaring only fifteen applications admissible in 2003.
44. Tatyana Glazkova, interview with authors. See also Judith Ingram, "Russian Judge Fights the System by Going to Court—Abroad," Associated Press, February 26, 2001. Glazkova's application to the European court was ultimately rejected because she did not have legal grounds to go to Strasbourg.
45. *Gusinsky vs. Russia,* issued by the European Court of Human Rights on May 19, 2004. The case focused narrowly on Gusinsky's detention and the pressure put on him to sign away his media holdings in exchange for being released from prison but generally did not address subsequent events.

46. Karpova interview, July 6, 2004.

47. The jury deliberations were reconstructed through interviews with half of the twelve members of the jury in the days after the trial ended.

CHAPTER 13: BACK IN THE USSR

1. Viktor Cherkesov, interview with authors, May 17, 2001.

2. Boris Pustintsev of the human rights group Citizens' Watch told Jen Tracy and Matt Bivens in "Putin's Patronage Elevates Cherkesov," *St. Petersburg Times*, February 25, 2000, that Cherkesov was the last KGB officer ever to open a case under Article 70 for political crimes. "It was in 1988 against [artist] Yuly Rybakov and others," Pustintsev said. "The case was closed by Moscow, against Mr. Cherkesov's will."

3. Cherkesov not only compared the current presidential envoys to tsarist governors-general, he said the precedent for Putin appointing *siloviki* to the job also came from the autocratic prerevolutionary model. "In an overwhelming majority, the former Russian governors-general of the past were professional military men. So here also the decision of President Putin to choose five out of seven plenipotentiary representatives from various military institutions coincided with what used to be traditional for Russia in former times," he told us in the 2001 interview.

4. Senior Russian official, interview with authors, September 2003. This official spoke on condition of anonymity.

5. Viktor Cherkesov, interview with authors, August 18, 2004.

6. Olga Kryshtanovskaya, interview with authors, September 2003. See also Olga Kryshtanovskaya and Stephen White, "Putin's Militocracy," an academic article. "The increasingly dominant position of military and particularly of security officials is likely in turn to strengthen the neo-authoritarian thrust of public policy under the Putin presidency," they concluded.

7. Putin was first shown joking about no former chekists on Rossiya television in 1999 not long before becoming prime minister; he repeated the line in 2001.

8. Kryshtanovskaya interview. Russian newspapers and magazines frequently ran listings of top government officials with KGB backgrounds, such as "Chekists in the Corridors of Power," *Novaya Gazeta*, July 2003, which listed several dozen prominent KGB alumni with top jobs.

9. Stalin's famous quote "*kadry reshayut vsyo*" (the cadres decide everything) was made at a graduation ceremony for the Red Army Academies on May 4, 1935. Historians consider it a forewarning of the harsh repressions to come in the following years by its signaling a new emphasis on the loyalty and personal characteristics of cadres rather than the earlier goals of industrialization and collectivization of agriculture that Stalin had previously stressed.

10. All of the envoys emphasized their efforts to cancel unconstitutional laws in the regions. In the central region of Russia, for example, which includes the capital of Moscow, Putin aides claimed to have forced the withdrawal of 729 regional and local laws in conflict with federal laws just in 2000 and 2001. Cherkesov told

us he had managed to overturn 500 of 600 conflicting laws in the northwest region by the spring of 2001; in the Volga region in the center of Russia, envoy Sergei Kiriyenko boasted of canceling nearly all of the 884 unconstitutional laws.

11. Cherkesov interview, May 17, 2001.

12. Nikolai Petrov, interview with authors, September 2003.

13. Cherkesov interview, August 18, 2004.

14. Vadim Bakatin, speech to "The KGB: Yesterday, Today, and Tomorrow," February 19, 1993, transcribed and translated, Official Kremlin International News Broadcast.

15. A useful history of the post-Soviet history of the Russian secret services is Amy Knight's book *Spies Without Cloaks: The KGB's Successors* (Princeton, NJ: Princeton University Press, 1996). The book, however, only covers the period before Boris Yeltsin's reelection in 1996.

16. Sergei Grigoryants, interview with authors, August 11, 2004.

17. Bakatin speech.

18. Grigoryants interview.

19. Bakatin speech.

20. Six name changes recounted on the FSB's official Web site, at *http:// www.fsb.ru/history/organi.html,* cited in Human Rights Watch Briefing Paper, "Russia's Spy Mania," October 2003, at *http://www.hrw.org.*

21. *Moskovsky Komsomolets,* April 7, 1995, cited in Knight, *Spies,* 220.

22. Knight, *Spies,* 4, 244.

23. Igor Goloshchapov, interview with authors, August 5, 2004.

24. Gennady Gudkov, interview with authors, July 14, 2004.

25. Aleksandr Lebedev, interview with authors, August 3, 2004.

26. Ibid.

27. Andrei Przhezdomsky, interview with authors, August 4, 2004.

28. Nikita Petrov, interview with authors, September 17, 2004.

29. Grigoryants interview.

30. Georgy Poltavchenko, interview with authors, August 18, 2004.

31. Gusinsky was not the only oligarch targeted by the tax police; police early in Putin's tenure also raided the car maker Avtovaz, linked to exiled tycoon Boris Berezovsky, and staged very public raids and allegations against officials at oil firms Lukoil and Sidanco.

32. Poltavchenko interview.

33. Frank Brown, "Return of the KGB," *Newsweek,* November 24, 2003. According to Brown, Kulakov was involved in one case in 1984 when KGB provocateurs tried to entrap a British exchange student several times—including by offering him the sexual services of a twelve-year-old girl. When he rebuffed their recruitment attempts, they arrested him and expelled him from the country.

34. Unless otherwise noted, the material on Governor Viktor Maslov and his election in Smolensk comes from interviews conducted there in September of 2003, some of which first appeared in Susan B. Glasser, "KGB Veterans Bring Tradecraft to Elected Office," *Washington Post,* September 24, 2003, A18.

35. Poltavchenko interview.
36. Leaflet obtained by authors.
37. Glasser, "KGB Veterans."
38. According to Smolensk journalist Gennady Kosenkov, the former governor, Prokhorov, was convicted and sentenced to three years in prison, then given amnesty. He later ran for mayor of the city of Smolensk and finished second. Makarenko, his former deputy, was convicted and sentenced to three years.
39. Glasser, "KGB Veterans."
40. Ibid.
41. Ibid.
42. Ibid.
43. Stanislav Lekarev, interview with authors, August 10, 2004.
44. Sharon LaFraniere, "Putin Gives Security Service New Powers," *Washington Post*, March 12, 2003.
45. Gudkov interview.
46. Goloshchapov interview.
47. Vladimir Kovalyov, "Zhirik Drinks at Starovoitova's Grave," *Moscow Times*, November 22, 2004.
48. Lev Ponomaryov, interview with authors, March 5, 2004. Konstantin Remchukov, interview with authors, March 5, 2004.
49. See, for example, Human Rights Watch report "Russia's Spy Mania."
50. Sergei Ivanov, interview with authors, March 5, 2004.
51. Tatyana Trepashkin, Mikhail's wife, interview with authors, March 5, 2004.
52. Peter Baker, "Young Men Vanishing in Russian Region; Prosecutor Probing Role of Secret Police Is Among Missing in Ingushetia," *Washington Post*, June 6, 2004.
53. Cherkesov interview, August 18, 2004.
54. Vladimir Pribylovsky and other interviews in this section for Susan B. Glasser, "Russian Drug Unit Criticized Over Dubious Tactics, Priorities," *Washington Post*, September 22, 2004.
55. Cherkesov interview, August 18, 2004.
56. Glasser, "Russian Drug Unit."
57. Ibid.
58. Ibid.
59. Ibid.
60. Kevin O'Flynn, "Paul McCartney Finally Back in the U.S.S.R.," *Moscow Times*, May 26, 2003.
61. Senior Russian official interview.
62. Ilya Bulavinov, "Russia's Deck of Cards," *Kommersant Vlast*, December 1, 2003.
63. Kim Murphy, "Russia's New Elite Draws from Old KGB," *Los Angeles Times*, November 10, 2003.
64. Vladimir Pribylovsky, "Oligarchs Toy with Their 2008 Options," *Moscow Times*, February 25, 2005. Pribylovsky reported signs that Sechin and Ivanov each wanted to lead separate factions of the *siloviki* headed toward 2008, with Ivanov

touting the political prospects of Duma speaker Boris Gryzlov and Sechin pro-moting Defense Minister Sergei Ivanov.

65. Pavlovsky interview for Glasser, "KGB Veterans." In the August 2003 report, posted on the Internet and reported widely in Russian media, Pavlovsky also fin-gered Sergei Pugachyov, the founder of Mezhprombank and a member of the Federation Council, as the chief outside funder for the Kremlin's *siloviki* faction, along with state-controlled natural gas monopoly Gazprom and state oil firm Rosneft. Pugachyov, often referred to by Russian reporters as "Putin's banker" and the "gray cardinal," sued Pavlovsky for libel and won an initial judgment from a Moscow court in late 2003 requiring Pavlovsky to pay him $1 million. Pavlovsky appealed.

CHAPTER 14: TWILIGHT OF THE OLIGARCHS

1. Aleksandr Batanov, interview with authors, October 6, 2004.
2. *Fortune* magazine survey, released in September 2002. The only person under forty richer than Khodorkovsky was American computer magnate Michael Dell. Khodorkovsky was the world's twenty-sixth richest person overall.
3. Batanov interview.
4. Khodorkovsky interview with Volga TV in Nizhny Novgorod, October 24, 2003.
5. Russian media reports on arrest, plus interviews with Batanov and Khodor-kovsky attorney Anton Drel.
6. Igor Bunin, *Forty Stories of Success* (Moscow: Center for Political Technologies, 1994), 169–78, as cited in David E. Hoffman's *The Oligarchs: Wealth and Power in the New Russia* (New York: Public Affairs, 2001), 118.
7. Peter Slevin, then a reporter for the *Miami Herald,* conducted the interview with Khodorkovsky. Many years later, he gave notes of the interview to Hoff-man, who used some of the previously unpublished material in *Oligarchs,* 116.
8. Hoffman, *Oligarchs,* 315–18.
9. Chrystia Freeland, *Sale of the Century: Russia's Wild Ride from Communism to Capitalism* (New York: Crown Publishers, 2000), 335.
10. Ibid., 157.
11. Study conducted in 2002 by Peter Boone, research director of Brunswick UBS Warburg brokerage house, and analyst Denis Rodionov.
12. Pyotr Aven, interview with authors, October 8, 2002.
13. Oleg Deripaska, interview with authors, October 21, 2002.
14. Robert Dudley, interview with authors, July 29, 2004.
15. Ibid.
16. Sabrina Tavernise, "Merger Creates Russian Oil Giant with Big Dreams," *New York Times,* April 23, 2003.
17. Ibid.
18. Clifford Kupchan, interview with authors, July 22, 2004.
19. Mikhail Khodorkovsky, interview with authors, August 22, 2002.

20. Ilya Ponomaryov, information director of the Communist Party, interview with authors, March 2, 2004. When we asked about the practice of selling slots on party candidate lists, Ponomaryov said, "Of course it happens. The party needs funds." Usually, he said, large businesses paid to have a representative in the Duma. "The corporation pays so he would be on the party list."
21. Pyotr Aven, interview with authors, June 8, 2004.
22. Source close to Khodorkovsky, interview with authors. This person spoke on condition of anonymity.
23. Gleb Pavlovsky, interview with authors, October 2003.
24. Senior Russian official, interview with authors. This official spoke on condition of anonymity.
25. Rosneft purchased the Severnaya Neft firm from a member of the Federation Council, the upper chamber of parliament, Andrei Vavilov. The confrontation between Putin and Khodorkovsky was shown on Russian television.
26. Igor Yurgens, interview with authors, July 2, 2004.
27. Aleksei Kondaurov, interview with authors, July 29, 2004.
28. Senior aide to Putin, interview with authors. This aide spoke on condition of anonymity.
29. Source close to Khodorkovsky.
30. Senior Russian government official, interview with authors. This official spoke on condition of anonymity.
31. Another senior Russian official, interview with authors. This official spoke on condition of anonymity.
32. Pavlovsky interview.
33. Putin news conference, June 20, 2003, as translated and transcribed from Rossiya television by BBC Worldwide Monitoring service.
34. Khodorkovsky spoke to a group of Western correspondents at Ambassador Alexander Vershbow's annual Fourth of July celebration at Spaso House, the ambassador's Moscow residence.
35. Chrystia Freeland, "A Falling Tsar," *Financial Times Weekend Magazine*, November 1, 2003.
36. Khodorkovsky made the remarks on TV-Tsentr television on July 20, 2003.
37. Senior Russian official interview.
38. Igor Yurgens, interview with authors, October 2003.
39. Putin session with American correspondents at Novo-Ogaryovo, September 20, 2003.
40. Ibid.
41. Mikhail Fridman, interview with authors, September 20, 2004.
42. Yevgeny Kiselyov, interview with authors, November 26, 2003.
43. Freeland, "Falling Tsar."
44. Remarks shown on Russian television, October 3, 2003.
45. Kondaurov interview.
46. Senior Russian official interview.
47. A. John Pappalardo and Sanford M. Saunders Jr., both partners at the U.S. law

firm Greenberg Traurig, recounted the conversation during several interviews with the authors from 2003 to 2005.

48. Aleksandr Dobrovinsky, interview with authors, October 28, 2003.

49. Anton Drel, interview with authors, July 9, 2004. Khodorkovsky also has a fourth child by a previous marriage, a grown son who was at the time studying in Boston.

50. Ibid.

51. Boris Nemtsov, interview with authors, October 25, 2003.

52. Historical records of the Russian Trading System, or RTS, index can be found on its Web site, *http://www.rts.ru.*

53. Senior aide interview.

54. Putin's remarks on Russian television were translated and transcribed by Federal News Service, October 27, 2003.

55. Kasyanov's comments were shown on NTV, October 31, 2003.

56. Pavlovsky commentary for *Vremya Novostei* newspaper, October 28, 2003.

57. Pavlovsky said this on the Russian news Web site *http://www.gazeta.ru* the same day.

58. Bush administration official, interview with authors. This official spoke on condition of anonymity.

59. Senior U.S. diplomat, who spoke on condition of anonymity.

60. Yurgens interview, July 2, 2004.

61. Oleg Kiselyov, interview with authors, October 5, 2004.

62. Fridman interview.

CHAPTER 15: AGITATION

1. Marat Gelman, interview with authors, August 17, 2004.

2. Under the Russian constitution, the State Duma is composed of 450 seats, all of them up for reelection in 2003. The rules stipulated that 225 seats would be allocated on the basis of national party-list voting, while the remaining 225 seats were decided by individual district contests (known in Russian as single-mandate districts). To secure official representation as a party faction in the State Duma, a party was required to win 5 percent of the national party-list vote. Heading into the 2003 elections, five parties were represented: United Russia (the merger of Unity and the Yevgeny Primakov–Yuri Luzhkov party Fatherland–All Russia), the Communist Party of the Russian Federation (known by its initials KPRF), the ultranationalist Liberal Democratic Party of Russia (LDPR), and the two Western-oriented liberal parties, the Union of Right Forces (SPS) and Yabloko.

3. Surkov mentioned his Richard Gere aspirations in an interview with David E. Hoffman for *The Oligarchs: Wealth and Power in the New Russia* (New York: Public Affairs, 2001), 123. "I wanted to be like a hero in the movie *Pretty Woman*. I wanted to be a big businessman who's sitting in a big hotel, supervising big events," Surkov said in 1999.

4. Sergei Markov, interview with authors, September 30, 2004.

5. The participant was Marina Litvinovich, an aide to Gleb Pavlovsky who attended

the sessions until February 2003, when she became campaign manager for the Union of Right Forces. Interview with authors, September 27, 2004.

6. Steven Lee Myers, "On Russian TV, Whatever Putin Wants, He Gets," *New York Times*, February 17, 2004.
7. Gelman interview.
8. Aleksandr Oslon, interview with authors, autumn 2003.
9. Vyacheslav Nikonov, interview with authors, autumn 2003.
10. Sergei Popov, interview with authors, September 30, 2004.
11. Interfax, September 20, 2003.
12. Markov interview.
13. Susan B. Glasser, "Russia's Party for One; Putin Hopes to Use Body to Consolidate Power," *Washington Post*, December 6, 2003.
14. Markov interview.
15. Glasser, "Russia's Party for One."
16. Ibid.
17. Ibid.
18. Ibid.
19. Ibid.
20. Gelman interview.
21. Parts of this section first appeared in our story "How Nationalist Party Became a Powerhouse; Putin Had Blessed Effort to Weaken Communists," *Washington Post*, December 16, 2003. We conducted interviews at the time with Gelman, Glazyev, Rogozin, Pavlovsky, and other key players, which are used unless otherwise cited.
22. Ivan Melnikov, interview with authors, September 30, 2004.
23. Gleb Pavlovsky, interview with authors, autumn 2003.
24. Vyacheslav Nikonov, interview with authors, August 23, 2004.
25. Gennady Gudkov, interview with authors, July 14, 2004.
26. Markov interview.
27. Sergei Glazyev, interview with authors, September 23, 2004.
28. Markov interview.
29. Sergei Butin, interview with authors, September 28, 2004.
30. Ibid.
31. Dmitri Rogozin, interview with authors, December 8, 2003.
32. Glasser and Baker, "Nationalist Party."
33. Ibid. A source close to Deripaska, however, said he had stopped financing at the campaign's end, when he found out how much oligarch-bashing was responsible for Motherland's success.
34. Markov interview.
35. Butin interview.
36. Malik Saidullayev, interview with authors, September 2003.
37. Aslambakek Aslakhanov, interview with authors, September 2003.
38. Putin interview with American correspondents at Novo-Ogaryovo, September 20, 2003.

39. Peter Baker, "Chechens Vote, but Outcome Seems Clear; Kremlin-Appointed Cleric's Main Rivals Were Not on Ballot," *Washington Post,* October 6, 2003.
40. Glasser, "Russia's Party for One."
41. Konstantin Titov, interview with authors, October 21, 2003.
42. Alla Startseva, "United Russia Makes Campaigners of Cashiers," *Moscow Times,* November 26, 2003.
43. Glasser, "Russia's Party for One."
44. Public Opinion Foundation polls, *http://www.english.fom.ru.*
45. Yekaterina Yegorova, interview with authors, September 27, 2004
46. "New Center-Left Force in Russia Campaigns on Anti-Tycoon Ticket," Agence France-Presse, September 14, 2003.
47. Gelman telephone interview with authors, December 2003.
48. Grigory Yavlinsky, interview with authors, September 23, 2004.
49. Boris Nemtsov, interview with authors, September 22, 2004.
50. Irina Khakamada, interview with authors, September 22, 2004.
51. Gelman interview.
52. The Berezovsky "plot" allegation was made by former FSB director Nikolai Kovalyov, now a member of the Duma. According to Interfax, November 13, 2003, he said, "Berezovsky is intending to bring certain people to power using Yukos and the Communist party's money." On businessmen running as Communists, see, for example, Francesca Mereu, "Capitalists Signing Up as Communists," *Moscow Times,* December 2, 2003.
53. Gennady Zyuganov, interview with *Vedomosti,* December 3, 2003.
54. Anatoly Laptev, interview with authors, December 11, 2003.
55. We spent the day, November 20, 2003, in St. Petersburg at the events for Starovoitova.
56. Fred Hiatt, "Russia's Iron Lady," *Washington Post,* November 26, 1998.
57. Sergei Mitrokhin, interview with authors, November 2003.
58. Yavlinsky interview.
59. Litvinovich interview.
60. Yavlinsky interview.
61. Yegorova interview.
62. Nemtsov interview. Recriminations over the ad would go on for months. Well into the new year, the Chubais group quietly commissioned a consulting firm to conduct focus groups to evaluate the now-infamous airplane ad. Not surprisingly, responses were extremely negative. "The first response was—they have flown out of the country, emigrated," recalled Yegorova, the consultant tapped to run the focus groups. "The second was—they are on high and they are looking down on us. But of course afterwards it was useless to conduct an audit, after you had already lost the election." Yegorova interview.
63. Sergei Gaidai, interview with authors, November 20, 2003.
64. Gennady Seleznyov, interview with authors, November 26, 2003.
65. Gaidai interview.
66. Olga Starovoitova, interview with authors, November 20, 2003.

67. Markov interview.
68. Putin, for example, chided Nemtsov for seeking "PR on blood" after the Moscow theater siege and received his rival Yavlinsky in a televised meeting.
69. Rogozin interview.
70. Leonid Grozman, interview with authors, December 2003.
71. Rogozin interview.
72. Public Opinion Foundation poll, *http://www.english.fom.ru.*
73. Voter interviews, November 20, 2003.
74. Russian television, monitored December 7, 2003.
75. Ibid.
76. "Chubais Worried About Election Outcome," Interfax, December 7, 2003.
77. Michael McFaul, the Stanford University scholar on Russia, was the guest who spoke with Gaidar. Interview with authors, December 8, 2003.
78. Yavlinsky interview.
79. Oslon interview.
80. Glazyev interview.
81. Khakamada spoke on Russian television.
82. Interfax, December 8, 2003.
83. Organization for Security and Cooperation in Europe, news conference in Moscow, December 8, 2003. Also see monitoring reports on Russian election at *http://www.osce.org/odihr.*
84. Marat Gelman, interview with *Nezavisimaya Gazeta,* February 17, 2004. He said he had resigned on December 8, the day after the elections, though he didn't speak publicly about it until two months later in the midst of the presidential campaign.
85. Gelman interview with authors.

CHAPTER 16: PUTIN'S RUSSIA

1. Mikhail Khromov and Katya Khromova shared dozens of hours of their time and opened up their lives to the authors during two extensive trips to the city of Ivanovo in the runup to the 2004 presidential election.
2. Candidate debate, Channel One, February 12, 2004.
3. Sergei Mironov, interview with authors, February 10, 2004.
4. Dmitri Rogozin, interview with authors, February 2004.
5. Irina Khakamada, interview with authors, February 12, 2004.
6. What had happened to Rybkin remained a mystery. Russian media speculated that Boris Berezovsky, the exiled Putin foe who'd bankrolled Rybkin, had staged the disappearance; Rybkin held to his claims.
7. Putin speech at Moscow State University, February 12, 2004.
8. Sergei Markov, interview with authors, September 30, 2004.
9. Maria Danilova, "Zhirinovsky Announces Presidential Bid," Associated Press, December 10, 2003.
10. The criticism was made by Harvard economist Jeffrey Sachs, who blamed him for stoking Russian inflation in the 1990s.

11. Sergei Glazyev, interview with authors, September 23, 2004.
12. Ibid.
13. Sergei Butin, interview with authors, September 28, 2004.
14. Markov interview.
15. Grigory Yavlinsky, interview with authors, September 23, 2004.
16. Boris Nemtsov, interview with authors, September 22, 2004; and Vladimir Ryzhkov, interview with authors, October 25, 2004. Told of Nemtsov's comment, Ryzhkov responded, "Of course I was afraid. Any politician in Russia who's in opposition always faces a threat."
17. Irina Khakamada, interview with authors, September 22, 2004.
18. Senior Russian official, interview with authors. This official spoke on condition of anonymity.
19. Khakamada interview.
20. Mari El memo obtained by authors. Local official Dzheppar Ablyazov in Mari El confirmed he was told of the orders for 80 percent turnout and 75 percent Putin vote mentioned in the memo, though other officials disavowed specific knowledge of the memo.
21. Vyacheslav Nikonov, interview with authors, August 23, 2004.
22. Khakamada interview.
23. Peter Baker, "Putin Woos, Warns to Get Out the Vote," *Washington Post*, March 14, 2004.
24. Glazyev, Khakamada interviews.
25. Khakamada interview.
26. Marina Litvinovich, interview with authors, September 27, 2004.
27. Markov interview.
28. Senior Russian official interview.
29. Butin interview.
30. Glazyev interview.
31. Butin interview.
32. Sergei Baburin quoted by *Vedomosti*, March 5, 2004. The actual ouster happened on March 4, according to a Glazyev aide in an interview, when Motherland faction members in the State Duma were called to Rogozin's office and asked to sign a letter rejecting Glazyev and endorsing Rogozin; twenty-three out of thirty-eight members did so.
33. Glazyev interview.
34. Litvinovich interview.
35. This account of Kasyonov's firing comes from the senior Russian official.
36. Caroline McGregor, "Putin Fires Kasyanov 18 Days Before Vote," *Moscow Times*, February 25, 2004.
37. This account of Putin's Krasnoyarsk trip comes from interviews conducted there during his visit February 26 and 27, 2004.
38. Svetlana Shportenko, briefing for reporters, February 26, 2004.
39. Senior Kremlin official, conversation with authors, February 27, 2004.
40. Peter Baker, "Russian Missile Launch Flops," *Washington Post*, February 18, 2004.

Only NTV under the control of state gas monopoly Gazprom mentioned the failed missile tests and it put on independent military analyst Pavel Felgenhauer to discuss them. Felgenhauer, though, told us later that NTV producers pleaded with him not to say anything to offend Putin. "I saw they were afraid so I decided I would not make big trouble," he recalled.

41. Mara D. Bellaby, "Far East Russia Aims to Boost Votes," Associated Press, February 27, 2004.
42. Putin shown on Russian television.
43. Nina Yomshina, interview with authors, February 27, 2004.
44. Vladislav Yurchik, interview with authors, February 26, 2004.
45. Sergei Zhabinsky, interview with authors, February 26, 2004.
46. Fradkov has not acknowledged working with the KGB, but experts familiar with the Soviet secret services said Fradkov's résumé is in keeping with an intelligence-related job. The future prime minister had a one-year gap in his official biography between graduating from university and being posted to the Soviet embassy in New Delhi as a trade diplomat at a time when India was a key Cold War spying battleground.
47. The only known reference to Fradkov as a possible prime minister came in the December 7, 2001, dispatch by the Political News Agency (known by its Russian initials APN), headlined "Kasyanov's Successor Found; He Works at the Tax Police." The agency is a project of the National Strategy Institute, run by Kremlin-connected political analyst Stanislav Belkovsky. Its dispatch pegging Fradkov as the next prime minister was later pointed out to us by a Western diplomat.
48. Putin election-night remarks, March 15, 2004, at *http://www.kremlin.ru*.
49. Mari El produced a below-average 67.3 percent for Putin in the final tally, suggesting the imperfections, or at least imprecision, of managed elections. On the missing million voters, see Caroline McGregor, "Election Numbers Do Not Add Up," *Moscow Times,* March 19, 2004.
50. Putin shown on Russian television.
51. Marat Gelman, interview with authors, August 17, 2004.
52. Mikhail Margelov, interview with authors, March 15, 2004.
53. Putin inaugural address, May 7, 2004, at *http://www.kremlin.ru*.

CHAPTER 17: SCAM OF THE YEAR

1. Khodorkovsky interview with Volga TV on October 24, 2003.
2. The authors spent time in Nizhny Novgorod with Aleksandr (Sasha) Markus over several weeks in July and August 2004, interviewing him, his ex-wife, business partner, employees, and friends.
3. William F. Browder, interview with authors, October 26, 2003.
4. Boris Kuznetsov, interview with authors, November 6, 2003.
5. Prosecution documents were posted at the time on the Internet.
6. A copy of Vladimir Ustinov's April 28, 2003, letter, was obtained by the authors.
7. Eric Kraus, "Truth and Beauty," desknote for investors, Sovlink, October 27, 2003.

8. Participant at cabinet meeting, interview with authors. This participant spoke on condition of anonymity.
9. Ibid.
10. Khodorkovsky's letter, available in Russian at his Web site, *http://www.khodorkovsky.ru*.
11. Ibid.
12. Arkady Ostrovsky, "Chubais Rejects Call to Repent Russia Sell-Offs," *Financial Times*, April 16, 2004.
13. Boris Nemtsov, interview with authors, April 21, 2004.
14. Andrew Kutchins, interview with authors, April 21, 2004.
15. Grigory Yavlinsky told this joke at the tenth anniversary celebration of the Carnegie Moscow Center, which was held in Moscow on April 22, 2004.
16. Boris Khodorkovsky told reporters this in the courthouse hallway on July 15, 2004.
17. Figures from the Russian Ministry of Justice Web site.
18. Khodorkovsky speech, per media pool report.
19. Lebedev speech, per media pool report.
20. Anton Drel, interview with authors, July 9, 2004.
21. Ibid.
22. Ibid.
23. Putin made the comments during a trip to Italy on November 5, 2003, and his remarks were broadcast that night on Rossiya television.
24. Data on market capitalization of Yukos and other Russian companies can also be found at the RTS Web site, *http://www.rts.ru*.
25. Investment analyst, interview with authors. This analyst spoke on condition of anonymity.
26. Arkady Volsky spoke on NTV on July 21, 2004.
27. Along with colleagues from other major Western news organizations based in Moscow, we eventually organized a permanent pool to cover the Khodorkovsky trial each day and provide all of us with a report of the arguments and testimony. Igor Malakhov, a Russian journalist who had previously worked for ABC News, German television, and other media organizations, was hired to produce these pool reports for us. Pool report by Igor Malakhov, October 12, 2004.
28. Malakhov pool report, October 11, 2004.
29. Malakhov pool report, October 12, 2004.
30. Leonid Fedun, interview with authors, July 15, 2004.
31. Vladimir Milov, interview with authors, August 2004.
32. Bruce Misamore, chief financial officer of Yukos, used these figures in a conference call with investment analysts on November 16, 2004.
33. Valuation conducted under contract with the Russian government by the German firm Dresdner Kleinwort Wasserstein, obtained by the authors. The firm gave the lowest possible valuation of $10.4 billion but then dismissed it as "overly conservative." To the extent that the firm's value was depressed, it was a direct result of the government's own tax charges against it.

34. Andrei Illarionov made the comments at a news conference on December 28, 2004. Within days, he was stripped of his responsibilities as Putin's chief economic adviser for Group of Eight (G-8) international summits, but he remained in the Kremlin.

35. Anton Drel, interview with authors, September 29, 2004.

CHAPTER 18: LENIN WAS RIGHT AFTER ALL

1. This chapter comes out of reporting over the 2003–4 school year at School Number 775 in Moscow. Thanks to the generosity and fearlessness of School Number 775's director, Elizaveta Chirkova, and deputy director, Irina Viktorovna Suvolokina, we were able to attend Suvolokina's history class whenever we liked, with no restrictions, and in the end visited more than a dozen lessons over the year. We taped each lesson but did not participate in class discussions. We also benefited from interviews outside the classroom with Suvolokina, Chirkova, and students Tanya Levina, Lyudmila Kolpakova, and Anton Tretyakov.

2. Putin was asked to assess Stalin's place in Russian history by the well-known Polish journalist and former Solidarity leader Adam Michnik. In the January 15, 2002, interview, a transcript of which was available in Russian at *http://www.kremlin.ru*, Putin refused to condemn Stalin and did not mention his mass murder of his own people. He did, however, state, "Stalin is of course a dictator. That goes without saying. This was a man guided to a great extent by the interests of keeping his personal power and that explains a lot, in my view. The problem is that it was under his leadership that the country won the Second World War, and the victory to a large extent is connected with his name. And it would be foolish to ignore this circumstance. So this is my incomplete answer, and it should satisfy you."

3. "Luzhkov Suggests Returning Dzerzhinsky Monument to Lubyanka Square," Interfax, September 13, 2002.

4. "Stalin's name back on Russian war monument," Reuters, July 23, 2004. The order, posted on *http://www.kremlin.ru*, said restoring Stalin's name was meant to "pay tribute to the heroism of the defenders of Stalingrad and to preserve the history of the Russian state." Putin has, however, so far stopped short of endorsing the city name change. In December 2002, he said the switch back to Stalingrad "could trigger suspicion that we are returning to the times of Stalinism. This would do us no good."

5. "Russia criticizes public debates on Warsaw uprising," Interfax, August 4, 2004.

6. Journalist Masha Lipman shared this observation with us. A Google search of the phrase "chaos of the 1990s" and Putin turns up twenty thousand references.

7. Gleb Pavlovsky, interview with authors, May 7, 2004.

8. Interfax, March 4, 2005.

9. Sarah E. Mendelson and Theodore P. Gerber, "Up for Grabs: Russia's Political Trajectory and Stalin's Legacy," PONARS Policy Memo 296, November 2003.

10. Galina Klokova, interview with authors, September 12, 2003.

11. Ibid.

12. Maria Danilova, "Russian History Books Accused of Bias," Associated Press, August 16, 2004.

13. Klokova interview.

14. Volobyev, O., V. A. Klokov, M. V. Ponomaryev, V. A. Rogozhkin, *Rossiya I Mir, XX Vek* (Russia and the World, 20th Century) (Moscow: Drofa, 2002).

15. Oleg Volobyev, telephone interview with authors, April 29, 2004.

16. *Rossiya I Mir,* 292.

17. Klokova interview.

18. Igor Dolutsky, interview with authors, April 28, 2004. His account was confirmed by an editor who asked to remain anonymous.

19. Dolutsky interview.

20. Natalya Konygina, "Education Minister Blasted 'Pseudoliberalism' in History Schoolbooks," *Izvestia,* January 27, 2004. Also Yelena Zinina, head of the Education Ministry textbook-publishing department, on Radio Free Europe/Radio Liberty, December 5, 2003.

21. "Putin Objects to Politicized History Textbooks," Interfax, November 27, 2003.

22. Dolutsky interview.

23. Ibid.

24. Quotes are from Dolutsky's textbook, *Otechesvennaya Istoriya: XX Vek* (National History: 20th Century), pt. 2 (Moscow: Mnemozina Publishing, 2003).

25. Dolutsky interview.

EPILOGUE: AFTER BESLAN

1. Elza Baskayeva, interview with authors, October 2004.

2. Vladimir Putin speech, aired on Channel One, May 17, 2000.

3. According to a source close to Kakha Bendukidze, who spoke on condition of anonymity. Budget figure from Erin E. Arvedlund, "An Oligarch Goes Home to Lift Georgia's Economy," *New York Times,* November 5, 2004.

4. RIA-Novosti, January 27, 2005.

5. Viktor Cherkesov, "Moda na KGB?" *Komsomolskaya Pravda,* December 29, 2004.

6. Steven Lee Myers, "Russian Military TV to Beat Patriotic Drum," *International Herald Tribune,* February 12, 2005.

7. Senior Russian official, interview with authors. This official spoke on condition of anonymity.

8. Francesca Mereu, "Liberal Ministers Take the Blame," *Moscow Times,* January 24, 2005.

9. "Russian Ex-PM Laments Lack of Democracy," Agence France-Presse, February 24, 2005.

10. Rossiya television, BBC Monitoring, February 24, 2005.

11. "Putin Strengthened," *Komsomolskaya Pravda,* September 29, 2004.

12. Vladimir Putin press conference, December 24, 2004, available at *http://www. kremlin.ru.*

13. Ibid.

14. Lilia Shevtsova has used the phrase "imitation democracy" in papers, interviews,

and lectures throughout the Putin era, including her book *Putin's Russia,* published in expanded form in 2005 by the Carnegie Endowment for International Peace.

15. Richard Pipes, "Flight from Freedom: What Russians Think and Want," *Foreign Affairs,* May-June 2004.

16. Senior Russian official interview.

17. Interview with *Itogi* magazine, October 2004.

18. Adviser to President Bush, interview with authors. The adviser spoke on condition of anonymity.

19. Jim Hoagland, "Reassessing Putin," *Washington Post,* March 13, 2005.

20. For transcript of the February 24, 2005, joint Bush-Putin news conference in Bratislava, Slovakia, see http://www.whitehouse.gov.

21. Khamid Magomadov, interview with authors, October 2004.

22. Vladimir Putin comment, staff TV monitoring, May 11, 2004.

23. Multiple Russian media outlets reported the formation of Nashi. Among the first articles was Mikhail Chevchyk and Dmitri Kamyshev, "Ordinary 'Nashism,'" *Kommersant,* February 21, 2005.

24. Mikhail Kozyrev, interview with authors, September 29, 2004. Lyrics from Nashe radio, reprinted with permission from Sergei Shnurov.

25. Andrei Norkin, interview with authors, November 5, 2003.

26. Senior Russian official interview.

27. Tatyana Shalimova, interview with authors, September 29, 2004.

SELECTED BIBLIOGRAPHY

There is an extraordinary body of literature on Russia, and we could not begin to list all the best. But this is a sampling of some of the books we relied on the most as we put together ours.

Albright, Madeleine. *Madame Secretary*. New York: Talk Miramax, 2003.

Andrew, Christopher, and Vasili Mitrokhin. *The Sword and the Shield: The Mitrokhin Archive and the Secret History of the KGB*. New York: Basic Books, 1999.

Applebaum, Anne. *Gulag: A History*. New York: Doubleday, 2003.

Baiev, Khassan. *The Oath: A Surgeon Under Fire*. With Ruth and Nicholas Daniloff. New York: Walter & Company, 2003.

Blotsky, Oleg. *Vladimir Putin: Doroga k Vlasti* (Vladimir Putin: The Road to Power). Moscow: Osmos Press, 2002.

———. *Vladimir Putin: Istoriya Zhizni* (Vladimir Putin: Life Story). Moscow: Mezhdunarodniye Otnosheniya, 2001.

Borovik, Artyom. *The Hidden War: A Russian Journalist's Account of the Soviet War in Afghanistan*. New York: Grove Press, 1990.

Butler, Richard. *The Greatest Threat: Iraq, Weapons of Mass Destruction, and the Growing Crisis of Global Security*. New York: Public Affairs, 2000.

Clarke, Richard A. *Against All Enemies*. New York: Free Press, 2004.

Coll, Steve. *Ghost Wars: The Secret History of the CIA, Afghanistan and Bin Laden, from the Soviet Invasion to September 10, 2001*. New York: Penguin Press, 2004.

Custine, Marquis de. *Empire of the Czar: A Journey Through Eternal Russia*. New York: Doubleday, 1989. Originally published as *La Russie en 1839*.

Dolutsky, Igor. *Otechestvennaya Istoriya XX Vek* (Fatherland History of the 20th Century). Moscow: Mnemozina, 2003.

Evangelista, Matthew. *The Chechen Wars: Will Russia Go the Way of the Soviet Union?* Washington, D.C.: Brookings Institution Press, 2002.

Freeland, Chrystia. *Sale of the Century: Russia's Wild Ride from Communism to Capitalism*. New York: Crown Publishers, 2000.

Fyodorov, Valery, and Avtandil Tsuladze. *Epokha Putina: Taini i Zagadki "Kremlevskovo Dvora"* (The Putin Era: Secrets and Mysteries of the Kremlin Palace). Moscow: Eksmo, 2003.

Gall, Carlotta, and Thomas de Waal. *Chechnya: Calamity in the Caucasus*. New York and London: New York University Press, 1998.

Golts, Aleksandr. *Armiya Rossii: 11 Poteryannikh Let* (The Army of Russia: 11 Lost Years). Moscow: Zakharov, 2004.

Goltz, Thomas. *Chechnya Diary: A War Correspondent's Story of Surviving the War in Chechnya*. New York: Thomas Dunne Books/St. Martin's Press, 2003.

Griffin, Nichólas. *Caucasus: Mountain Men and Holy Wars*. New York: Thomas Dunne Books/St. Martin's Press, 2001.

Hill, Fiona, and Clifford Gaddy. *Siberian Curse: How Communist Planners Left Russia Out in the Cold*. Washington: Brookings Institution Press, 2003.

Hoffman, David E. *The Oligarchs: Wealth and Power in the New Russia*. New York: Public Affairs, 2001.

Hughes, Karen. *Ten Minutes from Normal*. New York: Viking, 2004.

Jack, Andrew. *Inside Putin's Russia*. London: Granta, 2004. Later published in the United States by Oxford University Press.

Kaiser, Robert G. *Russia: The People and the Power*. New York: Atheneum, 1976.

Klebnikov, Paul. *Godfather of the Kremlin: Boris Berezovsky and the Looting of Russia*. New York: Harcourt, 2000.

Knight, Amy. *Spies Without Cloaks: The KGB's Successors*. Princeton, NJ: Princeton University Press, 1996.

Lieven, Anatol. *Chechnya: Tombstone of Russian Power*. New Haven and London: Yale University Press, 1998.

McFaul, Michael. *Russia's Unfinished Revolution: Political Change from Gorbachev to Putin*. Ithaca and London: Cornell University Press, 2001.

McFaul, Michael, and James M. Goldgeier. *Power and Purpose: U.S. Policy Toward Russia After the Cold War*. Washington: Brookings Institution Press, 2003.

McFaul, Michael, Nikolai Petrov, and Andrei Ryabov. *Between Dictatorship and Democracy: Russian Post-Communist Political Reform*. Washington, D.C.: Carnegie Endowment for International Peace, 2004.

Meier, Andrew. *Black Earth: A Journey Through Russia After the Fall*. New York: W. W. Norton & Co., 2003.

Mosse, W. E. *Alexander II and the Modernization of Russia*. New York: Collier Books, 1958.

Nedkov, Vesselin, and Paul Wilson. *57 Hours: A Survivor's Account of the Moscow Hostage Drama*. Toronto: Viking Canada, 2003.

Nivat, Anne. *Chienne de Guerre: A Woman Reporter Behind the Lines of the War in Chechnya*. Trans. by Susan Darnton. New York: Public Affairs, 2001.

Pipes, Richard. *Russia Under the Old Regime: The History of Civilization*. New York: Macmillan Publishing Co., 1976.

Politkovskaya, Anna. *A Dirty War: A Russian Reporter in Chechnya*. Trans. by John Crowfoot. London: Harvill Press, 2001.

———. *A Small Corner of Hell: Dispatches from Chechnya*. Trans. by Alexander Burry and Tatiana Tulchinsky. Chicago: University of Chicago Press, 2003.

Pope, Edmond D., and Tom Shachtman. *Torpedoed: An American Businessman's True Story of Secrets, Betrayal, Imprisonment in Russia, and the Battle to Set Him Free*. New York: Little, Brown and Co., 2001.

Primakov, Yevgeny M. *A World Challenged: Fighting Terrorism in the Twenty-First Century*. Washington: The Nixon Center and Brookings Institution Press, 2004.

Putin, Vladimir. *First Person: An Astonishingly Frank Self-Portrait by Russia's President*. With Nataliya Gevorkyan, Natalya Timakova, and Andrei Kolesnikov. Trans. by Catherine A. Fitzpatrick. New York: Public Affairs, 2000. Originally published in Russian as *Ot Pervovo Litsa: Razgovori c Vladimirom Putinim*. Moscow: Vagrius, 2000.

Rasputin, Valentin. *Siberia, Siberia*. Trans. by Margaret Winchell and Gerald Mikkelson. Evanston, Ill.: Northwestern University Press, 1991.

Remnick, David. *Lenin's Tomb: The Last Days of the Soviet Empire*. New York: Random House, 1993.

——. *Resurrection: The Struggle for a New Russia*. New York: Random House, 1997.

Sakwa, Richard. *Putin: Russia's Choice*. London: Routledge, 2004.

Salisbury, Harrison. *The 900 Days: The Siege of Leningrad*. London: Martin Secker & Warburg Limited, 1969. Reprinted in 2000 by Pan Books.

Satter, David. *Darkness at Dawn: The Rise of the Russian Criminal State*. New Haven: Yale University Press, 2003.

Shevchenko, Vladimir. *Povsednevnaya Zhizn: Kremlya pri Prezidentakh* (Everyday Life: The Kremlin Under the Presidents). Moscow: Molodaya Gvardiya, 2004.

Shevtsova, Lilia. *Putin's Russia*. Washington, D.C.: Carnegie Endowment for International Police, 2003.

Solzhenitsyn, Aleksandr. *Gulag Archipelago*. New York: HarperCollins, 1992.

Suskind, Ron. *The Price of Loyalty: George W. Bush, the White House and the Education of Paul O'Neill*. New York: Simon & Schuster, 2004.

Talbott, Strobe. *The Russia Hand: A Memoir of Presidential Diplomacy*. New York: Random House, 2002.

Telen, Lyudmila. *Pokoleniye Putina* (The Putin Generation). Moscow: Vagrius, 2004.

Topol, Edward. *Roman o Lyubvy i Terrorye* (A Novel about Love and Terror). Moscow: AST Publishers, 2002.

Tregubova, Yelena. *Baiki Kremlevskovo Diggera* (Tales of a Kremlin Digger). Moscow: Ad Marginem, 2003.

Truscott, Peter. *Kursk: The Gripping True Story of Russia's Worst Submarine Disaster*. London: Simon & Schuster UK, 2002.

——. *Putin's Progress*. London: Simon & Schuster UK, 2004.

Usoltsev, Vladimir. *Sosluzhivets: Neizvestnye Stranitsy Zhizni Presidenta* (Co-Worker: Unknown Pages from the President's Life). Moscow: Eksmo, 2004.

Woodward, Bob. *Bush at War*. New York: Simon & Schuster, 2002.

——. *Plan of Attack*. New York: Simon & Schuster, 2004.

Yakovlev, Alexander N. *A Century of Violence in Soviet Russia*. Trans. by Anthony Austin. New Haven & London: Yale University Press, 2002. Originally published in Russian as *Krestosev* (Crosses). Moscow: Vagrius, 2000.

Yeltsin, Boris. *Midnight Diaries*. New York: Public Affairs, 2000.

Yevtushenko, Yevgeny. *Fatal Half Measures: The Culture of Democracy in the Soviet Union*. Ed. and trans. by Antonina W. Bouis. Boston, Toronto, and London: Little, Brown, 1991.

DOCUMENTARIES

Assassination of Russia. Charles Gazelle, Transparences Productions. France, 2002.

Terror in Moscow. Producer-director Dan Reed, producer Mark Franchetti. Aired on Britain's Channel 4, May 12, 2003, and on HBO on October 23, 2003.

Self-Portrait: Ten Years on NTV. Aired on NTV, October 11, 2003.

ABOUT THE AUTHORS

PETER BAKER and SUSAN GLASSER were the Moscow bureau chiefs for *The Washington Post* from January 2001 to November 2004, responsible for covering Russia and the fourteen other nations that once belonged to the Soviet Union. During their overseas tour, they also covered the United States–led wars in Afghanistan and Iraq. Baker has been a reporter at the *Post* for seventeen years, including two stints as White House correspondent, first during Bill Clinton's presidency and now again covering George W. Bush. He is the author of the *New York Times* bestseller, *The Breach: Inside the Impeachment and Trial of William Jefferson Clinton* (Scribner, 2000). Glasser joined the *Post* seven years ago as deputy national editor and oversaw coverage of the Monica Lewinsky investigation, then became a national political correspondent, writing about money and politics. Today she is the paper's terrorism correspondent. Before coming to the *Post*, she was editor of *Roll Call*, the newspaper covering Capitol Hill. They live in Washington with their son, Theodore.

947.086   Baker, Peter.
BAK
           Kremlin rising.

$27.50

DATE